THE GLOBAL PUZZLE

Issues and Actors in World Politics

THE GLOBAL PUZZLE

Issues and Actors in World Politics

RICHARD W. MANSBACH

Iowa State University

HOUGHTON MIFFLIN COMPANY   BOSTON   TORONTO

Geneva, Illinois   *Palo Alto*   *Princeton, New Jersey*

Editor-in-Chief   Jean Woy
Senior Associate Editor   Fran Gay
Project Editor   Susan Lee-Belhocine
Production/Design Coordinator   Jennifer Waddell
Senior Manufacturing Coordinator   Marie Barnes
Marketing Manager   George Kane

Cover Designer   Ron Kosciak

Cover Photo   Ron Lowery/The Stock Market

Credits: A list of text credits follows the index.

Printed in the U.S.A.

Library of Congress Catalog Card Number: 93-78639

ISBN: 0-395-52580-2

123456789-DH-96 95 94 93

Contents

Maps

Figures and Tables

Preface

The dramatic changes that have transformed global politics in recent years, especially the end of the Cold War, and the failure of our theoretical lenses to keep pace with those changes have inspired me to write this text. If we steep new generations of students in old ideas, we will prepare them for a world that has disappeared. Many scholars and practitioners continue to rely on a power-politics approach to international relations. "Sovereign states," "military power," and "national interest" are among the key features of that approach, and they are ill suited and perhaps even dangerous to the new world.

In contrast, *The Global Puzzle* explores the following themes. First, global politics consists of a variety of issues that may be linked yet involve different actors. For example, although rising oil prices place special burdens on the poorest societies by increasing the cost of fertilizer for agriculture and energy for industrialization, the issues of economic development in the third world and of oil price regulation do not involve the same set of actors. Second, the cast of global actors is large and includes both state and nonstate groups. Giant corporations like Sony and Texaco, terrorist groups like the Abu Nidal faction, international organizations like OPEC, and even private organizations like Amnesty International play important supporting roles in the dramas of global politics. Third, the cooperative and social features of global politics have received insufficient attention in the literature. Relations between Arabs and Israelis, Bosnians and Serbs, and Somali warlords feature a high degree of conflict and violence, but much of global politics is actually stable and cooperative. Fourth, contemporary global issues have important historical and, often, non-Western roots. And finally, such issues increasingly transcend the capacity of states to cope with them.

The text consists of four parts. The first, "Setting the Stage," offers students comparative theoretical prisms through which to view the dramas of the real world. The introduction and four chapters in this section examine the historical evolution of global politics and take issue with the Eurocentric bias of traditional approaches. The section also introduces students to the key concepts that the text uses to make sense of global politics—political systems, power, actors, and issues. The first chapter ("The Richness of Historical Experience") emphasizes the critical role of the past in understanding the present and future, illustrating this by looking briefly at ancient Greece, imperial China, medieval Islam, and medieval Europe. The second chapter ("Systems in Global Politics") looks at the "big picture" of the global system and examines the role of global structure in shaping human behavior, especially the importance of resource and attitude distribution. Chapter 3 ("The Puzzle of Power") introduces the elements of power-politics approaches—power and the territorial state—and evaluates the evolution, virtues, and limitations of these concepts. The final two chapters in this section ("Issues and Actors in World Politics" and "Beyond the Nation-State? A World of Many Actors") elaborate an alternative approach to global politics that paints a more complex and richer portrait. They describe the variety of issues and actors in global politics and the manner in which issues arise and evolve.

Part Two, "The Changing Balance of Cooperation and Conflict," consists of five chapters that collectively examine the mix of conflict and cooperation in global politics. Chapter 6("Anarchy and Society in World Politics") focuses on the balance between anarchical and social elements in the global system. The difficulty actors have in trusting each other in the absence of world government is one anarchic feature, while the proliferation of informal rules and international regimes is an element of global society. Chapters 7 and 8 ("The Changing Role of Force in World Politics" and "War and The Nuclear Age") evaluate the changing nature and role of war in global politics, and Chapter 9 ("The Many Paths to Cooperation") introduces some of the ways in which actors cooperate with one another through such organizations as the United Nations. Chapter 10 ("International Political Economy: Where Economics and Politics Meet") focuses on the growing role of economic factors such as trade issues in global politics, and on the pressure that the global economy exerts upon actors to coordinate their goals and policies.

The four chapters in Part Three, "Old and New Issues" move beyond the theoretical perspectives of the previous sections and illustrate them in the context of key substantive issues. Chapter 11 ("The Janus Face of Issues—Foreign Policy"), for example, illustrates how the barriers between international and domestic politics are falling. Chapter 12 ("The Changing Security Dilemma: The End of the Cold War") examines how alternative theoretical lenses explain the outbreak and resolution of the Cold War. Chapter 13 ("Friendly Economic Adversaries: The United States, Japan, and Europe") looks at relations among the United States, Japan, and the European Community as it shows how the economic dimension of global politics is growing. Finally, Chapter 14 ("The Middle East Cauldron") examines the violence-prone Middle East to show the continuing impact of history on global politics and the tangled relationships in a diverse universe of actors and issues.

The final section of the book, "The Search for Solutions," sets out to show how confining is the cage we call the state in understanding global politics. Chapter 15 ("The State versus the Species: Environmental Dilemmas") focuses on a series of environmental issues that threaten the survival of everyone and that individual states cannot resolve, and Chapter 16 ("States versus the Individual: Human Rights") examines the relationship between the state and individual citizens in the context of human rights. The final chapter ("Solving the Puzzle: Some Alternate Futures") concludes the book by depicting two dramatically different scenarios for the future—one an optimistic vision of growing global cooperation and the other a bleak vision of intensifying conflict within and among states.

To help students understand the complexities of global politics, the text employs a variety of visual and pedagogical aids. The extensive use of maps, not merely locates peoples in a conventional sense but reflects the changing global distribution of phenomena like population and conflict. A variety of tables and figures provides students with contemporary data that reinforce and illustrate substantive points such as the extent of environmental damage suffered by the planet. Photographs with instructive captions bring to life some of the people and issues described in the text. Substantive footnoting provides students with the background to key issues and with additional sources to consult if they wish to do so. Finally, lists of key terms at the end of chapters and a glossary at the end of the text serve as an additional resource to help students understand the basic concepts in the text.

An accompanying Instructor's Resource Manual will make it easier for instructors to use this text effectively. To facilitate preparation of lectures, it includes chapter summaries and detailed lecture outlines. It also includes a number of illustrative syllabi that suggest how the text can be used in both introductory and more advanced settings. These syllabi contain additional suggested readings as well as suggested activities that I have found useful. The manual also provides essay and multiple-choice questions, which are also available on disk. Additionally, a set of transparencies features maps and other visual aids from the text.

My thanks go to many colleagues and students whose advice and assistance over the years have informed this book. Thanks go, too, to those at Houghton Mifflin who have been so generous with their time and effort, including Susan Lee-Belhocine, Jean Woy, Margaret Seawell, Greg Tobin, and Lance Wickens, and to those who, in reviewing this manuscript, have improved it by their suggestions and emendations: W. Craig Bledsoe, David Lipscomb University; Steven J. Breyman, Rensselaer Polytechnic Institute; Harvey B. Feigenbaum, The George Washington University; John Lovell, Indiana University; Donald F. Megnin, Slippery Rock University; Robert B. McCalla, University of Wisconsin-Madison; Karen A. Mingst, University of Kentucky; Kenneth A. Rodman, Colby College; Claudena Skran, Lawrence University; Daniel H. Unger, Georgetown University; Thomas J. Volgy, The University of Arizona.

As this book nears completion, it remains unclear whether or not the end of the long nightmare of Cold War will usher in a dawn of peace and progress or a new night of nationalist violence and ecological decay. Atrocities in Bosnia, Angola, and South Africa conjure up images of fascist barbarism. Yet, there are contrary clues—a decline in the Chinese birthrate, an international rescue operation in Somalia, and the spread of democracy in Russia. Perhaps it has always been like this, evidence of atavism and progress side by side. We approach the twenty-first century, as our ancestors approached earlier centuries, with a mix of hope and fear.

Sadly, we still understand little about the forces that shape global politics and thus our prospects for survival. Ignorance, even more than malice, explains the failure to realize our best aspirations; and as the pace of change accelerates, our ability to understand the world around us likely will lag still further behind events. Must we despair at fathoming global politics and so surrender control of our destinies? The answer is "no" if we turn away from obsolete theories and seek new perspectives that can illuminate what is important. It is no less critical in global politics than in other fields of human endeavor to throw off old ways of thinking that have become stale and worn. Recognizing that our fates are linked, we must find new ways to look at old phenomena and fashion new lenses to help us see what is new in the world.

In closing, it is important to observe that neither sentimental optimism nor paralytic despair will serve our ends. It takes courage to confront the daunting issues of global politics that threaten our survival not merely as individuals but as a species. Let us show that courage so that our children and our children's children can say that we did what we could to make their lives better than ours. It is for this reason I dedicate this book to my daughter, Rachael Alexandra.

Richard W. Mansbach

A World Turned Upside Down

Imagine you have boarded a machine that can instantly accelerate you backward or forward in time. At first, you lurch back to the year 1945; next, you slowly move forward a few years and observe the changing world, and then you surge ahead to the present. The worlds you will have observed even in that short a time will look markedly different from each other. Most people may see their problems as the same in all periods, but differences in style of dress, level of technology, and social and economic conditions will be evident as well.

For students of global politics, this journey would be even more startling. In 1945, shortly after World War II, the world was divided between two superpowers—the United States and the Soviet Union. Virtually all of global politics revolved around the interaction between these two states and their relations with others. As the 1940s ended and the 1950s began, the tense and dangerous standoff between the communist East (the Soviet Union and its allies) and the capitalist West (the United States and its allies) governed global politics. Each side expended vast resources on their respective military establishments, funneled military and economic assistance to friendly states, and built competing alliances. This struggle would last almost forty years.

As recently as 1983, President Ronald Reagan called the Soviet Union an *evil empire* as Washington engaged in a massive arms buildup aimed at closing a perceived "missile gap," which the president called *the window of vulnerability* between the two states. President Reagan blamed heightened tension on the Soviet deployment of a new generation of large and highly accurate intercontinental ballistic missiles (ICBMs).[1]

---

[1]Although Soviet deployment of these missiles was permitted under arms-control agreements, the Reagan administration feared that America's arsenal of land-based missiles had become vulnerable to a sneak Soviet attack. The window of vulnerability was an excellent rationale for conservatives who wanted a larger defense budget. The revelation that the Soviet nuclear arsenal peaked in 1986 at

1

Responding to this "evil empire," the U.S. government deployed intermediate-range nuclear forces (INF) in Western Europe and provided assistance to the "contras" in Nicaragua, the Mujahedeen in Afghanistan, Jonas Savimbi's UNITA rebels in Angola, and other insurgents in Mozambique, Cambodia, and Ethiopia who were rebelling against Soviet-supported governments or clients. The purpose was to bleed the Soviet Union, much as Moscow had bled the United States by supporting "national liberation movements" in Vietnam and elsewhere. In this respect, the mid-1980s world looked little different from that of the 1940s and 1950s.

By the end of 1991, the *Cold War* had been formally and practically ended by agreements between the two sides, climaxing in the dissolution of the Soviet empire and then the U.S.S.R. itself. Bargains reduced many points of friction and promised dramatic cuts in the superpowers' nuclear arsenals and their troops and tanks in Central Europe. Agreements for reducing and eventually eliminating chemical and biological weapons were also signed. Ultimately, a nonaggression pact between two opposed alliances — the *North Atlantic Treaty Organization* (NATO) and the *Warsaw Treaty Organization* (WTO) — was signed late in 1990, just four months before the latter collapsed.

The most dramatic symbol telling the end of the Cold War was the collapse of communist party rule in the Soviet "satellite" states in Eastern Europe — East Germany, Poland, Czechoslovakia, Romania, Bulgaria, and Hungary — beginning in 1989 and continuing into 1991. The new governments in these countries sought to dismantle the single-party system and the highly centralized political and economic controls that had dominated their societies and to move toward political democracy and market economies. These new governments sought close ties with and assistance from the United States and Western Europe. Within three years, the Soviet empire had dissolved and its members had been transformed.

Even more remarkable, the Communist Party of the Soviet Union (CPSU) — the party of Lenin, Trotsky, Stalin, Khrushchev, and Brezhnev — voluntarily surrendered its constitutionally-guaranteed monopoly over political power early in 1990. That party had been discredited by a failed hard-liner coup against Soviet President Mikhail Gorbachev in August 1991. An unforgettable image from those tense days showed Russian leader Boris Yeltsin atop a Soviet tank promising to resist hard-line efforts to turn back the clock. Few observers realized that Yeltsin was taking advantage of events to outmaneuver Gorbachev and rush the dissolution of the CPSU and the U.S.S.R. Immediately after the abortive coup, the three Baltic states — Estonia, Latvia, and Lithuania — were granted independence.[2] Other republics quickly sought to use the political chaos in Moscow to reshape their relationship with the central Soviet government. The rigidly

---

45,000 warheads — 12,000 more than believed and twice the U.S. number suggests, however, that there was reason for concern. See William J. Broad, "Russian Says Soviet Atom Arsenal Was Larger Than West Estimated," *The New York Times*, September 26, 1993, Section 1, pp. 1, 7.

[2]Stalin seized the three countries in 1940 as security for the U.S.S.R. from Nazi Germany. In fact, they were quickly overrun when the Germans invaded the Soviet Union in June 1941. The United States continued to recognize the independence of the three Baltic states.

The toppling of the statues of Lenin in the former Soviet Union and Eastern Europe was a fitting symbol to the death of communism and the end of the Cold War.

centralized Soviet structure was soon dissolved into a loose union of republics, but even that reform proved insufficient for most of the constituent states. By early December 1991, the remaining Soviet republics, with a vastly weakened central Soviet government, were seeking a new order. On Christmas day 1991, the Soviet Union was formally disbanded. Soviet President Mikhail Gorbachev, who had initiated reforms beginning in 1985, had no country to rule.

Russia, principal successor to the Soviet Union, and three other republics still held nuclear weapons and other significant military capability. Still, the economic and social problems faced by the former Soviet states sharply reduced the prospect that global politics would soon return to the tense world of only a decade earlier. Seven decades of Marxism–Leninism had left consumers in the former Soviet Union with long queues, poor services, empty shelves, inadequate housing, shoddy goods, rampant underemployment, a degraded environment, and "hidden" inflation. Year after year, despite highly publicized achievements in space and science, the Soviet society and economy fell further and further behind the United States, Western Europe, and Japan in critical areas of high technology. Addressing pent-up consumer demands, yearnings for democracy, and revived ethnic rivalries would occupy the leaders of these new states more than involvement in foreign adventures.

The most vivid single symbol of the sea change in global politics occurred two years prior to the collapse of the Soviet Union—the Berlin Wall opened, accompanied by pictures of Germans hacking pieces from it. The wall was erected by the communist-controlled East German government in August 1961 to keep its people from fleeing East Germany for West Berlin. Construction of the Wall and the killing of those seeking to flee the East symbolized the gulf between East and West and the apparent permanence of the Cold War. When the Wall opened November 9, 1989, it foretold change in Germany—where the Cold War began—in Eastern Europe, and in the Soviet Union itself. About four months later, in March 1990, the communists were voted out of power in East Germany's first free election, and German reunification was under way. It was completed by October 1990, and reunified Germany had its first democratic elections in December.

Since the Cold War ended the world has actually become more complex. In these chapters, we describe the pieces of the global puzzle and suggest how they fit together. Who will be the major political actors in the world of the 1990s and beyond, and what will their relationship be like? Which are the major issues in this new world? How has power changed? How are economic and political issues related? What will the global political system and structure be like? For the moment, let us review briefly how we got here and illustrate how world politics has indeed been turned upside down by events in the past few years.

The Old World

British foreign minister George Canning boasted that, by persuading the U.S. government to issue the Monroe Doctrine in 1823, he had "called the New World into existence to redress the balance of the Old." We are entering an era in global politics that differs as much from the old as frontier America differed from cosmopolitan Europe early in the nineteenth century. We are leaving behind a long, intense, and hostile competition between the United States and the Soviet Union and their allies. For more than forty years, international crises like the 1962 Cuban missile crisis, the use of *proxies* in local conflicts, the arms race, and competition in other realms substituted for direct military conflict between the two protagonists. Despite the limited but "hot" conflicts such as the Korean (1950–1953) and Vietnam (1960–1976)[3] wars, the two main players were able to avoid direct military confrontation that might have escalated into World War III.

The Cold War is usually said to have begun when the Grand Alliance of World War II—the United States, Great Britain, and the Soviet Union—broke down, but the seeds of the conflict were planted much earlier. The 1917 Bolshevik Revolution in Russia and Russia's withdrawal from World War I made the Western democracies suspect the Soviet Union. Mutual suspicions were intensified by Soviet efforts to foster

---

[3]Two Vietnam wars were fought. The first, against French colonial rule, lasted from 1945 until 1954. The second, climaxing in the 1976 unification of North and South Vietnam, began in 1960. Between 1965 and 1973, the United States heavily intervened in the war.

revolutionary activities in Europe and Western military intervention in Siberia and northern Russia. A fundamental ideological division separated those who followed Lenin and Stalin, believing in *economic socialism* and denying political democracy, from Western elites, who advocated *free-market capitalism* and *political democracy*.

Rising *fascism* in Germany, Italy, and Japan intensified mutual suspicion. The European democracies and the Soviet Union believed each was prepared to let the dictators Hitler and Mussolini devour the other. Suddenly all that changed when the Nazis invaded Western Europe and, a year later, attacked the Soviet Union. These events, along with the Japanese attack on Pearl Harbor and Europe's colonial possessions in Asia threw the United States, Great Britain, and the Soviet Union together in an alliance of convenience, even survival.[4] With their enemies crushed in 1945, the bond that had united them disappeared, and their changed circumstances revived old grudges and aroused new ones.

The most profound change was the emergence of the United States and the Soviet Union at the apex of the global hierarchy. Their resources, populations, industrial bases, and military might elevated the two above others like colossi. That each alone could harm the interests of the other produced perceptions of threat. By 1945, Germany, Japan, and Italy had been devastated by the war; most of Western Europe had been occupied, and, along with Britain and France, was an economic shambles. Much of China had been occupied. Even as the Japanese occupiers withdrew, that country found itself engulfed by civil war. An enfeebled Europe also loosened its grip on the colonial empires in Asia and Africa.

The war was not yet over when misunderstandings began. Stalin, Roosevelt, and Churchill, meeting at *Yalta* in February 1945, agreed to establish "democracies"[5] in the Eastern European countries that were being occupied by the Red Army as it advanced toward Berlin. But Moscow rapidly imposed communist dictatorships in those countries to ensure that they would be governed, as agreed at Yalta, by "friendly regimes."[6] Romania (1945) and Bulgaria (1946) were the first to succumb, and Hungary (1947)

---

[4]Stalin cooperated with Hitler in dividing Poland in September 1939 but less than two years later found his country the victim of a surprise Nazi invasion. During World War II, the allies remained suspicious of each other. Stalin accused Franklin Roosevelt and Winston Churchill of delaying a "second front" in the hope that Germany and Russia would bleed each other to death, and the Anglo-Americans and Soviets suspected that the other side was negotiating a separate peace.

[5]Marxists believed economic equality was integral to achieving "democracy"; they saw free elections without economic equality as a sham. His political enemies, especially in the Republican Party, repeatedly accused Roosevelt of having been duped by Stalin at Yalta and having sold out Eastern Europe. In fact, Roosevelt understood that because the Red Army was there, Stalin had no need to make concessions. From Roosevelt's point of view, Stalin's willingness to participate in a United Nations was itself an important concession.

[6]In October 1944, Churchill and Stalin agreed to spheres of influence in Eastern Europe, but Roosevelt was appalled by the deal.

and Czechoslovakia (1948) were the last. Although Yugoslavia remained beyond the Red Army's reach, a radical communist and pro-Soviet regime under Marshal Josif Broz (Tito) took power.[7]

Americans felt that imposing communism on Eastern Europe betrayed the wartime alliance and threatened the security of Western Europe. Poland's fate was symbolic because Hitler's invasion had marked the beginning of World War II. He struck only after concluding a nonaggression pact with the U.S.S.R. including a secret protocol dividing Poland into German and Soviet spheres of influence. United States voters of East European extraction, especially the many Polish-Americans in such cities as Chicago, Buffalo, and Pittsburgh, were incensed. The fall of Czechoslovakia also weighed heavily on U.S. public opinion. The West had failed to help that country resist Hitler's demands at the Munich conference of 1938 for the Sudetenland and then in the following year when the Nazis occupied the rest of Czechoslovakia. The United States had provided the Soviet Union with billions of dollars in military and economic assistance through "lend lease" in the war against Hitler, and British and American women had spent long evenings "knitting socks for Uncle Joe," and Soviet actions in Eastern Europe and elsewhere were not the gratitude Americans expected.

Defeated Germany, however, was the crucible in which the Cold War was forged. Germany had been the most powerful state in Europe, both sides believed it could be so again. Control of Germany was seen as the key to control of Europe as a whole. Until 1947, both sides paid lip service to a united Germany but for incompatible reasons. Stalin wanted to make sure that Germans would never again threaten his country and would pay as much as possible for the havoc they had wrought. By contrast, the United States, Great Britain, and France, also uneasy about a German resurgence,[8] felt it necessary to restore the German economy as quickly as possible so that Germany could lead European economic recovery and could reduce bankrupt Germany's economic burden on Western taxpayers.

At the *Potsdam* Conference (August 1945), Stalin, President Harry Truman,[9] and British Prime Minister Clement Attlee[10] agreed to divide Germany into zones of occupation reflecting the location of the conquering armies,[11] but to administer the country as one economic unit. Berlin, located well within the Soviet zone, was to serve

---

[7]When Stalin tried to exert control over the Yugoslavs, Tito broke with Moscow in 1948, and Yugoslavia became the first "national" communist society.

[8]The French and others in Western Europe who had suffered at the hands of the Nazis were especially disturbed about Germany, and the Americans and British supported the formation of the Brussels Pact in 1948 to meet these fears. This pact was the precursor of NATO.

[9]Franklin Roosevelt had died suddenly from a stroke in April. Truman saw much less need than Roosevelt to maintain unity among the wartime allies and was determined to stand up to the Russians.

[10]Winston Churchill and his Conservative Party were voted out of office while the conference was under way, and he was replaced by his Labour foe, Clement Attlee.

[11]At U.S. urging, the French were later granted a zone of occupation (carved from the U.S. zone), even though France had only a small role in liberating Europe.

as headquarters for the Big Four. This agreement quickly broke down as the Soviets sought large reparations from the Germans, and the Americans and British tried to reinvigorate the moribund German economy.

This contest, along with a growing communist insurgency in Greece, were the first acts in the Cold War drama and triggered, by early 1947, a new U.S. policy toward the Soviet Union—containment.[12] This policy, transformed into a global doctrine by President Truman in a dramatic speech before the U.S. Congress, was to assist "free peoples" everywhere who "must choose between alternative ways of life," one "based upon the will of the majority" and the other "based upon the will of the minority forcibly imposed upon the majority." The president's announcement of the "Truman Doctrine" and his request for economic assistance to aid tottering governments in Greece and Turkey was closer than any other single act to an official declaration of Cold War.[13]

With this declaration, the division in Europe deepened. The United States initiated the Marshall Plan to help Western Europeans recover economically and thereby resist the attraction of communism. The former World War II allies established separate West and East German governments in the areas they occupied. In 1949, the North Atlantic Treaty Organization (NATO) was established to combat potential Soviet expansionism. Other steps in partitioning Europe included the beginning of West European economic integration and establishing the Warsaw Treaty Organization (WTO) among the Soviet Union and its East European allies in 1955.

With the division of Europe complete, Americans and Russians continued to confront each other warily. And, even as armies and armaments grew, the two sides came to understand that direct military engagement would be mutually suicidal and that neither could dislodge the other from its sphere of interest.[14] Appreciating the risks of escalating conflict—that a relatively minor incident might get out of hand—Russians and Americans continued to threaten each other across the line separating them but each resisted the temptation to meddle in the other's sphere of influence.

Features of the Old World

What were the outstanding features of this pre-1991 *old world? First, the Cold War subsumed most other issues, and the game of global politics was played according to the rules set by East–West confrontation.* With stalemate in Europe, the Cold War spread into Asia,

---

[12]See Chapter 12, pp. 408–409.

[13]For the East, the equivalent took place in September 1947 with establishment of the Cominform by representatives of the Soviet, East European, French, and Italian communist parties to act on behalf of the international communist movement in the struggle against "imperialism."

[14]The major *anomaly* was Berlin, east of the main East-West line of demarcation. The Soviet Union and the United States experienced repeated crises (1948, 1959, 1960, 1961) over the disputed city as the U.S.S.R. sought to use Berlin's vulnerability to bring pressure on the West and as the latter tried to ensure the integrity of West Berlin as an "outpost of freedom."

the Middle East, Africa, and the Caribbean and infected most other issues in global politics. Both Washington and Moscow saw the world almost entirely through the lens of this issue and questioned how this or that event might affect East–West relations and the relative power of the two sides.

Abortive alliance groups such as SEATO (Southeast Asia Treaty Organization) and the Baghdad Pact (later called CENTO) unsuccessfully tried to extend containment into Southeast and Central Asia respectively. The critical postwar conflicts in Korea and Vietnam pitted the United States and its clients against Soviet clients and were the bloodiest U.S. efforts to restrain "communist expansion." Regional and local strategies were largely designed to weaken the other superpower.

When one side backed a party to a local crisis, the other supported that party's adversary. If a local leader declared himself Marxist (whatever that might mean in the local context), Moscow would rush to his side; and, if he declared himself anti-Marxist or anti-Soviet, he could depend on U.S. aid. In Asia, Stalin backed Mao Tse-tung and the communists after 1945, ensuring U.S. assistance to Chiang Kai-shek and the Kuomintang. Quarrels between allies could lead to shifts in alignments. Starting in the 1960s, the Sino-Soviet rift began a thaw in Sino-American relations. In the Middle East, Soviet leaders after 1955 vigorously wooed Egypt, first under Abdel Gamal Nasser and then Anwar Sadat, but in 1972 Sadat expelled the Russians and the United States became Egypt's main benefactor. A similar game of musical chairs took place in sub-Saharan Africa. Prior to the overthrow of Emperor Haile Selassie in Ethiopia in 1974, Washington supported the Ethiopians in their quarrel with Soviet-supported Somalia and secessionist rebels in Eritrea. After the emperor was overthrown and a revolutionary Ethiopian government sought Soviet assistance, the United States began to assist the Somalis.[15] Such behavior was frequent.

Second, leaders on both sides believed the adversary was somehow responsible for all their woes and problems. Each side believed the other was at the center of a planned conspiracy and, like a giant puppeteer, could pull strings all over the world and manipulate events. United States leaders assumed that anyone who resisted U.S. policies—at home or abroad—were part of a "communist conspiracy." Setbacks for U.S. policy, such as the "fall of China" to Mao in 1949 or the Soviet Union's exploding a nuclear weapon in the same year, had to be the result of "treason." Led by a previously little-known senator from Wisconsin, Joseph McCarthy, this belief led to witch hunts in the early 1950s against Americans in government and outside who might be engaged in "un-American" activities.

Belief in the enemy's responsibility (and apparent omnipotence) routinely led to decisions based on dubious assumptions. President Truman decided that America should intervene in Korea in June 1950 because he believed that North Koreans were

---

[15]The civil war that erupted in Somalia after General Muhammed Siad Barre's overthrow in January 1991 was fought with the vast stores of modern weapons left behind by the competing superpowers.

puppets of Moscow and that their attack on the South was an effort to test U.S. resolve; if unanswered, the next step would be invasion of Western Europe. In the 1980s, President Ronald Reagan spoke as though terrorism directed at Americans and American interests by radical groups and governments around the world originated in Moscow.[16] Such beliefs made it difficult for leaders on either side to respond appropriately to challenges. Instability caused by nationalism, poverty, or ethnic rivalries was often misperceived as intentionally inspired by Americans or Soviets.

A *third feature of this old world was a perception that a gain for one side or its sympathizers was equivalent to a loss for the other*. The world was perceived to be *bipolar* (divided into two blocs), and East and West were engaged in a *zero-sum game* (a loss by one side is equaled by the other's gain). United States and Soviet leaders were prepared to become involved in situations in which their only interest was to harm the adversary and from which it was difficult to extricate themselves because admitting defeat might give heart to the enemy.

America's commitment to maintaining a client government in South Vietnam dramatically increased with passage by Congress in 1964 of the Gulf of Tonkin Resolution.[17] That act partly resulted from President Lyndon B. Johnson's belief that the communists must learn that "wars of national liberation" did not pay. A series of American presidents, including Dwight D. Eisenhower, John F. Kennedy, and Johnson, failed to recognize the power of Vietnamese nationalism and, more important, failed to realize that nationalism was as much an enemy of the Soviet Union as of the United States. The Soviet invasion of Afghanistan in 1979 and the decade of struggle that ensued was compelling evidence that Soviet leaders wore the same blinders.

Just as American leaders translated the fall of the "friendly" military government in Saigon as a gain for the Soviet Union, so Soviet leaders viewed the overthrow of an Afghan Marxist leader in the late 1970s as a triumph for Western capitalists. Viewing the world through Cold-War lenses, Soviet leaders believed their only choice was to intervene in order to prevent an American gain. That intervention led to a protracted civil war in Afghanistan in the 1980s and ultimately a humiliating defeat for the U.S.S.R. The parallels with American action in Vietnam are striking; leaders on both sides were victims of a perception of reality that made a dangerous world still more dangerous.

A *fourth feature of this old world was that security was strictly defined in military terms*. Immediately after World War II, the U.S. military establishment was reduced, but the Cold War reversed this trend. The major impetus militarizing the Cold War was the Korean War. The North Korean invasion of the South on June 25, 1950, was a shock

---

[16]The odd mix of assumption and fact that led to such conclusions is illustrated in Claire Sterling, *The Terror Network: The Secret War of International Terrorism* (New York: Holt, Rinehart and Winston, 1981).

[17]American troops had been in Vietnam since 1961, but alleged attacks by small North Vietnamese vessels on American aircraft carriers in the Gulf of Tonkin provided an excuse for a major buildup of U.S. military power in Southeast Asia.

to Americans. United States leaders believed the invasion was the first step in worldwide Soviet military expansion, and they argued that failure to resist would whet the appetite of a dictator as had the effort in the 1930s to appease Hitler. Unwittingly, the North Koreans provided legitimacy for a rapid American rearmament that had been recommended in a secret study by the Truman administration.[18]

Even after the Korean War, military expenditures remained high, and the United States encouraged militarizing the NATO alliance and rearming Europe. Originally, NATO had been a political alliance, in which the United States provided its allies with a unilateral guarantee based on American possession of atomic weapons. The panic caused by the Korean invasion changed all that. To deter conventional war, conventional forces, it was believed, were necessary. On this assumption U.S. troops were sent back to Europe and America's European allies (including West Germany) rapidly rearmed, making NATO the most formidable peacetime military alliance in history.

A final step in militarizing the Cold War took place after the U.S.S.R. became the first to launch a space satellite and an intercontinental missile that could deliver nuclear warheads. Americans, believing they were falling behind the Russians, feverishly began to compete in developing nuclear weapons and increasingly sophisticated delivery systems. An unprecedented arms race ensued. Each side, seeking a technological breakthrough, devoted more and more resources to stockpiling and improving weapons of mass destruction.[19] The climax of this race was reached with President Reagan's idealistic fervor for the strategic defense initiative (SDI) or Star Wars, which at vast cost would prevent Soviet missiles from reaching American cities. Efforts to slow the arms race were repeatedly stymied by mutual fear and suspicion.

As the features of the Cold War era have faded, we can dimly see the outlines of a *new world* of global politics. Whether this world will be better or more peaceful is not clear. Certainly it will seem unsettling to those accustomed to the old. And the intellectual tools that served us well in the old world need to be revised to understand the new one.

The New World

As the old world comes to an end, different global participants (actors) and different global preoccupations (issues) that do not fit the old mold will come to the fore. Overwhelming dominance of global affairs by the two superpowers has ended. The Soviet Union has collapsed, and the United States, still a major player, cannot command its former massive influence. The extent of American decline is debated, but the United

---

[18] An April 1950 classified report, prepared by Truman's advisers and called NSC-68, had proposed a dramatic military buildup to control the U.S.S.R. threat.

[19] The exploration of space, ostensibly a peaceful pursuit by the two superpowers, has constantly been driven by military exigencies.

States no longer enjoys global preeminence, especially in the economic realm. Germany and Japan have risen from the ashes of defeat and occupation at the end of World War II and are pivotal in global economic and political life.

States are not the only major actors. Regional organizations, like the European Community (EC), the Association of South East Asian Nations (ASEAN), and such new regional trading pacts as the proposed North American Free Trade Agreement (among the United States, Canada, and Mexico), are leading participants in global affairs as well. Global intergovernmental organizations are also in a position to play a new role in world affairs. The United Nations as a peacekeeping and collective-security instrument has been reinvigorated by its role in the 1990–1991 Persian Gulf crisis. Further, with consensus growing among permanent members of the Security Council on some vital issues, this organization's influence has been enhanced. Global economic organizations like the International Monetary Fund (IMF) and the World Bank (IBRD), are also in a position to assume larger responsibilities in world affairs. And finally, some nongovernmental groups, from Amnesty International, General Motors, and Sony to the Palestine Liberation Organization, are participating in global politics as never before.

Just as the cast of *global actors* is changing, so too is the range of *global issues*. Global politics has been moving away from overriding preoccupation with military security and that departure is likely to accelerate during the next decade. New issues and old ones dormant during recent decades are moving to center stage. Economic and environmental questions in particular are demanding and receiving greater attention from actors everywhere.

The state of the global economy and the role played by actors and groups of actors in that economy are leading issues for the 1990s. Global recession and economic development are fundamental and include efforts to integrate Western Europe's economies more fully, create market systems in the former communist areas of Central and Eastern Europe and the Soviet Union, stimulate more growth and development in industrial societies, and face continuing poverty in Asia, Latin America, and Africa. Such issues are as likely to shape world politics in the near future as traditional political and military interests.

The new world is also recognizing that it must preserve planet earth. Environmental questions are now challenging political–military rivalries for a place on the global agenda. These issues were dramatically brought to the world's attention by the exploding nuclear reactor at Chernobyl in the former Soviet Union in 1986, the conflict in Brazil between developers and environmentalists over cutting the rainforests late in the 1980s, and the U.N. summit on the environment and economic development (the Rio Summit) in 1992.

The collapse of communism in Eastern Europe also brought to light the environmental disaster that befell the region under communist rule. Communist regimes set out to industrialize their societies as quickly and inexpensively as possible, and the results were devastating. Across East Germany, Czechoslovakia, and Poland lie "barren plateaus . . . with the stumps and skeletons of pine trees. Under the snow lie thousands of acres of poisoned ground, where for centuries thick forests had grown."[20] Air and groundwater grow toxic as acid rain is produced by industries without effective scrubbers burning lignite, a highly sulfurous coal. The air is also laden with poisonous nitrogen oxide and heavy metals like lead, mercury, and zinc that are linked to cancer in humans. Such environmental tampering has produced a chain reaction. The forests now gone; the birds that used to eat mice have disappeared, exploding mouse populations. In turn, the mice consume tree seedlings and prevent reforestation. Such conditions also have created serious health problems.[21] In Hungary, as many as 10 percent of the deaths are believed to be directly related to pollution, and clinics have set up inhalitoriums, small booths in which individuals with lung problems can breathe clean air. In the former East Germany, air pollution appears to be related to abnormal levels of aggression and reduced life expectancy. One Hungarian woman said, "In this part of the world, nobody takes breathing for granted."[22]

These issues, too, are a legacy of the old world that require attention in the new world of the late 1990s and beyond.

Features of the New World

Environmental degradation in Eastern Europe is one of many issues rising to the top of the global agenda. *One feature of these issues is that no one government can cope with them.* "With prevailing winds blowing east, Czechs blame East Germans for half their pollution and Poles blame both neighbors for as much. Poland's fallout is also felt in the Ukraine and in Sweden."[23] When the Chernobyl nuclear power plant caught fire and started to release nuclear debris into the atmosphere in April 1986, it poisoned land, animals, and crops as far away as Ireland. To reduce the threat to health, cattle and sheep were slaughtered and milk was dumped throughout Europe. The nomadic Laplanders in Scandinavia who depend on herds of reindeer for survival, were among the most severely affected. The grass upon which the reindeer forage was made toxic, so that their owners could not consume the animals and their milk. Indeed, the global effects of this disaster — including higher rates of cancer in Europe — will not be known for decades.

No one government can cope with such issues because *they involve values that must be shared and made available to everyone if they are to be enjoyed by anyone.* In other words, it is difficult for individual actors to prosper at the expense of others. In earlier centuries,

[20]Marlise Simons, "Pollution's Toll in Eastern Europe: Stumps Where Great Trees Once Grew," *The New York Times* March 19, 1990, p. A9.

[21]Mark M. Nelson, "Darkness at Noon: As Shroud of Secrecy Lifts in East Europe, Smog Shroud Emerges," *The Wall Street Journal*, pp. A1, A13.

[22]Cited in Nelson, p. A1.

[23]Marlise Simons, "Pollution's Toll," p. A9.

nomadic tribes could enrich themselves by stealing cattle and other goods from each other, and states could prosper by seizing each other's territory. By contrast, many of today's sources of prosperity and welfare cannot be acquired in such a predatory manner. Each society prospers only when other societies are able to buy its products, and the economic health of any actor depends heavily on the health of the global economic system as a whole. This was brought home shortly after the 1973 Arab–Israeli war when the Organization of Arab Petroleum Exporting Countries (AOPEC) imposed an oil embargo against the United States and the Netherlands and reduced deliveries to other nations because they supported Israel. This action dramatically forced up the price of petroleum in 1973–1974. A similar shock came at the end of the decade when oil prices soared to more than $30 a barrel, ten to fifteen times the price at the beginning of the 1970s.

Although higher prices initially increased wealth in oil-producing states, the price increases had four additional effects. Economic *stagflation* (combined inflation and recession) reduced Western purchases of all goods (including petroleum), stimulated increased oil production and exploration around the world, encouraged energy conservation and the search for petroleum substitutes, and reduced the value of the U.S. dollar (the currency widely used to purchase petroleum). The combined global economic slowdown and fall in the dollar meant that AOPEC began to suffer the consequences of the policy it had initiated. Matters grew even worse for AOPEC when the world market was glutted with oil in the 1980s.

This example also illustrates that *issues are increasingly placing actors in situations in which they win or lose jointly.* Instead of zero-sum situations, these are *positive-* and *negative-sum games* in which all players win or lose together. In international economics, individual actors tend to enjoy prosperity or suffer pain jointly, and rarely are able to profit at each other's expense.[24] This is also the case in the more traditional security matters. The U.S. and Soviet governments saw more clearly after their traumatic head-to-head confrontation in the Cuban missile crisis in 1962 that nuclear war between them would lead to mutual annihilation; both would lose. As we shall see in Chapter 6, this recognition led first to "rules of interaction" between the superpowers and, more recently, contributed to the end of the Cold War as a whole.

As leaders recognize that they and their peoples share the same fates as others, they also slowly redefine *security* and the ways in which it can be secured. The traditional view emphasized safeguarding the state and its citizens from direct military threat. As a consequence, governments routinely channeled enormous resources into building their

---

[24]This dependence is more evident in relations among wealthy societies. The connection also applies, however, to relations among more and less developed societies. If the less developed prosper, they can purchase more from highly developed societies. The same is true for the highly developed states toward the less developed, though not equally so, because the demand and price of primary commodities on which many poor countries depend are not elastic. Thus, the highly developed countries may end up purchasing less from the less developed.

own military establishment, regarded as the most important source of influence in world politics. Military threats, such as fear of a North Korean invasion of the South and the Indian threat to Pakistan, still strongly influence government calculations, and enormous resources are poured into building military power; but we also recognize nonmilitary threats to security and appreciate the limitations on military force. Threats to the environment such as global warming, scarce resources because of overpopulation, rapid spread of diseases like AIDS (acquired immune deficiency syndrome), proliferating illicit drugs, and enmities caused by racial and economic inequalities are threats to security—even survival—against which military force can provide little protection.

Another way of looking at this change is to consider nuclear weapons. As we shall see in Chapter 8, nuclear weapons dramatically changed the world, providing a few governments with the means to incinerate each other almost instantaneously. It is now apparent, though, that the influence such weapons provide those who possess them is less than had been believed. Nuclear weapons clearly can be used effectively for only one purpose—to deter an adversary from using such weapons first. Nuclear weapons probably are not even of much use in fighting conventional conflicts, as the United States discovered to its frustration in Korea and Vietnam. Finally, it appears that, if a nuclear war were ever fought, such unintended results as dust particles in the atmosphere might bring about an unprecedented environmental disaster.[25]

Our new world also finds *new or reawakened local and regional quarrels that had been suppressed during the Cold War.* As we recognize more and more global issues that entail widespread cooperation, it is paradoxical that the Cold War's end reveals a host of bitter local contests and historical hatreds formerly hidden. Many of these grow out of ancient national and ethnic animosities, as in Central and Eastern Europe. As long as the Soviet Union controlled its satellites, quarrels that might siphon resources away from the Cold War confrontation were not permitted to surface. As Soviet authority receded, bitter local enmities came back to life. The area known as Transylvania, for example, inhabited by both Romanians and Hungarians, has long caused contention between the two countries and is doing so once again.

Indeed, from Germany to the Balkans, hostility is again breaking loose among the mosaic of ethnic minorities which live cheek-to-jowl. The enmities are the same which helped start World War I in 1914 and which Hitler manipulated to produce tensions in the years leading up to World War II in 1939. These kinds of differences will continue to be one of the great threats to world peace as we approach 2000.

A final feature of this new world is the decline of some states and groups as global leaders and the rise of new ones. The Soviet Union's collapse and Russia's uncertain role in the new global hierarchy are the best example of this transformation. As we saw, the Soviet government and the Communist Party of the Soviet Union, though they controlled great military force, were unable to survive. The United States remains a military and

---

[25]See Carl Sagan, "Nuclear Winter and Climatic Catastrophe: Some Policy Implications," *Foreign Affairs* 62:2 (Winter 1983/84). pp. 257–292.

economic superpower, but exercises less global clout than it did in the years after World War II. More important, overall U.S. ability to control global events continues to decline. Economically, Japan, Germany, and a number of smaller countries known as NICs *(newly industrializing countries)* — South Korea, Singapore, and Taiwan — are growing in power. If Western Europe forges a closer economic and political relationship, it will rival in importance any other global economic entity.

The Economic Community (EC) is a reminder that many major participants or actors in this new world are not states or their surrogates. In economics, giant transnational corporations and banks control more assets than many countries and determine the prosperity of many societies. In some issues, international civil servants, private nonprofit organizations, and even secretive terrorist groups wield disproportionate influence. For instance, the World Bank, an international organization affiliated with the United Nations, works with a network of public and private bureaucrats to facilitate efforts to aid countries and people seeking to improve their economic condition.

At the Cusp of Old and New Worlds: The Gulf War

With improved East–West relations and the Cold War over, former President George Bush enthusiastically spoke of the coming *new world order*. Within months, however, the United States was at war with Iraq over Saddam Hussein's invasion of Kuwait, a contest suspiciously like the old world of force and violence. In fact, the Iraqi issue may be something of a transition. It has characteristics that we associate with the old world but also provides clues to the new world that is beginning to unfold.

On the one hand, the Iraqi invasion appeared to mirror traditional world politics in a number of ways. First, Iraq used *force* to annex Kuwait and the U.S.-led coalition used force to undo that annexation. An incentive behind opposition to Saddam may have been the traditional sense that an aggressor was amassing great power and threatening a regional balance of power. The allied coalition opposed to Iraq was determined that the Middle East balance of power would not be upset and that the violation of state sovereignty would be reversed. Finally, the major actors in the drama were the governments of states. In all, twenty-eight allied states took the field against Saddam Hussein. At first blush, then, the issue appeared to be one of *power politics*, and the absence of central authority in global politics produced a bloody conflict among rivals for power in the Middle East.

On the other hand, aspects of the Kuwait issue reflect a departure from the international system of the previous four decades. First, in this dispute superpower politics were muted. Although Iraq had been a close ally of the Soviet Union and had received enormous amounts of Soviet military assistance, by late 1990 and early 1991, the Soviet Union was on the verge of collapse, and Soviet leaders were disenchanted with their former client. Warming U.S.-Soviet relations meant that Baghdad could no longer depend on its patron for protection.

Second, this dramatic shift in Soviet–Iraqi relations had another effect: the United Nations could now respond to Iraqi aggression in a manner intended by its founders yet almost unprecedented since its establishment. Because the Soviet Union was no longer inclined to veto actions by the United Nations, that country proved to be a helpful, if cautious, partner of the United States in steering resolutions through that organization demanding Iraq's withdrawal from Kuwait. That cooperation ultimately led to a U.N. resolution late in November 1990 calling on allied forces to use force against Iraq.

Third, behind the response to Iraqi aggression lay recognition of a significant feature in contemporary global politics — *economic interdependence*. Saddam Hussein's control of Kuwait not only threatened the territorial and political integrity of neighboring states, but Iraq also appeared about to gain a stranglehold on the global economy. As we shall see in Chapter 10, that economy is characterized by a high level of *interdependence* and every individual's prosperity is to some extent linked to others' well-being. Were one leader or state in a position to determine oil production and therefore oil prices, it might prove possible to bully the rest of the world to carry out a political agenda.[26] Arrangements governing oil production and pricing, already under stress from different sources, would be in danger of collapse. Rapid change in oil prices could throw the world economy into chaos. The cost of manufactured goods and of agricultural products[27] depends on energy prices. Recognizing this face of the crisis, the members of the allied coalition were determined to end this threat to the stability of the global economic system.

Saddam Hussein himself appreciated some of the new global interdependencies when he caused a giant oil spill to befoul the Persian Gulf in January 1991. Whatever his military purpose in this act (perhaps to shut down desalinization plants in Saudi Arabia that provided fresh water to coalition forces as well as Saudi citizens), he must have known that such *eco-terrorism* would frighten the world and conjure up visions of environmental catastrophes to come. In effect, Saddam said "I, too, recognize the fragility of the global environment and the manner in which it is linked to the future survival of all of us; and, if you continue this war against me, I can do harm to the world as a whole."

A fourth feature of the new world was the extent to which the traditionally bifurcated domestic and international spheres of political life were united during the Iraqi crisis. In Chapter 11 we evoke the *Janus face of politics* — the idea that foreign

[26]Such a scenario recognizes that manipulation of prices would prove costly to the bully as well as to its victims but assumes that the bully is prepared to accept those costs to achieve a political agenda.

[27]Much of the world's agriculture depends on petroleum-based fertilizers. Modern agricultural techniques also rely on combines and other vehicles that consume large amounts of oil. As a consequence, agricultural societies in Africa and Asia are as sensitive to shifts in oil prices as are regions that have large manufacturing economies.

policy is produced by forces within and outside a country—an aspect that was evident throughout the crisis.[28] In the United States, attitudes toward the conflict were shaped by an economic recession, memories of the Vietnam quagmire, and calculations of partisan political gain and loss. Conventional wisdom about foreign policy failed: politics did *not* stop at the water's edge. Among the domestic groups that became involved were defense contractors,[29] oil corporations, military reservists, peace activists, and others who recognized their interests in events taking place thousands of miles away. That the issue was domestically sensitive was reflected in the importance attached to the positive vote by both houses of Congress authorizing the president to use military force. Those votes were taken shortly before the United States resorted to force against Iraq and were regarded as something of a domestic equivalent of the U.N. authorization.

Finally, as implied, the issue mobilized a panoply of *nongovernmental actors*. Among those directly or indirectly involved were private arms suppliers and defense industries—"merchants of death"—in Germany, France, Sweden, and elsewhere who had provided Iraq with information and material necessary for producing chemical, biological, and even nuclear weapons. A number of terrorist groups were sheltered by the Iraqi dictator and offered their services to him. Transnational corporations, especially oil firms like Aramco and Exxon, saw their profits soar as the price of crude oil jumped after Iraq occupied Kuwait. The International Red Cross encouraged both sides to observe international law, including humane treatment of prisoners of war. The role of such groups was not trivial.

The Gulf War illustrates that we may be in a transition in global politics. Some of the elements of the old world—force, the role of states, balance of power—continued. Yet, some of the elements of the new world—great-power cooperation, global interdependence, and the enhanced role of nonstate actors—are revealed. We aim to explain this transition, describing where global politics has been and where it is going.

Plan for The Global Puzzle

The four parts in *The Global Puzzle* are designed to display the changes that have swept world politics in recent years. These parts also bring into sharp relief the changes we need to make in our way of looking at and thinking about world affairs. Part I is a review and critique of traditional concepts and theories in the study of global politics and offers an alternative lens through which to view events. Part II consists of five chapters that extend our conceptual lenses of global politics by focusing on the balance between

[28]Janus was the Roman god of beginnings and of the rising and setting of the sun and was depicted with two faces looking in opposite directions.

[29]The apparent success of some U.S. high-tech weapons, such as the Patriot missile, rapidly enhanced the stock of corporations like Raytheon that built them. The use of such weapons in the war renewed calls for investment in the moribund Star Wars program and for protecting the defense budget from further cuts.

cooperative and conflictual world behavior. Traditional theorists have viewed international politics as an arena for competition and conflict. For the most part, they understate the social and cooperative elements and ignore the communitarian fabric that binds actors even without central authority. Part III consists of four chapters that flesh out the ideas about global politics presented in Part II. They illustrate these ideas in the context of historical and contemporary global issues—onset and decline of the Cold War, development and consequences of economic competition among the United States, Japan, and Europe, and the Middle East political cauldron. The final section, Part IV, consists of three chapters in which we explore environmental and human-rights issues that increasingly challenge global politics and human survival as we approach the twenty-first century. The first of these chapters addresses issues that challenge all human beings, whatever their nationality or partisan preferences. In the second we discuss issues in which nation-states are actually pitted against their own citizens. We conclude this final part by thinking briefly about prospects for the future and projecting alternative scenarios of global politics at the birth of the twenty-first century. With this brief glimpse at the old and new worlds of global politics, let us raise the curtain.

Key Terms

evil empire
Cold War
old world
proxies
economic socialism
political democracy
market capitalism
fascism
bipolar
zero-sum game
new world
global actors
global issues
stagflation
positive sum games
negative sum games
newly industrializing countries

power politics
economic interdependence
interdependence
eco-terrorism
the Janus face of politics
nongovernmental actors
new world order
window of vulnerability
Yalta
Potsdam
anomaly
security
North Atlantic Treaty Organization
    (NATO)
Warsaw Treaty Organization
    (WTO)

PART ONE

Setting the Stage

Part I of The Global Puzzle is a review and critique of concepts in the study of global politics and offers an alternative lens through which to view world affairs. These chapters provide the building blocks for understanding a world in flux. We open by briefly examining the historical evolution of global politics and then evaluate several concepts—political systems, power, actors, and issues—on which we can build an understanding of what is happening in the world around us.

Chapter 1 demonstrates how we need to know the past if we are to understand the present and the future. It provides a window onto several important and unique political systems that preceded the territorial state system in seventeenth- and eighteenth-century Europe. This chapter emphasizes how recent Western experience is only a small portion of global political relations over human history.

In Chapter 2 we address the most encompassing level of analysis—the global political system—and suggest how to make sense of global politics by looking at the attributes of whole systems, especially the distribution of resources and attitudes. Global systems have traditionally emphasized how tangible resources determine behavior. We suggest that the subjective dimension of political life, though elusive, is critical and insufficiently attended to in most discussions.

In Chapter 3, we examine how the state system evolved from the Treaty of Westphalia in 1648, and how this historical system shaped the views of scholars and practitioners who adopt a traditional power-politics approach to global politics. Here, we raise questions about the contemporary and historical utility of this Eurocentric model with its pronounced emphasis on states as actors and conflict among them.

Chapters 4 and 5 elaborate a nonrealist lens through which to interpret contemporary global politics. They reveal the world to be more complex and multifaceted than the traditional model suggests. Both the multiplicity of actors and issues and the relationship among them form the elements upon which to build further analysis of global politics.

CHAPTER ONE

The Richness
of Historical Experience

In a moment of contemplating history, the American naturalist Henry David Thoreau observed, "To the philosopher, all news is gossip." Deluged as we are with a flood of startling news about world developments, we are prone to forget that those events have their origin in the past, a past sometimes only dimly recalled. The present is only a bridge between past and future, and there is no future without a past. And yet, our propensity is to assume that the world as we see it at any moment has always existed and will continue to do so.

Why Study History?

Generations of students are accustomed to thinking of Soviet-American hostility as a paramount and permanent feature in world politics. With that as context, we see that many scholars and practitioners also feel the military power wielded by a few governments is the overriding factor in world politics and the key to explaining and predicting behavior. The story of world politics has rarely had so simple a plot; mostly it has not been limited to a few powerful states engaged in life-and-death struggle, and the world after the Cold War is likely to be even more complex.

Indeed, it has taken a series of extraordinary events at the end of the twentieth century to remind us that the global arena is always in flux: Marxism-Leninism collapsed in Eastern Europe, the Communist Party surrendering its monopoly of power in the Soviet Union, Germany reunified, reconciliation of whites and blacks in South Africa, "democracy" an explosively powerful symbol for peoples all over the world, and the breakdown of order in several states. Global politics reflects continuity as well as change, however. Many of these

The end of the Cold War was accompanied by the demise of authoritarian regimes in the East bloc and elsewhere and an explosion of democratic and nationalist demands around the world.

events have earlier parallels, recognition of which helps us interpret and respond to them. Many of these historical roots grew in very different cultural and social milieus, making it imperative that we understand these cultures and societies if we hope to respond wisely to the events they have produced. If we apply recent Western experience parochially to make sense of the world around us, we are doomed to misunderstand and react inappropriately to events.

We need to appreciate Chinese culture and politics, for example, to understand and explain that country's defensive reaction to the critical international response to the massacre of prodemocratic demonstrators in Beijing's Tiananmen Square in June 1989. Similarly, acquaintance with the national and religious cleavages that have divided Europe for centuries—Germans versus French, Catholics versus Protestants—helps make sense of the difficulties Europeans experience in achieving closer unity today. In the same way, the savage conflict between Serbians and Muslim Bosnians makes sense only when we are aware of ancient rivalries between Turkey's Ottoman Empire and the states forming in seventeenth- and eighteenth-century Europe. Whether we are preoccupied by conflict in Northern Ireland—its roots dating back at least as far as King Henry VIII's efforts to pacify Ireland in the sixteenth century—or communal violence in India—its roots in the sixteenth-century Mogul conquest of that country—contemporary problems make little sense without a historical and cultural context. Past social arrangements and global politics directly affect contemporary politics.

Let us briefly turn to several historically unique systems and explore how world politics was conducted then. We shall get a sense for the varied actors and issues that have occupied center stage in global politics as well as watershed events that continue to influence the world. We start by examining how competition and interaction among the small Greek city-states in the fifth century B.C. illuminate interaction in global politics today. Then we turn to a very different system: the highly centralized Chinese Empire. We focus next on the development and expansion of medieval Muslim society and examine how the clash between decentralization and centralization in that context continues to echo in the modern Middle East.

In the second half of the chapter we consider how global politics evolved in Europe, from the collapse of the Roman Empire, through the Middle Ages, to the emergence of modern states. Examining Europe's transformation from a centralized political system during the Roman Empire to a decentralized one in the Middle Ages, climaxing in competitive territorial states illuminates the impact the past on our thinking today and provides clues about evolving global politics. Although the European model of territorial states was only one form of international organization, it became especially significant because of Europe's outward expansion beginning late in the fifteenth century. "The global international society of today," declare Hedley Bull and Adam Watson, "is in large part the consequence of Europe's impact on the rest of the world over the last five centuries."[1]

Five Assumptions Critical to Understanding Global Politics

Before we set out to survey these historical settings, we list five assumptions necessary for understanding contemporary global politics and the vast changes taking place in the global system.

1. *During much of history, human beings have lived all but isolated from most of their fellow people.* Through much of history, isolated pockets of people interacted only with those living close by, in ignorance of others elsewhere on the globe. These pockets evolved their own cultures, religions, and political and moral beliefs, and inevitably felt superior to those who did not share their mores. The ancient Greeks, to whom subsequent Western civilization owes much, coined the word *barbarian* for those who did not speak their language because they considered them uncivilized.[2] The ancient Chinese had much the same attitude toward those who spoke other tongues and regarded their empire as the center of the universe.

[1]Hedley Bull and Adam Watson, Introduction, in Bull and Watson, eds., *The Expansion of International Society* (New York: Oxford University Press, 1984), p. 1.

[2]To Greek ears, non-Greek speakers sounded as though they were saying "bar-bar-bar."

Contact with foreigners was episodic, impeded by geography, primitive transportation, and vulnerability to unaccustomed diseases.[3] Most cultures were agrarian, tying inhabitants to the land. Few knew anything about the world beyond their immediate vicinity, and fewer cared. People in such *traditional societies* more easily accepted such natural catastrophes as drought, flood, famine, and disease than we do today. Progress or change had little influence in their lives. Only a few lived above the subsistence level.

When previously isolated cultures came in contact, the mixture frequently was explosive, as during the medieval crusades between Christians and Muslim Saracens. Most of the global interconnectedness that we take for granted was produced by European imperialism and colonialism, reinforced in recent decades by revolutions in transportation and communication. We cannot begin to appreciate and understand the misperceptions and suspicions of disparate peoples today without recognizing that they retain beliefs and customs inherited from earlier centuries and that they persist in believing that their ways are superior to all others.

Tensions between Shi'ite and Sunni Muslims, Jews and Arabs in the Middle East, Chinese and Malays in Southeast Asia, Christians and Muslims in Lebanon, Arabs and black Africans in the Sudan, Tamils and Sinhalese in Sri Lanka, and between many other groups are held over from collisions and conflicts in earlier centuries. So, too, is Japanese reluctance to buy foreign goods or accept immigrants and the Chinese sense of cultural superiority, characteristics that annoy, even infuriate Westerners. Despite rapid communications and transportation, many people remain isolated and rarely come in contact with foreigners, or do so fleetingly when foreigners arrive as tourists.

2. *The Western experience, though it helps us understand global politics, is not the only valid guide to world politics.* Bull and Watson write, "Europeans have never had any monopoly of knowledge or experience of international relations."[4] The traditional power-politics model of global politics, in which sovereign states are the principal actors and military issues dominate, derives from European historical experience. Elements of that model, especially those dealing with power, are also found in writings by non-Western philosophers and theorists,[5] but the *state-centric* bias of our thinking about world politics comes mainly from European history and philosophy. That is, the idea of world politics as the study of interactions among centralized *territorial states* is especially European. However well this tradition served us in the past, it is now less relevant to understanding global politics after the Cold War.

Scholars and practitioners also typically point to examples and our leaders recite "lessons" of world politics largely drawn from Western experience. Even our understanding of ethics and morality in politics is adduced from the Judeo-Christian tradition

---

[3]See, for example, William H. McNeill, *Plagues and People* (New York: Anchor Books, 1976).

[4]Bull and Watson, Introduction, p. 1.

[5]See especially, Chanakya Kautilya, the fourth-century B.C. Indian Brahman who wrote the *Arthashastra*, outlining strategies for leaders that closely resemble balance-of-power politics, and the Chinese legalist philosophers of the same period. The importance of force in early China is reflected in Sun-tzu, *The Art of Warfare*, trans. by Roger Ames (New York: Ballantine Books, 1993).

in the West. Our ignorance of other cultures and traditions makes this bias inevitable, but it also heightens the likelihood of misunderstanding when Westerners come in contact with non-Westerners. Until recently, the insights non-Western history might provide were often ignored. Only in the past decade have American schools and colleges routinely introduced us to non-Western ideas, history, and literature. Our leaders have often seen the world through *Eurocentric* eyes.

Western colonialism throughout Africa, Asia, and Latin America and Western dominance of global economics and politics during the nineteenth and twentieth centuries have led us to assume that Western mores and ideas are inherently better than those of other societies and regions. Ideas like economic and political development have too often meant becoming more like "us in the West." Yet, it is increasingly clear that blind emulation of economic, political, and social policies that worked in the West perhaps a hundred years ago may be inappropriate for societies elsewhere confronting challenges that eighteenth- and nineteenth-century Europeans and Americans could hardly have imagined. Indeed, the *modern state* consisting of a government's centralized and exclusive control over a defined population in a clearly defined territory, is a European invention, and efforts to impose this form of political organization on areas like Africa, with competing tribal and ethnic traditions, have sometimes been disastrous. When the colonial powers imposed state structures on peoples with different tribal loyalties they have often contributed to authoritarian rule and periodic civil strife. The bloody struggles among groups like the Hutu and Tutsi in Burundi; the Burman, Karen, and Shan in Burma; the Ibo, Yoruba, and Hausa in Nigeria, and others illustrate the consequences of trying to force diverse *tribes* and ethnic groups into Western-style state boxes.

3. *Human beings have organized themselves into a rich variety of groups other than territorial states.* As the tribal experience suggests, the territorial state with an elaborate bureaucracy is only one of many political organizations. Indeed, the modern state is a relatively recent European invention. For a number of reasons, especially its capacity to mobilize large numbers of people with significant resources, the state has proved a durable participant in global affairs. Where it collided with other forms of organization in recent centuries, such as tribal groups in Africa and North America, it has triumphed.

The state is not, however, inherently superior to other forms of political organization. Other types of actors have also been effective and successful. Nomadic tribesmen—Arabs under the banner of Islam in the seventh century and Mongols in the twelfth century—swept across their worlds. One writer observes that the Arabs "conquered the civilized world from Spain to India, destroying one empire in the process and severely mutilating another, in some 50 years, while the Mongols destroyed states of every kind from eastern Europe to Burma, narrowly missing the conquest of Egypt in the west and Japan in the east, in less than a century."[6]

---

[6]Patricia Crone, "The Tribe and the State," in John A. Hall, ed., *States in History* (New York: Basil Blackwell, 1987), p. 71.

Although the state remains the dominant political organization in global politics, it is not the exclusive or even primary object of human loyalty in large parts of the world. If history is a guide, we cannot assume that the state *as we know it*—a clearly defined territory with central government control—will remain dominant in the future. Indeed, other global actors such as *transnational corporations* (General Motors or Exxon) federations of states (the North Atlantic Treaty Organization [NATO]), and even *supranational* organizations (the High Commission of the European Community) may well grow in prominence to cope with regional and global issues.

4. *Political organization, ideological fervor, economic vitality, and technological capability are major factors in explaining the waxing and waning of global influence.* History also reveals that a number of factors account for the epochal shifts that occur from time to time in global power centers.[7] Such shifts include decline of the classical Greek *city-states* and their absorption by Rome, expansion and subsequent division of Islam, expansion of the Chinese Empire south of the Han River, erosion of the Holy Roman Empire and medieval papacy, and emergence of U.S.–Soviet bipolarity after World War II.

Political organization is one factor in explaining these great shifts. European organization into states with efficient bureaucracies that could extract taxes from citizens and invest those funds in economic and technological growth was a large element in successful expansion into tribal America and Africa. *Ideologies*—deeply anchored sets of beliefs of individuals or groups that guide behavior—like those of Islam and Christianity, nationalism, or, more recently, capitalism and Marxism are another great factor in these shifts.

Finally, *economic vitality* and *technology* are critical in explaining major shifts in power centers. One leading historian argues that the decline of "great powers" can be traced to their being overtaken and surpassed by others in economic and industrial performance and that their decline is accompanied by overexpenditure on nonproductive military ventures and underinvestment at home.[8] Thus, competitive market economies took root in Western Europe comparatively early, a major reason Europeans were able to take advantage of and dramatically improve military technologies including gunpowder and cannon that had been invented elsewhere. Without comparable weapons, such non-Europeans as the Aztecs of Mexico and the Incas of Peru were unable to resist European imperialism. The recent collapse of communist regimes in Eastern Europe and the Soviet Union under faltering economies again bears witness to the power of economic factors.

5. *Important theories of global politics are rooted in historical conditions.* The way we think about the world around us is determined mainly by the real conditions we confront. In other words, political theories and philosophies—however abstract they seem—are *not* produced by dispassionate analysis of thinkers laboring in ivory towers.

---

[7]In contemporary theory, such centers of power are often called hegemons and their weakening is called the decline of hegemony.

[8]Paul Kennedy, *The Rise and Fall of the Great Powers* (New York: Random House, 1987).

Instead, they represent efforts by people actively working to change those conditions in a manner consonant with their preferences.

We can distinguish between two major branches of theory—*empirical* and *normative*. The first entails the search for knowledge by experiment and experience, and the second a search for that which is moral and right. A theory that stipulates the causes of war is empirical, and one addressing the goodness or badness of war is normative. Scientific knowledge is empirical, and scientists argue for maintaining the boundary between the two branches of theory. The study of politics is not the same as the study of physics, however, even though some political scientists wish to emulate the physicist's certainty and precision.[9] Although it is desirable to keep the empirical and normative aspects of problems as clearly separated as possible, political practitioners are so involved in the real world and are so interested in changing it that the boundary is sometimes difficult to sustain.[10]

Consider the great Florentine Renaissance writer Niccolò Machiavelli. Machiavelli is famous among scholars of global politics for his treatise *The Prince*. Dedicating the work to and writing it as practical advice for a statesman, he argues that, because conditions make it impossible for leaders to trust each other, it is necessary, even laudable, for them to act in ways that most of us would consider immoral. His analysis is regarded as an important contribution to the power-politics approach to global politics because of its insistence that preserving and promoting the state were and ought to be the overriding objectives of global actors. To this day, he is widely read by political practitioners.

Far from being a disinterested scientist and observer of human nature, Machiavelli was a deeply committed statesman and Italian patriot. At the same time, *The Prince* faithfully depicted how small Italian city-state politicians in the fifteenth and sixteenth centuries behaved and was a primer for a leader who might unite the country to cast out the French and Spaniards who had invaded it. "So now," he concludes, "left lifeless, Italy is waiting to see who can be the one to heal her wounds, put an end to the sacking of Lombardy, to extortion in the Kingdom and in Tuscany, and cleanse those sores which have been festering for so long."[11]

Few modern writers on world politics are so publicly passionate about their beliefs, but most are as deeply committed as Machiavelli. Their beliefs vary but we cannot understand their work unless we recognize those beliefs and ideals. Thus, those who study the causes of interstate war are simultaneously often scientists seeking truth and idealists trying to end the scourge they are studying. Inevitably, empirical theory is infused with normative values.

---

[9]See Klaus Knorr and James N. Rosenau, eds., *Contending Approaches to International Politics* (Princeton: Princeton University Press, 1969). For a reconsideration of these issues two decades later, see Ernst-Otto Czempiel and James N. Rosenau, eds., *Global Changes and Theoretical Challenges: Approaches to World Politics for the 1990s* (Lexington, Mass.: Lexington Books, 1989).

[10]See Yale H. Ferguson and Richard W. Mansbach, *The Elusive Quest: Theory and International Politics* (Columbia: University of South Carolina Press, 1988), pp. 32–48.

[11]Niccolò Machiavelli, *The Prince*, trans. by George Bull (Baltimore, Md.:Penguin Books, 1961), p. 134.

FIGURE 1.1

The Politics of Classical Greece

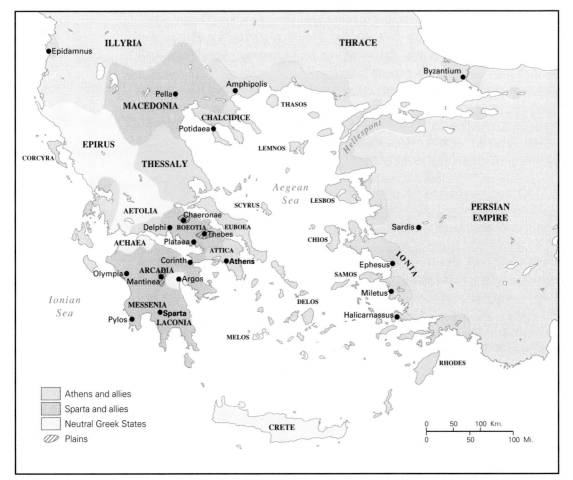

This map, which shows the alignment of states during the Peloponnesian War, vividly illustrates the large scale of the war and its divisive impact.

Systems of Classical Greece, Imperial China, and Theocratic Islam

Today's *global politics* owes much not only to modern Europe, in which the sovereign state was born, but to other systems that flourished in antiquity and in other regions. Those systems had their own cast of actors and their own issues, some of which have reappeared in contemporary global politics.

Politics in Classical Greece

The Greek city-states, which gave birth to much of Western culture and many of its political ideas, lay in and around the Aegean Archipelago, with additional settlements along the Mediterranean shore to the east in Asia Minor and to the west in Italy, Sicily, southern France, and northern Africa. One observer declares that they are important both because they "organized their external relations in very innovative and significant ways" and because they "exercised great influence on the European system, out of which the present system has developed; and for several centuries aspects of Greek practice served as models for the European society of states."[12]

Individual city-states were much smaller than modern states[13] and frequently were in conflict. Resources were widely distributed, although Athens and Sparta came to dominate the other city-states. Individual Greeks nevertheless felt a sense of community with each other that was reinforced by their tongue, their gods, their extensive trade, and their culture. Such rudimentary "international" institutions as the shrine to Apollo at Delphi and the Olympic Games further strengthened the sense of Greekness. Their perception of a common identity proved potent when the Persian Empire sought to conquer the Greeks between 490 and 478 B.C. For a brief time the city-states were able to unite and defeat the common enemy. This we–they perception was recognized in the conflict as one between Greeks from Europe and aliens from Asia. Successive efforts by the Persians to subdue Greece, culminating in an invasion led by Xerxes, were thrown back in the battles of Marathon (490 B.C.),[14] Salamis (480 B.C.), and Plataea (479 B.C.) by an alliance of Greek city-states.

Unfortunately, once the Persians had been repelled, the Greek city-states returned to their quarrelsome ways. Without the bond provided by a common enemy, too little remained to keep them together. If Greeks viewed themselves as united by blood and culture, they were divided by type of political system and territorial jealousies. The city-states also suffered divisions between rich and poor that each exploited. After defeating the Persians, Athenian influence grew, and an Athenian empire arose on the oars of a powerful navy. A countervailing alliance lead by Sparta, which possessed the leading army in Greece, was formed to limit Athenian influence. Other key actors included Corinth, a commercial rival of Athens, and Argos, long a rival of Sparta. The ensuing Peloponnesian War (431–404 B.C.) between the two alliances dragged on for almost three decades. It nearly eliminated Athens as a factor in world politics and so enfeebled the Greek universe that the Persians reasserted their control over the Greek communities in Asia Minor.

---

[12] Adam Watson, *The Evolution of International Society* (New York: Routledge, 1992), p. 47.

[13] The population of fifth-century B.C. Greece was a few hundred thousand.

[14] The marathon, a foot race of just over 26 miles, originated with the run Pheidippides made to carry the news of the Greek victory to Athens.

FIGURE 1.2

International, National, and Transnational Politics in Classical Greece

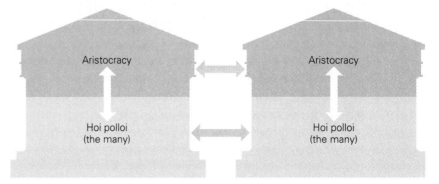

Like modern actors, the city-states of ancient Greece were divided internally and interacted among themselves both at an official and unofficial level. Leaders, soldiers, and politicians regularly changed sides.

The activities of these small Greek city-states have much in common with today's world politics and seemed to offer insights into the causes of war between states. In the years leading up to war in Greece, resources and attitudes were divided into competing and exclusive alliances, one headed by Athens, the other by Sparta. This competition seemed to resemble the evolution of global politics after 1945, when much of the world divided into two rival camps. Many observers feared that, just as world war engulfed Greece in 431 B.C., the Cold War would end in tragedy, but one of nuclear proportions. The idea that war can be prevented if power is divided among several participants and no alliance or state is allowed to amass too much power is still propounded by some statesmen and theorists.[15]

Another important parallel for today was division between domestic and international politics. *Internal politics* seemed hierarchic and international relations horizontal. Behavior between these city-states was global politics, but within them it was not. A good deal of *transnational* behavior also appeared between Greek city-states as leaders and soldiers frequently betrayed their city-state and changed sides. (See Figure 1.2.)

Chinese Imperial System

China is home to the oldest continuous historical tradition and one of the richest and most ancient civilizations. That tradition, as it applies to world politics, differs significantly from the Western experience. Chinese ideas about global politics took their own

[15]See, for example, Morton Kaplan, *System and Process in International Politics* (New York: Wiley, 1957), pp. 22–36.

FIGURE 1.3

The Chinese Imperial System

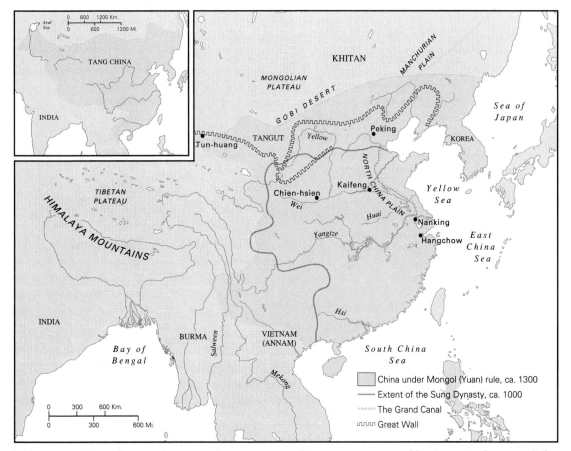

This map and inset illustrate how the T'ang Dynasty and its successors were able to sustain the expanded frontiers of the Han Dynasty, although their hold in the west was always somewhat tenuous.

shape, differing from Western ideas as those evolved from classical Greece. This divergence has contributed to incomprehension and misunderstanding between the Chinese and other peoples.

"The monumental Chinese achievement in the field of statecraft," declares Adam Watson, "is usually held to be the more or less effective imperial unity that has assured domestic peace and order for most of Chinese history."[16] The distinctive Chinese

---

[16]Watson, *Evolution of International Society*, p. 85. Watson points out that this unity was achieved only after some 500 years of war among rival polities. Nevertheless, as in Greece, disunity did not prevent the growth of an inclusive cultural sense of being "Chinese."

outlook on foreign affairs was forming long before the Greek historian Thucydides recorded the Athens–Sparta conflict in the fifth century B.C. "The ethical system that has largely determined the Chinese view of life, and therefore also the Chinese approach to foreign affairs," declares one observer, "was already well established in its broad outlines in the first centuries of the Chou period [1027–221 B.C.] — long before it was restated and amplified by Confucius in the sixth century B.C."[17] We associate this outlook mainly with the philosopher-sage Confucius, writing at a time of political turmoil in China.

The Chinese outlook on foreign affairs was built on the conviction — reinforced by the age, continuity, and isolation of the Chinese empire and the sophistication of Chinese civilization — that the Middle Kingdom (as China referred to itself) was the center of the world and that the Son of Heaven (as the emperor was called) was the ruler of the universe. The Chinese empire "remained the center of the world known to it, only vaguely aware of the other ancient centers to the west" and "never lost its sense of all-embracing unity and cultural entity."[18] The arrogance of this self-perception is apparent in a letter sent from the emperor to British King George III in the eighteenth century:

> Swaying the wide world, I have but one aim in view, namely, to maintain a perfect governance and to fulfill the duties of the state. . . . It behooves you, Oh King, to respect my sentiments and to display even greater devotion and loyalty in the future, so that by perpetual submission to our throne, you may secure peace and security for your country hereafter. . . . I do not forget the lonely remoteness of your island, cut off from the world by intervening wastes of sea, nor do I overlook your excusable ignorance of the usages of our Celestial Empire. . . . Tremblingly obey and show no negligence.[19]

The practical consequence of this egoistic view of the world was a belief that the political universe was centrally and hierarchically organized and that all peoples were subjects of the Son of Heaven. Such a perspective, of course, contrasted vividly with theories of international politics that evolved in the West beginning with Thucydides. These viewed the political universe as consisting of numerous independent and competing entities with no superior to govern them all. The Chinese view provided a basis for organizing China's relationship with small neighbors like Korea that were treated as subject peoples. Such peoples had to provide symbolic tribute to the emperor, and their representatives had to perform the kowtow (ritual bow) when coming before the Son of Heaven.

With its imperial experience, the Chinese view of world affairs, unlike the classical Western tradition, was unable to distinguish, at least in theory, between international and domestic politics. The Chinese felt that the world did not consist of autonomous

---

[17]Adda B. Bozeman, *Politics and Culture in International History* (Princeton: Princeton University Press, 1960), p. 134. See also pp. 133–146.

[18]John K. Fairbank, "A Preliminary Framework," in Fairbank, ed., *The Chinese World Order* (Cambridge: Harvard University Press, 1968), p. 5. Owing to shared culture, this sense of unity persisted even during periods in which the empire was divided among warring competitors.

[19]Cited in Bozeman, *Politics and Culture*, pp. 145–146.

actors. Instead, all peoples were under the rule of heaven, and the emperor of China was charged with governing them all, whether Chinese or not. The emperor's subjects, whether Chinese or barbarian (non-Chinese), should be treated in the same manner in accord with the norms of Confucianism, and all subjects should obey and respect the emperor. The Chinese knew that theory and practice were in conflict and that the emperor could not govern foreigners as effectively as those who lived in China. Nevertheless, they tried to force non-Chinese who wished to trade or negotiate with China to follow the rituals of submission to the emperor. Occasionally, these efforts created tension with foreigners, especially when the latter were more powerful than the Chinese.

The quality of rulership, taught Confucius, depended on adherence to traditional moral principles. As a consequence, Chinese theories of world politics were infused with a strong normative element; classical Chinese views of the world were as preoccupied with what ought to be as with explaining and predicting what really was. John Fairbank writes, "Adherence to the correct teachings would be manifested in virtuous conduct and would enhance one's authority and influence. . . . Right principles exhibited through proper conduct . . . gave one prestige among others and power over them."[20] In other words, moral behavior had the utilitarian consequence of increasing the emperor's power. Right, one might say, makes might. By contrast, policy failures could be traced to the rulers' lack of virtue and their loss of the Mandate of Heaven.

Although the emperor of China, in theory at least, was ruler of the world, he had to exercise his authority in accord with Confucian moral principles. China's ruler was obliged to educate barbarians in the ethical precepts of Confucianism and extend to them the benefits of Chinese culture and learning.[21] The Son of Heaven was expected to behave toward foreigners as he did toward his own people, in accord with the benign universal morality of heaven. If he did so, the natural harmony of heaven would prevail. Thus, the traditional Chinese perspective viewed harmony, rather than conflict, as the natural condition of the political universe.[22]

Global harmony might be viewed as a natural condition, but the Chinese did *not* assume that such harmony would be automatic. "In the very nature of human relations," declares one observer, "superiors cannot expect automatic obedience from their inferiors. But since neither father nor husband, older brother nor emperor, was supposed to enforce subservience by reliance on the power that he inherited in his superior status, the exercise of control was traditionally viewed as an art requiring consummate

[20]Fairbank, "Preliminary Framework," p. 6.

[21]After Genghis Khan and his Mongol warriors conquered China and established their own imperial dynasty in the twelfth century, they were seduced by Chinese mores and in time were themselves "conquered" and absorbed by Chinese culture.

[22]The major exception was the legalist school of thought in the fourth century B.C. which viewed domination and conquest as the major objectives of foreign policy. Perhaps the most famous advocates of legalist doctrine were Lord Shang and Li Ssu, who served as advisers to the rulers of the Ch'in state during an era of Chinese disunity and conflict. Using policies that they advocated, Ch'in conquered its competitors a century later, but the victory was temporary.

knowledge and skill."[23] Moral suasion and patience, not coercion, were, Confucians believed, the way to gain obedience and maintain order. This outlook was reinforced by the pacifist strains in the teachings of Taoist philosophers emphasizing inner virtue in contrast to the trappings of the external world.[24]

China's sense of virtue and superiority and its rulers' effort to isolate the country from the barbarians became sources of conflict with the Europeans and Japanese, especially in the nineteenth century, when they acquired the economic and military clout necessary not only to disobey the emperor but to impose imperial rule over large sections of the country. The British,[25] Germans, Japanese, Russians, and others established trading zones in Chinese cities over which they exercised exclusive control. Chinese efforts to oust the "foreign devils," including the Boxer Rebellion (1900), were unsuccessful until after World War II.

This Chinese self-perception still is somewhat reflected in foreign-policy attitudes. Japanese economic power and Western military prowess are regarded as less important than Chinese cultural superiority. Chinese leaders still believe they have special rights and responsibilities toward neighboring states in Asia over which they had once exercised dominion. Chinese refusal to embrace democratic reform or abandon communism and the leadership's rejection of foreign interference in their affairs after the massacre in Tiananmen Square in June 1989 reflect the belief that China has little to learn from the West. Chinese suspicions of the West are also intensified by the century of imperial interference in their internal affairs.

Rise and Decline of an Islamic Empire

Another historical imperial system that continues to influence events was based on Islam. Like the Chinese Empire, the adherents of Islam sought to gain universal allegiance

[23]Bozeman, *Politics and Culture in International History*, p. 136.

[24]China was not without its own tradition of power politics. The Legalists of the fourth and third centuries B.C., many of whom were practitioners as well as scholars, advocated an aggressive ethic of power politics, especially in order to unify China.

[25]The British prevented Chinese authorities from disrupting the lucrative opium trade that helped finance British rule in India, the source of much of the opium.

FIGURE 1.4

Medieval and Modern Islam
Political weaknesses in the territories they conquered, as well as superior fighting skills, help explain the speed with which the Muslims expanded. Initially spreading outward from Arabia into Persia and Egypt, Arab armies thereafter spread across North Africa and into Asia Minor, gaining a foothold in Europe in Spain and conquering the Byzantine and Sassanid (Persian) empires in the process.

Although the Islamic heartland remains the Middle East and North Africa, Islam is growing steadily in black Africa and is the faith of heavily populated Indonesia.

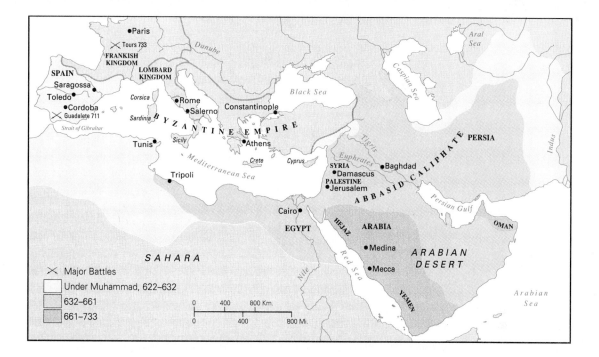

Paris
✕ Tours 733
FRANKISH
KINGDOM
Danube
SPAIN
LOMBARD
KINGDOM
Saragossa
Toledo
Corsica
Rome
Salerno
Constantinople
Black Sea
Aral Sea
Cordoba
Guadalete 711
Sardinia
BYZANTINE EMPIRE
Caspian Sea
Strait of Gibraltar
Tunis
Sicily
Athens
Crete
Cyprus
Euphrates
Tigris
Baghdad
PERSIA
Mediterranean Sea
SYRIA
Damascus
PALESTINE
Jerusalem
ABBASID CALIPHATE
Indus
Tripoli
Cairo
Persian Gulf
OMAN
EGYPT
HEJAZ
ARABIA
Red Sea
Medina
ARABIAN DESERT
SAHARA
Nile
Mecca
Arabian Sea
YEMEN

✕ Major Battles
Under Muhammad, 622–632
632–661
661–733

0   400   800 Km.
0   400   800 Mi.

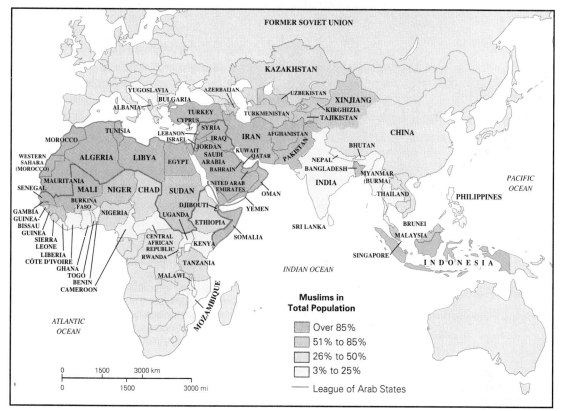

FORMER SOVIET UNION

KAZAKHSTAN

YUGOSLAVIA
AZERBAIJAN
UZBEKISTAN
XINJIANG
BULGARIA
ALBANIA
TURKEY
TURKMENISTAN
KIRGHIZIA
TAJIKISTAN
CYPRUS
SYRIA
IRAN
AFGHANISTAN
CHINA
MOROCCO
TUNISIA
LEBANON
ISRAEL
IRAQ
JORDAN
PAKISTAN
BHUTAN
WESTERN
SAHARA
(MOROCCO)
ALGERIA
LIBYA
EGYPT
SAUDI
ARABIA
KUWAIT
QATAR
BAHRAIN
NEPAL
BANGLADESH
MYANMAR
(BURMA)
PACIFIC
OCEAN
MAURITANIA
UNITED ARAB
EMIRATES
OMAN
INDIA
THAILAND
PHILIPPINES
SENEGAL
MALI
NIGER
CHAD
SUDAN
YEMEN
GAMBIA
GUINEA-
BISSAU
GUINEA
SIERRA
LEONE
LIBERIA
CÔTE D'IVOIRE
GHANA
TOGO
BENIN
CAMEROON
BURKINA
FASO
NIGERIA
DJIBOUTI
UGANDA
ETHIOPIA
CENTRAL
AFRICAN
REPUBLIC
RWANDA
KENYA
SOMALIA
SRI LANKA
BRUNEI
MALAYSIA
SINGAPORE
INDONESIA
TANZANIA
MALAWI
MOZAMBIQUE
ATLANTIC
OCEAN
INDIAN OCEAN

**Muslims in
Total Population**

Over 85%
51% to 85%
26% to 50%
3% to 25%
League of Arab States

0   1500   3000 km
0   1500   3000 mi

and to extend their influence worldwide. The empire expanded with unprecedented speed, at its height stretching from western Asia and the Middle East, through northern Africa, and into southern Europe. Slowly, internal disintegration eroded imperial unity, and outside challengers weakened the empire. The consequences of that expansion and of developments within Islam, however, remain very much a part of the world. Today, almost a billion Muslims live in the Arabic Middle East, Turkey, Iran, Afghanistan, North Africa, India, Pakistan, Indonesia, Malaysia, central Asia, and even parts of the Philippines and sub-Saharan Africa. And many devoted Muslims still believe that the world is divided "into the *dar al Islam*, the area of acceptance (of the will of God) or the area of peace, and the *dar al harb*, the area of war, where conflict with non-Muslim powers was to be expected and where war to expand the *dar al Islam* . . . was not only legitimate but positively virtuous."[26]

Islam was founded in the seventh century A.D. by the prophet Muhammad, who claimed that a message from Allah (God) had been revealed to him. Muhammad shared Allah's message with the Arabs of Mecca, and that message was recorded in the Quran (*Koran*). To understand the history of Islam or the politics of an Islamic society, we must realize that "Muslims have always believed in the completeness of the Quran; it is not to be supplemented by recurrent messages. . . . Among the Quran's truths is a prescription for regulating the political and social affairs of man. Islam makes no distinction between the state and the realm of believers. . . ."[27] In other words, Islamic authority tended toward *theocracy* — that is, government by religious leaders according to religious precepts. All Muslim behavior is guided by religion, and all Muslims are united by their faith regardless of national or class differences. The expansion of Islam illustrates the potency of religion whether or not its adherents are organized into territorial states.

By the middle of the eighth century, Muhammad's successors, the Umayyad caliphs, with their capital in Damascus, had transformed Islam's religious fervor into a workable Muslim empire. These caliphs often could not meet the principles of government and law as required by the theologians from the holy city of Medina, yet they were able to establish the needed political institutions for an expanding empire.[28] In time, they succeeded in conquering Afghanistan, parts of central Asia, parts of the Indian subcontinent, North Africa, and Spain. During the ensuing hundred years, Arab caliphs completed the conquest of Spain and Sicily and came into conflict with the European Christians led by Charlemagne. This Abbasid empire was the high-water mark of Islam's spread as a united religion.[29] Under the Abbasid

---

[26]Watson, *Evolution of International Society*, p. 113.

[27]James A. Bill and Carl Leiden, *Politics in the Middle East*, 2nd ed. (Boston: Little, Brown, 1984), p. 40.

[28]Sydney Nettleton Fisher, *The Middle East: A History* (New York: Alfred A. Knopf, 1970), pp. 69–70, 77–81.

[29]It also witnessed the flowering of a culture far more sophisticated than anything in Europe at the time. The revival of Greek classicism, great advances in mathematics, and imaginative architecture (e.g., the Alhambra in Granada, Spain) were features of the empire.

caliphs (750–1250 A.D.), Islamic society reached its height. Greek, Roman, Persian, and Hindu works were translated into Arabic and became part of Muslim culture. The works of ancient theology, jurisprudence, philosophy, science, and the humanities were preserved in Muslim culture and the Arabic language. Baghdad, too, became a center of intellectual and cultural life.

Thereafter, the Islamic empire began to pull apart. Rivalries grew among competing caliphs. The Seljuk Turks, hired as mercenaries to preserve the empire, gained independent influence. Western Christians invaded the empire to recapture the Holy Land and controlled parts of the region for more than two hundred years (1094–1294). More important, Mongols from the east and Mamluks from Egypt made inroads as well. Eventually, the remains of the Muslim empire were conquered by the Ottoman Turks.[30] Of the once great Islamic empire, one analyst concludes:

> [O]ne must conclude that the Muslims were more successful than their Christian rivals in winning the allegiance of men. . . . However, the remarkable success of [Islam] as an international association of coreligionists was offset by its equally remarkable failure as a political commonwealth. . . . The only pattern of political coalescence on the international level that Islamic history suggested was that of the unconsolidated empire-in-motion. It is not surprising to find, therefore, that expansion became the principal international policy of each separate Islamic sovereignty after the unified Empire had ceased to be a reality.[31]

In 1453, the Ottoman Turks conquered Constantinople, destroying the last vestiges of Christian Byzantium and producing panic in Europe. The Christian-Muslim conflict that had flared earlier began in earnest, and some of its consequences remain with us as hostilities in the Middle East, Bosnia, and elsewhere. Christians retook most of Spain by 1492, and expelled the country's Muslims and Jews. During the ensuing two hundred years, the Ottomans conquered much of the Middle East and, until repelled, extended their rule into Greece and the Balkans and to the borders of Austria and Hungary.

Although the Islamic tide had slowly receded from its crest, it was still felt socially and politically. During the nineteenth century, European conflicts with the declining Ottomans and with one another for the spoils of that empire were endemic.[32] Ottoman power retreating from the Balkans late in the nineteenth century produced power vacuums in which Russia and Austria-Hungary repeatedly collided until World War I erupted in 1914. During that war the Ottomans fought along with Germany. They were driven from their possessions in the Middle East by the British and French in a campaign that earned Lawrence of Arabia his reputation. The Ottoman Empire came to an end in 1919.

---

[30]George A. Kirk, *A Short History of the Middle East* (New York: Praeger, 1964), pp. 50–56.

[31]Bozeman, *Politics and Culture*, p. 385.

[32]For an analysis of European-Ottoman relations during this later phase, see Thomas Naff, "The Ottoman Empire and the European States System," in Bull and Watson, eds., *Expansion of International Society*, pp. 144–169.

Global politics today is witnessing a revival of *Islamic fundamentalism* demanding that people be ruled solely in accordance with religious doctrine.[33] Under the Ayatollah Khomeini and his successors, Iran is perhaps the most militant in this movement toward theocratic Islamic rule, but other societies as well have been pushed in that direction. In Egypt, Sudan, Lebanon, Algeria, and Afghanistan some are trying to level secular institutions and govern according to Muslim principles that transcend individual states. Iran apparently is training, arming, and financing militant fundamentalists throughout the Middle East.[34] The idea of a stateless Islamic world remains very much alive.

Medieval Europe to Westphalia: Birth of the State System

The system of sovereign states that dominated much of global politics in the nineteenth and twentieth centuries evolved mostly in a European context. That evolution was gradual and far from predictable, culminating in the great powers of Europe and their conquering much of the rest of the world.

Statelessness in Medieval Europe

If classical Greece was an age of small city-states and ancient China the model of a centralized empire, then medieval Europe reflected characteristics of both. Over the centuries it enfolded several empires, great traditional religions, independent city-states, successful trading companies, mixed classes, competing monarchies, and other independent or semi-independent groups that defy easy classification. In many ways European global politics during the Middle Ages (roughly the fifth to the fourteenth centuries) may seem more puzzling and remote to those who study contemporary world politics than that of Greece, medieval Islam, or ancient China. Nevertheless, medieval Europe is the portal through which the European territorial state appeared, and it has features that are again appearing in world politics.[35]

If we think of contemporary world politics as unfolding in an arena without a superordinate authority, in which various overlapping groups compete with one another for human loyalties, and in which the potential for violence is present, then the politics of medieval Europe may not seem so alien after all. If, on the other hand,

[33]Islamic law is set out in the *shari'ah* (the sacred law). See James Piscatori, "Islam in the International Order," in Bull and Watson, eds., *Expansion of International Society*, pp. 309–321.

[34]Youssef M. Ibrahim, "Arabs Anxiously Accuse Iran of Fomenting Revolt," *The New York Times*, December 21, 1992, pp. A1, A9.

[35]See Watson, *Evolution of International Society*, pp. 142–144. Medieval Japanese society featured similar feudal relationships.

we limit global politics to interactions of states clearly demarcated by territorial frontiers, then the medieval period will be almost unrecognizable to contemporary observers. (See Figure 1.5.)

In contrast to today's world, divided into territorial units (states), medieval Europe was organized around social groups: nobles, burghers, and peasants. This sociopolitical organization, known as *feudalism*, appeared in Europe after the Roman Empire collapsed and was built around an agrarian economic system based on landed wealth. Peasants owed obedience to a few powerful nobles who, at least in principle, held their landed estates in return for obedience to the Roman Church and the Holy Roman Empire. During the Middle Ages these two institutions were the principal political successors to centralized rule by Imperial Rome.[36] For the church, Christianity's triumph was proof that the pope was God's earthly agent. Secular authority, the church argued, could exist only with God's approval (as provided by the pope). The German-based Holy Roman Empire was heir to Charlemagne's Frankish empire and dates from 962, when a Saxon king, having invaded Italy and assisted the papacy, was designated Roman Emperor by the pope. The Italian poet Dante Alighieri defended the Holy Roman Empire by arguing that God had sought to create all things in His image and that, because God was universal and unitary, humanity would most resemble Him "when it is united wholly in one body, and it is evident that this cannot be except when it is subject to one prince."[37]

Theory and practice were not the same, however, and the powerful nobles, who were the society's military caste and were often high church officials as well, enjoyed considerable independence from both pope and emperor. Although the Church was unquestioned spiritual leader of the time, it discovered that transforming spiritual authority into secular authority was difficult. The emperor discovered that his secular authority was circumscribed. Compared to Imperial Rome at its peak, with an emperor who could command obedience by dispatching his legions to the farthest corners of the realm, medieval Europe was politically decentralized and the emperor's power was limited by local rulers.[38]

With overlapping authorities, conflict was frequent in medieval Europe. Life for peasants and nobles alike might well be described, as English political philosopher Thomas Hobbes did later, as "nasty, brutish, and short." Subjects of the Roman Empire might have expected their lives to be peaceful and orderly, but inhabitants of medieval

---

[36]The Roman or Catholic Church continues to influence millions of the faithful. It is no longer a territorial or military power, however, as it was in the Middle Ages. The Holy Roman Empire lingered on until Napoleon Bonaparte "officially" declared it at an end in 1806. Long before that it had ceased to exercise influence, and the French philosopher Voltaire satirically exclaimed: "This agglomeration which was called and still calls itself the Holy Roman Empire was neither holy, nor Roman, nor an Empire."

[37]Dante Alighieri, "De Monarchia," in William Ebenstein, ed., *Great Political Thinkers*, 4th ed. (New York: Holt, Rinehart and Winston, 1969), p. 252.

[38]Marc Bloch, *Feudal Society*, trans. by L. A. Manyon (Chicago: University of Chicago Press, 1961), p. 443.

Europe had no such assurance. One observer writes, "[I]nsecurity became general; no region was able to claim immunity from war."[39] The absence of clear centers of authority also erased the distinction between domestic and international politics for most people. "Each individual, every social or family group, had to look to their own security. . . . The differences were obliterated between public warfare and private violence, between the feud or vendetta and a conflict waged by the king in the name of his people."[40]

From the tenth through the twelfth centuries, confronting an absence of law and order, some tried to institute variants of arms control. These efforts—the Peace of God and the Truce of God—supported by early peace movements, were clerics' attempts to pacify their unruly flock by restricting the times (such as the Sabbath day and religious holidays) and places (such as churches) for combat and by protecting classes of persons (unarmed clerics, merchants, and pilgrims). One cleric wrote, "Because we know that without peace nobody will see the Lord, we warn men in the name of the Lord that they should be sons of peace."[41] The code of *chivalry*, obliging knights to help the innocent was another effort to limit the depredations associated with war.

Another characteristic of Europe at this time were conflicts between the empire and the papacy. The church itself was divided among those who wished to purge it of venality and corruption, others who wished to assert papal primacy over earthly as well as heavenly affairs, and still others who wished to grow rich by cooperating with the Holy Roman Empire. The empire, on the other hand, was torn by ducal families competing for the throne and by local nobles striving to exercise authority. In the end, neither pope nor emperor triumphed. Instead, both gave way to the territorial monarchs of France and England and the commercial city-states of Italy that took advantage of economic and military developments—money and firearms—and of the papal-imperial contest to assert their own independence and authority. From the collision between these actors the states in Europe arose in a form that is familiar to us.

Territorial States in Europe

The European territorial state did not emerge full-blown overnight. It was the product of a process that began with the fall of ancient Rome and continued in subsequent centuries. The construction continues with Germany unifying in 1990, older states reappearing after the Soviet Union broke up, and new states such as Ukraine and

[39]Philippe Contamine, *War in the Middle Ages*, trans. Michael Jones (Oxford: Basil Blackwell, 1984), p. 15.
[40]Contamine, *War in the Middle Ages*, p. 15.
[41]Contamine, *War in the Middle Ages*, p. 271.

FIGURE 1.5

The Holy Roman Empire of Medieval Europe with Major Vassals, ca. 1200

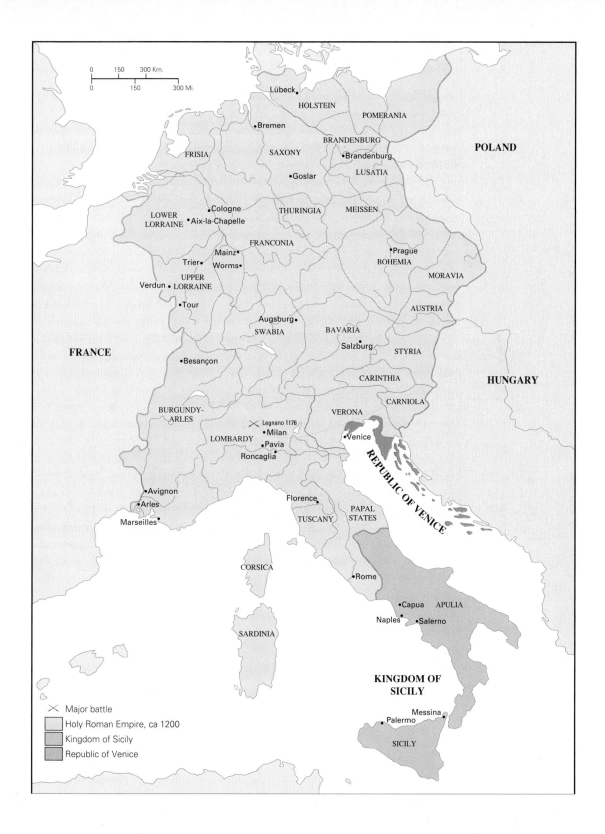

0 150 300 Km.

0 150 300 Mi.

POLAND

•Lübeck

HOLSTEIN

POMERANIA

•Bremen

BRANDENBURG

FRISIA

SAXONY

•Brandenburg

•Goslar

LUSATIA

•Cologne

LOWER
LORRAINE

•Aix-la-Chapelle

THURINGIA

MEISSEN

FRANCONIA

•Prague

Mainz•

BOHEMIA

Trier•

•Worms

MORAVIA

Verdun•

UPPER
LORRAINE

•Tour

AUSTRIA

Augsburg•

SWABIA

BAVARIA

Salzburg•

STYRIA

FRANCE

•Besançon

CARINTHIA

HUNGARY

CARNIOLA

BURGUNDY-
ARLES

VERONA

✕ Legnano 1176

•Milan

•Venice

LOMBARDY

•Pavia

Roncaglia•

REPUBLIC OF VENICE

•Avignon

Florence•

•Arles

PAPAL
STATES

Marseilles•

TUSCANY

CORSICA

•Rome

•Capua

APULIA

Naples•

•Salerno

SARDINIA

**KINGDOM OF
SICILY**

✕ Major battle

Messina•

Holy Roman Empire, ca 1200

•Palermo

Kingdom of Sicily

SICILY

Republic of Venice

Georgia. Many contemporary states (including Hungary and Croatia) are pale shadows of older centrally governed kingdoms (such as the Austrian–Hungarian Empire). The European territorial state was unique, however, and, as a consequence of Europe's colonial conquest over much of the world, that state came to be thought a model for others and even (quite mistakenly) a universal phenomenon.

With the waning of the Middle Ages and the church and Holy Roman Empire growing impotent, two different types of states appeared. One was the commercial city-state that grew up in Italy, and the other the territorial monarchic state that thrived in Spain, France, and England. The city-states of Italy were already prosperous independent entities by the eleventh century. The feudal system had never been deeply rooted in Italy, and the Holy Roman emperors were unable to exert lasting authority south of the Apennine Mountains.[42] These city-states, which controlled the countryside around them, were home to a new middle class whose wealth, accumulated by commerce, proved a challenge to feudal lords whose wealth was based on land. Gradually, this commercial class overthrew the local nobility, seized control of the countryside, and began to employ mercenaries to protect themselves. Newly available gunpowder and artillery undermined the feudal knights' military power; their stone castles and armor were less and less dominant.

These developments dramatically changed politics. "The relative protection which the sway of certain moral standards and the absence of destructive weapons had afforded groups and individuals in the earlier Middle Ages," argues one observer, "gave way to total insecurity under the dual impact of the breakdown of common standards and the invention of gunpowder."[43] These Italian urban centers, rediscovering ancient Greek and Roman learning (the Renaissance) gained intellectual leadership that complemented their technological and financial power. As they grew wealthier and more independent, the city-states of Italy, especially Florence, Venice, Milan, Naples, and the papacy began to compete among themselves for power and engage in elaborate *balance-of-power politics*. For almost two hundred years (1300–1494), they combined diplomacy, alliances, and limited wars to augment their security and spheres of interest and prevent any one or group from achieving preponderance over the others. They all, declares one historian, "eagerly observed the slightest move on the political chess board and made a great fuss whenever the smallest castle changed its ruler."[44] The Venetians, on the Adriatic Sea, grew rich from commerce and invented modern diplomatic techniques, including permanent diplomatic missions.[45]

---

[42]The German emperors did control Sicily and southern Italy for a time.

[43]John H. Herz, *International Politics in the Atomic Age* (New York: Columbia University Press, 1959), p. 45.

[44]Felix Gilbert, "Machiavelli: The Renaissance of the Art of War," in Edward Mead Earle, ed., *Makers of Modern Strategy* (New York: Atheneum, 1967), p. 8.

[45]Bozeman, *Politics and Culture*, pp. 457–477.

The Italian city-states were quite small. Although their use of balance-of-power is cited as an example of how states behave in a system lacking central authority, it is probably a mistake to generalize from their behavior to the larger new states that emerged in Europe and elsewhere later. Most important, "domestic" and "interstate" politics in the city-states were not really separate. Adversaries constantly meddled in each other's local affairs, cultivating local supporters and helping them to seize power, encouraging conspiracies, and aiding local factions. Few rules limited these struggles as adversaries routinely tried to assassinate each other.[46]

At the same time as the city-states of Italy were flowering, a second type of state was forming in Europe. Local monarchs were asserting independence from empire and papacy and developing bureaucracies to unite and exert control over large territories. These new monarchies traced their boundaries to those of the provinces in the Roman Empire, and ruling monarchs were the heirs of noble families who had increased their property holdings at the expense of neighbors. During the Middle Ages they had taken advantage of the papal–imperial quarrel to assert their independence and, especially in England, France, and Spain, had evolved effective ways of collecting taxes from subjects and mobilizing them into large bodies of infantry that could hold their own against mounted knights. They also created alliances with the growing commercial class that wanted its activities protected and was willing to lend money and pay taxes for the privilege.[47]

These new monarchs had to overcome both external and internal impediments to their independence. The sixteenth-century struggle of England's Henry VIII against the Catholic Church illustrates how Europe's kings sought to assert prerogatives *simultaneously* against external and internal challengers. One of the Catholic Church's most loyal servants, in 1521, Henry had been named Defender of the Faith. To strengthen England's Tudor dynasty, he sought to divorce his wife, Catherine of Aragon, who had borne him no male heirs to the throne. The pope refused to grant Henry the annulment he sought, then excommunicated the English king when he remarried. In retaliation, Henry forced the English Parliament to pass the Act of Supremacy (1534) naming him Protector and Only Supreme Head of the Church and Clergy of England. Having declared his independence from the papacy's external control, the king went on to confiscate the English monasteries, took control of their income, and made the clergy dependent on him. By identifying the Catholic Church with such enemies of England as Spain and exaggerating their threat, Henry fostered English nationalism.[48] He thus increased his own resources and acquired authority over the English clergy.

---

[46]Machiavelli provides a window through which to view the behavior of Renaissance politicians, and the names Cesare and Lucrezia Borgia are synonymous with political immorality.

[47]Holland's rise in the sixteenth and seventeenth centuries vividly revealed the importance of the new middle class and of capitalist enterprise as factors in world power.

[48]See F. H. Hinsley, *Sovereignty*, 2nd ed. (New York: Cambridge University Press, 1986), p. 118.

The movement toward independent states in Europe was also aided by the political and religious sentiment described as the *Protestant Reformation*. The Reformation began with Martin Luther's rejecting the Catholic Church's authority in religious matters (1517). Once the church had been stripped of the awe in which it had been held in matters of faith, rejecting its authority in politics was easier. Local princes, especially in Germany, took advantage of the ensuing century and a half of religious strife to encourage a national consciousness among subjects and assert practical independence of both pope and Holy Roman emperor.

The idea of *sovereignty*[49] was a prerequisite to legitimizing independence for the young states. Monarchs like Henry VIII were known as sovereigns, and in time their states—originally territories that the king owned by personal conquest, dynastic inheritance, and marriage—were granted the unique legal status of being sovereign. Like the state itself, the idea of sovereignty evolved slowly. This development, however, was a final step carrying the monarchic state to the center of political consciousness. In the midst of French political turmoil, the lawyer Jean Bodin provided a modern notion of sovereignty. Bodin was a member of a group of political moderates seeking to restore the French monarchy to its majesty, enfeebled by the fractious extremists, both Protestant and Catholic. In 1576, in *Six Books on the State*, Bodin defined sovereignty as "the absolute and perpetual power of the state, that is, the greatest power to command." The state, in the person of the monarch, was, Bodin declared, supreme within its own territory, independent of any higher authority, and the legal equal of other states. Sovereignty was, then, an attribute of the state itself rather than of an individual or a government. That the French state at the time did not possess "the greatest power to command" mattered little to Bodin; it *should* have such power to bring an end to chaos.

Peace was not to be restored to Europe for another seventy-five years. Indeed, the period from 1618 to 1648—the *Thirty Years' War*—was one of atrocity and violence that laid waste much of northern Europe and ended feudal political organization. The European state system is commonly dated from the Peace of Westphalia, which ended the war, but, as we have seen, that system had already been evolving for many years. The Peace confirmed the *idea of a system of independent and legally equal territorial states* and abandoned the idea of a universal Christian commonwealth governed by pope or Holy Roman emperor. The Peace also regularized the system of permanent diplomatic missions, encouraged the growth of *international law among* legally equal states rather than divine law *above* them, and encouraged a balance of power and a system of rules governing diplomatic etiquette. These rules were beyond question until just recently.

[49]See Chapter 4, pp. 117–119.

Conclusion

The present and future have little meaning apart from the past. "The Peace of Westphalia," declares one scholar of international organization, "for better or worse, marks the end of an epoch and the opening of another. It represents the majestic portal which leads from the old into the new world."[50] The new world was that of the sovereign state. Much of human history reflects this movement through portals, from old-world thinking to new.

The new era of the sovereign state engaged this same kind of attention among notable seventeenth- and eighteenth-century theorists of international law. Albericus Gentili (1552–1602), Hugo Grotius (1583–1645), and Emmerich de Vattel (1714–1767) sought to justify this new world and to explain to what, if any, limitations these new "leviathans" were subject. These young sovereign states, limited only by expedience and operating according to the dictates of prudence, became the basis for much of global politics over the succeeding centuries.

As we have seen, however, the European experience of territorial states is only part of the story. Other places and epochs have much to teach us, especially as actors other than sovereign states proliferate, many with non-European roots. Even more important is that issues and passions that were born in these settings continue to influence behavior in contemporary global politics or are resurfacing.

Key Terms

barbarian
traditional societies
modern state
tribe
transnational corporations
supranational organizations
city-states
political organization
ideology
economic vitality
technology
empirical theory
normative theory
theocracy
internal politics

global politics
transnational
feudalism
territorial state
sovereignty
international law
state-centric
Protestant Reformation
balance-of-power politics
chivalry
Islamic fundamentalism
Koran
Eurocentric
Thirty Years' War

---

[50]Leo Gross, "The Peace of Westphalia, 1648–1948," in Robert S. Wood, ed., *The Process of International Organization* (New York: Random House, 1971), p. 42.

CHAPTER TWO

Systems in Global Politics

The *global political system* is the most comprehensive level at which to analyze global politics and allows us to see all the pieces of the global puzzle and how they fit together. Once we have looked at the forest, we can turn to the trees in later chapters.

Our ancestors were nomadic hunters and gatherers who lived in small groups. Individuals might help each other, but these groups had little impact on one another. They had no organized warfare or commerce.[1] Improvements in agriculture gradually provided food to support larger populations, including concentrations in cities. People living in towns manufactured tools and clothes that they traded for food and raw materials with those living in the country. Some, specializing in violence, became soldiers organized by local rulers to protect cities and trade routes and raid others' cities and farms. In this way, groups began to specialize and depend on each other. Some began to travel great distances to sell their wares.

Nevertheless, until recent centuries, people living in one part of the globe had little connection with those elsewhere. Contacts among Chinese, Europeans, and Arabs, for example, were episodic, limited to intrepid individuals like the Venetian traveler Marco Polo (1254–1324), who returned to Europe with tales of the great Mongol Khubilai Khan and with the recipe for pasta. Although Chinese explorers sailed the Indian Ocean and beyond before the birth of Christ, and Viking Norsemen traveled to North America, it was not until European explorers like the Portuguese Vasco da Gama (1460–1524) and the Italian Christopher Columbus (1446–1506) sailed on their epic voyages of

---

[1]See, for example, Allen W. Johnson and Timothy Earle, *The Evolution of Human Societies: From Foraging Group to Agrarian State* (Stanford, Stanford University Press, 1987), pp. 19–20.

discovery that regular contact became possible between Africans and Americans, on the one hand, and Europeans, on the other.

More than ever, the states of Europe after the Treaty of Westphalia experienced how the behavior of people and groups — even those separated by great distances — affected each other's well-being and prosperity. The English poet John Donne expressed it best when he wrote early in the seventeenth century, "No man is an island entire of itself. Any man's death diminishes me because I am involved in mankind." In contemporary world politics, the decisions and actions of Americans, Asians, Europeans, and Africans enhance one another's opportunities for happiness or deprive them of those opportunities.

We may think people affect one another only when they try to do so, but in fact the fates of human beings, even those remote from and unaware of each other, are linked. Farmers in one country may have a large harvest, driving down the world price of grain and reducing profits for farmers on the other side of the earth. Wealthy consumers in North America use vast amounts of oil to drive cars, making it more expensive for the poor in Africa to obtain petroleum-based fertilizers to grow food and contributing to environmental problems that affect everyone. In the aggregate, individuals' decisions about which car to buy or where to travel can enhance or reduce the prospects of individuals living thousands of miles away whom they have never met and almost certainly never will meet. Links such as these create political systems.

Attributes of the Global System

In short, the concept of a political system is intended to convey the reality that people everywhere, wittingly or unwittingly, affect people everywhere else and that the way in which global resources and attitudes are distributed determines the kind of world in which we live.

System Defined: Parts and Wholes

The abstraction *system*, which came to political science from the natural sciences, expresses the idea of sustained and predictable patterns of action and reaction among individuals or groups of individuals. The *parts of a system* are individuals and groups, and what each of those parts does influences each other and the whole, whether intentionally or not. A system, then, consists of *interdependent units*; the welfare of any one depends on the others' actions and vice versa. The *interaction* of a system's parts determines the characteristics of the system as a whole. Imagine a number of peaceful countries, each developing an army solely for defense. Will the system *as a whole* be peaceful? That depends on how the individual countries — the parts — interact. If each perceives its neighbor's army as threatening, the system may be warlike even though no one seeks war.

FIGURE 2.1

Parts and Wholes: Domestic Pressures and Global Consequences

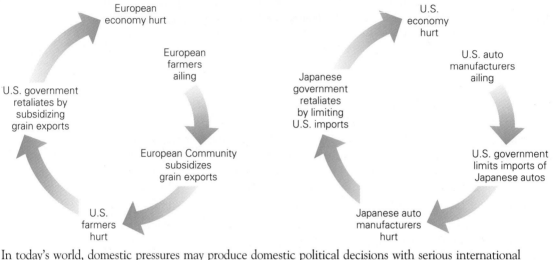

In today's world, domestic pressures may produce domestic political decisions with serious international consequences, and foreign-policy decisions will affect the domestic arena in other societies. This is illustrated by hypothetical policies fashioned to aid European farmers and U.S. auto manufacturers.

The *system* idea, then, helps explain why outcomes in global politics are often unexpected. Consider world trade. Leaders recognize that an open trading system, without impediments to free movement of goods and services, benefits everyone. And yet, when one country tries to aid a domestic group, it may set off a chain reaction unwittingly producing an economic disaster that no one seeks. American leaders may seek to protect U.S. auto manufacturers or farmers by limiting imports of Japanese autos or subsidizing U.S. grain exports. Such actions will harm Japanese auto manufacturers and European farmers, who may pressure their leaders to retaliate against vulnerable U.S. enterprises. A sequence of tit-for-tat actions may ensue that can threaten a trade war in which all will suffer as fewer people around the world buy each other's products.

Such interaction is a sequence in which one actor does something that affects others. The consequences of the initial action provide *information* that conditions the response of those whom the initial action affected. Responses are neither random nor mechanical. They are purposeful reactions to others' initiatives. The North Korean invasion of South Korea in 1950 seemed to inform U.S. leaders that efforts to deter communism had failed, and U.S. troops were sent to South Korea to remedy that failure. Such information is called *feedback*.

If information reinforces existing policies, it is *positive* or *amplifying feedback*. Cases of *escalation* and *panic* involve positive feedback. Escalation is a policy of intensified military action like that adopted by the United States in Vietnam between 1961 and 1968 in the belief that more of the same will achieve one's goals. Sometimes, as in panics, positive feedback can be pathological. In the Great Depression of 1929, massive selling in the stock market led to panic, which led to further selling of stock, inducing a stock-market collapse. Those who panicked also sought to get their money out of banks and triggered a run on the banks and a collapse of the U.S. banking system. As rumors spread that people were withdrawing money, others sought to do the same until the banks ran out of cash.

By contrast, information that changes the direction of policy is *negative* or *corrective* feedback. Leaders who recognize that policy has failed may take steps to change ("correct") those policies. Thus, as it became clear that escalation could not achieve U.S. objectives in Vietnam after 1972 or Soviet objectives in Afghanistan in 1986, leaders took steps to reduce their military effort. If genuine learning leads to change in goals rather than simply change in policies, we may speak of *second-order feedback.*[2]

Actors, Issues, and Systems

Actors.   As people interact in patterned ways, they join collective groups with whom they have something in common. Those others may be members of the same family; then the group is based on kinship and involves values such as affection. Others with whom they interact may purchase goods or sell their wares; such groups are based on economic exchange and entail values like prosperity and well-being. When such groups become so highly organized that the individuals can act together to achieve joint ends, they are called political *actors.*[3] Actors cooperate or compete in larger systems that cluster around matters of common interest. We call such matters *issues.*[4]

Issues.   Historically, issues expanded geographically to link persons and places far apart. Local and regional trading networks expanded to become global trading networks, and local security issues acquired global scope. It then became possible to speak of a *global political system.* Today, the economic health of a corporation like General Motors (and the millions of Americans and foreigners who directly or indirectly depend upon GM for prosperity) is related to such factors as petroleum production and prices in the Middle East; security in the Persian Gulf; labor-union decisions in the United States, Mexico, and Japan that determine labor productivity in those countries; and a budget deficit in Washington that helps set interest rates enabling people to borrow money to pay for GM products. In other words, the fate of GM is determined by the global system of which it is a small part.

[2]See Karl W. Deutsch, *The Nerves of Government* (New York: Free Press, 1963), pp. 92–93.
[3]For more on actors, see Chapter 4, pp. 114–116.
[4]For more on issues, see Chapter 4, pp. 109–114.

Subsystems.   Within the global system, selected actors interact intensely with each other in specific issues. We designate these very intense relationships *subsystems*. Such interaction is, of course, not always friendly. A subsystem may be sustained by high levels of hostile, even violent, action and reaction, and war may erupt among participants with appalling regularity. The patterned interaction that sustains subsystems, then, may be either hostile or cooperative.

Many of the most significant subsystems seem to be geographically based, and so we give them regional names, such as the Middle East subsystem. In fact, few subsystems are based on geography alone. The problems of peace and war between Arabs and Israel involves many actors who are geographically proximate; others, such as the U.S. and Russian governments, are not. Also, many Arab and Islamic governments and groups, like Kuwait or Algeria, are just peripherally involved in Arab–Israeli quarrels. And, if one thinks also about access to energy and oil prices, actors like Texaco and the governments of Indonesia and Nigeria could also be considered important players.

Subsystem boundaries.   By identifying which actors are members of a subsystem and which are not, we are deciding the subsystem's *boundaries*, but, as our example suggests, this is no simple task. The decision is subjective, determined by the original definition of the issue. Just as no signs hang in space to demarcate the heavenly bodies we call our solar system, so there are no objective criteria for determining which actors are part of the Middle East system and which are not. The system concept is an intellectual tool intended to focus attention and facilitate analysis. It is not a tangible and objective reality.

In sum, geography is not the basis for a political system, but it can facilitate or inhibit formation of such a system. Throughout history, people have tended to interact with those with whom they were close to geographically, so that systems often reflect geographic reality. Geographic barriers such as mountain ranges and oceans typically limited the possibilities for systems and, still do somewhat. War and trade are possible only if people are physically accessible to each other. The ancient Greek city-states were unable to unite partly because of mountains that inhibited communication. Isolation has saved from invasion island nations including Great Britain and Japan, as well as the North American and Australian continents, and have fostered isolationist policies for lengthy periods.

Growing Interdependence of the Global Political System

Technological changes are producing greater interaction than ever before and allowing more specialization around the world. Interaction and specialization, in turn, have produced *interdependence* among actors. People can, massively and almost instantly, alter the lives of those living on the other side of the globe. Ideas and images travel at the speed of light, and weapons of mass destruction can span oceans in minutes. Indeed, growing interdependence, perhaps more than any other development, provoked political scientists to borrow the system idea from the biologists who had originally conceived it.

Systems and subsystems vary significantly in the tightness of their weave, and therefore the interdependence of their participants. Sometimes interdependence is modest. Each actor's activity affects others, but only after much time and then marginally. In other systems, though, each member's action instantly affects the fate of others and does so profoundly. The Cold War illustrated how interdependent actors had become in world politics. Not only did Soviet and U.S. survival depend on the other's restraint and good sense, but neither could ensure its own security without the other's cooperation. Military planners on each side tried to take into account decisions made by the other in drawing their own plans. And, whatever the real motives behind military recommendations, they were inevitably justified on both sides by referring to the threat posed by the other. When either side increased its defense effort, the other felt compelled to do the same; and, when either deployed a new weapons system, the other followed.

Actors' interdependence extends beyond single subsystems. Actors interact in various issues, some of which overlap, and they participate together in various subsystems. The same actors may find themselves tightly linked in some subsystems and loosely connected in others. Where issues overlap, interdependent actors can trade across system boundaries, as by surrendering something to a rival on one issue in return for a concession on another. Recognize, then, that interaction in one subsystem is likely to have consequences—intended or unintended—in others. The global economy illustrates interdependence of issues across subsystems.[5] If the Federal Reserve Board lowers U.S. interest rates to stimulate the domestic economy by increasing consumer spending and borrowing, wealthy Japanese investors may be less inclined to invest in U.S. securities. Yet those are the funds the Treasury relies upon to pay the costs of the U.S. budget deficit. Here, as on other issues, an action taken for one reason in one realm of policy has immediate, though perhaps unforeseen, consequences in another.

Sometimes we are not aware how closely our fates are linked. All of us are involved in a global environment or ecosystem, yet only in recent decades have we been made aware of such a system. When Brazilians clear their Amazon jungle, they reduce the oxygen in the world needed by all; when Americans use air conditioning, they quicken depletion of the world's ozone layer; and when any of us drives an automobile, it exacerbates acid rain and the greenhouse effect.[6]

Leaders' success depends on recognizing their interdependence. Each depends on others in distant lands for cooperation on policies to make them succeed. Russian President Boris Yeltsin would fail in trying to reform the Russian economy and society without economic cooperation by Western governments and corporations. If they failed

---

[5]In Chapter 10 we deal with this subject in detail.
[6]See Chapter 15, pp. 523–524.

to extend aid and expertise to Russia, domestic resistance to Yeltsin's efforts to impose a free market would intensify. Runaway inflation, spiraling unemployment, and a decline in production would encourage former communists unhappy that the Soviet empire and its centralized system had collapsed and would like nothing better than to do away with Yeltsin. If Yeltsin and Russian reformers needed the West for success at home, Western leaders needed Yeltsin to accomplish their aims, especially to end the arms race and enhance global stability. Nuclear disarmament imposed financial and technological burdens on Russia, however. No country had ever undertaken nuclear disarmament, and disposing of nuclear wastes is complex. Russia, Ukraine, and Kazakhstan (heirs to the Soviet nuclear arsenal) probably could not accomplish this task without infusions of aid and advice from the West, and the West could not reduce the nuclear threat without cooperation from these countries. Indeed, as the 1992 Russian sale of submarines to Iran revealed, without economic assistance from the West, Russia might exchange its sophisticated arsenal to others for hard currency. Such sales are destabilizing because they proliferate sophisticated weapons.

System interdependence is the reason it is imperative for leaders to view the world through the eyes and ears of those with whom they must deal. If they assume that others think as they do, their policies are likely to fail. President Lyndon Johnson's efforts to force North Vietnam to capitulate between 1965 and 1968 failed partly because he assumed the Vietnamese perceived the world in the same way as Texans did. He assumed wrongly that they would compromise to protect their country's infrastructure from destruction. More recently, Japan's efforts to acquire higher political status has been undermined by its failure to appreciate Asians' sensitivity to anything that reminds them of the World War II Japanese "Co-Prosperity Sphere." Japanese decisions to send troops to Cambodia to aid the U.N. in that country, to transport enriched nuclear fuel by ship from France, and to increase economic cooperation with members of the Association of Southeast Asian Nations (ASEAN), however innocent, heightened fears in Asia of resurgent Japanese ambitions.

Table 2.1 summarizes our discussion thus far of the global system. We began by focusing on the factors that define a political system—parts, wholes, interaction, interdependence, and feedback, then explained how issues and actors constitute the building blocks of political systems and the subsystems within them. The manner in which the parts are arranged mainly defines a political system, and that arrangement is expressed by the structural properties of systems—the distribution of resources and attitudes—the subject to which we now turn.

Structural Properties of Global Systems

All systems have a framework within which actors' interaction takes place, and understanding that structure provides valuable clues about why actors behave as they do. Leaders, for example, often explain their behavior toward the Middle East as an

TABLE 2.1

Characteristics of a Political System: Key Concepts

A. Defining Characteristics	
Parts	Basic components of a system.
Wholes	Result of interaction among the system's parts.
Interaction	Sequence of actions in which one actor's behavior elicits a response from others.
Interdependence	Linked fates in which any unit's welfare depends on decisions by other units.
Feedback	"Information" from previous interaction that structures responses to future actions.
B. Political Features	
Actors	Individuals, groups, states, international organizations that act jointly toward the same ends.
Political issues	Matters of common interest and concern over which political actors contend and bargain.
Political system	Issues that link actors.
Subsystems	Extensive interaction among actors within a larger system over specific issues.

effort to maintain a balance of power between Israel and the Arab states. This explanation implies a *system structure* that determines what is possible and what is probable in that system. Presumably, such leaders believe that a change in the system's distribution of power will have negative consequences, such as outbreak of war or disruption of energy supplies.

In describing the structure of the Middle East system, we start by outlining how military resources are distributed among main actors, including the number of army divisions each has, the relative strengths of their air forces, how modern their equipment is, how good their training and mobilization plans are, and so on. If we believe that one side may be tempted to start a war if it acquires a military advantage, we try to determine what would be necessary to maintain equality between adversaries. We also examine how strong the actors' economies are, how high is the quality of their education systems, how easily available critical raw materials are, how much skilled labor they have, how skilled the leaders are, and other data that could tell us how resources are distributed in the region. From such data we could paint a picture of the Middle East system. But the image would still be incomplete, lacking color and tone. Our knowledge of resources tells us little until we learn about the intentions, loyalties, and historical memories of those in the region. After all, another set of actors, located elsewhere, would probably behave differently even though their system's resources were similarly distributed.

Resources are created to serve actors' objectives and goals, and such attitudes explain how the resources are likely to be used. What do people think of each other? Do they like or trust each other? What are their memories of each other, what do they intend to do to one another, and what do they expect others to do to them? If Arab–Israeli memories and expectations could somehow be altered, the framework of Middle Eastern politics would differ dramatically from the one that has prevailed since 1948, regardless of resources.

How resources are distributed and redistributed of course affects the distribution and redistribution of attitudes and vice versa. Third-World states and leaders are often jealous of Western wealth, and such jealousy produces hostility. Efforts to provide economic assistance rarely inspire gratitude. Instead, beneficiaries may resent those on whom they depend. As societies grow wealthier, they may turn more conservative in outlook, seeking to guard what they have from the have-nots. Consequently, once we have examined how resources and attitudes are distributed, we must discern how they are related to each other in a system.

The Importance of Distribution

The structure of a political system tells us what is possible and what is probable in that system. Specifically, its distribution of resources tells us what can happen, and its distribution of attitudes tells us what is likely to happen within the possible. Before defining "resources" and "attitudes," let us consider why we pay attention to distribution and redistribution rather than absolute level. The absolute *quantity* of India's resources matters less in understanding politics in the Indian subcontinent than recognizing that Indian capabilities are greater than those of other actors in the region, including Pakistan, Sri Lanka, Nepal, Afghanistan, and Burma. That fact produces fear in India's neighbors and hostility when India throws its weight around.

Weapons of mass destruction — nuclear, chemical, and bacteriological — also illustrate how distribution matters more than absolute level. Such weapons enable any actor who possesses them and the means to deliver them to annihilate adversaries. But that information alone tells us little until we know how these weapons are distributed globally. Indeed, a leading reason neither the United States nor the Soviet Union ever used nuclear weapons against the other is that each had them and could retaliate.[7] Knowing that two governments controlled incomparably large and sophisticated nuclear arsenals explains a remarkable and nonobvious paradox: The two actors who held the greatest potential military threat over each other were very unlikely to attack each other. The Cold War never became a hot war partly because of the distribution of weapons of mass destruction.

[7]See Chapter 8, pp. 253–258, for a discussion of how nuclear deterrence evolved.

Peace between the two leading actors in the system, then, was an *emergent property*—that is, peace grew from the interaction of two hostile actors who were deterred from attacking each other by their possessing nuclear weapons. We use the label emergent property because the outcome—peace—was not expected by most observers, who feared U.S. and Soviet hostility would sooner or later lead to World War III. Although neither superpower was inherently peace-loving, the system's structure, particularly the nuclear stalemate, prevented either from initiating war against the other. And, as the distribution of such weapons changes, we expect the probability of peace will also change. If more actors acquire sophisticated nuclear forces, the system's growing complexity and uncertainty will make it difficult for any actor to plan a rational defense budget or strategy. Now the question is: What would be the emergent properties of a system in which nuclear weapons were widely available? One possibility is that an actor might try to prepare itself against all possible enemies. If it did so, the rest would see that actor as a grave threat. They, in turn, might seek to add to their armaments (or ally with each other), and an *arms race* would be on. Under conditions of uncertainty and fear, the risk of conflict between some or all the actors would increase dramatically. In this example, an arms race and war would be emergent properties of the system. Alternatively, the spread of nuclear weapons might make those possessing them feel more secure, increasing the general feeling of security and the probability of peace, a very different set of emergent properties.

An actor tends to arm only against those it fears, and here the distribution of attitudes come into play. If Pakistanis were to wake up tomorrow morning to the news that one of their major military bases had been destroyed in a nuclear bombing, perpetrator unknown, many would conclude that India was the attacker. After all, Pakistan and India have gone to war repeatedly since their partition and independence in August 1947, have been fearful of each other for many years, and are divided by disputes such as the disposition of Kashmir. By contrast, few Pakistanis could imagine that the attack might have been carried out by the United States or China (even though both have the capability to do so) because for years both have been Pakistan's friends and allies.

We can see that *attitude distribution* is vital. If Pakistanis knew about nothing more than *distribution of resources*—nuclear weapons—they would have no reason to suspect India more than any other country that had nuclear weapons. Judging by distribution of resources, it would have been *possible* for any of them to carry out the attack. Knowing attitudes such as affect is critical in transforming knowledge about what is possible into conclusions about what is *probable*. For the observer of global politics, understanding how attitudes are distributed provides useful clues just as understanding motives is critical to a detective trying to solve a murder.

Systems have other emergent properties besides their propensity to conflict. *Distribution of influence*, to which we turn in Chapter 3, is one such property, and it is the consequence of interaction, the redistribution of resources and attitudes, and other systemic factors such as changes in technology. Another includes *compatibility of goals*, which reflects how the actors perceive their interests, others' interests, and their own experience. Third-World goals are incompatible with those of Western societies to the extent that the have-nots and the haves have very different needs and pursue very different values. The former seek change that will permit redistribution of wealth in their favor, and the latter seek stability to safeguard their prosperity.

A third emergent property in a system is *alliances* and *alignments* — actors cooperating by pooling their strength to achieve political or military objectives. Such groupings are conditioned by such attitudes as expectations, affect, and identities. Thus, the British–American relationship is facilitated by a history of cordial relations, sharing traits like language, perceiving shared interests and common enemies, and expecting continued amicable relations in the future.

Stability, a fourth emergent property, is *the ability of other structural features of the system to maintain themselves over time.* A system is stable to the extent that redistributing resources and attitudes does not trigger massive and rapid changes in the distribution of influence, compatibility of goals, or alliances. Stability thus is a propensity — systems are more or less stable, not stable or unstable. The system of two dominant superpowers after 1945 — the Cold-War system — was relatively stable. Influence remained more or less evenly distributed between the two poles, Soviet–U.S. goals remained in competition, and alliance systems remained intact despite arms races, regional conflicts, several large wars, and major technological and economic changes. By contrast, global politics was unstable after 1918 when the German, Austro-Hungarian, Russian, and Ottoman empires collapsed; new states appeared in Central Europe; the British and French empires were enfeebled; and waves of nationalism were unleashed, climaxing in the outbreak of World War II. One worry in global politics is declining stability in a number of regions since the Cold War ended.

We now examine in greater detail how resources are distributed in global politics, emphasizing differences among types in resources, the problem in harnessing them to international goals, and limitations on ways of using them. Thereafter, we will look more closely at attitudes to see how they affect the structure of global systems and how they are related to resources.

Distribution of Resources in Global Politics

Only resources that actors can use to achieve their goals and objectives or prevent others from doing so matter in global politics. Guns and uranium count more heavily than stamps. Resources can be either tangible, like precious metals, or intangible, like citizens' morale or skilled diplomacy: the list of vital resources endlessly changes to keep pace with technological, economic, and other innovations. For many centuries, land was the major source of wealth, and population indispensable to military victory. Today, though, technological skills and entrepreneurship contribute more to wealth than land and more military weight than manpower.

Tangible and Intangible Resources

Tangible resources such as population, land, and wealth are easy to see and count, and get more attention from political officials than such elusive *intangible resources* as popular satisfaction, citizens' morale, and leader's experience. Because dependable and accurate information about intangible resources is difficult to acquire, decision-makers often disregard them in their calculations or resort to wishful thinking in estimating them.

One leader who failed to recognize how important intangible resources were was Soviet dictator Josef Stalin. He did not appreciate the barrier that Catholicism posed to communist rule in Eastern Europe after World War II. Warned that Soviet influence in Eastern Europe might be attenuated by the pope, Stalin responded sarcastically, "How many divisions has the pope got?" If the pope had no armies at his disposal, then, Stalin believed, he could not resist Soviet power. In fact, as Stalin and subsequent Soviet leaders discovered and as many secular leaders could have told them earlier, the pope's intangible resources—prestige and moral authority—enabled him to mobilize Catholics in Eastern Europe. The communist regime in Poland made a similar mistake in the 1980s by underestimating the moral authority of the labor union Solidarity.

As a rule, leaders overestimate friends' and allies' intangible resources (as Americans did with Mikhail Gorbachev) and underestimate their enemies' intangible resources. They may assume that those who lead countries with which they are allied are popular and that public morale is high. Thus, U.S. leaders consistently overestimated popular support for "their man"—Chiang Kai-shek—during the Chinese civil war that pitted Chiang's Kuomintang (Nationalist Party) against Mao Tse-tung's communists. Soviet leaders erred similarly in steadfastly supporting Dr. Sayid Mohammed Najibullah as president of Afghanistan from 1986 to 1991, when an Islamic Interim Government replaced his regime. The opposite tendency is evident in the U.S. belief that Cubans were itching to overthrow Fidel Castro after his successful revolution toppled the American-supported regime of Fulgencio Batista in 1959. As a result, the U.S.-sponsored Cuban émigré invasion of the Bay of Pigs in 1961 was doomed to failure.

Failure to account for intangible factors can cause policy errors and disasters. For example, Hitler decided to launch a bombing blitz against British cities in 1940, assuming that it would undermine British morale. In fact, it had the opposite effect. The communist hard-liners' coup d'état to overthrow President Mikhail Gorbachev in August 1991 reflected similar ignorance of intangible resources. Assuming that many Soviet citizens and officials, especially Soviet military leaders, yearned for the good old days, the hard-liners discovered too late that they were wrong. Their plot collapsed and actually hastened the demise of the Soviet Communist Party and dismemberment of the Soviet Union—precisely the end they had sought to prevent.

Knowing how global resources are distributed, we have some idea about what actors *can* do to each other—their *capability*—not what they *will* do. Most governments actively ferret out information about others' capabilities. Intelligence agencies use spies, informants, diplomats, radio intercepts, and sophisticated space satellites to collect such data. Although some information about capabilities is hard to get, it is far more difficult to fathom an adversary's *intentions*. To do so with confidence may require planting a mole (an agent) in the adversary's inner councils.[8]

Because it is almost impossible to be sure about an adversary's intentions, leaders infer them from known capabilities. They assume the worst and, too often, prepare for it. Late in 1992, it was revealed that Iran was purchasing modern submarines from Russia. The Iranians may have meant them for defending Iranian oil-loading platforms in the Persian Gulf if hostilities reignited with Iraq, or they may have had no mission but were purchased because Russia was selling the equipment inexpensively. United States' military leaders, however, dispatched nuclear attack submarines to the Persian Gulf because Iran's new submarines would enable that country to wreak havoc on Western oil tankers, perhaps even closing the narrow Strait of Hormuz, through which ships leaving the Persian Gulf must pass.

Nevertheless, Iranian acquisition of modern weapons meant that the country's Muslim fundamentalist leaders *might* have sinister intentions toward the West and Arab oil producers in the region. Because certainty was impossible, the Pentagon quickly made a conservative assessment and took steps to prevent Iran from carrying out its worst-case objectives. In all likelihood, Teheran saw Washington's decision to send nuclear submarines as provocative and threatening.

Putting Resources to Work

Merely possessing resources does not mean that an actor can or will achieve its objectives and goals. Resources are "things" which may be helpful in pursuing those objectives but which the actor may not use or may use inefficiently. When wealth is employed to provide military or economic assistance it is a resource that is used directly to achieve foreign-policy objectives. But wealth may be used for other purposes and so may be irrelevant to an actor's international aspirations.

Prior to Iraq's invasion in August 1990, Kuwait's ruling emir and government had spent much of the country's huge wealth on raising citizens' standard of living. Much had also been squandered on luxuries or invested overseas, and little had been spent to develop Kuwait's military capability. Kuwaiti displays of wealth merely goaded the neighboring Iraqis to jealousy. Where the Kuwaitis had expended wealth in pursuing foreign-policy objectives, they had done so foolishly, essentially trying to bribe Iraq by granting it huge loans during its war with Iran (1980–1988). Indeed, one factor that triggered the Iraqi decision to invade was Kuwait's refusal to forgive such loans after the Iraqi–Iranian war ended. The wealthy may have greater potential for achieving foreign-policy objectives and goals than do the poor, but wealth alone does not ensure that they will do so.

[8]A mole is a spy who spends years working into an enemy's confidence.

Resources are not equally useful for all objectives; political leaders tend to overlook this limitation, assuming that, if resources are useful in some cases, they are useful in all. This error may have tragic consequences. Humbling experiences in Vietnam and Afghanistan made it clear to the United States and the Soviet Union that military force has limited utility if the objective is to win the local population's hearts and minds and thereby prop up friendly governments. That lesson is difficult for politicians to learn, and the United States continues using its military resources to achieve objectives for which such resources may be ill suited, such as suppressing cocaine production and export in Peru and Colombia and halting illegal immigration from China and Mexico. In all likelihood, military resources will mean less in a world less disturbed by traditional territorial quarrels and more attentive to cleavages based on economic, environmental, and even gender differences.

Resources are effective only for a limited number of people and types of behavior. A medical doctor's resources consist mostly of knowledge and experience, and the doctor's influence is limited to patients (number of people) and health issues (type of behavior). Similarly, resources of transnational corporations like Toyota or IBM are not especially useful in achieving objectives unrelated to issues of international economics. Wealth, experience, and expertise make such giant banks as Citibank or Barclays major players in settling the problem of how debtor countries including Brazil, Argentina, Mexico, and Russia will repay their enormous loans, but the banks have little leverage in other world issues.

In fact, barriers to mobilizing resources and applying them effectively and efficiently are numerous, as we see in the guns versus butter dilemma. It is difficult to convert consumer industries to a "war effort" or to convert military resources to serve civilian economic needs. Automobile factories may be used to produce tanks, hosiery companies may make parachutes, and chemical industries may turn out poison gas. Some industries, however, can serve few military purposes and may have to go out of business until the conflict is over.

The opposite problem — going from military to civilian use — is even trickier, as the United States and Russia discover in seeking to reduce their armaments. Retraining and housing hundreds of thousands of unemployed troops withdrawn from Eastern Europe and the Baltic Republics threaten Russia's political stability.[9] Few novel uses can be found for nuclear warheads, though some of the material can be reprocessed and used for civilian energy. In the United States too, converting resources from military to civilian purposes has caused economic dislocation and unemployment, a controversial issue during the 1992 presidential campaign. The Clinton administration appropriated funding to help regions adjust to defense conversion and also sought to cushion Russia's effort to do so. It also decided to close down military bases inside and outside the United States despite strong local resistance.

[9]As part of the agreement that reunified Germany, the German government agreed to underwrite some of the cost of resettling withdrawn Soviet forces.

Geographic Location

Location may be an actor's chief resource. Before this century, geography could provide advantages or disadvantages. Relative isolation from continental power in Europe and Asia gave Britain and Japan security, whereas Poland, lying between Germany and Russia, and Korea's, between China and Russia, left them insecure.

Geopolitics involves analyzing the relationship between politics and geography. This discipline was especially in vogue during the nineteenth-century heyday of imperialism when imperialist ambitions began to collide at the fringes of Europe and beyond. Among the most celebrated geopolitical analysts was a studious U.S. naval officer, Alfred Thayer Mahan, who argued that global influence is determined by control of the sea, especially strategic geographic chokepoints astride the great sea-lanes of international commerce. These included the Straits of Gibraltar[10] between Europe and Africa at the Atlantic entrance to the Mediterranean; the Strait of Malacca between Sumatra and the Malay Peninsula (connecting the Pacific and Indian Oceans); the Dardanelles (guarding the mouth of the Black Sea); the English Channel between British and French coasts (linking Atlantic Ocean and North Sea); the Skaggerak between Denmark and Norway (providing an outlet from the Baltic into the North Sea); and the Suez Canal (linking the Mediterranean and Red Seas). Mahan believed the United States, to become a world power, had to acquire and protect both a canal across the Isthmus of Panama and the Hawaiian Islands.[11]

Just before World War I, a British student of geopolitics, Sir Halford J. Mackinder, fearful of German land power, expressed doubt that naval power could ensure British security. Mackinder's nightmare was an alliance between Germany and Russia, because their geographic position would give them control of the "world island" — Europe, Asia, and Africa — and therefore global supremacy. Mackinder's view of geopolitics was summed up in an aphorism:

> Who rules East Europe commands the Heartland;
> Who rules the Heartland commands the World Island;
> Who rules the World Island commands the World.[12]

Both Mahan and Mackinder saw geography as determining global influence. We should not conclude, however, that geography determines destiny. That a country is an island does not guarantee it will become a sea power. Although Great Britain did become a marine power, Japan only left its isolation to do so late in the nineteenth

---

[10]Antiquity knew this narrow strait was critical, and the promontories on either side of this waterway — the Rock of Gibraltar in Europe and the Jebel Musa in Africa — were together known as the Pillars of Hercules.

[11]Philip A. Crowl, "Alfred Thayer Mahan: The Naval Historian," in Peter Paret, ed., *Makers of Modern Strategy from Machiavelli to the Nuclear Age* (Princeton: Princeton University Press, 1986), pp. 444–477.

[12]Cited in Harold Sprout and Margaret Sprout, *The Foundations of National Power* (Princeton: Van Nostrand, 1951), p. 155.

century, and some islands — Iceland, Australia, Cuba — have never done so. Nor does a long, shared border necessarily produce conflict, as U.S.–Canadian relations and postwar Franco–German relations indicate.

Moreover, advances in technology now enable people to interact at almost any distance, reducing the political significance of geography. With jet bombers, intercontinental missiles, and nuclear submarines, countries can destroy each other at vast distances. Modern computers, facsimile printers, and telephones provide instant communication around the world; corporations and banks can move billions of dollars across oceans in seconds.

Size and Development

The absolute level of resources controlled by an actor or to which it has access reflects its *size* and indicates its potential oomph or clout in global politics. The individual citizen's access to resources though, reflects an actor's *social and economic development* and indicates how effectively it can use the resources it has. Neither indicator alone adequately measures an actor's capabilities or the success it will enjoy in pursuing objectives. Two observers write, "Big states act differently than small states. Rich states behave in ways that poor states cannot."[13]

Some years ago Bruce M. Russett, using factor analysis, a statistical technique, concluded that combining an actor's *total population,* *total gross domestic product,* and *total land area* yielded a measure for size.[14] A large population is the raw material for big armies and plentiful labor; total GDP reflects the overall size of an actor's economy; and total land area is the space it has for everything from agriculture to homes and cities. Of course Russia and China rank high on all three and are "big" actors. As in football, countries like Russia and China are the big players in the game of world politics. Others that are big include India, Brazil, Indonesia, and Iran. When such countries act, everyone, at least in their region, notices, and many are affected by their action.

Russia, China, and the other big actors mentioned above are not economically advanced, and poverty and inadequate technology limit how effectively their leaders can use their size to achieve what they want. Although the former Soviet Union created an immense military machine, it could not provide its citizens with basic consumer goods, including food and housing, or compete with other modern societies in such high-technology fields as computers. The communist regime collapsed because it failed to deal with the country's economic crises, as the tsarist system had failed to modernize Russia seven decades earlier.

Socioeconomic development is reflected by other indicators: number of people per physician, number of radios per capita, gross national product per capita, number of

[13]Charles Lewis Taylor and Michael C. Hudson, *World Handbook of Political and Social Indicators,* 2nd ed. (New Haven: Yale University Press, 1972), p. 283.

[14]Bruce M. Russett, *International Regions and the International System: A Study in Political Ecology* (Chicago: Rand McNally, 1967), pp. 16–17, 41–46.

students in higher education per capita, literacy rate, ratio of population living in cities, and percentage of labor force in agriculture.[15] Combined, these indicators reveal that some smaller countries — Canada, Belgium, New Zealand, the Netherlands, Sweden, Switzerland, Israel, and Denmark — are nevertheless highly "developed." With some notable exceptions like the United States, Japan, and Germany, those that rank highest on one scale are not identical to those on the other, as illustrated in Table 2.2.

As in football again, often the biggest players are not the most skilled. The United States, Germany, and Japan are the rare big players who are also highly skilled. Size alone tells us little about relative wealth and modernity. People in small countries like Switzerland and Norway enjoy a far higher standard of living than do people in China and India, and a number of small countries are significant in global politics because they provide vital technical services to others — in effect, exporting skills. Singapore, little more than a city-state on an island off the Malay Peninsula, has achieved influence throughout Southeast Asia because it provides varied skills, from medicine to business training to its larger neighbors.

In our economic and technological sense, *modernity* is neither inherently superior nor inferior. Some praise it because they equate it with physical comfort and leisure; others decry its accompanying pollution and erosion of spiritual values. Undeniably, societies increasingly need *brains* rather than *muscle* to satisfy human needs. Good health requires doctors; high technology requires knowledge and therefore education and literacy; supplying adequate food and clothing for a growing population depends on technological know-how. Military security and economic competitiveness also depend on science and technology. Populations that are well educated and highly trained have the skills to provide products and services that are in demand at home and abroad. Today wealth is partly the product of skills, and wealth, in turn, is necessary to gain such skills.

Such data are important to observers of global politics because they tell us how effectively a society can apply the basic resources that make "size" to achieve their objectives. Education is needed to use technology effectively, and highly skilled soldiers are needed for modern weaponry. Literacy and education are critical for managing complex government, military, and corporate bureaucracies, and such bureaucracies — international, transnational, national, and even local — are crucial in dealing with the complex issues that confront societies. When the U.N. seeks to ferry food to end famine in Somalia, supervise a peaceful transition in Cambodia, oversee elections in Angola, or operate a sea blockade against Serbia, it recruits highly trained civil and military administrators.

Modernity, as we use it, also means a mental outlook or way of looking at the world with scientific and secular lenses. Citizens in modern societies believe problems can be overcome by applying science and technology rather than accepting them fatalistically as divinely ordained. Such citizens build dams to deal with floods and spend huge sums

---

[15]Russett, *International Regions*, p. 16–17, 41–46.

TABLE 2.2
Top 25 Countries 1990[a]

Per Capita (Development)	Total GDP (Size)
1. Switzerland	1. United States
2. Finland	2. Japan
3. Japan	3. Germany
4. Sweden	4. France
5. Norway	5. Italy
6. Germany	6. Great Britain
7. Denmark	7. Canada
8. United States	8. Spain
9. Canada	9. Brazil
10. United Arab Emirates	10. China
11. France	11. Australia
12. Austria	12. Netherlands
13. Netherlands	13. India
14. Australia	14. Mexico
15. Italy	15. South Korea
16. Great Britain	16. Sweden
17. Belgium	17. Switzerland
18. New Zealand	18. Belgium
19. Hong Kong	19. Austria
20. Singapore	20. Finland
21. Spain	21. Denmark
22. Israel	22. Iran
23. Ireland	23. Indonesia
24. Saudi Arabia	24. Norway
25. Greece	25. Turkey

[a]Data unavailable for the U.S.S.R., Kuwait, Oman, Libya, and Iraq.

SOURCE: World Bank, *World Development Report, 1992*, Table 1, pp. 218–219 and Table 3, pp. 222–223.

to build laboratories like the National Institutes of Health in Washington to deal with diseases like AIDS. They are also trained to think and behave independently and to act as individuals in coping with problems.

Thus, military personnel today are trained to cope with various exigencies and how to assume command and continue to fight effectively after losing senior officers. By contrast, soldiers in traditional societies, however brave, are ill prepared to fight effectively if their leaders are out of action.[16] Recognizing this dependence facilitated the British conquest of South Africa and the European expansion across North America in the nineteenth century. Both the indigenous Zulus in South Africa and the American Indians showed ingenuity and courage in defending their lands, but their well-armed enemy could reduce their military effectiveness by intentionally killing their chiefs. During this century, too, those with traditional values have found it difficult to fight effectively against modern foes. The Russian army's catastrophic defeat at the hands of the Germans in 1914 owed much to the Russian peasant soldiers' inability to use effectively the modern equipment they were given — field radios, trains, and so on.[17]

As we shall see in Chapter 15, education, technological training, and social change are necessary for citizens of traditional societies to overcome the challenges of overpopulation and poverty (sometimes exacerbated by technological advances, as in medicine). Traditional value systems provide spiritual and psychological sustenance but do not foster an outlook conducive to economic growth or scientific discovery. They encourage identification with family and locality but discourage participation in economic markets and social systems. Finally, they emphasize collective rather than individual behavior and rewards.

Capability and Status in Global Politics

The distribution of resources in the global system is highly unequal. More than a third of 125 countries in 1990 — with almost three billion people — had a per capita GNP of less than $600 a year. More than half had per capita GNP of less than $1,500, and more than two-thirds — four billion plus — had per capita GNP of less than $2,500. Fewer than 20 percent of these countries — 816 million people — enjoyed per capita GNP in excess of $9,000 a year.[18] The world after the Cold War still has relatively few top dogs, more middle dogs, and many underdogs.

It is a world in which the cleavage between rich and poor is exacerbated by regional and racial differences. Of the twenty-five top dogs, as measured by per capita GNP, four-fifths are predominantly European or populated by those of European descent. Three are Asian (Japan, Singapore, Hong Kong), and two are sparsely populated Arab oil-producing countries (United Arab Emirates and Saudi Arabia). By contrast, eighteen of the poorest twenty-five countries in the world are sub-Saharan African, six are Asian, and one, Haiti, is in the Caribbean.

And the growing diffusion of television, radio, motion pictures, glossy magazines, and tourism makes the underdogs increasingly aware of their relative deprivation. This

---

[16]Marxist-Leninist regimes seek to uproot traditional value systems, and, in doing so, they are often able to improve their soldiers' fighting capacity. The military success of communist guerrilla forces in China and later in Vietnam attest to this.

[17]See Alexander Solzhenitsyn, *August 1914* (New York: Farrar, Straus and Giroux, 1978).

[18]The World Bank, *World Development Report 1992* (New York: Oxford University Press, 1990), Table 1, pp. 218–219.

FIGURE 2.2

Global Pyramid of Wealth

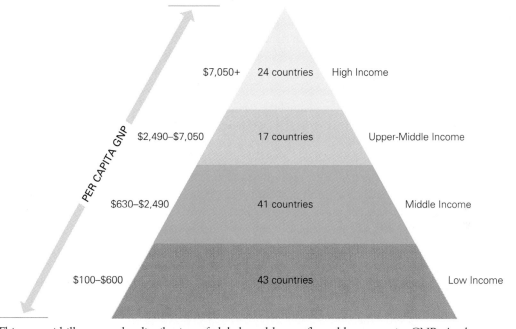

$7,050+	24 countries	High Income
$2,490–$7,050	17 countries	Upper-Middle Income
$630–$2,490	41 countries	Middle Income
$100–$600	43 countries	Low Income

PER CAPITA GNP

This pyramid illustrates the distribution of global wealth as reflected by per capita GNP. At the top are a small number of wealthy countries and at the bottom a large number of very poor countries.

is a world in which the many are envious of the few but unable to do much about it. Amid this acute frustration the poor may resort to violence and will seek the means, even weapons of mass destruction, to force redistribution of resources and get a more equitable share of the world's wealth. The gap and resulting frustration will keep growing because the world's poorest societies also have the world's highest birth rates.[19]

Inequality *within* poor societies is also sharp.[20] In Brazil, El Salvador, and the Philippines, for example, enormous concentrations of land and wealth are held by tiny elites, but the many live in poverty in urban shanties or on small rural plots. Cycles of chronic instability and spasms of political violence, extremism, and military authoritarianism are the companions of such inequality. Such a cycle has plagued Latin America,

[19]See Chapter 15, pp. 512–515.

[20]Two useful measures of income inequality are the Lorenz curve and the Gini coefficient. The first combines income distribution and population to measure the shares of income enjoyed by sectors of the population. The second is an arithmetic measure of the area between absolute income equality and the Lorenz curve. Using these tools, one recent study of 127 countries concludes that income inequality between countries is considerably greater than inequality within most countries. Reuben P. Mendez, *International Public Finance: A New Perspective on Global Relations* (New York: Oxford University Press, 1992), p. 96.

as in the civil war that engulfed El Salvador throughout the 1980s until the peace agreement of 1992. The main causes were such inequalities, intensified by a growing population of landless peasants. In this world relatively few individuals or actors enjoy high status.

The *status* or *prestige* of an actor may be defined as where other actors think it ranks in the global hierarchy. Actors thought to be important are treated accordingly. The marks of status are many. One of the most public for national governments is permanent membership on the U.N. Security Council, and this is why Germany and Japan have expressed interest in such membership. Other marks of status include visits by major leaders,[21] media coverage, and invitations to participate in major conferences. The leaders of high-status actors are routinely consulted by other important leaders and have a big part in global decisions. We pay attention to actors who have clout because they can affect our lives. By contrast, we pay little attention to the poor or weak because, with few resources, they seem unable to affect us greatly. They are low-status actors.

In earlier centuries, diplomatic missions were carefully graded to reflect the relative status accorded recipients. Ambassadors (not lower-ranking diplomats) were assigned only to capitals of countries regarded as great powers. Even today, governments, especially those which cannot afford to maintain embassies everywhere, do maintain them in countries like the United States that have high status (just as corporations of Honda's status have branch offices in wealthy countries). And, if we carefully observe ambassadorial appointments and the size of embassy staffs, we get an idea about which actors enjoy high status. United States' presidents appoint political donors to plum posts like Tokyo, Paris, and London, and the United States supports its largest embassies in Japan and Germany. Other countries appoint their most experienced diplomats to the United States, as befits the world's only remaining superpower.

The leaders of important actors—whether prime ministers or CEOs—are sensitive to the status they are accorded. When they are guests at state dinners they hope to get prestigious seats near their host, and when something significant arises they wish to be consulted. Former president of France Charles de Gaulle was prickly on matters of protocol and was sensitive to his role as representative of France. Aware of de Gaulle's sensitivity, President John F. Kennedy sent former U.S. Secretary of State Dean Acheson to speak with the French leader at the height of the Cuban missile crisis in 1962. In one account of their meeting, "De Gaulle raised his hand in a delaying gesture that the long-departed Kings of France might have envied. 'May we be clear before you start,' he said. 'Are you consulting or informing me?' Acheson confessed that he was there to inform, not consult."[22] Countries demand respect and may go to war over perceived insults. In 1739 war actually broke out between Britain and Spain after a British captain named Jenkins displayed what he claimed was his ear amputated by the Spanish.

[21]When a new U.S. president takes office, foreign leaders compete to be the first to visit Washington and persuade the new president to visit their country.
[22]Elie Abel, *The Missile Crisis* (New York: Bantam Books, 1966), p. 96.

Actors with greater resources usually enjoy high status, so that status and resources are in balance. Often, however, a time lag separates redistribution of resources from status of actors. Actors may lose significant resources yet continue to enjoy high status for some time. Two world wars and decolonization reduced Great Britain from being the center of a great empire and an industrial giant to very modest circumstances. Nevertheless, after 1945, London continued to participate in global decision making at the highest levels and to enjoy a "special relationship" with the United States. In the same period, Japan and Germany became economic giants,[23] yet because of the shadow cast by their superpower ally they have just recently begun to receive the attention that their economic muscle merits.

Such imbalance is called *status inconsistency*, and it can be dangerous.[24] Like an aging gunfighter in the old West, a high-status actor with a declining share of resources may be challenged by upstarts, and, like Austria-Hungary in 1914, it may behave rashly to reverse its growing weakness. Repeatedly challenged by adversaries in the Balkans and elsewhere, the creaking empire sought to avoid its fate with one throw of the dice. When the heir to the imperial throne, Archduke Francis Ferdinand, was assassinated in Sarajevo, Austria-Hungary took the opportunity to humiliate upstart Serbia. The result was World War I and dissolution of the empire. More recently, the 1982 Argentine challenge to British rule of the Falkland Islands (known to the Argentines as Islas Malvinas) seemed an upstart's effort to challenge a declining but still prestigious actor. When a declining actor is challenged by upstarts, war is always a risk.

Actors who are accorded lower status than they think they deserve may rock the boat until attention is paid them. Germany under Kaiser Wilhelm II behaved in this way between 1890 and 1914, repeatedly causing crises over such issues as the fate of Morocco. Soviet behavior after 1945 can be explained at least partly as an effort to force others to treat Moscow as a superpower, the status its leaders believed it merited, especially after its sacrifices first to industrialize and then to win World War II. The Soviet leaders' desire for respect illustrates how crucial attitudes are in global structure, the topic to which we now turn.

[23]On paper, Japan became the world's wealthiest country in 1987. For the first time its national assets were valued higher than those of the United States. *The New York Times*, August 22, 1989, p. 43.

[24]For a summary of research on the relationship between status inconsistency and war, see Michael P. Sullivan, *Power in Contemporary International Politics* (Columbia: University of South Carolina Press, 1990), p. 134. For a theoretical and historical analysis of the importance of a balance between status and resources for actors in a system, which the author calls systemic equilibrium, see Charles F. Doran, *Systems in Crisis: New Imperatives of High Politics at Century's End* (New York: Cambridge University Press, 1991), pp. 117–140.

Distribution of Attitudes in Global Politics

If the distribution of resources in world politics tells us what is possible, the *distribution of attitudes* informs us of what is *likely* to take place. Significant attitudes include *identities, expectations, beliefs, and goals.* These attitudes condition how actors will utilize resources toward each other. Answers to questions such as whether actors like each other, expect friendly acts from each other, and share goals are critical if we are to make sense of why actors behave as they do.

Identities

Identities help determine whether people like each other. Most individuals have loyalties to various groups and identify with them—government, gender, employer,[25] church, ethnicity, and so on. If Americans were asked to describe themselves, some of the answers might be American, Afro-American, Catholic American, Jewish American, college student, Californian, or farmer. A person in France, describing himself as French, might identify with a feminist group seeking equality for women, a farm association trying to hold on to European agricultural subsidies, a consumer who would like to reduce such subsidies and so lower the price of food, the Catholic Church petitioning for state funds to support parochial schools, or even a right-wing political party seeking to expel France's immigrant population. In complex societies, such multiple identities are common.

The crucial aim in looking at multiple identities is to discern how people rank them and whether or not they are compatible. What relative importance do we accord to various objects of our loyalty (*ranking*), and do those entail conflicting interests? Do we think of ourselves as Americans first or as something else, and do our loyalties clash? Shared identities produce psychological affinity, but conflicting identities produce psychological distance; and the presence or absence of such affinity will reinforce or undermine effects of geographic distance. Thus, the major conflicts in global politics are anchored more in attitudes than in geography. Yugoslavs are located in a small geographic area but are separated by an abyss, the product of incompatible self-identities as Serbs, Croats, Moslem Bosnians, Slovenians, Albanians, and Macedonians. Individuals who identify themselves as Jewish or Palestinian feel loyalty to one another that overcomes their living in remote communities around the world.

One identity that was believed to defy geography was economic class. In 1848, Karl Marx and Friedrich Engels brought the Communist Manifesto to a stirring conclusion:

[25]Candidly expressing such a loyalty, Charles Wilson, chairman of General Motors, declared, during a Senate hearing on his nomination to become Secretary of Defense under President Eisenhower, that "what is good for our country is good for General Motors, and vice versa." *Hearings before the Committee on Armed Services, U.S. Senate, 83rd Congress, 1st Session, January 15–16, 1953* (Washington, D.C.: Government Printing Office, 1953), p. 15.

The communists disdain to conceal their views and aims. They openly declare that their ends can be attained only by the forcible overthrow of all existing social conditions. Let the ruling classes tremble at a communistic revolution. The proletarians have nothing to lose but their chains. They have a world to win. Workingmen of all countries, unite![26]

Marxists interpreted historical development as a struggle among classes and tried to ignite a world revolution that would overthrow the bourgeoisie.

Repeatedly, however, Marxists have overestimated the strength of class loyalties. In 1914, the Russian revolutionary Vladimir Ilych Lenin mistakenly believed that workers would identify with their class rather than with their country and would refuse to fight in World War I. In 1917, when the Marxists seized power in Russia, they believed world revolution was imminent. They were wrong, and in the 1920s the Soviet Communist Party spent its energy in the struggle between those allied with Leon Trotsky, who wished to pursue the goal of world revolution, and those backing Stalin, who sought to build a power base in the U.S.S.R. before exporting revolution. Although Stalin won the battle, the Soviet Union kept trying to export revolution until its collapse early in the 1990s.

Countries are able to act in a unified way only if citizens view them as the ultimate repository of loyalty. Where citizens identify strongly with other actors, the state may be torn by conflict. At one extreme is a relatively homogeneous country like Sweden with few rivals for citizens' loyalties. Belgium, on the other hand, is split into rival language groups: the Flemish-speaking population in the north and the French-speaking population in the south. Although Belgians are divided over education and other issues, they have contained language-based conflicts by a variety of ingenious political devices, and for the most part citizens see themselves as Belgian patriots.

Things are not so simple in former colonial territories in Africa, Asia, the Middle East, and even Canada, where Europeans imposed boundaries that did not reflect actual identities. Even today citizens in these countries identify more intensely with groups other than their country, and the result is civil strife. Nigerians think of themselves as Hausa, Ibo, and Yoruba, not Nigerian, and these tribal loyalties exploded into bloody civil war between 1967 and 1970, when the Ibos in the east sought to secede as the Republic of Biafra. Even where civil war is avoided, the governments of these countries may provide ways for one tribal, language, or religious group to repress or exploit another. In Kenya, for example, members of the Kikuyu and Kalenjin tribes have enjoyed political power at the expense of the Luo since national independence in 1963.

Fortunately, citizens do not usually have to make hard choices among the groups with which they identify. One can be a good American and also be loyal to other groups at home and abroad. There is nothing disloyal about an American whose views on reproductive issues are influenced by loyalty to the Catholic Church or whose views on

[26]Karl Marx and Friedrich Engels, "Manifesto of the Communist Party," in Lewis S. Feuer, ed., *Marx and Engels: Basic Writings on Politics and Philosophy* (Garden City, N.Y.: Doubleday, 1959), p. 41.

the Middle East are influenced by identity with Israel and Judaism. Their efforts to influence the American political process are legitimate, and myriad actors participate directly or indirectly, often by employing paid lobbyists to look after their interests. Sometimes, however, issues force individuals to make difficult choices among deep loyalties. The American Civil War forced people to choose between the United States and the Confederacy, a regional loyalty. This choice was especially painful for the many southerners who had attended the U.S. Military Academy at West Point and were officers in the U.S. Army. One such, General Robert E. Lee, became commander of the Confederate Army.

Governments sometimes fear that divided loyalties will engender treason. In the Middle East and North Africa, such governments as those of Egypt, Syria, Tunisia, Algeria, and Morocco fear fundamentalist Muslims, whose loyalty they suspect. In Asia, the governments of Malaysia and Indonesia look with suspicion on communities of "overseas" Chinese, whose loyalties, they suspect, lie elsewhere, and the Indian government is constantly alert for Sikh, Muslim, and fundamentalist Hindu loyalties that might undermine the unity of the multilingual Indian state.

Identities count as heavily between collective actors as within them. Collective actors, like individuals, may identify with, feel kinship with, and sympathize with each other's goals. Group identities may result from shared historical experience (fighting a war against the same foe) or such traits as language, religion, political ideology, type of political system, and political values.

During the French Revolution and subsequent wars between republican France and the monarchic states of Europe, democratic America sympathized with the French struggle. Partly this was in gratitude for French assistance to the colonies during their war for independence and sympathy for another people with similar political institutions. Thomas Jefferson and Alexander Hamilton disputed whether or not the United States should side with France. Jefferson argued that bonds of friendship and ideology required the United States to ally with France. Hamilton cited the principle of balance of power to disagree, arguing that the United States was too weak to provide effective assistance and would merely invite British attacks on American commerce.[27] In short order, this dispute infected domestic politics and divided Jefferson's partisans (the Democratic Party) from Hamilton's (the Federalist Party).

In recent years, the United States and Britain have closely identified with each other owing to their shared experience in World Wars I and II, their common language, and their common heritage. United States–British identities have been reinforced by generations of Americans, including President Bill Clinton, Justice Byron White, and Senator Bill Bradley (N.J.), who studied at British universities, and by other forms of people-to-people contact. When war erupted between Britain and Argentina over the Falklands in 1982, a debate erupted in the United States about which country to

---

[27]Fearing that U.S. interference would help the French little but that it could harm the United States, especially trade and shipping, George Washington issued the Neutrality Proclamation of 1793.

support. One prominent group of Americans led by U.N. Ambassador Jeanne Kirk-patrick favored supporting Argentina because it was in the Western Hemisphere and because it was a growing power. At first, the Reagan administration tried to take a neutral position in the war, but most Americans sympathized with the British and the United States finally supported the successful British war effort.

Expectations

What actors expect of each other is a consequence of combining identities and previous interaction, and such expectations inspire either suspicion or trust. Americans would not expect British hostility but would not be surprised by Libyan or Iranian attacks on U.S. interests. After all, Americans identify with the British, and the two peoples have long enjoyed cooperation and friendship. Most Americans, though, have little in common with the Iran shaped by the Ayatollah Khomeini and his successors or Libya under Muammar Qaddafi, and the hostility of these two societies toward the United States readied Americans to expect the worst from them.

When Pan American Airways flight 103 blew up over Lockerbie, Scotland, in December 1988, Americans suspected that Iranian agents were responsible. The Iranian government not only had a reputation for supporting international terrorism but had specifically vowed to avenge itself for the U.S. Navy downing of an Iranian civilian jetliner over the Persian Gulf earlier in that year. As the investigation of the Lockerbie incident continued, suspicion fell on Libya. Colonel Qaddafi had repeatedly aided international terrorists and had reason to wish to avenge himself for U.S. air raids in April 1986 against Tripoli and Benghazi that had killed one of his children.[28] Such cycles of violence are fueled by negative expectations.

As these examples suggest, the past is a large factor in determining expectations about the future. Actors who have been involved in conflict expect such conflict to recur. Actors who have enjoyed good relations in the past may be surprised if relations sour. In general, people expect the future to resemble the past. Thus, between 1870 and 1913, Europe experienced repeated crises and limited wars. The climate of tension, fear, and frustration these incidents produced made many believe war was inevitable. Ultimately, this "psychology of inevitability" as much as anything else was responsible for the great conflagration in 1914.

Beliefs

What people believe and especially what they regard as right and wrong powerfully shape behavior. Closed sets of beliefs, *ideologies*, resist change. Ideological cleavages form durable conflicts such as those separating East and West during the Cold War, and may

[28]The U.S. raids followed terrorist attacks by Palestinians at the Rome and Vienna airports in December 1985 in which Libyan involvement was suspected.

prolong such conflicts long after the original impetus is irrelevant and the idealism that inspired the ideologies has faded. Ideological conflicts are especially difficult to compromise and inspire fervor in their adherents. Unlike land and money, ideas cannot be divided fairly. Territory can be apportioned between rivals, but it is difficult to become half Christian and half Muslim. One may depersonalize ideological enemies and declare them anathema, and enemies may seek to extirpate ideological antagonists. Abraham Lincoln feared the threatened clash between incompatible ideologies when he declared that no nation could exist "half slave and half free." In contemporary politics, "isms," such as Islamic fundamentalism make it difficult for adversaries to find common ground and solve disputes.

At the same time, ideology makes available to rulers potent new energy. When China's communist rulers took power in 1949, they could apply Marxist-Leninist principles to mobilize China's masses more effectively than previous leaders of the country had done. Eighteenth-century French revolutionary leaders effectively used democratic and nationalist ideologies to rally the masses and defend their country. With his country in greatest peril in 1941, Nazi armies at the gates of Moscow and Leningrad, Soviet dictator Josef Stalin abandoned appeals to Marxist ideology for the more powerful Russian nationalism.

Indeed, since the French Revolution, *nationalism*—exclusive attachment to a national or ethnic group—has probably been the most intensely felt "ism" in world politics. Nationalism can be benign, encouraging interest in language and literature, or it can be malignant. It has contributed to starting wars and to the ferocity with which they were fought. Repeatedly, politicians whip up popular fervor for their policies by posing as defenders of the nation. Napoleon almost succeeded in conquering Europe by stirring up French nationalism, and, late in the nineteenth century, Germany's Iron Chancellor, Otto von Bismarck, used nationalism as a cover for repressing opponents at home and carrying out German unification abroad.

Growing nationalism, as we shall see in Chapter 3, reduces the diplomat's independence and the flexibility of the government's policy. Politicians find it difficult to compromise with adversaries lest they be accused at home of selling out the nation. And, during the hard times when flexible policy is needed, nationalism may intensify and grow ugly. Thus, during the 1920s and 1930s, extreme nationalists ended democratic experiments in Italy, Germany, and Japan, as people sought simple solutions to social and economic ills. Indeed, part of nationalism's potency as an ideology is its simplicity. It does not depend on complex economic or social theories; it merely identifies a heritage (sometimes mythical) shared by a group of people that distinguishes them from others.

Nationalism has resisted challenges by Marxism and liberalism and has survived the Cold War. It remains potent in many parts of the world and may be used to justify violence, as among the peoples of Yugoslavia, the successor nations to the U.S.S.R., and exploding antiforeign violence in Germany. Indeed, political scientist John Mearsheimer triggered a lively debate by arguing that the revival of nationalism might help make conflict more likely in Europe than it was during the Cold War. He denies "the common view":

The yearning for democracy with the Cold War seemed universal, even reaching Beijing, capital of the last major communist state. The statue of liberty in Tiananmen Square revealed Chinese aspirations to achieve American-style democracy, but their aspirations were crushed beneath the treads of tanks.

The profound changes now under way in Europe have been widely viewed as harbingers of a new age of peace. With the Cold War over, it is said, the threat of war that has hung over Europe for more than four decades is lifting. . . . Harmony can reign among the states and peoples of Europe. Central Europe, which long groaned under the massive forces of the two military blocs, can convert its military bases into industrial parks, playgrounds, and condominiums.[29]

Mearsheimer feels that "the decline in nationalism in Europe since 1945 has contributed to the peacefulness of the postwar world."[30] Withdrawing U.S. and Soviet troops, ending the nuclear threat, unifying Germany, and ending communism may all stimulate dangerous nationalism.

[29]John J. Mearsheimer, "Back to the Future: Instability in Europe After the Cold War," *International Security* 15:1 (Summer 1990), p. 5.

[30]Mearsheimer, "Back to the Future," p. 7.

On the whole, it is not clear whether ideological divisions cause war or leaders use them to justify war. The answer is probably a bit of both. Many conflicts (as between Catholics and Protestants in Northern Ireland) are clothed in the language of ideology. Leaders can also use ideology to *depersonalize* an enemy and justify atrocities.[31] The enemy is not a person like you and me but is a communist, a heretic, or a member of some other hated category.

Goals

Actors' beliefs help determine what they wish to accomplish — their goals. If goals are compatible, actors can cooperate; if not, they may find themselves in conflict. The French revolutionary ideology after 1789 led them to seek to overthrow the conservative monarchies of Europe, and the Soviet leaders' communist ideology after 1917 led them to help communists elsewhere to overthrow capitalism.

In the abstract, goals are efforts to increase human satisfaction — prosperity and peace — and reduce deprivation — poverty, disease, and insecurity. As a rule, people who feel they are deprived of things that they need to survive and be happy will make demands on their leaders and others in the global system to satisfy those needs. People who are relatively satisfied with their lot will seek to retain what they already have. Conflicts between haves and have-nots are common in global politics, both past and present. In the 1970s, many of these demands were aggregated under pressure exerted in the U.N. for a New International Economic Order (NIEO).[32] In this contest, wealthy states have sought to preserve their privileged position, and the poor have sought redistribution of resources.

Disputes between haves and have-nots are one example of a larger problem: incompatible goals. Actors assign different priorities to objects that they value. People who are reasonably satisfied with their lives rank peace highly, but for those who are starving or are enslaved, peace may be a luxury they cannot afford. Those who sought to appease Hitler in the 1930s were accused of wanting "peace at any price." Every day, South African blacks, Palestinians, and others said by their deeds that they were willing to sacrifice peace for equality and national independence. The patriot Patrick Henry eloquently proposed this sort of trade-off, thunderingly challenging his fellow Virginians to cast off British rule: "Give me liberty, or give me death!"

Different ordering of what people think is important is a major source of misunderstanding in global politics. People who do not share our sense of what is

---

[31] The power of ideology as justification for leaders' behavior is portrayed by George Orwell in his novel *1984*.

[32] See Chapter 10, pp. 336–358.

important in similar situations are not necessarily irrational. If we cannot make sense of the values they cherish, we must recognize the cultural and psychological distance that may separate us from them. For Shi'ite Muslims, unlike Americans, ensuring the purity of Islam matters most; for Israelis it may be secure borders; for others it may be a loaf of bread. Value priorities do change, however, driving people's goals further apart or bringing them closer together. North Americans and West Europeans, many of whom have not only satisfied basic material needs but enjoy a high standard of living are increasingly interested in "post-material" goals, including a clean and healthful global environment. The poor inhabitants of the Third World, though, hope to achieve prosperity by industrialization, exacerbating by their determination a number of environmental crises. Inevitably, such differences in hierarchies of values lead to disagreements over such issues as deforestation, conservation of energy, and disposal of hazardous wastes.

Conclusion

You have now encountered the system, subsystem, and the components of a system's structure. When we study systems, we look at the big picture to see how the parts of the global puzzle fit together. Because viewing the whole clarifies how the pieces fit, it is useful to begin here. The system's structure, though mostly invisible to individuals, determines that which is possible and probable in global politics. The possible is circumscribed by resources, and the probable is conditioned by attitudes. Their distribution and redistribution, not their absolute level, are critical to understanding the interaction of actors in the system.

Defining and measuring resources and attitudes is neither simple nor easy. Use of resources may or may not be directed toward achieving political objectives and goals and may or may not be appropriate for attaining those goals. Some resources contribute to overall clout and others help us use what we have effectively. Resources are also related in complex ways to an actor's status. But we are likely to study resources and ignore attitudes. Ultimately, the relationship between resources and attitudes is reciprocal.

Still, resources are not the same as power, our next subject. Power is one of our most elusive concepts but is the basis for the traditional view of global politics. That interpretation has dominated theory and practice in Western international relations for hundreds of years; it also sees the state and the state system as they evolved in Europe as the foundation for global politics. In Chapter 3, we look more closely at this view and the historical reality on which it is based. We also consider power and the pitfalls it poses for the unwary.

Key Terms

global political system

interaction

system

positive or amplifying feedback

negative or corrective feedback

second-order feedback

subsystems

boundaries

system structure

emergent property

distribution of resources

distribution of influence

compatibility of goals

alliances

stability

tangible resources

intangible resources

geopolitics

size

social and economic development

modernity

status

status inconsistency

distribution of attitudes

identities

expectations

beliefs

goals

nationalism

parts of a system

interdependent units

information

interdependence

ideologies

capability

intentions

escalation

panic

actors

issues

weapons of mass destruction

arms race

depersonalize

CHAPTER THREE

The Puzzle of Power

The stronger do not always enjoy the spoils of victory. During the Vietnam war, half a million American and more than a million South Vietnamese troops, supported by a naval armada including aircraft carriers and battleships and air forces flying B-52 bombers, spent nearly a decade (1965–1973) in a frustrating effort to keep the Saigon government from collapsing and Vietnam from unifying under communist rule. America's enormous nuclear arsenal and much of its high-technology weaponry were less useful in the Vietnam war than the Vietcong and North Vietnamese low-tech bicycles and small arms, with which they fought as guerrillas in the jungles of Southeast Asia. Despite U.S. military might, the last American soldiers were forced to flee Saigon helter-skelter in helicopters on April 30, 1975, the day the city fell to the communists.

Sometimes, the strong do not know their own strength. Following the Iraqi invasion of Kuwait in August 1990, the United States assembled a coalition of twenty-eight countries and more than half a million troops equipped with the most modern weapons in America's arsenal.[1] The allies took no chances with the large, battle-hardened Iraqi army, armed with up-to-date Soviet and Western weapons and concealed in deep fortifications along the border with Saudi Arabia. Allied forces commanded by U.S. General Norman Schwarzkopf waited through a month of intense air bombardment before launching, on February 23, 1991, a ground invasion (Operation Desert Storm). Within 100 hours, President George Bush was able to announce that Kuwait was liberated. Iraq suffered as many as 400,000 casualties,

---

[1] Among the weapons the allies used for the first time in combat in the Persian Gulf War were sea-launched cruise missiles, Patriot anti-missile missiles, and the Abrams tank (M-1). The array of modern U.S. aircraft included Stealth fighters and B-52s equipped with precision-guided "smart" bombs.

The end of the Cold War did not bring an end to force, and a multinational army, spearheaded by U.S. units, was needed to reverse Iraqi dictator Saddam Hussein's invasion and occupation of oil-rich Kuwait.

including 100,000 dead, and lost 4,000 of its 4,200 tanks. Western losses were a few hundred, mostly from "friendly fire." Despite the "elephantine estimate" of Iraqi military resources, "the Iraqi army," declared one observer, "put up almost no defense at all. . . . The sides were so mismatched that it was hardly a war at all."[2]

Although the first conflict was a policy disaster and the second a triumph, they have in common the failure to assess an enemy's power well enough to guide policy. Despite the most advanced intelligence apparatus in history, the United States woefully *under*estimated the power of North Vietnam — a "third-rate" country — to endure hardship, absorb military blows, and defeat a superpower in a contest for Vietnamese political loyalties. Having learned the "lesson" of Vietnam — perhaps too well — the United States drastically *over*estimated Iraq's power following its seizure of Kuwait.

These military miscalculations only begin to tell the story of the puzzle of power. Consider efforts to exert economic power. By the early 1970s, the Organization of Arab Petroleum Exporting Countries (OAPEC)[3] controlled much of the world's oil — an

[2]Theodore Draper, "The True History of the Gulf War," *New York Review of Books*, January 30, 1992, pp. 41, 42.

[3]The OAPEC consortium, established by Kuwait, Libya, and Saudi Arabia at a 1968 meeting in Beirut, recognized the special need for coordination among Arab members of OPEC.

all-but irreplaceable raw material — and seemed to enjoy a stranglehold on the West's energy supplies. Following the 1973 Arab-Israeli war, OAPEC sought to use its oil power to force the West to change its Middle-Eastern policies. Yet the resulting embargo on OAPEC oil to the United States and the Netherlands and threat of an embargo against others such as Japan affected their policies little.[4] Again, ineptly estimating and applying power kept its wielders from their objectives.

Power is indeed a puzzling, elusive, concept, difficult to define and even harder to measure. Nevertheless, power is at the heart of a major tradition in international-relations scholarship — variously called *realism*, *Realpolitik*, and *power politics* — wedding the idea of power to that of the territorial state in Europe. We begin with a general definition and follow by briefly sketching how the European state system evolved and the *balance-of-power* theory and practice that accompanied it. Thereafter, we consider more recent theories of global politics growing out of the power-politics tradition. Finally, we return to our definition and some problems in measuring power. The phenomenon changes, of course, before our eyes. A source of power in one historical period may vanish in another.

Power: A General Definition

Although many would agree with the Italian political theorist Niccolò Machiavelli that a prince "before engaging in any enterprise should well measure his strength, and govern himself accordingly,"[5] carrying out his advice is not simple. How tempting it is to conceptualize power as a thing, a tangible object the possession of which permits an actor to do as it wishes. Some such assumption lies behind facile claims such as "countries with nuclear weapons are powerful." But making nuclear weapons equivalent to power confuses the capabilities that might contribute to power with power itself. Those who make this error may then be surprised when a gigantic country with nuclear weapons — a *superpower* like the United States — fails to achieve its aims in Vietnam, or the Soviet Union is forced to withdraw ignominiously from Afghanistan.

Such observers are caught by surprise because, first, power is not a tangible thing, nor does it inhere in one actor. *Power is a psychological relationship in which one actor influences another to behave differently than it would have if left to its own devices.* When we speak of an actor as powerful, we really mean it can exercise influence over someone or something.[6] In a position of power an actor can *cause* another actor to do what it

---

[4]Roy Licklider, *Political Power and the Arab Oil Weapon: The Experience of Five Industrialized Nations* (Berkeley: University of California Press, 1988), p. 279.

[5]Niccolo Machiavelli, *The Prince and The Discourses* (New York: Random House, Modern Library College Edition, 1950), p. 308.

[6]We use *power* and *influence* interchangeably. *Power* is the more popular, but *influence* — unlike power — can be used as a verb and so connotes more fully that the phenomenon is relational.

wishes.[7] The first actor's power over the second does not necessarily extend to other actors. Indeed, the first actor may take power from conditions that apply to that relationship and no other: a common frontier, unusually high dependence on an imported resource, or a personal relationship among leaders.

A corollary of the first reason is that the influence relationship is not general but *exists only in particular contexts*. An actor's capabilities or resources may prove useful for creating power in one context but not in another.[8] In other words, any influence relationship is limited and has a specific *domain* (the persons whose probable behavior is subject to it) and *scope* (the aspects of behavior that are subject to it).[9]

The Japanese government holds greatest influence over actors who depend on Tokyo for trade and high technology—the domain of its power. Japanese influence is greatest in countries that are single-mindedly preoccupied by economic development; it is less in countries like Russia in which nationalist sentiment is high. Strong Russian nationalism prevents Moscow from giving back to Japan the tiny northern islands of Kunashiri, Etorofu, Habomai, and Shikotan in the Kurile chain. Annexed after World War II, they could be swapped for the economic and technological assistance that Russia desperately needs. Japanese influence is much less where military force is necessary because its constitution forbids a large army, and memories of Japanese aggression in World War II make other countries nervous about Japanese troops overseas.

The fact that power is a relationship limited by its context makes it easier to explain why measuring it has proved so elusive. After all, how do we tangibly capture a psychological relationship? Instead, we must infer the relationship by analyzing its consequences (output) or looking at what goes into it (input).

The Power-Politics Tradition

Power politics is an intellectual tradition from classical Greece and the Italian Renaissance. Many of its ideas appear in the monumental *History of the Peloponnesian War* written by a discredited Athenian general Thucydides, and in *The Prince*, by the Florentine politician Niccolò Machiavelli.

---

[7]Defining power as a causal relationship is complicated because the influencer can have power without taking any action. An actor may either refrain from behaving in certain ways or may undertake some action because it *anticipates* that this is the behavior a more powerful actor would wish. Then the cause of the actor's behavior is invisible, but a power relationship exists.

[8]See Chapter 2, pp. 58–59.

[9]Karl W. Deutsch, *The Analysis of International Relations*, 2nd ed. (Englewood Cliffs, N.J.: Prentice-Hall, 1978), pp. 32, 38, 40. Emphasis in original.

Thucydides

Thucydides depicts Athens declining from wealth, power, and glory to indigence and dependence. Analyzing the conflict between Athens and Sparta that engulfed Greece in 431 B.C., Thucydides sought to understand the general causes of war: "It will be enough for me . . . if these words . . . are judged useful by those who want to understand clearly the events which happened in the past and which (human nature being what it is) will . . . be repeated in the future. My work is not a piece of writing designed to meet the taste of an immediate public, but was done to last for ever."[10]

Like a physician diagnosing an illness, Thucydides identifies a cause that can be treated. "What made war inevitable," he writes, "was the growth of Athenian power and the fear which this caused in Sparta"[11] — in other words, a breakdown in the balance of power. Spartan fear of Athenian power stirred suspicion and hostility, sparking war during a crisis. Thucydides illustrates that the key may not be how power is distributed at one moment but whether redistribution takes place so quickly as to destabilize the system. He reports that many city-states in Greece came to fear Athens because, after the Greeks defeated the Persians, the Athenians *rapidly* increased their empire and their economic and naval strength. Changing the system's distribution of resources left uncertainty about the future and made old expectations and identities obsolete. Sparta sought to balance Athenian power, and its effort made Athens and its allies suspicious of Spartan motives. Amid mutual fear and recrimination, it took only a spark to produce a conflagration.

Thucydides is regarded as a father of the power-politics tradition in international relations. First, distribution of power seems to him to determine events. He also *appears* to discount morality in global affairs. In the famed *Melian dialogue* he recounts how Athens demanded assistance from the small island of Melos and how the Athenians rejected the Melians' appeal to justice and fair play. "[W]e recommend," declare the Athenians, "that you should try to get what is possible for you to get . . . ; since you know as well as we do that . . . the standard of justice depends on the equality of power to compel and that in fact the strong do what they have the power to do and the weak accept what they have to accept."[12] Some see Thucydides' analysis as no more than praise of power at the expense of justice ("might makes right"), but they miss his most eloquent contributions. He narrates the tragedy of Athens, a great city-state, and how power and glory made its citizens arrogant and insensitive. In their arrogance they overextended the empire until a disastrous expedition to Sicily, culminating in defeat of the city and decline for classical Greek civilization.

Describing that decline, Thucydides argues that democracies are poorly equipped to make foreign policy because people turn for leadership to zealous demagogues. In his description of overextended Athenian power and the subsequent decline in civic virtue,

[10]Thucydides, *The Peloponnesian War*, trans. by Rex Warner (Baltimore: Penguin Books, 1954), pp. 24–25.
[11]Ibid., p. 25.
[12]Ibid., p. 160.

some readers see an uncanny parallel to the United States in Vietnam. Echoing Thucydides's analysis, critics of the U.S. intervention saw a close relationship between overextended capabilities abroad and political and social turmoil at home.[13] America's leaders, they said, were victims of overweening pride, and, like Athenian leaders, they were undermining democracy at home to repress criticism of an overseas adventure.

Machiavelli

Like Thucydides's *History*, Machiavelli's *Prince* is recognized as a major contribution to the power-politics tradition. Machiavelli distinguishes clearly between a prince's *private* duties and obligations and their *public* role as surrogate for the citizens of a state, declaring that a prince "must not flinch from being blamed for vices which are necessary for safeguarding the state" and will find "that some of the things that appear to be virtues will, if he practices them, ruin him, and some of the things that appear to be wicked will bring him security and prosperity."[14]

This idea—called *reason of state* (*raison d'état* or *ragioni di stato*) because it was the direction an actor would take if its leaders behaved rationally—implied that the citizens of a state *collectively* have interests that are greater and different than the mere sum of their individual interests. In other words, each state had a national interest, as it would be called later, which reflected its relative power, geography, and other factors that determined its survival and prosperity.[15] Both Thucydides and Machiavelli seemed to regard power and its distribution as the most important determinants of *national interest*, which presumably was the source of an actor's goals and actions.

Machiavelli, like others in the power-politics tradition, rested his analyses on the belief that the world is a dangerous place. The source of danger, some in this tradition felt, was inherent in the defective nature of human beings, who were naturally aggressive and acquisitive.[16] Others emphasize human nature less and point to the absence of central authority in world politics—*anarchy*—that they believe makes trust impossible and forces actors to rely on their own devices—the practice of self-help. Still others emphasize both, but whatever the source of danger, all stress the central role of power in ensuring states' survival.

If conflict is an inevitable consequence of human nature or global anarchy, questions arise: why are we not constantly at war with each other, and how can war be prevented and its consequences mitigated? For many in this tradition, the answer is to

---

[13]The economic inflation in the 1970s, upsurge in use in drugs, and decay in the inner cities are at least in part viewed as the inheritance of the Vietnam war.

[14]Niccolò Machiavelli, *The Prince*, trans. by George Bull (Baltimore, Md.: Penguin Books, 1961), p. 92.

[15]See Friedrich Meinecke, *Machiavellism* (New Haven: Yale University Press, 1957).

[16]There are variations on such human nature claims. Christian theologians refer to man's fallen nature and to original sin. Some psychologists in the tradition of Sigmund Freud speak of a death instinct. Some anthropologists think human aggression has become dangerous because of incomplete evolution combined with mastery of weapons.

be found in the use of power to thwart others who seek power. This is the basic idea of the *balance of power*. A brief look at the evolution and flowering of the state system in Europe will help us understand this concept.

The Halcyon Era of the Sovereign State

The emphasis on power in global-relations theory partly grows out of scholars' and practitioners' preoccupation with lessons drawn from the crowded system of competitive European territorial states that dominated world politics between the seventeenth and nineteenth centuries. These "sovereign" states sought to guard their internal affairs from external interference and vigorously competed among themselves for advantage in foreign affairs. During that same period, the territorial states of Europe conquered much of the rest of the world, and their ideas of world politics accompanied them.

The restless competition among European states encouraged observers to emphasize power and its distribution in the system. The heirs to this tradition—scholars and practitioners—remain transfixed by a belief that global politics is little more than a struggle for power among sovereign states. Although the classical tradition of power politics or Realpolitik seems curiously dated in some ways, it does correspond to a historical reality in Europe. The perceptions and maxims of many contemporary theorists and practitioners reflect this bygone era, and often their illustrations are from that era. Some are also drawn to the period because, one observer writes, it "was a period of order and progress." "An international society of states, or princes, functioned well, with rules and institutions and underlying assumptions which its members accepted."[17]

Power and the Evolution of the European State

Although the idea of organizing people within defined and stable boundaries governed from the center by complex, autonomous, and anonymous bureaucracies had many historical precedents, it reached its zenith and was idealized in Europe when territorial kingdoms formed. The European system as it evolved after the Renaissance was unusual in that numerous independent states coexisted next to each other and none was able to dominate the others. By contrast, important regional systems elsewhere were dominated by one bureaucratic state, as mainland Asia was by China after its unification, and, as a result, rivalries were less intense and continuous than in Europe.

The many small states in a limited space with no authority to regulate their behavior meant that rivalry and war were endemic among the European kingdoms, and that custom and law evolved to keep participants from each other's throats. The eighteenth-century French political philosopher Jean-Jacques Rousseau captured the spirit of states living cheek-by-jowl when he wrote that "they touch each other at so

[17]Adam Watson, *The Evolution of International Society: A Comparative Historical Analysis* (New York: Routledge, 1992), p. 198.

many points that not one of them can move without giving a jar to all the rest; their variances are all the more deadly, as their ties are more closely woven; their frequent quarrels are almost as savage as civil wars."[18] In fact, the almost continuous conflict among Europeans compelled them to compete in developing the economic and technological innovations (especially military) that enabled them to conquer other peoples.

By the eighteenth century, the European monarchs had achieved nearly absolute power within their territories and had built a protective barrier around them. John Herz captures the essence of the sovereign state during this "halcyon era":

> What is it that ultimately accounted for the peculiar unity, compactness, coherence of the modern nation-state . . . ? It would seem that this underlying factor is to be found neither in the sphere of law nor in that of politics, but rather in that substratum of statehood where the state unit confronts us, as it were, in its physical, corporeal capacity: *as an expanse of territory encircled for its identification and its defense by a "hard shell" of fortifications.* In this lies what will here be referred to as the "impermeability," or "impenetrability," or simply the "territoriality," of the modern state.[19]

The model sovereign state of the age was France under King Louis XIV (1643–1715). Assisted by the great cleric-statesmen Cardinals Mazarin and Richelieu, the king ensured the *external* security of his realm with a professional army of unprecedented size, the administrative and technological skills of an increasingly prosperous middle class, an economic system developed specifically to increase military power, and a series of fortifications along the French frontiers.[20] France was a genuine *great power* in an age when the label meant a state that could not be conquered even by the united efforts of the other states.[21] It was not the army alone that wove a *hard shell of impermeability* around France and the other great powers of the time. All pursued an economic system known as *mercantilism*—the opposite of free trade—the aim of which was to become self-sufficient in manufactures and agricultural products necessary to wage war. No ruler wished to depend on imports from another, and all aided domestic industries by

---

[18]Jean-Jacques Rousseau, "Abstract of the Abbé de Saint-Pierre's Project for Perpetual Peace," in M. G. Forsyth, H. M. A. Keens-Soper, P. Savigear, eds., *The Theory of International Relations* (New York: Atherton Press, 1970), p. 136.

[19]John H. Herz, "Rise and Demise of the Territorial State," in Herz, ed., *The Nation-State and the Crisis of World Politics* (New York: McKay, 1976), pp. 100–101. (Emphasis added.) It is doubtful that states were ever fully impermeable. Peter Gourevitch says, "The same hopelessly inter-penetrated quality of foreign and domestic issues was also present in the Revolt of the Netherlands, the Thirty Years' War, and indeed all the wars of the sixteenth and seventeenth centuries . . ." ("The Second Image Reversed: The International Sources of Domestic Power," *International Organization* 32:4 (Autumn 1978), p. 908.)

[20]See Henry Guerlac, "Vauban: The Impact of Science on War," in Peter Paret, ed., *Makers of Modern Strategy* (Princeton: Princeton University Press, 1986), pp. 64–90.

[21]If France and Britain were the leading great powers of their age, Prussia under King Frederick the Great was the smallest. Yet, Frederick's Prussia proved its credentials in the Seven Years' War (1756–1763), surviving against the united effort of France, Austria's Habsburg Empire, and Russia, each of which had a population more than four times that of Prussia.

imposing import duties, providing state support for inefficient industries, and building state-owned monopolies. Mercantilism meant that states sought self-sufficiency by encouraging exports and discouraging imports.[22] Mercantilist states hoarded precious metals to pay for armies and weapons and sought empires in which they would enjoy exclusive trading rights. Though less efficient in cost and quality from a *global* perspective than free trade, mercantilism served the purpose of expanding power for *individual states.*[23]

Louis XIV, known as the Sun King, reinforced the *internal* side of French sovereignty by centralizing authority at his court in Versailles and forcing French nobles to reside there. In this and other ways, the king made the formerly rebellious nobility dependent on him and his corps of central administrators.[24] Increasingly, the king bound his realm together by appointing to administrative positions prosperous members of the French middle class, who depended on and were loyal to the monarchy. Although limited communications and transportation made Louis XIV less of an absolute monarch than is often thought, his web of administrators successfully tamed the independent nobles, economic guilds, and cities throughout France.

Europe's Classical Balance of Power

Eighteenth-century Europe is even more an object of attention because of a relationship that evolved among the great powers known as *the balance of power.*[25] The idea of such a balance did not, of course, originate in eighteenth-century Europe. The historian Thucydides implied a balance among the Greek city-states, and balance-of-power politics characterized the city-states of Renaissance Italy as well as the princely states in ancient India and the warring states in ancient China.[26] Nowhere, however, did the

[22]As we shall see in Chapter 10, economic interdependence has made it costly for actors to pursue mercantilist policies today. Nevertheless, actors sometimes make the effort. Until recently the Soviet Union, China, and the countries of Eastern Europe isolated themselves from global economic institutions and the "capitalist" international economic system.

[23]Free trade was encouraged by entrepreneurs and corporations, and its growing popularity in the nineteenth century was a consequence of global economic dominance by one state—Great Britain—that could profit from it. The growth of free trade also reflected the eroding power that states held over their citizens.

[24]This practice has been referred to as the "Courtization of Warriors." Norbert Elias, *State Formation and Civilization,* trans. by Edmund Jephcott (Oxford, Eng.: Basil Blackwell, 1982), pp. 258–270.

[25]See Edward Vose Gulick, *Europe's Classical Balance of Power: A Case History of the Theory and Practice of One of the Great Concepts of European Statecraft* (New York: W. W. Norton, 1955).

[26]However, the Italian balance of power deteriorated into a "theater in which the conflicts of the European powers were acted out." Winfried Franke, "The Italian City-State System as an International System," in Morton A. Kaplan, ed., *New Approaches to International Relations* (New York: St. Martin's Press, 1968), p. 448. And the Hindu system lacked "stable patterns of collaboration" and was characterized by "rudimentary and unregulated" diplomacy. George Modelski, "Kautilya: Foreign Policy in the Ancient Hindu World," *American Political Science Review* 58:3 (September 1964), p. 556.

balance-of-power metaphor and model become so embedded in the thinking of states-men and philosophers as in Europe.[27]

During the eighteenth century, Europe was dominated by a few major powers which competed for limited political and economic advantage. None was sufficiently powerful to dominate the rest, and each respected the right of the others to survive. Mutual respect among the great powers did not extend to small countries. Indeed, the fate of small countries was a source of conflict among the great powers, and settlements among them often meant fair division of the spoils — that is, countries like Poland.[28] Each participant felt obliged to do what was necessary — including joining and shifting alliances, increasing armaments, and going to war — to prevent any of them from dominating or threatening the others. This aim is reflected in a treaty between England and Spain that permitted the French king's grandson to become king of Spain but forbade union of the French and Spanish kingdoms:

> Whereas the war . . . was at the beginning undertaken . . . because of the great danger which threatened the liberty and safety of all Europe, from the too close conjunction of the kingdoms of Spain and France; and whereas, to take away all uneasiness and suspicion concerning such conjunction out of the minds of people, and to settle and establish the peace and tranquillity of Christendom by an equal balance of power (which is the best and most solid foundation of a mutual friendship . . .); as well the Catholic King [of Spain] as the most Christian King [of France] have consented, that care should be taken . . . that the kingdoms of Spain and of France should never come and be united under the same dominion, and that one and the same person should never become king of both kingdoms.[29]

Wars occurred frequently among states, but they were usually short and had limited objectives. Those who were defeated were welcomed back into the system by the winners and were treated as potential allies in future conflicts. Peace was not an objective of balance-of-power politics, and one observer writes that peace "was no more essential to equilibrist theory than the barnacle to the boat."[30] In fact, maintaining the balance depended on the threat of large-scale war. The powers used that threat—

---

[27]The balance-of-power idea was deeply rooted in the eighteenth-century mind and reflected the principles of the science of mechanics that were in vogue. Leaders even viewed their states as having a defined role in the "game" — a game often likened to chess. British statesmen thought of their country as a *balancer* that would intervene to tip the scales of the balance in the direction of the weaker alliance.

[28]Poland was partitioned among the great powers on three occasions — 1772, 1793, and 1795.

[29]Cited in Watson, *Evolution of International Society*, p. 199.

[30]Gulick, *Europe's Classical Balance of Power*, p. 35.

supplemented by flexible alliances,[31] compensations,[32] and armaments races—to prevent any of them from upsetting the balance and dominating the others.

Recalling the indiscriminate slaughter that accompanied religious conflicts in the previous century, the conservative rulers of eighteenth-century Europe wished to avoid major war which would destroy the system that was so beneficial to them and their class or which would disrupt the national economies that were bringing them prosperity. In a word, the policy of balance of power aimed to maintain the status quo among the great powers and therefore the stability of the system as a whole.[33] In other words, rulers recognized that rapid and unguided changes in the system's structure might endanger their hold on power as well as the independence of their realms.

The balance-of-power system *seemed* to work, and theorists of the time regarded it almost reverentially. The Swiss scholar of international law Emmerich de Vattel described it as a product of the "common interest" of the European monarchies, united "for the maintenance of order and the preservation of liberty."[34] Rousseau declared that the balance flowed from a Europe "united by identity of religion, of moral standard, of international law,"[35] and the English radical Henry Lord Brougham likened it to a scientific breakthrough: "It was as much unknown to Athens and Rome, as the Keplerian or Newtonian laws were concealed from Plato and Cicero. . . . It has arisen, in the progress of science, out of the circumstances of modern Europe. . . . "[36] The balance was also loudly praised by thinkers as diverse as David Hume, Immanuel Kant, Edmund Burke, and Friedrich von Gentz.

Prerequisites for Balance of Power

The balance of power, one observer states, "became a feasible practice for eighteenth-century statesmen . . . because Louis XIV's bid for hegemony was broken by a coalition of states in which no one was dominant. There was no successor to Louis's claims, and no state felt strong enough to challenge the prevailing assumptions against hegemony and in favour of balance."[37] Yet, if balance-of-power theory was germane to Europe at

[31] See, for example, Hans J. Morgenthau, *Politics Among Nations*, 6th ed. rev. by Kenneth W. Thompson (New York: Knopf, 1985), pp. 209–213.

[32] If one actor increased its power, it might maintain the balance (and peace as well) by compensating the other great powers. In some cases, *compensation* was used as the basis for policies of *appeasement*, which entailed using rewards to conciliate a potential adversary. German Chancellor Otto von Bismarck's effort to propitiate the French in 1881 by dangling Tunisia as "a ripe plum ready to be plucked" illustrates the policy of appeasement.

[33] Gulick, *Europe's Classical Balance of Power*, pp. 37–42.

[34] Emmerich de Vattel, "The Law of Nations," in Forsyth et al., *Theory of International Relations*, p. 118.

[35] Jean-Jacques Rousseau, "Abstract of the Abbé de Saint-Pierre's Project for Perpetual Peace," in Forsyth et al., *Theory of International Relations*, p. 133.

[36] Henry Brougham, "Balance of Power," in Forsyth et al., *Theory of International Relations*, p. 269.

[37] Watson, *Evolution of International Society*, p. 199.

a moment in its history, the conditions that allowed it to flourish had already begun to disappear by the end of the eighteenth century with the French Revolution and Napoleon's conquests. After all, Gulick says, the "theory was adjusted to work best through absolutism and under the warm sun of cosmopolitanism, since it demanded both flexibility and moderation."[38] What were these conditions; why were they necessary for the balance to function effectively; and what brought them to an end?

The first condition for a balance of power is the existence of a system of competitive states the leaders of which are aware of their linked fates.   The states that constituted the European system of the seventeenth and eighteenth centuries were tightly linked, and their leaders were conscious of those links. Lord Brougham saw the connection between a successful balance-of-power system and "the perpetual attention to foreign affairs which it inculcates; the constant watchfulness which it prescribes over every movement in all parts of the system . . . ; the unceasing care which it dictates of nations mostly remotely situated, and apparently unconnected with ourselves; the general union . . . of all the European powers in one connecting system. . . ."[39] In contemporary jargon, we might say that eighteenth-century Europe was highly interdependent and that leaders' understanding of how each state affected all other states in the system permitted the balance to work effectively.

The system requires a limited number of leading actors relatively equal in power.   The eighteenth-century European balance comprised five great powers—Britain, France, Austria, Russia, and Prussia—second-ranking states like Ottoman Turkey, Sweden, Spain, and the Netherlands, and such smaller *pawns* as Poland, Bavaria, Saxony, and Denmark. Although the military and economic capabilities of the great powers differed, they were sufficiently equal that, by adroitly shifting from one alliance to another, each could make a significant difference. In a system with numerous relatively equal actors, their number alone would dilute the balance because no one of them would be felt. In a system with very few great powers and many minor actors (such as the bipolar system that formed after 1945), a balance cannot function because no one can restrain a superpower except another superpower.

Those states and their leaders must share an interest in preserving the system itself, and ideology must not reduce flexibility.   The participants must be generally conservative and interested in preserving the status quo; neither ideology nor intense antipathy must impede communication and negotiation. An effective balance of power depends on rapid shifts in alliances. Once a potential threat to the balance has ended, actors must be willing and able to reverse alliances, even allying with former enemies. Actors must

---

[38]Gulick, *Europe's Classical Balance of Power,* p. 298.
[39]Brougham, "Balance of Power," p. 269.

have no permanent friends or enemies, and former adversaries must not be excluded from the system after their defeat. If ideological differences or nationalist passions bar cooperation, behavior will not be moderate, and political flexibility will vanish.

When ideology, and especially *nationalism*, intrude in relations, the system becomes rigid and timely shifts in alliances become difficult. After the Franco-Prussian War of 1870, intense French nationalism aroused by France's defeat and loss of the frontier provinces Alsace and Lorraine to Germany prevented Franco-German reconciliation and produced the conditions out of which a rigid alliance system evolved. This system greatly contributed to starting World War I. And, in the years following the war, French and British nationalism isolated Weimar Germany and contributed to the German climate of opinion that brought Hitler to power in 1933. Ideological antipathy between Bolshevik Russia and the capitalist West also prevented an alliance among Britain, France, and Russia to balance Hitler.[40]

The states in seventeenth and eighteenth-century Europe, though, were dominated by like-minded monarchs and aristocratic elites who, whatever their differences, were bound by class interest in maintaining the system and the dynasties they represented. They were also bound by ties of marriage, language, similar education, and friendships and sympathy. All "civilized" Europeans of the age spoke French, just as all civilized Europeans in the Middle Ages had spoken Latin.[41] Europe's rulers understood that dominance by any one of them or unrestrained warfare could threaten the survival of those *dynastic interests*. Consequently, their objectives and their wars remained relatively moderate and limited.

Both soldiers and diplomats were prepared to shift allegiances. And, if soldiers did not wish to struggle too fiercely against potential employers, diplomats could be persuaded to see virtue in each other's positions when provided with a nice fat bribe. The durable French statesman, Charles Maurice de Talleyrand, reflects the ideal of his age. He was flexible, serving King Louis XIV as minister of foreign affairs, the revolutionaries who beheaded Louis, Napoleon Bonaparte who overthrew the revolutionaries, and the new king who was installed after Napoleon's defeat. Talleyrand also died the wealthiest man in Europe from the bribes he received. By the lights of his time he was an honest man; he never accepted a *sou* unless he could keep his end of a bargain.

The *French Revolution* unleashed forces of nationalism that rapidly made the balance of power obsolete. These forces erected new psychological barriers between peoples and rulers. The revolutionary leaders in France were pioneers in manipulating political symbols to intensify nationalist fervor emphasizing the barriers dividing states. The very word for "state" in French (*l'état*) was replaced by "fatherland" (*la patrie*),

---

[40]British and French leaders were so blinded by ideology that in the moment of their greatest peril, just before the invasion of France, they were trying to help Finland resist "Bolshevik" aggression.

[41]In fact, some of Europe's rulers, including the Russian tsars, spoke their country's language indifferently. Modern Russian still reflects that influence in words such as "royal" (meaning piano) that was the name of the French grand piano played by the tsar.

implying that all citizens were part owners of their country. A new flag with the nation's colors—red, white, and blue—replaced the old one with the Bourbon monarchy's fleur-de-lis. A new national anthem—*La Marseillaise*—stirred the nationalist spirit of the masses.[42] The common form of address, "sir" (*monsieur*), was replaced by "citizen" (*citoyen*).[43]

Foreign policy should be in the hands of professional diplomats.   As we observed in Chapter 2, there was another side to these symbols of popular nationalism—growing rigidity in *diplomacy*. The conduct of foreign affairs was increasingly conducted with an eye on domestic politics, and the role of dispassionate professionals, so important to the system's smooth functioning, was diminished. When the balance of power functioned effectively, diplomacy was in the hands of a few professionals who, like Talleyrand, understood how the balance worked, were alert to threats to it, and were willing to bargain effectively with representatives from other countries. Such diplomats were independent of domestic pressures (except, of course, the whims of their royal masters) and were responsive *only* to external conditions.[44]

Following the defeat of Napoleon, a remarkable group of such diplomats gathered in Vienna (September 1814–June 1815) to rebuild the shattered eighteenth-century balance by erecting a *Concert of Europe*. These diplomats—Talleyrand of France, Prince Metternich of Austria, Viscount Castlereagh of Great Britain, and Tsar Alexander I of Russia—appreciated, one observer reports, "that something new and different must be devised to mitigate the increasingly chaotic and warlike balance-of-power system of the previous century."[45] In accord with balance-of-power principles, the assembled diplomats agreed to readmit France to their community and redistributed a number of European territories to equalize the power of the leading states. More important, the victors (plus France) agreed that they should regulate Europe's affairs through periodic summit conferences and should prevent any new revolutionary excesses that might, as the French Revolution had, imperil the status quo.[46]

The professional diplomats who made the European balance work and who created the Concert of Europe were agents of the *state*, not the *nation*. And they could not function effectively and the Concert could not survive the surges of public passion that inhibited policy or drove it in directions that were incompatible with principles of the balance. "State"

[42]Fans of old films may recall the scene in *Casablanca* when the anthem is played, and all the French in "Rick's" stand to attention and sing, disgusting the Nazi onlookers.

[43]Similar symbolism characterized Russia after the 1917 Bolshevik Revolution when "comrade" (*tovarich*) replaced "mister" (*gospadin*).

[44]See Inis L. Claude, Jr., *Power and International Relations* (New York: Random House, 1962), pp. 90–91.

[45]Richard B. Elrod, "The Concert of Europe: A Fresh Look at an International System," *World Politics* 28:2 (January 1976), p. 161.

[46]See René Albrecht-Carríe, *The Concert of Europe* (New York: Harper & Row, 1968), p. 48.

and "nation" are different. Often states consist of peoples who identify with different nations, such as Austria-Hungary, which consisted of German-speaking Austrians, Magyar-speaking Hungarians, Serbian-speaking Slavs, and even Italians. Sometimes, nations do not possess a homeland and must struggle to make one and create a state.

Nationalism forces leaders to gain and maintain popular approval for their actions. One principle of the balance is, of course, that wars should have only limited ends or should be undertaken to preserve the balance itself. Statesmen designed the balance and the later Concert to prevent "unlimited" conflicts such as the *Thirty Years' War* and the *Napoleonic Wars*. The merging of nation and state undermined this principle. Nationalism enables leaders to whip up *nationalist* fervor at home to draw attention away from the country's problems, and, if war erupts, diplomats have a tough time limiting them because of national passions. As U.S. leaders discovered in the Korean and Vietnamese conflicts and in the Somali intervention, it is hard to wage limited wars for limited ends or to reverse popular passions and make friends with former enemies.

If nationalism has reduced the diplomat's autonomy, technology has exacerbated the problem. In the eighteenth century, ambassadors were pretty much on their own. They received instructions from their masters sporadically and had to base most decisions on local conditions. *Revolutions in communication and transportation* undermined diplomats' autonomy: they are now in constant contact with superiors back home. Those superiors are often more responsive to domestic polls, electoral considerations, and bureaucratic pulling and hauling than to conditions overseas, As a result, many ambassadors have become little more than messengers and cocktail-party hosts.

Some observers argue that diplomatic competence and independence have declined most precipitously in countries like the United States and France where democracy and nationalism have been united. For the balance of power to function well, they contend, diplomats must not only be independent, but must be able to negotiate secretly and make deals without caring about moral conventions. Diplomacy cannot flourish where policies are made in public because impatient publics may be unwilling to sacrifice virtue to expediency. This is the problem President Clinton faced when, after taking office, he cited national interest to justify a retreat from his earlier pledge to aid Bosnia's beleaguered Muslims. The nineteenth-century French political observer Alexis de Tocqueville summed up the general problem for democratic societies:

> Foreign politics demand scarcely any of those qualities which are peculiar to a democracy. . . . [A] democracy can only with great difficulty regulate the details of an important undertaking, persevere in a fixed design, and work out its execution in spite of serious obstacles. It cannot combine its measures with secrecy or await their consequences with patience.[47]

[47] Alexis de Tocqueville, *Democracy in America*, vol. 1 (New York: Vintage Books, 1959), p. 243. See also Walter Lippmann, *The Public Philosophy* (New York: Mentor, 1955) and Hans J. Morgenthau, *Politics in the Twentieth Century*, abridged ed. (Chicago: University of Chicago Press, 1971), pp. 390–400.

It must be possible to estimate power and its distribution accurately.   The eighteenth-century balance functioned well partly because leaders kept a close eye on changes in distribution of power and reacted quickly to those changes.[48] They carefully tracked the distribution of resources that contributed to a state's military potential, such as numbers of men, horses, and cannon, amount of territory, and size of harvest. Differences in power were *quantitative*, making it relatively easy to determine who should join with whom to maintain a balance. By the nineteenth century, estimating distribution of power had become exceedingly complex. *Qualitative* or step-level differences in capabilities became critical, and the pace of technological change accelerated. Technological improvements in weapons systems and proliferation of specialized weapons made quantitative comparisons unreliable and complicated comparisons of military power. If it was simple to add soldiers and cannons and come up with precise estimates of military capability in the eighteenth century, it has become difficult to do so in today's global politics. As a result, the calculations necessary for balance-of-power politics are close to impossible, and leaders find it difficult to recognize when a balance is in danger.

As the pace of technological change quickens and qualitative differences among armies widen, it will become even more difficult to assess military balances. If one cannot calculate precisely the distribution of power, it is, therefore, impossible to determine global or regional balances except in the roughest fashion.

War and the threat of war must be usable instruments of diplomacy.   The historian Edward Vose Gulick reminds us that "the ablest theorists universally accepted the connection and thought of war as one more corollary of the balance of power."[49] In other words, the successful operation of the historical balance depended on war being "imaginable, controllable, usable."[50] Otherwise, how could one persuade ambitious actors that efforts to disrupt the system will not succeed? The great powers' objectives in the eighteenth century remained limited partly because each recognized that pursuing grandiose goals would lead to war in which a preponderant coalition would form to prevent their attainment.

War has, however, changed in recent centuries. Since the Napoleonic Wars early in the nineteenth century, armies and the firepower available to them have increased dramatically. The great military strategist and contemporary of Napoleon, Karl Maria von Clausewitz, understood the meaning of these changes: "War is an act of force, and to the application of that force there is no limit. . . . [A] reciprocal action results which in theory can have no limit."[51] As Table 3.1 shows, wars have grown bloodier. The two world wars in this century suggest that contemporary warfare may embroil and threaten entire societies. And with nuclear weapons, wars could threaten the survival of

[48]Claude, *Power and International Relations*, p. 91.

[49]Gulick, *Europe's Classical Balance of Power*, p. 89.

[50]Claude, *Power and International Relations*, p. 91.

[51]Karl Maria von Clausewitz, *On War*, trans. by O. J. Matthijs Jolles (New York: Modern Library, 1943), p. 5.

TABLE 3.1

The Bloodiest Interstate Wars Between 1816 and 1988

War and dates	Estimated battle deaths
1. World War II (1939–1945)	15,000,000
2. World War I (1914–1918)	9,000,000
3. Korean War (1950–1953)	2,900,000
4. Vietnam War (1965–1973)	2,058,000
5. Iran-Iraq (1980–1988)	1,500,000
6. Sino-Japanese War (1937–1941)	1,000,000
7. Russo-Turkish War (1877–1878)	285,000
8. Crimean War (1853–1856)	264,200
9. Franco-Prussian War (1870–1871)	187,500
10. Chaco War (1932–1935)	130,000
10. Russo-Japanese War (1904–1905)	130,000
10. Russo-Turkish War (1828–1829)	130,000

SOURCES: J. David Singer and Melvin Small, *The Wages of War 1816–1965: A Statistical Handbook* (New York: John Wiley, 1972), Table 4.2., pp. 60–69; and Michael J. Sullivan III, *Measuring Global Values: The Ranking of 162 Countries* (New York: Greenwood Press, 1991), Table V1.1a, pp. 35–38.

entire civilizations. It is difficult to imagine anyone resorting to such weapons to "restore a balance of power"; as a result, war is less and less "imaginable, controllable, usable."

Realism and Balance of Power in the Twentieth Century

Even though the historical balance of power ceased to function by the end of the eighteenth century, the revival of the power-politics tradition in the United States after World War II by those calling themselves *realists* also reawakened interest in the balance as a mechanism for maintaining order in a disorderly world. Their leading spokesman was Hans Morgenthau, and publication of his book *Politics Among Nations* in 1948 was a big step in popularizing the tradition in the United States. In his view, "the balance of power and policies aiming at its preservation are not only inevitable but are an essential stabilizing factor in a society of sovereign nations."[52]

[52]Hans J. Morgenthau, *Politics Among Nations: The Struggle for Power and Peace*, revised by Kenneth W. Thompson, 6th ed. (New York: Alfred A. Knopf, 1985), p. 187.

George Kennan and Henry Kissinger are two other American scholar-statesmen who reflect the influence of the European tradition of power politics. Kennan, a prolific scholar of European and Russian history and politics and architect of America's postwar policy of "containing" the Soviet Union,[53] was a career diplomat who served as ambassador to the U.S.S.R. and Yugoslavia and as director of the Policy Planning Staff of the State Department. For much of his career, Kennan decried what he believed to be America's refusal to confront the realities of power and the irrelevance of moral niceties to global politics. "I see the most serious fault of our past policy formulation to lie in something that I might call the *legalistic-moralistic approach* to international problems."[54] Americans, he believed, "tend to underestimate the violence of national maladjustments and discontents elsewhere in the world"[55] and try to make over the rest of the world in the image of U.S. democracy and respect for human rights.

Henry Kissinger, a Harvard University political scientist, served as National Security Adviser between 1969 and 1975 and as Secretary of State between 1973 and 1976. Kissinger is a European, steeped in the tradition of power politics, and his doctoral research dealt with early nineteenth-century European diplomacy.[56] Like Kennan, Kissinger looked askance at America's tradition of moralism and legalism and deprecation of power and order. "It is part of American folklore," he observed sarcastically, "that, while other nations have interests, we have responsibilities; while other nations are concerned with equilibrium, we are concerned with the legal responsibilities of peace. We have a tendency to offer our altruism as a guarantee of our reliability."[57] Like Kennan, too, he sought to prevent America from trying to export its domestic values, and as a practitioner he forged policies similar to those of the European diplomats he studied, in which force and diplomacy were wedded to achieve objectives.

A Confusing Concept

The efforts of realists such as these to popularize balance-of-power policies in this country were hampered because conditions for it to function effectively were lacking. Also the concept has so many (often contradictory) meanings.[58]

Perhaps the most common usage of balance of power is to describe *any existing distribution of power*. When political leaders argue that the movement of large numbers

---

[53]See Chapter 12, p. 408.

[54]George F. Kennan, *American Diplomacy 1900–1950* (New York: Mentor Books, 1952), p. 82.

[55]Ibid., p. 84.

[56]Kissinger's doctoral dissertation was published under the title *A World Restored: Metternich, Castlereagh and the Problems of Peace* (Boston: Houghton Mifflin, 1957).

[57]Henry A. Kissinger, *American Foreign Policy*, expanded ed. (New York: W. W. Norton, 1974), pp. 91–92.

[58]Claude, *Power and International Relations*, p. 13. Claude argues that the concept is used to refer to a "situation," a "policy," and a "system" (pp. 13–25). See also Ernst B. Haas, "The Balance of Power: Prescription, Concept, or Propaganda?" *World Politics* 5:4 (July 1953), pp. 442–477.

of Russian Jews to Israel or the Iraqi invasion of Kuwait will overturn the Middle East balance of power, they mean merely that Israel or Iraq will become relatively stronger. Neither usage corresponds to the eighteenth-century sense. Another common use of the phrase is to describe the *purposive policy* of actors, which is closer to its original meaning. In this usage, actors follow a policy of forming flexible defensive alliances to prevent dominance by one of their number. One expression of such a policy was British Foreign Secretary George Canning's explanation in 1826 of how after the French occupation of Spain he had restored Europe's balance of power without having to go to war. He had done so, he declared, by recognizing the independence of the Latin American states formerly part of the Spanish Empire and by having persuaded the Americans to issue the Monroe Doctrine. "If France occupied Spain, was it necessary, in order to avoid the consequences of that occupation that we should blockade Cadiz? No. I looked another way—I saw materials for compensation in another hemisphere. . . . I resolved that if France had Spain, it should not be Spain 'with the Indies.' I called the New World into existence, to redress the balance of the Old."[59]

Yet a third use of balance of power is to denote *a relatively equal distribution of power* among a limited number of actors that ensures the system's stability. In this usage, the actors' intent or policy is relatively unimportant. What counts is how power is distributed system-wide. The structural condition of the system as a whole, not the policy of its members, automatically brings about the desired outcome. Structure, in this version, determines behavior.[60] Structural determinism is probably misleading as well as dangerous, however. Frederick the Great of Prussia, a leading exponent of and participant in balance-of-power politics, recalled ruefully in his Political Testament (1768) the importance of chance in human affairs, which he illustrates by discussing the young King of Denmark:

> How can one foresee all the ideas that might pass through that young head? The favorites, mistresses and ministers, who will take hold of his mind. . . . A similar uncertainty, although every time in another form, dominates all operations of foreign policy. . . . [61]

Power and Neorealism

Many power theorists today recognize that the balance-of-power idea is no longer as usable as in the past. Often called *neorealists*, they retain the idea of countervailing power but articulate it in a more sophisticated manner than their realist predecessors and take into account a greater variety of factors that produce power. As with the realists who preceded them, differences appear among neorealists.

[59]Cited in Morgenthau, *Politics Among Nations*, p. 211.

[60]See Morton A. Kaplan, *System and Process in International Politics* (New York: John Wiley, 1957), pp. 22–36.

[61]Cited in Morgenthau, *Politics Among Nations*, p. 225.

Some, like Kenneth Waltz, are called *structural realists* because they emphasize the structure of the global system as determining actors' behavior. Waltz considers important the distribution of capabilities in the system, the hierarchic or nonhierarchic arrangement of the actors, and the *functional similarity* or *diversity* of the units.[62] In contrast, Robert Gilpin emphasizes the rationality of states in designing policies in pursuing their interests. "[A]ctors," he argues, "enter social relations and create social structures in order to advance particular sets of political, economic, or other types of interests." Conflict ensues, and power determines which interests are satisfied: "Because the interests of some of the actors may conflict with those of other actors, the particular interests that are most favored by these social arrangements tend to reflect the relative power of the actors involved."[63] As a group, neorealists acknowledge their debt to the past and the tradition from which they are descended, and they believe global politics remains a struggle for power under conditions of anarchy. Gilpin writes, "international politics still can be characterized as it was by Thucydides."[64]

Although neorealists retain much of the balance-of-power language, its meaning has been changed. The idea of power distribution remains prominent, but balance involving a number of states has just about disappeared. Both Waltz and Gilpin argue—though for different reasons—that a bipolar distribution of power like that existing between the United States and the Soviet Union after World War II provides world politics with stability and limits the probability of war. "It is to a great extent due to its bipolar structure," declares Waltz, "that the world since the war has enjoyed a stability seldom known where three or more powers have sought to cooperate with each other or have competed for existence."[65]

Waltz has argued repeatedly that *bipolarity* is the safest condition because responsibility is clear, and the leaders of the two poles need only observe each other closely while safely ignoring other actors. Waltz viewed the periodic crises that punctuated U.S.–Soviet relations in the 1950s and 1960s as healthy signs of bilateral attention, and he believed (correctly as it turned out) that leaders would work out tacit procedures for resolving crises peacefully. Unlike the balance-of-power system, the two were so much more powerful than anyone else that they could also ignore all but the most important shifts in power.

[62]Kenneth N. Waltz, *Theory of International Politics* (Reading, Mass.: Addison-Wesley, 1979).

[63]Robert Gilpin, *War and Change in World Politics* (New York: Cambridge University Press, 1981), p. 9.

[64]Ibid., p. 228.

[65]Kenneth N. Waltz, "The Stability of a Bipolar World," in David Edwards, ed., *International Political Analysis* (New York: Holt, Rinehart and Winston, 1970), p. 340. See also Waltz, *Theory of International Politics*, pp. 163–173. Gilpin declares that "Waltz's argument that bipolar systems are more stable and less subject to abrupt transformations than multi-polar structures has an impressive logic to it" (*War and Change in World Politics*, p. 89), but he suggests that Waltz overemphasizes "the static distribution of power in the system" at the expense of "the dynamic of power relationships over time" (ibid., p. 93).

As a concept, bipolarity (and *polarity* generally) suffers from some of the same confusion as balance of power. For some, it means dividing the world into two ideological camps, thereby equating the bipolar division with an attitudinal cleavage between the forces of communism and capitalism. For others, it means that two countries (or alliances) enjoyed significantly more resources than others. Complicating matters is disagreement over which resources matter. Waltz emphasizes raw military power, especially distribution of nuclear weapons. But this interpretation has at least three problems. The first is that military capabilities, especially nuclear weapons, provide power only in some contexts. A second is that distribution of military power between the two poles may be relatively equal or unequal.[66] The third is that if we count other capabilities — economic resources, for example — countries like Japan and Germany must be regarded as major powers and Russia, despite nuclear weapons, as a declining one. As a result, it is difficult to agree on whether the world is bipolar, multipolar, or something else.

Waltz believes that *multipolarity* — the existence of three or more power centers (however defined) — is a dangerous condition for two reasons:

> There are too many to enable anyone to see for certain what is happening, and too few to make what is happening a matter of indifference. . . . Second, in the great-power politics of a multipolar world, who is a danger to whom, and who can be expected to deal with threats and problems, are matters of uncertainty. Dangers are diffused, responsibilities blurred, and definitions of vital interest easily obscured.[67]

Although not all neorealists agree with Waltz's view of bipolarity, most share his belief that conditions of uncertainty generated by changes in status and power increase the likelihood of major *hegemonic war* — war between great powers for control of the system — in which "the declining power destroys or weakens the rising challenger while the military advantage is still with the declining power."[68]

[66]During most of the Cold War the United States enjoyed marked military superiority over the Soviet Union.

[67]Kenneth N. Waltz, "Will the Future Be Like the Past?" in Nissan Oren, ed., *When Patterns Change: Turning Points in International Politics* (New York: St. Martin's Press, 1984), p. 17. An alternative argument is that multipolarity is more stable than bipolarity because the presence of more major actors permits more complex interactions that produce crosscutting pressures, moderating conflict. In addition, in multipolarity actors cannot pay each other sufficient attention to go to war. Karl W. Deutsch and J. David Singer, "Multipolar Power Systems and International Stability," in James N. Rosenau, ed., *International Politics and Foreign Policy*, rev. ed. (New York: Free Press, 1969), pp. 315–324. See also Richard N. Rosecrance, "Bipolarity, Multipolarity, and the Future" in ibid., pp. 325–335.

[68]Gilpin, *War and Change in World Politics*, p. 191. Some realists reverse this theory, arguing that it is the rising challenger who starts the conflict.

By any standard, bipolarity is a thing of the past. The Soviet Union has broken into pieces. Those who believed that this change would make the world unipolar with an "unchallenged superpower, the United States, attended by its Western allies"[69] are beginning to doubt this prediction, for the United States has become the world's leading debtor and confronts intractable problems everywhere. Global power, however defined and measured, is becoming more dispersed. All in all, the end of the Cold War, a source of optimism for so many observers, is viewed by neorealists as a potentially dangerous development. They believe the retreat of superpowers from global leadership can only produce power vacuums that new powers will be tempted to fill. For neorealists, the paradox is that the breakup of Cold War alliances and loss of control formerly enjoyed by the superpowers over the rest of the world is frightening rather than comforting, and events in the former Yugoslavia provide evidence for this view.[70]

Defining and Measuring Power

If concepts like the balance of power or bipolarity are to be of use or if any theory of power distribution is to provide guidance, we must have a working definition of power and a means to measure it. Yet, we saw when the chapter began, a satisfactory and consensual definition of power has proven elusive, and efforts to measure power accurately continue to defy scholars and practitioners. Some agreement seems to gather, however, around the deceptively simple ideas that *power is the ability to get people to do what you want, that it is specific to particular contexts and issues, and that it is a relationship between specific actors at a particular time rather than an attribute of any one actor.*[71] Even if there were agreement about defining power, serious impediments to its measurement would remain.[72] At least two general approaches have been used to identify and measure power.

Inferring Power from Results

Inferring a power relationship by looking at "output" means observing the degree to which one actor is able to change the behavior of a target of influence as a result of the actor's effort. Presumably, a powerful actor is able to alter the behavior of those it seeks to influence, whereas a weak one is not able to effect such change. Analysis that appears simple in theory, however, is complex in practice. In the first place, even when one

[69]Charles Krauthammer, "The Unipolar Moment," *Foreign Affairs* 70:1 (1990/91), p. 23.

[70]See, for example, John J. Mearsheimer, "Back to the Future: Instability in Europe After the Cold War," *International Security* 15:1 (Summer 1990), pp. 5–56.

[71]See David A. Baldwin, *Economic Statecraft* (Princeton: Princeton University Press, 1985).

[72]Michael P. Sullivan, *Power in Contemporary International Politics* (Columbia: University of South Carolina Press, 1990), pp. 102–109.

observes changes in an actor's behavior, it is difficult to ascertain the cause of those changes and thereby confirm the presence of influence. The German chancellor may try to persuade other European leaders to accept a German proposal for dealing with civil war in Yugoslavia. Even if those leaders do accept the proposal, however, we cannot be certain that the chancellor *caused* the change. Perhaps the other leaders were influenced by their advisers, fear of domestic upheaval, some third party like the U.N. Secretary-General, or some factor about which we remain in the dark. Whatever the reason, it is difficult for an observer to confirm the cause of a change in behavior *in any one case*. By contrast, an observer can have greater confidence in concluding that a power relationship is present if a *pattern* is observed such that every time one actor seeks to alter another's behavior the latter does so.[73]

A second problem in measuring output arises because a power relationship may exist even without an observable change in behavior. We cannot infer that the German chancellor has no power simply because his efforts to influence a foreign leader appears to bear no fruit. Prior to the chancellor's efforts, the leaders of Germany's neighbors may have been adamantly opposed to changing their behavior in the direction the chancellor wishes. His exertions may have increased significantly the probability of a change in behavior, perhaps as high as 50:50, yet in the end other leaders continued in the same old way.

In other words, power may be conceptualized as one actor's ability to alter the *probability* that another actor will behave in a preferred way.[74] The initiator will require greater power to change a target's behavior if the autonomous probability of such change starts out very low and the absence of change does not signify the absence of power. By contrast, if the probability of a desired outcome is high at the start, that it does take place after an actor's effort does not mean that the actor has great power. If the German chancellor exerted great effort to force other European leaders to accept German economic assistance, we would not conclude that the chancellor was powerful because they elected to accept the funding.

[73]Even when such a pattern is present, the observer must exercise care. It is entirely possible for one actor to predict correctly what a second actor will do and to do it first. The first actor would then *appear* to be influencing the second when no influence was present. This phenomenon is called the *chameleon effect* after the small lizard that changes color to blend with its surroundings. The *satellite phenomenon* is akin to the chameleon effect. Two actors may act in tandem, and it is possible for an observer to mistake which of the two is powerful. Consider how the Ukrainian, Byelorussian, and Soviet delegates to the U.N. General Assembly always voted on the same side of issues during the Cold War. If one knew nothing else about the three, one might erroneously infer that the Ukrainian or Byelorussian delegates had exercised power over the Soviet delegate when the reverse was true.

[74]Objective probability in a mathematical sense exists only in reference to a series of events. The use of probability when referring to one event is pretty much metaphorical.

Inferring Power from Capabilities

Because inferring power from outcomes is difficult in global politics, scholars and practitioners lean heavily on the input side of the power equation—*capabilities*—in trying to estimate power. Capabilities are resources available to an actor that could be used to influence other actors.

In turning from results of interaction to capabilities, we are trying to predict outcomes by observing *potential power* because it is not clear whether capabilities will be dedicated to producing influence and, if so, whether the capabilities at hand are suitable. For example, the Soviet Union continued to control enormous military capabilities throughout the 1980s but discovered that such power did not provide economic prosperity or satisfy citizens' yearnings for political democracy. It also discovered that its military capabilities were of limited use in generating influence. By contrast, both the Europeans and Japanese, though they controlled enormous economic assets, discovered that they still had to depend on the United States to provide the military clout necessary to protect oil supplies after Iraq invaded Kuwait in August 1990. For its part, the United States discovered it needed financial support to carry out its military role and obtained it from Japan, Germany, Saudi Arabia, Kuwait, and South Korea.

As this case suggests and as we saw earlier, capabilities are situation-specific. All capabilities are useful in providing an actor with influence in *some* contexts but may be of little value in others. This variability explains why general comparisons of power can be misleading. Repeatedly leaders err by concluding that amassing more capabilities will make an actor more influential. In fact, the opposite may occur. One actor's acquiring greater capabilities may frighten others into acquiring more themselves. In this way an actor's acquiring greater capability may actually reduce its ability to achieve its objectives. The paradox is that greater capability produces *reduced* influence.

German behavior following the country's first unification is an illustration. Between 1870 and 1914, Imperial Germany sought a goal its leaders called "a place in the sun." Germany wished greater influence in world affairs, commensurate with its growth as a major military and industrial power. As part of this effort, the German government began to increase military capabilities, especially its navy. A strong navy, the leaders reasoned, would enhance growth of an overseas empire, provide protection for German commerce, and in general allow Berlin to show the flag around the world. The naval effort confirmed as one historian puts it, "important elements of British opinion in dark suspicions: expanding Germany was looking toward the day when it would openly defy Britain, and was preparing to challenge it on the seas. . . . [W]hat was basically a German gesture of self-assertion was construed, and indeed could only be construed, as a threat to Britain."[75] The British and other Europeans responded to the German challenge by intensifying their own

---

[75]Laurence Lafore, *The Long Fuse: An Interpretation of the Origins of World War I*, 2nd ed. (New York: Lippincott, 1971), pp. 131–132.

FIGURE 3.1

The Power Relationship

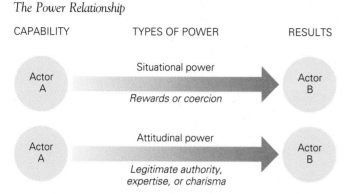

CAPABILITY   TYPES OF POWER   RESULTS

Power is illustrated here as a relationship between specific actors in particular contexts. The two diagrams show the two major types of power—situational and attitudinal—and the sources of each.

armament effort and forming an alliance that encircled Germany. As 1914 approached, Germany possessed significantly greater capabilities than it had before yet suffered from greater insecurity.

United States–Soviet relations during the Cold War reflected the same paradox. Each side sought to increase its armaments and achieve technological military breakthroughs that would increase its security in relation to the adversary. The technological advances of each were emulated by the other in a growing spiral of insecurity. In the costly technological seesaw, neither superpower gained a significant military advantage over the other, and the arms race itself generated greater mutual insecurity.

The *paradox of power* is that actors with the greatest capabilities (like Germany before 1914 and the United States and Soviet Union after 1945) may generate fear, envy, and even hatred in others. They sometimes find it more difficult than their weaker brethren to influence other actors, and they may even have negative influence in the sense that their initiatives are almost automatically resented and opposed by those who fear them.

Types of Power

In discussing power, several distinctions should be kept in mind. The first is between power that arises from ability to manipulate the situation (*situational power*) of a target and ability to alter the target's attitude (*attitudinal power*). Situational power has two major sources: *rewards* (positive incentives) and *coercion* (negative incentives). Attitudinal power has at least three major sources: *legitimate authority*, *expertise*, and *charisma*. (See Figure 3.1.)

Situational Power. In global politics, actors typically promise to reward or threaten to coerce each other in order to achieve objectives. If a target submits, it does so not because it is convinced that the initiator is correct but because it feels compelled to do so. In other words, rewards and coercion generate power by altering the *situation* of a target, not by altering the latter's opinion. Rewards improve a target's situation contingent on obedience, and coercion involves a deterioration of that situation contingent on disobedience. If a target capitulates to the threat of force, it does so unwillingly because failure to obey would worsen its existing situation.

Although we associate military force with coercion and economic assistance with reward, the distinction depends less on the capability being used than on *how* it is used. Rewards improve the target's situation, and coercion deteriorates its situation. In practice, however, the distinction can be murky. Suppose one actor promises to provide another with economic assistance if the latter votes in favor of its proposal in the United Nations. Such apparent generosity certainly sounds like a reward, but are we sure? The answer is not clear until we learn more about the original situation. We may discover that the first actor had routinely provided the second with such assistance for years without making it contingent on such support. What sounds like a reward is actually a threat. By contrast, an offer to reduce punishment—to cease military action or end an economic embargo—in return for a target's vote actually involves promising a reward because the reduced punishment would improve the target's situation.

Attitudinal Power. Power in global politics is not entirely based on control over a situation. Sometimes it is generated by ability to persuade others of a policy's correctness; that is, to get the target to change its mind rather than influence it to do something involuntarily. Many governments have accepted the compelling need to act quickly to avoid such potential environmental disasters as global warming and depletion of the ozone layer less because of rewards or coercion than because of a genuine shift in opinion following persuasive scientific analysis.

The bases of attitudinal influence are mainly quite different from the bases for rewards or coercion. One is *legitimate authority*, a belief that the actor has the right to demand a change in behavior. Thus, one might obey one's parent or an elected official because the position conferred authority. *Expertise* is a second source of attitudinal influence. Just as a doctor commands obedience in medical matters because of knowledge of medicine, so a scholar of international relations might influence the beliefs of students who study global politics. Finally, attitudes may be changed because of some *charismatic quality* that makes others wish to emulate or follow an individual. The "star power" of famous actors and actresses in advertising and political campaigning illustrates charismatic influence, as did the profound political influence of such great religious leaders as Jesus, Moses, and Muhammad.

Costs of Power

The exercise of power may entail various *costs*, including the opposition that exercising of influence tends to arouse. Significant costs are also associated with producing and maintaining capabilities such as modern military forces. And resources expended for one purpose (such as military forces) are not available for others (such as domestic welfare). Defense budgets give an idea of what it takes to be a modern military power. In 1989, the Soviet defense budget was about $311 billion and the U.S. budget $304 billion, or an average $1,222 for each American and $1,077 for every Russian. The *relative* burden on the Soviet economy was greater than on the American economy, which helps explain President Gorbachev's effort to lighten the load after 1985. In 1989, the Soviet Union still spent almost 12 percent of its GNP on defense, compared to the United States, which spent less than 6 percent of its GNP for military purposes.[76] We can begin to appreciate how big a burden such expenditures are by looking at Figure 3.2, which depicts the military burden of defense expenditures in GNP (total and per capita) for different regions.

Countries in the Middle East bear the highest burden in military manpower with almost eighteen persons per thousand serving in the armed forces.[77] By this measurement the U.S. burden was lower than the Soviet. Manpower burdens can prove especially difficult for economically developed societies with smaller populations. Skilled individuals who are drafted are not available for nonmilitary purposes, which can prove costly to the domestic economy. During World War II, many countries, including the United States, trained women to take over the jobs men were leaving to join the armed forces.

There are also invisible costs, such as the time spent by decision makers. Time spent on one issue is time unavailable to spend on others. During the final months of his presidency in 1974, for example, Richard M. Nixon was so preoccupied with the Watergate scandal that he had little time to attend to the nation's business. In foreign affairs, Nixon, like his predecessor Lyndon B. Johnson, spent much of his time agonizing over Vietnam. As a consequence, inadequate attention was paid to the Middle East, where a war erupted between Egypt and Israel in 1973 that threatened a superpower confrontation. More recently, one reason President George Bush lost the 1992 election was that he was viewed as spending so much time on foreign affairs that he was paying too little attention to domestic problems.

Perhaps the most important costs associated with exerting power are future expenditures. If efforts to exert influence in the present offend and alienate others, it will prove difficult to cooperate with them in the future. If, though, current behavior seems

---

[76]U.S. Arms Control and Disarmament Agency, *World Military Expenditures and Arms Transfers 1990* (Washington, D.C.: U.S. Government Printing Office, 1991), p. 36.

[77]The range here is from Jordan, with 57.9 soldiers per 1,000 people to Iceland and Costa Rica, which do not have armies.

MILITARY EXPENDITURES AS PERCENTAGE OF GNP

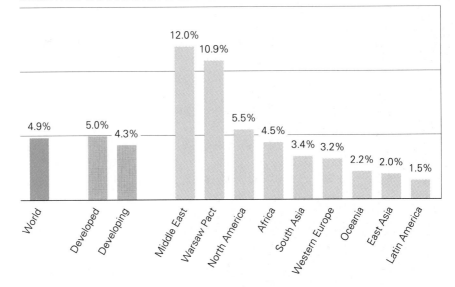

MILITARY EXPENDITURES PER CAPITA

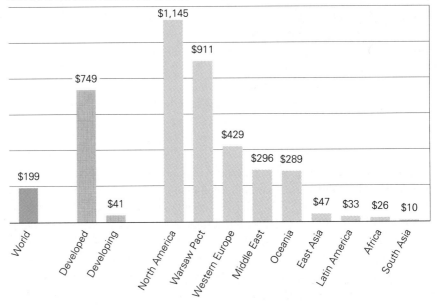

just and reasonable, future costs are likely to be low. Most leaders therefore honor treaties and other agreements with each other. Were they to violate agreements regularly, they would find that few would trust them in the future.

Conclusion

Power is, indeed, a puzzle. Though difficulties in definition and measurement have complicated efforts to build the discipline around it, many contemporary scholars and practitioners — realists — have not been deterred from placing the concept of power at the center of their analyses of global politics. Realists continue a power-politics tradition with roots in European history that can be traced back to the classical Greek city-states and the Italian Renaissance. Many territorial states evolved in a European context, finding themselves competing for scarce resources in limited geographic space. Under these conditions, conflict was common and theorists and practitioners focused on questions of power.

For many of these specialists, the balance-of-power theory was the key to preventing unlimited conflict and competition that would destabilize their system. It also prevented any one of them from gaining power over the rest. The balance-of-power system, for all its flaws, worked tolerably well in the eighteenth century. For better or worse, all of the conditions that allowed it to do so disappeared in the centuries that followed. Among the most important of these conditions was the ability to estimate and accurately compare the relative power of actors. Without that ability it is impossible to determine when a balance has been achieved and what to do if it begins to collapse. A number of factors, however, especially technology and the various capabilities that can contribute to power, make accurately assessing relative power a complex task.

Although power is difficult to define, there is some consensus that it is about relationships among particular actors in specific contexts and is not a general attribute. Measuring power is even more arduous than defining it. We cannot see power any more than we can see electricity. Like electricity, however, we can infer it from its results or consequences. We can also infer it from the resources that are invested in creating it. Having done so, and realizing that power cannot be applied indiscriminately means that

---

FIGURE 3.2

Military Burdens 1989

The burden of providing military security is not evenly distributed. When measured as a percentage of GNP, it appears that countries in the Middle East and in the former Warsaw Treaty Organization bore the heaviest defense burdens during the Cold War. When we use military expenditures per capita, we discover that Americans and citizens in Warsaw Treaty Organization countries like the Soviet Union spent the most on defense as recently as 1989.

we must be alert to differences between using rewards and coercion to achieve goals and applying persuasion to that task. We must also remain alert, realizing that efforts to use power produce costs that can indeed be high.

Our observation that power is contextual leads directly to chapter 4, focused on issues and actors in global politics. Different types of actors differ in capabilities and objectives and are, therefore, willing and able to exert influence under varying circumstances. Indeed, it is the failure of the power-politics tradition to recognize the diversity of issues and actors in global politics more than any other factor that limits its utility. Its almost exclusive focus on competition among sovereign states seems out of place in a world wracked by terrorism, globe-girdling macroeconomic forces, civil wars, and looming environmental disaster.

Key Terms

power
realism
realpolitik
power politics
balance of power
superpower
domain of power
influence
scope of power
Melian dialogue
reason of state
national interest
anarchy
great power
hard shell of impermeability
mercantilism
compensation
pawns
dynastic interests
l'état
la patrie
Concert of Europe
French Revolution
nation
Thirty Years War
Napoleonic wars
revolution in communication
revolution in transportation

diplomacy
quantitative power difference
qualitative power difference
legalistic-moralistic approach
neorealists
structural realists
functional similarity
functional diversity
bipolarity
polarity
multipolarity
hegemonic war
capabilities
potential power
paradox of power
situational power
attitudinal power
rewards
coercion
legitimate authority
expertise
charisma
costs of power
state
balancer
nationalism
probability

CHAPTER FOUR

Issues and Actors in World Politics

In our discussion in Chapter 3, we saw that the contemporary world is dramatically different from the European world in which the power-politics tradition was born. History is always in flux, and eighteenth-century European lenses are not adequate to make sense of events today. We next review the claims made in the power-politics tradition that global politics is dominated by a single issue and one type of actor, suggesting instead that global politics features a rich galaxy of actors interacting on a host of issues, each forming a separate arena. Like William Shakespeare's vision of the world: "All the world's a stage, and all its men and women merely players." In that world there are many theaters, each with its own stage and unique cast of actors, and each drama has its own plot. Some are violent, like the confrontations between fanatical Hindus and Muslims in India or the slaughter of Croatians and Bosnian Muslims in Yugoslavia, and others — like negotiations to stop destroying the earth's ozone layer — are conducted peacefully.

Actors and Issues in the Power-Politics Tradition

The tradition of power politics that is associated with such scholars as Thucydides, Machiavelli, the English political philosopher Thomas Hobbes and, more recently, those called realists and neorealists, sees little distinction among issues, arguing that everything is tied together by the "key concept of interest defined as power."[1] They believe

[1]Hans J. Morgenthau, *Politics Among Nations: The Struggle for Power and Peace*, 6th ed. revised by Kenneth W. Thompson (New York: Alfred A. Knopf, 1985), p. 10.

that there is only one type of issue, and it necessarily "relates to peace and war."[2] The attraction of this claim is its simplicity, reducing everything in global politics to "the struggle for power and peace."[3] Not only do the followers of this tradition believe in just one script and plot line for the dramas of global politics, they also argue for only one cast of players, "sovereign" states. In their view, the sovereign territorial state that formed in post-Westphalian Europe remains the main and inescapable actor in world politics. K. J. Holsti writes,

> Nation states are the essential actors, not only because they share the legal attribute of sovereignty and because many norms and practices are designed to protect their independence, but because they are the actors that *engage in war and are essential in organizing the norms and institutions which provide more or less stability, security, order, and/or peace for the system.*[4]

This and similar analyses encourage those in the power-politics tradition to focus on the few great powers among the almost two-hundred territorial states that have been recognized as sovereign by the global community.[5] The realist case is presented by Hans Morgenthau:

> Today, no less than when it was first developed in the sixteenth century, sovereignty points to a political fact. The fact is the existence of a person or a group of persons who, within the limits of a given territory, are more powerful than any competing person or group of persons. . . . Thus the absolute monarch of the sixteenth and the following centuries was the supreme authority . . . within his territory, not as a matter of theoretical speculation or legal interpretation, but as a political fact.[6]

The power-politics tradition is sometimes referred to as *state-centric* not only because it emphasizes states but also because it regards states as *unitary actors*, which reach decisions in a unified manner in response to external factors in the same way regardless of domestic differences. All are assumed to behave identically, responding in a unified way to a "national interest" that is "defined in terms of power." Statesmen, defined "as trustees of the national interest,"[7] are presumed able to discern that interest through *rational analysis*. In a frequently cited passage, Morgenthau argues:

---

[2]K. J. Holsti, *The Dividing Discipline: Hegemony and Diversity in International Theory* (Boston: Allen & Unwin, 1985), p. 9.

[3]John A. Vasquez, *The Power of Power Politics: A Critique* (New Brunswick, N.J.: Rutgers University Press, 1983), p. 18.

[4]Holsti, *Dividing Discipline*, p. 9. Emphasis in original. John Vasquez summarizes this view, "Nation-states or their decision makers are the most important actors for understanding international relations." *Power of Power Politics*, p. 18.

[5]In recent years, U.N. membership has jumped to 183, mostly from the broken-up U.S.S.R. and Yugoslavia. New members included Armenia, Azerbaijan, Bosnia-Herzegovina, Croatia, Georgia, Kazakhstan, Kirghizstan, Moldova, San Marino, Slovenia, Tajikistan, Turkmenistan, and Uzbekistan.

[6]Morgenthau, *Politics Among Nations*, p. 335.

[7]Holsti, *Dividing Discipline*, p. 9.

We assume that statesmen think and act in terms of interest defined as power, and the evidence of history bears that assumption out. That assumption allows us to retrace and anticipate, as it were, the steps a statesman — past, present, or future — has taken or will take on the political scene.[8]

In this model, states have interests greater than the sum of their citizens' interests and domestic factors are mainly regarded as irrelevant to state action.[9]

Issues in Global Politics

Imagine for a moment that throughout the world audiences are observing different dramas. Each drama is an *issue*, and each player is an *actor*. Every issue involves actors contending with one another to achieve outcomes that they believe will bring them benefits. Conflict occurs when actors perceive they cannot all attain their preferences, and cooperation results when they perceive they can get what they wish by working together. The range of issues on the global agenda at any time is enormous.

The Global Agenda

At any moment, a number of issues compete for the attention of leaders who must necessarily ignore other issues. President George Bush tended to pay attention to a number of crucial global issues such as nuclear arms control, the collapse of the Soviet Union, and Iraq's invasion of Kuwait, generally ignoring domestic economic issues. The leaders of most countries ignored the civil war in Somalia that erupted in 1991 and the spread of anarchy in that country until pictures of starving children forced the world community to sit up and take notice. The issues that attract most attention sit atop the global agenda.

The *global agenda*, like any other, consists of matters which attract attention and to which participants are prepared to devote resources. Roger Cobb and Charles Elder describe an agenda as "a general set of political controversies that will be viewed at any point in time as falling within the range of legitimate concerns meriting the attention of the polity."[10] Although we have no accurate way to determine which issues are on the global agenda at a particular time, reading prestigious newspapers and journals like *The New York Times*, *The Times* (London), or *Le Monde* (Paris) (which are also read by leaders) can provide a reasonably accurate picture. Some issues remain in the headlines for long periods and reappear on the front pages or on television news repeatedly. These are issues of high salience. Other issues are seven-day wonders that enter our consciousness with dramatic quickness and disappear almost as suddenly.

[8]Morgenthau, *Politics Among Nations*, p. 5.

[9]See Chapter 11, pp. 370–373.

[10]Roger W. Cobb and Charles D. Elder, *Participation in American Politics: The Dynamics of Agenda Building* (Boston: Allyn & Bacon, 1972), p. 14.

Because attention and resources are limited, at any moment issues compete for a place on the agenda. Major issues do not just suddenly appear or disappear; instead, their appearance and disappearance are part of a discernible and identifiable pattern.[11] An issue surfaces owing to changes in the global environment or in the behavior of specific actors that redistribute resources in ways that produce conflicts. Events occurring in the global environment—the catastrophic oil spill by the *Exxon Valdez* in Alaska's Prince William Sound late in March 1989 or reports of a growing hole in the ozone layer above the North Pole in February 1992—pushed the issue of global ecology higher on the political agenda. Similarly, actors' behavior—Chinese authorities crushing prodemocracy demonstrators in Tiananmen Square in June 1989—restored the human-rights issue to the attention of the world community, posing deep problems for the Bush administration, which preferred to play down human rights in its dealings with Beijing.

Once an issue gains attention, it is still not assured of a place sufficiently high on the global agenda to merit action by world leaders who have access to substantial resources. Individuals are drawn to issues because they affect those individuals directly, perhaps because of nationality, profession, or gender. Individuals who are sufficiently motivated may actively seek to bring "their" issues to the leaders' attention. Such efforts include writing letters to politicians, participating in demonstrations, or even performing acts of civil disobedience to get attention for the "cause."

The environmental group Greenpeace has been unusually effective in getting publicity for its causes. On occasion, its members have sailed into an area of the South Pacific in which France was to test nuclear weapons specifically to interrupt these tests. On other occasions, Greenpeace vessels interfered with Japanese and Norwegian whaling ships to publicize their opposition to further hunting of whales, some species of which are endangered. Greenpeace has even cut the nets of fishermen whose methods for catching tuna also result in death for dolphins. Whatever one may think of the methods Greenpeace uses, the group succeeds in making issues that it deems important visible to those in positions of leadership who have the authority and capacity to publicize and deal with them. An issue becomes salient for an actor when it is seen as producing costs and is perceived as likely to affect the actor's fate significantly.

The Issue Cycle

Entry to the agenda is only the first of several stages that form the *issue cycle*. The cycle has four stages: (1) *genesis*, that is, placing an issue on the global agenda; (2) *crisis*, moment(s) of danger in which adversaries seek to determine the rules of the game; (3) *ritualization*, during which routinized patterns of behavior and rules evolve among the actors to address and manage the issue, and the heat of controversy cools; and (4) *resolution*, when final agreement is reached or the issue loses key actors' attention.

[11]This section draws on Richard W. Mansbach and John A. Vasquez, *In Search of Theory: A New Paradigm for Global Politics* (New York: Columbia University Press, 1981), pp. 87–142.

Genesis. During *genesis,* an issue moves from the foreign-policy agendas of individual actors to those of other main actors in global politics. High-status actors are important because they have access to global media and international organizations and because what they say or do catches the attention of the entire cast of global actors. Minor actors seek to interest major ones in their issues because, once the mighty have become interested, an issue will become salient. In a few instances, such as the Cold War, an issue may so predominate that other issues are obscured by or subordinated to it.

As an actor of very high status, the U.S. government is constantly lobbied by other actors who have issues that they want Washington to take up. Poor countries try to press U.S. leaders to attend to redistribution of resources; Arab countries pressure Washington to pay attention to the Middle East; environmental, corporate, and human-rights actors have issues that they want Washington to promote; and so on. Because even small countries have access to the United Nations and other international organizations, efforts are often directed toward getting these organizations to take up an issue and place pressure on large countries to act.

Crisis. During the *crisis* phase, an issue assumes urgency — the belief grows that unless something is done quickly, matters will deteriorate. The issue comes to be recognized as entailing a high threat to a number of actors. It surprises them with its implications for the future of global politics; and it seems to demand rapid decisions to address it.[12] The crisis phase of an issue further produces a change in behavioral interactions among the actors.[13] The frequency of interactions among leading players increases; new alignments form; and political activities change their content. Most important, this stage involves a frantic search by actors for stable expectations and workable policies to ensure security.

The crisis stage is dangerous because actors do not know what to expect of each other and do not know the consequences of their own actions. One actor may make a decision that it views as justified or harmless, perhaps provoking another to retaliate. If care is not taken, the spiral of hostility may get out of hand with harm to everyone. Trade wars begin in this way. One actor, perhaps under pressure from such vocal domestic industries as U.S. steel manufacturers or Japanese rice farmers, raises tariffs on imports from other countries, and those countries do the same.

Ritualization. If adversaries survive the dangerous recurrent crises that pit them against each other, an issue may enter the stage of *ritualization.*[14] Having groped with each other to reach acceptable and stable relations, actors may acquire patterned and

[12]On these familiar components of crisis, see Charles F. Hermann, *Crises in Foreign Policy* (Indianapolis, Ind.: Bobbs-Merrill, 1969), pp. 21–29.

[13]Mansbach and Vasquez, *In Search of Theory,* p. 114.

[14]The term is intended to convey the sort of conflict in many animal species with much sound and fury but very little physical harm.

Intro, 1, 4

stable mutual expectations about how they sh
They have learned what they can safely do
spirals. Their actions may be downright unfri
adversaries, are regarded as posturing, and are c
of conflict, actors are able to satisfy constitu
out of hand.

For many years Israeli–Jordanian relatior
highly ritualized. Jordanian leaders could not a
population, especially the many Palestinian re
relatively moderate King Hussein from bein
militant leader. Each side routinely denounced the other while carefully keeping the
level of conflict stable. Israel kept the border between the West and East Banks of the
Jordan River open as much as it safely could, and Jordan did what it could to discourage
terrorist raids across the frontier by militant Palestinians.

Resolution.   A final possible stage in the cycle is *resolution* or removal of an issue
from the agenda. Resolution can take several forms. An issue may be resolved by formal
or informal agreements among competing actors. For a complex issue, such as the Cold
War, formal resolution may be required so that leading actors can revise deep beliefs and
reorient durable policies and practices. Alternatively, an issue may remain unresolved,
but, because it loses its salience for leaders, it may fall dormant. It may lose its salience
either because global conditions change or because new issues arise to compete with the
original one for time and attention. Although the old issue may remain unresolved, it
will receive little attention and generate little heat.

The 1919 *Versailles Conference* was an international assembly that formally resolved
an issue: World War I. In contrast, the 1962 *Cuban missile crisis* between the United
States and the Soviet Union was informally resolved by a trade—withdrawing Soviet
missiles in return for Washington's promise not to invade Cuba and withdrawing U.S.
missiles from Turkey at a later date. The civil war in Afghanistan is an issue that
gradually became less salient. Between December 1979, when Soviet troops first
marched into the country and February 1989, when the last of those troops were
withdrawn, Afghanistan was near the top of the global agenda. Although the civil
war continued after the Soviet withdrawal, most world leaders pushed the issue to
the back burner.

Types of Issues

As we observed earlier, actors seek power, not for its own sake but to satisfy basic
goals—prosperity, happiness, freedom, justice, equality, peace, security, and knowledge—that reflect human aspirations for a better life.[15] Each of the many dramas in

[15]See Mansbach and Vasquez, *In Search of Theory*, pp. 57–58.

world politics that we call issues involves actors' efforts to achieve greater satisfaction in one or more of these basic goals. Those who live in fear seek security, and those in poverty seek prosperity and respect. Those who lack freedom wish it, and those who live in turmoil seek order and peace.

Global politics, then, has many kinds of issues. Some, such as U.S.–Russian negotiations on nuclear arms control or territorial disputes in the Middle East — involve the quest for security. Others, such as the General Agreement on Tariffs and Trade (GATT) negotiations on global tariffs — focus on economic questions. Still others, like controversies about acid rain, are about threats to the environment. In other words, the enormous range of issues in world politics covers diverse topics. Increasingly, the global agenda is attracting nontraditional issues that either produce cooperation or necessitate collaboration if disaster is to be avoided.[16]

Every issue is unique. Each has its own cast of actors and geographic domain. Some are global in scope, such as environmental questions including global warming. Others are regional, including U.N. efforts to stabilize Cambodia. Finally, some issues are local. The same actors may deal with each other in a number of issue arenas. Each actor, however, is likely to ascribe different weight to what is at stake on an issue. Thus, U.S. relations with Ukraine are dominated by U.S. preoccupation with the nuclear arms that Kiev inherited when the U.S.S.R. dissolved. Ukrainian relations with the United States, though, are dominated by Kiev's economic needs and fear of its Russian neighbor. Such differences mean that the way in which the same actors behave toward each other will also vary by issue.

For example, the U.S. and French governments increasingly cooperate in responding to Third World crises, and both sent troops to deal with crises in the Persian Gulf in 1990–1991 and Somalia in 1992–1993. At the same time, however, their relations were strained by trade differences, especially on subsidies provided to farmers on each side. Thus, at the very moment when French troops from Djibouti were coordinating their entry into Somalia with U.S. landings in Mogadishu, French farmers were burning American flags and attacking French McDonald's outlets in protest against U.S. pressure for reducing subsidies to French and other European farmers.

This case illustrates how two actors can interact in dramatically different ways in different issue arenas. It illustrates, too, how actors can find themselves cooperating and competing at the same time. Finally, it illustrates how issues can remain relatively isolated from each other. Sometimes, however, issues become entangled, as when actors agree to make trades among them. One actor may change its position on an issue that is relatively unimportant to it but is important to a second actor in return for a similar concession on another issue that the first actor regards as important. Issues may also become linked if relations between actors so deteriorate

[16]See Chapter 15, pp. 507–509.

in one arena that it infects their relations in other issue arenas. This linkage is essentially what took place in U.S.–Soviet relations in the early years of the Cold War.

In this way, issues evolve and change their character. New actors become involved, and old ones leave the fray. The stakes may grow more or less important to some of the players, and issues may become entangled. The Vietnam issue arrived on the global agenda after 1945 as a matter of decolonization, with U.S. President Franklin Roosevelt seeking to promote Vietnamese independence. After his death and the onset of the Cold War, the issue was transformed into a civil war against French colonialism; but, with growing U.S. assistance to the French struggle in the 1950s, it began to assume the characteristics of a Cold-War issue. After the French defeat in the decisive battle of Dienbienphu in 1954 and French withdrawal from Indochina, U.S. involvement increased, in turn eliciting greater "fraternal" aid to Ho Chi Minh's North Vietnam from the U.S.S.R. and China.

Actors in World Politics

Perusing our daily newspapers makes it clear that geographic maps dividing the world into the neat territorial compartments we call states do not exhaust political reality. The news repeatedly features terrorist groups like the one that blew up Pan American flight 103 over Lockerbie, Scotland. We see also repeated references, especially in the financial section, to globe-girdling corporations like Toshiba and Shell Oil, banks like Barclays and Chase Manhattan that control vast and highly fluid assets, and authoritative international organizations like the World Bank. We also contribute time, energy, and money to dedicated and influential private organizations like Amnesty International and Greenpeace and a rich galaxy of other nonstate actors who affect our daily lives in myriad ways. Finally, our attention is increasingly drawn to dissatisfied and often violent ethnic and national groups like the Kurds in Iraq, the Basques in Spain, and the Tibetans in China. Indeed, the disintegration in Yugoslavia becomes less surprising when we see the patchwork quilt of quarreling nationality groups that live next to one another in that country.

Of course, states, too, are in the headlines. When we see references to Russian arms-control proposals, Iranian–American hostility, Greek opposition to Macedonia, and the like, we think of entities that occupy territorial spaces on geographic maps. Such headlines are deceptive, for it is not those territorial entities that are acting but rather some individual or group—the premier or the government—in the name of the state. And, as we shall see, groups often claim that they are acting on behalf of an entire state and all its citizens when, in reality, they are acting only for themselves or for a small segment of the population.

FIGURE 4.1

Nationalities in the Former Yugoslavia Prior to the Eruption of Civil War (1990)

This map shows the degree to which the former Yugoslavia (Union of the South Slavs) is a patchwork of ethnic groups.

In many of these reports we are observing the actions of government bureaucracies—the U.S. State Department, the Russian Ministry of Agriculture, the Argentine Army—and such actions sometimes have approval from other bureaucracies in the same government and sometimes they do not. Some states may house competing governments, as in Cyprus, which is divided into Greek and Turkish enclaves, with rival authorities claiming to represent the Cypriot state.

Inevitably, those who claim to represent the nation-state have access to only part of the state's resources and command the loyalties of only a portion of its citizens. Unless some group (such as a *government*) controls the bulk of the resources and population within a state's territorial boundaries and can do so on a regular and sustained basis, it is probably deceptive to think of "unified" state-actors in world politics. Therefore, when we think of the United States or France as actors in world politics we are anthropomorphizing (ascribing human form or attributes to a thing not human). As long as we keep in mind that people, not states, act, we can avoid this trap. Thus, when the names of states are mentioned, we should ask ourselves who is really acting and on behalf of whom.[17]

Each state has only one legal government, though as we have observed, several may contend for this status, and that government may or may not act in a unified manner. Some governments may consist of fragile coalitions of different political parties or ethnic groups in which individual ministers regard each other as political enemies and are actually working to undermine the opponent's faction. Early in the 1990s, coalition governments in Israel reflected such a situation as ministers from the Likud and Labor parties sought to weaken each other. Sometimes, even ministers from the *same* political parties may sabotage each other as they compete to lead the country. In such countries we must also distinguish between the partisans who have been elected to govern the country and the professional bureaucrats who staff the ministries and are expected to serve their country in a nonpartisan manner regardless of which political party holds power. As we shall see in Chapter 11, however, even those bureaucrats may work against each other to serve the interests of "their" bureaucracy or ministry.

Finally, a territorial state may be coterminous with a single society or may consist of several societies and even nations (or parts thereof). The former—such as Denmark and Iceland—are *homogeneous states*, and the latter—like the United States and India—are *heterogeneous*. In fact, most of the world's states are ethnically diverse, producing social cleavages of which governments must take account. This category includes even some of the world's stablest countries. The population of Canada is divided into several ethnic groups that speak different languages. Consequently, the politics of the country follows the efforts of each group, especially the French in Quebec, to guard jealously its cultural and linguistic prerogatives.

---

[17]As we ask ourselves these questions, we should try to avoid the common confusion among *state*, *government*, and *society*. *States* are territorial entities with *governments* that are empowered to act authoritatively on their behalf. A *society* is a group of individuals who perceive themselves as united by a culture that distinguishes them from others. If members of a society share language, ethnicity, history, and, most important, a sense of destiny, they may regard themselves as a *nation*. Shared creation myths may help produce national self-perception. The ancient Roman Republic fostered the myth that Rome had been founded by the twins Romulus and Remus. Emperor Augustus, wishing a more vigorous creation myth, commissioned the poet Virgil to write the *Aeneid* about how Rome had been founded by the hero Aeneas on his flight from the city of Troy after its destruction by the Greeks.

Decline of Sovereignty

The idea of *state sovereignty* as we understand it appeared in Europe several hundred years ago. As the concept evolved, it came to mean that states, each with a defined territorial area and a government, were legal "persons" equal to each other under international law. States, therefore, enjoy legal supremacy within their territory.[18] Each is supreme internally and subject to no higher external authority. In this way, sovereignty erects a barrier between the domestic and international political arenas. Because states are regarded as supreme within their own realm, they are forbidden to intervene in each other's domestic affairs. In fact, Article 2 of the U.N. Charter enshrines sovereignty by stating that the organization is based "on the principle of *sovereign equality*," prohibiting "the threat or use of force against the territorial integrity or political independence of any state," and, most important, forbidding U.N. intervention "in matters which are essentially within the domestic jurisdiction of any state."

We have observed how those in the power-politics tradition argue that sovereignty continues to define the actors in global politics even though it was invented several hundred years ago for a particular political purpose. In effect, international law transformed the reality of the monarch's personal property into the legal fiction of the sovereign state. Again, Morgenthau captures the original idea, observing that the "doctrine of sovereignty" elevated the political realities of the age "into a legal theory and thus gave them both moral approbation and the appearance of legal necessity. The monarch was now supreme within his territory not only as a matter of political fact but also as a matter of law. He was the sole source of manmade law . . . but he was not himself subject to it."[19] But has the global system changed so much and become so complex that the concept of sovereignty has lost much of its usefulness?

When Is an Entity Sovereign?

One problem in contemporary world politics is the vast differences in actors' autonomy and power. How, then, can we identify when entities are sovereign and when they are not? The answer is that sovereignty is not a quality that inheres in an actor but is bestowed upon it by the governments of other states, especially large ones, which "recognize" it as sovereign. *Recognition*, however, is mostly a political act and may or

[18]Disagreement remains over which entities should be counted as sovereign. Should *microsovereignties* like Monaco and Andorra be counted as sovereign states? What about groups like the Palestine Liberation Organization (PLO), which aspire to become the governments of states and are recognized by some as having this status but which for many years do not control the territory or people they claim as theirs? What about the "tribal homelands" of Bophuthatswana, Ciskei, Transkei, and Venda that were granted independence by the Republic of South Africa between 1963 and 1981 but were recognized by almost no one else?

[19]Morgenthau, *Politics Among Nations*, p. 329.

may not reflect in some real change in the condition of the "new" state. As a result, some actors may be deemed sovereign because they find favor with more powerful actors, but others may never become sovereign, even though they seem to have the same attributes. In recent years, tiny states like Lithuania, Latvia, Estonia, Bosnia, and Slovenia have been recognized as sovereign, but other entities such as Macedonia have found it difficult to gain recognition.[20] And, in past years, entities like Tibet and Manchukuo (Manchuria) were denied recognition, the first (after 1950) to avoid offending China, and the second (after 1931) to indicate disapproval of Japanese aggression in China.

Recognition for the sovereign status of many Third-World states reflects the expedient recognition of actors who were poorly prepared to become and remain independent. During the era of decolonization in the 1950s and 1960s, many European colonies in Africa and Asia declared independence from their mother countries—Great Britain, France, Portugal, and the Netherlands. At the strong urging of the U.S. and Soviet governments that were competing for influence in the Third World, the "sovereign" independence of these new states was widely recognized by the global community. They were then admitted to international organizations like the United Nations and were accorded diplomatic recognition by other sovereign states.

Israel, though, achieved international recognition only after much effort, and some of Israel's Arab neighbors for many years refused to recognize the sovereign independence of the Jewish State. When the British Mandate[21] in Palestine came to an end on May 15, 1948 and the Jewish Agency in Palestine declared the sovereign independence of Israel, it was not clear whether the global community as a whole would recognize the new state. A critical moment came when President Harry S Truman declared American recognition of the new state. At the time of this recognition, there was little consensus about Israel's territorial boundaries, and the new government still did not enjoy control over its own frontiers or events within them. In other words, Israel did not look very sovereign.

The failure of a secessionist movement to attract external recognition of its statehood may contribute to its ultimate failure. This was the fate of the Confederacy during the American Civil War (1860–1865). It was also the fate of Biafra, the name assumed by the eastern region of Nigeria during the bloody civil war that was waged in that country between 1967 and 1970. Biafra, consisting mostly of Christians who were members of the Ibo tribe that was resisting dominance by the Yoruba and Hausa tribes in Nigeria, was recognized by four small African states—Gabon, the Ivory Coast, Tanzania, and Zambia. Although the Biafrans fought with skill and courage and

---

[20]Greece objects to the name Macedonia, which it claims for one of its own regions and fears that an independent Macedonia would create unrest among Macedonians living in Greece. Thus, the country was admitted to the U.N. with the awkward name "The Former Yugoslav Republic of Macedonia."

[21]"Mandates" such as Palestine were territories formerly owned by the losers in World War I (1914–1918). They had been taken over by the League of Nations, which, in turn, had entrusted their administration to particular governments. Palestine had been occupied by the Ottoman Turks, who were allied with Germany and Austria-Hungary.

received assistance from the French and South African governments, the limited recognition accorded by the global community was a significant factor in defeating the rebellion. One should not, however, assume that had the Confederacy or Biafra been recognized as sovereign states, they would have survived. Indeed, despite widespread recognition of the sovereign independence of Bosnia-Herzegovina, that state has been carved up by Serbian and Croatian militants and may not survive as an independent entity.

Differences Among Sovereign States

Despite the legal equality conferred by sovereignty, in practice states are neither equal in all respects nor independent, and their governments vary dramatically in their capacity to protect and command citizens. In other words, unlike the great powers in eighteenth-century Europe, some states are more "sovereign" than others. If Russia occupies more than 17 million square kilometers stretching from the shores of the Baltic Sea in Europe to the Pacific Ocean, the prosperous city-state of Singapore consists of small islands totaling about 625 square kilometers off the south coast of the Malay Peninsula. And if China has a population of more than one billion, countries like Mauritius and Gabon have populations that are scarcely above one million. All are equal from a legal perspective, but states with large populations, territories, and gross national products as a rule have a larger voice than those which are smaller. Indeed, two observers suggest that many recently independent states, unlike their European predecessors, "are not states in the strict sense, but only by courtesy."[22] They are *quasi-states*, declares Robert Jackson, "a parody of statehood indicated by pervasive incompetence, deflated credibility, and systematized corruption."[23]

These paragraphs only begin to tell the story of the differences among today's states. The governments of many older states, especially in the West, where the state tradition dates back centuries, are a primary object of most citizens' loyalties. When asked to identify their primary affiliations, citizens will list their state almost immediately, calling themselves French, Japanese, Brazilian, or American. Such patriotic citizens are more likely to obey and trust their government, pay taxes voluntarily, serve in their country's armed forces, and rally around their leaders in moments of crisis.

Citizens in many of the new states in Africa and Asia since World War II are quite different from those described above. For one thing, unlike the gradual and natural evolution of the state in Europe, these states were built quickly, and, upon independence, had few resources and skills to carry out the job. As a result, citizens in such states

[22]Hedley Bull and Adam Watson, Conclusion, in Bull and Watson, eds., *The Expansion of International Society* (New York: Oxford University Press, 1984), p. 430.

[23]Robert H. Jackson, "Quasi-States, Dual Regimes, and Neoclassical Theory: International Jurisprudence and the Third World," *International Organization* 41:4 (Autumn 1987), pp. 526, 527.

may identify principally with groups other than the state. Their loyalties may be directed first toward a tribe, a locality, an ethnic group, a race, or a religion; and these affiliations may, for many issues, place them in opposition to their own governments. The state's frontiers are sometimes only arbitrary lines on a map that may have been drawn by colonial governors and have little meaning for inhabitants, especially if others with whom they identify live on the other side of the frontier or if it interrupts traditional economic and social patterns. The maps in Figure 4.2 illustrate the discontinuity between these frontiers and preexisting ethnic and tribal identities.

Sometimes an ethnic group is spread among several states and seeks to carve its own state in their midst. One prominent example is the Kurds, who live in Iran, Iraq, and Turkey and whose efforts to establish an independent Kurdistan have been brutally repressed by authorities in all three countries. During the bloody Iraq-Iran war (1980–1988), both combatants tried to use the Kurds against each other, and, once the war ended, the Iraqi regime of Saddam Hussein turned with ferocity on Iraqi Kurds, forcing thousands to flee the poison gas that was used against their villages. Iraqi Kurds currently enjoy a precarious existence, protected from the Iraqis only by the threat of Western intervention. To preserve their status, they have cooperated with Turkish authorities against their Turkish brethren.

Frequently dissatisfied ethnic, tribal, and religious groups try to achieve either independence or greater political power, and such efforts — culminating in civil strife — have been among the bloodiest events in recent world politics.[24] Indeed, since 1945, many more lives have been lost in civil wars than in interstate conflicts. And, as shown in Table 4.1, the most violent civil wars since 1945 have all been fought in the Third World, especially Asia and Africa.[25] The Nigerian conflict, the violent confrontations between the Tutsi and the Hutu in Burundi, and clashes in many other African countries such as South Africa, Mozambique, Angola, and Zimbabwe illustrate the ferocity of intertribal warfare. Ethnic struggles are endemic in the developing world, though ethnic problems rage elsewhere as well. The Kurds, the Basques in Spain and France, and the Karen and Shan in Burma are only a few of the dissatisfied ethnic minorities that have resorted to violence against majorities in their countries. Violence in India, Northern Ireland, Iran, and Lebanon and tensions in other countries reflect the volatility of religious animosities. Finally, the cruelties of apartheid in South Africa and the urban explosions that rock American cities like Los Angeles from time to time reveal the depth of racial mistrust that undermines national unity. Figure 4.3 illustrates how widespread major civil strife has been in global politics since 1945.

The problems of India epitomize the centrifugal forces facing many Third-World states. The British Indian empire included today's India, Pakistan, and Bangladesh. When independence was granted in 1947, fierce clashes between Muslims and Hindus

---

[24]See Chapter 5, pp. 143–144 for a discussion of the difference between strong and weak states.

[25]The civil war that raged in the former Yugoslavia was the first in Europe since World War II.

FIGURE 4.2

Africa: State Frontiers vs. Tribal Identities

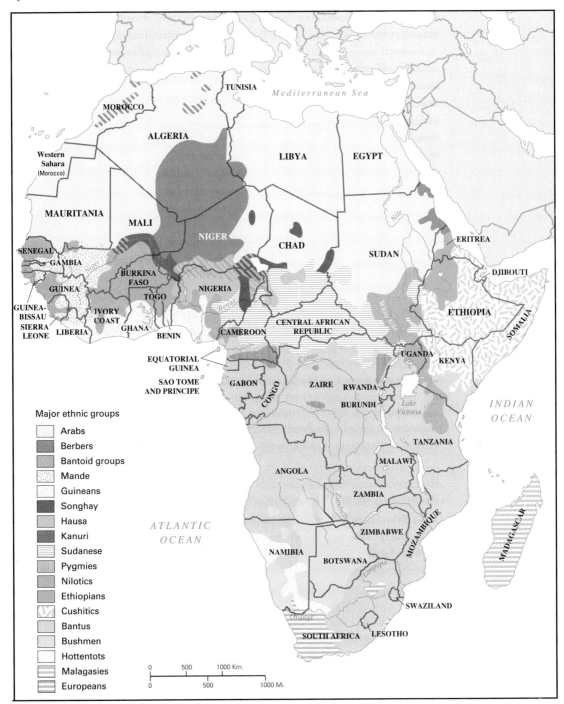

Major ethnic groups

- Arabs
- Berbers
- Bantoid groups
- Mande
- Guineans
- Songhay
- Hausa
- Kanuri
- Sudanese
- Pygmies
- Nilotics
- Ethiopians
- Cushitics
- Bantus
- Bushmen
- Hottentots
- Malagasies
- Europeans

This map illustrates the degree to which the frontiers of African states—largely imposed by European colonial authorities—are incompatible with the realities of tribal affiliations.

T A B L E 4.1

Bloodiest Civil Wars Since 1945

Civil War	Deaths
1. China, "Great Leap Forward"(1957–1962)	2.5–5,000,000
2. Nigeria (1967–1970)	2,000,000
3. Afghanistan (1979–1989)	1,300,000
4. Cambodian "Killing Fields" (1975–1978)	1–1,500,000
5. Sudan (1955–1972, 1983–)	1,006,000
6. China civil war (1946–1949)	1,000,000
6. China (government versus landlords) (1950–1951)	1,000,000
7. Ethiopia (1978–1990)	600,000–1,000,000
8. Mozambique (1978–1993)	400,000–900,000
9. Uganda (1971–1978, 1981–1986)	500,000–700,000
10. Chinese "Cultural Revolution" (1966–1968)	500,000
10. Indonesia (1965–1966)	500,000
10. Vietnam (1959–1965, 1973–1975)	500,000

SOURCE: Michael J. Sullivan III, *Measuring Global Values*, p. 34, Greenwood Press, an imprint of Greenwood Pulishing Group, Inc., Westport CT. Reprinted with permission.

forced the country to divide into India and Pakistan. India was established as a secular state with a Hindu majority and Muslim minority,[26] and Pakistan as a Muslim state. This partition did not end religious tension in India; it resurfaces with deadly regularity, as in the bloody riots that swept the country following the razing by Hindu extremists of a sixteenth-century mosque in December 1992. The Hindu–Muslim cleavage is only one of many that threaten the Indian state's integrity. Demands by the Sikhs of the Punjab for a separate state called Khalistan have led to repeated cycles of terrorism and civil violence, as has separatist agitation in northern tribal regions — Arunachal Pradesh, Mizoram, Assam, Nagaland, Tripura, and, most important, Kashmir and Jammu. With people speaking 1,600 languages, vast socioeconomic gaps, and continued caste discrimination against "untouchables," the forces pulling India apart are strong indeed.

Nonstate loyalties to *ethnic* or *tribal* groups may undermine a state's capacity to govern itself, reducing the sovereign condition of the sovereign state. In sum, emphasizing sovereignty may distort our view of the world, especially if we confuse its sweeping *legal* connotations with its limited *practical* consequences. Sovereignty entitles states to

[26]Even after secession by Pakistan, Muslims were still 11 percent of India's population, making it the third-largest Muslim country in the world after Indonesia and Bangladesh. Bangladesh was created by the secession of East Bengal from Pakistan in the early 1970s.

FIGURE 4.3

Victims of Major Civil Strife Since 1945

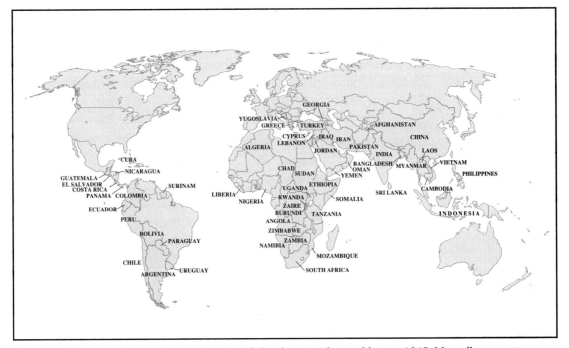

This map illustrates where widespread civil strife has been in the world since 1945. Virtually no region except North America and Oceania has been left unscathed.

SOURCE: Sullivan, *Measuring Global Values*, Table V1.1a, pp. 35–38.

legal privileges in international organizations and tribunals and in national courts of law. It also provides those who are regarded as the legal surrogates for the state with a measure of authority that others may lack. Thus, we tend to regard representatives of the sovereign state (even if they originally attained their positions by fraud and bloodshed) with awe, and they try to enhance this image by surrounding themselves with symbols of authority and power. Such symbols include music ("Hail to the Chief" is played whenever a U.S. president appears in public), uniforms (dictators often dress up in gaudy military uniforms), and all the other accouterments of pomp and circumstance.

In many ways, then, sovereignty is something of a historical curiosity with declining importance for world politics. Although it continues to confer benefits, these have become less valuable. French recognition of the sovereign independence of the United States during its revolution against Britain late in the eighteenth century was an enormous asset to the new republic. More recently it has been argued that the very existence, continued independence, and territorial integrity of many weak states in

Africa owe much to *juridical statehood*.[27] However, events such as the 1971 overthrow of Uganda's President Idi Amin by the Tanzanian Army, the 1990 intervention in Liberia by peacekeeping forces of the Economic Community of West African States (ECOWAS), and landing of U.S. forces in Somalia in December 1992 weaken even this argument. Indeed, the United Nations, which authorized intervention in Somalia, finds itself less able than ever before to obey Article 2 of its charter and, from Cambodia to Bosnia, it intervenes in "domestic" affairs that are recognized as threats to peace.

None of this activity means that the concept of sovereignty is disappearing. Actors continue to invoke sovereignty to prevent outsiders from dealing with such issues as the environment, human rights, drugs, and public health. The United Nations is still hampered by what two critics describe as the "talisman of 'sovereignty.'"

> That ill-defined and amorphous notion of international law has been used to denote everything from a state's political independence . . . to the more extreme view that all the internal affairs of a state are beyond the scrutiny of the international community.[28]

But the barriers posed by sovereignty are beginning to fall. Thus, U.N. Secretary General Boutros Boutros-Ghali observed in his June 1992 report that "the time of absolute and exclusive sovereignty . . . has passed; its theory was never matched by reality."[29]

The National-Interest Concept

National leaders routinely justify their actions and elicit popular support for them by appealing to the *national interest*. Hitler declared that the decision to invade Poland in 1939, starting World War II, was taken to further Germany's national interests, and yet six years later German cities were in flames and Hitler had committed suicide. More recently, with the end of the Cold War, a debate has raged in the United States about whether the American national interest is better served by maintaining an active presence overseas or by concentrating on the country's domestic problems.

Is there a common or collective interest that binds the inhabitants of nation-states, differentiates them from citizens of other states, and can guide their behavior? And, if so, is there some rational and objective way of determining what that interest is? As we have seen, adherents of power politics argue that each nation-state has a

---

[27]Robert H. Jackson and Carl G. Rosberg, "Why Africa's Weak States Persist: The Empirical and the Juridical in Statehood," *World Politics* 35:1 (October 1982), p. 21; and Robert H. Jackson, "Quasi-States, Dual Regimes, and Neoclassical Theory: International Jurisprudence and the Third World," pp. 529–533.

[28]Gerald B. Helman and Steven R. Ratner, "Saving Failed States," *Foreign Policy* 89 (Winter 1992–93), p. 9.

[29]Cited in ibid., p. 10.

unique national interest that rational leaders will or should follow. Such interests are thought to arise out of the relative power of states. Powerful and weak states have different opportunities and are confronted by different constraints and perils and should, as a result, use different strategies and tactics adapted to their position in the world. The problem is that, at this level of abstraction, the idea of a national interest can be translated into little more than agreement on the importance of survival, independence, and security.

If rationality gets us little beyond such abstractions, it is even more difficult to use the concept of the national interest to determine the policies that should be followed to enhance it. Although many (though not all) inhabitants of large or rich states are apt to perceive the world differently than those of small and poor ones, the real question is whether or not those perceptions of common interest are strong enough to overcome the interests they associate with being rich or poor, urban or rural, male or female, and employed or unemployed. In other words, are the interests of "their group" sufficiently compatible with the interests of other groups to produce a consensus about the state as a whole? On this logic, the national interest might be attacked as a rhetorical device that legitimizes whatever it is leaders wish to do. It might also be attacked, as did Marxists, as identical with the interests of the group(s) of which leaders are members—class, gender, profession, income bracket, and so on. Far from determining national interest in the deductive and rational manner described by power-politics theorists, it appears that the national interest is determined by the rough and tumble of groups and individuals striving to be heard and to have their interests served.

If there were an objective standard for determining national interest, we could probably give a straightforward answer to this question: Is it in the U.S. interest to raise tariffs and limit foreign imports or to lower tariffs and remove limits? In fact, the answer is that it depends. Owners and workers in industries that are suffering at the hands of foreign competition believe that limiting free trade is in the national interest and passionately oppose the proposal for a North American Free Trade Agreement. But stockholders and employees in industries that are exporters, and consumers who want to buy products at the lowest price find it obvious that limitations on free trade are against the national interest. Even if we had a standard that could determine the condition that the English utilitarian Jeremy Bentham called the greatest good for the greatest number, there would be winners and losers. The losers—whether a majority of the population or a minority—are unlikely to agree that the policy reflects the national interest. Cogent and persuasive arguments can "prove" that any policy is in the national interest, but saying it is so does not make it so. Honest people can reach opposite conclusions about what is in the national interest, and, as the violent demonstrations and counterdemonstrations in the United States during the Vietnam War showed, such disagreements can elicit great passion.

The government itself rarely agrees completely about what constitutes the national interest or how it can best be served. Bureaucrats commonly identify the national interest with what they believe to be in their agency's interest. Those responsible for defense rarely believe that cuts in defense spending are in the national interest, just as

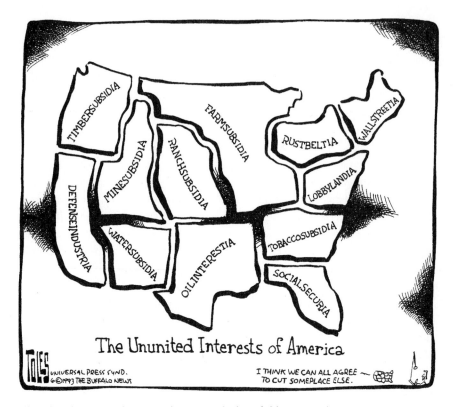

The idea that states have a coherent and identifiable national interest is a
fiction—instead, groups identify their interests with the interests of the state and
seek to justify policies that they prefer.

those responsible for agriculture, diplomacy, or the urban poor usually argue that greater
investments in their sector will benefit the country as a whole. This bias will apply in all
countries, whether rich or poor, socialist or nonsocialist, large or small. The propensity
for officials, both public and private, to merge parochial with general interests is probably
universal and is expressed by the bureaucratic adage: Where one stands depends upon
where one sits.

The national interest seems to change quickly even though it is thought to be
determined by a system-wide distribution of power that changes slowly. The changing
definitions by leaders of the national interests reflect changing popular moods, swings in
public opinion, and shifting political conditions and coalitions. During the late 1940s

and early 1950s when the American public was aroused against the "Red menace," the young Richard Nixon was a virulent anticommunist who believed a hostile policy toward the Soviet Union and the People's Republic of China was in America's national interest. As president, though, Nixon was responsible for détente with the Soviet Union and renewed American ties with "Red" China.

In the end, the national interest, like sovereignty, is a fiction with an important function. Leaders use it as a symbol to gain citizens' acquiescence and support on issues and to produce unity. The symbol is especially effective during times of crisis but can also be used by unscrupulous authorities to justify almost anything. The symbols of the national interest, and its close relative, *national security*, were used in the United States to justify the illegal activities of Colonel Oliver North and his associates in their dealings with Iran and the Nicaraguan *contras* in the 1980s. The same symbols had been brandished by Senator Joseph McCarthy during his anti-communist witch hunts in the 1950s to smear professional foreign-service officers and by cronies of President Nixon during the Watergate affair in 1972 to justify such bizarre activities as burglarizing the office of Daniel Ellsberg's psychiatrist. In the words of two political commentators: "Watergate . . . widened the fissures which the Vietnam War opened. . . . It . . . raised in bold type the biggest foreign policy issue of them all—what is 'national security'?"[30]

National-interest arguments have also been used by U.S. leaders to justify supporting brutal and corrupt governments and leaders who turn around and justify their own actions as necessary because of alleged dangers to the state. The anticommunist credentials of dictators like Francisco Franco in Spain (1936–1975), Antonio Salazar (1932–1968) in Portugal, Syngman Rhee (1948–1960) in South Korea, Ngo Dinh Diem (1955–1963) in South Vietnam, General Anastasio Somoza Debayle (1967–1972; 1974–1979) in Nicaragua, and Ferdinand E. Marcos (1965–1986) in the Philippines were sufficient justification for many Americans to turn a blind eye to their repressive policies. Thus, the national interest can serve to justify almost anything.

The Transnational Challenge to the State

The very independence of states that the idea of national interest was invented to serve is circumscribed by the proliferating links among people around the world which cross national frontiers and which can be severed only at great cost. Such limitations on states and their dependence on each other contrast with the relative

---

[30]Leslie H. Gelb and Anthony Lake, "Watergate and Foreign Policy," *Foreign Policy* 12 (Fall 1973), p. 177.

self-sufficiency of eighteenth-century European states. John Herz says, "Self-contained, centralized, internally pacified, they could rely on themselves for a high degree of external security."[31]

The concept of national interest is further muddied by trends and problems that are common to peoples in different states. Not only are these problems that defy solution by individual governments, but they will be exacerbated if actors fail to cooperate and merely seek to increase their relative power. Such problems limit the independence of individual actors and dilute the belief that one actor can further its interests without taking account of others' interests. State frontiers and the traditional preoccupation with political autonomy and military security begin to pale before the challenges of nonstrategic and nonnuclear issues that are brought home by food and energy crises and pollution of the environment in which we live.[32] Failure to cope with such crises will harm the interests of all states.

Technology and Diminishing Independence

The revolution in technology contributes to the decline in actors' autonomy. Military security is threatened by technology that, in Herz's words, enables "belligerents to overleap or bypass the traditional hard-shell defense of states."[33] The frontiers of *all* states—from the most insignificant like the Maldives and the Comoros to the largest, such as Russia and the United States—are more penetrable in today's world than ever before. High-speed jet aircraft, space shuttles, spy satellites in space, and intercontinental ballistic missiles (ICBMs) are only a few of the revolutionary developments that make the frontiers of states more permeable than ever before. In some ways, the computer, the facsimile machine, television, the copying machine, and radio have even less respect for legal boundaries. Thus, it is possible for bankers to move huge sums of money almost instantaneously from continent to continent, influencing national and global economic policy. And, during the Chinese government's brutal suppression of student efforts for democracy in 1989, students in China used fax machines to stay in touch with sympathizers overseas. Most governments cannot prevent radio broadcasts and television images from being beamed down from satellites, and some actors' efforts to prevent the spread of subversive ideas are challenged by broadcasts from the BBC (British Broadcasting Company), Radio Liberty, and other sources of information.

---

[31]John H. Herz, *International Politics in the Atomic Age* (New York: Columbia University Press, 1959), p. 96.

[32]See John H. Herz, *The Nation-State and the Crisis of World Politics: Essays on International Politics in the Twentieth Century* (New York: David McKay, 1976), p. 19.

[33]Herz, *International Politics*, p. 97.

Television is especially powerful in breaking down national frontiers. In the two decades after 1965, the number of television transmitters globally exploded from 8,550 to 60,570 and the number of receivers from 55 to 137 per thousand inhabitants.[34] Stations like Cable News Network (CNN) give access to remote corners of the world, and the pictures they send have roused publics against starvation in Somalia and brutality in Bosnia. Indeed, Iraqi dictator Saddam Hussein kept abreast of the effort to oust his forces from Kuwait by watching CNN, and CNN allowed us to watch Boris Yeltsin attack his parlimentary enemies in Moscow's "White House" in October 1993. People all over the world can witness dramatic events anywhere else, and they tend to imitate what they have seen (the *demonstration effect*). Thus, students who were publicly demonstrating for democracy in China in 1989 were influenced by events in the U.S.S.R. surrounding Mikhail Gorbachev's steps to introduce democratic elements in his country.[35] Public opinion in one part of the world can influence public opinion elsewhere, sometimes so quickly that in, the colorful metaphor of one observer, U.S.–European perceptions "have become as closely linked as their financial markets, creating a political stock market with dramatically reduced reaction times."[36] As a result of technology, states can control only in part the movement of things, ideas, and people entering and leaving their territory.

Mobilizing the Masses and the Growing Global Society

The immense technological changes described above are not the only reasons for the state's declining independence. The growing desire of private citizens to become directly involved in world politics and their refusal to leave foreign-policy decisions to government elites have produced a *participation explosion*.[37] Earlier, mass publics were either ignorant of or uninterested in foreign policy, and their inertia was captured by Karl Marx's sarcastic description of the French peasantry as "homologous multitudes, much as potatoes in a sack form a sack of potatoes." As a result, the masses "cannot represent themselves, they must be represented. Their representative must at the same time appear as their master, as an authority over them, as an unlimited government power that protects them against the other classes and sends them rain and sunshine from above."[38]

[34]James N. Rosenau, *Turbulence in World Politics* (Princeton: Princeton University Press, 1990), pp. 339, 340.

[35]Two particularly powerful images from the turbulent events in China were a photograph of a student wearing a T-shirt with the words "We Shall Overcome" in English (the title of the unofficial anthem of the U.S. civil-rights movement) and a picture of a replica of the Statue of Liberty in Tiananmen Square in Beijing.

[36]Stephen F. Szabo, "Public Opinion and the Alliance: European and American Perspectives on NATO and European Security," in Stanley R. Sloan, ed., *NATO in the 1990s* (Washington, D.C.: Pergamon-Brassey's, 1989), p. 144.

[37]See Rosenau, *Turbulence in World Politics*, pp. 141–177.

[38]Karl Marx, "Excerpts from the Eighteenth Brumaire of Louis Bonaparte," in Lewis S. Feuer, ed., *Marx and Engels: Basic Writings on Politics and Philosophy* (Garden City, N.Y.: Doubleday, 1959), pp. 338, 339.

This condition began to change with the revolutions late in the eighteenth century that resulted in growing *democratization* of Europe and America. Nevertheless, most human beings remained preoccupied by personal survival and had neither the time nor information to participate in political life. The absence of mass participation in politics in much of Asia, Africa, Latin America, and the Middle East facilitated their conquest and pacification by relatively few European soldiers. The imperialists needed only to corrupt and co-opt the small local elite or defeat relatively primitive local armies to win the day. Thus it took only a few thousand British soldiers and administrators to control hundreds of millions of Indians at the height of the British Raj.

Higher standards of living, wider education, and improved communication have combined during this century to make many citizens throughout the world politically conscious. Once this awakening took place, it became possible to mobilize their energies, first to oust the colonial authorities and later to resist external control of their affairs. Thus, the French in Indochina (1946–1954) and in Algeria (1954–1962) and the Americans in South Vietnam (1965–1973) were unable to retain control despite having committed far more troops than had their colonial predecessors. Formerly passive populations have been transformed into intensely participant publics, willing to die if necessary to resist aggression. Thus conquest and occupation of one state by another has become extremely difficult and expensive even though, as we have seen, frontiers are porous. In sum, mobilizing the masses intensified nationalism and, by combining nation and state, propelled the nation-state to the forefront of human loyalties.

But this is only part of the story of the participation explosion. The more important part is that, even while providing the raw material for nationalism, mass *political consciousness* has reduced governments' ability to shield foreign affairs from domestic passions, isolate the domestic arena from global politics, or manage international affairs without interference. Consider, for a moment, how each of us participates in world politics. Every day we make conscious and unconscious decisions with implications for the world around us. We are constantly deciding whether to purchase products made overseas, and those decisions affect the domestic and international economies and, indirectly, the political stability of the societies involved. Shall we buy a Toyota or a Chevrolet? Shall we use Italian olive oil or American vegetable oil? Indeed, it is staggering to realize just how much of what we eat, wear, and use is either partly or wholly foreign. In fact, many products which we think of as American have parts that are made outside the United States or which we think of as Japanese are made in North America.

We are also constantly exposed to cultural influences from abroad, whether rock stars, BBC television programs, French and Italian clothing designs, or sports stars. Similarly, U.S. cultural influences are constantly bombarding other societies, exasperating local leaders because such influences erode traditional mores and patterns of obedience, especially among the young. Jeans and pop music are now part of the youth culture from New York to Bombay, and from Lagos to Moscow. Thus, McDonald's became part of the local scene in Moscow by opening the largest eating establishment in that city, and a Euro-Disney theme park near Paris produced local controversy. Fear that such influences will dilute national culture or undermine local values fuel Islamic fundamentalism in Iran, separatism in Canada, authoritarianism in China, and *xenophobia* in Burma. Indeed, in Iran gangs of religious vigilantes roam the streets of cities searching for signs of western culture.

Cultural exchange is also produced by growing numbers of people traveling and studying abroad. Expanding tourism, student and sports exchanges, foreign films, business and professional travel — facilitated by increased speed and capacity in global communications and transportation — lead to homogenized lifestyles, especially among urban youths, business and professional classes, and political elites. Such exchanges may have great political consequences such as increasing consciousness of vital issues and greater sensitivity for other peoples' customs, and they have done much in mobilizing transnational environmental and feminist movements and in creating a global economic market.

Occasionally, a news story is potent enough to persuade us to try to change a country's foreign policy. We might merely write our member of Congress, contribute to an organization working to achieve international aspirations that we share, or boycott foreign goods. Thus, some Irish-Americans contribute liberally to a group called Noraid to assist those seeking to oust the British from Northern Ireland, and others boycott Japanese goods because they believe imports take American jobs. We might even demonstrate for our cause, as many have in recent years, to pressure U.S. and European firms to divest their holdings in South Africa and in opposition to apartheid or against advertising baby formula in the Third World.[39] Such passions produce political pressures on foreign-policy elites that would have been unthinkable in earlier centuries. On a few issues, individuals travel overseas to advance causes about which they feel strongly. In the 1930s, numbers of idealistic young Americans and Europeans fought for the Spanish Loyalists against General Francisco Franco's Fascists, and others joined Britain's Royal Air Force (RAF) to fight the Nazis in 1939 and 1940. In recent years, Muslims from around the world have gone to fight alongside coreligionists in Afghanistan and Bosnia.

Other massive movements of people across frontiers are caused by economic necessity, famine, or war. "*Guest workers*" who migrated from such poor countries as Turkey, Vietnam, and Romania to wealthier countries like Germany which had shortages of labor later found themselves targets of right-wing xenophobia. Illegal aliens from Mexico and Central America have created resentment among those in the United States who believe they compete for scarce jobs or place demands on scarce public

---

[39]It has been argued that advertising such formula contributes to malnutrition because mothers do not rely on their own milk and, when it is too late, discover they cannot afford expensive formula. In Third World societies, the water that is mixed with powdered formula is often impure.

resources. Huge numbers of people have fled wars in Afghanistan, Bosnia, Mozambique, Cambodia, Iraq, Vietnam, and, elsewhere and impose economic and political burdens on such host countries as Pakistan, Austria, Jordan, Thailand, and Iran and on international organizations like the International Red Cross.[40] Indeed, the sagas of Vietnamese "*boat people*" who were victimized by pirates and then refused entry into countries like Hong Kong, Singapore, and Thailand or of Albanians and Haitians fleeing hardship and tyranny being turned away by Italy and the United States respectively create global political controversy.

Finally, individuals have organized themselves in a host of ways that defy confinement by state frontiers. As we shall see in Chapter 5, actors such as corporations, terrorist groups, political movements, and ethnic movements challenge the integrity of national frontiers and form the basis of transnational society.

Transnational Relations

According to the traditional model, direct interactions in world politics take place *solely* between and among governments of sovereign states (interstate interaction), as depicted in Figure 4.4. Nonsovereign groups or individuals were believed not to affect global politics except indirectly, as by voting, lobbying, demonstrating, writing letters, or in other ways trying to persuade governments. It is apparent, however, that many interactions involve nongovernmental actors, and such interactions are *transnational*.[41] Figure 4.5 illustrates how the traditional model of global politics changes when one takes account of *direct* involvement by nonstate actors—corporations, drug cartels, terrorists, nonprofit organizations, and so on—that are players in global political issues, sometimes even despite opposition by governments.

Rather than a global hierarchy with sovereign states at the top, we can increasingly speak of a "web of world politics,"[42] in which flows of goods, people, and ideas across national frontiers produce interdependence—a concept to which we turn shortly. This is surely the model of world politics that the president of the IBM World Trade Corporation had in mind when he declared,

> For business purposes, the boundaries that separate one nation from another are no more real than the equator. They are merely convenient demarcations of ethnic, linguistic, and cultural entities. They do not define business requirements or

[40] An equally huge problem is posed by internal refugees who flee one part of a country for another to escape war and famine. Pictures of starving refugees in camps in Somalia, Ethiopia, Iraq, and the Sudan suggest the size of the problem.

[41] Joseph S. Nye, Jr. and Robert O. Keohane, "Transnational Relations and World Politics: An Introduction," in Keohane and Nye, eds., *Transnational Relations and World Politics* (Cambridge: Harvard University Press, 1971), p. xii.

[42] See Richard W. Mansbach, Yale H. Ferguson, and Donald E. Lampert, *The Web of World Politics: Nonstate Actors in the Global System* (Englewood Cliffs, N.J.: Prentice-Hall, 1975).

FIGURE 4.4

Traditional Restricted Model of State-Centered Politics

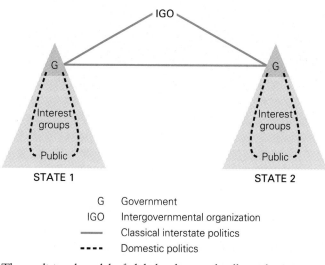

G	Government
IGO	Intergovernmental organization
——	Classical interstate politics
----	Domestic politics

The traditional model of global politics only allows domestic groups to influence the outside world *indirectly* by pressuring their government. The sum of global politics in this model is interaction among governments or between governments and IGOs like the United Nations. Copyright © 1971. Reprinted with permission of the MIT Press.

consumer trends. . . . The world outside the home country is no longer viewed as a series of disconnected customers and prospects for its products, but as an extension of a single market.[43]

Transnational activity reduces governments' ability to carry out their own policies. During the early 1990s, the government of Germany under Chancellor Helmut Kohl sought to maintain high interest rates to reduce inflation, keep the value of the mark high, and attract investment from German and foreign sources to pay for reconstructing the former East Germany. At the same time, Great Britain and France sought to reduce interest rates to stimulate their domestic economies and reduce unemployment during recession. The German policy unintentionally undermined these efforts and also put pressure on currencies such as the British pound and the Italian lira as speculators sought to dump them and buy marks in the belief that the value of the German currency would continue to rise. A speculative frenzy engulfed Europe in October 1992, and anger at home forced the British and Italian governments to abandon the European

[43]Cited in Richard J. Barnet and Ronald E. Muller, *Global Reach: The Power of the Multinational Corporations* (New York: Simon and Schuster, 1974). See Christopher Bartlett and Sumantra Ghoshal, *Managing Across Borders* (Cambridge: Harvard University Press, 1989).

FIGURE 4.5

Expanded Model of International and Domestic Policy Links

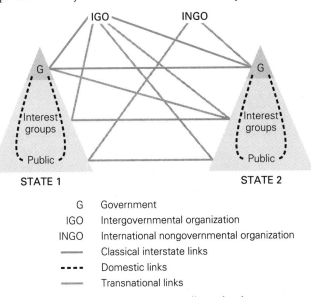

G	Government
IGO	Intergovernmental organization
INGO	International nongovernmental organization
——	Classical interstate links
- - - -	Domestic links
~~	Transnational links

The expanded model of global politics allows for direct transnational interactions between societies, between societal groups and governments, and between societal groups and IGOs and INGOs. This model permits nongovernmental organizations like the PLO to behave as autonomous actors. Copyright © 1971. Reprinted with permission of MIT Press.

Monetary System (EMS), dealing a blow to European unification. The role of private speculators and investors illustrates the power of *transnational relations*. Governments thought they could maintain the value of their currencies as they had in the past by ordering their central banks to buy and sell currencies. In fact, the central banks had little idea how much cash was in private hands or how quickly it could be moved, and their resources were overwhelmed by the flows of private funds.

In sum, transnational relations are increasingly vital to global politics. Indeed, some issues are really transnational rather than interstate. One dramatic illustration of this direction is the global drug problem and the role played by organized crime. "In many Latin American countries," writes one observer, "drug-trafficking organizations, rather than the government, now represent the ultimate power in portions of a country if not the country as a whole."[44] To some extent, this description applies to states including Burma, Bolivia, Colombia, and Peru. For its part, the U.S. government—notwithstanding the creation of "drug czars," use of the military, and investment of large amounts of money—seems helpless to control its own frontiers against imported cocaine and heroin.

[44]Ethan A. Nadelmann, "U.S. Drug Policy: A Bad Export," *Foreign Policy* No. 70 (Fall 1988), p. 87.

Efforts to eradicate the sources of drugs are either unsuccessful or simply lead to their being moved to another region or country, and efforts to interdict the import of drugs are as good as useless. Figure 4.6 illustrates the transnational extent of the narcotics problem by showing the circuitous routes from cultivation areas in South America, the Middle East ("the Golden Crescent"), and Southeast Asia ("the Golden Triangle") to the lucrative markets in North America and Western Europe.

The Meaning of Interdependence

What we have been describing suggests how difficult it is in contemporary politics for any state to close its frontiers to the movement of persons, ideas, and things or to shield citizens from the consequences of events far from home. From time to time states try to shield their inhabitants from foreign influences, but the costs inevitably are very high in modernization, prosperity, and human welfare. They are cut off from the economic, technological, and informational benefits that accompany international trade, foreign investment, tourism, overseas education, international media, and other transnational and international activities. In other words, nation-states can retain a measure of sovereign independence, but they will pay a steep price for doing so.

Whether we like it or not, we live in an *interdependent* world.[45] An actor is *dependent* if it is significantly affected by external forces. *Interdependence* is a situation of mutual dependence. In earlier centuries, interdependence was relatively low. People were mainly self-sufficient and interacted infrequently with others outside their immediate locality. Today, *all* human beings depend, to some extent, on others outside their community for the necessities of survival. Thus, the price Americans and Europeans pay for coffee and other primary products depends on events in Latin America and Africa, and prosperity in those regions depends upon demand for their products in the developed world and the availability of substitutes from elsewhere that may depress prices for these products.

It has been suggested that there are two sides to interdependence — *sensitivity* and *vulnerability*.[46] Sensitivity is the *speed* with which changes in one part of the world affect other parts of the world and the *magnitude* of those effects. Farmers in the United States are more sensitive than most to changes in oil prices because oil and oil-based products are indispensable in running farm machinery and producing fertilizers. Vulnerability refers to the alternatives actors have in seeking to limit the effects of change. Can farmers find a substitute for oil to limit their costs? If not, their vulnerability to oil price changes is high. Do commuters have access to mass transit, or can they do their work at home if oil becomes unavailable for their automobiles? In fact, commuters in Los

---

[45]See Robert O. Keohane and Joseph S. Nye, *Power and Interdependence*, 2nd ed. (Glenview, Ill.: Scott, Foresman, 1989).

[46]Ibid., pp. 11–19.

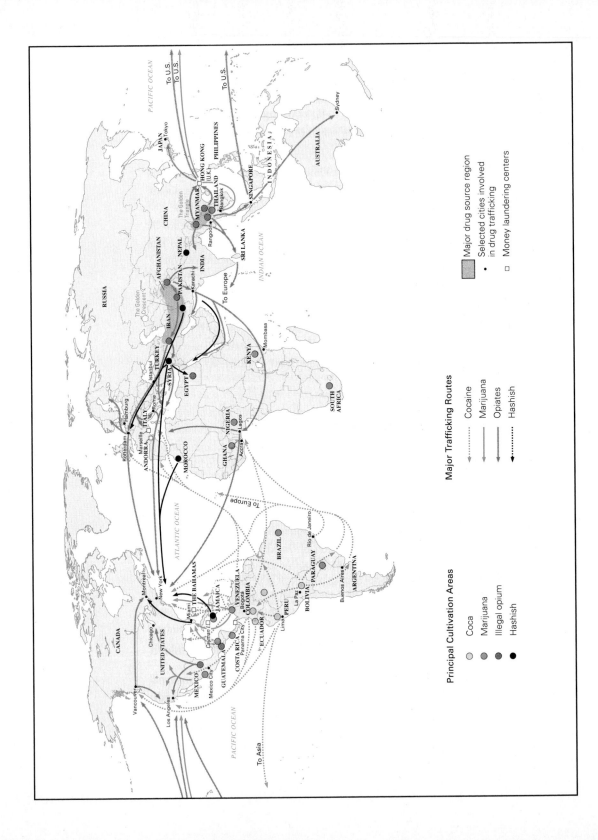

Principal Cultivation Areas

● Coca
● Marijuana
● Illegal opium
● Hashish

Major Trafficking Routes

┈┈ Cocaine
→ Marijuana
→ Opiates
┅┅ Hashish

▨ Major drug source region
● Selected cities involved in drug trafficking
□ Money laundering centers

PACIFIC OCEAN

To U.S.
To U.S.
To U.S.

JAPAN
•Tokyo

HONG KONG
|U.K.|

PHILIPPINES

SINGAPORE

INDONESIA

AUSTRALIA

•Sydney

MYANMAR
THAILAND
•Bangkok

The Golden
Triangle

CHINA

•Rangoon

NEPAL

SRI LANKA

INDIA

INDIAN OCEAN

AFGHANISTAN

PAKISTAN
•Karachi

The Golden
Crescent

IRAN

RUSSIA

To Europe

TURKEY
•Istanbul

SYRIA

EGYPT

KENYA
•Mombasa

•Rome
ITALY
ANDORRA□
Marseille
MOROCCO

Hamburg□
Rotterdam

NIGERIA
•Lagos

GHANA
•Accra

SOUTH
AFRICA

ATLANTIC OCEAN

To Europe

CANADA

•Chicago

•Vancouver

•Montreal

•New York

UNITED STATES

Miami•
THE BAHAMAS□

JAMAICA

•Cayman□

GUATEMALA

MEXICO
•Mexico City

COSTA RICA
Panama City□

ECUADOR

VENEZUELA
•Bogotá
COLOMBIA

PERU
•Lima
•La Paz
BOLIVIA

BRAZIL
•Rio de Janeiro

PARAGUAY

ARGENTINA
•Buenos Aires

•Los Angeles

PACIFIC OCEAN

To Asia

Angeles are more vulnerable than commuters in New Jersey to fluctuations in the price and supply of oil because they have no access to mass transit and must travel greater distances to work.

Many quantitative *indicators* point to relative interdependence and can help us to measure it. The ratio of international to national trade is one measure of how involved or embedded a people are in the global system. This ratio has increased for most actors, especially the United States, which until recently was relatively self-sufficient economically. Figure 4.7 illustrates the dramatic increase in U.S. foreign trade as a percentage of GNP, especially since the early 1970s, and shows how thoroughly the U.S. economy has been integrated into the global market. A similar conclusion becomes apparent from Figure 4.8, which shows the dramatic increases in U.S. investment overseas and foreign investment, especially direct rather than portfolio investment, in the United States since the 1950s. Such indicators, according to one observer, reveal "rapid acceleration in the development of ties linking nations, their institutional components, and the individuals who populate them" and "a general tendency for many forms of human interconnectedness across national boundaries to be doubling every ten years."[47]

Such indicators of interdependence should not, however, be confused with interdependence itself. Changes in factors like technology and trade create links across national boundaries and make it more expensive to go it alone in the world today. If, however, people are prepared to pay a price, they can escape dependence.[48] A society can sever economic and political ties to others if people are prepared to accept a lower standard of living, higher unemployment, and isolation more generally. Moreover, if a society is cohesive and a government popular, citizens may be willing to bear high costs to escape dependence on others.

During World War I, Germans were cut off from the oil imports necessary to maintain their economy and run their war machine. Although Germany produced no oil at home and could not break the British naval blockade, the country did not

[47]Alex Inkeles, "The Emerging Social Structure of the World," *World Politics* 27:4 (July 1975), p. 479.

[48]Some observers argue that the idea of a "national" economy is obsolete. See Robert Reich, *The Work of Nations* (New York: Alfred Knopf, 1991).

FIGURE 4.6

Narcopolitics: A Transnational Issue
This map illustrates the transnational and global nature of narcopolitics. It shows the principal sources and markets of narcotics and the major trafficking routes from one to the other. As the drug trade has grown, the area of production has greatly expanded from the traditional Asian centers—the Golden Crescent and the Golden Triangle—to include many Third World countries. Poverty provides the drug lords with an army of drug runners.

FIGURE 4.7

U.S. Foreign Trade as a Percentage of GNP

This table reflects the growing importance of foreign trade to the U.S. economy and the growing participation of the United States in the interdependent global economy. By 1990, foreign trade accounted for 25 percent of the U.S. GNP.

capitulate. Instead, Germans found imaginative substitutes for oil, including vegetable-derived alcohol — beets and turnips — and animal energy, which they used even though the substitutes were less efficient and more expensive than oil. Fidel Castro's regime in Cuba — one of the few hard-line communist regimes in the world — refused to accept the consequences of its Soviet protector's collapse. Deprived of inexpensive Soviet oil and hard currency from subsidized Soviet purchases of Cuban sugar, Cubans abandoned cars for bicycles and sought substitutes for other imports.

As these cases suggest, dependence and interdependence are subjective phenomena. Indicators such as those above are not the same as interdependence; they merely reflect the costs that have to be paid for independence. The question is: *How high a cost are people prepared to bear to assert their independence?* Those who are prepared to bear higher costs in seeking alternatives to circumstances in which they are vulnerable are less dependent than those who are not.

FIGURE 4.8

U.S. Private Investment Abroad, Foreign Private Investment in the U.S. as a Percentage of U.S. GNP

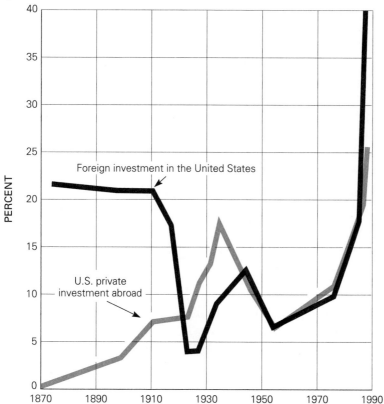

Although foreign investment fueled U.S. economic growth in the nineteenth century, it played a relatively minor role in much of this century until the 1970s and 1980s. During recent decades, foreign investment in the United States, especially direct investment, grew dramatically, outstripping the growth of U.S. investment overseas. From *World Politics: The Menu for Choice* by Bruce Russett and Harvey Starr. Copyright © 1992 by W.H. Freeman and Company. Reprinted with permission.

Conclusion

The traditional approach helps make sense of issues that involve military security, in which actors' interdependence is low or negative, and in which the main players remain the governments of states. An increasing number of issues, however, do not involve military security in the traditional sense and do involve various actors other than governments who find themselves highly interdependent. Such issues have always been present but remained in shadow, receiving insufficient attention from scholars and practitioners. They are poorly understood when viewed through the lens of the power-politics approach.

In sum, traditional scholars and practitioners limit their attention mostly to issues characterized by:

1. A dominant and authoritative role for the governments of states.
2. Clear differentiation between domestic and international political activity.
3. A direct or indirect military aspect with implications for national power and balancing of power among states.
4. Deep conflict in which the gains (national interest) of one actor or set of actors are roughly equal to the losses of another.
5. A propensity for actors to evaluate their gains and losses *relative* to the gains and losses of others.

An alternative perspective on global politics would focus on issues with these features:

1. A variety of governmental and nongovernmental actors who have direct and indirect influence in determining political outcomes.
2. Muddling and merging of distinctions between the international and domestic arenas so that it becomes unclear whether issues fall mainly into one or the other.
3. The declining value of military force for resolving issues.
4. The reduced utility of national interest for understanding policy.
5. Growing recognition of the presence of "public goods" so that no one actor or group of actors can profit (or lose) unless all do and recognition that profit depends upon cooperation.
6. A propensity for actors to evaluate gains or losses in *absolute* terms.

In sum, we live in an interdependent world. "Almost every day," writes James Rosenau, "incidents are reported that defy the principles of sovereignty. Politics everywhere, it would seem, are related to politics everywhere else."[49] One major consequence of actors' autonomy being eroded by transnationalism and interdependence, as this quotation suggests, is that the domestic and international aspects of issues are increasingly fused. In Chapter 5, we turn to the rich variety of actors who have important roles in a complex and interdependent universe.

---

[49]James N. Rosenau, "Introduction: Political Science in a Shrinking World," in Rosenau, ed., *Linkage Politics: Essays on the Convergence of National and International Systems* (New York: Free Press, 1969), p. 2.

Key Terms

unitary actors	political consciousness
rational analysis	xenophobia
global agenda	cultural exchange
issue cycle	transnational
genesis	guest workers
crisis	boat people
ritualization	transnational relations
resolution	interdependence
government	dependence
homogeneous states	sensitivity
heterogeneous states	vulnerability
state sovereignty	state-centric
sovereign equality	issue
recognition of states	actor
quasi-states	microsovereignties
tribe	*contras*
ethnic group	Versailles Conference
juridical statehood	Cuban missile crisis
national interest	nation
national security	society
participation explosion	demonstration effect
democratization	indicators

CHAPTER FIVE

Beyond the Nation-State?
A World of Many Actors

We live in a world in which many actors compete for the individual's loyalty and resources.[1] As we saw in Chapter 4, the state itself has evolved gradually but dramatically in recent centuries and is more varied than in the past. In sum, we are "witnessing a movement away from a system dominated by a single type of actor and toward a system characterized by extensive interactions among several qualitatively different types of actors."[2]

In this chapter we survey the varied actors in world politics, especially those other than the state. We begin, however, by picking up one strand of the earlier argument about the state—that there are weak and strong states and that the presence of weak states makes actors other than states more important than they once were. Nonstate actors include *subnational* groups such as political parties, *transnational* entities like corporations that operate across national frontiers, *intergovernmental* organizations like the United Nations that consist of the representatives of states, and even a few tentative *supranational* entities. Depending on the issue, these actors may challenge the traditional prerogatives of sovereign states in different ways. Giant corporations challenge their economic independence, small bands of terrorists challenge the security of their citizens and diplomats, and dissatisfied ethnic groups challenge their territorial and political integrity. James Rosenau believes such actors are responsible for a multi-centric

---

[1]The title is from Ernst B. Haas, *Beyond the Nation-State: Functionalism and International Organization* (Stanford, Calif.: Stanford University Press, 1964). Haas is one of the few international-relations scholars who consistently thinks beyond the state-system model.

[2]Oran R. Young, "The Actors in World Politics," in James N. Rosenau, Vincent Davis, and Maurice A. East, eds., *The Analysis of International Politics* (New York: Free Press, 1972), p. 139.

world that he contrasts to the state-centric world.[3] The governments of states remain the dominant actors in world politics, but the number of strong states in world politics is declining as weak states continue to increase.

Strong and Weak States

As we use the labels "strong" and "weak" here, we do *not* mean the indicators of power such as size described in Chapter 3. *Strong states* are those whose governments enjoy *autonomy* and *capacity*. An autonomous state can formulate and pursue goals that "are not simply reflective of the demands or interests of social groups, classes, or society."[4] Capacity is the state's ability to tap and make use of its citizens' resources in ways that it wishes.[5] In a strong state, powerful autonomous bureaucracies can ensure citizens' security and well-being, command their loyalties and resources and, if necessary, overawe other groups within its frontiers. In a *weak state*, government bureaucracies are mainly controlled by or responsive to a segment of society—a class or a political elite. Also, the *administrative capacity* of a weak state is poorly developed, and the government can be manipulated by outsiders.

Two small neighbors in Central Europe—Switzerland and Austria—illustrate the differences between weak and strong states. Switzerland is a weak state. Its government structure is decentralized and has few powers; instead, most powers are reserved to the cantons (or provinces) in the federal system. The country has a small bureaucracy that has grown slowly during the past forty years. Popular referenda have restricted the central government's taxing power, limiting the revenue available to it, and the government has only a modest ability to intervene in the country's economy compared to governments elsewhere, as illustrated by the absence of regulation of Swiss banks. One analyst feels that reliance on the banks' self-regulation "illustrates the weakness that characterizes the Swiss state generally."[6] Although Switzerland is a weak state, the country's prosperity, history, and social stability have enabled it to avoid some of the debilitating consequences associated with weak states elsewhere.[7]

Austria, by contrast, can be classified as a strong state. Government power is centralized and it inherited a tradition of a "strong bureaucratic state" from the Austro-Hungarian Empire. The Austrian government has steadily expanded and now

[3]James N. Rosenau, *Turbulence in World Politics: A Theory of Change and Continuity* (Princeton: Princeton University Press, 1990), especially pp. 40–42.

[4]Theda Skocpol, "Bringing the State Back In: Strategies of Analysis in Current Research," in Peter B. Evans, Dietrich Rueschemeyer, and Theda Skocpol, eds., *Bringing the State Back In* (Cambridge: Cambridge University Press, 1985), p. 9.

[5]Ibid., p. 17.

[6]Peter Katzenstein, "Small Nations in an Open International Economy: The Converging Balance of State and Society in Switzerland and Austria," in Evans, Rueschemeyer, and Skocpol, *Bringing the State Back In*, p. 233.

[7]By contrast, Italy is a weak state in which the government often appears to be paralyzed.

employs the largest number of officials per capita in Europe.[8] The government is deeply involved in the economy, owning all or a major part of such industries and services as tobacco, salt, transportation, communication, and the largest commercial banks and insurance companies.[9] In all, government involvement in Austria contrasts dramatically with that in Switzerland.

Strong and weak states are all around the world. In the Western Hemisphere, states like Argentina and Bolivia, and, more recently, El Salvador and Haiti that have experienced endemic government instability owing to coups and revolutions, are weak. Other states in this region, including Costa Rica and Mexico, enjoy greater stability, stronger central bureaucracies, and greater governmental capacity and are strong. In Asia, such small countries as Singapore, South Korea, and Taiwan are strong. They have dynamic central governments and bureaucracies that help maintain dynamic economies. In this sense, they have autonomy and capacity. Other states in Asia including India, Sri Lanka, the Philippines, and Cambodia, are weaker. Despite its size, India, as we saw earlier, is hobbled by ethnic, religious, and linguistic cleavages. Although the country benefits from a strong bureaucratic tradition inherited from the British colonial authorities, the powers of the central government are limited by the strong powers retained by local states.

Overall, no region has as great a proportion of weak states as sub-Saharan Africa. Unlike other regions where governments are able to make some progress in raising standards of living, sub-Saharan Africa is losing ground. Between 1980 and 1991, per capita gross domestic product declined annually in many African states including Tanzania, Mauritania, Rwanda, Togo, Ethiopia, Somalia, Nigeria, Madagascar, Niger, and Mozambique.[10] Not only are such states unable to meet inhabitants' basic demands but, for reasons discussed earlier, many must share citizens' loyalty with either tribal groups or neighboring states. As a result, many people in Africa are coming to depend on outsiders for the essentials of survival and security.

Lebanon as a Weak State

Lebanon is an extreme example of how weak states may lose control of their own fate and how their weakness can involve the global community. Lebanon's government is less an autonomous actor than a reflection of the country's divisions. The country is so deeply divided that for more than a decade, its president and prime minister hardly spoke to each other, its cabinet rarely met, its army simply melted away and was parceled up among competing factions, and presidents were routinely assassinated. Although this era was ended by outside intervention, the cost was continued foreign occupation. Currently, the southernmost region is controlled by Israel and its Christian Lebanese allies. Parts of Beirut and the Bekaa Valley are occupied by the Syrian army, and much of the

---

[8]Katzenstein, "Small Nations," p. 234.

[9]Ibid.

[10]World Development Bank, *World Development Report 1993*, (New York: Oxford University Press, 1993), p. 238.

remainder of the country is under Syrian influence. Other influential players include militant Palestinians concentrated in overcrowded refugee camps, Islamic fundamentalists beholden to Iran, and various religious sects.

The basic division in Lebanon is between Christians and Muslims. The original 1943 pact that was the basis of Lebanese independence from French rule called for the two communities to share power, including an election system that guaranteed division of seats in parliament, a Muslim prime minister, and a Christian president. This arrangement broke down in the mid-1970s owing to the growth and poverty of the Muslim population, which demanded a greater share of political power. Christian–Muslim divisions were further complicated by cleavages within the two communities. Conflict within the Muslim community periodically erupts among the several Islamic sects—Sunni, Shi'ite, and Druse. The Christians too were divided, among Greek Orthodox, Maronites, and Armenian Catholics. These competing divisions set the stage for a bloody civil war that lasted from 1975 to 1990, and outside interventions by Israel, Syria, and, briefly, the United States and France.

Somalia as a Weak State

Somalia, on the Horn of East Africa and bordering on the Red Sea and the Indian Ocean, became a focus of world attention in 1992 as its central government melted away and civil war and famine engulfed the country. So desperate was its condition that in November 1992 the United Nations authorized force to restore order and provide humanitarian relief to those in need. In December, an international force led by American marines landed in Somalia to carry out that mission, some of whom remained as part of a multinational U.N. army established in April 1993. By autumn of 1993, U.S. troops continued to be stymied in their aim to end clan violence, and calls grew in the United States to end the operation.

Somalia achieved independence in 1960 by merging the British Somaliland Protectorate and the Italian Trusteeship Territory of Somalia. The Somali state was weak even prior to its 1991 civil war, for its government was little more than an agent for one of the country's dominant clans. At least two factors help account for the deteriorating Somali state, however, and, more generally, for the difficulties faced by many Third-World states. First, Somalia was the setting for superpower rivalry in the 1970s. The country had been wooed during the 1960s and 1970s by the U.S.S.R., which coveted a deep-sea naval base on the Red Sea. When, in the mid-1970s, a Marxist regime took power in Ethiopia, Somalia's neighbor and long its rival, the U.S.S.R. transferred its support to that regime and the United States began to aid Somalia. Both the Soviet Union and the United States poured weapons and other aid into Somalia, but, when the Cold War ended, the Somali government was left to its own devices.

Second, the Somali government's corrupt and authoritarian policies did little to overcome the weakening of the state. That government, long led by Siad Barre, became increasingly unpopular and ineffective. Finally, in 1991, Barre was ousted and fled the country, and Somalia was left without a government. This void was filled by the militias of rival clans, especially in the south. Instead of order, their competition produced anarchy. Despite efforts by foreign governments and other groups to end the suffering in Somalia, they were unable to prevent looting of relief supplies by the rival clans, and 350,000 Somalis died from starvation in 1992.

Many other countries are divided in ways that reduce state authority. The strength of a state helps determine how effectively it can cope with the variety of global actors that can affect its citizens' well-being and prosperity. For example, strong states are better able than weak ones to force foreign corporations on its soil to serve its citizens' interests as well as those of stockholders thousands of miles away. Strong states, too, are affected by such actors, but their relationship is less one of dependence and more one of interdependence.

The Variety of Global Actors

States are only one type of important actor in contemporary global politics. A brief typology of actors will guide our discussion. In addition to states, we distinguish between *intergovernmental organizations* (IGOs) and *nongovernmental organizations* (NGOs). Inter-governmental organizations (such as the United Nations) are actors in which states are members. The IGOs and the civil servants who manage them try to wrestle some control away from member states and, in this way, challenge their autonomy. By contrast, NGOs (such as Greenpeace) are composed of individuals or groups that are not members of governments. In other words, IGOs are organized *among* states, and NGOs are organized *across* states. There are also a few *supranational organizations*. Just as governments have authority over their citizens, such organizations enjoy authority *over* states.

Number and Distribution of IGOs and NGOs

The number of intergovernmental organizations has grown dramatically during this century. In 1909, there were only 37 IGOs. By 1960, they had increased to 154 and doubled again by 1981 to 337. By 1992, owing to mergers among some of these organizations, the total had declined slightly to 286. About three-quarters are "regionally oriented membership organizations"; that is, their membership is confined to one region. The other 25 percent are "universal" or "intercontinental" in membership.[11] Overall, intergovernmental organizations have a greater role in global politics and affect our lives more directly than ever before.

The pattern is much the same for nongovernmental organizations over this century. In 1909, there were only 176 NGOs worldwide. Half a century later, there were 1,255. By 1981, the total had reached 4,265, and, by 1992, it had risen to 4,696. Like IGOs, NGOs

[11]These data are from the *Yearbook of International Organizations 1992/93*, Vol. 1. (München: K. G. Saur, 1992), pp. 1668–1669.

are primarily "regionally oriented membership organizations" (3,457 of the 4,696 total). Fewer (1,239) are "universal or intercontinental" in scope. The NGOs too are involved in a growing range of global issues and have become important actors in world politics.

Unlike IGOs and NGOs, there are few supranational actors in global politics. One mostly unsuccessful effort to institute supranational principles has been that of the International Court of Justice (ICJ) in the Hague, which failed to gain *compulsory jurisdiction* over international-law cases. For the most part, states must agree to accept ICJ jurisdiction case by case and often do not do so. A more successful effort involved establishing the Higher Authority as the governing body of the European Coal and Steel Community in the 1950s. This agency shaped policy for its member states on coal and steel production.

The current European Community has supranational elements.[12] Its executive body, the *European Commission*, employs almost 14,000 bureaucrats in Brussels with authority over governments in a variety of matters, and, in an effort to eliminate trade barriers, the Commission is trying to harmonize and standardize the regulations of member states. These efforts have created fears among European publics and businesses that somehow supranationalism will erase national customs, threaten national culture, and place the people's fate in the hands of "faceless bureaucrats" in Brussels. So far the Commission's supranational power is limited, but this condition could change. One satirical evaluation of events summarizes matters:

> Brussels is, if you would believe the press, about to take away British prawn-cocktail crisps, German beer, French cheese, Danish apples, the Spanish tilde (the squiggle over the "n") and Italian pasta. . . . Take the question of foam-filled furniture, a subject of little interest to anybody except the British. For some reason, Britons are particularly apt to be killed by the fumes from flaming sofas. Britain now has laws requiring fire-retardant chemicals in furniture foam, and fears the import of dangerous foreign foam. . . . The British government says it will ban the import of foreign foam-filled furniture; and so, in one area, the single market will not exist. . . . The Germans will resist. Although they do not seem to get killed by their sofas, they are worried by the idea of pumping chemicals into their furniture which—who knows?—could do dreadful things to their babies' health.[13]

Thus, resistance is considerable, at least in Europe, to efforts to weaken states' authority.

In sum, almost no area of human activity is untouched by an intergovernmental organization or a nongovernmental organization.[14] To illustrate the range and significance of these actors in global politics, we survey significant types of NGOs and IGOs. Keep three considerations in mind as we undertake this survey. First, similar groups have operated historically, although they were not as prominent as today. Second, such actors are everywhere and are being asked to do more and more in the post-Cold War era.

---

[12]See Chapter 13, pp. 446–451.

[13]"Why Brussels Sprouts," *The Economist*, December 26, 1992–January 8, 1993, pp. 70, 72.

[14]See *Yearbook of International Organizations 1992/93*.

Third, each type of actor assumes varied forms. Some are regional and others global. Some specialize in one issue, and others are multipurpose. Along with states, however, IGOs and NGOs create the mosaic of actors that constitute contemporary global society.

Transnational Corporations

A useful point to begin with is the especially prominent nongovernmental organizations called *transnational (TNC)* or *multinational corporations*.[15] These corporations—economic enterprises with their headquarters in one country that are active in other countries[16]—are among the most important economic actors on the world stage. They span the globe, control immense economic resources, and their names are household words. Table 5.1 depicts the fifty wealthiest economic entities in the world. The economic size of states is measured by gross domestic product and corporations by total sales.[17] It shows how transnational corporations like General Motors rank just behind some of the largest states in the world and ahead of most states today. Indeed, corporations account for roughly one quarter of the largest economic entities in global politics.

Although there are significant historical examples of transnational corporations and trading groups—for instance, the British and Dutch East India companies[18] and the Hanseatic League[19]—and although companies like Singer and Nestlé have operated internationally for much of this century, the global role and influence of such corporations have expanded dramatically in recent decades. With economic issues globalized, proliferating linkages among national economies, and revolutions in communication, transportation, and computer technologies, transnational corporations have become leading global actors. Such actors enjoy greater flexibility than most states. In the words of one observer:

> While multinational companies can invest or disinvest, merge with others or go it alone, rise from nothing or disappear in bankruptcy, the state seems stodgy and stuck in comparison, glued more or less to one piece of territory, fighting off entropy

[15]Some authors differentiate between transnational and multinational corporations, and some do not. We regard the two as equivalent but prefer the former because it conveys the sense of global mobility characteristic of many economic enterprises.

[16]Robert S. Walters and David H. Blake, *The Politics of Global Economic Relations*, 4th ed. (Englewood Cliffs, N.J.: Prentice-Hall 1992), p. 108.

[17]This measure actually inflates the relative ranking of states because GDP data include corporate sales in those countries.

[18]Founded in 1600, the British East India Company at its height commanded an army and administered large areas of India. In a real sense it was responsible for the British conquest of India.

[19]The Hanseatic League was a consortium of 200 northern European trading towns. See John Conybeare, "Trade Wars: A Comparative Study of Anglo-Hanse, Franco-Italian, and Hawley-Smoot Conflicts," *World Politics* 38:1 (October 1985), pp. 152–155.

TABLE 5.1

The World's Top Fifty Economic Entities[a]

	U.S. Dollars (Billions)		U.S. Dollars (Billions)
1. United States	5,610.8	26. Saudi Arabia	108.6
2. Japan	3,362.3	27. Norway	105.9
3. Soviet Union	2,664.0	28. **Royal Dutch/Shell**	103.8
4. West Germany	1,574.3	29. **Exxon**	103.2
5. France	1,199.3	30. Iran	97.0
6. Italy	1,150.5	31. Turkey	95.8
7. United Kingdom	876.8	32. Thailand	93.3
8. Spain	527.1	33. South Africa	91.2
9. Canada	510.8	34. **Ford Motor**	89.0
10. Brazil	414.1	35. Yugoslavia	82.3
11. China	369.6	36. **Toyota Motor**	78.1
12. Australia	299.8	37. Poland	78.0
13. Netherlands	290.7	38. Hong Kong	67.6
14. South Korea	283.0	39. **IBM**	65.4
15. Mexico	282.5	40. Portugal	65.1
16. Switzerland	232.0	41. **IRI**	64.1
17. India	221.9	42. Israel	62.7
18. Sweden	206.4	43. **General Electric**	60.2
19. Belgium	196.9	44. **British Petroleum**	58.4
20. Austria	164.0	45. Greece	57.9
21. **General Motors**	123.8	46. **Daimler-Benz**	57.3
22. Indonesia	116.5	47. **Mobil**	56.9
23. Argentina	114.3	48. **Hitachi**	56.1
24. Denmark	112.1	49. Venezuela	53.4
25. Finland	110.0	50. Peru	48.3

[a]Countries are measured by total GDP and corporations by total sales.

SOURCE: Total GDP from Table 3 of the *World Development Report 1993: Investing in Health* (New York: Oxford University Press, 1993), pp. 242–243 and are for 1991. The data for Germany are for West Germany only, and the data for the U.S.S.R. were for 1989 and were taken from *World Military Expenditures and Arms Transfer 1990* (Washington, D.C.: US Arms Control and Disarmament Agency), p. 81. Corporate data are for 1991 and are from *Fortune*, July 27, 1992, p. 179.

and budget crises, the national community usually assessing the latest foreign attacks upon a condition of declining competitiveness and the vulnerability in its domestic markets.[20]

As a result, governments may find themselves at a disadvantage in dealing with such actors.

Global Reach of the TNC

A genuine transnational corporation is centrally organized but has no home. Whatever its national origin, it seeks to maximize its own interests rather than those of any country. Such corporations now span the globe and operate in all sectors in both developed and developing countries. Although many of these corporations, such as Exxon, Mitsubishi, British Petroleum, and Volvo, originate in economically-advanced countries, some are now appearing in newly industrializing countries, such as Samsung and Hyundai in Korea and even in some developing countries, such as Pemex in Mexico.

Corporations have a number of motivations for expanding overseas. First, they may seek access to new markets. By establishing subsidiaries in a region, they may avoid tariffs and other import barriers. Second, corporations may expand to gain access to local capital markets, raw materials, or low-cost labor. American corporations have established facilities in countries like Mexico and Hong Kong to keep down the cost of labor and maintain a competitive edge.[21] Since 1965, U.S. firms have established 1,700 plants called *maquiladoras* (mills) just across the border in Mexico, which employ 500,000 Mexicans at wages about 40 percent as high as those in the United States.[22] Japanese firms have expanded significantly into Southeast Asia in recent years for the same reasons. Third, corporations may leave a country and settle elsewhere because they decide they can no longer compete in a market or because of technological advances elsewhere, a poor business climate locally, or local labor unrest. In the 1980s, some U.S. television manufacturers moved operations to Japan because technological developments there were more attractive than in the United States. Whatever their motivation, the flexibility of corporations helps them to play off states against each other.

Corporations, of course, become transnational in varying degrees. Some remain *ethnocentric*, reflecting the values and interests of the country in which they were born. Such corporations usually organize to maximize control by managers in the home rather than the host country. Although they may have worldwide operations, such corporations are still American, French, or Japanese in spirit. Other corporations—akin to holding companies—are organized more loosely, giving local affiliates latitude in making

[20]Robert A. Isaak, *International Political Economy: Managing World Economic Change* (Englewood Cliffs, N.J.: Prentice-Hall, 1991), p. 160.
[21]Sometimes governments will offer corporations concessions to attract them.
[22]"Hi, amigo," *The Economist*, December 12–18, 1992, p. 21.

major decisions and allowing local managers to enjoy authority. Subsidiaries are managed locally but receive advice and assistance from the center. Like franchise operations in the United States, such corporations benefit by marketing products of local firms.[23] Such arrangements help corporations mobilize local support and evade national restrictions on their activities.

One result of escalating foreign investment has been to internationalize production. Today, products like automobiles commonly include parts made in several countries. As a result, many large corporations that are publicly associated with a country have progressively fewer ties to that country. When America's Big Three automobile manufacturers—General Motors, Ford, and Chrysler—invoke patriotism in urging Americans to forsake Japanese cars and "come home," they do not publicize the fact that "American" cars are made from parts produced all over the world and that those cars are assembled in many countries. Indeed, the former host may find it must import what it formerly exported! In some respects, such "domestic" corporations as Chrysler are no more American than Nissan, Toyota, Honda, and Hyundai which have established subsidiaries in the United States and employ many American workers and managers.

TNC Influence Worldwide

The influence of TNCs has met little resistance from the governments of economically advanced states.[24] Mostly, the United States has considered their growth benign since World War II, partly because many of them had American roots and because they were regarded as engines of free enterprise on a global scale.[25] Consequently, few efforts have been made to regulate these economic giants. For economic opportunity, political stability, and a receptive political climate, corporate investment in recent decades has increasingly been directed toward advanced countries and away from less-developed societies.[26] Nor has there been a sustained global effort to regulate these corporations. In the 1970s, the United Nations established a Center on Transnational Corporations to gather data and a Commission on Transnational Corporations to develop a code of conduct for these corporations. And in 1980, the U.N. Conference on Trade and

[23]See Richard Robinson, "Beyond the Multinational Corporation," in John Fayerweather, ed., *International Business–Government Affairs* (Cambridge, Mass.: Ballinger, 1973), pp. 17–26.

[24]In Chapter 10, pp. 345–346, 351–353, we assess efforts to regulate transnational corporations.

[25]Criticism of transnational corporations in the United States has been voiced mainly by organized labor, especially the AFL-CIO, because of its fear that U.S. jobs and technology are being exported.

[26]According to one study: "In much of the 1980s, the major feature of the net transfer of financial resources of the industrialized countries was the large inflow of resources to the United States and to a lesser extent the United Kingdom." *World Economic Survey 1992: Current Trends and Policies in the World Economy* (New York: United Nations, 1992), p. 71.

FIGURE 5.1

The Globalization of Auto Production

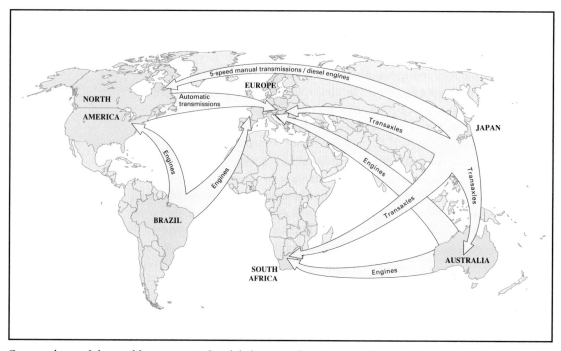

One attribute of the world economy is the globalization of production, illustrated here by automobile production. Globalization of production means that corporations become increasingly transnational and the world becomes increasingly interdependent.

SOURCE: Robert S. Walters and David H. Blake, *The Politics of Global Economic Relations.* 4th ed. (Englewood Cliffs, N.J.: Prentice-Hall, 1992), p. 114.

Development (UNCTAD) published guidelines to prevent limiting international competition. Overall, such efforts, lacking enforcement mechanisms, have had little effect on corporate behavior.

Transnational corporations enjoy greater economic and political leverage in less-developed countries (LDCs) than in wealthy ones, and their presence in the *Third World* has generated greater debate there than in advanced regions. The desperate need for capital, technology, skilled management, trained personnel, and employment opportunities for citizens often dissuades governments from limiting corporate freedom of operation. Corporations are sometimes able to enlist political aid from influential home countries. Corporate influence is also increased by control over assets like technology and global marketing and distribution networks. Furthermore, competition among governments for corporate investment worldwide and corporate threats to move operations elsewhere provide added corporate power. In recent years, the bargaining strength of such governments has been further weakened by the shift in corporate investment patterns away from the Third World to the more secure environment of the developed countries.[27]

Although the 1980s saw improvement in the climate for TNCs in the Third World, governments and publics in these countries remain suspicious of corporate motives and behavior. We return to these issues at greater length in Chapter 10, but briefly cite them here. Many believe that such corporations make unjustifiable profits that they do not share with host countries. It is also argued that relatively few citizens in host countries benefit from the operations of corporations, that those citizens spend their money on imports rather than domestic products, and that they create isolated enclaves of wealth and conspicuous consumption in poor societies. Still another allegation is that corporations overcharge for imported and often obsolete technology. The corporations also, it is argued, tend to make products for export rather than products that would be useful to local populations consisting of poor peasants and residents of teeming urban slums. Far from providing capital for local growth, some claim, the corporations compete for local capital, driving up rates for local enterprises and making it difficult for such enterprises to survive. These complaints are summarized by two observers:

> Overall, there seem to be three major sources of conflict provoked by the existence and actions of multinational corporations in host states. First, the international corporation is a foreign entity that behaves in a fashion that is unusual, different, or wrong, from the point of view of the host state. Second, the corporation is often perceived as an enterprise that is associated closely with a foreign country—the parent state—that is able to exert its influence on the host state through the mechanism of the corporation. Third, the multinational enterprise is an international entity able to take advantage of economic interdependencies among states without itself being subject to the rules and regulations of a comparable international agency.[28]

In practice, the influence of transnational corporations differs from country to country, depending on the kind of industry and the skill of local governments. Transnational corporations in extractive industries in developing countries—tin, silver, coal—are more easily subjected to local control because they cannot pick up and move. But TNCs in semiskilled manufacturing in developing countries have more bargaining leverage because they can pull up stakes and go elsewhere.

TNCs and Developing Countries: Union Carbide and ITT

Two cases illustrate how TNCs are not always model citizens. One deals with an environmental calamity caused by corporate negligence in India, and the other with a corporation's political meddling in the domestic politics of Chile.

[27]Growth in the number of TNCs looking for worldwide opportunities has provided some compensatory bargaining leverage for individual countries.

[28]Blake and Walters, *Politics of Global Economic Relations*, p. 111.

The chemical giant Union Carbide will be remembered for an environmental disaster in India in which more than 2,500 people died quickly and thousands more perished in ensuing weeks or suffered debilitating illness. In December 1984, the highly toxic chemical methyl isocyanate leaked from a Union Carbide pesticide factory in the city of Bhopal. According to one terrifying description:

> The vapor passed first over the shanty-towns of Jaiprakash and Chhola, just outside the walls of the plant, leaving hundreds dead as they slept. The gas quickly enveloped the city's railway station, where beggars were huddled against the chill. . . . Through temples and shops, over streets and lakes . . . the cloud continued to spread, noiselessly and lethally. . . . As word of the cloud of poison began to spread, hundreds then thousands, took to the road in flight from the fumes. . . . As in some eerie science-fiction nightmare people blinded by the gas groped vainly toward uncontaminated air. . . . [29]

For years, Union Carbide resisted efforts to force it to compensate victims, and, when it did so the funds provided were meager. The case illustrates how a developing country, needing a corporation's jobs and capital, may not have the resources to monitor its behavior and may be unable to enforce standards that the corporation has to observe at home.

International Telephone & Telegraph (ITT) is associated with efforts to prevent the election in Chile of a leftist government headed by Salvador Allende Gossens and then helping to create the conditions that led to his overthrow in 1973 by the Chilean army led by General Augusto Pinochet. Corporate memos "give us a picture of ITT operatives and executives, CIA leaders, and State Department people scurrying around in a strenuous 'effort' to stop Allende's assumption of power."[30] The corporation was consumed by fear that its Chilean subsidiary would be nationalized and sought to align itself with the internal and external enemies of Allende.[31]

The ITT case is often cited as evidence of corporate meddling in a sovereign state's affairs. Such meddling varies greatly among corporations and countries. Some corporations, including some under American ownership have routinely used bribery, campaign contributions to selected political candidates, or other corrupt practices to achieve their ends, though others have sought to be good citizens. Transnational corporations undoubtedly do enjoy economic clout in some developing societies and can use it to create political influence. Indeed, at the time of Allende's election in Chile, more than a hundred U.S.-based firms, including twenty-four of the largest U.S. TNCs, had operations in that country. Aside from Chile's copper and nitrate industries — at the time controlled by U.S. corporations like Anaconda — the sectors of the Chilean economy that were more than half controlled by foreign interests included:

[29]"India's Night of Death," *Time*, December 17, 1984, p. 22.

[30]Elizabeth Farnsworth, "More Than Admitted," *Foreign Policy* No. 16 (Fall 1974), p. 130. For a contrary view, see Paul E. Sigmund, "Less Than Charged," *Foreign Policy* No. 16 (Fall 1974), pp. 142–156.

[31]Even before, ITT had something of an unsavory reputation because it did business with both the allies and the Nazis during World War II. See Anthony Sampson, *The Sovereign State of ITT* (New York: Stein & Day, 1973).

Tobacco, 100 percent foreign control (e.g., British-American Tobacco Company).

Copper fabricating, 100 percent foreign control (e.g., Phelps Dodge, Northern Indiana Brass, General Cable).

Automotive assembly, 100 percent foreign control (e.g., GM, Ford, Chrysler).

Radio and television, nearly 100 percent foreign control (e.g., RCA, Phillips).

Pharmaceuticals, nearly 100 percent foreign control (e.g. American Cyanamid, Pfizer, Parke-Davis).

Office equipment, nearly 100 percent foreign control (e.g., Xerox, Sperry Rand, Remington).

Advertising, 90 percent foreign control (e.g., J. Walter Thompson, McCann-Erickson).

Metal products, 60 percent foreign control (e.g., Bethlehem Steel, ARMCO Steel, Koppers, Kaiser, Singer, Hoover).

Chemicals, 60 percent foreign control (e.g., Dow, Monsanto, W. R. Grace).

Oil and petroleum products, more than 50 percent foreign control (e.g., EXXON, Gulf, Mobil).

Machinery, 50 percent foreign control (e.g., Xerox, ITT, General Electric, National Cash Register).[32]

Such economic power such brings in its train political power and ambition.

Global Political Influence of TNCs

It is not clear whether or not TNCs can, in Raymond Vernon's apt phrase, keep "sovereignty at bay."[33] For the most part, corporations make important decisions over which governments have only partial control. Corporations view national impediments to trade and investment as providing advantages to competitors (which are not subject to such limitations) and do not want "politics" to interrupt the smooth transaction of business or their expansion into new markets. Consequently, tensions between governments and corporations are constant. Governments have various resources they can bring to bear against corporations, among them taxation, regulation, and nationalization. But TNCs have capabilities as well — wealth, flexibility, and governmental and nongovernmental allies. Because states need corporate investments and technology and corporations need a positive climate in which to do business, they may find themselves dependent on each other; when they collide, both may be losers. Ultimately, such contests may depend on the strength of the state, the type of corporation, and the context in which it takes place.

---

[32]See Dale L. Johnson, *The Chilean Road to Socialism* (Garden City, N.Y.: Doubleday, 1973).
[33]Raymond Vernon, *Sovereignty at Bay* (New York: Basic Books, 1971).

Even a superpower like the United States must take seriously the independent power of TNCs.[34] Corporations fiercely opposed the *Jackson-Vanik Amendment* to the Trade Act of 1974, which linked Soviet emigration policy to granting that country most-favored-nation trade status. They also disliked President Jimmy Carter's imposing sanctions on the U.S.S.R. after Moscow's invasion of Afghanistan in 1979, and President Reagan's efforts to limit Western exports of high technology to the Soviet Union after martial law was declared in Poland in 1981. Although the U.S. government had its way in the first two cases, it incurred political costs in doing so, and was forced to reverse its policy in the third case.

Finally, the developing countries' continued effort to attract TNCs suggests that, on balance, their governments view them in a positive light. Corporations bring scarce capital investment, train local managers, provide jobs, develop new products (which can be substituted for imports), and infuse new technology. They tend to be export-oriented and may be sources of needed hard and convertible currency. Most important, TNCs, it is argued, link relatively isolated societies to the global economy through global networks of production and distribution. From this perspective, they are the capitalist system's global engines of modernity. Walter Wriston, former chairman of Citibank, calls them "the principal agents for the peaceful transfer of technology from one part of the world to the other."[35]

Terrorist Groups

Terrorist groups impinge on global politics in a very different way than TNCs. *Terrorism* entails applying violence, usually against innocent civilians. Often individuals or groups use it to publicize a political cause if they are too weak to resort to conventional war. Terrorist violence gains publicity and attracts media attention, enabling perpetrators to air grievances before a wide audience. Although states[36]

---

[34]The legal right of the U.S. government to force U.S.-based corporations to obey its policy was established by the Supreme Court's decision in *U.S. v. Curtiss-Wright Export Corporation et al.* (1936). The Court upheld the enforcement of an embargo declared by the Roosevelt administration against the export of arms to belligerents in the Chaco War.

[35]Walter B. Wriston, "Agents of Change Are Rarely Welcome," in Jeffry A. Frieden and David A. Lake, eds., *International Political Economy: Perspectives on Global Power and Wealth*, 2nd ed. (New York: St. Martin's Press, 1991), p. 161. For an opposing point of view, see Richard S. Newfarmer, "Multinationals and Marketplace Magic in the 1980s," in ibid., pp. 192–207.

[36]State terrorism is typified by the Reign of Terror in France (1793–1794) in which a Committee on Public Safety was established to punish "the enemies of revolutionary France and to intimidate those it could not reach." Donna M. Schlagheck, *International Terrorism: An Introduction to the Concepts and Actors* (Lexington, Mass.: Lexington Books, 1988), p. 20. The U.S. government, like many others, has provided assistance to groups that use terrorism as we define it. United States-supported Afghan rebels used terrorism against their foes, as did groups supported by

HELP US FIND THE MISSING TERRORIST, BEFORE HE FINDS MORE INNOCENT VICTIMS.

The terrorists who bombed the World Trade Center murdered six innocent people, injured over 1,000 others, and left terrified school children trapped for hours in an elevator. Several prime suspects have been tracked down and arrested. Indicted terrorist RAMZI AHMED YOUSEF remains at large. As long as YOUSEF is free, more innocent lives could be at risk.

The U.S. State Department is offering a reward of up to $2,000,000 for information leading to his arrest. If you have any information, please contact the police, the FBI, or call us at 1-800-HEROES-1. Overseas, contact the authorities or the nearest U.S. embassy. Or write:

HEROES ■ P.O. Box 96781 Washington, DC 20090-6781 ■ U.S.A.

The bombing of New York's World Trade Center in 1993 was a vivid reminder of the risks to Americans posed by international terrorists. In response, the U.S. government offered a reward for the capture of one of the alleged terrorists and published this "wanted notice."

---

may also use terrorism, we are interested here in the nongovernmental terrorist groups that have proliferated in recent decades and whose routine resort to assassination and kidnapping violates international law and custom. Indeed, "terrorist" is a pejorative label that we apply to those we dislike.[37]

Washington in Angola, Cambodia, and elsewhere. Some states also sponsor or aid terrorist groups, and the U.S. government keeps a list of such "state sponsors of terrorism." In recent years, allegations of sponsorship have been made against Iraq, Iran, Libya, Syria, South Yemen, and others.

[37]Those whose cause we support we call freedom fighters.

Global Expanse of International Terrorism

Like transnational corporations, terrorism is not a new phenomenon. Terrorist violence has been used for political purposes in all epochs. The Roman historian Flavius Josephus chronicled the terrorist campaign of Jewish zealots against Roman control of Palestine at the time of Christ's birth. Various forms of terror were used in this campaign, "including assassinations and guerrilla attacks on Roman personnel and installations."[38] Indeed, the terror campaign continued more than a century, culminating in mass suicide by zealots at Masada to demonstrate their resolve. In this century, the most celebrated act of international terrorism was the assassination of the Archduke Francis Ferdinand, heir to the Austro-Hungarian throne, by Gavrilo Princip, a member of the Serbian terrorist Black Hand organization, which was the event that triggered World War I.

Terrorist groups may form wherever and whenever someone is intensely dissatisfied with the political, economic, or social status quo, but incidents of *international terrorism* appear to have increased consistently in recent decades. Among the reasons for this increase are the growing accessibility of weapons and explosives desired by terrorists and the revolutions in global travel and communication that facilitate their movement across national frontiers. State support for terrorist groups, and the propensity of individuals and groups to copy each other's behavior — the demonstration effect — have also contributed to the trend. Today, terrorism touches every corner of the world. During the 1980s, incidents of international terrorism rose sharply, exceeding 600 between 1985 and 1988.[39] As shown in Figure 5.3, Latin America, Western Europe, and the Middle East were the most frequent sites for international terrorism in 1992, and North America, though not untouched, was relatively safe.[40] Lax U.S. immigration procedures, growing numbers of political refugees, and easier access to the country may bring the United States into the front lines of global terrorism in coming years.

Motives and Tactics of Terrorists

International terrorists act from a variety of motives.[41] One powerful motivation is to achieve independence for an ethnic or national group. Palestinian terrorist groups — the

---

[38]Schlagheck, *International Terrorism*, p. 15.

[39]Walter Enders, Gerald F. Parise, and Todd Sandler, "A Time-Series Analysis of Transnational Terrorism: Trends and Cycles," *Defence Economics* 3 (1992), p. 306.

[40]U.S. Department of State, *Patterns of Global Terrorism: 1992* (Washington, D.C.: U.S. Department of State, April 1993), p. 56.

[41]See Schlagheck, *International Terrorism*, pp. 5–8.

FIGURE 5.2

International Terrorist Incidents over Time

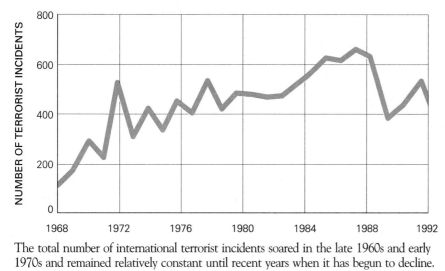

The total number of international terrorist incidents soared in the late 1960s and early 1970s and remained relatively constant until recent years when it has begun to decline.

Palestine Liberation Front (PLF) and the Popular Front for the Liberation of Palestine — General Command (PFLP-GC) to name a few — justify their behavior thus. In Europe, terrorist groups seek Basque, Breton, and Corsican independence. Perhaps the most prominent of such *national-liberation* groups is the Provisional Irish Republican Army (PIRA). Known as the Provos, this group, heir to earlier efforts to unite Ireland, has carried out terrorist acts in England, Northern Ireland, Belgium, and elsewhere for more than two decades to force Britain out of Northern Ireland.

Other groups are motivated by ideologies, sometimes obscure. In the 1970s, two notorious examples were the Red Brigades in Italy and the Baader-Meinhof Gang (later called the Red Army Faction) in West Germany. Acting in the name of anticapitalism, they staged attacks against corporations, businessmen, and prominent politicians to demonstrate their dislike for Western materialism. In one dramatic incident, the Red Brigades kidnapped a U.S. general, James Dozier, and held him five days until he was rescued by Italian counterterrorist forces. In another, the Red Brigades kidnapped the former Italian prime minister, Aldo Moro, murdered him, and left his body in a truck on a street in Rome.

Two other widely feared terrorist groups motivated by ideology are Hizballah (Party of God) and Sendero Luminoso (Shining Path). Hizballah, an Iranian-supported Shi'ite Muslim group, seeks to promote Islamic fundamentalism in the Middle East and rid the region of Western influence.[42] The group has been closely identified with the seizure of

[42]Other names used by Hizballah include Islamic Jihad, Party of God, Revolutionary Justice Organization, and Organization of the Oppressed.

FIGURE 5.3

International Terrorist Incidents by Region, over Time

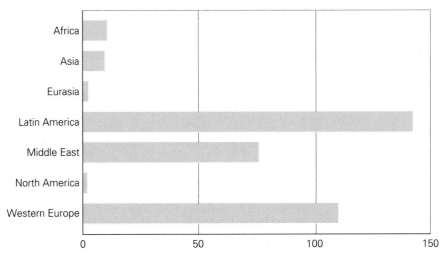

NUMBER OF TERRORIST INCIDENTS

Incidents of international terrorism are most frequent in Latin America, Western Europe, and the Middle East. In Latin America, such incidents as kidnapping foreign businessmen are common. The high rate in Western Europe reflects the propensity of outside groups, especially from the Middle East, to carry on the feuds there and to attack Western interests. Middle Eastern terrorism is dominated by attacks against Israeli targets.

U.S. and other Western hostages in Lebanon between 1985 and 1991. Shining Path's objective is usually described as vaguely Maoist (after the ideas of the Chinese communist leader, Mao Tse-tung) with the aim of transforming Peru into a communist society led by ethnic Indians. Shining Path works closely with and provides protection for cocaine growers and exporters, for which the group receives funds and provisions. Escalating violence in Peru had made large areas of the country ungovernable when President Alberto Fujimori declared a virtual dictatorship in 1992.[43]

International terrorists use many forms of violence and intimidation. *Skyjackings*, accompanied by demands for release of passengers, were popular in the 1970s, but they declined as airline security improved. Hizballah, for example, was involved in seizing TWA Flight 847 en route to Athens in June 1985 and held thirty-nine U.S. citizens hostage on the ground in Beirut for seventeen days. The Palestine Liberation Front (PLF) pioneered in hijacking ships. In October 1985, in an unprecedented act of contemporary piracy, Muhammad Abu al Abbas with other terrorists took control of the Italian cruise ship *Achille Lauro*. During the operation, a handicapped U.S. tourist was murdered in his wheelchair, and

---

[43] A third motive for terrorism is criminal greed. For a discussion of the Colombian drug lords, see Chapter 16, pp. 546–547.

his body was thrown overboard. In the notorious operation we have mentioned, Pan American Flight 103 was blown out of the sky over Lockerbie, Scotland in December 1988 by a terrorist bomb, killing 259 passengers and 11 local residents.

Some groups specialize in kidnapping those whom they view as symbols of their enemy, and others undertake suicide missions or random shootings and bombings to dramatize their views. The Red Brigades and Hizballah have used kidnapping extensively, as has Sendero Luminoso. Hizballah was also responsible for the *suicide bombing* of the U.S. marine barracks in Beirut in October 1983, driving a truck laden with explosives into the compound. Other groups try to stir fear by indiscriminate machine-gun or grenade attacks against innocent civilians. The Provos have repeatedly launched bombing campaigns in central London and elsewhere in Britain and used bombs to murder Louis, Earl Mountbatten, a war hero, last Viceroy of India, and a member of the British royal family (August 1979) and to try and assassinate British Prime Minister Margaret Thatcher and her aides in Brighton, England (October 1984).

Global Influence of Terrorism

The proliferation of terrorist groups and their expanded activity in recent decades has reduced the sense of security enjoyed by authorities and citizens around the world. State authorities everywhere find themselves under siege as they or their citizens are threatened by terrorist violence. Despite vigorous efforts to control skyjackings or increase security in public buildings, governments and the global community cannot entirely prevent such incidents. And whether we find ourselves in long lines at airports or prevented from traveling as freely as we did in the past, we are all affected in some way by global terrorism.

Another consequence of international terrorism has been to bring issues to the attention of the global community. Palestinian terrorism increased global awareness of the Palestinian cause. Whether terrorism advanced their goal—an independent Palestinian state—is difficult to determine. Similarly, although terrorism has increased the cost to Britain of retaining Northern Ireland, it is not clear whether terrorist acts have brought the issue any closer to resolution.

Ethnic and Tribal Actors

Ethnic and *tribal actors* are a third prominent type of NGO in contemporary global politics.[44] A shared ethnic or tribal heritage can be a source of unity for a state , but its absence can be a major challenge to a state's integrity. Through much of the world, ethnic or tribal loyalties collide with rather than reinforce nationalism. Recent examples appeared in the former Soviet Union, Yugoslavia, and Czechoslovakia. Not only did the

[44]A *tribe* is an entity the members of which claim they share an ethnic origin and in which kinship is a strong tie in political organization.

U.S.S.R. split into quarreling national groups, but a number of those are at each other's throats — Armenians and Azeris, Russians and Ukrainians, and Russians and Moldovians — and others are experiencing civil war, such as Georgians and Tajiks.

Perhaps even more than other nonstate groups, ethnic and tribal actors have deep historical roots. As the European state system evolved, state identities were often imposed on top of ethnic and tribal identities that were repressed or ignored by colonial authorities. When the European conquerors came to the New World they imposed their version of the territorial state on indigenous tribal groups. The Spanish conquest of the Aztecs in Mexico and Incas in Peru and the European conquest of native Indians all across North America reflect this process. Again, when the Europeans extended their empires into Africa, they came into conflict with indigenous tribal groups. Seldom were the earlier identities forgotten.

European colonial boundaries and the independent African states that shared them had little in common with tribal realities. Some African states consisted of numerous tribal entities that continue to battle for power. Elsewhere, tribes were divided by state boundaries. Regardless of the situation, many Africans continue to have greater loyalty to their tribe than to their state, and African governments are often the agents for tribal groups. Therein lies the weakness in many contemporary African states and the endemic violence that has convulsed much of the continent.

In 1990, Liberia deteriorated almost into anarchy owing to a civil war that pitted the tribal supporters of President Samuel Doe against rebel military units principally drawn from other tribal groupings. Another violent example is the small central African country of Rwanda and its neighbors. Formerly a Belgian colony, the Republic of Rwanda became independent in 1962. Since then it has experienced continual tribal conflict. Rwanda's population is 90 percent Hutu, 9 percent Tutsi, and 1 percent Twa (or pygmies). Before the European arrival, Rwanda had been a feudal monarchy ruled by the minority Tutsi, and Tutsi dominance of society continued during the colonial period and after. Hutu resistance grew in the 1950s, and a bloody rebellion in 1959 overthrew the monarchy. In the early 1960s, civil war slaughtered more than 10,000 Tutsis and forced several hundred thousand more to flee. Since then Hutu-Tutsi violence has recurred episodically, with Hutu émigrés living in neighboring Uganda seeking to restore Tutsi dominance.[45] In October 1990, 1,000 Tutsi warriors invaded Rwanda from Uganda, Tanzania, and Zaire, battling the Rwandan army and seeking to instigate an uprising among their fellow tribesmen.

[45]Hutu–Tutsi conflicts have produced tensions between the Rwandan government and those of Burundi and Uganda which have aided those who fled. Burundi also has a Tutsi minority and Hutu majority, but, unlike Rwanda, in Burundi the minority continues to dominate the majority.

Global Intergovernmental Organizations

Just as nongovernmental organizations take varied forms and deal with various issues, so, too, do intergovernmental organizations. Some IGOs enjoy large responsibilities on major issues and are autonomous actors. Other IGOs merely carry out states' commands. And still others seek to influence states to change policy. Thus, the actions of U.N. personnel in Bosnia such as General Philippe Morillon galvanized world public opinion against Serbian atrocities in that country. From a brief description of each type of IGO you will get a sense of the variety and role of such organizations in world politics today.

Multipurpose Global IGOs

Although modern intergovernmental organizations date from the Central Commission for the Navigation of the Rhine, established in 1815, the first great experiment in *multipurpose intergovernmental organization* was the League of Nations, established after World War I.[46] That organization, its operating principle of collective security, and its record are described in more detail in Chapter 9. The League ultimately failed to achieve its most important goal, preventing war, and after 1945 its successor, the United Nations, tried to create a universal organization to replace it. The structure of the U.N., its role in global politics, and its successes and failures are also discussed in Chapter 9.

Specialized Global IGOs

The League and U.N. ideas accelerated creation of *specialized IGOs* with nearly universal membership. (These came to be called the *specialized agencies* of the U.N. because of their close relationship to the U.N. system.) These IGOs share responsibility with states for particular issues in global politics and try to coordinate state policies toward these issues. As a result, several of the agencies are at the heart of international regimes that regulate issue areas described in Chapter 6. The tasks of the specialized IGOs range from mundane activities such as delivering the mail (Universal Postal Union), regulating airplane traffic (International Civil Aviation Organization), monitoring global weather (World Meteorological Organization), to confronting severe problems like increasing food for the world's hungry (World Food Program), improving global health (World Health Organization), and improving the global environment (U.N. Environment Program). Other agencies that are U.N. affiliates or offshoots respond to emergencies

[46]See Inis L. Claude, Jr., *Power and International Relations* (New York: Random House, 1962), pp. 94–149.

around the world, among them the U.N. High Commission for Refugees, which aids those displaced by political upheavals or natural disasters. These and other specialized agencies and their role in world affairs are treated more fully in Chapter 9.[47]

Regional Intergovernmental Organizations

On every continent, regional intergovernmental organizations are at work. Like global IGOs, some regional IGOs are multipurpose, and others are specialized. A complete list of such organizations is very long, but we can illustrate here their wide domain and diverse functions.[48]

Multipurpose Regional IGOs

Figure 5.4, which maps the extent of several *multipurpose regional IGOs*, suggests how varied are these organizations in world politics today. Almost every country is a member of at least one such organization, and many countries are members of several. The Organization of African Unity (OAU), the Organization of American States (OAS), the Association of Southeast Asian Nations (ASEAN), and the Arab League are among the most prominent regional intergovernmental organizations. The OAU has repeatedly and with considerable success sought to prevent alterations in the postcolonial frontiers of African states because of fear that the legitimacy of all African frontiers would then be open to question. For its part, the OAS has on occasion served to balance the influence of the "Colossus of the North," and at other times it has helped the United States to organize its friends in the Western Hemisphere against threats like the Soviet installation of nuclear missiles in Cuba in 1962. The ASEAN group, started initially to stimulate trade among the developing states of Southeast Asia, has expanded into a multipurpose actor that coordinates its members' activities for economic, social, and political issues.

Specialized Regional IGOs

There are also *many specialized regional intergovernmental organizations* in global politics. Again, some of these are familiar but others are not. The North Atlantic Treaty Organization (NATO) was the West's bulwark against the U.S.S.R. during the Cold War. With that conflict ended, this organization has come under careful scrutiny as to

[47]We discuss the major global economic IGOs—the World Bank, the International Monetary Fund, and the General Agreement on Tariffs and Trade—in Chapter 10.
[48]For a complete listing, see *Yearbook of International Organizations 1992/93*.

its purpose. Can it remain useful in coming years? Should it assume a new role in Central Europe to dampen the ethnic rivalries arising from communism's collapse? Should former adversaries be admitted to NATO? That organization illustrates how IGOs, especially those with a specialty, may outlive their purpose and must then change if they are to survive.

Indeed, new IGOs have sprung up in post-Cold War Europe and old ones have been revived. The Conference on Security and Cooperation in Europe (CSCE), originally established in 1975 among states of Central Europe and North America to provide a forum for adversaries, has tried since 1990 to enlarge its role so as to address security problems formally handled by NATO. The Western European Union (WEU), a treaty organization among the states of Western Europe that antedated NATO and fell dormant after NATO's establishment, has been revived as a potential regional alternative to NATO.

Perhaps the most important aspect in the growth of specialized IGOs has been the regional economic organization arising on almost every continent. Their model is the European Economic Community (EEC). Africa has an Economic Community of West African States (ECOWAS). Asia is the site of ASEAN and the more recent Asian Pacific Economic Cooperation (APEC). Central and South America are home to the Central American Common Market (CACM), the Latin American Free Trade Area, and the incipient Southern Common Market among Brazil, Argentina, Paraguay, and Uruguay. To the north, a treaty was signed establishing the North American Free Trade Agreement (NAFTA) among the United States, Canada, and Mexico; and finally in Oceania a free trade zone exists between Australia and New Zealand. The influence of these IGOs differs from region to region; as a group, their pervasiveness is impressive.

Influence of IGOs in World Politics Today

Global and regional IGOs are afforded fuller treatment later, but now we need some tentative observations about their effect on member states and on world politics. First, the evolving web of IGOs, and the interlocking memberships of states in them, have left some states less free to act on some issues but have provided states with additional capabilities to cope with other issues. Some argue that IGOs have already transformed global life, but others remain skeptical, believing that this network "has not yet radically transformed this [global political] system" but admitting that "the radical transformation may yet come."[49]

---

[49]Harold K. Jacobson, William M. Reisinger, and Todd Mathers, "National Entanglements in International Governmental Organizations," in Paul F. Diehl, ed., *The Politics of International Organizations: Patterns and Insights* (Chicago: Dorsey Press, 1989), p. 79.

FIGURE 5.4

International Organizations: A Sample

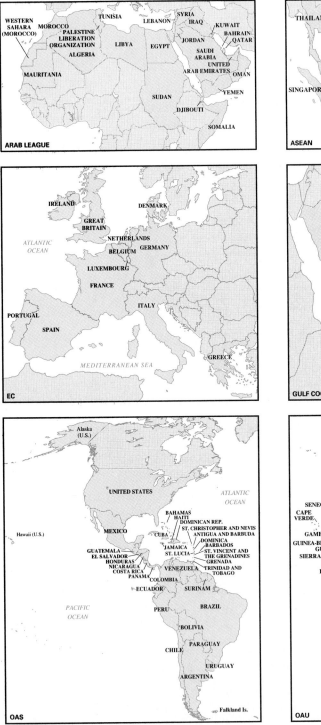

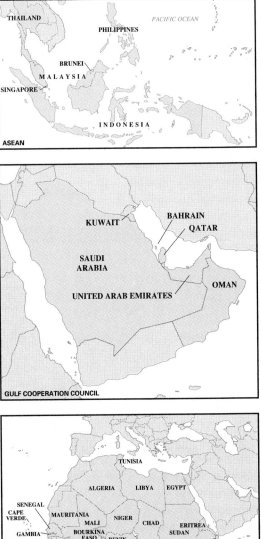

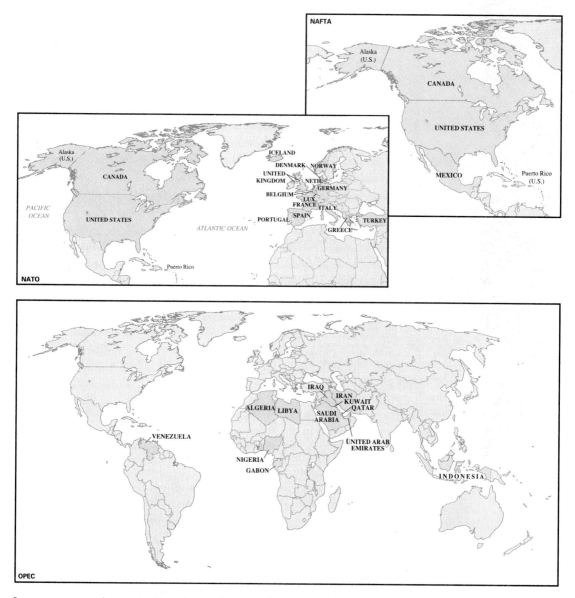

Intergovernmental organizations that perform a wide variety of functions exist in every region of the world. They include economic groupings (ASEAN, EC, NAFTA, and OPEC), security arrangements (Gulf Cooperation Council and NATO), and political forums (Arab League, OAU, and OAS). Some countries are members of several organizations.

The complexity of modern life creates many pressures for states to establish additional IGOs. What has happened so far demonstrates the overwhelming sense of governments throughout the world that states no longer provide enough frameworks for tackling pressing problems.[50]

In sum, international organizations are likely to enjoy even greater influence than at present owing to proliferating problems that require global attention, interdependence among peoples in many countries, and the enfeeblement of a number of states.

At the same time, a greater role for regional IGOs in general does not mean that all will remain operative or that they will continue to contribute to global cooperation and order. They may become obsolete and perhaps even disappear (as the Warsaw Treaty Organization did). They may be enfeebled by conflict among members (as OPEC has been), or they may be unable to achieve the objectives for which they were founded (like the Southeast Asia Treaty Organization).

In short, although IGOs have in some ways challenged the autonomy of the state while in other ways enhancing state capacity and so have altered world politics, their overall role continues to evolve. It remains to be seen which IGOs are likely to be most relevant to the issues in the coming decades.

A World of Many Actors: South Africa and Apartheid

We briefly review events in southern Africa, specifically South Africa and the *apartheid* issue (separation of the races) to illustrate how states and nonstate actors, including regional and global IGOs and NGOs, routinely interact and jointly determine outcomes of key events in contemporary global politics. From this review we can see how far reality diverges from a model of world politics focused exclusively on unitary states. This case also reveals how, as we saw earlier, issues are linked to and affect each other. Finally, we can see how far the barriers between the domestic and international arenas have tumbled.

Evolution of the South African Issue

To many, South Africa is a cruel symbol of racial oppression and injustice — a society in which for decades a white minority exercised power over a large black majority. Although this image remains partly correct, the South African situation has begun to change. The issue has involved a diverse cast of actors both within and outside of South Africa itself and is much more complex than the stark image of black versus white suggests.

[50]Ibid., p. 80.

South Africa grew from three colliding cultures—Protestant Dutch colonists, English imperialists, and tribal Africans. Settled originally by pious Dutch farmers in the seventeenth century, the Cape Colony became British in the political settlement that followed Napoleon's defeat. In 1836, the Dutch sought to escape British rule by fleeing northward. During their journey they clashed with and subjugated the native *Zulus* and thereafter declared the independent republics of Orange Free State and Transvaal.

The Dutch, known as *Boers*, were not destined to remain independent for long. The discovery of diamonds and gold attracted English adventurers, notably Cecil Rhodes, and friction between the British and Boers and the imperial ambitions of those like Rhodes culminated in conquest of the Boer republics during the bloody *Boer War* (1899–1902). That war, like the later Vietnam War, was mostly a guerrilla conflict, with the Boers holding at bay large numbers of British regulars.[51] The Boers were finally defeated, and in 1910, the Orange Free State and Transvaal were merged with British Cape Colony and Natal to form the Union of South Africa. Conquest of the Boers was the zenith of the British Empire and generated hostility between the ancestors of the Dutch and British that continues to divide the white community in South Africa today.

In 1934, South Africa became an independent member of the British Common-wealth, and South African soldiers fought alongside the British in both World Wars I and II. The link with Britain, however, progressively weakened as a result of South Africa's racial policies. A main source of these policies was the *National Party* (NP) which was elected to office in South Africa in 1948, promising to impose strict racial separation (*apartheid*). First, under Daniel F. Malan and then Hendrik F. Verwoerd, the Boer minority promoted separation of blacks and whites and white dominance over all aspects of life. Racial separation meant denying the black majority such basic rights as the vote. Facilities for blacks in housing, recreation, and education were routinely inferior to those for whites. Under apartheid, blacks held only low-skilled jobs; and, even if they worked in white areas of the country, they could not reside there. In other ways too, both important and petty, blacks were treated as inferior.

Boer efforts to enforce racial segregation and assure permanent white rule in South Africa produced agitation in the 1960s in black townships (including the Sharpeville incident, which left many black casualties) and the assassination of Prime Minister Verwoerd in 1966 (by a white assassin). Confronted with growing criticism overseas and intensified resistance at home, the South African government retaliated against its enemies with a coordinated domestic and foreign strategy.

---

[51]The comparison between the two wars is apt for other reasons as well. The Boer War was very unpopular in Britain, as the Vietnam War was in the United States. Like the United States, Britain was isolated internationally, and other countries aided the Boers. The United States, which at the time was in the midst of its own imperial expansion (including the Philippines, Hawaii, and Puerto Rico), was one of the few states to sympathize with the British.

FIGURE 5.5

South Africa, Its Black Homelands, and Its Neighbors

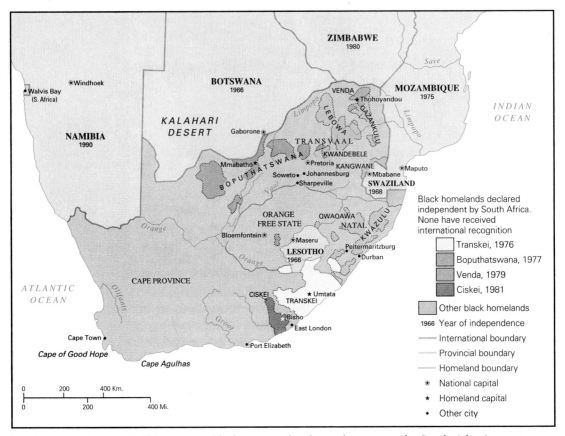

Despite repressive apartheid laws, many blacks managed to leave the reserves for South Africa's growing cities, where most Indians and coloreds already lived.

Apartheid: Variety of Actors

Because apartheid generated opposition both domestically and internationally, the efforts to maintain and change this policy have involved a host of political actors, including many that are nongovernmental.[52] Nevertheless, a useful beginning for our discussion is to consider the strategy and behavior of various states on the issue, starting with the South African government itself.

[52]For an assessment of the apartheid policy in South Africa upon which we draw, see "After Apartheid: A Survey of South Africa," *The Economist*, November 3, 1990, pp. 1–26.

TABLE 5.2

Per Capita GNP in Southern Africa 1991.

South Africa	2,560	Namibia	1,460
Botswana	2,530	Malawi	230
Zimbabwe	650	Tanzania	100
Lesotho	580	Mozambique	80

SOURCE: *World Development Report 1992* (New York: Oxford University Press, 1990), pp. 218–219.

States: Role of South Africa. One prong of the South African government's strategy was to assist white settlers or black allies in neighboring countries to maintain friendly *buffer zones* along its frontier and crush black liberation movements that could assist the opposition inside South Africa. Such assistance included advice, arms, intelligence, funding, and even intervention by South African troops helping supporters of white South Africa. The South African government repeatedly intervened in Zimbabwe (formerly Rhodesia), Namibia (the former South-West Africa), Mozambique, and Angola in an effort to maintain buffer zones on its border.

The government's justification for meddling in the affairs of neighboring states was to prevent the spread of "communism" in southern Africa. A number of black liberation movements, including the *African National Congress (ANC)*, the principal anti-apartheid group,[53] did receive military and economic assistance from the Soviet Union and its allies, notably Cuba. Although some ANC members were communists and the South African Communist Party also fought apartheid, the ANC accepted Soviet aid mainly because it was the only assistance available. South Africa's anticommunist rhetoric generated support in the West, however, and, like its other policies, was part of a concerted strategy to secure its minority position by maintaining military, political, and economic primacy throughout the region.

Another part of South Africa's strategy was to forge close economic ties with regional African states including Zambia, Botswana, Mozambique, and Malawi. By doing so, South Africa—the economic and military powerhouse in the region—fostered their dependence and discouraged them from cooperating with its enemies. For many years this effort proved effective, for these governments paid little more than lip service to the antiapartheid cause. Table 5.2 reflects South Africa's regional economic dominance. South Africans enjoy a per capita GNP of $2,560 and, at the other extreme, Mozambicans have the lowest per capita GNP in the world.[54]

[53]The founders of the ANC were Nelson Mandela, Oliver Tambo, and Walter Sisulu.

[54]These data undestimate South African dominance because they include the much lower incomes of the black majority in South Africa who are outside the country's economic mainstream.

Where economic leverage seemed insufficient, white South Africa sponsored its own black guerrilla movements to keep neighbors weak and divided. The most prominent examples were the Mozambique National Resistance, known as *Renamo*,[55] and the National Union for the Total Independence of Angola, known as *UNITA* and led by Jonas Savimbi.[56] The regimes in Angola and Mozambique both earned South Africa's wrath by proclaiming themselves Marxist and assisting the ANC. South Africa supported UNITA also partly in retaliation for the asylum Angola provided for *SWAPO*, the South-West African People's Organization fighting to achieve independence from South African rule for the area known as South-West Africa.

A final aspect of South Africa's strategy to maintain apartheid was creating "*Bantustans*" or tribal homelands that were intended to isolate much of the country's black population in small territorial "islands." Ten supposedly self-governing homelands were created of which four—Transkei, Bophuthatswana, Venda, and Ciskei—were granted independent status. In fact, no one except South Africa recognized the legal independence of these entities because they were viewed as part of a transparent effort to locate large numbers of blacks in relatively small and unproductive areas to keep them from living near white population centers.[57]

The Front-line States. The institutionalization of apartheid in South Africa accompanied independence for other black African states, and those states made the struggle against white South Africa a focus of their foreign policy. Most important were the *front-line states*, those bordering South Africa itself: Angola, Botswana, Malawi, Mozambique, Swaziland, Zimbabwe, and Zambia. Their governments opposed white rule in South Africa but were unable to do much. Not only were they dependent on South Africa economically, but some of their products had to transit South African territory to get to the sea for export. Aside from denouncing apartheid in the United Nations and the Organization of African Unity and quietly assisting South African blacks who sought to change the system, South Africa deterred them from hostile activity. Angola, Botswana, Mozambique, Zambia, and Tanzania did establish the Southern African Development Coordination Conference (SADCC) to reduce their dependence on South Africa, but its effect was marginal.[58]

[55]Renamo appears to have been created by the white government in Southern Rhodesia. South Africa became its main benefactor after Zimbabwe's independence in 1980.

[56]Guerrilla war was waged against the Portuguese authorities in Angola between 1961 and 1975, when Lisbon granted independence to its colony. UNITA had been one of three principal guerrilla groups. Following independence, the new Angolan government was dominated by the Popular Liberation Movement of Angola–Party of Labor (MPLA–PT), and UNITA, initially with Chinese as well as South African assistance, continued its rebellion.

[57]One of apartheid's cruelest aspects was forcing blacks who worked in white areas to live elsewhere and either to commute huge distances or live seasonally in primitive shanties.

[58]See Gavin G. Maasdorp, "Squaring up to Economic Dominance: Regional Patterns," in Robert I. Rotberg, Henry S. Bienen, Robert Legvold, and Gavin G. Massdorp, *South Africa and Its Neighbors* (Lexington, Mass.: Lexington Books, 1985), pp. 91–135.

Apartheid was imposed in South Africa at a time of racial conflict between black independence fighters and minority white communities in neighboring countries like Angola and Southern Rhodesia.[59] Angola was particularly important in the challenge to South Africa and was the scene of civil war, with South Africa and the United States supporting the insurgents and the Soviet Union and Cuba—including more than 18,000 Cuban troops—assisting the government. The Angolan government aided insurgents in South-West Africa, and Angolan territory was repeatedly raided by the South African army. An agreement reached in December 1988 provided for gradually evacuating Cuban troops and the U.N.-supervised transition of the area to independence early in 1990 as the country Namibia.[60]

IGOs and South Africa. International and domestic opposition to South African policies of racial domination intensified in the late 1970s as the South African government resorted to repressive police tactics to cope with mounting black discontent. Despite modest reforms and revoking some apartheid legislation, the early 1980s saw continued escalation of violence, climaxing in declaration of a state of emergency in July 1985 in many black areas.

The application of *sanctions* by intergovernmental organizations was one primary weapon in the global struggle waged against South African racial policies. In 1977, the United Nations embargoed the sale of military supplies to South Africa. In the 1980s, the European Community imposed stringent sanctions against South African exports and prevented participation by white South Africans in international events, including sports. The Organization of African Unity had long had a subcommittee that sought to coordinate action against minority rule in South Africa.

Urged by the United Nations and the international community as a whole, individual states imposed sanctions on South Africa. Perhaps most influential were actions by the United States and Great Britain, two major trading partners of South Africa. In 1985 antiapartheid agitation, long a feature of campus life in the United States and Western Europe, grew dramatically. Faced by student protests, many U.S. colleges and universities divested themselves, often at financial loss, of stock in corporations that did business in South Africa. Under pressure from Congress, President Ronald Reagan issued an executive order to impose limited sanctions against South Africa. In the following year, despite President Reagan's veto, the U.S. Congress passed the Anti-Apartheid Act forbidding U.S.-based companies or their subsidiaries to make new investments in South Africa. These sanctions ended only when agreement was reached to bring a multiracial government to power in 1993.

---

[59]In 1965, Rhodesian whites led by Ian D. Smith declared unilateral independence of Britain to maintain political power. For almost fifteen years the rebellious whites held out against U.N. condemnation, economic embargo, and a guerrilla war waged by the black independence movement.

[60]Under the agreement South Africa retained residual political and economic rights in Namibia.

NGOs Inside and Outside of South Africa.   For years, major transnational corpo-rations were also subjected to pressure to eliminate discriminatory practices that their South African subsidiaries might be following. Many U.S. firms voluntarily agreed to abide by the "*Sullivan principles*," authored by the American black activist Leon Sullivan. These committed corporations to ensure that their black employees in South Africa received the same treatment as white employees regardless of local apartheid laws.

Thereafter, as antiapartheid agitation grew in the 1980s, corporations were pres-sured by activists, church groups, and even stockholders to divest themselves of subsidiaries in South Africa and to cease doing business in that country. Major U.S.-based transnational corporations like Xerox, Ford, General Motors, and IBM were subjected to intense lobbying and were threatened with boycotts by consumer groups, and 141 U.S. firms, including IBM, divested themselves of investments in South Africa between 1984 and 1988. Most of those remaining changed their employment practices and did not further enlarge their investment in the country.[61]

Actions such as these and South Africa's heightened international political and economic isolation during the 1980s exerted growing pressure against white rule and began to take their toll on white South Africans. The omens of change became evident when South African Prime Minister R. F. Botha declared early in 1986 that "it would possibly become unavoidable that in future you might have black presidents in this country."[62] Although Prime Minister Botha was reprimanded by President P. W. Botha, white South Africans began to grapple with the prospect that conditions in their country had to change. White voters who refused to acknowledge the inevitability of change abandoned the ruling National Party in favor of the Conservative Party, which had been established by former members of the National Party opposed to further steps to dilute apartheid. Government concessions also contributed to growth in militant support for fascist groups such as White Com-mando and the Afrikaner Resistance Movement that threatened to use terrorism to prevent erosion of white dominance in South Africa.

Ironically, the prospect of change escalated the confrontation between militant blacks and the government until illness forced P. W. Botha to resign in 1989; he was replaced by Frederik W. de Klerk. After becoming President, de Klerk almost single-handedly moved his country in a new direction and showed how individual leaders could produce an impact on global politics that exceeds their formal role.[63] De Klerk

---

[61]Spero, *Politics of International Economic Relations*, p. 123.

[62]"Botha Rebukes a Key Minister," *The New York Times*, February 9, 1986, Section 4, p. 2E.

[63]Most often, individuals should be viewed as surrogates for collective political entities. On occasion, however, they exceed their role in some dramatic act that entitles them to special consideration. President Anwar al-Sadat of Egypt, who broke the deadlock between his country and Israel in a dramatic journey to Jerusalem on November 19, 1977, and President Mikhail Gorbachev of the Soviet Union, whose policies at home and abroad contributed to the end of the Cold War, are recent examples of such "heroic" individuals. Both received Nobel Peace Prize for their actions.

understood that, as one observer puts it, "South Africa confronts an inexorable logic. A coercively fragmented and stratified state of five million white citizens dominating some 28 million 'others' cannot hope to achieve and sustain healthy economic development."[64] For this reason, the South African business community became a force for change in that country. A clear relationship connects political events in South Africa and the confidence business has in the country's future.

To find a new road for his country, de Klerk began quiet negotiations with Nelson Mandela, for many years the imprisoned leader of the ANC. In February 1990, Mandela was released from prison and his organization was legalized. So began a gradual breaking down of apartheid's structure by concessions on both sides. Although the procedure went through fits and starts. Mandela came to be regarded as the informal co-leader, with de Klerk, of South Africa and as a probable future president of the country. Whether white rule in South Africa would end peacefully remained to be seen. It became clear, however, that the path would be a rocky one. Tribal and personal conflicts and violence among blacks with an eye toward future political power escalated after Mandela's release. The ANC and its Xhosa supporters were bitterly opposed by a Zulu[65] political movement called the *Inkatha Freedom Party* and headed by Chief Mangosuthu Buthelezi, which had enjoyed considerable autonomy under white rule and advocated traditional tribal rule for South Africa as a whole, and by the Pan African Congress and the Azanian People's Organization which opposed sharing power with whites and hoped to install a Marxist regime. In ten days in August 1990, more than 500 blacks died in fierce internecine violence. "For the near future," concluded one observer, "the outlook for South Africa is change but no solution."[66] Killings of supporters of these competing groups continued throughout 1992 and 1993, with government security forces on occasion providing clandestine assistance to Inkatha. Nevertheless, change was clearly in the air. In October 1993 a multiracial transitional council was created to guide the country until the first genuinely multiracial election of April 1994. A month later, agreement was reached on a new constitution that would balance majority rule with safeguards to reassure white South Africans.

Conclusion

South Africa reflects the rich galaxy of actors involved in contemporary global politics. As we observed at the outset of this chapter, the governments of states are neither alone nor unchallenged as the focus of human loyalty. The many weak states

[64]John A. Marcum, "Africa: A Continent Adrift," *Foreign Affairs* 68:1 (1988/89), p. 174.

[65]The Zulus are the largest tribal group in South Africa, and Xhosas the second largest. Despite an element of tribal conflict in the ANC–Inkatha collision, many Zulus supported Mandela and his leadership.

[66]Bill Keller, "South African Blacks Gain Share of Power in Months Before a Multiracial Vote," *The New York Times*, September 8, 1993, pp. A1, A4.

are especially vulnerable to penetration by other actors or need their assistance. Many of these states are being wrenched apart by centrifugal forces — hatred between ethnic groups and tribes like Serbs and Bosnians in the former Yugoslavia or Zulu and Xhosa in South Africa, secessionist nationalities like the Basques, and even hostile religious and language groups like Muslims and Hindus in India. If the division of Czechoslovakia on January 1, 1993 into the Czech Republic and Slovakia or Canadians' refusal in October 1992 to endorse a constitutional compromise between French-speaking Quebec and the country's other provinces are indications, the future will be one of ever-smaller territorial entities, struggling with each other for scarcer resources.

On the other hand, the behavior of many important nonstate actors like IGOs and transnational corporations not only help compensate for the weak states' reduced capacity but knit together peoples around the world. The evolution of the international economic system may provide clues for the future. The growing role of transnational corporations and common markets has accompanied decline in national economic autonomy and growth in global economic interdependence.

Probably both tendencies will continue simultaneously. Some areas, especially those which are more prosperous, will have more powerful interstate organizations. At the same time, fragmentation of states is likely to continue in the Third World and possibly in the former Soviet Union as well. Such actors as corporations and international organizations may reduce the chaotic consequences of such fragmentation. One observer writes that we are simultaneously witnessing a "retribalization of large swaths of humankind" and "an onrush of economic and ecological forces that demand integration and uniformity. . . . The planet is falling precipitately apart and coming reluctantly together at the very same moment."[67]

These first five chapters have set the stage for a more detailed look at global politics employing the variety of actors and issues identified thus far. Our task in Part II is to examine how changing issues and actors affect global politics, and in Chapter 6, we turn to the balance between anarchy and society in the global system, evaluating the factors that push the world in different directions.

[67]Benjamin R. Barber, "Jihad vs. McWorld," *The Atlantic*, no. 269 (March 1992), p. 53.

Key Terms

strong states
weak states
autonomy
capacity
administrative capacity
intergovernmental organizations
nongovernmental organizations
supranational organizations
compulsory jurisdiction
European Commission
transnational corporations
maquiladoras
ethnocentric
Third World
terrorism
subnational groups
ethnic actors
tribal actors
international terrorism
"national liberation"
skyjackings
multipurpose Global IGOs

specialized Global IGOs
"specialized agencies"
multipurpose Regional IGOs
specialized Regional IGOs
apartheid
buffer zones
Bantustans
front-line states
sanctions
Sullivan principles
ANC
Inkatha Freedom Party
Jackson-Vanik Amendment
suicide bombing
Zulus
Boers
Boer War
National Party
Renamo
UNTA
SWAPO

Cooperation and Conflict: A Changing Balance

Part Two consists of five chapters that will extend our conceptual lenses of global politics. The power-politics approach focuses on competition and conflict in understanding the field. It does not do justice to cooperation or to the social and communitarian fabric that binds actors even without central authority. Perhaps the reason for exaggerating the conflictual side of global politics is, that in the words of English novelist Thomas Hardy, people think "War makes rattling good history but peace is poor reading." In fact, much of global politics is peaceful and routine, and our survival depends as much on understanding cooperation as on conflict and war.

In Chapter 6, we challenge the dominant belief that the global system is governed by anarchy and conflict. Even without world government, norms and structures have evolved that regularize global life and create conditions for society. In Chapters 7 and 8, we depict the changing role of force in world politics and ask how useful it is in contemporary global politics. In these chapters we emphasize technological change and suggest that force must be used more selectively than in the past.

In Chapter 9, we turn from military instruments to examine the various paths available to actors to coordinate their activities peacefully. We argue that actors may choose to cooperate rather than compete for reasons of expediency as well as morality. In Chapter 10, we review the nexus of economics and politics, showing how the two fields are closely tied and how economic issues encourage cooperative solutions, and we describe economic relations among the rich, between North and South, and between East and West.

CHAPTER SIX

Anarchy and Society
in Global Politics

Is the global system filled with unbridled competition and *conflict*, or does it have enough *cooperation* and adequate common interests to make it resemble a society?[1] What is the balance between force and cooperation among the galaxy of actors and variety of issues discussed in Chapters 4 and 5? These are some of the questions to which we now turn.

Jean-Jacques Rousseau, the French Enlightenment philosopher, recognized that *both* anarchic and social attributes coexist uneasily in global politics. Describing eighteenth-century Europe, he painted the bonds that made Europeans members of one society:

> Princes are united by ties of blood, by commerce, by arts and colonies. Communication is made easy by countless rivers winding from one country to another. An inbred love of change impels her inhabitants to constant travel. . . . The invention of printing and the general love of letters has given them a basis of common knowledge and common intellectual pursuits. Finally, the number and smallness of her States, the cravings of luxury and the large diversity of climates . . . makes them all necessary to each other. All these causes combine to make of Europe . . . a purely imaginary assemblage of peoples with nothing in common save the name, *but a real community* with a religion and a moral code, with customs and even laws of its own. . . . [2]

[1]See Adam Watson, *The Evolution of International Society* (New York: Routledge, 1992), pp. 311–318.

[2]Jean-Jacques Rousseau, "Abstract of the Abbé de Saint-Pierre's Project for Perpetual Peace," in M. G. Forsyth, H. M. A. Keens-Soper, and P. Savigear, eds., *The Theory of International Relations* (New York: Atherton Press, 1970), p. 135. Emphasis added.

ontinuing: "Now look at the other side of the
the robberies, the usurpations, the revolts, the
ation to this venerable home of philosophy."[3]
lictions" are made possible because "[e]very
lers, every union formed and maintained by
ly fall into quarrels and dissensions at the first

al Politics

The concepts *anarchy* and *cooperation* summarize competing visions of global politics. Anarchy describes a world with no overarching authority to regulate individual actor's behavior—a world in which the possibility of war always exists. Those who believe anarchy is the dominant feature in world politics reason that, without central power, trust among actors is difficult to achieve and that, as a result, actors must rely on themselves for security (*self-help*). Under such conditions, conflict is normal and inevitable, and each actor must prepare to defend itself under ferociously competitive conditions. Because conflict is natural, human ingenuity can do little more than limit its scope and consequences.

Anarchy and Absence of Trust

Most theorists have focused on the anarchic side of world politics, ignoring the social bonds that moderate an otherwise harsh climate. They reason that, as independent actors with incompatible interests pursue their objectives, they will collide with others who seek the same objectives. Consequently, there can be no "natural" harmony of interests.[5] In the tradition of power politics, conflicts result from the equal status of acquisitive states and the absence of a central authority that can regulate their behavior, arbitrate their quarrels, or enforce agreements among them. States can make treaties or reach understandings with one another, but no one can ensure that they will abide by such agreements. In other words, anarchy results from *absence of trust*. A state can rely on no one but itself and its own capabilities.

The problem identified by power-politics theorists is structural—the absence of central authority—and it matters little whether people are good or evil by nature. Rousseau illustrates with a simple parable of five men in the "*state of nature*" who have

[3]Ibid.

[4]Ibid., p. 136. Emphasis added.

[5]According to the liberal tradition in economics associated with Adam Smith, the pursuit by individuals of selfish interests in a free market is transformed into general prosperity by an "invisible hand." The liberal tradition in economics and politics in which Smith was so influential stresses the individual and the primacy of private enterprise, and is optimistic about the prospect for progress.

acquired rudimentary ability to communicate. They recognize that they can satisfy their hunger by cooperating to capture a stag. But what, asks Rousseau, if "a hare happened to pass within reach of one of them"?[6] His answer is that "it must not be doubted that he pursued it without scruple, and that, having caught his prey, he troubled himself very little about having caused his companions to miss theirs."[7]

Unlike theorists who argue that the human propensity to engage in conflict arises from our evil nature,[8] Rousseau believed that human beings were benign by nature. He reasoned that each of the five hunters "certainly felt strongly that for this purpose he ought to remain faithfully at his post."[9] The problem grows out of the logic of the situation in which there was no way for the hunter to assure himself that his fellow hunters had not seen the hare and no way to be certain that they would not desert their post to take it and satisfy their hunger. Indeed, the hunter recognizes that if he cannot trust his fellow hunters, then they cannot trust him, and so on ad infinitum.

In seizing the hare, the hunter is pursuing his immediate interest at the expense of his long-term interest and is endangering the well-being of the group as a whole. His four comrades will no longer be able to catch the stag and are unlikely to cooperate with him again. And, if they catch him, they will certainly avenge themselves. A paradox is described by the realist Kenneth Waltz: "Reason would have told him [the hunter who catches the hare] that his long-run interest depends on establishing, through experience, the conviction that cooperative action will benefit all of the participants. But reason also tells him that if he foregoes the hare, the man next to him might leave his post to chase it, leaving the first man with nothing but food for thought on the folly of being loyal."[10]

The absence of trust and resulting pressure to pursue immediate at the expense of long-term collective interests lies at the heart of the *security dilemma*. This metaphor is intended to suggest that, without reliable enforcement, actors can trust each other only at their own peril. Moreover, efforts by each to augment its own security, perhaps by

[6]Jean-Jacques Rousseau, *Discourse on Inequality*, in Alan Ritter and Julia Conaway Bondanella, eds., *Rousseau's Political Writings*, trans. Julia Conaway Bondanella (New York: W. W. Norton, 1988), p. 36.

[7]Ibid.

[8]See, for example, Hans J. Morgenthau, *Politics Among Nations: The Struggle for Power and Peace*, 6th ed., rev. by Kenneth W. Thompson (New York: Knopf, 1985), p. 4. The English political philosopher Thomas Hobbes argued that human beings have a "perpetuall and restlesse desire of Power after power, that ceaseth only in Death." Hobbes, *Leviathan* (New York: E. P. Dutton, 1950), Part I, ch. XI, p. 79. Realist theologians, especially Reinhold Niebuhr, argue that original sin leads human beings to behave in evil ways. See Niebuhr, *Moral Man and Immoral Society* (New York: Scribner's, 1947). The founder of modern psychology, Sigmund Freud, hypothesized an instinct for aggression or "death wish" in human beings. See Freud, *Beyond the Pleasure Principle* (New York: Bantam, 1958). Some animal biologists have suggested that aggression is instinctive behavior that is in the interest of evolutionary survival. See Konrad Lorenz, *On Aggression*, trans. Marjorie Kerr Wilson (New York: Bantam, 1966) and Robert Ardrey, *The Territorial Imperative* (New York: Atheneum, 1966).

[9]Jean-Jacques Rousseau, *Discourse on Inequality*, p. 36.

[10]Kenneth N. Waltz, *Man, the State and War* (New York: Columbia University Press, 1959), p. 169.

FIGURE 6.1

Prisoner's Dilemma, Prisoner A and Prisoner B

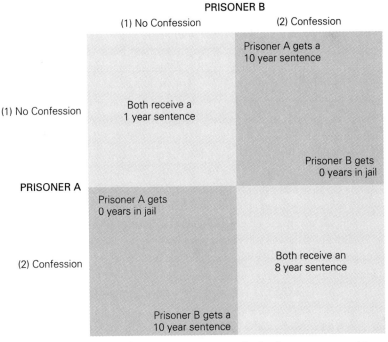

The prisoner's dilemma depicts a situation in which players cannot achieve the *mutually* best outcome ("no confession") because each fears that the other will confess to get off scot free. Both confess because they cannot trust each and receive 8-year sentences. The game illustrates the security dilemma in global politics under conditions of anarchy.

joining alliances or increasing defense spending, will be perceived as threatening by other actors and increase their insecurity. The dilemma can be illustrated by an analogy borrowed from *game theory*.[11] Two individuals are arrested for robbery. They are placed in separate cells, unable to communicate with each other, and interrogated separately. Each is informed that if neither confesses both will receive a light sentence: one year in prison. If both confess, they will receive relatively heavy sentences: eight years in prison. If only one confesses and the other does not, however, the first will be released, and the second will receive the heaviest possible sentence: ten years.

Figure 6.1 depicts the choices confronting both prisoners, and the numbers

[11]The two-by-two game is purely illustrative. The world is neither so simple nor so rational as game theorists would like.

("values") in the boxes of the matrix represent the joint payoffs each can receive from the available strategies ("no confession" or "confession"). The best joint solution would be for neither to confess (outcome 1:1). In doing so, however, each risks that the other may turn state's evidence and confess, in which case the one who does not confess will receive a ten-year sentence, and the "defector" will get off scot-free. Like actors in global politics, it appears that neither prisoner can trust the other. Each "must" confess to avoid the possibility that the other will do so. By confessing, each guarantees the best payoff under the potentially worst conditions. This is known as a *maximin strategy* because it assures each a maximum minimum. The paradox is that their joint payoff (outcome 2:2) is worse for both than they would have if they had trusted each other and cooperated (outcome 1:1).[12]

The maximin "solution" in the *prisoner's dilemma game* — confession — reflects the participants' unwillingness to place themselves in a situation where their well-being depends on the good will of someone else. With no *enforcement mechanism*, each player has an incentive to cheat, not for any positive benefit but as protection against cheating by the other player. Clearly, many observers argue, the problem of trust is even more acute in global politics because the penalty for error may be national extinction and the actors reflect disparate cultures and traditions. Under such conditions, the likelihood of misunderstanding is high.

Various situations resemble the prisoner's dilemma. In international trade, one state's government may impose obstacles to importing goods from others — tariffs, quotas, inspection requirements, and so on[13] — because they believe the latter will do the same. Each may seek to protect its industries from the *possibility* that others will seek to protect theirs. If one government fails to adopt safeguards and the other assists its industries, the former may wake up and discover that its industries have lost markets and are no longer competitive.

Arms-control issues also resemble the prisoner's dilemma. Figure 6.2 depicts the general problem confronting an actor who is deciding whether or not to agree to a disarmament proposal. If both actors continue to arm (outcome 2:2), they will pay a price in continued budgetary outlays and associated political tension. By contrast, mutual disarmament (outcome 1:1) eliminates economic and political costs and is the most advantageous mutual outcome. If actors agree to disarm, however, each runs the risk that the other will cheat either by hiding weapons or building new ones surreptitiously. Then the actor who disarmed might find itself at a real, even life-threatening, disadvantage.

---

[12]In reality, the widespread norm against squealing or ratting might lead to revenge against one who confessed. This norm serves for enforcement, reducing the "anarchy" in the situation.

[13]The incentive to pose such obstacles will grow as long as it is believed that such obstacles can be hidden or disguised.

The incentive is strong to avoid the risks associated with outcomes 1:2 and 2:1.[14] The possibility that one of the parties to an arms-control agreement, especially involving nuclear weapons, might cheat is frightening. As in the prisoner's dilemma, those involved in negotiating arms-control agreements must constantly ask themselves whether they can trust each other and what, if anything, could be done in the event of cheating. One observer declares, "states are trapped in the double-defection box of a prisoners' dilemma."[15] One can imagine the consequences of a situation in which the United States and Russia signed an agreement to destroy all nuclear missiles that one did not honor. If one carries out its end of the bargain but the other hides 100 missiles, the former would be at a terrible disadvantage. Trust requires something to back up the mutual pledge and provide both sides with confidence in the agreement. That is why means of *verification*—ability to monitor compliance with an arms-control agreement—has a vital role in arms-control negotiations.

For much of the Cold War U.S. and Soviet leaders vainly negotiated about arms control. Agreements like the Strategic Arms Limitation Talks I (1972), the Intermediate-Range Nuclear Forces Treaty (1987) and the Strategic Arms Reduction Talks I (1991) and II (1992) became possible only when Washington and Moscow could begin to trust each other. Such trust was less the product of warming relations than of improved means of verification. The possibility of reliable verification was enhanced by technological developments, including satellites and electronic surveillance, and by willingness on both sides to permit on-site inspection. Improved verification techniques also reduced the domestic costs of seeking agreements with the adversary and insulated negotiators from charges at home that they were "gambling with the country's national security."

As these agreements illustrate, there are ways of overcoming the dilemma in the prisoner's dilemma. As we shall see, some of the factors that promote cooperation in such situations include:

1. Long time horizons.
2. Regularity of stakes.
3. Reliability of information about the other's actions.
4. Quick feedback about changes in the other's actions.[16]

Without such factors, coordinating policy among autonomous actors is difficult.

[14]That incentive varies depending on the values of the *double-defection box* (2:2). If that outcome is just slightly better than the worst case in outcomes 1:2 and 2:1, players will be willing to take greater risks to get 1:1; this is a *weak prisoner's dilemma*. If the "worst case" is significantly worse than double defection—as in the disarmament game—it is a *strong prisoner's dilemma*, and players will be risk-averse.

[15]Glenn H. Snyder, "'Prisoners' Dilemma' and 'Chicken' Models in International Politics," *International Studies Quarterly* 15:1 (March 1971), p. 69.

[16]Robert Axelrod and Robert O. Keohane, "Achieving Cooperation Under Anarchy: Strategies and Institutions," *World Politics* 38:1 (October 1985), p. 232.

FIGURE 6.2

The Disarmament Game

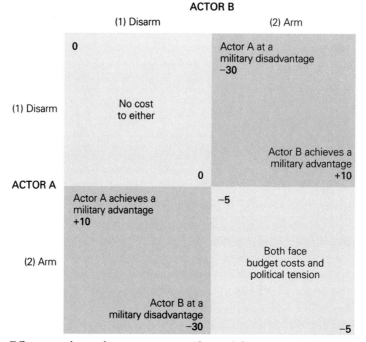

Efforts to achieve disarmament are a form of the prisoner's-dilemma game. Although players could benefit by disarming, each fears the other might "cheat." As a result both may continue to arm and face budget costs and continued political tension.

Consequences of Assuming the Worst

If global politics were anarchic, it would be rational for practitioners to exercise prudence and avoid risks. If many real-world situations are prisoner's dilemmas, then leaders will have little choice but to select risk-averse alternatives that minimize the mischief others can do to them. In other words, a logical inference from the assumption of anarchy is that leaders should determine the worst their adversaries can do to them, assume that it may happen, and take steps to prevent it. This is *worst-case analysis.*

As we saw in Chapter 2, the paucity of reliable information is one reason for selecting conservative strategies. If leaders do not know what their adversaries are planning, they must assume the worst. In many famous *"intelligence failures,"* the victim had information that the aggressor was able to carry out an attack but lacked specific intelligence about the adversary's intentions. Some of the best known are the U.S. failure to predict the Japanese attack on Pearl Harbor in 1941, Soviet surprise at the Nazi attack in 1941, and Israeli inability to predict Egypt's surprise attack in 1973. To avoid such disasters, actors prepare for the worst, assuming that, because they cannot get accurate information about adversaries' intentions, this is their safest course.

Unfortunately, worst-case analysis produces conservative thinking that is resistant to change. Resulting policies tend to produce the fear and suspicion they were supposed to counter; they often intensify the security dilemma. Actors may build weapons systems or conclude alliances in reaction to adversaries' capabilities—actions with defensive purposes. Yet almost every weapons system or alliance that can be used for defense can also be used aggressively. Because an opponent too is likely to employ worst-case analysis, it may reciprocate, triggering an arms race. Such interaction will, in time, make both sides feel less rather than more secure. Like the prisoner's dilemma, the adversaries may find that prudence produces a poor outcome for both. Each seeks to assure itself of minimal security that does not depend on trusting the adversary. But the resulting paradox is that efforts to increase security frighten and alienate the adversary and stimulate it to respond in kind.

Once such a spiral begins, the relationship between adversaries, especially during crises, may come to resemble a *game of chicken*.[17] This is a game, ascribed to teenagers in California decades ago, in which two cars speed toward each other, straddling the road's center line. The object of the game is to see which driver will "chicken out" and swerve first. If both drivers swerve (outcome 1:1), both suffer loss of reputation. If only one swerves, there is a loser and a winner (outcomes 1:2 and 2:1). If neither swerves, however, both are big losers in the inevitable collision (outcome 2:2). In global politics, crises like that involving the Soviet installation of missiles in Cuba in 1962 and spirals of threat and counterthreat such as that involving Iraq and Kuwait prior to Iraq's invasion August 2, 1990, resemble games of chicken. And sometimes disaster does occur, and both players lose. Thus, in 1992, the leaders of the Czech and Slovak republics sought to force each other to make important political and economic concessions to avoid collision—breakup of Czechoslovakia. Neither swerved, the country broke up, and both were losers.

In a prisoner's dilemma, disaster results from absence of trust and can be avoided only when each player is persuaded that the other will do what it promises. *Fear prevents the players from cooperating.* By contrast, disaster occurs in a game of chicken when both players believe the other is *bluffing* and can be dissuaded from carrying out its threat not to swerve. Disaster is avoided when each comes to believe that the other will actually carry out its threat and not swerve, thereby causing a life-threatening crash. *Fear forces the players to cooperate.*

The way to win a game of chicken is for one actor to persuade or trick the other to capitulate. The second actor will do so if it believes the first is sufficiently irrational

---

[17]See Thomas C. Schelling, *Arms and Influence* (New Haven: Yale University Press, 1966), pp. 116–125; and Glenn H. Snyder and Paul Diesing, *Conflict Among Nations* (Princeton: Princeton University Press, 1977), pp. 107–122.

FIGURE 6.3

Chicken

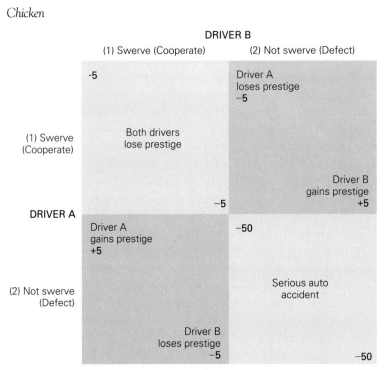

By contrast with prisoner's dilemma, the game of chicken reflects conflict spirals in global politics in which players fear that each will carry out its threats. In the game, two cars speed toward one another; whoever swerves first loses, but if neither do so catastrophe will ensue. There is great pressure for both to "bluff" but ultimately to swerve. The situation is analogous to crises in global politics in which actors engage in brinkmanship.

to risk its survival. Unlike the prisoner's dilemma, where each player wishes the other to trust him or her and cooperate, chicken entails an effort to produce fear. Indeed, this is the heart of the general problem of making credible commitments that underlies the strategies of deterrence and coercive diplomacy.[18] A number of tactics are available to a hotrodder (or a leader) in a game of chicken. You might throw the steering wheel out the window, making it impossible to swerve. This action makes your commitment not to chicken out, irrational though it may be a credible one.[19]

[18]See Chapter 8, pp. 260–261.

[19]A hotrodder who uses this tactic had better be certain to do so before his adversary does. If he waits to throw his steering wheel out the window until after the other driver does so, he will be committing suicide. Thomas Schelling refers to the principle of "last clear chance." He writes: "In strategy when both parties abhor collision the advantage often goes to the one who arranges the status quo in his favor and leaves to the other the 'last clear chance' to stop or turn aside" (*Arms and Influence*, pp. 44–45).

In global politics, the willingness of actors to behave in apparently irrational ways—assume risks with the prospect of little gain—is often based on a belief that behavior in one case will affect their *bargaining reputation*. In other words, actions and outcomes in one situation will affect actions and outcomes in others. As in a poker game, actors who gain a reputation for bluffing will have their bluff called. Robert Jervis explains: "The state must often go to extremes because moderation and conciliation are apt to be taken for weakness."[20]

Japanese–U.S. Relations Before World War II: "Chicken" and the Conflict Spiral

Relations between the U.S. and Japanese governments in the 1930s went into a negative spiral that culminated in the Japanese attack on *Pearl Harbor* on December 7, 1941. Disagreement between the two over major issues intensified hostility that came to be associated with racial, economic, religious, cultural, and other societal differences. Lasting disagreement and hostility set the stage for the cycle of reciprocally negative actions in the months before war broke out.[21]

Japan was a latecomer among the major powers. The country was dragged out of isolation in 1853 by a U.S. fleet under Commodore Matthew Perry. A treaty of friendship and trade relations between the two countries was followed in the next decades by rapid industrialization of Japan, and its leaders determined that the country should acquire an empire and achieve military and political equality with the Western powers. One consequence of rapid development was the country's growing dependence on imported food and raw materials. In 1895, Japan went to war with China and acquired the island of Formosa (Taiwan). Ten years later, in the first military victory of an Asian country over a European power, Japan defeated Russia and acquired new influence in Korea, South Sakhalin, and the Chinese province of Manchuria.[22] The latter was especially useful because of its industries and such natural resources as iron and coal and because it served as a buffer zone between Japan and Russia. In 1910 Japan annexed Korea. Having entered into a treaty with Great Britain in 1902 (the first between a major European power and an Asian country), Japan benefited from Germany's defeat in World War I by acquiring German concessions in China and German territories in the Pacific.

Despite these triumphs, the Japanese did not feel they were being treated equally by the West. One reason was a residue of racial animosity. Japanese efforts to include a clause affirming racial equality in the 1919 *Versailles Treaty* were thwarted by U.S.

[20]Robert Jervis, *Perception and Misperception in International Politics* (Princeton: Princeton University Press, 1976), p. 59.

[21]See Richard W. Mansbach and John A. Vasquez, *In Search of Theory: A New Paradigm for Global Politics* (New York: Columbia University Press, 1981), pp. 234–240.

[22]The Russo-Japanese War was a disaster for Russia's Tsarist government and triggered revolutionary currents in 1905 that were a foretaste of the 1917 revolution.

President Woodrow Wilson, who feared such a clause would invalidate U.S. immigration laws that excluded most Asians from America's shores. The Japanese were
especially aggrieved because Wilson advocated the rights of national minorities in
Central Europe. Japan's failure to gain tangible benefits from its policy of cooperation
with the West during the 1920s and economic difficulties at home during the depression
(1930), frustrated Japanese nationalists and military officers. Among these groups,
admiration was growing for Benito Mussolini and the fascists, who had seized power in
Italy in 1923. In September 1931, Japanese armed forces in Manchuria (the Kwantung
Army), threatened by growing Chinese nationalism, conquered the province.[23] Following Japan's conquest of Manchuria and creation of a puppet state called *Manchukuo* in
1932,[24] U.S. suspicions about Japanese intentions deepened, especially before the
military's growing influence in Japanese political life.[25] Japanese militarists saw Western
opposition to Japan's penetration of China as an effort to deny Tokyo an imperial destiny
already enjoyed by Western states. Suspicions were transformed into open antagonism
after the Japanese invasion of China in 1937 and the atrocities committed by the
Japanese Army in Shanghai and Nanking.

Tokyo felt that U.S. assistance to China was an effort to hamstring Japan, and
feared the U.S. Pacific fleet as the greatest military threat to Japan's national survival.
American opposition to Japanese expansionism in China and the Japanese belief that
this opposition was an effort to prevent Japan from realizing its destiny led to tit-for-tat
behavior and the upward spiral of mutual insecurity. For Japan to bring the war in China
to a successful conclusion, it needed secure access to raw materials, especially oil and
iron, for a modern military machine. This problem was part of a more general one: Japan
lacked most natural resources, and, if cut off from such resources, its industrial economy
would shrivel and die. Raw materials whetted Japan's interest in Southeast Asia, placing
it on a collision course with the colonial powers that still ruled the area.[26]

In June 1940 Japanese military observers were sent to Tonking in northern
Indochina, and in September additional troops followed. That month the Japanese
government entered into a military alliance — the *Tripartite Pact* — with fascist Italy and

[23]The Japanese were agreed about the need to maintain influence in Manchuria against the
forces of Chinese nationalism that had rallied around Chiang Kai-shek, but Japan's civilian cabinet
sought to use peaceful methods to do so.

[24]The puppet ruler of Manchukuo was Pu-yi, the "last emperor" of China, who is depicted
in a film with that name.

[25]Such suspicion grew so strong that U.S. Secretary of State Cordell Hull described Japan's
Foreign Minister Matsuoka Yosuke as "crooked as a basket of fishhooks." Cited in John K.
Fairbank, Edwin O. Reischauer, and Albert M. Craig, *East Asia: The Modern Transformation*
(Boston: Houghton Mifflin, 1965), p. 608.

[26]The major colonial powers in Asia were Britain (Singapore, Hong Kong, India, Burma,
Ceylon), France (Indochina), Holland (Indonesia), and the United States (the Philippines). Other
than Japan itself, Thailand was the only major Asian society that was not either colonized or
heavily penetrated by Western imperialism in the 1930s.

Nazi Germany. Japanese expansion into Southeast Asia especially engaged public attention in the United States, convincing observers that Tokyo was aggressive and was a threat to American interests and friends. In response, the U.S. government ended sales of aviation gasoline to Japan in July 1940 and in September placed an embargo on steel and scrap iron.

Just as Japan's actions had antagonized rather than cowed the United States, the U.S. response fueled anti-Americanism in Japan, creating fear that additional U.S. actions might be forthcoming and producing determination to secure additional sources of raw material and close down the southern supply routes to China. The lure of oil, rubber, and other resources needed by Japan grew rapidly. In July 1941, the die was cast as Japanese troops occupied southern Indochina. In response, the U.S., British, and Dutch[27] governments embargoed all oil exports to Japan, cutting off 90 percent of Japanese oil imports. By late 1941, U.S.-Japanese relations had acquired the characteristics of a game of chicken. Both sides blustered, threatened, and took steps to convince the other that they were willing to go to war rather than back down. Thus, in September 1941 Japanese Prime Minister Hideki Tojo argued that "The real purpose of the United States [is] the domination of the Far East. Consequently, to yield on one matter would be to encourage other demands, until there would be no end to the concessions required of Japan."[28]

Japan's leaders were under mounting pressure. Oil reserves were limited, and, in time, Japan's capacity to wage war would decline. Yet, any effort to seize oil resources in Southeast Asia had to take into account the U.S. Pacific fleet. On September 3, Japanese leaders decided to go to war against the United States if the oil issue remained unresolved by October. Tokyo simultaneously intensified diplomatic efforts and began to plan a secret attack on America's giant naval base at Pearl Harbor in Hawaii.[29] On Sunday, December 7, a day President Roosevelt declared "would live in infamy," the intensifying spiral of U.S.–Japanese hostility exploded in the surprise attack on Pearl Harbor.

United States–Japanese relations before World War II had the attributes of anarchy that some theorists believe apply to all global politics. Two actors with incompatible interests using the threat of force to increase their own security found themselves embroiled in a conflict spiral that climaxed in war. But, as we shall see, anarchy is only one side of the coin.

[27]By this time Holland itself had been occupied by the Germans, but Dutch administrators continued to govern the Dutch East Indies (Indonesia).

[28]Robert Butow, *Tojo and the Coming of War* (Princeton: Princeton University Press, 1961), p. 280.

[29]The operation at Pearl Harbor was a *preventive attack* with the aim of eliminating America's military capacity to oppose Japan's later military plans. It was not a *preemptive attack*; that is, an attack that is launched because of fear that the enemy is about to attack. Israel's attack on Egypt, Syria, and Jordan in June 1967 — the Six-Day War — was a preemptive attack initiated because of fear that Egypt was about to launch its own attack.

Social Side of Global Politics

World politics is not merely a condition of unrelieved anarchy, and war is an exception rather than the rule. Even those who are adversaries on some issues find it necessary to work together on others and share some interests. And even issues that entail conflict leave opportunities for players to lose or win together. Somehow things get done in world politics without a central government, and we take for granted such routine and predictable, but critical, matters as international trade, mail delivery, and safe travel.

In the remainder of this chapter we address the question of cooperation in the absence of overarching authority. First, we look at the role of *reciprocity*, which helps explain why it is expedient for actors to cooperate. Second, we consider how a *history of rewarding cooperation and shared values* may encourage cooperation. Third, we examine how *concern about the future* and the desire to avoid alienating those on whom future outcomes depend also encourage cooperation. Fourth, we look at how *learning* occurs in global politics as in other realms of life. Such learning is a prerequisite for evolving *norms and rules of behavior* that are necessary if cooperation among actors is to become habitual. Finally, where "principles, norms, rules, and decision-making procedures" are sufficiently clear to enable actors' expectations to "converge in a given issue-area,"[30] we may speak of an *international regime*. Such regimes may facilitate intensive and continuous cooperation among actors. Together, these factors permit a global society to function that is a far cry from the anarchic image of the state of nature depicted by Thomas Hobbes in his *Leviathan*:

> Hereby it is manifest that, during the time men live without a common power to keep them all in awe, they are in that condition called war, and such a war as is of every man against every man. . . . In such condition there is no place for industry, because the fruit thereof is uncertain: and consequently no culture of the earth; no navigation nor use of the commodities that may be imported by sea . . . ; no arts; no letters; no society; and, which is worst of all, continual fear and danger of violent death. . . . [31]

Reciprocity

Some of the most compelling metaphors used to illustrate anarchy, such as Rousseau's *stag–hare parable*, are flawed. What will happen to the hunter who grabs the hare and deserts his fellows if he meets them later? In all likelihood they will turn on him; at least they will not trust him again, and he will be ostracized. Rousseau's state of nature differs from the real world in that its inhabitants interact with each other rarely. Rousseau's hunter is like a fly-by-night business purveyor or con artist who cheats customers and then flees with the profits, hoping never to see them again. In fact, actors in world politics, like most reputable business leaders, keep faith with each other, not only from ethical considerations, but

---

[30]Stephen D. Krasner, "Structural Causes and Regime Consequences: Regimes as Intervening Variables," *International Organization* 36:2 (Spring 1982), p. 185.

[31]Thomas Hobbes, *Leviathan, Parts I and II* (Indianapolis: Bobbs-Merrill, 1958), pp. 106–107.

This engraving is from the frontispiece to the 1651 edition of *Leviathan* by Thomas Hobbes. It shows Hobbes's all-powerful sovereign brandishing a sword in one hand and the scepter of justice in the other. The sovereign watches over an orderly town, made peaceful by his absolute authority. But note that his body is composed of tiny images of his subjects. The sovereign exists only through them. Hobbes explains that such awesome governmental power can be created only if men "confer all their power and strength upon one man, or upon one assembly of men, that may reduce all their wills, by plurality of voices, unto one will." In Hobbes's view, only power could preserve peace.

---

because their interests are served by the golden rule—do unto others as you would have them do unto you. Despite the missing central authority, most promises are kept, most treaties are observed, and actors do not routinely cheat each other. Repeatedly we witness agreements—between governments and terrorists, even opponents in civil wars—that stick despite strong incentives for participants to disavow them and seek short-term advantages.[32]

The golden rule reflects *reciprocity*—an exchange in which each actor's behavior depends on that of the other and in which each actor's behavior emulates that of the other "in such a way that good is returned for good, and bad for bad."[33] The single

[32]If agreements are imposed rather than voluntary, the rate of defection will be higher.

[33]Robert O. Keohane, "Reciprocity in International Relations," *International Organization* 40:1 (Winter 1986), p. 8. Emphasis omitted.

interaction among the several hunters in Rousseau's stag-hare parable is an *end-of-the-world* or *one-shot game*; it takes place only once and does not permit reciprocity. By acknowledging that reciprocity is indispensable in creating common interest in not cheating, we recognize that global politics is not an end-of-the-world interaction but is a repeated interaction in which each actor's behavior conditions others' expectations for the future. Unlike the residents in Rousseau's state of nature, who presumably never expect to meet again, French and Germans and Russians and Chinese cannot hide from one another and must consider the eventual consequences of what they do to each other. An actor who regularly cheats will not be trusted. If it plays by the rules, it will probably receive similar treatment in return.

Our earlier discussion of the prisoner's-dilemma game, and indeed much of game theory, as a model for real-world situations, suffers from the same shortcomings as Rousseau's stag–hare parable. Although the game's structure forces both prisoners to confess on a *single* occasion, the situation changes if the game is replayed. In time, with an eye to the future, actors may be willing to take risks to achieve larger gains; unlike the stag–hare hunter, they will compare short-term and long-term interests. Whether or not cooperation evolves depends on the situation in which actors find themselves and on how other players respond to initiatives intended to promote trust. Axelrod and Keohane observe, "effective reciprocity depends on three conditions: (1) players can identify defectors; (2) they are able to focus retaliation on defectors; and (3) they have sufficient long-run incentives to punish defectors."[34] Where many actors are involved it may be difficult to recognize cheating or know who the culprits are. Actors may also lack the will to retaliate, hoping that someone else will do it for them.

The most important factor in overcoming a prisoner's-dilemma trap, however, is recognizing long-term interests. "The more future payoffs are valued relative to current payoffs," observe Axelrod and Keohane, "the less incentive to defect today—since the other side is likely to retaliate tomorrow."[35] The authors illustrate by referring to cooperation between international banks and governments in Latin America that are in debt to those banks:

> [C]ontemporary negotiations among banks, and between banks and debtor countries, are heavily affected by the shadow of the future. . . . [T]he banks know that they will be dealing . . . with the debtor countries . . . again and again. . . . Continuing relations between banks and debtor countries give the banks incentives to cooperate with the debtor countries, not merely in order to facilitate debt servicing on loans already made, but to stay in their good graces—looking toward a more prosperous future.[36]

---

[34]Axelrod and Keohane, "Achieving Cooperation," p. 235.

[35]Ibid., p. 232.

[36]Ibid., p. 233. See also Charles Lipson, "Bankers' Dilemmas: Private Cooperation in Rescheduling Sovereign Debts," *World Politics* 38:1 (October 1985), pp. 200–225.

This is why, when the same players are involved in repeated (iterated) prisoner's-dilemma games, they become increasingly able to cooperate and avoid the penalties associated with "confession."[37]

Weight of the Past in Cooperation

The context in which decisions are made is crucial, and *time* is a big part of that context. For better or worse, political leaders are influenced by both the past and "the shadow of the future." By "past," we mean both the history of the actors that leaders represent and the personal experiences of the leaders themselves. In "future," we include expectations and aspirations of the collectivities and of individual leaders.

A people's *historical experience* is relevant to current behavior in a number of ways. History is the basis for "myths" that are necessary for group solidarity and values. In the United States, stories about the revolution against British rule in 1776 and the subsequent Constitutional Convention; the Civil War (1860–1865) that ended slavery; and the "conquest" of the West are invoked to define American values — individualism, equality, tolerance, and hard work. The stories may be no more than partly accurate, but accuracy is not the point. They serve the purpose of providing a shared past and shared experiences to deepen unity and, like Biblical parables, they help define what each society regards as ethically acceptable.[38] In general, these values and the historical tales that justify them are ritualized and recalled on holidays.[39]

Historical experience helps to predict the future. If two actors have enjoyed warm relations in the past, leaders routinely assume they will continue to do so. They react sympathetically and are sensitive to each other's interests, thereby confirming their own assumption. And, if they find themselves in disagreement, leaders will make efforts to find common ground.[40] Thus, a history of cooperation facilitates future cooperation. The *special relationship* between the United States and Britain illustrates how a long history of good relations can influence the present. When the Argentine military seized the Falkland (Malvinas) Islands from Britain in 1982, there should have been little doubt that, once Washington failed to negotiate a peaceful resolution to the conflict, it would

---

[37]See Robert Axelrod, *The Evolution of Cooperation* (New York: Basic Books, 1984).

[38]Statesmen try to appear ethical and show that they remain faithful to their society's values to ensure that they will be well regarded by later generations. Attorney General Robert Kennedy may have had this purpose in claiming that, when someone proposed a surprise attack on Soviet installations in Cuba during the 1962 missile crisis, he passed his brother, the president, a note reading: "I now know how Tojo felt when he was planning Pearl Harbor." Robert F. Kennedy, *Thirteen Days* (New York: W. W. Norton, 1968), p. 9.

[39]If people cease believing such myths, unity will suffer. The debate over "multiculturalism" in U.S. education reveals growing doubts about America's myths; the collapse of the U.S.S.R. followed a long period in which the "heroes" of Bolshevism were shown to have feet of clay.

[40]If they fail to do so, however, the resulting schism may be more serious because of a mutual sense of betrayal by a long-time friend. Sino-Soviet relations in the late 1960s and 1970s saw such a sense of betrayal following their falling out after two decades of Marxist-Leninist "fraternal" cooperation.

tilt toward London. The British government showed similar sensitivity to U.S. interests in 1986 when it permitted U.S. bombers to use British air bases to bomb targets in Libya in retaliation for Libyan support of international terrorism and again in 1990 when the British government sent troops to stand alongside their American allies to reverse the Iraqi invasion of Kuwait.

It is because the past is assumed to be a reliable predictor of the future that leaders are caught by surprise when change occurs. Events like the overthrow of Shah Muhammad Reza Pahlavi in Iran by Muslim fundamentalist followers of Ayatollah Ruhollah Khomeini in 1979 following decades of close U.S.–Iranian cooperation[41] and the Iraqi invasion of Kuwait in 1990 following U.S. aid to Iraq during the Iraq–Iran war surprised the U.S. government despite evidence of their imminence. These events were simply not expected by observers because they did not fit past patterns. Expectations shaped by the past may be reinforced by leaders' unwillingness to perceive what they do not wish to happen, thereby inviting "intelligence failures."

Indeed, having incomplete information, leaders are prone to interpret the present through past events, especially those which they remember. In other words, personal experience is treated as equivalent to hard information. The problem, as one historian explains, "is that framers of foreign policy are often influenced by beliefs about what history teaches or portends. Sometimes, they perceive problems in terms of analogies from the past. Sometimes, they envision the future either as foreshadowed by historical parallels or as following a straight line from what has recently gone before."[42]

The attitudes toward the U.S.S.R. of Western leaders like U.S. President Harry Truman and British Prime Minister Winston Churchill after 1945 were influenced by their experiences in the 1930s when appeasement of the dictators Hitler and Mussolini, rather than ensuring peace, seemed to whet their appetites for greater conquest.[43] And those in power in the West in the 1930s, like Neville Chamberlain, who sought to appease Hitler and Mussolini, were influenced by their experiences during World War I and practiced appeasement partly because they were determined to avoid the carnage of that earlier war. Contemplating another imminent war with Germany, Chamberlain declared in a radio broadcast: "How horrible, fantastic, incredible it is that we should be digging trenches and trying on gas-masks here because of a quarrel in a far-away country between people of whom we know nothing."[44] Chamberlain, declares one historian,

---

[41]The Shah had been a close friend of the United States since 1941, and, in 1953, the CIA assisted in overthrowing Iran's leftist Premier Muhammad Mossadeq to restore power to the Shah.

[42]Ernest R. May, *"Lessons" of The Past: The Use and Misuse of History in American Foreign Policy* (New York: Oxford University Press, 1973), p. ix.

[43]See Chapter 8, pp. 546–547.

[44]Cited in Francis L. Loewenheim, ed., *Peace or Appeasement?* (Boston: Houghton Mifflin, 1965), p. 55.

"was so deeply, so desperately, anxious to avoid war that he could not conceive of its being inevitable."[45]

Superficial *analogies from the past* can be dangerous.[46] Though inappropriate, such comparisons may guide or rationalize policy and substitute for more relevant information. In all likelihood, too many differences separate past from present events for the one to provide lessons for the other. Another tendency is to misread the past or distort it so that it can serve the purposes of the present. President Lyndon Johnson and other U.S. leaders became embroiled in the Vietnam War (1965–1973) precisely because they "misunderstood past insurgency situations."[47]

Import of the Future

We have observed how concern for the future may enhance cooperation. Leaders may forego immediate advantage to reap long-term benefits and gain a reputation for trustworthiness. Under some circumstances, however, preoccupation with the future may also enhance pugnacity if actors worry about their reputation for keeping commitments.

Actors may invest considerable resources toward achieving minor objectives simply to maintain a reputation for toughness. The objectives themselves are symbolic, but crises over them may trigger conflicts that can be dangerous and costly. On two occasions (1954 and 1958), the U.S. government seemed willing to risk war with China over the tiny Taiwanese-occupied islands of Quemoy and Matsu. During the crises over these two specks off the coast of China, "[President] Eisenhower actually brought the country to the 'nuclear brink,' far closer to war than a distraught public feared in 1955, closer than Eisenhower acknowledged in his own memoirs, and closer than most historians have heretofore even suspected."[48] During the Cold War, the United States and the Soviet Union engaged in repeated crises over the isolated and indefensible city of Berlin (1948, 1960, 1961), a city whose value was almost entirely symbolic. Ultimately, the costs of maintaining a reputation for toughness may become disproportionate to the ends sought. United States intervention in Vietnam — "70 percent" of the aim of which, according to Assistant Secretary of Defense John T. McNaughton, was "to avoid humiliating U.S. defeat (to our reputation as a guarantor)"[49] — was one such instance.

[45]John W. Wheeler-Bennett, *Munich: Prologue to Tragedy* (New York: Viking Press, 1964), p. 269.

[46]See Richard E. Neustadt and Ernest R. May, *Thinking in Time: The Uses of History for Decision Makers* (New York: Free Press, 1986).

[47]D. Michael Shafer, *Deadly Paradigms: The Failure of U.S. Counterinsurgency Policy* (Princeton: Princeton University Press, 1988), p. 276.

[48]Gordon H. Chang, "To the Nuclear Brink: Eisenhower, Dulles, and the Quemoy-Matsu Crisis," *International Security* 12:4 (Spring 1988), p. 97.

[49]Neil Sheehan, ed., *The Pentagon Papers* (New York: Bantam, 1971), p. 432.

Preoccupation with the past and future also intrudes into the present by shaping the *roles* individuals play in their professional lives. Whatever individuals' personal preferences, their official behavior is shaped by expectations associated with the position they occupy.[50] As in the roles actors play upon the stage, those in official positions have something like a "script" to guide their actions. Thus, military officers are expected to seek larger defense appropriations and to oppose pacifist policies and cuts in defense outlays. The past and future affect the evolution of roles in the sense that leaders pay attention to the views of those who were responsible for placing them in the position. And, if officials wish to be promoted in the future, they must be sensitive to the views of those responsible for such promotion. Recognizing such obligations makes the behavior of those in such roles highly predictable on some issues. The past and the future conspire, then, to produce stable roles that help diminish the effect of personal idiosyncrasies. Such roles may make it difficult to bring about change, but they also enhance the stability and predictability of political systems.

Learning by Doing

As our earlier discussion of the prisoner's dilemma suggests, *learning* does take place in global politics. Time is so important because the way in which actors perceive a situation in which they find themselves and, therefore, the way in which they behave can change. In the language of game theory, the way in which one game is played affects the values attached to other games.[51] *It is this assumption that underlies leaders' willingness to forego immediate gain for long-term interests and to contest minor issues to maintain a reputation for upholding commitments.*

Learning the Hard Way: The 1930s

The steps leading up to World War II illustrate how the values that leaders attach to issues evolve with events. We have seen how Western leaders in the 1930s, including prime ministers Stanley Baldwin and Neville Chamberlain of Great Britain and Premier Édouard Daladier of France—repeatedly chose to appease the dictators of Germany, Japan, and Italy rather than risk war. None of the violations of international law and decency—the Japanese invasion of Manchuria (1931) and China (1937), Italian

---

[50]Personal and role preferences tend to merge because of self-selection. Individuals are rarely comfortable occupying roles that require them to behave contrary to personal beliefs, and they are likely to seek professional lives that are psychologically more satisfying.

[51]See Kenneth A. Oye, "Explaining Cooperation under Anarchy: Hypotheses and Strategies," *World Politics* 38:1(October 1985), p. 9 for a discussion of "strategies to alter the payoff structure." See also Glenn H. Snyder, "'Prisoner's Dilemma' and 'Chicken' Models in International Politics," *International Studies Quarterly* 15:1 (March 1971), pp. 66–103.

aggression against Ethiopia (1935), and German repudiation of the Treaty of Versailles (1935),[52] occupation of the Rhineland (1936),[53] Austria (1938),[54] the Czech Sudetenland (1938),[55] and the remainder of "rump" Czechoslovakia (1939)—triggered military resistance from the Western democracies.

The reasons for Western passivity in the face of provocation were complex—memories of trench-warfare horrors in World War I, fear of air power, public opposition to defense expenditures during economic hard times, and lack of military preparedness—among others. Perhaps most important, however, was that Western leaders were convinced that the dictators' demands were limited. The feeling was widespread that the Versailles Treaty, imposed on defeated Germany, was unfair and that, as British economist John Maynard Keynes wrote, "little has been overlooked which might impoverish Germany now or obstruct her development in future."[56] Many observers believed German efforts to regain equality with the other Europeans were justified.

Consequently, when Hitler claimed that his aims were limited—to restore Germany to the family of nations and unite German-speaking peoples in one state under national self-determination—Western leaders chose to take him at his word.[57] Although they denounced Hitler's actions, they believed the costs of war outweighed the value of individual stakes such as the Rhineland or the Sudetenland. This attitude changed dramatically, however, when Hitler occupied the ancient Czechoslovak provinces of Bohemia and Moravia where, unlike the Sudetenland, few Germans lived. British and French perceptions were suddenly altered. Clearly, the German leader was after more than unifying Germans; now his earlier actions seemed more sinister, part of a larger plot to give Germany control of Europe and perhaps even more. Those actions seemed akin to *salami tactics*, in which an actor makes small demands (like thin slices of a salami) that collectively add up to something more significant (the whole salami). Thomas Schelling writes,

> "Salami tactics," we can be sure, were invented by a child; whoever first expounded the adult version had already understood the principle when he was small. Tell a child not to go in the water and he'll sit on the bank and submerge his bare feet;

[52]This repudiation included the limitation on size of military forces that the treaty had imposed on Germany after 1919.

[53]The Rhineland, on the west bank of the Rhine River, was demilitarized to prevent Germany from again posing a threat to France.

[54]The political union of Austria and Germany—called *Anschluss*—was forbidden by the Versailles Treaty.

[55]The Sudetenland was ceded to Germany in the infamous Munich Treaty.

[56]John Maynard Keynes, *The Economic Consequences of the Peace* (New York: Harper & Row, 1971), pp. 111–112.

[57]That Hitler posed as an enemy of Bolshevism appealed to some of the West's leaders who were suspicious of Soviet dictator Josef Stalin. Furthermore, because they had supported the rights of nationalities to have their own state, it was difficult for Western leaders to oppose Hitler's alleged objective, uniting Germans.

he is not yet "in" the water. Acquiesce, and he'll stand up; no more of him is in the water than before. Think it over, and he'll start wading, not going any deeper; take a moment to decide whether this is different and he'll go a little deeper, arguing that since he goes back and forth it all averages out. Pretty soon we are calling to him not to swim out of sight, wondering whatever happened to all our discipline.[58]

On September 1, 1939, the Nazis attacked Poland. Within hours, the British and French declared war on Germany, and World War II had begun. In some respects, the British and French decision made little sense. A year earlier, they had decided not to fight for Czechoslovakia even though France and the Soviet Union had an alliance with that country and though it was a democracy. Czechoslovakia also had an excellent army, enjoyed strong natural defenses, and had the giant Skoda armaments works. Neither the British nor the French though, were allied to the authoritarian Polish government. The Polish army was mostly obsolete, and the Polish plain was ideal for mechanized warfare of the sort the Germans were equipped to wage. It seemed as though Western leaders had chosen to fight in the wrong place and at the wrong time. At another level, however, the Anglo-French decision makes a great deal of sense because their perceptions of Hitler had been altered by his own behavior.

Hitler was a radical who, along with his Italian and Japanese allies, sought to remake global politics; their behavior was governed by an ideology that was alien to other world leaders and their aims were almost unlimited.[59] Their actions repeatedly violated the expectations of other leaders, who believed those objectives were limited and traditional, not unlimited and radical. In time, the West "learned" from bitter experience that Hitler could not be trusted and was a danger to all.

Learning to Cooperate: the Cold War Ends

Unlike Hitler's provoking a hostile spiral in the 1930s, Mikhail Gorbachev, after assuming control of the Soviet Union in 1985, had a big hand in triggering a benign spiral that brought an end to the Cold War. He realized that Soviet policies were leading to economic and political bankruptcy. He also recognized that it was necessary to woo the West for economic and technological assistance to modernize the U.S.S.R. and to permit arms reductions that would free up resources for Soviet consumers. As a result, Gorbachev repeatedly initiated unilateral and *entirely unexpected* concessions to the

---

[58]Schelling, *Arms and Influence*, pp. 66–67.

[59]Hitler's views, virulent with racism, were available for anyone to read. During the year (1923–1924) when he was in prison for seeking to overthrow the German government, he wrote *Mein Kampf* (*My Struggle*). Yet few of his opponents chose to take him seriously, perhaps because, as one historian writes, his ideas were "written in a verbose style which is both difficult and dull to read." Alan Bullock, *Hitler: A Study in Tyranny*, rev. ed. (New York: Harper & Row, 1964), p. 121.

West on arms-control issues and in regional conflicts.[60] These were initially greeted with skepticism and disbelief: It's a Communist trick so that we will let down our guard.[61] Such skepticism was understandable considering Gorbachev's background as a loyal communist functionary or *apparatchik*. Gradually, however, Western leaders accepted Gorbachev's "new thinking" as genuine and started making reciprocal concessions as "partners in peace." In time, Presidents Reagan and Bush and British Prime Minister Margaret Thatcher came to regard Gorbachev as someone with whom they could do business.

Gorbachev's strategy was reflected in the concessions he made to the U.S. point of view in negotiations that led to the successful Intermediate-Range Nuclear Forces (INF) Treaty that he signed with President Reagan on December 8, 1987. A brief history of the affair is instructive. After 1979, U.S. and West European leaders sought to deploy a new generation of missiles in Western Europe that could strike at targets in Eastern Europe and the U.S.S.R. The military problem was caused by Soviet deployment of an accurate new mobile missile equipped with multiple warheads—the SS-20. Politically, deploying a comparable system of Western missiles seemed imperative to convey to Moscow a credible U.S. commitment on nuclear deterrence and to reassure the Europeans. The NATO plan was known as the *dual-track decision* because it committed the allies to negotiating with the U.S.S.R. at the same time as missiles were being deployed.[62] Such negotiation was, however, regarded as mostly cosmetic, to win public opinion, and few expected the negotiations to bear fruit.

To the chagrin of U.S. and allied leaders, however, the planned deployment was confronted by massive opposition among West Europeans and, less extensively, Americans. Soviet leaders launched an effective propaganda campaign against deployment of these missiles, seeking to assist the European "peace movement." In the end, the missiles were deployed, but public opinion in Western Europe had to be persuaded that NATO was seriously negotiating an arms-control agreement with the Soviet-dominated Warsaw Treaty Organization. The Reagan administration, influenced by such hawkish members of the Department of Defense as Caspar Weinberger, Fred Iklé, and Richard Perle, was not very interested in an arms-control agreement with Moscow; rather, it sought to reestablish military superiority over the U.S.S.R. It had, however, a public-relations problem.

[60]At the time Gorbachev assumed power, the U.S. and Soviet governments were supporting rival political factions in Nicaragua, El Salvador, Afghanistan, Angola, Ethiopia, and Cambodia. By the early 1990s, all those conflicts had been resolved or muted. In some cases, for instance Angola, they have been revived but without U.S. or Russian involvement.

[61]See, for example, James Schlesinger, "Reykjavik and Revelations: A Turn of the Tide?" *Foreign Affairs* 65:3 1987, pp. 426–446.

[62]NATO planned to deploy 572 Pershing 2 and ground-launched cruise missiles (GLCMs) in West Germany, Britain, Italy, Belgium, and the Netherlands. Even after their deployment, the U.S.S.R. would have continued to enjoy a marked numerical advantage in intermediate-range nuclear missiles.

To allay growing public fears about nuclear war, the administration in 1981 proposed the "*zero option*" — worldwide elimination of INF missiles. The administration believed this simple proposal would find public favor in the West but would be unacceptable to Moscow because it required the U.S.S.R. to eliminate a great number of missiles that had already been deployed but merely required the United States not to build the proposed NATO missiles. In other words, the Soviet Union was being asked to give up a significant advantage. At the time the ploy worked. In 1986, however, "when Gorbachev offered to eliminate all SS-20s in Europe, the West was trapped."[63] This limited version of the zero option was attractive to Western publics. It satisfied Western demands for verification by permitting on-site inspections even in the Soviet Union. Most important, it entailed a concession by Gorbachev because it committed the U.S.S.R. to eliminate far more weapons than the West. The Reagan administration was forced to go along or else pay a price in domestic and European support.

After the INF Treaty was signed in 1987, new arms-control initiatives got under way, especially on conventional arms in Europe and the U.S.-Soviet strategic nuclear balance.[64] Each step was encouraged by unilateral initiatives from the Soviet leader. Finally, sensing the need for dramatic U.S. action and prodded by an abortive coup against President Gorbachev by hard-liners in the U.S.S.R.,[65] President George Bush announced on September 28, 1991, that the United States would unilaterally eliminate its vast arsenal of short-range nuclear weapons. A few days later, Gorbachev announced that the U.S.S.R. would reciprocate and, in some arms categories, go even further.[66]

The dance, with unilateral concessions followed by reciprocal concessions, reflected in Soviet–U.S. relations after 1985 is a textbook illustration of the way in which adversaries with conflicting value systems can create trust.[67] This exchange resembles the proposal that psychologist Charles Osgood advanced: *graduated reduction in tension* (GRIT).[68] He argued that trust could be created in situations like the prisoner's dilemma if one side made significant unilateral concessions to the other and continued to do so

---

[63]Lynn E. Davis, "Lessons of the INF Treaty," *Foreign Affairs* 66:4 (Spring 1988), p. 727.

[64]See Chapter 12, pp. 417–418.

[65]Dramatic changes in the Soviet Union after the abortive August 1991 coup enhanced the independence of the U.S.S.R. republics. The Bush administration worried that short-range nuclear weapons stationed by the Soviet military on land and sea in the republics might fall into the wrong hands. The U.S. offer, it was believed, would make it possible for the Soviet Union to withdraw these weapons and eliminate this danger.

[66]Serge Schmemann, "Gorbachev Matches U.S. on Nuclear Cuts And Goes Further on Strategic Warheads," *The New York Times*, October 6, 1991, Section 1, p. 1.

[67]Psychologists and sociologists for years have sought to analyze this problem experimentally. One of the best known of such experiments involved two groups of boys placed in a competitive situation out of which grew mistrust and hostility akin to U.S.-Soviet relations during the Cold War. Gradually their hostility abated after they were assigned a cooperative task. See Muzafer Sherif et. al., *Intergroup Conflict and Cooperation: The Robbers' Cave Experiment* (Norman: University of Oklahoma Press, 1961).

[68]Charles Osgood, *An Alternative to War or Surrender* (Urbana: University of Illinois Press, 1962).

for a while. At some time, though, the other has to reciprocate. President Gorbachev seemed to understand instinctively how such a *peace race* could be launched when he reacted to President Bush's unilateral concession on short-range nuclear weapons: "I can say that this initiative, either by the United States or the Soviet Union, wouldn't have become possible if the Soviet Union hadn't adopted the policy of new thinking, if it hadn't said good-bye to the cold war and hadn't started moving towards a new type of international relations. These are all interrelated issues."[69]

Global Norms and Rules of the Game

Learning of the sort that transformed U.S.–Soviet relations is constantly taking place in global politics and is reflected in evolving norms that shape expectations and define what is proper and what is not. Despite those who believe global politics is unchangeable—an anarchic universe dominated by conflict—it appears that different eras and settings have very different norms. During the twelfth century it was perfectly acceptable for a conqueror like Genghis Khan to burn and loot cities and sell captives into slavery. By the nineteenth century, however, such behavior was regarded as depraved.[70] During World War II, Hitler violated most global norms, and the *Nuremberg Trials* of captured Nazis after the war were an effort to outlaw such behavior. More recently, atrocities committed by Serbians and Croatians against each other and against Bosnians have created speculation about the need for similar war-crimes trials in order to reaffirm the Nuremberg norms.

Norms, in the sense used here, apply to behavior that is regarded as appropriate by other significant actors. When such norms are widely understood and accepted, they provide *rules of the game* that actors follow out of habit and self-interest. They provide coherence even without central authority and thereby reduce anarchy. Awareness of such norms can be surmised from reasoning such as:

"Under conditions A and B, other actors expect us to do X."

"Under conditions A and B, action Y will violate the expectations of other actors and will produce unpredictable reactions."

"If we wish to avoid conflict and mutual harm, we should do X."

Actions communicate intent. If actors follow the rules of the game, their initiatives will probably be met by standard responses that have evolved for such situations and are anticipated by all participants. Where expectations are realized and actors limit themselves to standard repertoires of behavior, the probability is reduced that fear and surprise will trigger spiraling conflict. Mutual interests encourage actors to develop repertoires of

[69]"Excerpts from Gorbachev's Remarks on Cuts," *The New York Times*, September 29, 1991, Section 1, p. 8.

[70]The Geneva Convention of 1864 reflected this change by establishing rules for the humane treatment of prisoners of war and of the sick and those wounded in battle.

cooperative activities covering diverse issues. Norms that define for participants what is permissible and what is improper under different conditions underlie these cooperative endeavors. They permit activities that, like trade and travel, are critical to maintaining the fabric of global society. If all goes well these activities are conducted routinely and quietly and may go unnoticed by students of world politics.

Norms do not govern routine interactions only, and clear norms are as important in regulating adversaries' behavior as that of friends. Under the best of conditions adversaries find it difficult to maintain control over events and limit the negative consequences of their interactions. Only if norms inform them about what they can and cannot do is it possible for them to avoid catastrophe. Actor A may initiate an action that it knows will anger B but *only* so much that B will issue a protest. If norms are clear, B, although unhappy with A's action, should be able to recognize that A's objectives are limited. Actor B can then "retaliate" in a manner expected by A that will not trigger an uncontrollable spiral of action and reaction. If norms are murky and if A's initial action not only angers but shocks B and seems to violate the rules of the game, B may feel threatened. Such fear can trigger extreme, even unthinking, responses. The resulting spiral may lead to disaster.

When global norms are clear and are followed, global life is predictable and safe. But when norms decay or change rapidly or major actors persistently violate them, the resulting unpredictability makes global life perilous. In some instances, major wars may result. Indeed, assassination of the archduke in 1914 seemed as contrary to the norms of decency in that era as today's murder, maiming, and kidnapping of innocent civilians and diplomats by terrorists.

Thus, the French Revolution in 1789 that overthrew the monarchy also brought new norms of equality and democracy, which revolutionaries sought to export to others in Europe. The revolutionaries also set out to eliminate all vestiges of Europe's feudal past, dramatically altering laws, property rights, and social customs. In a word, they refused to play by the old rules of the game. Other European rulers saw revolutionary norms as dangerous to their security, and their fears were intensified by the French effort to imbue others with the new ideologies of nationalism and democracy. French actions at home and abroad violated the accepted rules of the time, notably balance-of-power politics and nonintervention in the domestic affairs of sovereign states. At home the king and his family were executed in January 1793, and the reign of terror ensued, featuring "Madame Guillotine," which terrified aristocrats in other countries.[71] Abroad, French armies occupied Belgium and the Rhineland, annexed neighboring territories, and declared war on England and Holland. Even France's way of waging war, with a huge army of conscripted citizens rather than a small force of mercenaries, was terrifyingly new.

[71]Charles Dickens in *A Tale of Two Cities*. (New York: Harper & Brothers, n.d.) wrote: "Above all, one hideous figure as familiar as if it had been before the general gaze from the foundations of the world—the figure of the sharp female called La Guillotine" (p. 289). And Baroness Orczy in *The Elusive Pimpernel* (New York: Buccaneer Books, 1984) depicted "Madame Guillotine" who stood "grim and gaunt, with long thin arms stretched out towards the sky, the last glimmer of waning light striking the triangular knife . . . where it was not rusty with stains of blood" (p. 245).

English philosopher Edmund Burke described the widespread fear and loathing that greeted the French Revolution, which "doubled the licence, of a ferocious dissoluteness in manners, and of an insolent irreligion in opinions and practices," "utterly disgraced the tone of lenient council in the cabinets of princes," "sanctified the dark suspicious maxims of tyrannous distrust," and gave rise to "treasons, robberies, rapes, assassinations, slaughters, and burnings throughout their harassed land." Burke added with disgust that "In the groves of *their* academy, at the end of every vista, you see nothing but gallows," and predicted that "learning will be cast into the mire, and trodden down under the hoofs of a swinish multitude."[72]

The conservative monarchs reacted with alarm to this threat against the old order of things, and Europe remained at war until the final defeat of French Emperor Napoleon Bonaparte in 1815. The conservative victors sought to restore the old rules of the game at the *Congress of Vienna*.[73] They sought to prevent a similar catastrophe by agreeing to restore the balance of power in Europe and, if necessary, in the future intervene in each other's domestic affairs to prevent a revolutionary outburst like that which had engulfed France.[74]

In the 1930s the Nazis challenged the rules of the game in much the same way as had the French Revolution. The outcome too was the same: war. Its effects were dramatic because the leading players — Germany, Great Britain, France, and Japan — were swept aside and replaced by two inexperienced superpowers, the United States and the Soviet Union. All of a sudden the two countries towered over the rest of the world like two Gullivers amid a host of Lilliputians. Following the defeat of Hitler in 1945, the major common interest of U.S. and Soviet leaders disappeared, and they had no norms to guide their behavior toward each other. The superpowers found themselves in confrontation, each with only a vague understanding of the other's intentions. Without shared norms, each tried to impose its norms on the other, and the sequence of moves and countermoves produced surprise, mistrust, and fear.[75] Almost inevitably the summit conferences at Yalta and Potsdam produced misunderstandings because the superpowers found themselves in command of a strange new world, facing new challenges that they understood only dimly. Fortunately, war did not result as they probed the limits of each other's tolerance in the crises that strained their relationship during the following years. In these crises, the two sides began to evolve rules for surviving together in a nuclear world — "basic rules of prudence."[76]

[72]Edmund Burke, *Reflections on the Revolution in France* (Garden City, N.Y.: Doubleday, 1961), pp. 50, 52, 91, 92. Emphasis in original.

[73]The Congress began in September 1814 but was interrupted by Napoleon's escape from exile on the island of Elba. After his final defeat at the Battle of Waterloo, Napoleon was removed to the remote Atlantic island of St. Helena, where he died.

[74]René Albrecht-Carrié, *The Concert of Europe* (New York: Harper & Row, 1968), p. 4. The agreement and the regular conferences among leaders in the years following are called the Concert of Europe.

[75]See Chapter 12, pp. 402–405.

[76]Joseph S. Nye, "Nuclear Learning and U.S.–Soviet Security Regime," *International Organization* 41:3 (Summer 1987), p. 392.

International Regimes

When norms governing actors' interaction on an issue become so systematic, habitual, and rule-like that behavior and outcomes become predictable, an *international regime* comes into existence. The concept denotes a political system defined by an issue that is managed by something which is more legitimate and institutionalized than norms or regularities but which is not a fully fledged government or international organization.[77] Although not constituting a government, regime-based activity is stronger and more durable than "temporary arrangements that change with every shift in power or interests."[78] In sum, an international regime mixes "multilateral systems of rules and procedures"[79] and "norms, rules, and procedures agreed to in order to regulate an issue-area."[80] Typically, the elements of a regime are some combination of treaties, international organizations, bureaucracies of states, and even international law — all of which reflect those norms, rules, and procedures.

Types of Regimes

International regimes have been identified for issues as varied as international food assistance, trade, whaling, ozone depletion, drug trafficking, telecommunications, banking, human rights, and piracy.[81] In these issues egoistic actors have not only learned to cooperate but have come to see their interests as served by binding norms and rules.[82] Regimes have even been identified in security, where one would least expect to find them because actors are unwilling to entrust their survival to others. Nevertheless,

[77]Rules are legitimate if participants regard them as right and proper. Legitimacy anchors rules more firmly than do interests or power alone.

[78]Robert O. Keohane, *After Hegemony: Cooperation and Discord in the World Political Economy* (Princeton: Princeton University Press, 1984), p. 64. Some scholars argue that the concept of international regimes is woolly, hardly distinct from international law and organization. See Susan Strange, "*Cave! hic dragones*: A Critique of Regime Analysis," *International Organization* 36:2 (Spring 1982), pp. 484–486.

[79]Vinod K. Aggarwal, "The Unraveling of the Multi-Fiber Agreement, 1981: An Examination of International Regime Change," *International Organization* 37:4 (Autumn 1983), p. 618.

[80]Ernst B. Haas, "Why Collaborate? Issue-Linkage and International Regimes," *World Politics* 32:3 (April 1980), p. 358.

[81]The literature on specific international regimes has grown huge. For some recent examples, see Peter F. Cowhey, "The International Telecommunications Regime: The Political Roots of Regimes for High Technology," *International Organization* 44:2 (Spring 1990), pp. 169–199; Ethan A. Nadelmann, "Global Prohibition Regimes: The Evolution of Norms in International Society," *International Organization* 44:4 (Autumn 1990), 479–526; Robert H. Bates, Philip Brock, and Jill Tiefenthaler, "Risk and Trade Regimes: Another Exploration," *International Organization* 45:1 (Winter 1991), pp. 1–18; Raymond F. Hopkins, "Reform in the International Food Aid Regime: The Role of Consensual Knowledge," *International Organization* 46:1 (Winter 1992), pp. 225–264.

[82]See Alexander Wendt, "Anarchy Is What States Make of It: The Social Construction of Power Politics," *International Organization* 46:2 (Spring 1992), p. 417.

writing in 1987, one observer defined U.S.–Soviet relations "as a patchwork quilt, or a mosaic of subissues in the security area, some characterized by rules and institutions we would call regimes and others not."[83]

Regimes vary in several ways.[84] For some, norms and rules are binding; others allow actors to opt out under special circumstances; and still others are merely hortatory, not binding at all. Thus, the prohibition against nuclear proliferation is regarded as binding on all who subscribe to the Nuclear Proliferation Treaty. In contrast, the European Community allows individual members to veto actions they regard as contrary to their essential interest. Enforcement regimes are unusually powerful and autonomous. The U.N. Security Council and, increasingly, the Council of the European Economic Community enjoy this relatively rare status. Somewhat weaker are regimes involved in international trade and finance.

Another important distinction is between regimes that can enforce obedience to rules and those which only monitor compliance. As Iraq discovered after invading Kuwait, the U.N. Security Council can enforce its decisions if it elects to do so. But the International Atomic Energy Agency (IAEA) and Amnesty International mostly monitor compliance with international norms and rules in nuclear proliferation and human rights respectively. Still weaker are regimes which can only bring participants together and facilitate cooperation without monitoring or enforcing, or which can only provide information about the content of norms and rules so that actors will know what is expected of them.

Regimes facilitate cooperation among independent actors by compensating for "*institutional deficiencies*,"[85] such as absence of information and a framework of conventional law. Imagine how much easier it would be for prisoner's-dilemma players to cooperate if they could freely communicate their intentions and had some way of penalizing each other for squealing. That is what an effective regime does for the actors participating in it. Without a regime, reciprocity would be less effective with more than two actors because of the difficulty in assigning responsibility when conflict occurs and coordinating sanctions against a defector. Regimes help overcome these difficulties by providing "information about actors' compliance; they facilitate the development and maintenance of reputations; they can be incorporated into actors' rules of thumb for responding to others' actions; and they may even apportion responsibility for decentralized enforcement of rules."[86]

[83]Nye, "Nuclear Learning," p. 376.

[84]For more on these distinctions, see Jack Donnelly, "International Human Rights: A Regime Analysis," *International Organization* 40:3 (Summer 1986), pp. 603–605.

[85]Keohane, *After Hegemony*, p. 85.

[86]Robert Axelrod and Robert O. Keohane, "Achieving Cooperation Under Anarchy: Strategies and Institutions," *World Politics* 38:1 (October 1985), p. 237. For an enlightening case study of how a regime served this purpose in getting banks to cooperate to solve the debt crisis in the Third World, see Charles Lipson, "Bankers' Dilemmas: Private Cooperation in Rescheduling Sovereign Debts," *World Politics* 38:1 (October 1985), pp. 200–225.

hegemon

An international regime with its rules and expectations governs an issue without a government. On issues for which regimes exist, actors are part of a society in the sense used by Hedley Bull, "that they conceive themselves to be bound by a common set of rules in their relations with one another, and share in the working of common institutions."[87] An issue governed by a regime is characterized by clear and consensual norms and regulated by binding rules that, though perhaps not legislated by actors, exist by virtue of actual practice.[88] Robert Keohane writes,

> [R]egimes . . . enhance the likelihood of cooperation by reducing the costs of making transactions that are consistent with the principles of the regime. They create the conditions for orderly multilateral negotiations. . . . They . . . improve the quality of the information that governments receive. . . . [T]hey help to bring governments into continuing interaction with one another, reducing incentives to cheat and enhancing the value of reputation. By establishing legitimate standards of behavior for states to follow and by providing ways to monitor compliance, they create the basis for decentralized enforcement founded on the principle of reciprocity.[89]

In international trade, for example, rules are clear on what individual actors are permitted to do to assist their exporters and protect home industries. Sometimes these rules are violated or tested to their limits. Nevertheless, they are observed surprisingly often by governments, when we consider the intense pressures placed on them by domestic industries and labor. Governments are constantly tempted to cheat for domestic reasons but are discouraged from doing so by factors like the advantages they would surrender by not being participants in the trade regime and probable retaliation by trading partners. Indeed, the regime has rules that stipulate how victims of cheating may retaliate against cheaters, making the costs of cheating clear and, if those costs are high enough, reducing the temptation to do so.

Some argue that international regimes take root because actors are sufficiently rational to recognize a long-term advantage in following rules and significant costs in not doing so. Others argue that regimes are created and survive only in the presence of superior power, a *hegemon* whose interests the regime serves and by whom it can be enforced. Finally, it is suggested that the real key to regime formation lies in hard bargaining among independent actors.[90] Related to the debate about how a regime is created is disagreement about how much structure rules and norms must have for a regime to exist. Some scholars believe a regime exists only when the norms and rules

[87]Hedley Bull, *The Anarchical Society: A Study of Order in World Politics* (New York: Columbia University Press, 1977), p. 13.

[88]Ibid., p. 148.

[89]Keohane, *After Hegemony*, pp. 244–245.

[90]See Oran R. Young, "The Politics of International Regime Formation: Managing Natural Resources and the Environment," *International Organization* 43:3 (Summer 1989), pp. 349–375.

that constitute it are incorporated in formal international organizations or legal documents such as treaties. In this view, a regime requires formal consent by those who are part of it, and power has more to do in creating it than rationality. Other scholars claim that a regime is virtually identical with any system, so that "a regime exists in every substantive issue-area where there is discernibly patterned behavior."[91] In this perspective, a regime requires no formal arrangements or agreements; custom and habit are sufficient. For those who hold this view, the rational pursuit of interest is sufficient to explain why actors form and maintain regimes; power has a smaller role.

In all likelihood, power, rationality, and bargaining all take part in creating and maintaining a regime. Power is involved because some actor or actors must provide leadership. Nevertheless, power, in the sense that one or a few actors is able to enforce obedience to the regime's norms, is probably not enough to maintain it in the long run unless it is perceived to serve common interests and unless its demise would produce significant costs. Finally, bargaining is essential if rules are to be sufficiently clear and consensual for the regime to endure and adapt to changing conditions.

This debate matters because some of the most critical regimes in global politics, especially those of an economic variety, were created with U.S. assistance immediately after World War II.[92] At that moment, the United States sat alone atop the global hierarchy, and was able to create and maintain the rules and norms it wished. Under U.S. leadership, agencies like the International Monetary Fund and the World Bank were created, and a liberal international economic order based on free trade was constructed. An international system dominated by one actor is called *hegemonic* — a system "in which one state is able and willing to determine and maintain the essential rules by which relations among states are governed. The hegemonical state not only can abrogate existing rules or prevent the adoption of rules that it opposes but can also play the dominant role in constructing new rules."[93]

In recent decades, U.S. hegemony has receded. What does this retreat mean for the future of regimes? If they require powerful hegemons to endure, then the complex norms that provide cooperation on such issues as international trade, nuclear proliferation, and pollution may decline, and the world will be a more dangerous place. By contrast, if hegemonic leadership is unnecessary, then we can expect arrangements that are useful to continue to flourish and new regimes to come into existence. The world is grappling with a host of complex problems, ranging from trade negotiations under the General Agreement on Tariffs and Trade (GATT) to whaling quotas that will test these divergent views. Only time will tell which perspective is correct.

---

[91]Donald J. Puchala and Raymond F. Hopkins, "International Regimes: Lessons from Inductive Analysis," *International Organization* 36:2 (Spring 1982), p. 247.

[92]See Chapter 10, pp. 325–327.

[93]C. Fred Bergsten, Robert O. Keohane, and Joseph S. Nye, "International Economics and International Politics: A Framework for Analysis," *International Organization* 29:1 (Winter 1975), p. 14.

Nuclear Proliferation and the Environment

A brief discussion of two regimes — one that has existed for some time and another only now forming — illustrates how they produce cooperation in the face of common global problems. An international regime to limit the spread of nuclear weapons (*horizontal nuclear proliferation*) has evolved slowly in the past thirty years. The first step involved an agreement to outlaw atmospheric testing of nuclear weapons (the Limited Test Ban Treaty). This limitation restricted the number of states permitted to test weapons and therefore develop their own. The next step involved creating several *nuclear-free regions* or *zones* where nuclear weapons could not be deployed. Nuclear weapons were prohibited in the Antarctic (the Antarctic Treaty of 1959), Latin America (the Latin American Nuclear Free Zone Treaty of 1967), outer space (the Outer Space Treaty of 1967), and the seabed (Seabed Arms Control Treaty of 1971). The most important step in creating a regime was a treaty prohibiting transfer of nuclear-weapons technology by the nuclear haves to states that did not have nuclear weapons and calling for international inspection of peaceful nuclear facilities to ensure that they were not being used surreptitiously to produce nuclear weapons (the Nuclear Non-Proliferation Treaty of 1968). Finally, several understandings, agreements, and prohibitions have been placed on transferring nuclear-energy technology and nuclear fuels among states.

Collectively, these agreements and understandings have established a broad global norm against nuclear proliferation. Although agreements are voluntary, the regime has largely worked. Only one state (India) has publicly joined the *nuclear club* since the regime was established. Nevertheless, it is not clear whether the regime is strong enough to prevent nuclear competition between such adversaries as India and Pakistan or Israel and its Arab adversaries. That North Korea and Iraq have been able to divert nuclear fuel from peaceful purposes to develop nuclear weapons suggests that the inspection system operated by the International Atomic Energy Agency (IAEA) is far from foolproof, and North Korea's defiance of the IAEA in 1993 was a challenge to the future of the regime.

More recently, a regime has been begun to protect and promote global ecology. The U.N. Conference on the Environment and Development (UNCED), held in Rio de Janeiro, Brazil, in June 1992, was a major step toward creating such a regime.[94] The results of the conference were encouraging, though hardly decisive. Two conventions were signed, and the conferees published three declarations. However, the norms they include may signal the beginning of an important international regime.[95]

The first agreement was a Declaration on Environment and Development stating twenty-seven principles that link efforts to protect the environment with the promotion of global economic development. The declaration recognizes that Third World countries must bear a special burden in protecting their fragile ecosystems while developing

[94]See Chapter 15, p. 532.

[95]The summary of the Rio Summit Accords is from "Accords for Nature's Sake," *The New York Times*, June 15, 1992, p. A5.

economically. A second declaration, entitled Agenda 21, was even broader, articulating a commitment to clean up the environment and leave it in better condition in the coming century. A third declaration was more specific and dealt with global principles to protect forests worldwide. It calls upon countries to evaluate the effect of economic development on forests and to take action to protect that valuable resource for the future. Although these declarations are nonbinding, they establish norms and expectations toward which countries must strive and which, if flagrantly violated, will elicit widespread disapproval.

The two conventions, a biodiversity treaty and a global warming treaty, entail more binding commitments for signatories, but they also leave room for extension and expansion in the future. The biodiversity treaty calls for assembling a world inventory of plants and animals and for making plans to protect endangered species. Under the agreement, the signatories must share "research, profits, and technology with nations whose genetic resources they use," a clause that the Bush administration invoked to explain America's refusal to sign the treaty.[96] The Clinton administration reversed this stand. The global-warming treaty recommends, but does not explicitly require, curbing the various "greenhouse gases" — carbon dioxide, methane, and chlorofluorocarbons. Again, not all countries signed the treaty or agreed on the target dates for reducing these gases.

Conclusion

The claim that global politics is anarchic, implying unpredictability and conflict, is only half accurate. Anarchy and cooperation are not exclusive properties. Cooperation requires only a mixture of common and divergent interests in which such factors as reciprocity and bargaining help actors identify what they have in common and overcome that which separates them. Nor does anarchy mean absence of coordination and organization.[97] Although global politics lacks a central authority that can monopolize coercion and coordinate behavior, much of what goes on in the global arena reflects cooperation and coordination. Large areas of global interaction are so routinized and function so smoothly that they are regarded as humdrum and make the front pages or the evening news only when something goes wrong.

Much of global politics is governed by informal norms defining what is proper and structuring stable expectations. Such expectations are crucial to cooperation and trust. When norms decay or are absent, global politics enters periods of peril and often violence. When norms and rules are legitimate and institutionalized, they may produce international regimes that can serve the interests of participants and prevent costly

[96]The Bush administration feared that the clause would undermine the exclusive patents held by U.S. pharmaceutical companies.
[97]Axelrod and Keohane, "Achieving Cooperation," p. 226.

breakdowns of trust. Where regimes prosper, force is dysfunctional and is rarely necessary (unless internationally sponsored). For this reason we explore in Chapter 7 the changing role of force in global politics. Force is the hallmark of anarchy and of self-help, and negates community and trust.

Key Terms

conflict

cooperation

anarchy

self-help

state of nature

security dilemma

game theory

maximin strategy

prisoner's dilemma game

enforcement mechanism

double-defection box

verification

worst-case analysis

intelligence failures

chicken game

bargaining reputation

bluffing

Versailles Treaty

Manchukuo

Pearl Harbor

reciprocity

Tripartite Pact

history of rewarding cooperation

concern about the future

learning

stag-hare parable

end-of-the-world game

historical experience

special relationship

analogies from the past

roles

salami tactics

apparatchik

dual-track decision

zero option

graduated reduction in tension

peace race

global norms

rules of the game

international regime

institutional deficiencies

hegemon

hegemonic system

horizontal nuclear proliferation

nuclear-free zones

nuclear club

preventive attack

preemptive attack

Nuremberg Trials

Congress of Vienna

CHAPTER SEVEN

Force in Global Politics:
A Changing Role

Although cooperation is more prevalent in global politics than many acknowledge, the study of conflict, especially war, has occupied students of global politics for centuries. This is a consequence of the widespread belief that violence will characterize a system lacking central authority. In this view, resort to force is to be regretted but should be expected as a consequence of the right of self-help. Because independent actors can depend on no one but themselves for survival, they must be armed and alert. Niccolò Machiavelli captured this perspective best: "The main foundations of every state . . . are good laws and good arms."[1]

> A prince, therefore, should have no other object or thought, nor acquire skill in anything, except war, its organization, and its discipline. The art of war is all that is expected of a ruler. . . . The first way to lose your state is to neglect the art of war; the first way to win a state is to be skilled in the art of war.[2]

Even political economist Adam Smith had to acknowledge that, "The one thing more important than opulence is defense."[3]

In the next two chapters we focus on force in global politics, how its use has changed, and its influence on the human condition. In this chapter we examine the use of force before nuclear weapons were introduced. We describe changes in the frequency and intensity of war, factors that contribute to outbreak of war, how technology affects the frequency and conduct of war, and some of the consequences of preparation for

---

[1]Niccolò Machiavelli, *The Prince*, trans. by George Bull (Baltimore, Md.: Penguin Books, 1961), ch. XII, p. 77.

[2]Ibid., ch. XIV, p. 87.

[3]Cited in Martin van Creveld, *Technology and War: From 2000 B.C. to the Present* (New York: Free Press, 1989), p. v.

defense on society. In Chapter 8, we address how warfare has changed with nuclear weapons and how the end of the Cold War may again alter the role of war. Let us begin by examining whether there have been changes in the number and magnitude of wars and by sampling several prominent explanations for the outbreak of war.

The Nature of War

Rarely has the world been free of *war* — organized violence between different societies — though the sort of global conflict that shatters a political order and remakes world politics has, thankfully, been infrequent. Examples of such global conflagrations over the past four centuries include the Thirty Years' War (1618–1648), the Wars of the French Revolution and Napoleon (1792–1815), World War I (1914–1918), and World War II (1939–1945). Despite the ideological competition that engulfed the world during the Cold War, we have been spared a similar cataclysm since, but past decades have not been peaceful or bloodless. Although recent years have witnessed fewer conventional interstate wars, there have been many bloody civil and anti-colonial conflicts. The Persian Gulf War, the violent collapse of Yugoslavia, and ethnic strife in the former U.S.S.R. during the early 1990s suggest that war is not a thing of the past.

Frequency of War: The Historical Record

To put the current period in perspective, we review briefly the frequency and magnitude of wars in recent centuries. Perhaps the best-known compilation of war-related data was developed by the *Correlates of War (COW) Project*, directed by J. David Singer at the University of Michigan. Singer and historian Melvin Small collected and coded data on *civil* and *interstate wars* in global politics from 1816 to 1980. These data allow some generalizations about the degree of change in war during this period.

Table 7.1 summarizes the number of wars during seven historical eras. The first — 1816–1849 — demarcates the era after the Congress of Vienna and prior to the period of revolutionary change that began in 1848. The second — 1850–1870 — was a period of flux in world affairs during which the Italian and German states were formed. The third — 1871–1890 — saw the ascendancy of Bismarck's Germany in global politics. The fourth — 1891–1914 — witnessed a hardening of alliance systems in Europe, culminating in World War I. The fifth period — 1919–1940 — witnessed the ascent of Hitler and Mussolini, and the final period — 1966–1980 — was the height of the Cold War.[4]

Although Table 7.1 seems to suggest a slight decline in wars, Singer and Small report that "no trend, either upward or downward, is evident. Whether concentrating upon frequencies, magnitudes, severities, or intensities, we do not find appreciably more

[4]These breakpoints are based on Melvin Small and J. David Singer, "Conflict in the International System, 1816–1977: Historical Trends and Policy Futures," in Charles W. Kegley, Jr., and Patrick J. McGowan, eds., *Challenges to America: United States Foreign Policy in the 1980s* (Beverly Hills: Sage Publications, 1979), pp. 94–95.

T ABLE 7.1

Frequency of International Wars

Period	Number of years	Number of wars
1816–1849	34	21
1850–1870	21	20
1871–1890	20	12
1891–1914	24	20
1917–1940	24	16
1945–1965	22	14
1966–1980	16	16

SOURCE: The number of wars in each period is calculated from Melvin Small and J. David Singer, "Patterns in International Warfare, 1816–1980," in Small and Singer, eds., *International War: An Anthology* (Chicago: Dorsey Press, 1989), Table 1, pp. 28–30.

or less war in any of the sub-epochs covered."[5] Although more people died from wars in the twentieth century than in the nineteenth, in a relative sense—considering population growth—the apparently greater severity of warfare for the current period disappears. What about civil wars during the same period? Again, Singer and Small provide systematic evidence, and, as Table 7.2 shows, they conclude that civil wars have neither increased nor decreased significantly during the period. Although the years after 1945 saw a growing number of civil wars, especially as part of decolonization, their absolute growth is not as great as it appears because more states were entering global politics and the opportunity for such civil unrest was greater.[6]

By extending our time horizon beyond the two centuries that Singer and Small consider, however, we reach a different conclusion. Over five centuries, the frequency of war has declined. And, if we count only wars involving great powers, the decline is even more pronounced. "The number of Great Power wars," declares Jack Levy, "declined continuously from the sixteenth to the nineteenth centuries, with a very slight increase in the twentieth century." In fact, the number of such wars "has been only one-fourth as frequent in the twentieth century as in the sixteenth century."[7] According to Levy's analysis, the sixteenth and seventeenth centuries were the most warlike, the eighteenth the least, and the nineteen and twentieth centuries roughly the same in

[5]Melvin Small and J. David Singer, "Patterns in International Warfare, 1816–1980," in Small and Singer, eds., *International War: An Anthology* (Chicago: Dorsey Press, 1989), p. 31.

[6]Small and Singer, "Conflict in the International System," pp. 100–101.

[7]Jack S. Levy, *War in the Modern Great Power System, 1495–1975* (Lexington: University Press of Kentucky, 1983), p. 117.

TABLE 7.2

Frequency of Civil Wars, 1816–1977

Period	Number of years	Number of wars
1816–1849	34	12
1850–1870	21	15
1871–1890	20	6
1891–1914	24	17
1919–1939	21	11
1946–1965	20	26
1966–1977	12	11

SOURCE: From Table 4 in Melvin Small and J. David Singer, "Conflict in the International System, 1816–1977: Historical Trends and Policy Futures," in Charles W. Kegley, Jr. and Patrick J. McGowan, *Challenges to America: United States Foreign Policy in the 1980s*. Copyright © 1979 by Sage Publications. Used with permission.

frequency of wars.[8] Although these data suggest a decline in the frequency of war, their severity (measured by war deaths) has remained about the same. Great-power wars, though less frequent, have actually become more severe. In sum, Levy's longitudinal analysis concludes that the frequency of war has declined somewhat but that the human costs of war have remained much the same or even increased in some instances.

War Since 1945

A closer look at the period since World War II provides additional clues about changing warfare. Between 1945 and 1990, 140 wars took 25 million lives.[9] Unlike previous eras, war since 1945 has been almost absent from developed regions like Europe and North America but has become endemic in the Third World. "[W]ar today (and certainly deaths related to war)," one observer writes, "is a phenomenon generally limited to the non-European (non-white) peoples of this planet."[10] As Table 7.3 shows, Asia has been

[8]Ibid., pp. 116, 139–140.

[9]Michael J. Sullivan III, *Measuring Global Values: The Ranking of 162 Countries* (New York: Greenwood Press, 1991), p. 27. Different sources provide different data depending on their definition of war. Sullivan (p. 25) observes: "It is difficult to identify clearly examples of belligerent states in this era of undeclared wars, revolutions without borders, military aid for probes by proxies, and other blurred distinctions between domestic and international conflict."

[10]Ibid. The outbreak of hostilities in the former Yugoslavia defies this generalization.

T ABLE 7.3

Wars Since 1945

Zone[a]	Wars	Interstate	Colonial	Civil	Deaths
Europe	5	3	0	2	0.2 million
Islamic	37	10	4	23	5.3 million
Africa	26	2	7	17	4.5 million
Asia	46	14	5	27	17.0 million
Latin America	27	6	0	21	0.6 million
Totals	141	35	16	90	27.6 million

[a]The five zones, taken from Sullivan, correspond to continental divisions with the exception of "Islamic," which includes the Arab Middle East (including Israel and Cyprus), northern Africa (including Chad, Sudan, Djibouti, and Somalia), and west Asia (including Iran, Afghanistan, and Pakistan).

SOURCE: From *Measuring Global Values* by Michael J. Sullivan III, pp. 35–38, Greenwood Press, an imprint of Greenwood Publishing Group, Inc., Westport, CT. Reprinted with permission.

the bloodiest region, including major wars in Korea and Vietnam. The Middle East, North Africa, and Muslim regions in South Asia have been almost as war-prone, with major conflicts involving the Arab states, Pakistan, and Afghanistan.

Although the number of interstate wars is declining, civil strife is growing.[11] They are also becoming bloodier as citizens turn against each other modern arms that were originally acquired to fight other armies. In 1992 and 1993 the civil war in the former Yugoslavia epitomized the destructiveness of modern weaponry in urban settings by devastating cities like Sarajevo, Mostar, and Dubrovnik. Cities such as Mogadishu in Somalia and Beirut in Lebanon were also all but leveled by civil war. Civil war has always been less restrained than interstate war. *International law*, embodied in instruments like the *Geneva Conventions*, applies only to interstate wars and places no limits on combatants in civil wars. Thus, after crushing the rebellion against the throne led by the Stuart pretender "Bonnie Prince Charlie" in 1745–1746, the English commander gave safe conduct home to troops who had been dispatched by King Louis of France but ordered execution for the native Scottish "rebels."

Atrocities of the sort committed in civil wars in Mozambique, Yugoslavia, Lebanon, Ethiopia, and Iraq would be unthinkable in wars between most states. Such episodes as the Nigerian civil war between 1967 and 1970 and the civil war in Cambodia between

[11]With the European colonial empires gone, colonial wars—frequent between 1945 and 1975—have ceased. A few colonial hotspots still remain, including East Timor's effort to liberate itself from Indonesia.

1975 and 1978 (as portrayed in the movie *Killing Fields*) are among the most savage conflicts since 1945. The first of these episodes is estimated to have cost 2 million lives and the second 1 to 1.5 million (in a population of 8 million).[12]

Causes of War

For social scientists, explaining why these wars occur is as elusive as medical researchers searching for a cure for cancer. In fact, there is probably more than one cause, and their effect is likely to vary depending on such factors as type of war, place, and time. In other words, no one explanation is likely to prove adequate for all wars. Recognizing that war has multiple causes, our review is not intended to be exhaustive. Rather, the aim is to give readers the flavor of the varied theorizing that goes on in global politics about this issue. For the sake of clarity, we organize these analyses into three clusters—those emphasizing the behavior of individuals, those dealing with societies and governments, and those focusing on the global system as a whole.[13] In practice, insights from all three are probably necessary to understand war.

Individuals and Aggression

The contention that the causes of war must be sought in individuals is not new. Political theorists including Hobbes long ago identified *human nature* as the source of violence in human affairs, and some religions maintain that "man's fallen nature," along with original sin, also contributes. More recently, biologists and psychologists have focused on aggressive behavior. The psychologist Sigmund Freud, in a pessimistic letter to Albert Einstein in 1932, posited a *thanatos* or *death instinct*:

> We assume that human instincts are of two kinds: those that conserve and unify . . . and . . . the instincts to destroy and kill. . . . [T]his latter instinct functions in every living being, striving to work its ruin and reduce life to its primal state of inert matter. Indeed it might well be called the "death instinct."[14]

Others have focused on the relationship between *aggression* and *frustration*. Aggressive behavior, one team of psychologists argues, "always presupposes the existence of frustration and . . . the existence of frustration always leads to some form of

[12]Sullivan, *Measuring Global Values*, pp. 36, 37.

[13]This roughly corresponds to the three "images" Kenneth N. Waltz employs in *Man, the State and War* (New York: Columbia University Press, 1959).

[14]Sigmund Freud, "Why War?" in Leon Bramson and George W. Goethals, eds., *War*, rev. ed. (New York: Basic Books, 1968), pp. 76, 77. Other early psychologists including William James and William McDougall thought that human instinct lay behind aggressive behavior.

aggression."[15] Some theorists have sought to link frustration and aggression to forms of behavior. A number of studies suggest that the aggression produced by frustration may be "displaced" onto innocent victims or *scapegoats*, such as minorities or foreigners.[16] Much of this thinking seems remote from war but, in fact, is not. Soldiers can be encouraged by war propaganda to displace aggressive feelings onto an enemy who is depersonalized, and they may not hesitate to commit acts in wartime that they would regard as repugnant in peacetime. Thus, Sergeant Alvin C. York, the most decorated American soldier in World War I, had been a pacifist as a civilian.

Most people do not question authority and are willing to obey orders (*the defense of superior orders* offered by Nazis accused of war crimes committed during World War II). Experiments conducted by Stanley Milgram to find out whether individuals would obey orders requiring them to inflict pain revealed that most were prepared to carry out superiors' orders. Although they varied, depending on such factors as proximity of authority and victim, the individuals who were tested routinely gave electric shocks to victims when ordered to do so. This result disappoints those who believe "it can't happen here" because the United States is a democracy in which individual liberties have legal protection. Milgram says,

> With numbing regularity good people were seen to knuckle under the demands of authority. . . . If in this study an anonymous experimenter could successfully command adults to subdue a fifty-year-old man, and force on him painful electric shocks against his protests, one can only wonder what government, with its vastly greater authority and prestige, can command of its subjects.[17]

Still others are convinced that aggression, whether of leaders or followers, is related to gender. Most societies have been controlled by males, and males are typically more aggressive than females. The roots of this difference may lie in early conditioning or in brain and hormonal factors. Dr. Helen Caldicott sums up this perspective:

> Men and women are psychologically and physiologically different . . . Typically . . . men . . . are always sure of themselves . . . above all, they are always tough and strong. . . . A typical woman . . . innately understands the basic principles of conflict resolution. . . . Women are nurturers. Their bodies are built anatomically and physiologically to nurture life. . . . [M]ost women care deeply about the preservation

---

[15]John Dollard, Leonard W. Doob, Neal E. Miller, et. al., *Frustration and Aggression* (New Haven: Yale University Press, 1939), p. 1.

[16]See Bernard Berelson and Gary A. Steiner, *Human Behavior: An Inventory of Scientific Findings* (New York: Harcourt Brace Jovanovich, 1964), pp. 267–269. The authors describe an earlier investigation that found that lynchings in the American South increased when the price of cotton declined.

[17]Cited in Roy L. Prosterman, *Surviving to 3000: An Introduction to the Study of Lethal Conflict* (Belmont, Calif.: Duxbury Press, 1972), p. 101. Military forces all over the world use similar methods to ensure obedience to authority to eliminate individualism—drills, uniforms, ranks, and so on.

of life. . . . I am sure that some aggressive behavior in men is conditioned, but some must also be hormonally controlled.[18]

Perhaps we should look less at "followers" than at those who give orders—"leaders." After all, politics involves struggles for status, and those who succeed may be more aggressive than those who do not. In recent years, greater use has been made of individual and social psychology to understand political elites.[19] Using Freudian insights, *psychobiographies* have been written delineating world leaders' unique personality attributes. A psychobiography of President Woodrow Wilson concludes that he was unwilling to compromise with political adversaries because of his childhood competition with his father. As a child, the authors argue, Wilson had been forced to repress his rebelliousness; consequently, as an adult, he "could brook no interference. . . . He bristled at the slightest challenge to his authority."[20]

Much research on leaders and their relationship to war has focused on impediments to rationality. Scholars have identified two sources of perceptual distortion that reduce capacity for rational behavior—*cognitive* and *affective causes.* Cognitive analysis focuses on the way in which leaders obtain and process information, and affective analysis emphasizes emotional factors like hostility in decisions.[21] Among scholars seeking the sources of cognitive distortion, some have focused on *ethnocentrism*—belief that one's own group is superior—as a factor behind misunderstanding.[22] Others emphasize *cognitive consistency*—the balance between feelings about and attitudes toward a phenomenon and the information that is being received about that phenomenon. It appears that psychological discomfort ensues when the facts seem to deny the validity of those feelings and that decision-makers may then skew the facts to make them compatible with affect. As Robert Jervis writes, "Evidence is being ignored, misremembered, or twisted to preserve old ideas."[23]

Although many observers believe that leaders' personality attributes influence the outbreak of war, little systematic research has been conducted on these factors. Psychologist Margaret G. Hermann has conducted research on forty-five leaders, including Charles de Gaulle of France, Ferdinand Marcos of the Philippines, Fidel Castro

[18]Helen Caldicott, *Missile Envy: The Arms Race and Nuclear War* (New York: Bantam Books, 1985), pp. 235–237.

[19]See Robert Mandel, "Psychological Approaches to International Relations," in Margaret G. Hermann, ed., *Political Psychology* (San Francisco: Jossey-Bass, 1986), pp. 251–278; and Charles A. Powell, James W. Dyson, and Helen E. Purkitt, "Opening the 'Black Box': Cognitive Processing and Optimal Choice in Foreign Policy Decision Making," in Charles F. Hermann, Charles W. Kegley, Jr., and James N. Rosenau, eds., *New Directions in the Study of Foreign Policy* (Boston: Allen & Unwin, 1987), pp. 203–220.

[20]Alexander George and Juliette George, *Woodrow Wilson and Colonel House* (New York: Day, 1956), p. 11.

[21]Mandel, "Psychological Approaches," p. 253.

[22]See, for example, Albert F. Eldridge, *Images of Conflict* (New York: St. Martin's Press, 1979), pp. 41–45.

[23]Robert Jervis, *Perception and Misperception in International Politics* (Princeton: Princeton University Press, 1976), p. 154.

of Cuba, and Chou En-Lai of China. Her results suggest that individuals can be divided into two political orientations and that each has a tendency to act in a particular way. Thus, "aggressive leaders are high in need for power, low in conceptual complexity, distrustful of others, nationalistic, and likely to believe that they have some control over the events in which they are involved. In contrast, . . . conciliatory leaders are high in the need for affiliation, high in conceptual complexity, trusting in others, low in nationalism, and likely to exhibit little belief in their own ability to control the event in which they are involved."[24] Personality traits of leaders, then, influence actions of states and ultimately questions of war and peace.

In contrast to the work of Hermann, much effort has been spent applying the assumption of *individual rationality* to decisions to initiate war. Perhaps the leading work was done by political scientist Bruce Bueno de Mesquita with his *"expected-utility" theory* of war. "That theory," the author writes, "is predicated on the belief that national leaders behave as if they are rational expected-utility maximizers. The broadest — and seemingly an obvious — generalization that emerges from the theory is the expectation that wars . . . will be initiated only when the initiator believes the war will yield positive expected utility."[25] Bueno de Mesquita and others have marshaled much evidence supporting this theory. In their view, war results less from irrational or nonrational factors than from rational decisions by policy-makers.

Societies, Governments, and War

Aggressive behavior and war occur more frequently in some cultures than in others, leading some to suspect that human nature and individual psychology are not the whole story. Little evidence appears of organized violence among prehistoric hunter-gatherers. Warfare may be a relatively recent phenomenon, dating from about 6500 B.C. in communities of herdsmen who found that "violent seizure of someone else's animals or pasture grounds was the easiest and speediest way to wealth and might be the only means of survival in a year of scant vegetation."[26]

Indeed, warfare may still not exist in some cultures. Anthropologist Margaret Mead describes societies that apparently neither know war nor have language to describe it: "warfare is an invention like any other of the inventions in terms of which we order our lives, such as writing, marriage, cooking our food instead of eating it raw, trial by jury, or burial of the dead . . . ." She continues: "[T]here are people even today who have no warfare. Of these the Eskimos are perhaps the most conspicuous examples, but the Lepchas of Sikkim . . . are as good. Neither of these peoples understands war. . . ."[27]

[24]Margaret G. Hermann, "Explaining Foreign Policy Behavior Using the Personal Characteristics of Political Leaders," *International Studies Quarterly* 24:1 (March 1980), p. 8. Hermann's research reveals links between these personality attributes and different types of foreign-policy behavior.

[25]Bruce Bueno de Mesquita, *The War Trap* (New Haven: Yale University Press, 1981), p. 127.

[26]William H. McNeill, *The Rise of the West* (Chicago: University of Chicago Press, 1963), p. 28.

[27]Cited in Prosterman, *Surviving to 3000*, p. 149.

Why should some societies be prone to war and others not? One answer was provided by Marxists who believe that acquisitive capitalist societies are inherently more violent than socialist ones. Karl Marx (1818–1883) in his theory of *class struggle* between the proletariat and bourgeoisie had little to say directly about global politics, but he did predict revolutions that would sweep away capitalist society itself. It was left to others to explain the link between this struggle and global politics. How was it that, despite Marx's predictions of spontaneous world revolution, the late nineteenth century proved to be an era of political stability in the developed capitalist states of Europe and North America in which Marx had expected the fires of revolution to burn first? An English economist, John A. Hobson (1858–1940), sought the answer in the growth of European and American *imperialism* in the Third World. [28] Hobson argued that a small wealthy minority and a large impoverished majority created a situation in which capitalist economies produced more than citizens could afford to consume. To deal with the *crisis of overproduction*, capitalists, Hobson suggested, invested overseas (where overproduction at home could be absorbed). Imperialism and wars of imperialism were the result.

Hobson's work influenced Vladimir Ilyich Lenin. Leader of the 1917 Bolshevik Revolution, Lenin declared that the world revolution had been delayed by imperialism, which allowed capitalists in advanced societies to exploit poor societies and provided them with resources to "buy off" workers at home with an improved standard of living and vicarious national glory. Imperialism was "the highest stage of capitalism,"[29] the result of the merger of banking and industrial monopolies and their quest overseas for raw materials and markets for surplus production. War was a result of clashes between expanding imperialists seeking exclusive control over overseas markets, cheap labor, and sources of raw materials. Only eliminating capitalism, Lenin contended, would end war.

Some theorists claim that type of government is the key to explaining war. Liberals believe that democracies with limited governments are less likely to go to war than authoritarian governments because the people, not the rulers, have to pay the price for conflicts. By contrast, authoritarian rulers can benefit from war, and not have to fear personal risk or hardship. Kenneth Waltz writes, "The transitory interests of royal houses may be advanced in war; the real interests of all peoples are furthered by peace. Most men suffer because some men are in positions that permit them to indulge their kingly ambitions."[30] Thus, Woodrow Wilson believed that peace could be secured only if governments were democratically elected.[31]

[28]John A. Hobson, *Imperialism: A Study* (Ann Arbor: University of Michigan Press, 1965).

[29]V. I. Lenin, "Imperialism, the Highest Stage of Capitalism," in Robert C. Tucker, ed., *The Lenin Anthology* (New York: W. W. Norton, 1975), pp. 204–274.

[30]Kenneth N. Waltz, *Man, the State and War: A Theoretical Analysis*, p. 98. The most influential liberal thinkers were the political philosophers Immanuel Kant and John Stuart Mill and the political economist Adam Smith.

[31]Empirical studies of this claim yield mixed results. See, for example, Steve Chan, "Mirror,

Finally, some scholars believe differences in propensity to war are related to conflict *within* societies. It is widely believed that domestic unity increases during external crises and that leaders sometimes provoke external tension to increase their popularity at home. Stalin, for example, sought to rally support at home by pointing to "*capitalist encirclement*" of the U.S.S.R. Typical of this perspective is Richard Rosecrance's claim of "a correlation between international instability and the domestic insecurity of elites."[32]

Systemic Theories of War

The power-politics tradition has mainly focused on the overall system in which actors behave as the principal source of war in global politics.[33] From this perspective, war is a property of interaction among actors, and the characteristics of individuals or groups are less important. That states are belligerent does not necessarily produce war; indeed, a balance of power or nuclear balance may prevent war in a system dominated by belligerent actors. By contrast, war may ensue even where none of the actors wishes it to happen. In this tradition, then, it is believed that the *whole* (the system) is greater than the sum of its *parts* (the actors). War may or may not result regardless of the characteristics of individuals or societies.[34]

As we have seen, the realist tradition considers absence of central authority and distribution of power as primary structural sources of war. Kenneth Waltz declares, "wars occur because there is nothing to prevent them," and, though this condition may suggest a need for world government, he, like other realists, dismisses this thought as impractical—"unassailable in logic" but "unattainable in practice."[35] Considerable research has been done on how distribution of power alters the probability of war. Does a system in which power is equally distributed produce more or less war than a system in which power is unequally distributed? One view is that as the global system moves toward

Mirror on the Wall . . . Are Freer Countries More Pacific," *Journal of Conflict Resolution* 28:4 (December 1983), pp. 617–648; Rudolph J. Rummel, "Libertarianism and International Violence," *Journal of Conflict Resolution* 27:1 (March 1982), pp. 27–71; and Erich Weede, "Democracy and War Involvement," *Journal of Conflict Resolution*, 28:4 (December 1983), pp. 649–664.

[32]Richard N. Rosecrance, *Action and Reaction in World Politics: International Systems in Perspective* (Boston: Little, Brown, 1963), p. 304. For a contrasting view, see Geoffrey Blainey, *The Causes of War*, 3rd ed. (New York: Free Press, 1988), pp. 71–86. The most ambitious effort to test the relationship between domestic instability and interstate conflict is the Dimensionality of Nations (DON) project. Its results have been inconclusive. See R. J. Rummel, *The Dimensions of Nations* (Beverly Hills, Calif.: Sage, 1972), and Rummel, *Field Theory Evolving* (Beverly Hills, Calif.: Sage, 1977).

[33]An excellent summary of alternate systemic approaches is in John A. Vasquez, "The Steps to War: Toward a Scientific Explanation of Correlates of War Findings," *World Politics* 40:1 (October 1987), pp. 108–145.

[34]This perspective is similar to the view of classical economists like Adam Smith that, under free-market conditions, an "invisible hand" transforms individuals' acquisitive behavior into a productive and benevolent economic system.

[35]Waltz, *Man, the State, and War*, pp. 232, 238.

equality, the likelihood of war is reduced.[36] The principal reason is that relative equality increases uncertainty about the outcome of war and that such uncertainty produces caution in the minds of political actors. Would the United States have initiated a war to free Kuwait in 1991 if U.S. leaders believed they had a 50–50 chance of losing the war?

Others believe *power preponderance* or *hegemony* ensure peace and that movement toward equality of power is dangerous. In a hegemonic system, the hegemon fears no one and has no reason to go to war, and the weak powers do not dare resort to war because of the certainty that they will face defeat. As a system moves toward equal distribution of power, however, the former hegemon grows more fearful for its security, and the weak powers grow more daring. The likelihood of war is thus enhanced.[37]

These arguments have been refined by introducing system *polarity* — the number of power centers in the system — as a major factor in producing war.[38] Waltz has consistently argued that *bipolarity* reduces the probability of war. Two superpowers "supreme in their power have to use force less often" and are "able both to moderate each other's use of violence and to absorb possibly destabilizing changes that emanate from uses of violence that they do not or cannot control."[39] An opposite argument was made by Karl W. Deutsch and J. David Singer, who claimed that, as predicted by theories of *political pluralism*, a system of many power centers — *multipolarity* — would produce crosscutting cleavages and loyalties that would attenuate any conflict. Adversaries in one issue might look to one another for support in another, and their attention would be divided among a number of participants rather than focused on one potential enemy.[40] Efforts to test these conflicting propositions have been inconclusive, and it is difficult to conclude that "decision-makers act as if they were significantly constrained by variations in the structural attributes. . . . "[41]

[36] A summary of the following two arguments is in Bruce Bueno de Mesquita and David Lalman, "Empirical Support for Systemic and Dyadic Explanations of International Conflict," *World Politics* 41:1 (October 1988), especially pp. 3–4.

[37] The preponderance argument is in A. F. K. Organski, *World Politics* (New York: Knopf, 1968). For a more recent exposition of this argument, see A. F. K. Organski and Jacek Kugler, *The War Ledger* (Chicago: University of Chicago Press, 1980).

[38] Polarity is a vague concept. Some scholars use it to mean the number of blocs or alliances in a system and for others it is synonymous with distribution of power.

[39] Kenneth N. Waltz, "International Structure, National Force, and the Balance of World Power," *Journal of International Affairs* 21:2 (1967), pp. 223, 220.

[40] Karl W. Deutsch and J. David Singer, "Multipolar Power Systems and International Stability," in James N. Rosenau, ed., *International Politics and Foreign Policy*, rev. ed. (New York: Free Press, 1969), pp. 315–324. Richard N. Rosecrance criticized both Waltz and Deutsch/Singer and argued that a system with features from both ("bimultipolarity") would be the safest. Rosecrance, "Bipolarity, Multipolarity, and the Future," in ibid, pp. 325–335.

[41] De Mesquita and Lalman, "Empirical Support," p. 20. The distribution of economic power is at the heart of the world-systems argument of Immanuel Wallerstein. See Chapter 10, p. 337. It is also the basis of "long-cycle theory," which sees war as related to the successive domination of world politics by leading trading states. See George Modelski, "The Long Cycle of Global

Whatever the role of structural features in war, we must recognize that identifying causes of war that cannot be altered (such as human nature or anarchy) are of little use to policy makers or theorists. If the factors that trigger war cannot be changed, then policies cannot be fashioned to prevent its outbreak. We might as well shrug our shoulders fatalistically, accept the idea that sooner or later we will find ourselves in another bloody conflict, and turn our energy to a more rewarding pursuit than studying global politics.

The suspicion is growing, however, that structural configurations like bipolarity matter less in triggering war than the rate and magnitude of change from one configuration to another. Unequal distribution of power may create envy in the weak and determination to overcome their inferiority; their temptation to avenge past grievances may grow as the distribution of power is equalized. In this view, "war is caused by differences in rates of growth among the great powers and, of particular importance, the differences in rates between the dominant nation and the challenger that permit the latter to overtake the former."[42] Some scholars posit a *power cycle* in which the danger of war is greatest at "critical points," when the power and role of pivotal states are changing rapidly.[43] States with growing power may demand a greater role in the system, and declining states may be reluctant to surrender their prerogatives.

The belief that changes in power distribution are important have focused some scholars on *arms races* as a factor in the outbreak of war. Shortly after World War I, British physicist Sir Lewis Fry Richardson, a pioneer in mathematical modeling, argued that war was related to such races and the fear that accompanies them. Richardson used differential equations to depict the manner in which the level of arms in two countries interacts with variables like threat perception to produce war. He did not view his equations as genuine models of reality. Instead, they were intended to illustrate "what people would do if they did not stop to think."[44] More recently, Michael D. Wallace found arms races to be associated with alliance formation (itself related to status inconsistency) and onset of war.[45] Wallace also found that in twenty-eight cases

Politics and the Nation-State," *Comparative Studies in Society and History* 20:2 (April 1978), pp. 214–235; and Joshua Goldstein, *Long Cycles: Prosperity and War in the Modern Age* (New Haven: Yale University Press, 1988). Long-cycle theory grew out of the Kondratieff theory of technological change and economic growth and contraction.

[42]Organski and Kugler, *War Ledger*, p. 61.

[43]See Charles F. Doran, *Systems In Crisis: New Imperatives of High Politics at Century's End* (New York: Cambridge University Press, 1991).

[44]Lewis F. Richardson, *Arms and Insecurity: A Mathematical Study of the Causes and Origins of War* (Chicago: Quadrangle, 1960), p. 12.

[45]Michael D. Wallace, "Status, Formal Organization, and Arms Levels as Factors Leading to the Onset of War, 1820–1964," in Bruce M. Russett, ed., *Peace, War, and Numbers* (Beverly Hills, Calif.: Sage, 1972), pp. 49–71.

between 1816 and 1965 in which there were arms races *and* serious disputes, twenty-three ended in war. [46]

Arms races partly grow out of changing technology. Such changes critically affect changes in global distribution of power, and that is one reason the relationship between technology and war has received close attention. To that issue we now turn.

Changing Technology and the Evolution of War

Actors' ability to adapt changing technology so as to achieve objectives has been a great factor in their rise and fall, and technological change is associated with the outbreak of war. Advances from the humble horse-drawn chariot of ancient civilizations and archers' use of stirrups to the splitting of the atom have provided some actors with military advantages over others. In this section, we briefly review the evolution of technology, examining its relation to changes in warfare. It is surprising how often statesmen have misunderstood the implications of technological change and planned for the future as though it were the same as the past. The consequences have sometimes been cata-strophic. Further, evolving technology has allowed some regions of the world to dominate others politically. The technological advances in Europe and the United States that allowed the West to dominate global politics by the eighteenth and nineteenth centuries continued into the twentieth century.

Arms, Politics, and the End of *Chivalry*

The changes in military technology between 1000 and 1500 A.D. brought great changes to global politics. The feudal system in medieval Europe depended on military domi-nation by a few mounted knights who could afford armor and horses. With the rise in commerce and the expansion of commercial cities in Italy and Holland from the eleventh to the fourteenth centuries, a middle class appeared that could afford to hire and equip large mercenary armies. The result was a change in warfare that ended the military and political dominance by aristocratic knights.[47]

The political and military revolution was completed by improvements in guns and artillery. By the middle of the fifteenth century, heavy artillery could reduce the walls of castles (or cities) to rubble in hours. On one occasion, a fortress in southern Italy, famous because it had withstood an earlier siege for seven years, was destroyed in eight hours.[48]

[46]Michael D. Wallace, "Arms Races and Escalation: Some New Evidence," *Journal of Conflict Resolution* 23:1 (March 1979), pp.14–15. See also Wallace, "Armaments and Escalation," *International Studies Quarterly* 26:1 (March 1982), pp. 37–56, in which the author shows that the relationship of arms races to war remains regardless of who is winning the race.

[47]William H. McNeill, *The Pursuit of Power* (Chicago: University of Chicago Press, 1982), p. 68. Mounted knights were especially vulnerable to the crossbows of foot soldiers.

[48]Ibid., p. 89.

Heavy artillery made defensive fortifications in general less effective, and facilitated territorial expansion. Historian William McNeill comments:

> Wherever the new artillery [of mobile siege guns] appeared, existing fortifications became useless. The power of any ruler who was able to afford the high cost of the new weapons was . . . enhanced at the expense of neighbors and subjects who were unable to avail themselves of the new technology of war.[49]

The availability of artillery, along with improvements in naval warfare and rapid growth in commerce, ushered in the era of the large territorial state and produced European military and political dominance.

War in Eighteenth-Century Europe

As the territorial state became the principal unit of social organization in the seventeenth and eighteenth centuries, global politics showed greater political stability. One reason was the state of military technology. Weapons and tactics provided few advantages for adopting offensive strategies. Armies lacked the logistical support to move quickly or far and could not get far ahead of their baggage trains. Muskets were inaccurate, could fire only a short distance, and were effective only when fired in volleys by large numbers of highly trained soldiers who stood together in mass formations. Warfare was a costly and indecisive enterprise.

The new technology was compatible with the economic, political, and social conditions of the time. Rulers did not wish to levy high taxes on subjects or interfere with economic activities that were the basis of their wealth and power. Dependent on professional soldiers recruited or impressed into service from the lowest classes of society, officers devised tactics meant as much to prevent desertion as to achieve victory. Brightly colored uniforms, so that officers could keep their eye on soldiers, and rigidly disciplined mass formations kept armies together better than achieving decisive victories. The low status of the military profession in Europe at the time was reflected in signs in cafés that read: "No dogs, lackeys, prostitutes or soldiers."[50] Because professional armies were expensive, neither commanders nor employers had an interest in needless bloodletting. All this fit an age in which kings, whatever their disputes, were conservative and had no wish for unrestrained war of the sort which had engulfed Europe between 1618 and 1648 and which might endanger their thrones. Most were related to one another by marriage or blood, and no king wished to do *too* much harm to a son-in-law or uncle.

Frederick the Great of Prussia was the most successful commander of this era, and his approach to war, as described by a historian, gives the flavor of the period:

[49]Ibid.

[50]Cited in R. R. Palmer, "Frederick the Great, Guibert, Bülow: From Dynastic to National War," in Paret, ed., *Makers of Modern Strategy*, p. 93.

Battle . . . was a methodical affair. Opposing armies were arrayed according to pattern, almost as regularly as chessmen at the beginning of a game. . . . Frederick . . . was not fond of full-size battles. . . . So Frederician war became increasingly a war of position, the war of complex maneuver and subtle accumulation of small gains; leisurely and slow in its main outlines. Of the gains to be expected from war, under conditions then existing, he became increasingly dubious. . . . He was a dynast, not a revolutionary or an adventurer.[51]

Napoleonic Revolution in Warfare

Much changed with the French Revolution and the wars of Napoleon. Awakened nationalism went hand in hand with new tactics and larger armies of aroused citizens. Artillery improved in accuracy and mobility, and its weight was reduced. Armies were organized into large units, each of which could maneuver separately. Technology and organization allowed large armies with greater firepower to move farther and faster than before. Popular fervor enlarged the objectives that leaders pursued through war even as it allowed more of the population to become directly or indirectly involved in the war effort. The proclamation in France of the *levée en masse* in August 1793 forecast the mobilization of entire populations for the war effort:

> From this moment until our enemies have been driven from the territory of the Republic, all Frenchmen are permanently requisitioned for military service. Young men will go forth to battle; married men will forge weapons and transport munitions; women will make tents and clothing; children will make bandages from old linen; and old men will be brought to the public squares to arouse the courage of the soldiers, while preaching the unity of the Republic and hatred against kings.[52]

Napoleon was able to send huge armies—more than a million in a population of twenty-five million[53]—into the field, and they were able to win crushing one-punch victories between 1800 and 1806 at Marengo, Ulm, Jena, Auerstadt, and Austerlitz.[54]

The lessons of the French Revolution and the power of the new nationalism were not lost on the greatest military intellectual of the age, the Prussian general Karl Maria von Clausewitz. Clausewitz, who had fought Napoleon for his native Prussia and then for the Tsar of Russia, was struck by the size and ferocity of the Napoleonic Wars. Unlike wars in the previous century, they seemed to bear little relation to objectives other than

---

[51]Ibid., pp. 99, 103–105.

[52]Cited in John Shy, "Jomini," in Paret, ed., *Makers of Modern Strategy*, pp. 144–145.

[53]Ibid., p. 145. For the first time in history, armies were too large for a commander to follow visually.

[54]The visitor to Paris can get a sense of these battles at a monument in the center of the Place Vendôme that was constructed from cannon captured by Napoleon.

destroying the enemy. The new wars seemed to him, as do nuclear weapons to us today, to threaten civilization itself. Such wars could get out of hand and become "total," deteriorating until the political objectives for which they had been initiated were forgotten and replaced by blind hatred, in which the only objective was destroying the enemy.

Clausewitz could imagine no political end that could justify "*total war*," and he wrote his unfinished masterpiece *On War (Vom Kriege)* "to iron out the creases in the heads" of the generals he feared might dictate the way wars were fought. As a professional soldier, Clausewitz recognized that war was a science, but he recoiled at the prospect of its being waged by military professionals according to technical principles rather than by political leaders according to political principles. Just as no battle should be undertaken without recognizing its implications for the overall war effort, no war should be waged without clearly understanding its implications for the combatants' long-term political situation.

Clausewitz had no doubt that the military requirements of war should be subordinated to civilian leaders' political needs. Wars, he reasoned, were not mindless outbreaks of violence. Rather, they were like games in which interacting chance and probability determine the outcome. And, though a general seeks to destroy the enemy's forces and will to fight, that is not the true objective of war. War might be violent, but it was not without purpose. "Force . . . is . . . the *means*; to impose our will upon the enemy is the *object*."[55] The aim was not to hurt the enemy but rather to coerce him to accede to political demands.

Because wars begin for political reasons, such reasons should be kept in mind even as the fighting rages. "Now if we reflect that war has its origin in a political object, we see that this first motive, which called it into existence, naturally remains the first and highest consideration to be regarded in its conduct."[56] If the original reasons for war were forgotten, disastrous confusion would ensue between *means* and *ends*. The amount of violence should be commensurate with the political objectives. If the objectives are limited, then, Clausewitz reasoned, the war should remain limited. "This explains how . . . there can be wars of all degrees of importance and energy, from a war of extermination down to a mere state of armed observation."[57] For Clausewitz, then, war, like diplomacy or trade, was a political instrument, albeit a violent one. It was "not merely a political act but a real political instrument. . . . "[58]

Clausewitz's influence on modern strategy is reflected in the work of theorists like Thomas Schelling, who writes: "Hurting . . . is not unconcerned with the

---

[55]Karl von Clausewitz, *On War*, trans. by O. J. Matthijs Jolles (New York: Random House, Modern Library, 1943), Book I, ch. I, p. 3. Emphasis in original.

[56]Ibid., Book I, ch. I, p. 16.

[57]Ibid., Book I, ch. I, p. 10.

[58]Ibid., Book I, ch. I, p. 16.

interest of others. . . . To inflict suffering gains nothing and saves nothing directly; it can only make people behave to avoid it. The only purpose, unless sport or revenge, must be to influence somebody's behavior, to coerce his decision or choice. . . . The power to hurt is *bargaining power*. To exploit it is diplomacy — vicious diplomacy, but diplomacy."[59] The idea of war as an extension of policy that can be used to coerce an adversary without escalating beyond control was reflected in the lengths to which American leaders went in Korea (1950–1953) to limit the conflict. The Americans neither invaded nor bombed China and avoided using nuclear weapons. Following Clausewitz's advice that generals must not take over the direction of war, President Truman fired his field commander, General Douglas MacArthur, in 1951 when the general was insubordinate and kept pressing to widen the war.[60] MacArthur was a war hero, and Truman had to pay political costs at home for asserting his authority.[61] More recently, the use of violence to convey a political message was clear in U.S. air strikes on selected Iraqi targets in early 1993 to persuade Saddam Hussein to submit to U.N. resolutions such as permitting U.N. personnel to destroy Iraq's stockpile of poison gas and oversee Iraqi weapons-testing facilities.

Technology and World War I

Clausewitz's nightmare seemed to come to life in World War I (1914–1918). The war was sparked by a conflict between Austria-Hungary and Serbia,[62] and, with the major countries of Europe linked by alliances,[63] it expanded rapidly. In time, the war, though remaining mostly European, spread to Africa, Asia, and the Middle East. Before it ended, one in every 28 Frenchmen, every 32 Germans, every 57 Englishmen, and every 107 Russians had been killed.[64] Statistics, however, fail to convey adequately the suicidal violence of trench warfare or how vast areas of Europe were turned into barren seas

---

[59]Thomas C. Schelling, *Arms and Influence* (New Haven: Yale University Press, 1966), p. 2. See also Schelling, *The Strategy of Conflict* (Cambridge: Harvard University Press, 1960). Emphasis added.

[60]At MacArthur's urging, U.S. forces had marched north of the 38th parallel and were sweeping toward the Yalu River border with China when Chinese forces intervened. The temptation to expand the war beyond its original objectives almost led to military disaster.

[61]Under growing voter dissatisfaction with American failure to "win" the war in Korea, the Republican Party chose another war hero, General Dwight D. Eisenhower, to run for the presidency in 1952. Eisenhower, vowing to visit Korea, defeated his Democratic opponent, Adlai E. Stevenson, by a landslide.

[62]The actual trigger was the assassination on June 28 of the heir to the Habsburg throne by a Serbian nationalist during a state visit to Sarajevo, capital of Bosnia-Herzegovina.

[63]On one side was the Triple Entente of Britain, France, and Russia (Serbia's protector). On the other was the Triple Alliance of Germany, Austria-Hungary, and Italy (which backed out of its obligation and later joined the war on the other side).

[64]Barbara Tuchman, *The Guns of August* (New York: Macmillan, 1962), p. 488n.

of mud in which nothing could survive. War in the modern age was not an affair of honor or individual valor. The English poet Wilfred Owen captured this truth by describing a gas attack:

> Bent double, like old beggars under sacks,
> Knock-kneed, coughing like hags, we cursed through sludge,
> Till on the haunting flares we turned our backs,
> And towards our distant rest began to trudge.
> Men marched asleep. Many had lost their boots,
> But limped on, blood-shod. All went lame, all blind;
> Drunk with fatigue; deaf even to the hoots
> Of gas-shells dropping softly behind.
>
> Gas! Gas! Quick boys! — An ecstasy of fumbling,
> Fitting the clumsy helmets just in time,
> But someone still was yelling out and stumbling
> And floundering like a man in fire or lime.
> Dim through the misty panes and thick green* light,
> As under a green sea, I saw him drowning.
>
> In all my dreams before my helpless sight
> He plunges at me, guttering, choking, drowning.
>
> If in some smothering dreams, you too could pace
> Behind the wagon that we flung him in,
> And watch the white eyes writhing in his face,
> His hanging face, like a devil's sick of sin;
> If you could hear, at every jolt, the blood
> Come gargling from the froth-corrupted lungs,
> Bitter as the cud
> Of vile, incurable sores on innocent tongues,
> My friend, you would not tell with such high zest
> To children ardent for some desperate glory,
> The old Lie: Dulce et decorum est
> Pro patria mori.†65

*Green was the color of mustard gas — $(ClCH_2CH_2)_2S$ — which produces burns, blindness, and death.

†"How sweet and fitting it is to die for one's homeland."

Perceptions about how military technology affects the relationship between the offense and the defense — and military plans reflecting these perceptions — were partly responsible for a war no one wanted.[66] Although many decades have passed since World

---

[65]Wilfred Owen, "Dulce et Decorum Est," in John Heath-Stubbs and David Wright, eds., *The Faber Book of Twentieth Century Verse* (London: Faber and Faber, 1953), p. 253. The title of the poem — "How Sweet and Fitting It Is" — is from an ode by the ancient Roman poet Horace lauding patriotism.

[66]That leaders neither wanted nor expected the war that erupted in 1914 is argued persuasively and systematically in Jack S. Levy, "Preferences, Constraints, and Choices in July 1914," *International Security* 15:3 (Winter 1990/91), pp. 151–186.

War I began, it is still not clear whether statesmen simply ignored the implications of technological change or did not understand those implications.[67] Politicians and generals planned for a quick war in which the offense would dominate and then found themselves in a war of attrition dominated by defensive tactics. Different technologies are responsible for this tragic result.

On the one hand, leaders were influenced by the German wars of unification (1863, 1866, and 1870),[68] and these wars became models for planning future wars. The unification wars were rapid affairs in which the outcome was settled in one decisive battle. At least two technological developments contributed to these decisive victories. The first was the railroad, enabling actors to assemble armies of unprecedented size at one location from which they could attack; the second was heavy artillery that could send huge projectiles twenty miles and more and could reduce defensive strong points.[69]

Other examples, if understood, might have led statesmen to adopt different models. The American Civil War (1860–1865) cost 500,000 lives and was mainly a deadly *war of attrition*, but it was dismissed with contempt by the chief of the German general staff as "movements of armed mobs."[70] The enormous toll in lives from frontal attacks on fixed positions during the Russo-Japanese War of 1904–1905 illustrated how technology had improved defensive prospects. Barbed wire and machine guns, combined with rows of trenches, made mincemeat of horse cavalry and frontal infantry assault. Massed attacks were also vulnerable to the greater accuracy and range of artillery and small arms that used high explosives rather than gunpowder as propellant. Long-range artillery was as deadly to concentrations of troops preparing to attack as to frontier fortresses.[71]

Instead, European observers concluded that the "real lesson of the Russo-Japanese War . . . was not technology but *morale*. . . ."[72] In other words, if soldiers were sufficiently imbued with the right spirit, they could overcome concentrated fire — mind over matter. Thus, French regulations in 1894 demanded that infantry advance "elbow to elbow in

---

[67]One unresolved issue is whether or not the state of technology determined the actors' tactical preferences. See Jonathan Shimshoni, "Technology, Military Advantage, and World War I: A Case for Military Entrepreneurship," *International Security* 15:3 (Winter 1990/91), pp. 187–215.

[68]The three conflicts were against Denmark, Austria, and France respectively.

[69]The long-range German artillery piece used in 1914 with great effect against Belgian and French fortresses was known as Big Bertha after the daughter of the head of Krupp armaments, which made the guns.

[70]Cited in Sigmund Neumann and Mark von Hagen, "Engels and Marx on Revolution, War, and the Army in Society," in Paret, *Makers of Modern Strategy*, p. 274.

[71]Michael Howard, "Men against Fire: The Doctrine of the Offensive in 1914," in Paret, *Makers of Modern Strategy*, pp. 517–518.

[72]Ibid., p. 519. Emphasis in original.

mass formations, to the sound of bugles and drums."[73] In short, the problem was not merely failure to recognize new technology, but lack of imagination in exploiting this technology.[74]

The "*cult of the offensive*" reached a peak in the German *Schlieffen Plan*.[75] Originally conceived in 1897,[76] the plan assumed that Germany would face a war on two fronts and would be outnumbered. German survival therefore depended on rapidly mobilizing and striking before Russian mobilization was completed. German forces were to be massed on the western front with only a screening force remaining in the east.[77] The main German blow was to fall on the French left flank in a preemptive strike, avoiding the French frontier fortresses, seizing French and Belgian ports to forestall British reinforcements, and sweeping behind French lines to rupture communications and smash the French army against the Alps. Then, taking advantage of Germany's internal lines of communication, forces would rush eastward to meet the Russian advance.[78] The plan's success depended on avoiding delay (including lengthy political negotiations) and on ruthlessly violating Belgian neutrality. In this way, contrary to Clausewitz's dictum, military considerations were allowed to dominate political decisions. Thus, in one famous episode in July 1914, the Russian foreign minister informed the chief of staff that he should "smash" his telephone so that Tsar Nicholas II could not again postpone declaring war in order to seek a political solution.[79]

Reality soon intruded in the plans of the general staffs, revealing that technology actually favored the defense. The German attack on France, the Russian advance against Germany, the Austro-Hungarian offensive against Russian Poland, and the French

[73]Cited in ibid., p. 514.

[74]This failure of comprehension is nowhere captured better than in Alexander Solzhenitsyn's fictional account of the Russian advance into East Prussia in 1914, which ended in disaster. The author describes how the Russian army was made to march all the way to the front, where they arrived exhausted, but horses were transported by rail, and how the Russian military failed to encode radio messages because they assumed the Germans would not be listening. Solzhenitsyn, *August 1914*, trans. by Michael Glenny (New York: Farrar, Straus and Giroux, 1971).

[75]See Richard Ned Lebow, *Nuclear Crisis Management: A Dangerous Illusion* (Ithaca, N.Y.: Cornell University Press, 1987), pp. 109–112. On the "cult of the offensive," see Stephen Van Evera, "Why Cooperation Failed in 1914," *World Politics* 38:1 (October 1985), especially pp. 83–84.

[76]The plan was the brainchild of Alfred von Schlieffen, chief of the German general staff from 1891 to 1906. Other countries had similar plans.

[77]See Jack Snyder, *The Ideology of the Offensive: Military Decision Making and the Disasters of 1914* (Ithaca, N.Y.: Cornell University Press, 1984), pp. 107–156.

[78]Ironically, Germany's greatest military triumphs of 1914 came against the Russians in the battles of Tannenberg and the Masurian Lakes. In a panic, German forces that might have brought victory in France were hurriedly sent east but arrived too late to play a role. Deprived of the forces envisioned in the Schlieffen Plan, the German offensive in the west came up short at the gates of Paris. Following the battle of the Marne, the war in the west became a defensive slugfest.

[79]Laurence Lafore, *The Long Fuse*, 2nd ed. (New York: Lippincott, 1971), p. 257.

World War I resembled the "total war" that Clausewitz had feared. Millions of Europeans and Americans died in trench warfare—a war of attrition in which machine guns and barbed wire destroyed hopes that the war might be ended quickly.

invasion of Alsace-Lorraine[80] all failed, with huge losses of life. Of the 1,500,000 French troops who marched off to war in August 1914, one in four were casualties within six weeks, and 110,000 were dead.[81] Rather than forcing a change in tactics, the toll simply hardened the resolve of generals on both sides to prove they had been correct in the first place. Time after time, following deafening artillery barrages, masses of troops went "over the top" only to be mowed down by an entrenched enemy. Michael Howard captures the futility and carnage of the war in his description of the British offensive on the Somme in summer 1916:

> By the end of June 1,437 guns had been assembled along an eighteen-mile front, and in a week-long bombardment they fired over 1,500,000 shells. . . . So the infantry went over the top on July 1 . . . expecting at worst to have to mop up a few dazed survivors. The result was one of the most terrible days in the history of

[80] Alsace-Lorraine had been severed from France by Germany after the Franco-Prussian War in 1870. It became a symbol of French nationalism. In 1880, the French leader Léon Gambetta said of the "lost" province, "Think of it always, speak of it never." Cited in René Albrecht-Carrié, *A Diplomatic History of Europe Since the Congress of Vienna* (New York: Harper & Row, 1958), p. 167. Visitors to Paris may observe that the Place de la Concorde at the center of the city is surrounded by statues of women representing the country's different cities. From 1870 until return of the province, the statues representing the Alsatian cities of Metz and Strasbourg were draped in black crêpe.

[81] Howard, "Men against Fire," p. 523.

the war. The barrage had not been heavy enough to reach the dugouts that the Germans had excavated deep in the chalk hills above the Somme. Appalling as the experience they suffered was, the German infantry were still able to set up their machine guns and mow down the advancing waves of British infantry. . . . Of the 120,000 men who assaulted, nearly half were casualties, and 20,000 were dead. The attacks continued until November, by which time the British and French armies engaged had lost nearly 500,000 men.[82]

Technology and World War II

If the offensive dominated preparations for World War I, fascination with the defensive dominated planning for World War II, at least among the British and the French. After World War I, French "security policies and doctrines," observe two historians, "naturally became defensive, and the 1920s witnessed a return to the traditional military credo of the Third Republic: faith in the trinity of a fortified eastern border, foreign alliances, and universal conscription."[83] This philosophy was reflected in a line of fixed fortifications constructed from Switzerland to Luxembourg—the *Maginot Line*.[84]

The Germans and Japanese proved more imaginative in employing new military technologies.[85] The Germans, to avenge the 1918 defeat, developed tactics that could exploit the new weapons, especially tanks and aircraft. Unlike the French and British, who thought of tanks as providing support for infantry, German planners had the idea of creating separate tank formations closely supported by aircraft that could move rapidly and break through enemy weak points, creating havoc in the enemy's rear.[86] The German doctrine—*Blitzkrieg* (Lightning War)—was different in another way: it wedded political indoctrination and ideology to mechanized warfare. Hitler's approach to war, one observer declares, made "the psychology of the enemy the primary target. It is his state of mind rather than his objective situation that one must focus on."[87] Prior to attack, the enemy was softened up by unconventional tactics aimed at lowering morale

[82]Ibid., p. 525.

[83]Brian Bond and Martin Alexander, "Liddell Hart and de Gaulle: The Doctrines of Limited Liability and Mobile Defense," in Peter Paret, ed., *Makers of Modern Strategy*, p. 598.

[84]These were named after André Maginot, the war minister who oversaw their construction. The Germans having outflanked the line in 1940, the fortifications were used to grow mushrooms during the war.

[85]Some of the most imaginative tactics did not require high technology at all. The Japanese used bicycles to move through the jungles of Malaya and spring from the rear upon the British naval fortress at Singapore in 1942. The British, believing Singapore could be attacked only from the sea, had guns pointed seaward, making little effort to fortify the Straits of Johore that separated the city from the Malay peninsula.

[86]A number of young British and French strategists, including Charles de Gaulle, understood the implications of the new weapons but were ignored by the military establishments in their countries. See ibid., pp. 600 ff.

[87]Andrew M. Scott, *The Revolution in Statecraft: Informal Penetration* (New York: Random House, 1965), p. 32.

and undermining the will to resist. Local Nazi parties or sympathizers were mobilized to undermine unity. Prior to their invasion of France, the Germans arranged to establish a news agency in that country to spread Nazi propaganda.[88] Other Nazi techniques included forging economic ties to increase dependency on Germany and recruiting local Germans to carry out assassinations and other terrorist acts.[89] Since World War II, these tactics have been emulated by others, and *political warfare* has become standard fare in world politics.

Hitler intuitively understood Clausewitz's idea of war as an extension of politics, and he used the threat of war to bully his adversaries into making concessions, always leaving them room to retreat and promising that he had no further ambitions. He unilaterally abrogated the disarmament provisions of the Versailles Treaty in March 1935. A year later, in a classic bluff and against the advice of his generals, Hitler sent his troops to reoccupy the Rhineland. Historian Alan Bullock writes:

> German rearmament was only beginning and the first conscripts had only been taken into the Army a few months before. France, together with her Polish and Czech allies, could immediately mobilize ninety divisions, with a further hundred in reserve. . . . Hitler did not dispute these facts; he based his decision on the belief that the French would not march—and he was right.[90]

Again and again, Hitler took advantage of his opponents' memories of World War I and their aversion to another conflict, as in pressuring them in a meeting held near Munich to abandon their commitments and help him force Czechoslovakia to surrender the Sudetenland.

After World War II, *Munich* became synonymous with *appeasement*. Appeasement had been regarded as a mechanism for avoiding unnecessary war and rectifying past injustices. Unfortunately, as practiced by British and French in the 1930s, the policy proved a disaster, as retreat followed retreat until no one believed any longer that Hitler's ambitions could be satisfied peacefully. Following the German invasion of Poland, September 1, 1939, the British and French declared war.

In the end, however, Hitler failed to limit his political objectives and waged war indiscriminately against civilians and soldiers. As one scholar says, "However skillfully individual battles and campaigns were fought, it was a war in which the expanding torrent of destruction became the main operational and tactical rationale. Its main and only operational goal was to inflict damage and destruction, to destroy the enemy state and to batter enemy societies and their armed forces into submission."[91] *The link between*

[88]Ibid., p. 36.

[89]In 1934, for example, Nazi sympathizers murdered the Austrian chancellor, and four years later Hitler gave serious consideration to ordering the assassination of his own ambassador to Austria to justify the Nazi takeover of that country.

[90]Alan Bullock, *Hitler: A Study in Tyranny*, rev. ed. (New York: Harper & Row, 1962), p. 343.

[91]Michael Geyer, "German Strategy in the Age of Machine Warfare, 1914–1945," in Paret, *Makers of Modern Strategy*, p. 593.

war and politics had been severed. Nazi policies of unlimited conquest, racial superiority, and genocide caused revulsion among civilized peoples everywhere and brought into existence the most powerful coalition in history—the United States, Britain, and the Soviet Union.[92]

Like the Germans, the Japanese used tactical ingenuity to exploit available military technology. The attack on Pearl Harbor was a tactical masterpiece fully revealing how useful the aircraft carrier was for the first time. Only the absence of America's aircraft carriers from Pearl Harbor at the time of the Japanese attack forced the United States into the carrier age.[93] On the other hand, like their German allies, the Japanese did not understand Clausewitz. The Japanese plan was to put the American fleet out of commission at Pearl Harbor, seize Southeast Asia and its raw materials, and then sit tight behind a barrier of island fortresses. In time, they believed, the Americans would become frustrated and give up the war. They failed to recognize America's enormous industrial potential and population and their own vulnerability to U.S. carrier forces. This power was brought home to them sooner than anyone expected when a U.S. air raid was launched against Tokyo led by General James H. Doolittle in April 1942 from the carrier *Hornet.* A few Japanese leaders understood what lay ahead, but those who directed Japan's fate paid them no heed.

As this review reveals, technology remains only a means to achieve political ends. Failure to learn and apply that lesson can have dire consequences. The question remains whether technology such as nuclear power can be harnessed and controlled for political—or ultimately, peaceful—ends, or whether it will produce total war.

Costs and Consequences of Military Security

Before turning to the nuclear issue in Chapter 8, we must identify the other costs and consequences that reliance on military force entails for actors. Four related consequences can be identified: (1) the burden of military expenditures and military forces, (2) the global arms trade, (3) the growth of military influence in countries, and (4) militarization of societies.

---

[92]Hitler repeatedly made the error of confronting new foes before defeating old ones, invading the U.S.S.R. ("Operation Barbarossa") in June 1941 before Britain had been defeated and declaring war against the United States shortly after the attack on Pearl Harbor.

[93]In World War I, airplanes had served primarily for observation. Nevertheless, a number of farsighted strategists understood the potential of airpower. In the United States, General Billy Mitchell was the leading exponent of tactical airpower, especially its potential effectiveness against surface ships. See Edward Warner, "Douhet, Mitchell, Seversky: Theories of Air Warfare," in Edward Mead Earle, *Makers of Modern Strategy,* 1st ed. (New York: Atheneum, 1967), pp. 497–501. See also David MacIsaac, "Voices from the Central Blue: The Air Power Theorists," in Paret, *Makers of Modern Strategy,* pp. 624–647.

FIGURE 7.1

World Military Expenditures

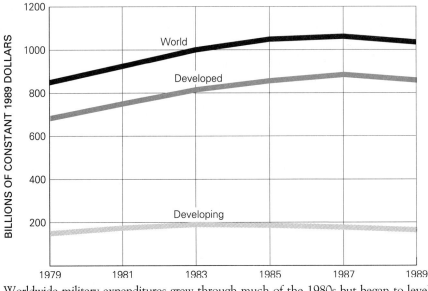

Worldwide military expenditures grew through much of the 1980s but began to level off and then decline as the Cold War came to an end. The military expenditures of economically developed states mirrored this trend.

Trends in Military Expenditures and Force Levels

The costs of the search for security have posed growing economic and social burdens in recent centuries. Although blood and treasure have always been consumed by actors pursuing security, costs have ballooned since 1945. With the end of the Cold War, are we likely to obtain a worldwide *peace dividend*? Or, like so many times in the past, will expenditures be kept high by vested interests? The opportunity costs associated with such military expenditures are considerable. By spending a large portion of scarce resources on the military, countries have less to spend on education and welfare, and economic growth is delayed.

As depicted in Figure 7.1, global military spending, despite inflation, finally began to slow. Worldwide, military expenditures reached more than $1 trillion in 1987 and then began to fall, as measured in *constant dollars*; that is, taking inflation into account.[94] Relatively few developed countries account for more than $800 billion of the total. The Cold War's influence is evident when we realize that, in 1989, members of NATO and

[94]U.S. Arms Control and Disarmament Agency, *World Military Expenditures and Arms Transfers 1990* (Washington, D.C.: U.S. Government Printing Office, 1991), p. 1.

FIGURE 7.2

Military Expenditure by Region

Region	Billions of 1989 Dollars
Warsaw Pact	365.7
North America	314.9
NATO Europe	147.4
East Asia	83.2
Middle East	53.2
Other Europe	22.4
Africa	15.3
Latin America	14.5
South Asia	11.5
Oceania	7.1

BILLIONS OF 1989 DOLLARS

As the Cold War came to an end, the bulk of global military expenditures were by the main Cold War contestants in the Warsaw Treaty Organization and NATO.

the Warsaw Treaty Organization accounted for 80 percent of global military expenditures. Although such expenditures were a burden on the West, they were even more of a problem for the smaller economies in the former Soviet bloc.[95] In 1980, that bloc accounted for close to two-fifths of global military expenditures, and by the end of the decade it was still responsible for more than 35 percent.

As the regional breakdown in Figure 7.2 and the growth rates in spending in Table 7.4 show, the defense burden is widespread. Several regions (South Asia, North America, Latin America, and Oceania) had a larger average annual growth rate in defense spending than the Warsaw Pact countries. The increase in U.S. defense expenditures during the Reagan years (1980–1988) accounts for much of North America's increase. The growing tensions and conflicts in South Asia account for that region's rapid yearly rise. The regional rivalry between India and Pakistan, the war in Afghanistan, and civil strife in Sri Lanka between Tamils and Sinhalese stimulated an average annual growth rate of more than 6 percent during the 1980s. In sum, the world's total military expenditures rose from more than $800 billion in 1979 to more than $1 trillion (in constant dollars) by 1989.

[95] In 1988, Soviet GNP was about half that of the United States. Michael Sullivan, *Measuring Global Values*, p. 101.

TABLE 7.4

Military Expenditures: Shares and Growth (in percentages)

| | World Share | | Real Growth Rate[a] |
	1979	1989	1979–1989
World	100.0	100.0	2.2
Developed	81.2	83.8	2.6
Developing	18.8	16.2	0.3
Region			
Warsaw Pact	39.1	35.3	1.4
North America	24.0	30.4	4.8[b]
NATO Europe	15.0	14.2	1.4
East Asia	8.1	8.0	2.0[c]
Middle East	6.8	5.1	−1.5
Other Europe	2.4	2.2	1.2
Africa	1.8	1.5	−0.7
Latin America	1.4	1.4	2.6
South Asia	0.8	1.1	6.4
Oceania	0.6	0.7	−1.5

[a]Average annual rate, calculated as a compound rate curve fitted to all points.

[b]Most of this increase was prior to 1985.

[c]Japan and South Korea accounted for most of the increase; Chinese expenditures declined.

SOURCE: U.S. Arms Control and Disarmament Agency, *World Military Expenditures and Arms Transfers 1990*, p. 2., Table 1.

The numbers of persons under arms reflect regional fears and rivalries as well as changes in global politics at the end of the Cold War. Thus, the world's armed forces declined from a 1986 peak of 28.9 million to 28.3 million in 1989.[96] The Middle East had far and away the largest proportion of population under arms, and Jordan, Iraq, Israel, South Yemen, and Syria — all in the Middle East — were among the world's leaders in proportion of population under arms. This region was the only one to experience growth in the number of soldiers per 1,000 population.[97]

Global Arms Trade

Although military spending is a drain on a country's resources, it benefits some economic sectors. Defense is a big industry, not only in the United States, but

[96]*World Military Expenditures and Arms Transfers 1990*, p. 5.

[97]Ibid., pp. 6–7.

everywhere else. Arms manufacturers employ many people in many countries, and arms sales, at home and abroad, are lucrative. Indeed, a standard theme in Marxist analysis is that arms manufacturers' search for profits is a cause of war. In fact, a U.S. Senate Committee looking into the causes of World War I concluded that a small group of profit-minded industrialists, referred to as *"merchants of death,"* was responsible for the conflict. Arms companies such as Vickers in Britain, Krupp in Germany, Schneider-Creusot in France, and Skoda in Austria-Hungary reaped great profits by selling arms to anyone who would buy them (including future enemies) in the years before 1914, and, more recently U.S. and European defense contractors sold Iraq weapons it used in the Persian Gulf War, as well as components for nuclear and chemical weapons.

The global traffic in arms among governments is a huge business, peaking at about $63 billion in 1987 before dropping to about $45 billion in 1989. For some governments, like that of Czechoslovakia before the overthrow of communism, arms sales were a vital source of hard currency, as well as political influence in the Third World. For Western countries, arms are a leading export industry and keep local defense manufacturers busy. For ambitious nonsuperpowers like China, Israel, North Korea, Brazil, and Spain, selling arms is a source of political influence and provides funds to maintain a defense industry at home. As shown in Figure 7.3, countries in the developing world, especially those in the Middle East and South Asia, account for more than three-quarters of global arms imports; and, as depicted in Figure 7.4, countries involved in conflicts such as Afghanistan, Iraq, Iran, and India were leading arms importers.

Although major arms importers are in the Third World, large exporters and beneficiaries from arms sales include Russia, the United States, and Western Europe. As depicted in Figure 7.5, the former U.S.S.R. was responsible for more than two-fifths of world arms exports between 1985 and 1989, selling to almost anyone who could pay in hard currency, including Libya and Iraq, which then made Soviet arms available to terrorist groups they supported. Others, including the United States, France, and China, were only marginally more scrupulous about whom they sold arms to. Little wonder that during wars between such foes as India and Pakistan, commentators wryly report whether U.S., British, Soviet, or French tanks and planes perform better. Perhaps some are merchants of death after all.

With the Cold War ended, are arms sales likely to grow or shrink? The U.S.S.R. broken up, a major supplier of armaments is gone. Although Russia continues to sell arms for hard currency to meet economic needs, its role in global arms sales has declined. Other states that emerged from the former Soviet Union have also tried to sell arms abroad, and the United States, France, and Great Britain became the leading sources of arms sales in 1992–1993. Furthermore, other arms suppliers, such as Brazil and China, are moving to fill the void left by the U.S.S.R. The end of the Cold War may only disperse arms suppliers and not reduce sales of weapons. As we shall see in Chapter 8, nuclear weapons and ballistic-missile transfers are prominent new dangers as we approach the next century.

FIGURE 7.3

Regional Shares of the World's Arms Import Market

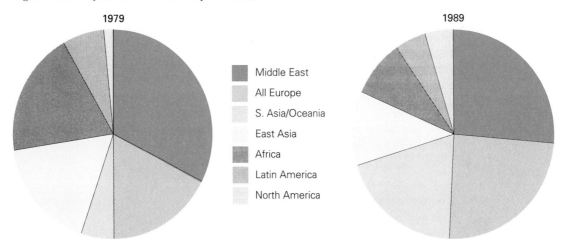

This graph illustrates that, despite some decline between 1979 and 1989, the countries of the Middle East were the largest importers of arms in the world. However, in the same period the share of arms imports in South Asia grew dramatically, reflecting conflicts and tensions involving Afghanistan, Pakistan, India, and Sri Lanka.

The Military in Politics

When defense is economically important and the perception of insecurity is great, military officials may acquire popularity, prestige, and political influence, at great cost to citizens' liberties. Political dominance by military leaders may undermine or distort civilian control of government and society. Again, this phenomenon is not new but has deep historical roots.

Sparta, the Greek city-state, under constant military threat from within and without for much of its history, organized its whole society according to military precepts. France, in the midst of revolution and at war with much of Europe in 1799, turned the country over to the young military hero, Napoleon Bonaparte.[98] Eighteenth-century Prussia, threatened on all sides by larger powers, transformed itself under Frederick the Great into a modern Sparta. And, in 1917, in the midst of World War I, the German government turned the country over to two senior military officers, Field Marshals Erich

[98]Bonapartism is still used to describe a military hero who seizes or is given political power often at the expense of democracy. Such leaders are also referred to as men on horseback, another allusion to Napoleon.

FIGURE 7.4

Leading Arms Importers

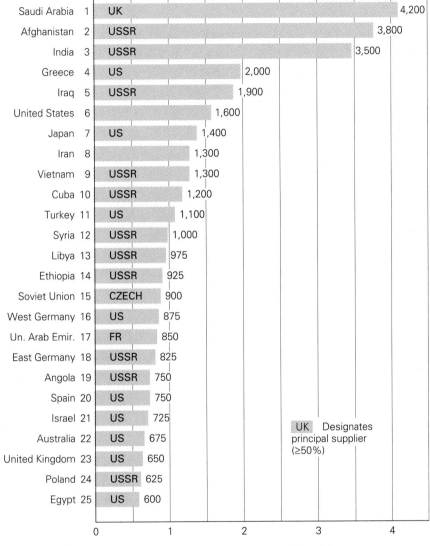

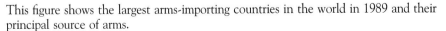

MILLIONS OF 1989 DOLLARS

This figure shows the largest arms-importing countries in the world in 1989 and their principal source of arms.

FIGURE 7.5

Arms Exporters

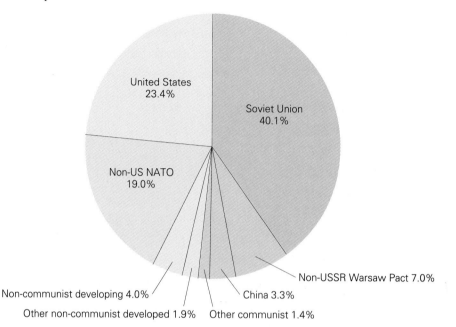

As the Cold War drew to a close, the Soviet Union was the world's leading exporter of arms the sale of which was a major source of hard currency. However, the United States and its NATO allies like Great Britain and France were also significant "merchants of death."

Ludendorff and Paul von Hindenburg. One historian writes, "Contemporaries likened their ascendance and their politics to the rise of total war."[99]

In this century, the military's takeover of Japan in the 1930s set the stage for World War II. For centuries, the military professionals—the *samurai*—had been admired in Japan and honored by Japan's official religion, *Shinto*. Although the Japanese political system in the 1920s was a multiparty parliamentary democracy, the armed forces remained independent of civilian control, and military officers without party affiliation were appointed ministers of the army and navy. Dissatisfaction with civilian rule was fueled by the world economic depression, Japanese dependence on imported raw materials, and Japanese perceptions of discrimination by the West. On September 18, 1931, Japanese

[99]Michael Geyer, "German Strategy in the Age of Machine Warfare, 1914–1945," p. 538. The failure of the Ludendorff–Hindenburg dictatorship in World War I contributed to Hitler's contempt for professional generals and his refusal to let them make major decisions during World War II.

army officers in China staged an "incident" in Mukden,[100] without the civilian government's knowledge or permission and used that episode as an excuse to conquer all of Manchuria. Edwin Reischauer describes what happened thereafter:

> The . . . change of mood within Japan soon brought an end to party cabinets. Small bodies of ultra-rightists among military officers and civilians had for some time been agitating for a military coup. The prime minister . . . was shot by a fanatic. . . . Other leaders were assassinated early in 1932, and the prime minister was killed by a group of young navy officers in May of that year. . . . Young army officers almost brought off a *coup d'état* on February 26, 1936 . . . and in 1937 all party participation in the cabinet was eliminated under a prime minister who was an army general.[101]

It was this military-dominated government that in 1937 launched a full-scale invasion of China and later planned the attack against Pearl Harbor.

Following Japan's defeat, an effort was made to eliminate the militarist spirit that had been so costly to the country and the world, and the new Japanese constitution that took effect in May 1947 renounced war forever. To this day, Japan continues to limit itself to "self-defense" forces, and has been reluctant to provide combat forces even for such multilateral operations as U.N. peacekeeping or the allied response to Iraq's occupation of Kuwait.

In contemporary global politics, "*leaders in mufti*" are common. Many of the world's governments are dominated by authoritarian military officers. In some countries, the military's purpose is less for providing security from external aggression than for maintaining *domestic* peace and keeping authoritarian regimes in power. Armies in Latin America have rarely fought wars with each other. Instead, they have functioned as political arbiters, deciding who should or should not remain in power, occasionally overthrowing civilian politicians and ruling directly, and forcing governments to pursue conservative policies at home. Although recent years have witnessed the military's retreat from politics in Latin America—Chile, Venezuela, Argentina, and Uruguay—civilian leaders continue to function in the soldiers' shadow.

Notorious military despots in recent years include Colonel Muammar Qadhafi of Libya (1969–), Major-General Idi Amin of Uganda (1971–1979), Major-General Joseph D. Mobutu of Zaire (1965–), General Alfredo Stroessner of Paraguay (1954–1989), General Muhammad Zia ul-Haq of Pakistan (1978–1988), General Augusto Pinochet of Chile (1974–1990), and the Panamanian "strongmen" Colonel Omar Torrijos (1969–1981) and General Manuel Noriega (1983–1989). Not all military leaders who seize power come from the higher ranks. Mobutu was a sergeant when he took control of what was then the Belgian Congo, and the governments of Ghana and Liberia were overthrown by Flight Lt. Jerry Rawlings (1979) and Sergeant Samuel Doe (1980) respectively. The military routinely

---

[100]See Chapter 13, p. 434.
[101]Edwin O. Reischauer, *The Japanese* (Cambridge: Harvard University Press, 1977), p. 99.

intervene in political life in Africa and Asia and even in Europe where military leaders used to govern Spain, Portugal, and Greece. In fact, regions like North America or Western Europe, with a tradition of civilian supremacy in politics, are rare.

Militarizing Society: Evidence from the U.S. Experience

Even where the military is barred from directly participating in governing, some have argued that its influence could become pervasive and in that way shape a society. Influenced by the militarization of German society in World Wars I and II and the military takeover of Japan in the 1930s, political scientist Harold D. Lasswell feared that a rise in tension among the major powers would thrust military leaders into power. Such "specialists in violence" might, he believed, seek to maintain global tension to preserve their status and privileges. Such societies Lasswell described as *garrison states*.[102] Despite the Cold War, the United States did not become a garrison state. Instead, it became a "*contract state*," which "extracted money and manpower for military purposes" but "at levels lower than Lasswell had anticipated."[103]

Of course, at a time when the Cold War triggered an explosive expansion of the American defense budget, interest groups proliferated, with the object of maintaining and even enlarging military spending. The Pentagon wishes to maintain spending not only to carry out its task of ensuring U.S. security but also to provide status and promotion for its personnel. Defense industries,[104] labor unions in which members' jobs depend on defense spending, and representatives of districts and states in which such industries are located are natural constituents of the Pentagon.[105] Other constituents include local districts with soldiers and dependents, which receive special government grants for their schools and where military spending aids the economy. The power of such interests is one reason those who expect a substantial peace dividend with the end of the Cold War may be disappointed.

Although reducing the defense budget to free up funds for pressing civilian needs may seem desirable,[106] such reductions entail wrenching dislocations as corporations lose business, jobs disappear, and communities find themselves losing business and

[102]Harold D. Lasswell, "The Garrison State," *American Journal of Sociology* 46 (January 1941), pp. 455–468. Lasswell's hypothesis applied in a Cold War setting can be found in Lasswell, "The Garrison State Hypothesis Today," in Samuel P. Huntington, ed., *Changing Patterns of Military Politics* (New York: Free Press, 1962), pp. 51–70.

[103]Aaron L. Friedberg, "Why Didn't the United States Become a Garrison State?" *International Security* 16:4 (Spring 1992), p. 113.

[104]Despite efforts to limit the practice, it is common for retiring military officers to take positions with defense contractors with which they had dealt in previous years.

[105]Senator Henry "Scoop" Jackson of Washington, who served thirty years in the U.S. Senate (1953–1983), was often referred to as the "Senator from Boeing" because that giant corporation was in his district and Jackson's support for military spending would benefit Boeing.

[106]It is difficult to show that defense reductions provide funds for other areas. See Alex Mintz, "Guns Versus Butter: A Disaggregated Analysis," *American Political Science Review* 83:4 (December 1989), pp. 1285–1293.

government money.[107] The Pentagon is already providing funds to such regions in an effort to facilitate life after defense spending. Communities such as Groton, Connecticut, where U.S. nuclear submarines are built, and their representatives in Congress have counterattacked to stave off painful reductions.

The cozy relationship among private defense interests, Congress, and the Pentagon has given rise to a belief that the United States has a *military-industrial complex*. This idea was elaborated by the sociologist C. Wright Mills, who argued that key political decisions in U.S. society are made by a small *"power elite"* that is held together by economic, social, and psychological factors. According to Mills,

> There is no longer, on the one hand, an economy, and, on the other, a political order, containing a military establishment unimportant to politics and to money-making. There is a political economy numerously linked with military order and decision.[108]

The warning uttered by President Dwight D. Eisenhower to the American public when he retired in 1961 reflects some of these worries:

> [T]his conjunction of an immense military establishment and a large arms industry is new in the American experience. The total influence—economic, political, even spiritual—is felt in every city, every state house, every office of the Federal Government. . . . In the councils of Government, we must guard against the acquisition of unwarranted influence . . . by the military-industrial complex. The potential for the disastrous rise of misplaced power exists and will persist.[109]

In fact, many prime military contractors in the United States are among the country's largest industrial corporations and, as shown in Table 7.5, 23 of the top 50 defense contractors in 1991 were drawn from the 100 largest corporations in America. Is it only coincidence that of 234 high-ranking officeholders Gabriel Kolko identified in the Departments of State, Defense, Treasury, and Commerce between 1944 and 1960 some 60 percent were "men who came from big business, investment, and law" so that "[a]t every level of the administration of the American state, domestically and internationally, business serves as the fount of critical assumptions or goals and strategically placed personnel"?[110] And, despite massive budget deficits and tight budgets, the Pentagon

---

[107]In 1992, the Philippines government decided not to renew the U.S. lease on the giant naval base at Subic Bay. This choice meant the end of orders placed with local businesses by the Navy for supplies and of the money sailors spent on shore leave.

[108]C. Wright Mills, "The Structure of Power in American Society," in Richard Gillam, ed., *Power in Postwar America* (Boston: Little, Brown, 1971), p. 55. Mills's full argument can be found in *The Power Elite* (New York: Oxford University Press, 1956).

[109]Dwight D. Eisenhower, "The Military-Industrial Complex," in Gillam, ed., *Power in Postwar America*, p. 158.

[110]Gabriel Kolko, *The Roots of American Foreign Policy: An Analysis of Power and Purpose* (Boston: Beacon Press, 1969), pp. 19, 26.

TABLE 7.5

Top Fifty U.S. Defense Contractors and Their Corporate Sales Rank for Fiscal Year 1991

Defense contract rank	Company	Corporate sales rank	Defense contract rank	Company	Corporate sales rank
1.	McDonnel Douglas Corporation	21	26.	GTE Corporation	a
2.	General Dynamics Corporation	50	27.	IBM Corporation	4
			28.	AT&T	a
3.	General Electric Corporation	5	29.	Allied Signal, Inc.	36
			30.	Harsco Corporation	a
4.	General Motors	1	31.	Olin Corporation	a
5.	Raytheon Company	51	32.	E Systems Inc.	a
6.	Northrop Corporation	97	33.	Exxon Corporation	2
7.	United Technologies Corporation	16	34.	Gencorp Inc.	a
8.	Martin Marietta Corporation	88	35.	Honeywell Inc.	83
9.	Lockheed Corporation	47	36.	Science Applications International Corporation	a
10.	Grumman Corporation	a	37.	Teledyne, Inc.	a
11.	Westinghouse Electric Corporation	30	38.	Dyncorp	a
12.	Rockwell International Corporation	35	39.	Oshkosh Truck Corporation	a
13.	Litton Industries, Inc.	99	40.	Arco Products Company	a
14.	FMC Corporation	a	41.	Mitre Corporation	a
15.	Unisys Corporation	58	42.	Foundation Health Corporation	a
16.	Loral Corporation	a	43.	Computer Sciences Corporation	a
17.	LTV Corporation	87	44.	Johns Hopkins University	a
18.	The Boeing Company	12	45.	MIT	a
19.	TRW, Inc.	62	46.	Aerospace Corporation	a
20.	Textron, Inc.	63	47.	World Rosen Key Amer et al. JV	a
21.	Texas Instruments, Inc.	77			
22.	ITT Corporation	a	48.	Coastal Corporation	49
23.	Bath Holding Corporation	a	49.	Royal Dutch Shell Group	a
24.	Federal Express, Pan Am, Northwest	a	50.	Hercules, Inc.	a
25.	Alliant Techsystems, Inc.	a			

aCompanies not listed in the top 100 in corporate sales.

SOURCE: Rankings of defense contracts are from *100 Companies Receiving the Largest Dollar Volume of Prime Contract Awards, Fiscal Year 1991* (Washington, D.C.: Department of Defense, Directorate for Information Operations and Reports, n.d.). Corporate ranks for 1991 are from "The 500 Largest U.S. Industrial Corporations," *Fortune*, April 20, 1992, pp. 220–222.

continues to spend millions to send weapons and personnel to trade shows around the world to help American defense contractors hawk their wares to the Third World.[111]

Fear of a garrison state has persuaded some that long periods of war or fear of war may undermine democracy. Thucydides described how democratic institutions in ancient Athens were eroded by the endless Peloponnesian War with Sparta and how demagogues ultimately brought Athens to disaster. The perversion of democratic institutions in Athens has been cited as an example of *"arrogance of power"*[112] and was compared with U.S. participation in an "unjust" war in Vietnam during the 1960s and 1970s. Indeed, intolerance of dissent at home, abuses of individual rights by the FBI and CIA in the name of "national security" and a pattern of government disregard for democratic traditions climaxed in the Watergate affair and resignation for President Richard M. Nixon in 1974. Later, during the 1970s and 1980s, suspicion about Soviet influence led to U.S. support of several covert operations worldwide, sometimes violating established congressional prohibitions, as in Angola. In Nicaragua, support for the anti-Sandinista *contras* resulted in the Iran-Contra Affair, an episode in which arms were illegally transferred to Iran and the profits used to fund the contras. Such challenges to the rule of law are the incidents Lasswell feared when he wrote of the garrison state.

Conclusion

Actors' willingness to resort to war and the manner in which wars are waged vary by time and place. The probability and nature of war at any moment reflect the underlying politics of the era's global system. As we have seen, changing technology is a large factor in determining political tension and in providing opportunities and setting limits on warfare. Memories of the past and expectations for the future condition leaders' willingness to resort to force and influence the types of wars they are prepared to fight. In this chapter we have reviewed the nature of war over the past six centuries. Disentangling the causes of those wars is very difficult. Although various theories of war are around, persuasive evidence is lacking on which are most accurate. Instead, it appears that causes vary by place and time. It is clear, however, that technology influences the probability and nature of war.

[111]R. Jeffrey Smith, "Guess Who's Paying to Hawk the Defense Industry Overseas?" *The Washington Post National Weekly Edition*, May 18–24, 1992, p. 31.

[112]This phrase was the title of a book by Senator J. William Fulbright of Arkansas criticizing U.S. involvement in Vietnam. Recalling the fate of Athens, Fulbright cautioned: "Other great nations . . . have aspired to too much, and by overextension of effort have declined and then fallen." Fulbright, *The Arrogance of Power* (New York: Vintage Books, 1966), p. 3. More recently, the idea that military overextension will erode power has been popularized by historian Paul Kennedy in *The Rise and Fall of the Great Powers: Economic Change and Military Conflict from 1500 to 2000* (New York: Random House, 1988).

The world wars profoundly affected a generation of leaders who found themselves at the helm during the Cold War. One additional factor intervened, however, altering everyone's calculations of the future. Nuclear weapons, introduced in 1945 forever changed warfare and global politics generally. In Chapter 8, we complete the story of war by examining the implications of these new weapons of mass destruction.

Key Terms

war
Correlates of War (COW) Project
civil wars
interstate war
Geneva Conventions
atrocities
human nature
death instinct
aggression
frustration
defense of superior orders
psychobiography
cognitive causes
affective causes
ethnocentrism
cognitive consistency
individual rationality
expected utility theory
crisis of overproduction
imperialism
class struggle
power preponderance
political pluralism
power cycle
arms races
chivalry
levée en masse
total war

means
ends
bargaining power
war of attrition
cult of the offensive
Schlieffen Plan
Maginot Line
Blitzkrieg (lightning war)
political warfare
appeasement
peace dividend
merchants of death
hard currency
samurai
leaders in mufti
garrison state
contract state
military-industrial complex
power elite
arrogance of power
Shinto
international law
scapegoats
capitalist encirclement
polarity
bipolarity
multipolarity
constant dollars

CHAPTER EIGHT

War in the Nuclear Era

On August 6, 1945, a lone U.S. B-29 Superfortress bomber, *Enola Gay*, dropped an atom bomb (called "Fat Man") on the Japanese city Hiroshima,[1] and the world would never be the same. Winston Churchill declared: "[W]hat was gunpowder? Trivial. What was electricity? Meaningless. This Atomic Bomb is the Second Coming in Wrath!"[2] The bomb, only 12 kilotons, was tiny by contemporary standards,[3] yet it killed 100,000 to 200,000 human beings by combining blast, raging fire, and radiation poisoning.[4] Three days later Nagasaki was struck, and soon thereafter World War II was over. Since 1945, nuclear weapons have not again been unleashed, but the threat of nuclear war has hung like the blade threatening Damocles. The nuclear age once born, global politics was forever changed.

The remarkable aspect of Hiroshima and Nagasaki was not the numbers who died but that so many could be killed so quickly and by one bomber and one bomb.[5] Thomas Schelling chillingly summarizes the nuclear revolution:

[1] Hiroshima was selected as the target partly because it had not been previously bombed: it would be easier to assess the atom bomb's effects.

[2] Cited in Herbert Feis, *The Atomic Bomb and the End of World War II* (Princeton: Princeton University Press, 1966), p. 87.

[3] Most current U.S. warheads range from .5 to 1 megaton. Russian warheads tend to be larger. The U.S.S.R. tested one device of 58 megatons. A *kiloton* is equivalent to 1,000 tons of TNT; a *megaton* to 1,000,000 tons of TNT.

[4] Similar numbers had died in the massive bombing of Tokyo in March 1945; there, incendiary bombs were chosen, not high explosives, because most Japanese lived in homes made of wood and thatch rather than brick. Most deaths were caused by firestorms so intense that people perished from suffocation because oxygen was burned away.

[5] Previously it would have taken 300 planes to cause as much damage. General H. H. Arnold, "Air Force in the Atomic Age," in Dexter Masters and Katherine Way, eds., *One World or None* (New York: McGraw-Hill, 1946), pp. 26–29.

A single bomb dropped from a single bomber on the Japanese city of Hiroshima destroyed the city and marked the beginning of the nuclear age.

Japan was defenseless by August 1945. With a combination of bombing and blockade, eventually invasion, and if necessary the deliberate spread of disease, the United States could probably have exterminated the population of the Japanese islands without nuclear weapons. . . . Against defenseless people there is not much that nuclear weapons can do that cannot be done with an icepick.[6]

Since Hiroshima, controversy has raged about whether the United States should have dropped the atom bomb. Although a nuclear device had been tested no one knew whether the bomb would work in combat. Suggestions that it be dropped on an unpopulated island, inviting Japanese witnesses, were set aside as impractical. President Truman and his advisers concluded that a demonstration would impress the enemy less than a real bombing and feared that, if invading the Japanese home islands were necessary, the cost in U.S. lives would be astronomical. Indeed, in the battles for Iwo Jima and Okinawa, Japanese defenders had shown themselves willing to fight to the

[6]Thomas C. Schelling, *Arms and Influence* (New Haven: Yale University Press, 1966), p. 19.

death. Finally, Truman wanted a quick end to the war to minimize the U.S.S.R.'s postwar role in governing Japan.[7]

In this chapter we review how nuclear weapons have changed warfare and, more generally, global politics. Has the nuclear weapon's destructive potential made war obsolete? Under what conditions can force be conceived of as a political instrument? How have these new weapons changed actors' calculations? What strategies have been designed to use these weapons for political ends, and how do *conventional weapons* fit into these strategies? What efforts have been made to control proliferation of weapons for mass destruction?

Needed: A New Military Strategy

The atom bomb grew from the discovery that enormous amounts of energy could be produced by splitting atoms in a chain reaction. The fission of uranium atoms releases neutrons and creates an atomic explosion. Scientists ran the first successful test of this theory at Alamagordo, New Mexico, July 16, 1945. For a time in the late 1940s, the United States enjoyed a monopoly on atomic knowledge. That era ended in September 1949, when the Soviet Union tested its own atomic bomb.[8] They did it earlier than U.S. experts had believed possible; as Americans became aware of the Soviet action, the first steps in a nuclear *arms race* had been taken.[9]

Vertical proliferation — competition between the United States and the Soviet Union to build more and better weapons — began immediately upon President Truman's decision (January 31, 1950) to develop a fusion bomb.[10] Instead of *nuclear fission* — splitting heavy atoms — the hydrogen bomb is based on *nuclear fusion*, combining light atoms. In fact, the hydrogen weapon requires an atomic bomb as a trigger. One major difference is the upper limit on the size of an atomic explosion; fusion weapons suffer no such limit. In 1952, the United States successfully tested its first hydrogen bomb, and two years later the U.S.S.R. did the same.

---

[7]At Yalta, the U.S.S.R. — previously neutral in the Pacific conflict — agreed to enter the war against Japan "two or three months" after Germany's surrender. The U.S.S.R. did declare war against Japan August 8, 1945, the day before Nagasaki was bombed. We can never know which event was more influential in persuading Japan to surrender. See Harry S Truman, *Memoirs*, vol. 1, *Year of Decisions* (Garden City, N.Y.: Doubleday, 1955), pp. 415–426.

[8]Peter R. Beckman, Larry Campbell, Paul W. Crumlish, Michael N. Dobkowski, and Steven P. Lee, *The Nuclear Predicament: Nuclear Weapons in the Cold War and Beyond*, 2nd ed. (Englewood Cliffs, N.J.: Prentice-Hall, 1992), p. 87.

[9]Peter A. Clausen, *Nonproliferation and the National Interest* (New York: HarperCollins, 1993), p. 23.

[10]Richard Smoke, "The Year of Shocks," in Jeffrey Porro with Paul Doty, Carl Kaysen, and Jack Ruina, eds., *The Nuclear Age Reader* (New York: Alfred A. Knopf, 1989), p. 51.

In the next years, proliferation was horizontal: weapons spread to additional countries. In 1952, the British tested their first atomic device,[11] and in 1960, France tested two in the Sahara Desert.[12] Not to hang back, the People's Republic of China joined the nuclear club in 1964, and in 1974, India, "for peaceful purposes," exploded a nuclear device and became the world's sixth nuclear power. With the U.S.S.R. dissolving in 1991, *horizontal nuclear proliferation* quickened. Four of the states created therefrom inherited Soviet nuclear weapons: Russia, Ukraine, Kazakhstan, and Belarus. Other states such as Israel and Pakistan may already have nuclear weapons, and still others, including Iran and North Korea, are seeking nuclear capability. Horizontal proliferation is a vital issue, but here we focus on the superpower relationship and the sustained competition to invent bigger, more accurate, and more destructive weapons.

America's nuclear monopoly after World War II and participation by civilian strategists in military planning made the United States the source of many strategic nuclear innovations. As additional states deployed atomic weapons, especially the Soviet Union, the superpowers found a new strategy — nuclear deterrence — on which to build superpower relations. To convey the flavor of this strategy and its evolution, we consider the late 1940s to the early 1960s, during which time the United States enjoyed strategic military superiority. We then turn to changes in the deterrence relationship in the 1960s and later, after Moscow achieved nuclear parity with the United States.

A Munich–Pearl Harbor Complex

As the Cold War dominated the global agenda,[13] two aspects of America's World War II experience increasingly structured the leaders' perceptions, deeply influencing their attitudes toward nuclear weapons. First, they believed that prewar *appeasement*, combined with U.S. *isolationism* between World Wars I and II, had whetted the dictators' appetites, encouraging further aggression. Second, they feared the Pearl Harbor attack might be repeated. For many postwar politicians, the searing 1930s and the subsequent war formed beliefs that would guide their decisions in the Cold War.[14]

The idea that appeasement had not satisfied but provoked Hitler, Mussolini, and Tojo became an axiom as the Cold War unfolded. For an American politician to be seen as an appeaser was political suicide. Stalin was just another dictator hungering for conquest, and Western leaders were determined not to make the same mistake again.

[11]C. J. Bartlett, *"The Special Relationship": A Political History of Anglo-American Relations Since 1945* (London: Longman, 1992), p. 68.

[12]Roy C. Macridis, "French Foreign Policy: The Quest for Rank," in Macridis, ed., *Foreign Policy in World Politics*, 8th ed. (Englewood Cliffs, N.J.: Prentice-Hall, 1992), p. 64.

[13]See Chapter 12.

[14]For an effort to reappraise prewar appeasement using new historical information, see J. L. Richardson, "New Perspectives on Appeasement: Some Implications for International Relations," *World Politics* 40:3 (April 1988), pp. 289–316.

President Truman recalled how he thought back to the 1930s, as he rushed back from Kansas City to Washington, D.C., after Secretary of State Dean Acheson told him about the North Korean invasion of South Korea:

> In my generation, this was not the first occasion when the strong had attacked the weak. I recalled some earlier instances: Manchuria, Ethiopia, Austria. I remembered how each time that the democracies failed to act it had encouraged the aggressors to keep going ahead. Communism was acting in Korea just as Hitler, Mussolini, and the Japanese had acted ten, fifteen, and twenty years earlier. I felt certain that if South Korea was allowed to fall Communist leaders would be emboldened to override nations closer to our own shores. . . . If this was allowed to go unchallenged it would mean a third world war, just as similar incidents had brought on the second world war.[15]

To avoid having to mobilize for war *after* it had broken out, as in 1917 and 1941, the United States had to devise a strategy built on advance *commitments* to keep potential aggressors from feeding vain hopes.[16] The policy must be erected from *positions of strength*. The nuclear-deterrence strategy fits both criteria. It is meant to avoid war by threatening retaliation, anchored by clear commitments.[17] One must have powerful military forces to carry out the retaliation.

For Americans, the *bolt from the blue* at Pearl Harbor, that day which would "live in infamy," according to President Roosevelt, was traumatic — an event that must not be permitted to recur. One consequence of the Pearl Harbor tragedy was U.S. construction of an elaborate system of human and technical intelligence organized in an *intelligence community* — the Central Intelligence Agency (CIA), the National Security Agency (NSA), and the Defense Intelligence Agency (DIA), among others — with the task of preventing a surprise attack.[18] A second consequence was the introduction of military

[15]Harry S Truman, *Memoirs*, vol. 2, *Years of Trial and Hope* (Garden City, N.Y.: Doubleday, 1956), pp. 332–333.

[16]Some empirical analysis suggests that the stuff of which commitments are made — alliances, weapons, and past performance — do *not* contribute to successful deterrence. Paul Huth and Bruce Russett, "What Makes Deterrence Work? Cases from 1900 to 1980," *World Politics* 36:4 (July 1984), pp. 496–526. For criticism of the assumptions, data, and methods Huth and Russett use, see Richard Ned Lebow and Janice Gross Stein, "Rational Deterrence Theory: I Think, Therefore I Deter," *World Politics* 41:2 (January 1989), pp. 208–224, and Lebow and Stein, "Deterrence: The Elusive Dependent Variable," *World Politics* 42:3 (April 1990), pp. 336–369. Lebow and Stein argue for the historical case method. Huth and Russett argue that "Lebow and Stein's conceptual imprecision and theoretical misunderstandings cause them to present a misleading critique of our work and to offer an alternative research strategy that fails to meet the standards of rigorous social science." "Testing Deterrence Theory: Rigor Makes a Difference," *World Politics* 42:4 (July 1990), p. 468.

[17]Historians point out that in 1914 Germany may have been deceived by the absence of a clear British commitment to come to the aid of France. This claim was popularized by the German Chancellor, who sought to excuse his own errors.

[18]The end of the Cold War created a crisis for U.S. intelligence agencies, forcing them to adapt to conditions in which the threat of a Soviet attack was no longer their first priority. The agencies instead began to focus on such issues as international terrorism and industrial espionage and sought ways of gathering information about economic and environmental trends.

technologies and tactics designed either to allow nuclear forces to retaliate before being struck or to survive such a strike and retaliate afterward.

The Doctrine of Massive Retaliation

During the U.S. nuclear monopoly, the American strategy was to use nuclear weapons just as heavy bombers had been applied in World War II, without recognizing the change nuclear weapons had caused in warfare.[19] In time, though, it became apparent to strategists that nuclear weapons posed new problems. Once the Soviet Union exploded its first atomic bomb in September 1949, fresh memories of Pearl Harbor and fears of a bolt from the blue, focused U.S. attention on preventing an attack on the American homeland. Assembling a credible threat to retaliate for such an attack seemed relatively simple for two reasons. First, no one doubted that Americans were committed to defending their own homes, and second, the nuclear balance favored the United States.

By 1954, the Eisenhower administration, venturing a New-Look policy, introduced the strategy of *massive retaliation*. The idea behind the policy—a policy never actually practiced—was to threaten a possible nuclear first strike against the U.S.S.R. or China if the communists initiated conventional or guerrilla war.[20] The doctrine's purpose was twofold—to provide a credible deterrent to such local probes as the invasion of South Korea and to contain mounting defense costs by finding an inexpensive substitute for the massive conventional forces that were believed necessary to cope with the U.S.S.R. and China. Like the Reagan administration twenty-five years later, the Eisenhower administration frightened observers by talking tougher than it acted.[21]

Secretary of State John Foster Dulles described massive retaliation as willingness to "retaliate, instantly, by means and at places of our own choosing."[22] The strategy did not mean the United States would use nuclear weapons in every case of aggression, although Dulles's rhetoric implied that the administration was prepared to use nuclear weapons in various contingencies.[23] It was hoped that the mere *possibility* of retaliation would prevent aggression. In 1954, Dulles wrote:

[19]Initial U.S. policy was to restrict nuclear sharing, even with its close ally Britain, and to turn nuclear technology over to the U.N. under the Baruch Plan. The British protested against their exclusion from this new technology, and the Soviets rejected the Baruch Plan. See Clausen, *Nonproliferation and National Interest*, pp. 9–22.

[20]See Lawrence Freedman, *The Evolution of Nuclear Strategy*, 2nd ed. (New York: St. Martin's Press, 1989), pp. 81–88.

[21]At the same time, U.S. conventional forces in Europe and Asia were equipped with short-range nuclear weapons such as atomic mines to compensate for disadvantages in numbers. The policy was dubious because fewer Americans were crowded into a smaller land area than their Soviet and Chinese opponents, and their supply lines, especially the European ports through which U.S. reinforcements would have to pour, were vulnerable to nuclear attack.

[22]Cited in Beckman, et al., *Nuclear Predicament*, p. 79.

[23]Discussion of a *rollback* policy to force the Red Army out of Eastern Europe reinforced this devil-may-care impression.

It should not be stated in advance precisely what would be the scope of military action if new aggression occurred. . . . That is a matter as to which the aggressor had best remain ignorant. But he can know . . . that the choice in this respect is ours and not his.[24]

The policy's real aim was to prevent a Soviet invasion of Western Europe.[25] In that goal, U.S. strategy succeeded. It was less successful in preventing aggression elsewhere, and U.S. nuclear power proved irrelevant in the Korean War (1950–1953), the Suez war (1956),[26] and the Soviet invasion of Hungary (1956).

America's Nuclear Monopoly Ends

Even as massive retaliation was being expounded, the real world conspired to make it obsolete. The controlling factor was the growing Soviet nuclear capability heightening the risk to continental America and challenging America's ability to ensure security for allies in Europe and Asia. Before the Soviet Union acquired the ability to strike North America, U.S. nuclear weapons had held Soviet cities and the Soviet public hostage to their government's good behavior.[27] In turn, the Red Army's conventional might held U.S. allies hostage to Washington's good behavior. Growing Soviet capabilities altered this equation. The U.S. threat to use nuclear weapons first in the event of a Soviet conventional attack on an ally lost *credibility* because it was difficult to believe that Americans (or anyone else) would risk their own survival for someone else.

By 1957, North America was vulnerable to attack, and a new military strategy was urgently needed. America's sense of vulnerability was heightened by Soviet deployment of new bombers — the Bison and the Bear — with the range to strike the United States.[28] More troubling, the Soviet Union successfully tested an intercontinental missile in August 1957 and then launched the first artificial satellite, *Sputnik* ("fellow traveler") I, in October. The United States was no longer invulnerable to a nuclear attack. The alleged missile gap became a presidential-election issue in 1960.

These events had three major strategic consequences. First, U.S. strategists began to consider the requirements of a nuclear force with second-strike capability — that is,

[24]Cited in Lawrence Freedman, *The Evolution of Nuclear Strategy* 2nd ed. (New York: St. Martin's Press, 1989), p. 86.

[25]Albert Carnesale, Paul Doty, Stanley Hoffmann, Samuel P. Huntington, Joseph S. Nye, Jr., and Scott D. Sagan, *Living with Nuclear Weapons* (New York: Bantam Books, 1983), p. 79. As the authors point out, the Soviet Union, even after acquiring nuclear weapons, lacked systems (long-range aircraft) for delivering these weapons (p. 79), leaving the U.S. with an effective nuclear monopoly. They in turn acquired this capability some years later.

[26]The U.S.S.R. threatened to use nuclear weapons against the British and French if they did not withdraw after they invaded Egypt.

[27]As early as 1946, President Truman threatened the U.S.S.R. with nuclear weapons if it did not withdraw troops from northern Iran.

[28]Carnesale et al., *Living with Nuclear Weapons*, pp. 82–83.

capable of absorbing an initial nuclear attack and retaliating afterward. Second, thought was given to a nuclear war-fighting strategy. What should the targets be? How should a nuclear war be fought? Third, attention was paid to the conditions under which nuclear war would be fought. Should nuclear war be an immediate option, as implied by the strategy of massive retaliation; should nuclear weapons be used only as a last resort; or should such weapons be part of a flexible-response strategy?[29]

These questions led to a strategy that took into account the superpowers' growing capabilities. Before turning to the details of that strategy—*mutual assured destruction (MAD)*—we must examine more closely the nuclear-deterrence concept on which that strategy was built.

Deterrence in Theory and Practice

Deterrence is not peculiar to the nuclear age, but nuclear weapons significantly changed the strategy.[30] The essential claim behind the strategy may be stated succinctly: A potential aggressor will not attack if it is persuaded that it will suffer "unacceptable" punishment from a defender as a result of its attack. The potential aggressor is deterred if it believes the defender has the *means* and the *will* to carry out its retaliatory threat and that the threat is *credible*. Assuming rationality, an actor will refrain from attacking because the expected costs will exceed expected gains.[31] If a potential aggressor is persuaded that the defender's means are inadequate or that the defender lacks the nerve to carry out its threat, it may attack. Deterrence succeeds if no attack occurs; it fails if the threat is discounted.[32] The theory also assumes that actors are "unitary" and ignores differences in cultural norms, propensity to take risks, psychological stability of leaders, or procedures for making decisions. We shall address these assumptions shortly, but let us first bring the weapons themselves into the discussion.

---

[29]Ibid., pp. 84–85.

[30]For an analysis of deterrence prior to nuclear weapons, see George H. Quester, *Deterrence Before Hiroshima* (New York: Wiley, 1966).

[31]For a defense of this debatable assumption, see Christopher H. Achen and Duncan Snidal, "Rational Deterrence Theory and Comparative Case Studies," *World Politics* 41:2 (January 1989), pp. 143–169. Deterrence theory originally evolved as an exercise in deductive logic with little empirical input, and it assumed that leaders are rational.

[32]Recognizing success or failure of deterrence can be a problem. Deterrence succeeds if no attack occurs, but, it might be argued that nothing happened because the target of the strategy never intended to attack in the first place. It is like the joke about a person who is standing on his head at one end of the Brooklyn Bridge. When a policeman asks why he is behaving so oddly, the person answers that he is keeping the elephants out of Manhattan. When the policeman says, chuckling, that there are no elephants in Manhattan, the person declares: "See? It works!"

First Strike, Second Strike, and Nuclear Deterrence

We must first understand *first-strike* and *second-strike capability*. First-strike capability is one actor's ability to initiate an attack that will destroy an enemy's capacity to retaliate. When a successful first strike is possible, the incentive is there to attack first and defeat the adversary before being attacked. If deterrence fails, an attack may be initiated without devastating military consequences for the attacker. The prospect that actors may have a crippling first-strike capability is dangerous. Under tense conditions, the security dilemma intensifies, for each adversary fears the other may be tempted to strike first, removing the threat to its survival in one fell swoop.

Once an actor gains the means to enable a significant portion of its nuclear forces to survive an enemy's first strike, it has a *second-strike capability*. That capacity is the way to reduce incentives to attack quickly or first, for a first strike would only induce a destructive retaliatory blow. Such capability can stabilize a nuclear relationship if the adversaries possess roughly equal capability. If one actor has a second-strike capability and the other does not, the first may still have some incentive for a first strike in a conflict. Once adversaries gain a substantial second-strike capability, though, little incentive remains for either to attack first. The result is a balance of terror, in which stability flows from the condition called mutually assured destruction. Although MAD had been around three decades, each side feared technological changes that might give the enemy a first-strike capability, and such worries fueled the nuclear arms race.

Maintaining Successful Deterrence

Successful deterrence depends on the "rationality of irrationality." It is rational to persuade an enemy that you are crazy enough to start a nuclear war, but it is probably crazy to carry out that threat. The problem with nuclear deterrence becomes clearer when it is viewed, Edward Rhodes writes, as "a relationship in which the rational and the irrational are inherently linked." He continues:

> On the one hand, nuclear threats create the potential for significant political power. . . . On the other hand, the mutual vulnerability . . . that stems from the existence of capabilities for Mutual Assured Destruction—MAD—threatens to make the actual execution of nuclear threats quite mad, at least for a state that values its own survival.[33]

Successful deterrence, then, is a psychological relationship[34] between two or more actors in which each threatens the other(s) with destruction even though the

[33]Edward Rhodes, *Power and MADness: The Logic of Nuclear Coercion* (New York: Columbia University Press, 1989), p. 1.

[34]Robert Jervis, "Introduction: Approach and Assumptions," in Robert Jervis, Richard Ned Lebow, and Janice Gross Stein, eds., *Psychology and Deterrence* (Baltimore: Johns Hopkins Press, 1985), p. 1.

threatening actor too may be annihilated. If actors have invulnerable[35] nuclear weapons, deterrence threats work only if each believes the other is prepared to commit suicide. It is rational to be deterred by such a threat if one accepts that the adversary is sufficiently irrational to carry it out. It is also rational to *pretend* either to be irrational enough to use nuclear weapons first or not to care whether the enemy does so. Before the Soviet Union acquired nuclear weapons, Stalin publicly discounted the importance of such weapons in war[36] to convince the West that he could not be blackmailed by them.

Extended Deterrence, Counterforce, and Nuclear Weapons

The issue of *extended deterrence*—providing nuclear protection to allies—sharpened the problem of credibility. With America vulnerable to Soviet nuclear attack and such Europeans as President Charles de Gaulle of France publicly expressing doubts about U.S. willingness to commit suicide for Europe, strategists in the 1960s began to accept, Thomas Schelling observes, "that it does not always help to be, or to be believed to be, fully rational, cool-headed, and in control of oneself or of one's country."[37] For extended deterrence to work, it was *not* necessary for the adversary to be absolutely certain that nuclear weapons would be introduced, only that the risk that they would was significant.

Uncertainty, not certainty, was the key to extended deterrence, and such uncertainty could be manipulated by actions that raised the cost of backing down in a crunch. Among such U.S. actions was stationing troops (along with their dependents) in Europe where their presence would raise the stakes if war with the U.S.S.R. came. The U.S. garrison in West Berlin was a *tripwire*. Surrounded by the enemy and far from help, the only role for that garrison in a U.S.-Soviet conflict would be to die, raising the stakes in the conflict.

It was not necessary to threaten immediate nuclear retaliation for an attack on Western Europe; it was enough merely to threaten escalation to any level necessary to halt aggression. During the early 1960s a version of this strategy, *flexible response*, provided extended deterrence. Beefed-up U.S. conventional forces would initially try to defend Europe against a conventional Soviet attack, but if they failed, NATO reserved the option of introducing nuclear weapons. Under such conditions, things might get out of control, a condition Schelling described as *brinkmanship*:

> It means exploiting the danger that somebody may inadvertently go over the brink, dragging the other with him. If two climbers are tied together, and one wants to intimidate the other by seeming about to fall over the edge, there has to be some uncertainty or anticipated irrationality or it won't work. . . . With loose ground,

---

[35] A weapons system is invulnerable if it is unlikely to be destroyed in an enemy attack.

[36] Stalin argued that wars would be determined by "permanently operating factors" like national morale. See H. S. Dinerstein, *War and the Soviet Union* (New York: Praeger, 1959).

[37] Schelling, *Arms and Influence*, p. 37.

gusty winds, and a propensity toward dizziness, there is some danger when a climber approaches the edge; one can credibly threaten to fall off *accidentally* by standing near the brink.[38]

Credibility is high because it is a "threat that leaves something to chance," in which "*the final decision is not altogether under the threatener's control*," and therefore nobody bears full responsibility for the disaster that may ensue.[39] Although the details of flexible response changed in subsequent decades, later NATO strategies were all variations on the original theme.

Ultimately, the dilemma posed by extended deterrence cannot be completely overcome because the guarantor has two audiences—its adversary *and* its allies. On the one hand, the guarantor must be tough and willing to take risks to convince the adversary that the threat is credible. On the other, the guarantor must appear judicious and prudent enough to persuade its allies that it will not trigger a war in which they will become embroiled against their will. The appearance of prudence, though reassuring to allies, may reduce an adversary's fear of the guarantor and so weaken deterrence. How to balance the need for a reputation for strength and risk-taking with an image of caution and reasonableness is an unsolved puzzle in the nuclear age.

From time to time the strategy of deterrence has been threatened by rival strategies that sought to move away from reliance on mutual assured destruction of population centers and toward including *counterforce* attacks on military targets. These rival strategies, proposed by both U.S. and Soviet leaders at various times, envisioned controlled conflicts in which escalation led to nuclear exchanges that could be terminated by political agreement short of all-out war. Such attacks, it was argued, could save lives by reducing an enemy's arsenal and would signal resolve. Counterforce strategies leave a number of questions unanswered, however. Do not nuclear weapons that are accurate enough for counterforce also create a first-strike capability and therefore destabilize the nuclear relationship? Is it possible during a nuclear exchange for leaders to remain sufficiently cool-headed and in control of their forces to prevent escalation to all-out war?

Problems in Nuclear Deterrence

Such doubts raise further questions about nuclear weapons and deterrence. *Stability* and *vulnerability* are at the heart of most of these questions. These in turn are related to the problems posed by technological change, especially missile and warhead accuracy.[40] A fundamental ethical question is: What good is a strategy that depends on nuclear threats to prevent war?

[38]Ibid., p. 99. Emphasis in original.

[39]Thomas C. Schelling, *The Strategy of Conflict* (Cambridge: Harvard University Press, 1960), pp. 187, 188. Emphasis in original.

[40]For a summary of such issues, see Ray Perkins, Jr., *The ABCs of the Soviet-American Nuclear Arms Race* (Pacific Grove, Calif.: Brooks/Cole, 1991).

Stability and Vulnerability

Strategic stability refers to leaders' incentives or disincentives to decide in haste and strike an adversary first. If actors fear their ability to retaliate is at risk, they may be tempted to use nuclear weapons quickly, especially during confrontations in which tempers and stress are high. Such a relationship is unstable. Conditions in which both sides feel that their own retaliatory systems are secure and that no one could reap a substantial advantage by striking first contribute to stability.

One of the paradoxes in a deterrence relationship is that stability, and therefore safety, actually *increase* if actors lack the means to defend themselves. As long as each side believes it can retaliate against an enemy no matter what that enemy does first, it will feel secure. This attitude may appear to turn common sense on its head. A serious civil-defense effort to construct antimissile missiles or air-raid shelters would reduce stability (even though it might save lives if war came). Although such shelters do not appear to be offensive in intent, constructing them would reduce the deterrent effect of a threat to retaliate. For this reason, in the logic of deterrence such shelters are regarded as highly provocative. If this logic appears convoluted, imagine your thoughts on awakening to a news report that during the night all Russian citizens had moved into air-raid shelters.

Vulnerability is closely related to stability and refers to the *survivability* of an actor's nuclear forces following an enemy first strike. Vulnerability and stability are inversely related: If nuclear-weapons systems are vulnerable to enemy attack, a deterrence relationship will be less stable; if such systems are invulnerable, stability will be enhanced. The superpowers took several steps to make their nuclear-weapons systems less vulnerable, including keeping forces on alert, dispersing and hiding weapons, "hardening" the weapons, and making forces mobile. Finally, arms-control and disarmament agreements were reached as part of the effort to stabilize the relationship.

The relationship was most dangerous in the 1950s and early 1960s when both superpowers depended on long-range bombers to deliver nuclear weapons, because airports and aircraft are relatively indefensible targets (as shown at Pearl Harbor). Under such conditions, both sides kept their forces in high readiness. Unidentified blips on radar screens (on occasion they turned out to be geese) sent crews scurrying to their aircraft.[41] During this period the Soviet Union depended on its gigantic land area to disperse and hide aircraft and missiles. In May 1960 an American U-2 spy plane, piloted by Francis Gary Powers, was downed near the Soviet city of Sverdlovsk. Soviet Premier Nikita S. Khrushchev, infuriated by the incident, canceled a summit conference he was about to hold with Western leaders. One reason for his anger was recognizing that the United States had the means to pinpoint Soviet bases, increasing Soviet forces' vulnerability.

---

[41] During crises, U.S. bombers took off and remained aloft, prepared to attack the U.S.S.R. when ordered to do so. This was the "fail-safe procedure."

The successful test of *Sputnik* I in 1957 and later of ballistic missiles raised new fears about vulnerability. The new technology meant that cities and weapons were now vulnerable to a first strike. The first generation of missiles on both sides sat in the open and had to be filled with liquid fuel just before launch. (The fuel was too volatile to be kept on board.) Such weapons were at once frightening and highly tempting targets. A second generation of missiles soon began to appear, using solid fuel and based in hardened underground concrete silos, making them difficult to destroy and easy to launch quickly. Even more revolutionary were submarine-launched missiles that were made invulnerable by combining concealment and mobility. In time, U.S. and Soviet nuclear-powered submarines with submarine-launched ballistic missiles (SLBMs) would spend months at a time lying silent and undetected under the polar ice pack, ready to retaliate if war began.

By the mid-1960s, the superpowers sought to ensure that their forces were invulnerable by simultaneously maintaining long-range bombers, nuclear-armed submarines, and land-based missiles. Efforts to maintain the several delivery systems in the United States were justified by the *triad* doctrine. Each leg of the triad was to provide an independent second-strike capability. The elements in each nation's triad differed: About 70 percent of the Soviet force were land-based missiles, but U.S. nuclear weapons were more evenly divided.

Destructiveness, Accuracy, and Stability

Destructiveness and accuracy of nuclear weapons strongly determine stability and vulnerability. *Destructiveness* is the extent of damage caused by weapons, and *accuracy* is their ability to hit targets. Since the 1960s, both superpowers have sought to create more destructive, more accurate weapons. The United States was able to create the more accurate weapons, obviating the need for more destructive power. The Soviet Union built weapons with greater destructive power, partly to compensate for the lower accuracy of some of its missiles.

The relationship connecting destructiveness, accuracy, and stability is illustrated by the consequences of a Soviet decision to deploy such giant missiles as the SS-8 and SS-9 and later the SS-18 and SS-19. Such missiles were thought to threaten U.S. land-based missiles, making one leg of the triad vulnerable to a Soviet first strike. The Americans too built new generations of missiles — Minuteman III and, later the missile experimental or MX — with improved accuracy that gave them a first-strike potential. The *MIRVed* (*multiple independently targetable reentry vehicles*) missile was a major destabilizing factor. The acronym MIRV meant that several nuclear warheads could ride on each missile and that each could be programmed to hit a different target. These MIRVed missiles were first-strike weapons and highly tempting targets for an enemy first strike. Such technological improvements fueled the arms race and reduced, rather than increased, the rival's security.

Even as the Cold War was winding down, the superpowers continued to upgrade their nuclear forces. Early in the 1980s, the Reagan administration committed the United States to modernizing all three triad components—MX missiles to improve the land-based leg, Trident-D submarines for the sea-based leg, and B-1 and Stealth bombers to improve the air leg. The Soviets continued to build heavy missiles (SS-18s and SS-19s) and deployed new missiles (SS-24 and SS-25). Both sides also introduced new intermediate-range missiles (less than 3,000 miles in range)—the Soviets had the SS-20 and the Americans the cruise missile and Pershing II. These missiles were accurate and hard to detect and could be used for a first strike against Western Europe or the U.S.S.R., respectively.

Cruise missiles are a special problem for stability because they are pilotless planes with precision guidance, and it is difficult to verify whether they carry nuclear warheads. The weapons can be launched from bombers, allowing the latter to stand off and fire at enemy targets without penetrating enemy airspace, from naval vessels, and from land.[42] On the one hand these missiles are relatively unthreatening because they are slow compared to ICBMs. However, their accuracy and ability to evade radar detection by flying at low altitudes make them potential first-strike weapons. They are also a relatively simple and inexpensive technology that is available to other countries, worsening the prospect of nuclear proliferation.

The most controversial technological innovation in the 1980s was President Ronald Reagan's proposal of March 23, 1983, for a *Strategic Defense Initiative* (SDI), also called "Star Wars."[43] The proposal was notable not simply because of the revolutionary technology that it required but because it was a giant step away from reliance on mutual assured destruction. Apparently, on assuming office President Reagan had been horrified to learn that the strategy for mutual survival depended on holding populations hostage and therefore on ensuring that they could be killed in a nuclear war. According to one source, the president "is alleged to have postponed his SIOP [Single Integrated Operations Plan—the list of enemy targets to be struck in the event of war] briefing for three years after assuming office," and that briefing "reportedly left him ashen-faced and speechless."[44] "Wouldn't it be better," Reagan asked, "to save lives than to avenge them?" "What if free people could live secure in the knowledge that their security did not rest upon the threat of instant United States retaliation to deter a Soviet attack, that we could intercept and destroy strategic

[42]A new generation of acronyms accompanied these developments: ALCMs (air-launched cruise missiles), SLCMs (sea-launched cruise missiles), and GLCMs (ground-launched cruise missiles). The SLCMs with conventional (not nuclear) payloads were used against Iraq as the 1991 war began in the Persian Gulf. Cruise technology begat a whole generation of precision-guided or "smart" weapons that revolutionized conventional warfare.

[43]The U.S.S.R. has had a modest anti-missile defense system ("Galosh") around Moscow since late in the 1960s.

[44]Lebow, *Nuclear Crisis Management*, p. 121.

FIGURE 8.1

Cruise Missile

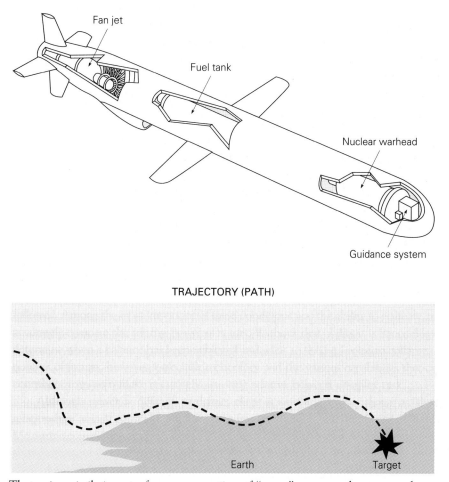

The cruise missile is part of a new generation of "smart" weapons that can evade enemy radar and deliver a nuclear payload precisely on its target.

ballistic missiles before they reached our own soil or that of our allies?" To this end he called for an antiballistic missile system that "could counter the awesome Soviet threat with measures that are defensive," and he offered to share the results of research with the U.S.S.R.[45]

[45] "'Peace and Security,'" President Reagan's Televised Address to the Nation, March 23, 1983," reprinted in *Realism, Strength, Negotiation: Key Foreign Policy Statements of the Reagan Administration* (Washington, D.C.: U.S. Department of State, May 1984).

The SDI program had several variants, but all depended on generating critical new technologies. Many billions of dollars later SDI appears to be an expensive illusion that is unlikely to be realized, and efforts by the U.S. Defense Department to doctor the results of SDI tests have been revealed. We will never know how it would have affected stability in the superpower deterrence relationship had it been available. A tentative conclusion is that if *only one side* had deployed such a system, it would have been destabilizing, permitting that side to act with impunity. If both sides had deployed such a system simultaneously, however (an idea implicit in the president's offer to share SDI technology), then stability need not have been endangered.

Nuclear Deterrence: Conceptual and Ethical Doubts

Other criticisms of nuclear deterrence focus on doubts about its assumptions and ethics. The strategy assumes that the actors are unitary and rational. In fact, as we see elsewhere, decisions may be determined by bureaucratic power struggles and bargaining or by the political pulling and hauling that takes place while decisions are reached.[46] And we can hardly assume that all leaders will evaluate costs and benefits in the same way or will perceive a situation correctly. The quality and amount of information and the amount of stress will vary and will affect perceptions.

Leaders differ in cognitive and cultural predispositions because their experiences and personalities differ. Prime Minister Chamberlain's experience in World War I conditioned him to believe that almost anything was preferable to war, whereas President Truman's memory of World War II prepared him to respond firmly to aggression. Some leaders may be victims of wishful thinking, group pressure, or a multitude of other factors that can distort judgment and perceptions of reality.[47] As one observer concludes "[D]eterrence is inadequate as an explanatory theory of international relations because the growing body of empirical evidence . . . indicates that neither leaders contemplating challenges nor leaders seeking to prevent them necessarily act as the theory predicts."[48]

[46]See Chapter 11, pp. 379–382.

[47]Extensive research has been done on perception and rationality in international crises. See, for example, Robert Jervis, *Perception and Misperception in International Politics* (Princeton: Princeton University Press, 1976); Alexander L. George and Richard Smoke, *Deterrence in American Foreign Policy* (New York: Columbia University Press, 1974); Richard Ned Lebow, *Between Peace and War: The Nature of International Crisis* (Baltimore: Johns Hopkins University Press, 1981); Richard Ned Lebow, *Nuclear Crisis Management: A Dangerous Illusion* (Ithaca, N.Y.: Cornell University Press, 1987); Glenn H. Snyder and Paul Diesing, *Conflict among Nations: Bargaining, Decision Making, and System Structure in International Crises* (Princeton: Princeton University Press, 1977); and John D. Steinbruner, *The Cybernetic Theory of Decision* (Princeton: Princeton University Press, 1974). Especially provocative is Irving L. Janis, *Victims of Groupthink: A Psychological Study of Foreign-Policy Decisions and Fiascoes* (Boston: Houghton Mifflin, 1972).

[48]Richard Ned Lebow, "Conclusions," in Jervis et al., *Psychology and Deterrence* p. 203.

Assumptions about deterrence have been criticized, and ethical objections have also been raised against the strategy. Is it moral to premise a military strategy on possible use of *weapons of mass destruction* (even for a "just" cause) that by their nature must violate international laws prohibiting attacks against undefended civilian centers, hospitals, and religious centers? And, though nuclear weapons have not themselves been outlawed, exploding them releases poisonous substances that are prohibited.[49] To what extent is use of such weapons "thinkable"?[50]

Some scientific analyses suggest that nuclear war cannot be waged without catastrophic consequences.[51] The blast and radiation of a single one-megaton weapon, detonated 3,000 feet up, would kill all unprotected people in a nine-square-mile area.[52] An electromagnetic pulse from that single weapon might destroy all electrical equipment in North America. Thermal radiation (heat and light) would blind anyone looking at it, cause fires out to eight miles, third-degree burns at ten miles, and second-degree burns up to thirteen miles away. A nuclear detonation would produce a blast wave that could destroy dwellings more than eight miles away. Finally, radioactive debris would be dispersed great distances from the blast, some carrying hundreds of miles and contaminating whatever it touched.

A group of American scientists has suggested that the environmental consequences of a nuclear war would be worse than ever imagined, perhaps leading to extinction of life itself. They argue that the four major environmental consequences of nuclear war—"obscuring smoke in the troposphere, obscuring dust in the stratosphere, the fallout of radioactive debris, and the partial destruction of the ozone layer"[53]—would cause a period of life-threatening darkness and cold on earth, a *nuclear winter*. Among its consequences, this "winter" might destroy almost all agriculture in the Northern Hemisphere and make water unavailable by freezing and contamination. Others challenge the nuclear-winter description, arguing that the effect would be closer to a "nuclear fall," but few dispute that nuclear war would have severe consequences for the planet.

---

[49]See, for example, Richard A. Falk, "The Shimoda Case: A Legal Appraisal of the Atomic Attacks upon Hiroshima and Nagasaki," *American Journal of International Law* 59 (1965), pp. 759–793.

[50]Herman Kahn, *Thinking About the Unthinkable* (New York: Horizon Books, 1962).

[51]Carl Sagan, "Nuclear War and Climatic Catastrophe: Some Policy Implications," *Foreign Affairs* 62:2 (Winter 1983/84), pp. 257–292.

[52]The following is based on Perkins, *ABCs of the Soviet-American Nuclear Arms Race*, pp. 25–31.

[53]Sagan, "Nuclear War and Climatic Catastrophe," pp. 263–264. Debate about the nuclear-winter hypothesis has raged since Sagan's article appeared. See, for example, "Comment and Correspondence," *Foreign Affairs* 62:4 (Spring 1984), 995–1002; Starley L. Thompson and Stephen H. Schneider, "Nuclear Winter Reappraised," *Foreign Affairs* 64:5 (Summer 1986), 981–1005; and "Comment and Correspondence," *Foreign Affairs* 65:1 (Fall 1986), pp. 163–178.

FIGURE 8.2

Effects of Bomb

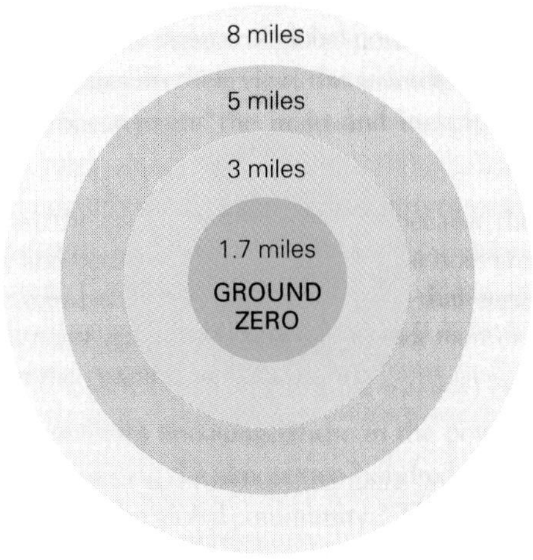

  98 percent of people are killed by flying debris, thermal radiation and fire storms. Few structures are left standing.

  50 percent of people are killed, and 40 percent are injured, half of whom may die. Only the strongest structures survive.

  50 percent of people are killed or injured. Most homes are blown out or leveled.

  20 percent of people are killed by injuries or burns; people in the open receive second- and third-degree burns or are blinded by flash. Most buildings are damaged.

The concentric circles illustrate the effect of a one-megaton nuclear bomb at a distance up to 8 miles from ground zero.

Debate over the morality of nuclear deterrence reached a crescendo as the "nuclear freeze" movement grew during the Reagan administration's nuclear buildup early in the 1980s. One observer identifies fifteen reasons that contribute to the "immorality of nuclear deterrence," including deliberate "killing of tens of millions of people" and holding "whole peoples as hostages."[54] A May 1983 pastoral letter of the American National Conference of Catholic Bishops accepted nuclear deterrence, conditioned upon rejecting nuclear war as an acceptable outcome, rejecting the search for nuclear superiority, and viewing deterrence as only a way station on the road to

[54]James A. Stegenga, "The Immorality of Nuclear Deterrence," *Arms Control* 4 (May 1983), pp. 65–72. The quotations are from pp. 65, 67, and 69.

negotiated disarmament.[55] They went on to recommend several steps that could be taken to move away from this strategy, including "support for immediate, bilateral, verifiable agreements," to stop development of new weapons systems, and "support for negotiated bilateral deep cuts in the arsenals of both superpowers."[56]

At about the same time, Harvard University's Joseph Nye, in *Nuclear Ethics*, also concluded that "nuclear deterrence is conditionally moral," using three assumptions. First, Nye argues that the means one uses and the consequences of those means should be proportionate to the cause of an action. Second, limits should be placed on the means one uses. Third, "a prudent consideration of consequences in both the near term and the indefinite long term" should inform policy.[57] Nye outlines these "maxims of nuclear ethics":

Self-defense is a just but limited cause.

Never treat nuclear weapons as normal weapons.

Minimize harm to innocent people.

Reduce risks of nuclear war in the near term.

Reduce reliance on nuclear weapons over time.[58]

Nye accepts limited extended deterrence but says targeting population centers (*countervalue strategy*) must be avoided. Instead, he proposes targeting "counter-combatants" or a more limited "counter-city targeting approach" to minimize harm to civilians. Nye also suggests that several steps be taken to avoid nuclear war in the short term: "improve conventional deterrence," "prevent and manage crises," and "invigorate non-proliferation efforts." Some of Nye's suggestions have been realized. The dramatic arms agreements ending the Cold War reduced the risks of nuclear war, but issues of nuclear ethics remain.

Vertical Proliferation: Controlling the Arms Race

When unilateral efforts by the superpowers failed to achieve nuclear superiority, *mutual* efforts to stabilize the arms race became more attractive to both. The idea of regulating changes in superpower nuclear-weapons technology is known as controlling vertical

[55]See "The Challenge of Peace: God's Promise and Our Response," reprinted as the appendix to Jim Castelli, *The Bishops and the Bomb: Waging Peace in a Nuclear Age* (Garden City, N.Y.: Doubleday, 1983), p. 241. The U.S. bishops were not the only religious leaders to question nuclear deterrence. See Joseph S. Nye, Jr., *Nuclear Ethics* (New York: Free Press, 1986) for a discussion of others, and Perkins, *ABCs of the Soviet-American Nuclear Arms Race*, pp. 146–147 for a discussion of the United Methodist Church response.

[56]These conditions and proposals are from "The Challenge of Peace: God's Promise and Our Response," in Castelli, *Bishops and the Bomb*, pp. 241–242. They are also discussed in Nye, *Nuclear Ethics*, pp. 97–98. For a sympathetic critique of the logic used to reach this conclusion, see Susan Moller Okin, "Taking the Bishops Seriously," *World Politics* 36:4 (July 1984), pp. 527–554.

[57]Nye, *Nuclear Ethics*, pp. 98–99.

[58]Ibid., p. 99.

proliferation. Efforts to control vertical proliferation mean constraining quantitative and qualitative improvements in nuclear arsenals of states already possessing such weapons. These efforts can take the form of either *arms control* or *disarmament.*

Those who favor disarmament argue that weapons themselves cause war and thus reducing the numbers of weapons and even eliminating them is necessary to stop war. Those who advocate arms control contend that some configurations of weapons are more likely to produce war than others and that the way to avoid war is not simply eliminating weapons wholesale but reinforcing stability in deterrence relationships. They further argue that conflicting political interests mean that arms-control measures are feasible where disarmament is not and that such measures are a prerequisite for disarmament.

Sometimes the two schools advocate the same policies, but even then they differ about why they advocate what they do. Disarmers favored eliminating short-range and theater (tactical) nuclear weapons in Europe in the 1980s because it would go far toward reducing nuclear stocks on the continent. Arms-control specialists also advocated eliminating such weapons, but for a different reason: they believed them to be destabilizing because, being vulnerable to enemy attack they must be used quickly in conflict or lost.

Sometimes the two schools' recommendations differ radically. Disarmers always seek fewer weapons, but arms-control theorists can envision situations in which increased numbers of weapons enhance stability. Instability might result, for instance, if both sides depended on only a few bombers or missiles for deterrence. Then it would be relatively easy for one side to eliminate the other's forces, and during a crisis the temptation to do so would grow. If both sides had many weapons, it would be more difficult to eliminate the threat of devastating retaliation, and so the incentive to try would be reduced. Most superpower negotiations have used arms-control logic.

Nuclear Arms-Control Agreements

Efforts to reach agreement on arms control between the United States and the Soviet Union at the height of the Cold War were frustrated by mistrust and animosity. Each side routinely made proposals with an eye toward wooing world public opinion rather than achieving substantive agreement. Each side advocated positions that it knew in advance would be unacceptable to the other.

By the early 1960s, a number of factors improved the prospects for arms-control agreements. Stalin's death in 1953 reduced Western fears of the U.S.S.R., and his successors communicated more openly with the West. Several dangerous U.S.-Soviet crises late in the 1950s and early in the 1960s, especially the Cuban missile crisis (1962), brought home to leaders on both sides that, however incompatible many of their interests were, they shared an overriding interest in surviving by avoiding nuclear war. Nowhere was this growing awareness more clearly reflected than in a letter Soviet

Premier Nikita Khrushchev wrote to President John F. Kennedy as the missile crisis peaked. Khrushchev used using the metaphor of a "knot" to describe their predicament:

> . . . Mr. President, we and you ought not to pull on the ends of the rope in which you have tied the knot of war, because the more the two of us pull, the tighter the knot will be tied. And a moment may come when that knot will be tied so tight that even he who tied it will not have the strength to untie it, and then it will be necessary to cut that knot, and what that would mean is not for me to explain to you, because you understand perfectly of what terrible forces our countries dispose. Consequently . . . let us not only relax the forces pulling on the ends of the rope, let us take measures to untie that knot.[59]

The Cuban crisis, during which the United States and the Soviet Union were close to nuclear war, had the ironic effect of stimulating efforts at nuclear arms control and crisis management.[60] Within a year, President Kennedy made a dramatic appeal for arms control in a speech at American University (June 1963), and two months later the first U.S.-Soviet arms-control agreement was signed—the Partial Test Ban Treaty (August 1963).[61] This agreement restricted testing of nuclear weapons to underground facilities and forbade testing in the atmosphere, underwater, or in outer space. Although the agreement addressed an environmental problem resulting from the release of nuclear materials into the air, it did not significantly alter the arms race. Still, it was an important first step.

As appreciation of the theory of deterrence stability deepened, and as the Soviet Union came to enjoy greater security, having attained *nuclear parity* or "essential equivalence" with the United States in the 1970s, serious arms-control agreements became possible. Nuclear superiority was seen increasingly to be illusory. As Henry Kissinger wrote some years later: "And one of the questions which we have to ask ourselves as a country is what in the name of God is strategic superiority? What is the significance of it, politically, militarily, operationally, at these levels of numbers? What do you do with it?"[62]

The first major steps toward nuclear arms control between the superpowers resulted from the strategic arms limitation talks, or *SALT*. The negotiations began late in the 1960s and concluded when the SALT I accords were signed in Moscow in May 1972. Negotiations were arduous. As in other arms-control negotiations, the participants sought to limit weapons in which they were inferior. The United States routinely sought to limit large land-based intercontinental ballistic missiles with multiple warheads, a

---

[59]Cited in Robert F. Kennedy, *Thirteen Days* (New York: W. W. Norton, 1969), pp. 67–68.

[60]Recent revelations show that the two superpowers were closer to the brink than many had believed, especially because local commanders of nuclear forces in Cuba at the time apparently had been given latitude in making decisions.

[61]The texts of the arms agreements discussed in this chapter appear in United States Arms Control and Disarmament Agency, *Arms Control and Disarmament Agreements: Texts and Histories of the Negotiations* (Washington, D.C.: U.S. Arms Control and Disarmament Agency, 1990).

[62]Cited in Freedman, *Evolution of Nuclear Strategy*, p. 363.

Soviet specialty, and the Soviet Union sought to limit long-range bombers, submarine-launched ballistic missiles, and, later, cruise missiles and strategic-defense weapons—all areas of American advantage. Similarly, U.S. negotiators repeatedly sought to reduce "throw weight" (the load that can be delivered aboard bombers and missiles) and numbers of launch vehicles (missiles and bombers), both areas of Soviet advantage. Soviet negotiators emphasized the U.S. advantage in numbers of warheads, including bombs.

TABLE 8.1

Major Arms-Control Agreements*

Anti-Proliferation Agreements

Antarctic Treaty (1959): Demilitarizes the Antarctic, prohibiting its use for military purposes.

Outer Space Treaty (1967): Prohibits weapons of mass destruction, military installations, or testing weapons in outer space.

Treaty of Tlatelolco (1967): Prohibits testing, using, manufacturing, or acquiring nuclear weapons in Latin America.

Nuclear Nonproliferation Treaty (1968): Prohibits transfer of nuclear weapons by nuclear countries to nonnuclear countries and forbids nonnuclear countries to acquire such weapons. Requires nuclear countries to seek disarmament. Up for renewal in 1995.

Seabed Treaty (1971): Prohibits placing nuclear weapons on the ocean bottom beyond the twelve-mile limit.

Confidence-Building Measurements

Hot Line Agreement (1963): Creates a direct U.S.-Soviet communications link for use during crises. Link improved in 1971 and 1984.

Nuclear Accidents Agreement (1971): Requires immediate notification of the other signatory in the event of an accident, unauthorized incident, or detonation involving a nuclear weapon.

High Seas Agreement (1972): Establishes rules of conduct to avoid collision among naval vessels and prohibits simulated attacks on each other's ships.

Agreement on Prevention of Nuclear War (1973): Agreement to do everything possible to prevent nuclear war. Revised in 1987 to establish nuclear-risk reduction centers in Washington and Moscow.

Conference on Security and Cooperation in Europe (1975): Agreement to give prior notice of major military exercises in Europe. Updated in 1986 to require advance notice of large troop movements and to allow aerial inspection of such movements.

Open Skies Treaty (1992): Agreement among the NATO countries, the successor states of the former Soviet Union, and the former members of the Warsaw Pact to permit surveillance flights over North America, Europe, and the Asian regions of the former Soviet Union to verify arms-control commitments.

Nuclear-Testing Limitations

Limited Test Ban Treaty (1963): Prohibits nuclear testing in the atmosphere, outer space, or underwater and commits signatories to seek a total test ban.

Threshold Test Ban Treaty (1974): Prohibits underground nuclear tests in excess of 150 kilotons.

Peaceful Nuclear Explosions Treaty (1976): Limits peaceful nuclear explosions to 150 kilotons.

Comprehensive Test Ban Treaty (?): Would end all nuclear testing.

Limitations on Nuclear Weapons

Antiballistic Missile Treaty (1972): Limits both sides to two ABM sites with 100 interceptors each. Reduced to one site in 1974.

Interim Agreement (1972)[a]: Froze the number of ballistic-missile launchers for five years. Both sides continued to observe the treaty after 1977.

SALT II (1979): Limited missiles and bombers for each side to 2,400, to be reduced to 2,250 by 1982. Limited MIRVed launchers to 1,320. Limited ICBM warheads to 10, SLBM warheads to 14, and cruise missiles on bombers to 20. The treaty was not ratified by the U.S. Senate and was breached by the United States in 1986.

Intermediate-Range Nuclear Forces Treaty (1987): Prohibits producing or deploying of missiles with a range of 300 to 3,400 miles. Required destruction of INF missiles within three years and on-site inspections for verification. Some 2,700 missiles eliminated by 1992 in this first agreement to *reduce* nuclear weapons.

START I (1991): Reduces the number of warheads from 11,600 to 8,600 for the United States and from 10,222 to 6,500 for the U.S.S.R. by the year 2000. After the U.S.S.R. collapse, these targets were reaffirmed among the United States, Russia, Ukraine, Belarus, and Kazakhstan.

Short-Range Commitments (1991): Commits the U.S. and U.S.S.R. (now Russia) to reduce short-range land, air, and sea-based nuclear warheads by varying numbers and takes nuclear forces off alert status.

START II (1992): Reduces the number of nuclear warheads on each side in two stages to 3,800–4,250 and then to 3,000–3,500 by the year 2003.

Nonnuclear Weapons Limitations

Biological Weapons Convention (1972): Prohibits developing, producing, and stockpiling biological weapons and requires that stockpiles be eliminated.

Environmental Modification Convention (1977): Prohibits efforts to modify the environment for military purposes.

Inhumane Weapons Convention (1981): Prohibits use of specified fragmentation bombs as well as using booby traps, incendiary weapons, and mines against civilians.

U.S.–Soviet Agreement on Chemical Arms (1990): Requires that stockpiles of chemical arms be cut to 5,000 tons by the year 2002 and bans production of chemical weapons.

Conventional Armed Forces in Europe Treaty (1990): Limits the numbers of tanks, combat vehicles, aircraft, and helicopters available to NATO and the Warsaw Pact in Central Europe, establishing parity in conventional forces.

---

[a]The Antiballistic Missile Treaty and Interim Agreement together constituted SALT I.

*Sources: Perkins, *ABCs of the Soviet-American Nuclear Arms Race*, pp. 175–177; "Fact Sheet: The CFE Treaty," *Dispatch*, November 26, 1990, p. 282; *The New York Times*, May 24, 1992, pp. 1 and 4; *The New York Times*, June 17, 1992, pp. A1 and A6; "Appendix B, Comparison of U.S. and Soviet Nuclear Cuts," in Dick Clark, *United States-Soviet Relations: Building a Congressional Cadre* (Queenstown, Md: Aspen Institute, 1992), p. 41; and *The Washington Post*, March 21, 1992, p. A18.

The *SALT I* accord consisted of two agreements. The first limited offensive missiles and the second antiballistic missiles (ABM treaty). The interim offensive arms pact of five years' duration was a *quantitative* agreement between the United States and the Soviet Union that sought to stabilize the number of land-based and sea-based delivery vehicles that each side could possess. In effect, it froze each side's quota at the number under production by July 1, 1972. The agreement provided for more delivery vehicles for the Soviet Union than for the United States. The matters not covered by this agreement are important, however, in understanding U.S. acceptance of it. It did not restrict qualitative improvements in nuclear forces, and long-range bombers as delivery vehicles (an area of U.S. advantage) were omitted. Because the United States already had the MIRV system, a vital improvement, the Nixon administration felt comfortable about signing the agreement.

The *ABM Treaty* sought to limit development of a weapons system that might degrade the stability of nuclear deterrence. If one side could protect its cities against enemy attack, that side would no longer have to fear retaliation if it was an aggressor. An ABM system would also invite development of additional offensive weapons to evade or defeat that system, intensifying the arms race. The 1972 treaty sought to eliminate these possibilities by restricting deployment of ABM systems to two sites — one around each nation's capital and the other around one of its land-based missile sites. It was believed that such limitations would discourage development of ABMs, stabilizing the superpower nuclear stalemate.[63] The ABM treaty, and some of the arguments surrounding it, were to be resurrected in the debate over the Strategic Defense Initiative (SDI) a decade later.

Although SALT I was a breakthrough in the effort to institutionalize the superpower balance of terror, it was only a first step. Not all nuclear delivery vehicles were included (bombers were omitted) and, more important, qualitative improvements too were excluded. As a result, a qualitative arms race ensued after SALT I was completed. The Soviet Union quickly developed a MIRV system and built larger missiles with more warheads, and the United States developed cruise missiles and moved toward modernizing all legs of its triad.

The *SALT II* Treaty, signed in June 1979 in Vienna, addressed both *quantitative* and *qualitative* issues. The treaty covered all types of delivery vehicles, including long-range bombers, set numerical limits on delivery vehicles and the MIRVed delivery vehicles that each side could have, and placed some restrictions on technological improvements that the Soviet Union and the United States were allowed to institute. But SALT II was never ratified because President Jimmy Carter withdrew it from U.S. Senate consideration after the Soviet Union invaded Afghanistan. Nevertheless, both sides agreed to

---

[63]Because of congressional opposition, no ABMs were permanently deployed in the United States.

adhere to its limits and did so until 1986, when the Reagan administration exceeded its limits after accusing the Soviets of violating the pact.

Confidence-Building Agreements

Another set of arms-control agreements involve *confidence-building measures*. The aim of such measures is to improve communication between foes to reduce the possibility of misunderstandings that might lead to crisis and war. The initial measure, like the Partial Test Ban Treaty, directly responded to the Cuban missile crisis. After that confrontation, the superpowers established a *hot line* between their capitals to reduce the risks of miscalculation or accident. The original teletype link between the two countries has been modernized twice, once in 1971 and again in 1984. These improvements included satellite communication beginning in 1971 and facsimile ("fax") equipment in 1984.

Additional confidence-building measures were incorporated into other agreements or were signed as stand-alone accords. In 1973, the two countries signed the "Agreement Between the United States and the Union of Soviet Socialist Republics on the Prevention of Nuclear War." The pact committed the two to act to prevent the development of situations, either with one another or with third parties, which could cause deterioration in their relationship. If such a situation developed, the agreement committed them "to enter into urgent consultations with each other."[64] Although the United States feared that the U.S.S.R. violated this agreement during the 1973 Yom Kippur War, it has worked well most of the time.

Other agreements have incorporated confidence-building measures. At the time SALT I was signed, political, cultural, scientific, and trade agreements were also completed, for example, a joint Apollo–Soyuz space mission. A few years later, the statement of principles of the *Conference on Security and Cooperation in Europe* (CSCE), an August 1975 meeting of thirty-five nations in Europe and North America, incorporated additional confidence-building measures. "Baskets" one and two of the Helsinki Accords (after Helsinki, Finland, where the accord was signed) provided for improved East–West cultural exchange, exchange of environmental information, and warning of military maneuvers. The Helsinki initiatives bore fruit at the 1986 Stockholm Conference on Confidence and Security-Building Measures and Disarmament in Europe, at which measures were adopted to reduce the risk of armed conflict in Europe. These included prior notification of military maneuvers, invitations to states to observe military maneuvers, exchange of information on future military activities, and the right to demand on-site inspection.[65]

[64]*Arms Control and Disarmament Agreements*, p. 180.
[65]Ibid., p. 322.

A more recent measure designed to enhance confidence is the *Open Skies Treaty* of March 1992. Observation flights can be conducted among states that are parties to the agreement. The treaty's aim is "to enhance mutual understanding and confidence" by allowing all signatories to gather "information about military activities of concern to them." The "transparency" of military activities and development is seen as an important mechanism in reducing regional tension and in preventing conflict.[66]

Agreements on Nuclear Disarmament

Although arms-control agreements and confidence-building measures were important, they did not alter the main contours of the arms race. Despite SALT I and II, nuclear arsenals remained large and loopholes permitted modernizing weapons systems. President Reagan ran for office on a commitment to close the *"window of vulnerability"* that he argued was a result of improvements in the Soviet nuclear arsenal that would enable Moscow to launch a successful first strike against U.S. land-based missiles. The Reagan administration took steps to ensure continued invulnerability of U.S. nuclear systems. This "nuclear modernization" program—an effort to improve all three legs of the triad—and the decision to introduce intermediate-range nuclear weapons in Western Europe to balance Soviet deployment of SS-20s, produced an outcry about the prospect of nuclear war and crystallized peace movements in Europe, the United States, and even the Soviet bloc. [67]

Liberal and pacifist opinion in the United States and Western Europe was roused by rhetoric that some regarded as reckless from the Reagan administration. On one occasion the president jokingly announced in a weekly radio broadcast that he believed had ended that he had ordered a nuclear attack on the U.S.S.R. On another occasion he appeared not to realize that, once launched, a missile could not be recalled. In another gaffe the president suggested that he could imagine a nuclear exchange in Europe that would not escalate to a superpower nuclear exchange, and he frightened observers with colorful phrases like "a nuclear shot across the bow."

Even more worrisome to some was speculation by experts with influence in the Reagan White House about how nuclear war could be fought and won. The United States and Soviet Union seemed to have enormous "overkill" capacity by the

---

[66]*Message from the President of the United States* transmitting the Treaty on Open Skies, with Twelve Annexes, Signed at Helsinki March 24, 1992 (Washington, D.C.: U.S. Government Printing Office, 1992), p. viii.

[67]The weapons proposed for deployment in Western Europe had a range of 300 to 3,400 miles, making them neither short-range nor intercontinental. Given strategic parity between the superpowers, it was feared that a Soviet advantage in theater nuclear weapons would allow Moscow to blackmail the Europeans, even forcing them to accept political neutrality. Many Western Europeans reacted negatively to the NATO proposal because of fear that their countries would become targets for Soviet nuclear attack.

mid-1980s.[68] The two controlled roughly 18,000 strategic nuclear weapons with a yield of about 10,000 megatons. Counting short and medium-range weapons, the superpowers had about 50,000 warheads between them with a yield of 15,000 megatons.[69] Never before in history had a military technology not been employed in actual war.

The outcry over nuclear weapons began to subside with two sets of U.S.-Soviet negotiations in the early 1980s. These differed from talks a decade earlier because the focus shifted from *arms control* to *arms reduction*. The first batch of negotiations over intermediate nuclear forces (INF) begun in November 1981, sought to limit or eliminate this class of nuclear weapons in Europe. The second, the strategic arms reduction talks (START), began in June 1982 with the aim of reducing the superpowers' long-range nuclear weapons. Both bore fruit by the end of the 1980s and early 1990s and produced the first nuclear arms-reduction agreements in history.

The 1987 *INF Treaty* was a dramatic step. It called for the superpowers totally to eliminate and destroy medium- and intermediate-range weapons within three years. It provided for on-site inspection by each country of dismantling and destruction and allowed for continued inspections for thirteen years after the treaty came into force to ensure compliance.[70] This pact was perhaps the most important single step in the history of disarmament. It eliminated an entire class of nuclear weapons and demonstrated that arms reduction, not just arms control, was a real possibility.

The crowning achievement of Soviet–American arms control was the conclusion of the Strategic Arms Reduction Treaty (START I) in 1991. The U.S.S.R. agreed to cut 3,722 of its 10,222 long-range nuclear warheads and the United States to reduce its 11,600 warheads by 3,000. Before the treaty could be ratified and carried out, however, the Soviet Union collapsed, and four of its successor states—Russia, Ukraine, Belarus, and Kazakhstan—retained a share of the Soviet arsenal. Under these conditions the treaty could not be ratified until all four agreed to the terms concluded by Presidents Bush and Gorbachev. Finally, in May 1992, the United States and the four former Soviet republics agreed to honor the treaty.[71] Ukraine, Belarus, and Kazakhstan agreed to destroy or turn over all nuclear warheads to Russia and to subscribe to the 1968 Nuclear

[68]The apparent excess of nuclear weapons was based on the premise that no retaliatory force was completely invulnerable and that large forces were needed to discourage an enemy from contemplating a first strike.

[69]One problem rarely discussed during the Cold War that is now contentious is how to dispose of the waste produced by reducing nuclear stockpiles. Russia has inadequate expertise and financial resources to dismantle and dispose of its weapons safely, and the United States has begun to assist Moscow in this effort.

[70]"The INF Treaty: What's in It?" *Arms Control Update* (Washington, D.C.: U.S. Arms Control and Disarmament Agency, January 1988), pp. 4–5.

[71]Barbara Crossette, "4 Ex-Soviet States and U.S. in Accord on 1991 Arms Pact," *The New York Times*, May 24, 1992, pp. 1, 4.

Nonproliferation Treaty.[72] Following ratification, the signatories were committed to carrying out the reductions in three stages over a seven-year period, but, thus far Ukraine has not carried out its obligations. However, in September 1993, as part of a deal by which Russia will buy Ukraine's share of the former Soviet Union's Black Sea fleet, Ukraine agreed to let Russia dismantle nuclear weapons on Ukrainian territory in return for the uranium taken from their warheads.[73]

Although *START I* entailed major reductions in both countries' nuclear arsenals, *START II*, which President Bush and Russian President Yeltsin completed at the end of 1992, was even more dramatic. START II called for a 50-percent reduction in U.S. and Russian nuclear arsenals, including the large MIRVed land-based Russian missiles that U.S. strategists feared were a first-strike threat. If START II is fully implemented, both sides would be allowed only 3,000 to 3,500 warheads. Figure 8.3 depicts the cuts in strategic warheads under START I and II.

Horizontal Proliferation: Nuclear Weapons Spread

Despite progress in vertical proliferation, the problem of horizontal proliferation — spreading nuclear-weapons technology to other actors — remains formidable. One reason for worry is sheer probability: the more fingers on nuclear triggers, the higher the probability that someone will use nuclear weapons intentionally or by accident. Proliferation also greatly complicates calculations of deterrence because each nuclear actor has to guess who might be its adversaries and arm accordingly. Does each prepare for *all* possible adversaries or for just the most dangerous ones? Actor A might increase its arms to counter Actor B, but this change will be destabilizing if Actor C concludes that the increase threatens its security. Finally, new nuclear powers have less sophisticated weaponry than that of the superpowers, and their relative vulnerability to a first strike creates unstable rivalries.

Technological change complicates the proliferation issue. The growing availability of peaceful nuclear reactors that yield plutonium is a danger because that metal can be reprocessed to make nuclear arms. Similarly, advances in miniaturization make it possible for nuclear weapons to be carried by hand, and fanatical terrorists straining to grab such ordnance can easily be imagined.

The United States, Russia, Ukraine, Kazakhstan, Belarus, Britain, France, India, South Africa, and China were nuclear powers by the early 1990s. Israel almost certainly had nuclear weapons by then, and Pakistan and North Korea were close to acquiring similar capability. Other societies had the capacity to do so if they wish.

[72]In February 1993, Belarus agreed to transfer its nuclear weapons to Russia and signed the Nuclear Nonproliferation Treaty.

[73]Celestine Bohlen, "Ukraine Agrees to Allow Russians To Buy Fleet and Destroy Arsenal," *The New York Times*, September 4, 1993, pp. 1, 5.

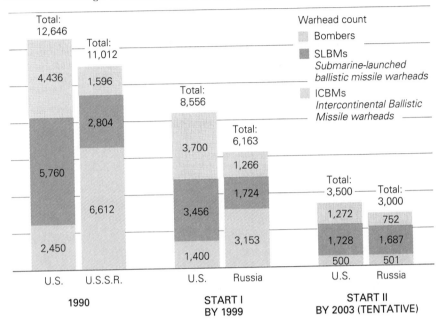

FIGURE 8.3

Reduction in Strategic Warheads under START I and II

The end of the Cold War has produced an end to the U.S.-Soviet nuclear arms race and a dramatic reduction in nuclear weapons. Between 1990 and 2003, total U.S. and Russian warheads will be reduced from 23,658 to 6,500 weapons.

Nuclear Nonproliferation Treaty

The global community has tried to do something about proliferation, however, by forging international agreements as building blocks for a regime to stop expanding nuclear-weapons technology. The most influential control for horizontal proliferation was the *Nuclear Nonproliferation Treaty* (*NPT*) of 1968, designed to dissuade any further nuclear-armed states. The treaty has four key provisions: (1) No nuclear power that has subscribed to the treaty is to transfer nuclear-weapons technology to nonnuclear states. (2) No nonnuclear-armed state that has agreed to the treaty is to develop nuclear-weapons technology. (3) All nonnuclear states that use nuclear energy are to have safeguards and to conclude an agreement with the International Atomic Energy Agency (IAEA) for inspecting such safeguards. (4) The nuclear-weapons states are to "pursue negotiations in good faith on effective measures relating to the cessation of the nuclear arms race . . . and to nuclear disarmament."[74]

[74]*Arms Control and Disarmament Agreements: Texts and Histories of the Negotiations*, p. 100.

Had this agreement gained universal acceptance, horizontal proliferation would, at least in theory, have ceased. Unfortunately, this achievement has not occurred, but acceptance has been high. As of 1993, 145 nonnuclear-weapons states and five nuclear powers had signed and ratified the agreement.[75] The NPT's principal shortcoming is that some "near-nuclear" states—those with the technology to produce nuclear weapons—had not signed the treaty and others who had agreed to it might not be in full compliance. Israel, India, Pakistan, and South Africa were in the first category, and Iraq, Iran, Libya, and North Korea in the second.

A second problem limiting the NPT's effectiveness has been expansion of nuclear fission as a source of energy. Safeguards to prevent transfer of nuclear fuels to nuclear weapons are inadequate. The International Atomic Energy Agency has primary responsibility for ensuring that this transfer does not happen, but it is a difficult task for an agency with few inspectors to watch over more and more nuclear power reactors. Moreover, countries still retain rights to refuse or restrict inspections. Thus, in 1993, North Korea refused to permit inspection of two suspected facilities and announced it would withdraw from the NPT. Failure to dissuade North Korea from its course of action led President Clinton to declare that "it is pointless for them to try to develop nuclear weapons, because if they ever use them it would be the end of their country."

Other Nonproliferation Agreements

Several other efforts also restrict the spread of nuclear weapons technology, although none is as comprehensive as the NPT. The Antarctica Treaty of 1959 was technically the first agreement of this kind. It limited use of Antarctica to "peaceful purposes only." No military bases, maneuvers, or "testing of any type of weapons" is permitted there. Moreover, the treaty prohibits "any nuclear explosions in Antarctica and the disposal there of radioactive waste materials."[76] About a decade later, another treaty modeled on the Antarctica Treaty was signed. The arena for the Outer Space Treaty of 1967 was different, but its aims were the same. This treaty prohibited placing in orbit around the earth nuclear weapons or other weapons of mass destruction. It also prohibited stationing such weapons in outer space and declared that space could be used only for peaceful purposes. Finally, as noted earlier, the Seabed Arms Control Treaty of 1971 prohibits emplacing nuclear weapons on the ocean floor beyond the twelve-mile territorial limit.

---

[75]See "Appendix I, Global Nonproliferation and Technology Transfer Regimes," in Leonard S. Spector and Virginia Foran, *Preventing Weapons Proliferation: Should the Regimes Be Combined?* A Report of the Thirty-third Strategy for Peace, U.S. Foreign Policy Conference, October 22–24, 1992, p. 32. France and China have just recently agreed to the NPT. Earlier, they had claimed that the treaty violated their sovereignty.

[76]See *Arms Control and Disarmament Agreements*, pp. 23–24.

Other agreements have focused on keeping specific regions free of nuclear weapons. The most successful has been the Latin American Nuclear-Free Zone Treaty, also known as the Treaty of Tlatelolco (1967).[77] This treaty commits signatories to apply nuclear energy for peaceful purposes only and prohibits use of their territories for manufacturing or storing nuclear weapons. The treaty was accompanied by two major protocols. Protocol I calls on states outside Latin America with territories in the area defined by the treaty to commit themselves to regional denuclearization. Thus, the United States cannot install nuclear weapons in Puerto Rico or the U.S. Virgin Islands. Protocol II calls on the nuclear powers to respect the nuclear-free status of Latin America and refrain from action that might violate the agreement.

Proliferation: A Continuing Problem

Despite efforts to keep nuclear-weapons technology from spreading, the problem remains severe despite the end of the Cold War. Indeed, the Cold War actually slowed the spread of nuclear weapons because many states felt comfortable under a superpower's nuclear umbrella and because the superpowers actively discouraged proliferation. At least four major developments are ominous.

First, efforts to keep delivery systems such as missiles from spreading have lagged behind efforts to stop disseminating nuclear weapons, and sales of nuclear reactors continue to grow. Figure 8.4 depicts the upsurging sale of nuclear and missile technology since the Cold War ended. Several states have been purchasing missiles and nuclear reactors, and these purchases raise questions about the future. Some of the sellers are not parties to the NPT (including India) and even those who are (such as North Korea) are not strong advocates of this control mechanism. And some of the buyers appear to be interested in acquiring nuclear weapons. Beginning in 1986, some effort was made to restrict transfer of missiles, but success was mixed. The *Missile Technology Control Regime* (MTCR) was originally assembled among some Western states, later joined by the U.S.S.R. and China, to restrict the transfer of missiles. An attempt to tighten these restrictions began after Iraq used Scud missiles in the 1991 Persian Gulf War.[78] In 1993, the United States applied strong pressure to prevent Russian missile sales to India but was less successful in persuading China to halt the sale of missile technology to Pakistan and Iran.[79]

Second, as more states use nuclear fuels to meet their need for energy, nuclear materials will grow easier to get. Although the NPT does not limit peaceful use of nuclear energy and the International Atomic Energy Agency conducts periodic inspections of nuclear facilities, several studies have questioned the effectiveness of such inspections. New and more sophisticated systems for monitoring compliance and detecting violations are necessary, and the global community must be prepared to act if violations are found.

[77]See ibid., pp. 64–67.

[78]See Spector and Foran, *Preventing Weapons Proliferation*, p. 8.

[79]Elaine Sciolino, "U.S. May Threaten China With Sanctions for Reported Arms Sales," *The New York Times*, July 20, 1993, p. A3.

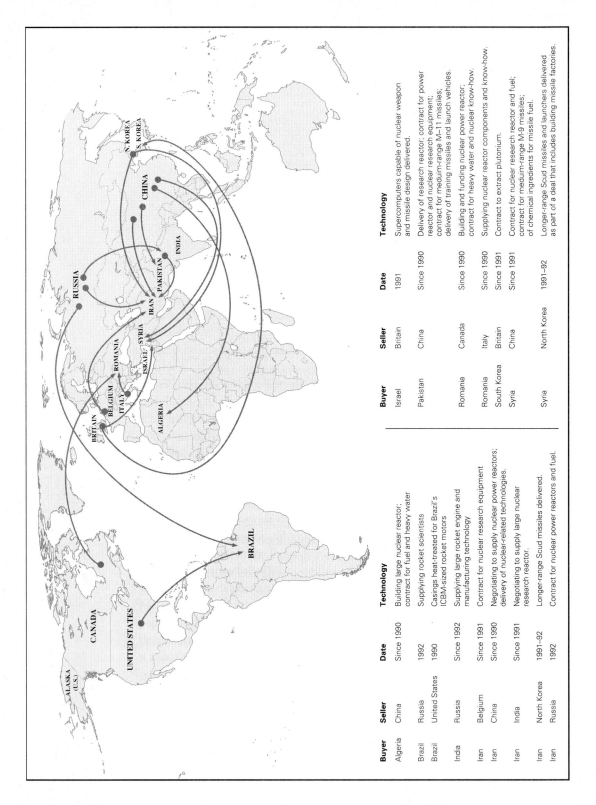

Buyer	Seller	Date	Technology
Algeria	China	Since 1990	Building large nuclear reactor; contract for fuel and heavy water
Brazil	Russia	1992	Supplying rocket scientists
Brazil	United States	1990	Casings heat-treated for Brazil's ICBM-sized rocket motors
India	Russia	Since 1992	Supplying large rocket engine and manufacturing technology
Iran	Belgium	Since 1991	Contract for nuclear research equipment
Iran	China	Since 1990	Negotiating to supply nuclear power reactors; delivery of nuclear-related technologies.
Iran	India	Since 1991	Negotiating to supply large nuclear research reactor.
Iran	North Korea	1991–92	Longer-range Scud missiles delivered.
Iran	Russia	1992	Contract for nuclear power reactors and fuel.

Buyer	Seller	Date	Technology
Israel	Britain	1991	Supercomputers capable of nuclear weapon and missile design delivered.
Pakistan	China	Since 1990	Delivery of research reactor; contract for power reactor and nuclear research equipment; contract for medium-range M-11 missiles; delivery of training missiles and launch vehicles.
Romania	Canada	Since 1990	Building and funding nuclear power reactor; contract for heavy water and nuclear know-how.
Romania	Italy	Since 1990	Supplying nuclear reactor components and know-how.
South Korea	Britain	Since 1991	Contract to extract plutonium.
Syria	China	Since 1991	Contract for nuclear research reactor and fuel; contract for medium-range M-9 missiles; of chemical ingredients for missile fuel.
Syria	North Korea	1991–92	Longer-range Scud missiles and launchers delivered as part of a deal that includes building missile factories.

Third, the agreements that call for destroying nuclear weapons systems (INF and START) and attempts by the former Soviet republics to discard or sell nuclear materials may make more fissile materials available for use by other actors. Coupled with the high levels of fissile stockpiles already available, better safeguard and storage systems will be required to prevent illegal and clandestine diversion of nuclear material.

Finally, the NPT, the main international agreement for preventing the spread of nuclear weapons, was due to expire in 1995, and its renewal was uncertain. The worries expressed in the signatories' periodic review conferences raise doubts about its future. One worry is the safeguards and inspection systems that allow the agreement to function properly. Greater attention to this aspect of nonproliferation may provide incentives for renewing this agreement among its signatories.

Limited Wars, Limited Force, and Nuclear Weapons

We have still barely touched on conventional war in the nuclear age. What place has force in a nuclear environment? If we are mired in a nuclear stalemate, how can force be used today to influence others and alter their behavior?

Compellance

Deterrence must be distinguished from what Thomas Schelling calls *compellance*. Deterrence involves preventing attack by threatening retaliation. The strategy works only if threats do not need to be carried out and force does not have to be used. Compellance, though, entails threatening to or using force to make an adversary do something it is not willing to do or to undo something it has already done.[80] If it works,

---

[80]Compellance is similar to the technique Alexander L. George calls "coercive diplomacy." See George, *Forceful Persuasion: Coercive Diplomacy as an Alternative to War* (Washington, D.C.: United States Institute of Peace Press, 1992).

FIGURE 8.4

Dangerous Transfers: The Traffic in Nuclear and Missile Technology Since 1990
The international market in missile and nuclear arms technology has been thriving in the 1990s. This is a list of transactions known to have taken place since Iraq invaded Kuwait, touching off the Gulf War. Any list of important participants in previous years would also have included France, Germany, and Switzerland, which were among the many nations trading in nuclear and missile technology with Iraq before the war; Germany also helped the nuclear programs of India, Pakistan, and South Africa.

deterrence is easier and less expensive than compellance. Schelling summarizes the differences between the two strategies:

> Deterrence involves setting the stage . . . and *waiting*. The overt act is up to the opponent. The stage-setting can often be nonintrusive, nonhostile, nonprovocative. The act that is intrusive, hostile, or provocative is usually the one to be deterred; the deterrent threat only changes the consequences *if* the act in question — the one to be deterred — is then taken. Compellance, in contrast, usually involves *initiating* an action . . . that can cease . . . only if the opponent responds. . . . To deter, one digs in . . . and waits. . . . To compel, one gets up enough momentum . . . to make the other act to avoid collision.[81]

Compellance may be linked to deterrence in the sense that an actor may use force on one occasion to bolster a reputation for toughness and prove that it is willing to carry out deterrent threats. Nevertheless, Schelling says, the two strategies are fundamentally different.

Compellance in Action

American policy during the 1962 Cuban missile crisis typifies a compellant strategy. The Soviet Union had secretly installed intermediate-range missiles in Cuba where they were being prepared for deployment when the United States became aware of their presence. United States leaders had two objectives: (1) to halt further shipments of offensive Soviet weapons to Cuba, and (2) to force the Soviet Union to withdraw the missiles it had already placed on the island. Both were compellant, not deterrent, objectives.[82] The first objective entailed coercing Moscow to cease an activity that was under way, and the second, forcing Moscow to undo a *fait accompli*. The first was accomplished by establishing a naval "quarantine" around Cuba with U.S. vessels instructed to interdict Soviet efforts to break the blockade. The second and more difficult objective was achieved by a U.S. ultimatum to attack the missile sites in Cuba if they were not dismantled. To make the ultimatum more palatable to the Soviet Union, the United States promised not to invade Cuba and tacitly agreed to withdraw missiles from Turkey (which Washington had planned to do anyway).

At least five factors favored using compellance during the Cuban crisis. American motivation to win was high, and the government had strong domestic support. The United States enjoyed both strategic and local military superiority. American objectives

---

[81]Schelling, *Arms and Influence*, pp. 71–72. Emphasis in original.

[82]Had the missiles become operational, U.S. leaders would have had the additional task of deterring their use against the United States. The United States was also faced with the problem of deterring Soviet action against targets such as West Berlin, which, it was feared, might be challenged in response to U.S. action against Cuba.

were clear and consistent throughout the crisis. The bargaining was simplified because only two main actors were involved in the crisis. Finally, the effect of America's use of coercion was intensified by the speed with which it was applied.[82]

By contrast, the U.S. effort to use compellance against North Vietnam between 1965 and 1973 was unsuccessful. Retrospectively, it is easy to understand America's failure. The U.S. government was divided over the war, and public opposition to the conflict grew after the 1968 Tet offensive.[83] During this period, the United States and the Soviet Union were military equals, and U.S. military power in Vietnam, though greater than its enemy's, was unsuited to waging an unconventional guerrilla war. United States objectives were murky. Were we there to prop up a pro-American government in South Vietnam, eliminate communism in all of Vietnam, teach the Chinese that guerrilla insurgencies would not weaken America's will, or reinforce America's bargaining reputation? At one time or another, all these reasons were cited to justify the United States presence in Vietnam. The bargaining situation was murky, too. Simultaneously, the United States was trying to influence communist rebels in South Vietnam (the Vietcong), the communist government in North Vietnam, and the governments of China and the Soviet Union. Dealing with each entailed different objectives and problems. Finally, the conflict escalated so slowly that the adversary was able to adapt to each increment of violence.

The United States also used a compellant strategy against Iraq in 1990–1991, following Iraq's occupation of Kuwait. This time the strategy produced, in the end, Iraqi withdrawal, though at considerable cost to the United States and its allies. Initial efforts to force Iraq's retreat by applying economic sanctions were unsuccessful, and so too was threatening to use force. Even overwhelming air power was insufficient in the allied bombing campaign in January and February, 1991. The Iraqis were thrown out of Kuwait only after a massive multinational ground attack launched from Saudi Arabia.

As in Cuba, U.S. motivation was high, but many feared getting bogged down in a land war. The United States enjoyed strategic military superiority, but achieving local military superiority proved a slow chore. The objective of America's compellant strategy — forcing Iraq to leave Kuwait — was again clear, though it became confused with desire to overthrow Saddam Hussein. Pressure was applied slowly to Iraq, allowing the Iraqis to adjust to each increment. Part of the reason for the delay was the complicated bargaining to construct and maintain an alliance that included the United Nations, the United States, the Soviet Union, Britain, France, Syria, Egypt, and Saudi Arabia. Added complications included persuading Israel not to intervene despite Iraqi missile attacks against Israeli population centers, and trying to persuade Jordan not to violate sanctions against Iraq.

[83]See George, *Forceful Persuasion*

[84]Tet is the Vietnamese New Year. The Vietcong offensive, launched on this holiday, seemed to show that even the half-million U.S. soldiers could not pacify the country.

The complications of using compellance against Iraq were replicated in U.N. efforts to compel Bosnian Serbians to stop their "ethnic cleansing" policy in Croatia and Bosnia in 1993. The limited force available to the United Nations and the limited success of economic sanctions against Serbia meant that Serbia was not intimidated. For several months the United States contemplated its own compellant strategy, including air strikes and perhaps ground forces. Reluctant to get mired in a situation without a clear prospect of success, however, the Clinton administration, despite campaign pledges to take more vigorous action, chose a strategy of first building an alliance and slowly raising the ante against Bosnian Serbs.

Conclusion

The strategies of deterrence and compellance as approaches to managing conflict face an uncertain future. The nuclear-deterrence strategy will need to be rethought because of the nuclear reductions brought about by START I and II and growing unease about nuclear proliferation. Although deterrence appears to have been stabilized at lower levels by agreements between the superpowers, new states with nuclear weapons and leaders who are less willing to accept the status quo may try to change the rules of the game. Deterrence will be further complicated by the growing availability of chemical and biological weapons and by new generations of highly destructive conventional weapons.

Compellance too may be less usable in the future. As the global community grows more diverse and alliances weaken, the prospect of one actor or group of actors successfully coercing others to adopt a course of action may grow more dangerous. Indeed, the unity shown by the global community in the Persian Gulf War of 1991 may prove an aberration. Without stabler institutions and regimes and with more states holding nuclear weapons, the strategy of compellance will be sorely tested.

Although the long night of Soviet–American nuclear confrontation has ended and strides have been made toward reducing nuclear arsenals, the threat of nuclear war is not over. Horizontal proliferation seriously threatens peace and stability. If the theory of nuclear deterrence is correct, new nuclear powers are likely to be dangerous for a number of reasons. In the first place, unlike the superpowers, they have little experience with flaming crises and do not yet have ways and practices for preventing escalation. Second, like first-generation U.S. and Soviet nuclear weapons, new weapons are likely to be vulnerable to a first strike, pressuring decision-makers in crises to "use them or lose them."

Nevertheless, the Cold War's end does offer tempting opportunities for cooperation in global politics, and we examine some of these in Chapter 9. The power-politics tradition has often ignored the social side of political life. Force is exaggerated partly because security narrowly defined neglects goals such as economic prosperity, social justice, and environmental health. Such goals are likely to be as important in the last years of the twentieth century as are more traditional aims, including territorial integrity and political autonomy. Finally, exaggerating military factors has the air of a self-fulfilling prophecy: leaders come to believe that force is the alpha and omega of global politics and act accordingly.

Key Terms

fission
fusion
arms race
horizontal proliferation
vertical proliferation
deterrence
compellance
Munich complex
Pearl Harbor complex
appeasement
isolationism
positions of strength
intelligence community
massive retaliation
bolt from the blue
credibility
conventional weapons
vulnerability of weapons systems
first-strike capability
commitments
tripwire
destructiveness
accuracy
hot line
second-strike capability
flexible response
mutual assured destruction (MAD)
extended deterrence
brinkmanship
counterforce strategy

countervalue strategy
strategic stability
survivability of weapons systems
triad doctrine
weapons of mass destruction
nuclear winter
verifiability
arms control
disarmament
nuclear parity
confidence-building measures
limited war
MIRVed
Strategic Defense Initiative (SDI)
SALT
SALT I
SALT II
ABM Treaty
Conference on Security and Cooperation in Europe (CSCE)
Open Skies Treaty
window of vulnerability
INF Treaty
START I
START II
Nuclear Nonproliferation Treaty (NPT)
Missile Technology Control Regime (MTCR)

CHAPTER NINE

Many Paths to
Political Cooperation

Global politics is traditionally identified with conflict rather than cooperation because the discipline itself grew from works by classic authors — Thucydides, Machiavelli, and Hobbes — who focused on conflicts among states caused by incompatible interests and states' readiness to resort to war to resolve those conflicts.[1] They rarely paid attention to situations in which actors enjoyed common interests or worked peaceably to overcome differences. *By cooperation, we mean actors trying to coordinate policies even though their interests diverge.*

Most issues actually feature actors working together.[2] Cooperation has had scant attention partly because observers assumed that conflict was the opposite of cooperation and that, where there is conflict, there is no cooperation.[3] *In fact, cooperation and conflict are separate aspects of behavior and may occur simultaneously between the same actors.* Thus, even as the Cold War raged, the United States and the Soviet Union coordinated policies in a multitude of ways to prevent World War III.

To be sure, a few observers of global politics have analyzed cooperation. These analyses are especially common in eras immediately following extended periods of war

[1]K. J. Holsti, *The Dividing Discipline: Hegemony and Diversity in International Theory* (Boston: Allen & Unwin, 1985), pp. 8–9.

[2]See James M. McCormick, "Intergovernmental Organization and Cooperation Among Nations," *International Studies Quarterly*, 24:1 (March 1980), pp. 75–98. From a sample of 35 nations between 1959 and 1968, the author concludes that 70 percent of interaction was cooperative.

[3]For notable exceptions, see Robert Axelrod, *The Evolution of Cooperation* (New York: Basic Books, 1984); Joshua Goldstein and John R. Freeman, *Three-Way Street: Strategic Reciprocity in World Politics* (Chicago: University of Chicago Press, 1990); and Kenneth A. Oye, ed., *Cooperation Under Anarchy* (Princeton: Princeton University Press, 1986).

as scholars and politicians propose schemes to prevent wars from recurring or try to outlaw barbarous practices. The Abbé de Saint-Pierre (1658–1743) outlined a utopian scheme for a federal union among European states after the "world" War of the Spanish Succession (1701–1714). Jean Jacques Rousseau (1712–1778) and Immanuel Kant (1724–1804), reacting to warfare in their time,[4] proposed schemes for interstate cooperation.

At the end of World War I, Woodrow Wilson, with his proposals for collective security and a League of Nations, ushered in a period of interest in international law and organization. This trend peaked in the interwar period (1919–1939) when numerous proposals were advanced for altering the structure of global affairs. Perhaps the most famous of these schemes, the *Kellogg-Briand Pact* (Pact of Paris) of 1928, sought to outlaw war. Such attitudes, which were collectively labelled *idealism*,[5] were short-lived. Shattered by the failure to prevent World War II, idealism was dethroned as realism reasserted itself.

In this chapter, we examine theoretical and practical approaches to cooperation in global politics. What motivates actors to cooperate with one another? With what strategies can they elicit greater cooperation from each other? What formal and informal modes of cooperation exist among political actors?

Cooperation and Conflict in International "Games"

In Chapter 6, we compared the relationship among actors to prisoner's-dilemma and chicken games to illustrate the challenges confronting actors entangled in a security dilemma or an acute crisis. Here, the game metaphor will again help us understand how deeply every actor's well-being depends on decisions made by others as well as by itself and to appreciate how global interactions combine conflict and cooperation. These are probably the most important lessons that leaders must learn to avoid disasters. When new leaders like Boris Yeltsin of Russia or Bill Clinton of the United States come to power, they often set out to change the world, only to discover that they cannot do so unless the world cooperates. They also discover that they share some interests with their country's worst enemies and that they will find conflict and competition even in dealing with good friends.

Value of the Game Metaphor

Politics is a dynamic interplay of competition and cooperation involving risky choices by actors. As in games, actors in global politics select among strategies and calculate others'

---

[4]Holsti, *Dividing Discipline*, pp. 21–30.

[5]See E. H. Carr, *The Twenty Years' Crisis 1919–1939* (New York: St. Martin's Press, 1962).

probable responses to their moves. The game metaphor reminds us, too, that an actor's fate depends as much on what other players do as on its own behavior. Actors in global politics may be involved in many games as well as many types of games.

Like all games, global politics has rules that determine who wins. In some games (such as war) winning requires one player to defeat other players; these are games with a great deal of conflict. Other games require individuals to coordinate their behavior to win (as in economic sanctions). Finally, in some games, no one can win unless everybody works together (as in confronting environmental problems). Some games have high stakes and some actors have the resources to play in many games. The manner of play in a game depends on contextual factors such as distribution of resources and attitudes. Consequently, a grandfather will play poker with his grandchildren very differently from a group of high rollers playing poker in Las Vegas.

Many apparently disparate global or regional games are so highly interdependent that gains or losses in one affect resources available for others.[6] Global issues inevitably affect regional politics, just as actions in a regional game may impinge upon global politics. The Vietnam War and the several Arab–Israeli wars between 1948 and 1973 involved regional issues that became entangled in the larger Cold War and were played against the backdrop of the global contest between the United States and the Soviet Union. If players forget that games are interdependent, the cost can be high. Western leaders dismissed the Italian invasion of Ethiopia (1935) and the German occupation of the Rhineland (1936) as having only local importance when, in fact, these early conquests whetted the appetites of Hitler and Mussolini.

Different games, different players, and different issues form a web of interaction encouraging actors to cooperate and compete at the same time. For games with apparently low stakes, cooperation may be relatively easy for actors. In games with high stakes, conflict may be more likely for some actors, but that very conflict may drive adversaries to cooperate. Thus, Israel and Syria found themselves on the same side in the Persian Gulf in 1991 because both were enemies of Saddam Hussein. Why should actors cooperate, especially with no central authority to enforce agreements? As we observed in Chapter 6, theorists have begun to examine various types of games in detail to learn how cooperation evolves.

Cooperation and Conflict in Games

Briefly, what elements of game theory do we need to begin our analysis? All games have *players, payoffs, rules,* and *strategies.* We assume that *players* are unitary actors rationally seeking to maximize their gains and minimize their losses — the *payoffs.* These assumptions, of course, are often inappropriate in the real world.

[6]For a cogent discussion of the "congruence and discontinuity" between regional and global systems in international politics, see Oran R. Young, "Political Discontinuities in the International System," *World Politics* 20:3 (April 1968), pp. 369–392.

Rules describe the structure and procedures governing how games are played (such as the time allowed for a move), and *strategies* are the set of moves that guide the players' actions in the game. The structure of a game helps to determine the players' strategies. A player will choose a different strategy for a game decided by one move than for a game in which players can make repeated moves as the game unfolds. Similarly, strategies differ in a game limited to two players from those in one with many. Thus, a game providing for no communication among players and allowing each only one move will probably produce a strategy designed to win as much for each as quickly as possible with no regard for the future than a game that permits communication and repeated moves.[7]

As we observed in the Introduction, a few games end in a *zero-sum* result — that is, one player's gains are equal to the other's losses so that they have no incentive to cooperate or compromise.[8] Zero-sum games are struggles for power, but most games are *variable-sum* (or non-zero sum) contests. Players can gain or lose more or less depending on the strategies they select. One player's gain is not equal to another's loss so that, as in prisoner's dilemma and chicken, they have incentives for cooperation — avoiding serious losses or gaining more for everyone.[9]

One flaw in the power-politics tradition is that it treats many situations in global politics as though they had zero-sum results. Although in a few zero-sum "survival" games one actor or another will settle for nothing less than annihilating its foe — the Nazis and the Jews, Saddam Hussein and the Iraqi Kurds, Serbian nationalists and Muslim Bosnians — most issues do not entail such stark choices. Actors may have incompatible interests and be separated by deep hostility, as are Israelis and Palestinians, but this division does not mean that no overlap occurs among those interests or that they cannot coordinate policy to overcome their differences. Strategies other than pure conflict offer all players possibilities for gaining some of what they desire or avoiding an even worse fate.

Creating and Sustaining Cooperation

Because most issues are variable-sum, compromise is possible even in the teeth of hostility. A territorial quarrel such as that dividing Israelis and Palestinians could have various outcomes in which one actor or the other does better and in which winning does not require that either actor gain or lose everything or annihilate its adversary. Once we recognize the variable-sum quality of most global politics, it becomes clearer why cooperation is possible for many issues.

---

[7]See Chapter 6, pp. 193–194.

[8]The phrase "zero-sum" means that the total of gains and losses equals zero.

[9]Many kinds of variable-sum games are known. In some, all players win (positive-sum games), and in others all lose (negative-sum games). In most, however, some players lose and others win.

Cooperation is sometimes possible simply because it entails few risks to actors. Situations such as economic coordination among industrial democracies may elicit cooperation because the difference in gains and losses between going it alone and cooperating are small. Other situations, such as reducing bilateral trade with a recalcitrant partner or engaging in an expensive arms race with a neighbor, provide less scope for cooperation because of the penalty that may be incurred by taking a chance that other players will also cooperate. Cooperative strategies are also encouraged if actors recognize the long-term effects of their behavior. What will future prospects be if an actor refuses to go along? For example, international banks that fail to cooperate with such countries as Russia and Mexico in rescheduling debt payments may suffer long-term losses if the debtors default. Finally, the more numerous the players, the greater the opportunities for cooperation. More players provide the possibility of trade-offs and coalitions among like-minded actors.

Sometimes a mix of "stick" and "carrot" is necessary to produce cooperation. During the Persian Gulf crisis, the United Nations voted economic sanctions against Iraq. Jordan, fearing Iraqi power and loss of Iraqi markets for its goods, failed to cooperate in enforcing those sanctions. Other actors quickly sought to force Jordanian cooperation by raising its costs for not doing so. The United States condemned Jordan's noncompliance and Saudi Arabia cut off oil shipments to Jordan. Nor were positive incentives ignored during the crisis in maintaining cooperation against Iraq. Japan and Germany provided financial aid to Arab countries whose economies were harmed by upholding economic sanctions. The United States took the unusual step of promising to forgive $7 billion in debt Egypt owed it to keep that pivotal state in the anti-Iraq coalition. Indeed, the U.S. lead in constructing and maintaining the coalition against Saddam Hussein reflects the claim by theorists who believe that cooperation among independent actors is made possible by "dominant, hegemonic, or core powers" because "would-be cooperators can elect to cooperate secure in the knowledge that the dominant power will prevent their exploitation; would-be defectors are deterred by the expectation that the dominant power will sanction defection."[10]

Eventually, cooperation seems to elicit more cooperation and positive incentives encourage cooperative responses more readily than do threats or force. Observing U.S.–Russian relations, Joshua Goldstein and John Freeman argue that beginning in 1985 Soviet leaders "launched a series of . . . cooperative initiatives toward both the United States and China," including a moratorium on nuclear tests in July, concessions to China on Asian security in the following year, withdrawal from Afghanistan, and promises of additional unilateral military cuts in 1988.[11] According to Goldstein and Freeman, only an extended strategy of cooperative initiatives such as that which Soviet

---

[10]Joanne Gowa, "Anarchy, Egoism, and Third Images: The Evolution of Cooperation and International Relations," *International Organization* 40:1 (Winter 1986), p. 174.

[11]Joshua Goldstein and John R. Freeman, *Three-Way Street: Strategic Reciprocity in World Politics* (Chicago: University of Chicago Press, 1990), p. 154.

leaders initiated in 1985 is likely to produce significant change in relations, though even it may not overcome "foreign policy inertia and . . . the overall political relationship that exists among the three countries."[12]

Institutionalizing Cooperation

Strategies such as reciprocity, tit-for-tat, and sustained-cooperation initiatives help actors ferret out the cooperative possibilities in variable-sum games. They help explain how egoistic actors can work together without higher authority; they achieve cooperation *despite* anarchy. Various proposals, however, have been aimed at overcoming the anarchic elements in global politics. Some theorists call for different kinds of states (such as republics and democracies) that they believe are naturally more peace-loving, and others advocate building international institutions that would obviate the need for self-help and would foster cooperation. We will review here some of these ideas and institutions.

Kant and Rousseau

Two eighteenth-century political philosophers, Immanuel Kant and Jean Jacques Rousseau, prescribed how states could reduce global anarchy and encourage cooperation. Born into Europe's Age of Enlightenment, they believed in the power of rationality and shared with modern game theorists the idea that people would pursue their rational self-interest if given adequate information. Unlike game theorists, however, they regarded individuals, not unitary states, as the primary actors in global politics. Their proposals touch on the perfectibility of individuals and states and on the means for overcoming the state system's anarchic properties. Both theorists are associated with the liberal tradition in global politics.[13] And in subsequent centuries their ideas contributed greatly to developing international law and organization.

Kant argued that human beings exist in two worlds — one the world of the senses (the phenomenal) and the other the world of reason (the noumenal).[14] Although both worlds guide and shape human conduct, the world of the senses often prevails over that

[12]Ibid., pp. 135–136. See Chapter 6, pp. 193–195 for a discussion of strategies such as reciprocity that sustain cooperation.

[13]For an assessment of the liberal tradition in the post–Cold War era, see Michael W. Doyle, "An International Liberal Community," in Graham Allison and Gregory F. Treverton, eds., *Rethinking America's Security* (New York: W. W. Norton, 1992), pp. 307–333. See also Mark W. Zacher and Richard A. Matthews, "Liberal International Theory: Common Threads, Divergent Strands," paper presented to the Annual Meeting of the American Political Science Association, 1992, for a recounting of this tradition.

[14]Kenneth N. Waltz, "Kant, Liberalism, and War," *American Political Science Review* 56:2 (June 1962), p. 332, and Kenneth W. Waltz, *Man, the State, and War* (New York: Columbia University Press, 1959), p. 163.

of reason. As a result, conflict often dominates human relations. For reason to prevail, human beings must enter civil society and create the civil state "in which," Kenneth Waltz says, "rights are secured, and with them the possibility of moral behavior."[15] But, according to Kant, only one kind of state can foster individual moral development and international peace: a *republic* that has representative institutions. Kant held that, unlike authoritarian states, republics enhance cooperation because they act in their citizens' interests, and cooperation and peace serve those interests.

Kant believed that states and their relationships were analogous to individuals in a state of nature. How can states escape this anarchic state? He had two answers. First, states should seek to improve internally and become republics so that "perpetual peace" is made possible. Second, republics should combine into a "voluntary combination of different States that would be *dissoluble* at any time"[16] so that reason can govern passion and ambition. Kant has been criticized for proposing a voluntary confederation rather than a supranational state because voluntarism seems to invite renewal of the problems associated with anarchy. Why then his preference for a voluntary arrangement? Kenneth Waltz argues that Kant had two reasons:

> States already have a legal constitution; it would be illogical to place them under another. . . . One suspects that his second reason for shying away from a world state is more important. He fears that such a state, once achieved, would be a greater evil than the wars it is designed to eliminate. It could so easily become a terrible despotism, stifle liberty, kill initiative, and in the end lapse into anarchy.[17]

Kant did expect that republics would voluntarily submit to the restraints imposed by global norms.

Rousseau's analysis parallels Kant's, though he reaches a different conclusion. Like Kant, Rousseau sees the condition of states as analogous to that of individuals in a state of nature. He also argues for the need to escape from that state into civil society and calls for establishing republican governments. But, whereas Kant thought that the existence of "good" states—republics—and a voluntary confederation would be sufficient to ensure perpetual peace, Rousseau believed that only a strong supranational state would overcome the conflict rising out of anarchy.[18] The reason for this difference is that, as we saw earlier, Rousseau believed conflict arose from the structure of the international system itself and the resulting security dilemma in which states found themselves, whereas Kant believed conflict was a result of defects within states. Rousseau, however, proposed a world state that "shall unite nations by bonds similar to those which already unite their individual members, and place the one no less than the other under the authority of the Law."

[15]Waltz, "Kant, Liberalism, and War," p. 332.
[16]Kant, as cited in ibid., p. 337. Emphasis in original.
[17]Ibid., p. 337.
[18]Waltz, *Man, the State, and War*, pp. 181–185.

It must have a Legislative Body, with powers to pass laws and ordinances binding upon all its members; it must have a coercive force capable of compelling every State to obey its common resolves whether in the way of command or of prohibition; and finally, it must be strong and firm enough to make it impossible for any member to withdraw at his own pleasure the moment he conceives his private interest to clash with that of the whole body.[19]

Woodrow Wilson's proposals for collective security and a League of Nations show the enduring influence of Kant and Rousseau on the liberal tradition in global politics.

Woodrow Wilson and Collective Security

President Woodrow Wilson's proposed *collective-security* system in reaction to World War I, which Wilson believed grew from the authoritarian domestic structure in Germany, Austria-Hungary, and Russia and their resort to balance-of-power policies.[20] Following Kant and Rousseau, Wilson believed war was caused by *both* the imperfection of states and the international system's structure.

Aggressive autocracy, according to Wilson, could be overcome by applying national self-determination and encouraging the spread of democracy. Whereas authoritarian leaders go to war for personal profit, glory, and power, democracy would prevent leaders from going to war without good cause. What if some states failed to become democracies, however, or did so and still behaved aggressively? The remedy, Wilson argued, was a new security structure to replace the balance-of-power system. And, as the last of his *Fourteen Points* (a statement of war aims made on January 8, 1918), Wilson proposed "a general association of nations . . . formed under specific covenants for the purpose of affording mutual guarantees of political independence and territorial integrity to great and small states alike."[21]

A collective-security system, according to Wilson, treated all nations as interdependent members of one community. Like the Three Musketeers, whose motto was "one for all and all for one," *all* states would help *any* state that was threatened by aggression. Aggressors would be deterred by the knowledge that punishment would be swift and effective.[22] Collective security, Wilson believed, could not rely only on the deterrent effect of one for all and all for one: it had to carry moral force. "Moral force," he declared, "is a great deal more powerful than physical."[23] Ultimately, peace could be assured only when states and leaders internalized the idea that aggression was wrong.

[19]Rousseau, *A Lasting Peace*, as cited in ibid., p. 185.

[20]The idea of collective security dates back at least to the Treaty of Osnabrück in the seventeenth century. See Inis L. Claude, Jr., *Power and International Relations* (New York: Random House, 1962), pp. 106–107.

[21]See a speech by President Woodrow Wilson to a joint session of the U.S. Congress, *Congressional Record*, January 8, 1918, p. 691.

[22]See Claude, *Power and International Relations*, p. 114. The earlier passage is also from p. 114, and the remainder of the discussion draws upon p. 111.

[23]Woodrow Wilson, "Collective Security vs. Balance of Power," in Frederick H. Hartmann, ed., *World in Crisis: Readings in International Relations*, 4th ed. (New York: Macmillan, 1973) p. 233.

Wilson was hardly naive, however, though some of his critics have so argued, and he did not dismiss the role of power in confronting power. In a speech in South Dakota on September 8, 1919, he declared: "You have either got to have the old system . . . or you have got to have a new system," and "[y]ou cannot establish freedom . . . without force, and the only force you can substitute for an armed mankind is the concerted force of the combined action of mankind. . . ."[24]

Functionalism and Neofunctionalism

After World War II, other ideas were advanced to make war less likely and encourage cooperation. Like Kant's *federalism*, some of these entailed moving beyond the state system by creating new loyalties and structures above states that would reduce anarchy. Two of the most durable ideas were *functionalism* and *neofunctionalism*, both arising from the idea that all societies have "functional needs" such as feeding and housing citizens that states seek to satisfy but may not successfully meet.

The origin of functionalism is often associated with David Mitrany's *The Working Peace System*, published during World War II.[25] Appalled by war's carnage, he called for new global arrangements to meet peoples' unsatisfied needs for economic and social welfare, which he believed led to conflict. Often, individual states were unable to meet these demands effectively. Assuming that states had to meet them, Mitrany argued that new institutions had to be built for the purpose. With those new structures, their response to global needs would be relatively spontaneous, involving the "binding together [of] those interests which are common, where they are common, and to the extent . . . they are common."[26] Mitrany could not specify those structures precisely because they would be determined by the functional needs. Nonetheless, his premise was optimistic — individuals are able to recognize their functional needs and will organize themselves to satisfy them effectively.

Functionalists believed a snowballing effect would occur once successful *functional organizations* had been built. Success would breed success, and new global institutions would be created to meet other functional needs. In time, the "functional alternative" would expand from a few areas into new and unexpected ones. Global efforts to address one demand (such as monitoring global food production) would stimulate additional demands to satisfy others (such as monitoring global weather). Functional agencies would be like "stones cast into a pond," each producing ever-widening ripples into new functional areas. According to functionalist theory, states would more readily surrender to functional organizations their apolitical technical and economic responsibilities than

---

[24]Woodrow Wilson, "Collective Security vs. Balance of Power," in Hartmann, ed., *World in Crisis*, pp. 232, 233.

[25]David Mitrany, *A Working Peace System: An Argument for the Functional Development of International Organization* (London: Oxford University Press, 1943).

[26]Mitrany, as quoted in James Patrick Sewell, *Functionalism and World Politics* (Princeton: Princeton University Press, 1966), p. 9.

security tasks. Nevertheless, state sovereignty would gradually erode, and a new global community would evolve. According to one observer, Mitrany's goal was clear: creating "a complex, interwoven network of cross-national organizations performing all the traditional welfare functions of the nation-state at the same time rendering war impossible."[27]

Functional organizations were not unknown at the time Mitrany wrote. They date from the International Telegraphic Union in 1865 and the Universal Postal Union in 1874. Indeed, the Central Commission for the Navigation of the Rhine River, created after the Congress of Vienna in 1815, antedates both and is often described as the first modern international functional organization. Proliferating functional organizations have not eroded state sovereignty as functionalists believed they would, and states have not surrendered significant powers to them. Even technical functions prove highly political, and one sees little evidence of an automatic extension of functional organization to meet human needs. Nevertheless, such organizations have reduced the anarchic side of global politics. One observer writes: "To call the thickening web of overlapping and intersecting functional institutions anarchical is to drain the term of all but a narrowly technical meaning."[28]

Some refinement in functionalist theory was clearly called for, and the form it took was neofunctionalism. Unlike its predecessor, neofunctionalism takes into account actors' interests and abandons the assumption that human needs will be met automatically or that functional areas are nonpolitical. In neofunctionalism, expanding global cooperation is no longer taken for granted. Instead, governments are pressured to cooperate by domestic interest groups and lobbyists who see an advantage to themselves in such cooperation.

Business groups in several countries may come to believe that eliminating interstate trade barriers will benefit them by stimulating greater sales and profits, and they may lobby their governments to form a common market. Thereafter, corporations may organize internationally to take advantage of the new opportunities and lobby for additional standardization of policy in taxes and welfare. This initiative in turn may provoke national labor unions to join one another to bargain effectively with the corporations. Because many economic policies are linked, creating a supranational agency to foster interstate cooperation on one issue may produce pressures for cooperation on others. Thus, negotiations among the United States, Canada, and Mexico for a North American Free Trade Agreement (NAFTA) could not be limited to reducing tariffs because wage and tax policies, environmental and health regulations, and labor laws all strongly influence distribution of costs and benefits among participants.

---

[27]Charles Pentland, *International Theory and European Integration* (New York: Free Press, 1973), p. 70.

[28]Richard Ullman, *Securing Europe* (Princeton: Princeton University Press, 1991), p. 145.

Neofunctionalists did not assume that any of this sequence was assured. Genuine progress required simultaneously extending supranational authority—the number of issues covered—*and* deepening that authority. And if this *spillover* went far enough it would lead to a shift in loyalties and political activities from states to a new political community.[29]

In sum, neofunctionalism shares characteristics with functionalism but also differs.[30] Like Mitrany and the functionalists, neofunctionalists rely on common welfare needs as a way of stimulating cooperation and depend on technocrats to facilitate this cooperation. Both approaches assume that cooperation confers more benefits than going it alone. On the other hand, neofunctionalists are more aware of just how political economic and technical issues are. They advocate selecting an issue that is technical but is also economically and politically important to a group of governments, and they are conscious that political institutions must be built to facilitate cooperation. Finally, neofunctionalists select areas with a potential for spillover into other sectors that can increase overall authority for supranational institutions. As we shall see shortly, neofunctionalist ideas remain relevant, especially in the evolving European Community.

The League of Nations

We have so far focused on theoretical approaches to cooperation in global politics. Some of these theories have been tested, and we now examine the major institutional mechanisms created to do so. It is widely believed that international organizations can anchor cooperative habits by overcoming the anarchic elements in global politics. Such organizations "*may* play roles in the creation and maintenance of [international] regimes" because they provide norms and rules for member states and forums for coordinating behavior among members.[31] The *League of Nations* and the *United Nations* are the two principal global organizations that have tried to promote cooperation by applying collective-security principles and meeting functional needs. Both were established at the end of world wars, and both had similar goals—maintaining peace and security, mobilizing the "collective" will of member states to do so, and addressing global social and economic needs.

---

[29]See Ernst B. Haas, *The Uniting of Europe* (Stanford: Stanford University Press, 1958), p. 16.

[30]This analysis draws upon Joseph S. Nye, *Peace in Parts: Integration and Conflict in Regional Organization* (Boston: Little, Brown, 1971), pp. 52–53.

[31]Margaret P. Karns and Karen A. Mingst, "The United States and Multilateral Institutions: A Framework for Analysis," in Karns and Mingst, eds., *The United States and Multilateral Institutions* (Boston: Unwin Hyman, 1990), p. 3. Emphasis in original.

The League: Origins and Characteristics

Among League of Nations predecessors were the *Hague Conferences* in 1899 and 1907 sponsored by the Tsar of Russia whose achievements included a convention specifying peaceful ways to settle disputes and a Permanent Court of Arbitration. The League was mainly a U.S. and British idea that evolved during World War I. In 1915, a group of idealistic Americans who belonged to the Century Club in New York and British pacifists who formed the Bryce Group in London offered alternate plans for a League of Nations.[32] These plans were brought to President Wilson's attention; he embraced the idea of a "general association of nations" as the last of his Fourteen Points.

Wilson envisioned the League as a means for enforcing collective security, but disputes erupted at Versailles about the form the organization should take.[33] The British and the Americans argued about how much the League should encourage change, the Americans hoping the organization would become a means for altering the global status quo. Small states were unhappy with their proposed representation in the organization. The French wanted the *League Covenant* to provide a stronger role for the use of force with an eye toward preventing restoration of German power. Finally, the Japanese sought, but failed before American and Australian opposition, to have a statement on racial equality added to the Covenant. Despite these controversies, the Covenant was ratified at Versailles in April 1919.

The League consisted of a Council, an Assembly, and a Secretariat, with a Permanent Court of Justice added in 1921. The Council was made up of the "Principal Allied or Associated Powers" (the victorious coalition) and four additional members selected by the Assembly. The Assembly, composed of all League members with equal voting rights, could deal with any issue "within the sphere of action of the League or affecting the peace of the world." The Secretariat, headed by a Secretary General, would serve as the League's executive and bureaucracy.

The Council was to be the principal mechanism for dealing with threats to peace. Among its options if a dispute arose were arbitration, judicial settlement, or investigation. If the Council became involved, it was obligated to investigate the dispute and issue a report, and it could refer the issue to the Assembly for similar action. If an actor still resorted to war, the Covenant specified the members' collective obligations. The offender would "be deemed to have committed an act of war against all other Members of the League" and be subject to "severance of all trade or financial relations" by other states. If necessary, says Article 16 of the Covenant, "it shall be the duty of the Council . . . to recommend to the several Governments concerned what effective military, naval or air force the Members of

---

[32]F. S. Northedge, *The League of Nations: Its Life and Times, 1920–1946* (Leicester, Eng.: Leicester University Press, 1986), pp. 26–27.

[33]Ibid., pp. 43–46.

the League shall severally contribute to the armed forces to be used to protect the covenants of the League." In other words, aggression would be met by collective sanctions and, if necessary, by collective force.

Evaluating the League's Effectiveness

The obligations outlined in the Covenant were voluntary and limited, ultimately undermining collective security. States could join or leave the League as they wished, and universal membership was never achieved, varying from thirty-two members in 1920 to sixty-three at its peak. Seventeen states withdrew or were expelled, including great powers Germany, Italy, Japan, and the Soviet Union. Some never joined, most important the United States, where the Senate, dominated by a Republican majority led by Senator Henry Cabot Lodge, refused to confirm the Treaty of Versailles.[34] Indeed, the U.S. policy of *isolationism* during the 1920s weakened the collective-security principle and is still cited to justify U.S. activism in global politics. Another source of weakness was institutional: most League decisions required unanimity, and even then they were only recommendations. Procedures for moving from recommending an action to implementing it were not fully spelled out. Finally, and most important, when challenges arose, major members acted unilaterally and failed to meet their collective-security obligations.

In the temperate 1920s' political climate, the League seemed to work. It helped solve disputes between Turkey and Iraq, Greece and Bulgaria, and Poland and Lithuania. The Greek–Bulgarian question reflected the League at its best. A border conflict between the two broke out in October 1925. Within days, Bulgaria asked for the League's help. The Council met, called for a cease-fire, sent observers, and started a formal inquiry. By December, a report was made to the Council, an indemnity was awarded to Bulgaria, and the issue was resolved.[35] *The League could succeed in relatively minor quarrels in which none of the great powers were directly involved.*

In the 1930s, the League proved helpless in coping with intense conflicts in which great powers were major players. Three episodes spelled the doom of the League as an effective collective-security organization—the Japanese seized Manchuria in 1931, the Italians invaded Ethiopia in 1935, and the Germans occupied Austria and Czechoslovakia in 1938. After the Japanese invaded Manchuria, China appealed to the League, seeking to have Japanese forces removed from its territory. After a delay, the Council passed resolutions requesting Japanese withdrawal and establishing a formal commission of inquiry. It took a year before the commission's report was adopted by the League Council and Assembly. Known as the *Lytton Report*, after the committee's chairman,

---

[34]Lynn H. Miller, *Organizing Mankind* (Boston: Holbrook Press, 1972), p. 38, and Northedge, *League of Nations*, pp. 47–48.

[35]Ibid., pp. 111–112. Even at this time the League's failure to grapple with issues like the Polish seizure of Vilna from Lithuania (1920), the French occupation of the Ruhr (1923), and the Italian bombardment of the Greek island Corfu (1923) boded ill for its future.

Lord Lytton, it supported Chinese claims against Japan and suggested that Japan had been provoked. Its recommendations — that China and Japan sign trade and nonaggression treaties and set up a joint "special administration" over Manchuria — were, one analyst says, "well-intentioned daydreaming."[36] Japan refused to accept even these timid recommendations and withdrew from the League.

The League had failed to meet its first big challenge, and the reasons for that failure show how difficult it is to elicit cooperation among powerful states with competing interests.[37] First, Manchuria was geographically and psychologically remote from the great powers. Second, Britain and France, the leading powers in the League, were ill prepared to challenge Japan militarily, and the United States, which did have military weight in Asia, preferred to invoke moral suasion against Japanese aggression. Third, the Great Depression reduced any interest in vigorous international action. Finally, the League's leading members preferred conciliation to sanctions in dealing with fellow members.

Italy's invasion of Ethiopia in October 1935 was an even clearer challenge to collective security. The Haitian representative to the League declared: "Great or small, strong or weak, near or far, white or coloured, let us never forget that one day we may be somebody's Ethiopia."[38] The case was made more compelling by Italian use of poison gas and high-level bombing against Ethiopians armed with spears. Economic sanctions were actually applied, but with little effect.[39] Although Britain supported sanctions, it refused to close the Suez Canal to Italian shipping or halt the flow of oil that was necessary for the fascist war machine to function. And, when it was clear sanctions would not work, the League refused to go further.

The Ethiopian case revealed a fundamental difficulty in applying the collective-security principle consistently. Britain and France were less interested in stopping Mussolini than in making him an ally against Hitler. These biases became stronger during the Ethiopian crisis when Hitler announced in March 1936 that he was unilaterally reneging on the Locarno Treaty of 1925 and remilitarizing the Rhineland. Of British Prime Minister Stanley Baldwin, Winston Churchill wrote, "The Prime Minister had declared that sanctions meant war; secondly, he was resolved that there must be no war; and, thirdly, he decided upon sanctions."[40] In their eagerness to avoid war with Italy, British Foreign Secretary Sir Samuel Hoare and French Foreign Minister Pierre Laval secretly offered Mussolini a deal in December 1935, giving him most of what

---

[36]Northedge, *League of Nations*, p. 159.

[37]See ibid., pp. 161–164 and in Miller, *Organizing Mankind*, pp. 37–41.

[38]Cited in F. P. Walters, *A History of the League of Nations*, vol. 2 (London: Oxford University Press, 1952), p. 653.

[39]Evan Luard, *A History of the United Nations. Volume 1: The Years of Western Domination, 1945–1955* (London: Macmillan Press, 1982), p. 7.

[40]Winston S. Churchill, *The Gathering Storm* (Boston: Houghton Mifflin, 1948), p. 175.

he demanded.[41] Both countries were absorbed by events in Europe, not Africa, contradicting the collective-security assumption that any aggression against anyone was equally important. Competing political games divided the actors' attention and resources, and they decided to sacrifice principle in one to strengthen their hand in another. The requirements of collective security and the demands of European politics at the time could not be reconciled.

That collective security was bankrupt showed in the League's failure to resist Hitler's aggression against Austria and Czechoslovakia in 1938.[42] Indeed, amid these crises, the League Assembly was debating whether to weaken the obligation of states to resist aggression.[43] In one last foolish act, the League expelled the Soviet Union in 1939 for invading Finland at the very moment when Hitler mortally threatened the rest of Europe. As World War II began, League operations were scattered to other countries, keeping only a small staff in Geneva. After the war, the Assembly held a final session in April 1946 before formally ending its own existence. The world's first experiment with collective security had failed dismally. In constructing a successor, conscious efforts were made to avoid the League's mistakes.

The United Nations

The idea for a new international organization was again born in wartime — in a 1942 declaration by twenty-six nations (the "United Nations"). By 1943, the notion of a new organization had become a regular agenda item at the major powers' wartime conferences. These discussions led the United States to invite Great Britain, Russia, and China to meet in Washington in August 1944. The Dumbarton Oaks Conference drafted proposals that became the basis for the *U.N. Charter* less than a year later.[44] In April 1945, at a conference in San Francisco, the Charter of the United Nations was signed.

The United Nations Begins and Grows

The goals and structure of the new international organization resembled those of the League, but the *U.N. Charter* also had provisions intended to address deficiencies in the League Covenant. Although maintaining peace and security remained a basic goal for

[41]The deal was leaked, and in the ensuing public outcry Hoare was dismissed and the French cabinet was replaced.

[42]The Soviet government's efforts to mobilize the League against Hitler especially by Foreign Minister Maxim Litvinov after 1934, were ignored.

[43]Walters, *History of League of Nations*, vol. II, pp. 780–782.

[44]Luard, *History of United Nations*, pp. 17–32. For an excellent overview of the United Nations, see Amos Yoder, *The Evolution of the United Nations System*, 2nd ed. (Washington, D.C.: Taylor & Francis, 1993).

the new organization, the U.N., more than the League, emphasized meeting the global community's economic and social needs. In this sense the U.N. Charter more fully reflected the functionalist belief that conflict arises from poverty.

The number and responsibilities of U.N. organs reflected these ideas. The Charter established six major organs: a General Assembly, a Security Council, an Economic and Social Council, a Trusteeship Council, a Secretariat, and an International Court of Justice. Three of these — the Security Council, the Secretariat, and the International Court — were intended primarily to address peace and security, and the other two were to be responsible for the organization's functional activities. The *General Assembly* was to shoulder responsibilities in both areas. Every member was represented in the General Assembly, and each was given one vote. The Assembly could take up any issue, but its resolutions would be only recommendations. Other organs were to be responsible to the General Assembly. Unlike the League, the United Nations has become a genuinely universal body. Fifty-one states were charter members, and thereafter membership expanded dramatically, fueled by incoming independent states in the 1960s and 1970s and, more recently, by the U.S.S.R. and Yugoslav successors. By late 1993, membership had reached 184.

Though analogous to the League Council, the *Security Council* differs from its predecessor in a number of ways. In matters of peaceful settlement and peacekeeping, the Security Council's authority is greater than that of the League Council. Under the Charter, the Security Council enjoys "primary responsibility for the maintenance of international peace and security." The Council also has authority to "investigate any dispute, or any situation which might lead to international friction or give rise to a dispute," and, unlike the League Council, it does not have to wait for a dispute to be brought before it. Under Chapters Six and Seven (Articles 33–51)[45] of the Charter, the Council may order a spectrum of actions to end a threat to peace. These range from inquiry, mediation, and conciliation to "complete or partial interruption of economic relations and of rail, sea, air, postal, telegraphic, radio, and other means of communication." In recent years the Council has imposed such sanctions against South Africa, Iraq, Serbia, and Libya. If such measures prove inadequate, the Council "may take such action by air, sea, or land forces as may be necessary to maintain or restore international peace and security. Such actions may include demonstrations, blockade, and other operations by air, sea, or land forces of Members of the United Nations." This provision was the basis for U.N. military action against Saddam Hussein.

Two big differences between the Charter and Covenant merit attention here. First, the Charter strengthened all states' obligations to carry out the Security Council's decisions before threats to the peace. Chapter Seven states categorically that all members "shall join in affording mutual assistance in carrying out the measures decided

---

[45]Chapter Seven deals with the "Pacific Settlement of Disputes" and is relevant to conflicts caused by misunderstanding. Chapter Eight — "Action with Respect to Threats to the Peace, Breaches of the Peace, and Acts of Aggression" — deals with intentional acts of aggression.

FIGURE 9.1

The United Nations System

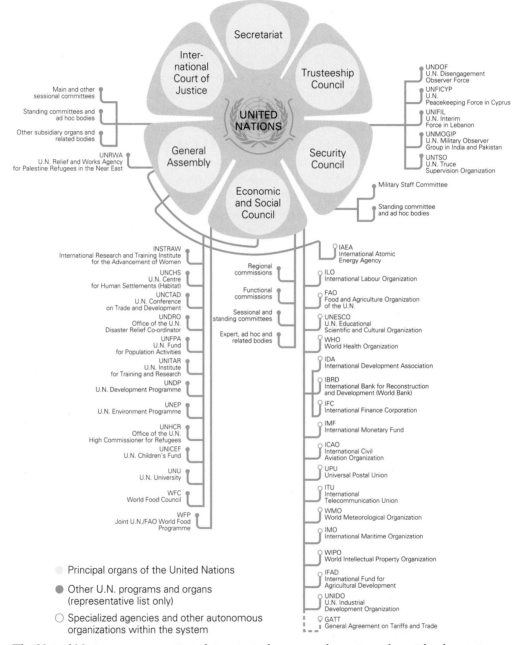

The United Nations system consists of six principal organs and a variety of specialized agencies and groups.

upon by the Security Council." Second, the Charter provides a stronger statement about the possible use of force to carry out a Security Council decision. In the end, however, despite the Charter's strong language, compliance by members remains voluntary, and the Council, like its predecessor, depends on members' willingness, especially that of the great powers, to provide resources. That is why the post-Cold War willingness of Russia and China to permit vigorous U.N. action have contributed to accelerated U.N. intervention around the world and why U.N. efforts to stop Serbian aggression in Bosnia failed.

The structure of the League and U.N. Councils also differ significantly. Membership in the League Council was divided between the permanent "Principal Allied and Associated Powers" and several appointed states. Each had one vote, and voting generally required unanimity. The Security Council has the same blend of permanent and temporary members, but with a major difference in voting procedure. Under the Charter, the United States, the Soviet Union, China, France, and Britain were designated permanent members and six (later ten) states were to be elected to serve in rotation as nonpermanent members.[46] Voting on procedural matters require a majority of nine of fifteen, but votes on substantive action by the Council require that the majority include *all* permanent members, giving each permanent member a veto on Council action.

That the *veto power* was limited became clear when the Soviet representative's absence from the Council when the Korean War began in June 1950 was not regarded as a veto. Previously, Council action was believed to require positive votes by all permanent members. The Korean case meant that absence or abstention did not imply either consent or disagreement. Permanent members that might be skeptical about a Council action could thus dissociate themselves from that action without being obstructionist. In recent years, China has adopted this posture toward several key matters.

Following Chinese intervention in Korea, the General Assembly at U.S. urging took additional action to circumvent the veto. The General Assembly adopted a *Uniting for Peace Resolution* permitting it to meet in emergency session within twenty-four hours to make "recommendations to Members for collective measures, including in a case of breach of the peace or act of aggression the use of armed forces when necessary" if the Security Council was unable to act. At the time the U.S.S.R. protested, but it invoked the provisions of this resolution in June 1967 during the Six-Day War, and the Uniting for Peace Resolution has been used on other occasions.[47]

[46] After the Soviet Union collapsed in 1991, Russia was given the permanent seat on the Council. The People's Republic of China gained China's permanent seat in 1971 from Taiwan after years of conflict over who would represent that state. United Germany and Japan indicated interest in becoming permanent members of the Council.

[47] A. Leroy Bennett, *International Organizations: Principles and Issues*, 5th ed. (Englewood Cliffs, N.J.: Prentice-Hall, 1991), p. 60.

The veto entails both advantages and disadvantages. Its main advantage is ensuring that Council recommendations will have support from the principal powers. One lesson from the Ethiopian and Czechoslovak cases in the 1930s was that the pivotal powers must be willing to support actions if collective action is to work. The disadvantage of the veto is that one permanent member can frustrate the Council. In a sense, the veto provision was an admission that "collective security" was not workable and that there was no point in trying to run roughshod over the major powers' objections. In practice, a superpower like the United States can thwart the Security Council, with or without the formal veto, by withholding resources or opposing Council action. Such actors enjoy a *tacit veto* regardless of the language in the U.N. Charter.

The *Secretariat* is the principal U.N. executive organ and is directed by a Secretary General, the prime U.N. "civil servant." The Secretariat manages the organization's global bureaucracy and finances and oversees operation of all U.N. organs and personnel, from technicians and policemen to doctors and soldiers. Initially, the United Nations had 1,500 employees; in 1993 it had close to 52,000. The Secretary General is appointed by the General Assembly after a recommendation by the Security Council and serves for a renewable five-year term. Because the Secretary can take a major part in the U.N.'s peacekeeping aspect, having the power to "bring to the attention of the Security Council any matter which in his opinion may threaten the maintenance of international peace and security," his selection involves delicate negotiations among members to ensure that their interests are looked after. The Secretary, too, is charged with carrying out recommendations by the Council. The United Nations has had only six Secretaries General—Trygve Lie of Norway, Dag Hammarskjöld of Sweden, U Thant of Burma, Kurt Waldheim of Austria, Javier Pérez de Cuellar of Peru, and Boutros Boutros-Ghali of Egypt. Their varied personalities and skills have determined the organization's effectiveness. Hammarskjöld became a target of Soviet wrath for his activism and alleged pro-Western bias. By contrast, Waldheim and Pérez de Cuellar were accused of being anti-Western, and Boutros-Ghali is an active spokesman for Third World interests.

The fourth major organ, the *International Court of Justice (ICJ)*, was established as successor to the Permanent Court of Justice in the Hague. The fifteen justices, appointed for nine-year terms, reflect geographic and political diversity. By the Charter, the Court is authorized to decide cases brought to it or to provide advisory opinions when asked by the Council or the Assembly. Few states have accepted the "compulsory jurisdiction" of the Court, however, and most have repeatedly decided, case by case, whether to allow the ICJ to render a binding decision. Thus, the United States refused to accept the ICJ's 1984 judgment in a case brought against it by the Sandinista government of Nicaragua because of U.S. support for the *contras*.[48]

---

[48]See Table 8.1 in Bennett, *International Organizations*, pp. 173–177 for a list of ICJ cases and advisory opinions between 1947 and 1988.

The remaining two organs are the *Economic and Social Council* (ECOSOC) and the *Trusteeship Council*. Both were intended for important work in carrying out functional responsibilities of the United Nations. ECOSOC, consisting of fifty-four members elected by the General Assembly, has for its principal tasks reporting on global "economic, social, cultural, educational, health and related matters." It may make recommendations to the Assembly and to the "specialized agencies" on these matters. The *specialized agencies* (such as the World Health Organization and the Food and Agricultural Organization) are semi-independent international agencies with specific functional responsibilities.

The Trusteeship Council was established to monitor the economic, social, and political progress of former colonial territories placed under United Nations trust as a result of World War II, previous League mandates, or voluntary actions. Most of these territories have now gained independence and self-government, and the Trusteeship Council is just about out of business. Some suggest, however, that the agency be given new responsibilities for countries like Somalia in which government has broken down.

U.N. Effectiveness in Maintaining Peace and Security

Although its record is mixed, the United Nations has been more successful than the League. It has survived fifty years and has used many mechanisms to manage or ease tensions. These include nonbinding resolutions, inquiries and fact-finding missions, observers to monitor cease-fires, economic and military sanctions, peacekeeping forces, and, on a few occasions, military force to combat aggression. By one count, the United Nations took up more than 180 disputes between 1946 and 1988.[49] Most U.N. involvement in these disputes involved identifying, debating, and seeking to resolve disputes by negotiation and mediation. Relatively few cases have entailed more extensive measures. Although the United Nations has enjoyed signal successes, its inability to resolve some of the most intransigent global political disputes and its failure to deal with others (especially at the height of the Cold War), also point to its limitations.

One impediment was use of the veto by the superpowers in the Security Council. During the early decades, the Council was dominated by the United States and its allies, and, for that reason, the Soviet Union cast many vetoes. Between 1946 and 1990, the U.S.S.R. was responsible for about half (116 out of 238).[50] Although many were cast to prevent admission of new pro-Western members (until an agreement was reached on joint admission for both East- and West-bloc members in the mid-1950s), several prevented actions that the U.S.S.R. believed harmful to its cause in the Cold War.

[49]See Table 6-1 in ibid., pp. 103–111, listing disputes "debated by the Security Council and General Assembly" (p. 102).

[50]John G. Stoessinger, *The United Nations and the Superpowers: China, Russia, and America*, 4th ed. (New York: Random House, 1977), p. 6, for Soviet vetoes through 1975. For the veto record through 1990, see U.S. Department of State, *Report to Congress on Voting Practices in the United Nations, 1990* (Washington, D.C.: Bureau of International Organization Affairs, March 1991), p. 78.

In the euphoria that accompanied the end of the Cold War, the United Nations assumed more and more peacekeeping burdens, but the world community was not prepared to provide the organization with the resources and authority it needed to cope successfully with all its new challenges.

The United States cast its first veto only in 1970, but thereafter, as the General Assembly came to be dominated by the Third World and the United States found itself unable to prevent the Council from passing resolutions that it believed contrary to its interests, Washington increasingly resorted to the veto.[51] Figure 9.2 depicts how the United States progressively found itself voting in the minority in the General Assembly. After 1960, U.N. voting majorities coalesced around the poor states in the Third World with strong interests in redistributing global resources, opposing South African apartheid, and appeasing Arab oil producers. The initial U.S. vetoes were used to prevent U.N. action against the white minority government of Rhodesia, and stop resolutions condemning Israel and U.S. control of the Panama Canal. More recently, the United States passed the U.S.S.R. in applying the veto. Between 1970 and 1990, the United States used its veto sixty-nine times, and the Soviet Union cast none after 1984.[52] In

---

[51]Stoessinger, *United Nations and Superpowers*, pp. 16–17.

[52]*Report to Congress on Voting Practices in the United Nations 1990*, p. 78. For a different scoring, see Anjali V. Patil's *The UN Veto in World Affairs, 1946–1990* (Sarasota, Fla.: UNIFO Publishers, 1992). Prior to 1970, Britain and France cast vetoes to protect Western interests and

FIGURE 9.2

U.S. and Soviet Union Percentage Agreement with the Majority

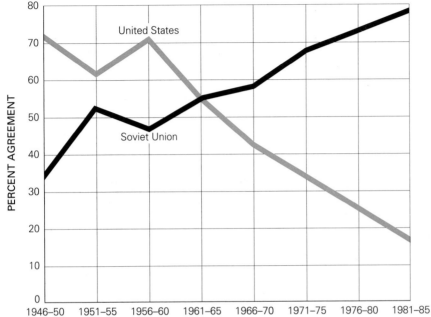

Until the mid-1960s, the United States found itself in the majority on most issues while the Soviet Union was in the minority. The growth in the U.N. membership, especially Third World states, accompanied the progressive isolation of the United States in the General Assembly after 1970.

addition to the actual use of the veto, the threat that it might be used acts as a deterrent to prevent issues from being brought to the Council unless the purpose is to embarrass the state that is threatening the veto.

The veto is one reason the Security Council has authorized the use of force to stop aggression only twice. The first occasion was in Korea in 1950 and the second in 1990 when member states were authorized to use force to implement U.N. resolutions to end Iraqi occupation of Kuwait.[53] On both occasions, unusual circumstances prevailed.

to save the United States from having to use its veto power. In 1993, Russia vetoed a resolution to make funding for peacekeeping contributions mandatory.

[53] The Korean case was not a pure case of collective security because U.N. forces were mostly American and South Korean troops and contingents sent by NATO and other U.S. allies. The operation against Iraq came closer to the ideal of collective security, though again relatively few states sent troops; others did provide financial assistance. United Nations imposition of "no-fly" zones over Iraq and Bosnia are somewhat more limited authorizations of the use of force.

When the Council authorized military action in Korea, the Soviet representative was boycotting its sessions. Forty years later, the U.N. authorization to use force against Iraq coincided with the end of the Cold War and increasing cooperation between Moscow and Washington.

Unable to *enforce* peace between these two occasions, the United Nations early devised the less-demanding techniques of *peacekeeping* and *preventive diplomacy*. Unlike the operations in Korea and the Persian Gulf, peacekeeping does not identify an aggressor. The objective is not to defeat an aggressor but to separate warring parties, contain violence by interposing U.N. forces, and cool off adversaries. The idea that such peacekeeping could prevent local disputes from escalating or expanding was expressed by calling it "preventive diplomacy." In the words of Secretary General Dag Hammarskjöld who coined the expression,

> Preventive action . . . must, in the first place, aim at filling the vacuum so that it will not provoke action from any of the major parties, the initiative from which might be taken for preventive purposes but might in turn lead to a counter action from the other sides. . . . Temporarily . . . the United Nations enters the picture on the basis of its non-commitment to any power bloc, so as to provide to the extent possible a guarantee in relation to all parties against initiatives from others.[54]

One example of peacekeeping forces used for preventive diplomacy took place when troops were dispatched to the former Belgian Congo (Zaire) in 1960, where it was feared that a breakdown in law and order would embroil the United States and Soviet Union in a dangerous confrontation.

United Nations peacekeepers, as shown in Table 9.1, have been sent to every continent.[55] The first peacekeeping force was the U.N. Emergency Force (UNEF) that was sent to the Middle East in 1956.[56] Operations range from a few peacekeepers — 20 to monitor the Greek border in 1947 — to large-scale military exercises — the 1992–94 Somali relief operation carried out by more than 30,000 U.S., French, Pakistani, Italian, and other troops. Although peacekeepers cannot address underlying disputes, they demonstrate that a relatively small U.N. presence can defuse tensions among adversaries. Their presence — and associated U.N. action — helps states extricate themselves from difficult situations without losing "face." These forces remain at the pleasure of the combatants, however. When they are no longer welcome, they can do little except leave.

---

[54]*Introduction to the Annual Report of the Secretary-General on the Work of the Organization*, June 16, 1959, to June 15, 1960, General Assembly, Official Records, 15th sess., supp. no. 1A, p. 4. On the role of Hammarskjöld in creating these mechanisms, see Miller, *Organizing Mankind*, pp. 104–105.

[55]See Ann Florini and Nina Tannenwald, *On the Front Lines: The United Nations' Role in Preventing and Containing Conflict* (New York: U.N. Association of the United States of America, 1984).

[56]UNEF was authorized under the Uniting for Peace Resolution because of British and French threats to veto any Security Council action.

TABLE 9.1
UN Peacekeeping and Observer Team Operations, 1948–1993

Name of force, *Location, and date* *Size of force, mission*

1. UN Truce Supervision Organization (UNTSO),
   Middle East, 1948–
   572 personnel; to supervise observance of truce in Palestine.
2. U.N. Military Observer Group in India and Pakistan (UNMOGIP),
   State of Jammu and Kashmir and border between India and Pakistan, 1949–
   102 personnel; to supervise the cease-fire between India and Pakistan in the states of
   Jammu and Kashmir.
3. First U.N. Emergency Force (UNEF I)
   Suez Canal, Sinai Peninsula, Gaza Strip, 1956–1967
   6,073 personnel; to secure and supervise the cessation of hostilities, withdrawal of
   French, Israeli, and British armed forces from Egyptian territory, and, thereafter, to
   serve as a buffer between Egyptian and Israeli forces.
4. U.N. Observation Group in Lebanon (UNOGIL)
   Lebanese–Syrian border, 1958
   591 personnel; to prevent illegal infiltration of personnel or arms across the Lebanese
   borders.
5. UN Operation in the Congo (ONUC)
   Congo (now Zaire), 1960–1964
   19,828 personnel; to ensure withdrawal of Belgian forces, help maintain law and order,
   and provide technical assistance; later, to maintain territorial integrity and political
   independence of the Congo by preventing recurrence of civil war and securing removal
   of foreign military, paramilitary, and advisory personnel and all mercenaries.
6. U.N. Temporary Executive Authority and U.N. Security Force in West
   New Guinea (West Irian) (UNTEA/UNSF), West New Guinea, 1962–1963
   1,576 personnel; to maintain peace and security under the U.N. Temporary Executive
   Authority (UNTEA) established between Indonesia and the Netherlands.
7. U.N. Yemen Observation Mission (UNYOM)
   Yemen, 1963–1964
   189 personnel; to observe and certify implementation of the disengagement agreement
   between Saudi Arabia and the United Arab Republic.
8. U.N. Peacekeeping Force in Cyprus (UNFICYP)
   Cyprus, 1964–
   6,411 personnel; to preserve peace and security and restore law and order; since the
   1974 war, to supervise the cease-fire and maintain a buffer zone between the Cyprus
   National Guard and the Turkish and Turkish Cypriot forces.
9. Representative of the Secretary General in the Dominican Republic (DOMREP)
   Dominican Republic, 1965–1966
   2 personnel; to observe and report on breaches of the cease-fire between the two de
   facto authorities.

10. U.N. India-Pakistan Observation Mission (UNIPOM)
    India-Pakistan border, 1965–1966
    96 personnel; to supervise the cease-fire along the India–Pakistan border, except
    Jammu and Kashmir, and withdrawal of all armed personnel to the positions held
    by them before August 5, 1965.
11. Second U.N. Emergency Force (UNEF II)
    Middle East, 1973–1979
    6,973 personnel; to supervise cease-fire between Egyptian and Israeli forces and
    assist in implementing the 1974 and 1975 disengagement agreements between
    the two countries.
12. U.N. Disengagement Observer Force (UNDOF)
    Syrian Golan Heights, 1974–
    1,450 personnel; to supervise the cease-fire between Israel and Syria and help im-
    plement the Israeli-Syrian Disengagement Agreement of 1974.
13. U.N. Interim Force in Lebanon (UNIFIL)
    Lebanon, 1978–
    7,000 personnel; to confirm withdrawal of Israeli forces from southern Lebanon,
    to restore peace and security to the area, and to help the Lebanese government
    regain effective authority.
14. U.N. Good Offices Mission in Afghanistan and Pakistan (UNGOMAP)
    Afghanistan and Pakistan, 1988–1990
    50 personnel; to help implement the Agreements on the Settlement in Afghani-
    stan and to investigate and report any violations of the Agreements.
15. U.N. Iran–Iraq Military Observer Group (UNIIMOG)
    Iran and Iraq, 1988–
    399 personnel; to verify and supervise the cease-fire and withdrawal of all forces
    to internationally recognized boundaries, pending a comprehensive settlement.
16. U.N. Angola Verification Mission (UNAVEM)
    Angola, 1989–
    70 personnel; to verify the redeployment northward and the phased withdrawal
    of Cuban troops from the territory of Angola in accordance with a timetable
    agreed to by Angola and Cuba.
17. U.N. Transition Assistance Group in Namibia (UNTAG)
    Namibia and Angola, 1989–1990
    4,493 personnel; to help the Special Representative of the U.N. Secretary General
    secure the independence of Namibia through free and fair elections.
18. U.N. Observer Group in Central America (ONUCA)
    Costa Rica, El Salvador, Guatemala, Honduras, and Nicaragua, 1989–
    1,098 personnel; to verify compliance with the security aspects of the Esquipulas
    II Agreement on cessation of aid to irregular forces and insurrectionist movements
    in the region and to help demobilize Nicaraguan resistance forces and monitor the
    cease-fire between the Nicaraguan parties.
19. U.N. Iraq-Kuwait Observer Mission (UNIKOM)
    Kuwait, 1991–
    500 personnel; to monitor a demilitarized zone along the Iraq–Kuwait boundary
    and observe any hostile action mounted from the territory of one state against
    the other after the Persian Gulf War.

20. U.N. Angola Verification Mission (UNAVEM II)
    Angola, 1991
    876 personnel; to verify that the two joint monitoring groups, representatives of
    the Angolan Government and representatives of the National Union for the Total
    Independence of Angola (UNITA) carry out their responsibilities under the Ango-
    lan Peace Accords of May 1991.
21. U.N. Observer Mission in El Salvador (ONVSAL)
    El Salvador, 1991–
    1,146 personnel; to monitor human-rights observance in El Salvador, making rec-
    ommendations for eliminating violations and reporting to the Secretary General
    and the Security Council.
22. U.N. Mission for the Referendum in Western Sahara (MINURSO)
    Western Sahara,1991–
    2,095 personnel; to implement the U.N. resolution on holding a referendum in
    Western Sahara.
23. U.N. Transitional Authority in Cambodia (UNTAC)
    Cambodia, 1991–
    15,000 personnel; to reestablish a functioning government in Cambodia with re-
    sponsibility to foster respect for human rights, exercise direct control over civil
    administration, organize and conduct an election, verify and monitor withdrawal
    of the various forces, and maintain law and order during the transition.
24. U.N. Protection Force (UNPROFOR)
    Yugoslavia, 1992–
    20,000 personnel; to help create conditions of peace and security required for an
    overall settlement in the former Yugoslavia; to provide that the three U.N.-
    Protected Areas will be demilitarized and protected from attack.
25. U.N. Operation in Somalia (UNOSOM)
    Somalia,1992–
    32,800 – 10,300 + 22,500 personnel; to ensure that relief supplies reach the
    needy and that law and order is restored.
26. U.N. Operation in Mozambique
    Mozambique, 1992–
    8,000 personnel; to monitor an agreement ending the civil war and prepare the
    country for elections.

Sources: The name, location, maximum size of the force and its function are from *The Blue Helmets: A Review of United Nations Peace-Keeping* (New York: United Nations Department of Public Information, 1990), pp. 419–449 for operations initiated until 1990. For more recent operations, data are from *United Nations Peace-keeping Operations Information Notes* (United Nations: Department of Public Information, September 1992), Eric Schmitt, "American Marine Killed in Somalia," *The New York Times,* January 13, 1993, p. 3A, and "United Nations: Peacekeeping Around the World," *The New York Times,* January 25, 1993, p. A6.

Because peacekeepers cannot solve underlying disputes, peacekeeping alone is not
enough—"peacekeeping is a means to an end, not an end in itself."[57]

Following authorization of UNEF in 1956, peacekeeping efforts were directed at
some of the most intractable problems in global politics. Several of these operations-
continue to this day. In 1960, the U.N. Congo Operation (ONUC) was sent to pacify

[57]Florini and Tannenwald, *On the Front Lines*, p. 18.

the former Belgian Congo and end the chaos that had engulfed that country immediately after independence. Though ONUC remained until 1964, it was controversial because of its effort to impose a particular solution. Civil-war situations such as that in the Congo are especially delicate because it may appear that the United Nations favors one side. In 1964, the Security Council also approved establishing the U.N. Force in Cyprus (UNFICYP) to separate the warring Turkish and Greek communities on that island. Following the 1973 Yom Kippur War, UNEF II was sent to the Sinai Peninsula to separate Egyptian and Israeli forces and oversee a cease-fire between the two. In 1978, the Security Council authorized a U.N. Interim Force in Lebanon (UNIFIL) to separate Israelis and Palestinians who were fighting in southern Lebanon. The U.N. Operation in Somalia and in the former Yugoslavia, which were authorized in 1992, ran the same risk of appearing to tilt toward one side or another in a civil war, as did the earlier U.N. operation in the Congo, and the U.N. Secretary General was the target of hostile demonstrations in Mogadishu and Sarajevo in January 1993 by groups that claimed that the United Nations was favoring their adversaries.

A variant of peacekeeping is the unarmed observer team sent to monitor agreements and verify that they are faithfully carried out. Such teams have been especially useful in recent decades. One of the earliest examples was the U.N. Truce Supervision Organization in Palestine (UNTSO), dispatched to oversee the cease-fires between Israel and its Arab enemies after the 1948 war. Since then, similar teams have served in various situations. In 1958, the U.N. Observer Group in Lebanon (UNOGIL) was sent to monitor border violations between Lebanon and Syria. More recently, U.N. observer groups have been used to monitor disengagement agreements in the Sinai Peninsula between Egypt and Israel and between Syria and Israel in the Golan Heights. Following the Persian Gulf War, U.N. observers were sent to monitor Saddam Hussein's compliance with U.N. resolutions on treatment of the Kurds in northern Iraq and on Iraq's destruction of weapons of mass destruction.

In Asia, too, observer teams have been valuable. In 1949, a U.N. Military Observer Group in India and Pakistan (UNMOGIP) was set up to monitor a cease-fire between those two new nations in their dispute over the contested territory of Kashmir.[58] United Nations observers have been in Korea since 1953 to monitor the armistice that ended the war. In 1992, a new team of U.N. observers — the U.N. Transitional Authority in Cambodia (UNTAC) — was sent to Cambodia to monitor the cease-fire among the warring parties in that country, demobilize the combatants, operate several important domestic ministries for a time, and supervise elections.[59] Repeated violations of the cease-fire, however, seriously complicated UNTAC's task.

[58]In 1947, British India was given independence after a long struggle waged by Mahatma Gandhi and the Indian Congress Party. Rioting between Hindus and Muslims forced partition of the subcontinent into mainly Hindu India and Muslim Pakistan. Kashmir was one of the princely states of India that were allowed to choose which country to join. Although most of its population was Muslim, the local prince chose to join India, and the two countries have contested the region ever since.

[59]William Branigin, "UN Influx Livens Phnom Penh Nights," *Washington Post*, June 22, 1992, p. A11.

Africa, Latin America, and Europe have also hosted U.N. observer missions. Two of these, the U.N. Observer Group in Central America (ONUCA) and the U.N. Observer Mission in El Salvador (UNONVSAL) — were sent to monitor cease-fire and peace arrangements in Nicaragua and El Salvador early in the 1990s. In October 1993, a U.N. force of 1,300 was sent to Haiti to oversee that country's return to democracy under President Jean-Bertraud Aristide. In southern Africa, the U.N. Transition Group (UNTAG) was responsible for supervising elections in Namibia and assisting that territory to independence. And in June 1993, the Security Council authorized dispatching an observer force to the border between Rwanda and Uganda. In the former Yugoslavia, an observer team, the U.N. Protection Force (UNPROFOR), was created in March 1992 to supervise repeated cease-fires reached among Serbian, Croatian, and Bosnian factions in Bosnia-Herzegovina and monitor U.N. economic sanctions imposed on the Serbians. These observers also tried to get relief supplies to besieged Bosnian communities in Sarajevo and elsewhere and establish havens for Bosnian Muslims. Another U.N. observer team including American soldiers was sent to the Serbian border with Macedonia to prevent the spread of war to that country.

The end of the Cold War was accompanied by growing optimism about expanding the U.N. peacekeeping role and even, for the first time since World War I, evolving a genuine collective-security system. Security Council cooperation during the Persian Gulf War and later efforts to make Iraq carry out its cease-fire obligations, U.N. sanctions against Serbia and Libya, and the more expansive use of U.N. observer missions generated hope about the organization's future. In fact, Secretary General Boutros Boutros-Ghali asked the Security Council to consider establishing a permanent U.N. peacekeeping contingent. Under his proposal, as many countries as possible would make available to the United Nations a force of about 1,000, available on twenty-four hours' notice, for peacekeeping. The U.N. also worked out arrangements with NATO by which the Western alliance could assist the United Nations achieve its peacekeeping aims. As a result, future peacekeeping efforts could begin quickly after Security Council decisions and the U.N.'s collective-security capacity could be strengthened.[60]

Generally, U.N. prospects are good, but the first flush of optimism that accompanied the end of the Cold War and the Persian Gulf War has diminished. Rivalries among powerful states and actors outside the U.N. structure will frustrate peacekeeping efforts. This difficulty was evident in problems confronting U.N. forces in Somalia in 1993 and the U.N. failure to bring a halt to Serbian aggression in Bosnia, an experience that may prove comparable to that of the League in the 1930s. U.N. efforts to protect Bosnian Muslims by enforcing a "no fly zone" over the country and designating Muslim towns

[60]Paul Lewis, "UN Chief Asks for 1,000-Troop Units," *The New York Times*, June 20, 1992, p. 5, and "Excerpts from U.N. Report," *The New York Times*, June 20, 1992, p. 5. Events in Bosnia and Somalia cooled U.S. enthusiasm for U.N. operations. Elaine Sciolino, "The U.N.'s Glow Is Gone," *The New York Times*, Oct. 9, 1993, pp. 1, 4.

as "safe areas" were fruitless exercises that could not save the country from being carved into three ethnically-based areas with the Muslims receiving the least desirable piece of the pie.

The United Nations continues to rely on leading members' goodwill and financial contributions. United Nations peacekeeping costs for 1993 exceeded $3 billion for 13 missions with more than 90,000 peacekeepers around the world, and for a time the United Nations was unable to reimburse countries for troops sent to Cambodia and Yugoslavia. The United States was in arrears by $830 million ($313 million for peacekeeping) until it repaid part of its debt in October 1993, and few states were fully paid up.[61] Because the organization cannot do more than its leading members let it do, it cannot expand its role unless members provide financial support.

Even as the United Nations was being praised in the early 1990s for renewed vigor in peacekeeping, the organization appeared to be the victim of mismanagement and corruption.[62] Negligence by U.N. personnel caused many deaths from starvation among refugees in Africa, and abuses were covered up. The organization and its peacekeeping operations were afflicted by financial waste and poor fiscal management, and some U.N. offices — such as a regional disarmament center in Katmandu, Nepal[63] — were almost worthless. Functional agencies were sometimes directed by poorly qualified managers who were subject to little oversight and who expended resources lavishly for things that did little to help those most in need. And efforts to reform the giant U.N. bureaucracy were met with resistance. One report says:

> [A]buses within the organization persist and often go unpunished. Chiefs of some autonomous U.N. agencies rule their fiefdoms like autocrats, answering to no one. Regional mafias of bureaucrats have consolidated their power through favoritism in hiring and promotions. Recipient governments routinely plunder U.N. programs, diverting aid from intended beneficiaries. . . .[64]

Some members, including the United States, assail the United Nations for failing to control its budget and institute personnel reforms and have withheld funding to pressure the organization to improve its management and auditing practices. These countries are frustrated because they pay most of the U.N.'s budget but have the same vote as others that pay little. Thus, between 1946 and 1992, the United States contributed

---

[61]Paul Lewis, "U.N. Is in Arrears on Peace Efforts," *The New York Times*, May 16, 1993, p. 9, and Julia Preston, "The U.N.: Spread Too Thin and Strapped for Cash," *The Washington Post National Weekly Edition*, July 5–11, 1993, p. 18. The ratio of U.S. spending for defense to U.S. spending for U.N. peacekeeping is $2,016 to $1. For other countries, the ratio is $1,877 to $1. As of October 1993 the United States still owed $472 million ($284 million in regular dues and $188 million for peacekeeping). Overall, the U.N. was owed $1.7 billion. See *The New York Times*, Oct. 7, 1993, p. A9.

[62]William Branigin, "United Frustrations: The U.N. Is Tripping Over its Own Bloat and Corruption," *The Washington Post National Weekly Edition*, November 30–December 6, 1992, pp. 6–7.

[63]Ibid., p. 6.

[64]Ibid.

FIGURE 9.3

U.N. Secretariat Expenditures

U.N. expenditures began to rise dramatically in the 1960s and now exceed one-billion dollars.

more than $20.3 billion to the United Nations. The United States is responsible for one quarter of the U.N. budget while almost half the member states are assessed the minimum of one one-hundredth of 1 percent of that budget. Some are disturbed also about the organization's Third World bias, which is reflected in U.N. resolutions condemning Israeli occupation of territories conquered in 1967 while paying little attention to the bloodier policies of Third World dictators in Africa and the Middle East.[65]

The United Nations has gone through several stages that reflect the organization's changing membership and changing conditions in global politics. During its first decade it was heavily influenced by the West and served American interests in the Cold War. The many newly independent Third World states entering in the 1950s and 1960s gave the organization a different coloration. Increasingly, it reflected this new majority's views, and, on issues such as the Middle East and South Africa, coalitions were forged between Third World states and members of the Soviet bloc that isolated the United States and its allies. The end of the Cold War broke the logjam that had prevented the United Nations from becoming an effective factor in global politics. And nowhere was this change more evident than in the upsurge in U.N. peacekeeping activities around the

[65]Ibid., p. 7.

FIGURE 9.4
Which Country Pays Most?

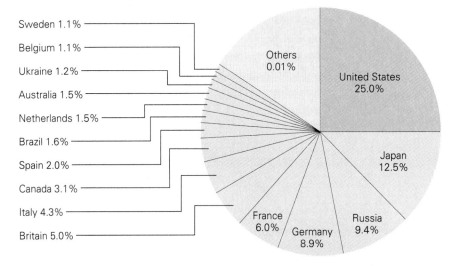

Sweden 1.1%
Belgium 1.1%
Ukraine 1.2%
Australia 1.5%
Netherlands 1.5%
Brazil 1.6%
Spain 2.0%
Canada 3.1%
Italy 4.3%
Britain 5.0%

Others 0.01%
United States 25.0%
Japan 12.5%
Russia 9.4%
Germany 8.9%
France 6.0%

The United States pays one-quarter of the U.N. budget, twice as much as Japan which pays the second largest share.

world: Angola, Namibia, Cambodia, Kuwait, Iraq, Croatia, Bosnia, Central America, Mozambique, Haiti, and Somalia. The Bosnian and Somali operations may augur a new role for U.N. forces—humanitarian intervention intended to save civilian lives endangered by civil strife. Such operations will pose complex problems, including the need to serve as a *de facto* government for countries without law and order.[66]

Functionalism in Action

Following World War II, greater attention was paid to the putative economic and social sources of conflict. The United Nations and other international organizations reflected the assumption that violence arises from conditions such as poverty, illiteracy, and disease.

The Functional Side of IGOs and NGOs

The Economic and Social Council coordinates its activities with sixteen semiautonomous specialized agencies that are described in Table 9.2. Among their functions, these

[66]See, for example, Paul Lewis, "Painting Nations Blue," *The New York Times*, December 9, 1992, p. A17.

TABLE 9.2

Functionalism in Action: Specialized Agencies Affiliated with the United Nations

1. Food and Agricultural Organization (FAO)
Seeks to increase food production, raise rural standards of living, and help cope with emergency food situations.

2. International Civil Aviation Organization (ICAO)
Facilitates and promotes safe international air transport by setting binding international standards.

3. International Fund for Agricultural Development (IFAD)
Lends money on concessionary terms for agricultural development projects, primarily to increase food production for poor rural populations.

4. International Labor Organization (ILO)
Formulates international labor standards and provides technical-assistance training to governments.

5. International Maritime Organization (IMO)
Promotes cooperation on shipping and provides a forum for discussing and adopting conventions and recommendations on such matters as safety at sea and control of pollution.

6. International Monetary Fund (IMF)
Provides technical assistance and financing to countries experiencing difficulty in balance of payments.

7. International Telecommunication Union (ITU)
Promotes global cooperation in telecommunications, allocates bands in the radio frequency spectrum, and collects and disseminates telecommunications information.

8. United Nations Educational, Scientific and Cultural Organization (UNESCO)
Coordinates cooperation in education, science, culture, and communications.

9. United Nations Industrial Development Organization (UNIDO)
Serves as an intermediary between developing and developed countries in industry and as a forum for consultations and negotiations to further industrialization.

10. Universal Postal Union (UPU)
Sets international postal standards and provides technical assistance to developing countries.

11. International Bank for Reconstruction and Development (IBRD)
Along with the IFC and IDA, forms the World Bank. Lends funds to governments and some private enterprises (with government guarantees) for specific projects.

12. International Finance Corporation (IFC)
Lends funds to private corporations in developing countries that do not have government guarantees.

13. International Development Association (IDA)
Provides interest-free credits to the world's poorest countries for fifty years, with a ten-year grace period.

14. World Health Organization (WHO)
Conducts immunization campaigns, promotes and coordinates research, and provides technical assistance to improve public-health services.

15. World Intellectual Property Organization (WIPO)

   Promotes protection of intellectual property rights (e.g., patents and copyrights). Encourages adherence to relevant treaties, provides legal and technical assistance to developing countries, encourages technology transfers, and administers the International Union for the Protection of Intellectual Property and the International Union for the Protection of Literary and Artistic Works.

16. World Meteorological Organization (WMO)

   Promotes exchange of meteorological information through its World Weather Watch and conducts research and training programs.

Source: *The United Nations at a Glance* (New York: United Nations Association of the United States of America, n.d.).

agencies provide global postal service, enhance economic development, foster health, and protect intellectual property rights.

Much of ECOSOC's work is carried on by its six Functional and five Regional Commissions. It has functional commissions for various global issues: Human Rights, Narcotic Drugs, Social Development, the Status of Women, and Population. The sixth—the Statistical Commission—is responsible for promoting collection of data by states and maintaining collections of data for economic and social development. The regional commissions for Africa, Europe, Latin America and the Caribbean, Asia and the Pacific, and Western Asia seek to stimulate economic activity and encourage economic ties among states. Each commission is relatively autonomous and has its own habits and procedures. The Economic Commission for Africa (ECA) has emphasized food production and agricultural self-sufficiency to reduce the specter of famine that haunts many African countries. The Economic Commission for Europe (ECE) focuses on environmental protection and coordinating policies on transportation and energy. Usually these commissions have tried to uphold the nonpolitical spirit of functionalism, but sometimes, as in the 1977 decision by the Economic and Social Commission for Western Asia (ESCWA) to grant membership to the Palestine Liberation Organization, they may dabble in highly charged political issues.

ECOSOC coordinates its activities with more than 300 interest-based nongovernmental organizations (NGOs) and consults with them.[67] Some 35 NGOs known as Category I enjoy special privileges such as adding items to ECOSOC's formal agenda. An additional 300 NGOs in Category II may submit written and oral statements to ECOSOC and its commissions. Finally, about 500 additional NGOs are on the ECOSOC roster and can attend Council meetings as observers.[68]

[67]NGOs are discussed at length in various contexts in this book. In Chapter 5, we elaborate on several types of NGOs and survey several of the most important: transnational corporations, terrorists, and ethnic/tribal groups. Transnational corporations are discussed in Chapters 10 and 14, and terrorists in Chapters 14 (in the context of the Middle East) and 16 (along with human rights groups). Individual NGOs such as environmental groups make cameo appearances in other chapters.

[68]Bennett, *International Organizations*, p. 280.

In addition to ECOSOC, several forums have been created in the U.N. framework to deal with functional issues. Some of the most important are the U.N. Conference on Trade and Development (UNCTAD), which was created in 1964 to address developing countries' concerns about trade relations; the United Nations Children's Fund (UNICEF), which tries to meet children's needs worldwide; and the United Nations Environmental Program (UNEP).

Regional Organizations and Neofunctionalism

The neofunctionalism ideal is best reflected in the *European Community*, a group of twelve countries in Western Europe.[69] These countries have turned over significant authority for their economies to this pan-European organization, headquartered in Brussels, Belgium. We discuss the EC in greater detail in Chapter 13, but suggest the outline here.

In line with neofunctionalist expectations, the EC has evolved since several specialized arrangements were merged. It has grown in membership over the years and has assumed an expanding array of functional tasks for its members. It originated in the European Coal and Steel Community (ECSC) in 1951, which was the product of a French proposal to integrate the coal and steel facilities of six states: France, Germany, Italy, Belgium, the Netherlands, and Luxembourg. Encouraging German industrial reconstruction in a European, rather than a national context, ECSC stimulated cooperation among Europeans and reduced the prospects of regional conflict. A remarkable feature of the ECSC was a supranational "government" known as the Higher Authority, which was authorized to make decisions about producing and distributing coal and steel.

Prodded by advocates of functional integration, the ECSC became a launching pad for extending functional cooperation into other areas, notably trade and peaceful nuclear energy. In 1965, these tasks were placed in one institutional context called the European Community, and institutional growth was accompanied by expanding community membership. In recent years, as we shall see, an effort has begun to complete the economic integration of Western Europe and also transform the community into a political union. This effort has *not* proceeded smoothly, and it is unclear whether further functional integration will occur. Nevertheless, it is now possible to travel among the member states of the EC without a passport, and customs barriers and other impediments to free movement are disappearing.

The difficulties the EC has faced reflect the barriers to regional integration. *Low politics*, as social and economic issues are described, do elicit strong national passions, and efforts to move into the realm of *high politics* — foreign and defense policy — generate national resistance. Spillover is neither as automatic nor as rapid as functionalists and neofunctionalists had hoped. The experience of two other regional groups, the Central American Common Market (CACM) and the East African Common Market (EACM),

---

[69]That number is likely to change as more applicants approach the EC, especially since the end of the Cold War.

suggests that the success of the EC may be more the exception than the rule. CACM was established in 1960 and by 1963 had five members: Guatemala, Nicaragua, El Salvador, Honduras, and Costa Rica. Like the EC, CACM's initial goal was to create a free market and a customs union. At first the experiment was successful, trade among members rising dramatically between 1960 and 1968. By 1968, however, it was clear that some members were benefiting more than others and that eliminating tariffs had reduced government revenues in some member countries.[70]

Growing friction between Honduras and El Salvador turned violent in June 1969 after soccer matches in both countries. The so-called Soccer War had less to do with sport than with population growth and with economic and social rivalries brought on in part by CACM. Hondurans believed El Salvador was flooding their market with products and encouraging its poor to emigrate to their country. Salvadorans, on the other hand, argued that Hondurans discriminated against Salvadoran nationals who sought to settle in Honduras. These frustrations led to a military conflict that required the Organization of American States to send a fact-finding mission.[71] Following the Soccer War, in the course of which invading Salvadoran forces inflicted heavy casualties on the Honduran defenders, CACM limped along, and, by the late 1970s, local elites were sufficiently satisfied with the status quo that they were unwilling to go beyond commitments already made.[72]

Originally formed among Kenya, Tanzania, and Uganda in 1963, EACM met with a similar fate. Efforts to kindle integration there were stymied by a host of political and economic rivalries among members.[73] Kenya, with a more highly developed market economy than its partners, was better placed to benefit from EACM, and Tanzania and Uganda grew envious of their neighbor. This jealousy led Tanzania to close its border with Kenya, and the ensuing economic friction was worsened by political differences among elites in the three countries. An ideological gulf separated Kenya and Tanzania, and personal animosity between Uganda's leader Idi Amin and Tanzania's Julius Nyerere militated against compromise.[74] In sum, as these cases show, integration requires a high level of economic and political compatibility among members.

[70]See Royce Q. Shaw, *Central America: Regional Integration and National Political Development* (Boulder, Colo.: Westview Press, 1978), pp. 6–9.

[71]Nye, *Peace in Parts*, pp. 121–123, 146–147.

[72]Shaw, *Central America*, p. 226.

[73]See Domenico Mazzeo, "The Experience of the East African Community: Implications for the Theory and Practice of Regional Cooperation in Africa," in Mazzeo, ed., *African Regional Organizations* (Cambridge, Eng.: Cambridge University Press, 1984), pp. 150–170.

[74]In 1979, following reports of atrocities committed by President Amin, Tanzanian troops invaded Uganda and helped the Uganda National Liberation Army (UNLA) overthrow Amin, who fled to Libya.

Conclusion

In this chapter you see some of the possibilities for cooperation in global political life. We have reviewed how and why actors cooperate with each other and various historical proposals for reducing conflict in global politics, including those of Kant, Rousseau, and Woodrow Wilson. Finally, we turned to a number of recent proposals for improving interstate cooperation, especially functionalism and neofunctionalism. We also addressed several organizational efforts to reduce interstate conflict and enhance cooperation: the League of Nations, the United Nations, the specialized agencies, nongovernmental organizations, and the European Community. In short, global cooperation takes various of forms and, though perhaps not as exciting as conflict, dominates global politics.

In Chapter 10, we explore the nexus between global politics and economics. Economic issues place great pressure on actors to cooperate lest all suffer together, but it is not always easy for them to do so. We will, therefore, describe some of the economic issues in global politics and the changing policies and international regimes that have dealt with them.

Key Terms

collective security
idealism
players
payoffs
rules
strategies
functionalism
neofunctionalism
functional organization
Fourteen Points
League Covenant
Kellogg-Briand Pact
zero-sum game
variable-sum game
cooperation
Secretariat
European Community
Trusteeship Council
Economic and Social Council
    (ECOSOC)

spillover
veto power
tacit veto
specialized agencies
peacekeeping
preventive diplomacy
high politics
low politics
League of Nations
Lytton Report
United Nations
U.N. Charter
republic
federalism
Hague Conferences
isolationism
Uniting for Peace Resolution
Security Council
General Assembly
International Court of Justice (ICJ)

CHAPTER TEN

International Political Economy: Where Economics and Politics Meet

Traditional approaches to global politics have neglected global economics. The renowned realist Hans J. Morgenthau argued that "the concept of interest defined in terms of power . . . sets politics as an autonomous sphere of action and understanding apart from other spheres, *such as economics (understood in terms of interest defined as wealth).* . . ."[1] Nevertheless, economic events invariably affect the political arena, and politics conditions the economic sphere. Although *political economy* was a widely used phrase in eighteenth- and nineteenth-century Europe, it was mostly ignored in the United States until recently.[2]

This lapse betrays ignorance of history. The Peloponnesian War between the Greek city-states Athens and Sparta was fought in part over the closing of ports to members of the Athenian-led Delian League. The leaders of the Persian Empire, enemy of ancient Greece, routinely used gold to bribe other states.[3] The practice of slavery and the American Civil War were linked to economic relations between North and South, and European colonial expansion between the seventeenth and twentieth centuries had economic motives.

---

[1] Hans J. Morgenthau, *Politics Among Nations: The Struggle for Power and Peace*, 6th ed., revised by Kenneth W. Thompson (New York: Alfred A. Knopf, 1985), p. 5. Emphasis added. The first edition of the book appeared in 1948.

[2] Adam Smith (1723–1790), author of *Wealth of Nations* and acknowledged father of modern capitalism, held a chair in political economy at the University of Glasgow, and Karl Marx (1818–1883) and his followers referred to themselves as political economists.

[3] Robert Gilpin, *The Political Economy of International Relations* (Princeton: Princeton University Press, 1987), p. 4.

One can hardly avoid reflecting on how interdependent politics and economics are whether describing sanctions against Iraq after it invaded Kuwait, friction between the United States and Japan, or U.S. efforts to make loan guarantees to Israel contingent on that country's policy on settlements in the West Bank. Such cases are at the intersection between politics and economics. One observer even declares, "economic power is the new determinant of international stature," and another argues, "economics will be the key to world affairs."[4]

In this chapter we examine the relationship between economics and politics. We begin by describing the actors and issues involved in creating the liberal economic order at the end of World War II and then turn to several issues that help determine political relations among global actors today. We point then to some trends in global political economy, especially the new trading blocs that are being created.

Politics of the Liberal Economic Order

The current economic order has its roots in decisions Western leaders made as World War II ended. They aimed to induce reconstruction and foster a global market system based on the principles of liberal capitalism. They sought to create institutions that would increase efficiency and growth[5] and would prevent adoption of the competitive and destructive *beggar-thy-neighbor policies* that had intensified the Depression in the 1930s and contributed to the rise of fascism. [6] As liberals, they assumed that actors seek to maximize efficiency and growth and that the purpose of economic institutions is to allocate resources for these ends. Such allocation, in their view, is best achieved by an open system without impediments to trade or capital flows. In such a system, states focus on producing what they can most efficiently and enjoy "comparative advantage." That system, liberals believe, if allowed to operate without interference, will lead to prosperity for all — rich and poor, industrialized and agrarian.

The Bretton Woods System

The first steps in building a *liberal economic order* were taken at a 1944 conference at *Bretton Woods*, New Hampshire. The conferees agreed to create three organizations to manage the global economy: the International Monetary Fund (IMF), the General Agreement on Tariffs and Trade (GATT), and the International Bank for Reconstruction and Development (the IBRD or World Bank).

[4]The first comment is by Indiana Congressman Lee H. Hamilton, "A Democrat Looks at Foreign Policy," *Foreign Affairs* 71:3 (Summer 1992), p. 34, and the second is by the president of the Economic Strategy Institute, Clyde V. Prestowitz, Jr., "Beyond Laissez Faire," *Foreign Policy* No. 87 (Summer 1992), p. 67.

[5]Gilpin, *Political Economy of International Relations*, p. 28.

[6]Robert S. Walters and David H. Blake, *The Politics of Global Economic Relations*, 4th ed. (Englewood Cliffs, N.J.: Prentice-Hall, 1992), pp. 13–14.

The IMF.   The IMF was expected to promote economic health by regulating monetary policy. International trade and investment require payment in money, which is possible only when rules determine the value of different national currencies. The IMF's main task was to stabilize *exchange rates* by assisting states with *balance-of-payments* difficulties. Such stability, it was believed, was critical to inspire confidence in the system. To meet its task, the IMF would provide short-term loans and set up a system of *fixed monetary exchange rates* and *currency convertibility* that would enable countries to use their own currency to purchase "international" currencies like the U.S. dollar and British pound that are acceptable everywhere.[7] The United States provided much of the initial IMF funding, and other currencies were pegged to the value of the dollar. As a result, the health and stability of the U.S. economy were crucial to the health and stability of the global economy. Adding another element of stability to the system, the United States fixed and guaranteed the value of the dollar against gold: U.S. dollars could be converted to gold at $35 an ounce. The Bretton Woods accord worked well from the 1940s through the early 1970s even as it continued to evolve.[8] Still, not until December 1958 was full currency convertibility achieved and funding obtained for the IMF. Simultaneously, agreement was struck to maintain gold at $35 an ounce.

The GATT.   A second element of Bretton Woods was movement toward a liberal trading order. Although the original conferees envisioned an ambitious International Trading Organization, the product was the General Agreement on Tariffs and Trade (GATT). The GATT became the focus after the U.S. Congress failed to ratify the Havana Charter and its goal of rapidly eliminating tariffs.[9] The GATT sought to reduce trade barriers (whether tariffs or quotas) on manufacturing, and to establish the principle of *most-favored-nation (MFN) status*. The MFN principle requires that actors treat each other equally by according the same (lowest) tariff rates on imports to *all* countries. At first, GATT membership was drawn mainly from the West, but in time it has expanded its membership to about 100 and continues to grow. The GATT has sponsored a series of "negotiating rounds" to remove other obstacles to free trade, and, by 1980, world trade had quintupled but average industrial tariffs were about one-tenth of what they had been when the GATT was started.[10] After 1980, the task of liberalizing trade became more complex. As the GATT turned from the relatively simple task of reducing industrial tariffs to knottier issues such as reducing nontariff barriers and liberalizing trade in services and agriculture, it became the forum for laborious negotiation.

[7] Walter LaFeber, *The American Age* (New York: W. W. Norton, 1989), pp. 410–411; and Robert O. Keohane and Joseph S. Nye, *Power and Interdependence*, 2nd ed. (Glenview, Ill.: Scott, Foresman, 1989), pp. 78–82.

[8] Keohane and Nye, *Power and Interdependence*, p. 81.

[9] The Havana Charter was negotiated in 1947, and final agreement was reached on it, incorporating an ambitious scheme for an International Trade Organization (ITO) in the following year. Congressional opposition, however, led to three years of delay followed by a Truman administration decision not to submit the treaty for ratification.

[10] Peter Calvocoressi, *World Politics Since 1945* (New York: Longman, 1991), p. 153.

The World Bank. The third leg of the Bretton Woods system was the World Bank. The Bank's initial aim was to aid reconstruction, but it soon turned to economic development. The Bank is funded by member states' contributions and by borrowing on international capital markets. Its lending decisions are based on market principles: current loan rates and prospects for repayment. About a decade after the World Bank was established, the *International Finance Corporation* was created to provide loans to private enterprises whose activities would contribute to development for poor countries. In 1960, the *International Development Association* was established to provide capital to poor countries at rates more favorable than those of the World Bank. The IDA grants interest-free credits on a long-term basis (usually fifty years). All three banking institutions are overseen by a Board of Governors, consisting of all member states, and twenty-two Executive Directors, five of whom are appointed by the largest contributors. In practice, these requirements mean that a few wealthy states, led by the United States, enjoy significant influence in these institutions.

With these institutions — and the shared rules and norms they promoted — Bretton Woods created a liberal international monetary and trading regime to guide and manage the global economy for more than three decades. It was able to do so for three reasons.[11] First, the system enabled wealthy countries in North America and Western Europe to gather economic power in their hands, and mostly excluded the command economies of Eastern Europe and Asia. Second, these states shared a commitment to market principles, albeit mixed with limited government intervention. All espoused a philosophy of economic freedom, which they were prepared to promote by cooperating with one another.

Third, and most important, the United States was willing to provide hegemonic stability to the system, both politically and economically. The IMF and World Bank had their headquarters in Washington and the United States assumed a lead in both. As the strongest postwar economic power, it was in an ideal position to assume this role. Both the U.S. dollar and domestic market were major elements in reviving the global economy, and U.S. leaders were prepared to make economic sacrifices to achieve political stability.

The Collapse of Bretton Woods

The Bretton Woods system fell apart in the early 1970s, beginning with a dramatic announcement by the Nixon administration.[12] To combat inflation and a spiraling balance-of-payments deficit, the administration decided that the United States could no longer afford to subsidize global trade by maintaining a strong dollar that encouraged imports to the United States but discouraged U.S. exports. On August 15, 1971, the United States announced it would no longer maintain a system of fixed exchange rates, that the convertibility of U.S. dollars into gold would cease, and that a 10 percent

[11]Joan E. Spero, *The Politics of International Economic Relations*, 4th ed. (New York: St. Martin's Press, 1990), pp. 21–24.

[12]The following discussion draws on Spero, *Politics of International Economic Relations*, pp. 23–27, and Gilpin, *Political Economy of International Relations*, pp. 134–140.

surcharge would be levied on all imports. The *"Nixon shock"* was followed by an agreement among the major trading partners reached at the Smithsonian Institution in Washington in December 1971 to try to maintain fixed exchange rates and dollar convertibility after agreeing to devalue the dollar in relation to gold. By March 1973, however, this effort too had collapsed, and all convertible currencies were permitted to "float" in relation to one another.

Why did the Bretton Woods system fall apart so quickly? Most explanations reveal how tightly politics and economics are enmeshed. First, as monetary interdependence deepened, it became increasingly difficult to coordinate so many actors' policies. International banks and corporations had learned how to take advantage of even slight fluctuations in interest and currency rates. Their actions — for example, purchasing "cheap" gold and selling dollars in the belief that the dollar was overvalued — were beyond effective control by the Bretton Woods regime and placed enormous pressure on the system.

Second, the increasingly prosperous Western European states and Japan were no longer happy with the privileged policymaking position of the United States. On the one hand, they resented how closely American economic health determined the health of their economies. United States spending to wage the Vietnam war and simultaneously combat poverty at home stimulated global inflation that harmed Europe and Japan. American inflation meant that U.S. dollars were worth less, but adjustment was impossible with fixed exchange rates. Politically, too, the Europeans and the Japanese had begun to chafe under U.S. dominance. Their economies were vigorous, and they had recovered much of the self-confidence they had lost during World War II. As a result, America's allies were able to reduce their dependence on the United States and seek a greater political role for themselves.

The Nixon administration sought to stem the decline in America's worldwide trading position. Under Bretton Woods, the United States could not devalue the dollar and so reduce the cost of U.S. exports to others while increasing the cost to Americans of imported goods. A strong dollar reduced U.S. competitiveness worldwide. Previously, Washington had absorbed this cost to open U.S. markets to allies' goods, helping their recovery and stimulating the global economy. By 1973, however, devaluation was seen as necessary to reduce America's growing payments deficits, and the government had come to resent what it believed was discrimination against U.S. goods by the Japanese and Europeans. The only way to confront these issues, the administration believed, was to move decisively away from a system of fixed exchange rates.

Issues in the Global Economy: The Developed States

Since the collapse of Bretton Woods, several economic issues have continued to plague political relations among developed states. These include trade protectionism, fluctuating currency exchange rates, global energy prices, and national budget deficits and unemployment rates. In recent decades, several strategies have been proposed to deal with these issues, but none has been entirely satisfactory. We briefly review these issues and the strategies used to cope with them.

Floating Exchange Rates

Since *floating exchange rates* were adopted early in the 1970s, the developed countries have tried to muddle through,[13] responding to crises in an ad hoc way—in managing monetary problems and stabilizing exchange rates. The issue is contentious because it directly affects domestic economic health in most countries. Under a system of floating exchange rates, the value of a currency depends on economic, political, and psychological factors at home and abroad. Economic factors such as a country's trade balance and its overall economic performance, as reflected by rate of growth and level of inflation, help determine the strength of its currency. However, the perceptions of those at home and abroad who buy and sell currency (thereby determining its value) are also influenced by other factors, such as political stability, confidence in political institutions, and long-term economic trends. In effect, those who speculate in currency are trying to predict an economy's future health. If the currency they purchase loses value, they will lose money; if it increases in value, they will profit.

Although the U.S. dollar is no longer the global benchmark currency it was when pegged to gold, stabilizing the dollar has remained a principal objective of the developed countries because of its importance in world trade. A wildly fluctuating dollar would harm the world trading system because it would create instability as trading partners were unable to predict the prices of the goods they wished to buy or sell.

In the 1970s, the dollar weakened—its value fell—because of high inflation in the United States and mushrooming U.S. trading deficits abroad and budget deficits at home. Thus other countries' goods were more expensive in the United States, fueling domestic inflation, and the dollars they received for their goods could buy less. Furthermore, as energy prices, calculated in dollars, soared in the 1970s, other countries suffered a double whammy: rising energy costs and less-valuable dollars with which to purchase expensive oil. The weak dollar was a thorn to the United States for other reasons as well. As the dollar's value declined, other countries sold dollars and bought stronger currencies like Japanese yen, which in turn further weakened the dollar (because demand for them was declining but the supply of dollars was growing). For Americans, this weakness meant that everything from overseas cost more and therefore they would have a lower standard of living.

In the 1980s, conditions changed, and the opposite problem appeared—a strong U.S. dollar—which made it difficult for Americans to sell their products overseas and opened a yawning trade deficit between the United States and its trading partners. The

[13]See Charles E. Lindblom, "The Science of 'Muddling Through,'" *Public Administration Review* 19 (Spring 1959), pp. 79–88.

strong dollar owed much to a lower rate of inflation (especially a lower price for oil), high interest rates, and restored confidence in the management of the American economy. As America's trade deficit grew and U.S. interest rates remained high, foreign investors bought dollars and invested them in the United States to gain high returns. These investments, especially by the Japanese, were used to pay for American budget deficits during the Reagan–Bush years. Although European and Japanese export industries thrived, the flight of capital to the United States drained resources that were vital to domestic business expansion and employment in Europe and elsewhere.

Thus, a weak or strong dollar or rapid fluctuation in its value have great consequences for everyone, at home and abroad. For this reason the monetary issue, though apparently "technical," generates strong passions, which in turn frustrate efforts to manage currency exchange according to nonpolitical criteria.

Political Efforts to Manage Monetary Problems

A number of European states undertook an imaginative regional effort to stabilize currencies by establishing the *European Monetary System* (EMS) in 1978. This system, as one observer described it, "was first and foremost a means of strengthening the EC in the medium term through introducing a kind of flexible Bretton Woods system for the member states." Specifically, it sought to create a system of predictable exchange rates among members to stimulate trade within Europe and to compete more effectively with "American monetary and exchange rate policy."[14] The EMS created a new unit of currency, the European Currency Unit (ECU) whose value reflected a "basket" of European currencies. Each national currency would be tied to the ECU, and the ECU would serve as the basis for calculating exchange rates. Under the European system, currencies would be allowed to fluctuate in a narrow range (2.5 percent), before a state could intervene in foreign-exchange markets to protect its currency.[15] More dramatic currency adjustments could be made if the EC Council of Ministers agreed.

Although the EMS provided temporary monetary stability in Europe, it was not wholly successful because some countries refused to join and others were less than fully committed to it. Portugal and Spain remained outside the system, though Spain finally joined in 1989. Britain and Greece, on the other hand, refused to accept the EMS exchange-rate mechanism and effectively remained outside as well. The British refusal to join fully was particularly troubling because the British pound sterling served as a *reserve currency*—a currency that countries hold because of its strength and stability. London worried about the possibility of German economic dominance owing to the strength of the mark and sought to shield Britain's economy from decisions made

[14]Derek W. Urwin, *The Community of Europe* (London: Longman, 1991), p. 183.

[15]Ibid. European currencies would continue to fluctuate freely in relation to non-European currencies.

elsewhere. As we shall see in Chapter 13, the EMS virtually collapsed in the tumultuous events in the autumn of 1992 and the following summer.

Another strategy was reflected in the multilateral and unilateral efforts the United States undertook at about the same time as the EMS was created. To prop up the weak dollar in the late 1970s, the Carter administration first sought to coordinate macroeconomic policy with its allies. Specifically, it urged other developed states, especially Germany and Japan, to pursue *expansionist economic policies* to encourage demand for U.S. goods and services in those countries and so strengthen the dollar. When this effort failed, partly because of U.S. unwillingness to make sensitive domestic budget cuts and impose energy-conservation measures, the U.S. Federal Reserve Bank began to intervene actively in the foreign-exchange markets, buying dollars to prop up their value and reducing the money supply at home to reduce inflation.[16]

Although the Reagan administration rejected the interventionist approach its predecessor adopted, it continued to pursue a unilateralist or nationalist approach, promoting U.S. economic interests even to the detriment of some of its traditional allies. In the end, the efforts of Presidents Carter and Reagan did increase the value of the U.S. dollar. The dollar, two observers declare, "appreciated, with temporary pauses and reversals, throughout the first Reagan administration," and "the President and the Secretary of the Treasury came to celebrate it."[17] Although a strong dollar dampened U.S. inflation and helped allied economic growth, it also had negative effects, including skyrocketing U.S. trade and budget deficits. Elsewhere, dollars were purchased, and capital investment fled to American shores, shrinking economic growth. By the mid-1980s, a real monetary-management crisis produced an effort to achieve a multilateral solution.

In September 1985, the finance ministers of the United States, Japan, Germany, France, and Great Britain—the so-called G-5 nations—gathered at the Plaza Hotel in New York City to address the problems posed by a strong U.S. dollar. Those present agreed that "further orderly appreciation of the main non-dollar currencies against the dollar is desirable."[18] Shortly thereafter the United States dumped large numbers of dollars in return for yen and marks, forcing down the dollar's value, a trend that continued until early in 1987. Following the *Plaza accord*, additional multilateral steps were taken to confront monetary instability. In rapid succession, four other informal and formal commitments were reached to stabilize exchange rates. In October 1986, U.S. Secretary of the Treasury James Baker and Japanese Finance Minister Kiichi Miyazawa agreed to try to stabilize the yen–dollar exchange rate and increase Japan's domestic demand for imports to stimulate trade between the two countries. In February 1987, a

---

[16]Spero, *Politics of International Economic Relations*, pp. 56–58.

[17]I. M. Destler and C. Randall Henning, *Dollar Politics: Exchange Rate Policymaking in the United States* (Washington, D.C.: Institute for International Economics, 1989), pp. 22, 26.

[18]Robert D. Hormats, "The World Economy Under Stress," in William G. Hyland, ed., *America and the World 1985* (New York: Pergamon Press, 1986), p. 469.

broad agreement was reached at the Louvre Palace in Paris among the G-6 (the original five plus Canada) (the specifics of which remain secret), which called for maintaining exchange rates among the dollar, the yen, and the deutsche mark within a narrow range.[19] Two additional agreements later in 1987 refined the commitment by the G-7 nations (now including Italy) to multilateral exchange-rate stability.[20]

These multilateral efforts have not wholly stabilized global exchange rates, but they have spread responsibility for doing so more widely. Since 1987, fluctuations in rates have occurred, although they have remained more modest than those of the late 1970s and early 1980s. Successful multilateral management of monetary affairs will continue to depend on negotiation and goodwill. Stability will be continually challenged by new events, and individual governments will always be tempted to go their own way. As a result, monetary management remains fragile.

Thus, between 1990 and 1992, the Bush administration tried to stimulate the American economy by letting the value of the dollar fall. Unfortunately, this fall was accompanied by lower U.S. interest rates at a time of high German interest rates, creating a rush to sell dollars, buy German marks, and invest at higher rates in German securities. High German interest rates were intended to attract capital that would assist in reconstructing the eastern region of the country. The difference in U.S. and German policies, however, created intense pressure on the dollar. High German interest rates and a strong German mark also undermined the efforts of other European countries like France and Britain to stimulate their own depressed economies. Their effect was to reduce German consumer spending, especially for imports, and place downward pressure on the franc and the pound. These events show the limits of unilateral action in the global economy.

Trade Issues and the Developed States

A second set of issues involves trade relations, such as using *nontariff barriers* like quotas to impede imports and the effort to move toward a free market in services and agriculture. The importance of trade to the developed states shows in Figure 10.1, depicting the growing role of trade in the economies of major states in recent decades. Trade in the U.S. economy, though historically small compared to countries like Great Britain and Japan, has grown dramatically in recent years and illustrates how overseas markets are gaining in importance to U.S. producers. As Figure 10.1 shows, the volume of trade among developed countries is huge, obviously being vital to their economic health. The leading trading partners of the United States are Canada, Japan, and Mexico, and the United States is Japan's and Europe's leading trading partner.

[19]This accord is described in Yoichi Funabashi, *Managing the Dollar: From the Plaza to the Louvre*, 2nd ed. (Washington, D.C.: Institute for International Economics, 1989), pp. 183–187.

[20]Destler and Henning, *Dollar Politics*, pp. 61–67.

FIGURE 10.1

Trade in Goods and Services as a Proportion of GNP

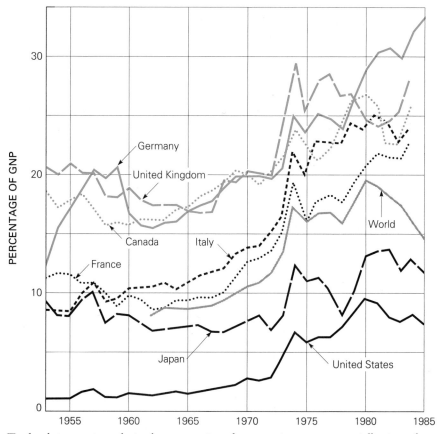

Trade plays a major role in the economies of most major states, especially since the 1970s. Countries like Germany, Great Britain, Canada, and Italy are especially dependent on international trade in comparison with the United States.

Events that disrupt or alter these trade patterns or even change relative amounts of trade among partners can create significant economic *and* political turmoil for individual countries. It is the inevitable political dimension of trade issues, such as Japanese refusal to permit entry to foreign rice exports, which so frustrates economists. One economist captures this feeling:

> On the one hand, we have our theory, descended from Adam Smith and David Ricardo, which stresses all the benefits of open markets and unrestricted exchange between nations based on underlying differences of comparative advantage. On the

other hand, we have the real world, where forces of . . . protection always seem rampant. . . . Rarely in the economics profession do we encounter greater disso-nance between what we are taught in principle and what we observe in practice. And try as we might to find logical reasons for all this in the tenets of our own discipline, ultimately we are tempted simply to throw up our hands and proclaim "It's all politics!"[21]

Since the late 1960s, turmoil in trading relations has been the rule. As Western Europe and Japan regained prosperity after 1945 and assumed the lead in the global economy, they were less prepared to accept U.S. leadership passively. As the threat of international communism receded, the United States, Germany, Japan, and others were less willing to compromise economic differences to maintain political solidarity. As a result, changes in the global political environment have directly influenced the global economic environment.

Managing Trade Relations Politically

Three strategies have been used to manage trade differences among the major developed countries.[22] The first has been global, involving the *General Agreement on Tariffs and Trade* (GATT). This strategy has involved coordinated efforts to reduce tariffs by multilateral negotiations (or "rounds") among members. A second strategy has been to use multilateral economic summits among the Western allies and Japan to coordinate economic activities. These summits have been held yearly since 1975 and reflect recognition that economic issues are growing in political salience. A third strategy to which we turn in Chapter 13 has been to use bilateral negotiations to overcome friction.

Negotiations on the GATT have passed through eight rounds.[23] The *Dillon* and *Kennedy Rounds* in the 1960s successfully reduced tariff and nontariff barriers for several industrial sectors and agricultural commodities.[24] The *Tokyo Round* (1973–1979) made deeper cuts in tariffs and launched a search for agreement on new subjects such as providing favorable treatment for poor countries and eliminating subsidies and coun-tervailing duties. The *Uruguay Round* set out in 1986 to take GATT a step further by addressing such nettlesome issues as agricultural subsidies, trade in services (such as insurance), rules for governing *intellectual property rights*, and nontariff barriers. Few

[21]Benjamin J. Cohen, "The Political Economy of International Trade," *International Organization* 44:2 (Spring 1990), pp. 261–262.

[22]See Beth V. Yarbrough and Robert M. Yarbrough, "Cooperation in the Liberalization of International Trade: After Hegemony, What?" *International Organization* 41:1 (Winter 1987), pp. 1–26.

[23]For a discussion of negotiating strategies at GATT, see Bernard M. Hoekman, "Deter-mining the Need for Issue Linkages in Multilateral Trade Negotiations," *International Organization* 43:4 (Autumn 1989), pp. 693–714.

[24]Named respectively after former U.S. Secretary of the Treasury Douglas Dillon and President John F. Kennedy.

global issues are as enmeshed in domestic politics as these are, complicating attempts to reach agreement.[25] Any effort to reduce agricultural subsidies is violently opposed by Japanese and European, especially French, farmers and raises grave doubts in the electorally important U.S. Midwest. This issue, exacerbated by global recession, remains the major barrier to completion of the Uruguay Round. In 1992, the United States and Europe narrowly avoided a trade war because of U.S. retaliation (increasing tariffs on selected European exports, including white wines) for French unwillingness to limit acreage growing subsidized oilseeds. The EC is still reluctant to accept a phased reduction in subsidies, and there is no assurance that the issue will soon be resolved.[26]

If the GATT is a permanent forum for trade negotiations, the regular *economic summits* among the leading industrial democracies are an innovative multilateral mechanism for sustaining the international trading regime. The idea was proposed by French President Valéry Giscard d'Estaing in 1975 in response to events that were challenging the economic well-being of the developed countries, especially the collapse of the Bretton Woods system and the 1973 Arab oil embargo.[27] The first summit was held at the Château of Rambouillet near Paris, and was attended by the heads of government of the United States, Britain, West Germany, Italy, Japan, and France. The Canadian prime minister and the president of the EC Commission were invited to the summits beginning in 1976 and 1977 respectively.[28] Summits have been held yearly, rotating among the participants—Puerto Rico, London, Tokyo, Bonn, Ottawa, Versailles, Williamsburg, and Munich, among others.

These summits have proved to be a significant way of managing the global economy. The meetings are small and allow for both formal and informal discussion among the world's most influential leaders. Bureaucratic and technical impediments to agreement that arise at lower levels are avoided at the top, encouraging flexibility with personal rapport. Second, the summits treat global economic problems as important political issues. Third, the heads of government are in a unique position to implement agreements they reach with one another.[29] Finally, the summits also focus on other issues—Soviet intervention in Afghanistan, INF deployment in Western Europe, global terrorism—to coordinate policy. The economic summits have had a mixed record. Two observers judge that, of the first twelve, only six meetings earned a grade of B or better for cooperation, and they say six achieved little, including three that accomplished

---

[25]See Charles E. Hanrahan, "The Uruguay Round: Impact on Agriculture," in *Trade and Investment: The Changing International Framework* (Washington, D.C.: Congressional Research Service, February–March, 1992), p. 8.

[26]See Chapter 13, p. 460. French farmers continued to demand that their government veto the EC-U.S. agreement.

[27]Robert D. Putnam and Nicholas Bayne, *Hanging Together: Cooperation and Conflict in the Seven-Power Summits*, rev. ed. (Cambridge: Harvard University Press, 1987), p. 25.

[28]Ibid., pp. 34, 151.

[29]Ibid., pp. 29–31.

"nothing significant."[30] With one exception, the summits that accomplished least were held in the 1980s, and those which achieved most in the 1970s. Summits in the early 1990s were also disappointing, even though they began to address economic reform in Eastern Europe and the former Soviet Union.

To get a taste of the summits, let us review some of their accomplishments. The 1978 Bonn summit was judged a success because it completed a comprehensive plan for dealing with pressing global economic problems: Japan and West Germany agreed to expand their economies; France agreed to cut its deficit; and the United States committed itself to find a more effective energy policy. The 1979 summit, held after a dramatic rise in oil prices earlier in the year, set a target for the participants' oil imports for the following years.[31] Finally, the 1991 and 1992 summits achieved some coordinating of relief efforts to Russia, Ukraine, and the other Soviet Union successor states. The 1993 Tokyo summit did reach preliminary agreement on eliminating tariffs in eight industrial sectors, including farm equipment, trying to breathe new life into the flagging Uruguay Round of the GATT.

Finally, the developed states have acted bilaterally and unilaterally in managing trade issues. In Chapter 13, we address these efforts in more detail, but suffice it to say that, despite some negotiated agreements, the developed countries still differ about trade relations.

Issues in the Global Economy: North versus South

The economic gulf between the developed and developing worlds is wide and continues to grow. In fact, some would identify the gap as the most challenging issue in world affairs. Ultimately, unmet economic (and social) problems may lead the poor to "desperate politics" versus the rich.[32] The poor have little reason to be satisfied by the liberal international economic system, which, in their eyes, perpetuates their poverty. Alternative approaches to global economics thus have found greater favor in the Third World than in the developed West. By the early 1970s, more and more states in Africa, Asia, and Latin America found the global economic system intolerable and inimical to their interests and called for a "new international economic order."

[30]Ibid., Table 11.1, p. 270.
[31]Ibid., pp. 73–92, 116–118.
[32]Richard Falk, "What's Wrong with Henry Kissinger's Foreign Policy," *Alternatives* 1 (1975), p. 99.

The Radical and Nationalist Alternatives

Liberal market theory contrasts with *radical*[33] *explanations* of how the global economy works. For the radicals, equality and political autonomy matter as much as productivity and efficiency. Free trade, they believe, works to the advantage of rich states and perpetuates dependence by poor states, especially primary producers, on the rich. Foreign investment and open markets do less to benefit or develop poor states than to open their human and natural resources to plundering. As a result, the system actually prevents development in the Third World; widening economic disparities reinforce political inequality.

Perhaps the most fully developed radical analysis is *Modern World System theory*.[34] World system theorists believe that political life revolves around class struggle that is reflected in relations between rich and poor states. Global capitalism, represented by a wealthy "core" (societies that are the source of capital), perpetuates economic under-development at the expense of an impoverished "periphery" (societies with little economic clout), whose wealth is exploited. This relationship, in which the "international division of labor imposes class and state structures on the periphery and dependent economies that prevent their economic development,"[35] it is argued, has its roots in the birth of Western capitalism in the sixteenth and seventeenth centuries and has remained essentially unchanged. The forces of modern capitalism are seen as running the global economy in their own interest, and "uneven" development results as profits and resources are siphoned from the periphery to the core.

Economic nationalists, on the other side, believe that "economic activities are and should be subordinate to the goal of state building and the interests of the state,"[36] and should be subordinated to national security. Economic radicals, arising from a Marxist tradition, believe in the primacy of economic over political forces, but the nationalists (sometimes called *neomercantilists*) reverse this relationship, arguing that wealth is the basis of political and military power. Their aim is to reduce the influence of market forces, accumulate economic resources within the state, and make the state as economically self-sufficient as possible. Economic nationalists believe domestic political demands are more crucial in global economic decisions than do liberals.

[33]Walters and Blake, *Politics of Global Economic Relations*, pp. 8–11. The radical perspective has evolved from Marxist assumptions.

[34]See, for example, Paul A. Baran, *The Political Economy of Growth* (New York: Monthly Review Press, 1967); André Gunder Frank, *Latin America: Underdevelopment or Revolution* (New York: Monthly Review Press, 1970); and Immanuel Wallerstein, *The Modern World System: Capitalist Agriculture and the Origins of the European World-Economy in the Sixteenth Century* (New York: Academic Press, 1974); and Wallerstein, *The Modern World-System II: Mercantilism and the Consolidation of the European World-Economy, 1600–1750* (New York: Academic Press, 1980).

[35]Gilpin, *Political Economy of International Relations*, p. 69. See also pp. 50–53, 67–71.

[36]Ibid., p. 31.

Economic nationalism can assume several forms. It ranges from efforts to shelter and isolate infant industries from global competition to policies that directly challenge the global economic order. High tariff barriers, nontariff impediments to trade (such as quotas or orderly marketing arrangements), and import-substitution arrangements are among the devices of economic nationalism.[37] More aggressive forms — "malevolent nationalism"[38] — include imperial expansion and economic warfare. Embargoes — refusing to sell goods or commodities to another state — or boycotts — refusal to buy goods or commodities — are forms of economic warfare.

All three economic perspectives have been subjected to criticism. Liberals retain an idealistic belief in separating politics from economics. For their part, radicals fail to recognize the substantial domestic political constraints against capitalist societies' sustained economic expansion, and nationalists underestimate how pervasive and important the market is in producing efficient and competitive economies. Nevertheless, the nonliberal variants do shed light on some issues in political economy and bring into relief the problems that confront actors in the Third World. Indeed, some of the issues that radical and nationalist critiques of economic liberalism raise provide insights into the tensions between the *North* (rich) and *South* (poor) and between developed capitalist states such as the United States and Japan.

The Poverty Gap

Several indicators illustrate how the economic disparity between rich and poor has grown in recent decades. Figure 10.2 portrays the average per capita GNP for the developed and developing countries. A striking fact is that, while average incomes for both worlds have increased, *the gap between them has actually widened during the most recent decade.*

Closer examination reveals that the worst poverty is in Africa and Asia. As Figure 10.3 (see p. 340) illustrates, countries like Burundi and Somalia in East Africa, Burkina Faso and Chad in West Africa, and Bangladesh and Sri Lanka in South Asia have the lowest per capita GNP (less than $610) and most of the high-income countries (more than $7,620) were European or their people of European ancestry. It is especially discouraging that the poorest regions also experienced some of the smallest increases in per capita GNP in recent decades. While the rest of the world was growing, these regions were not.[39]

[37]W. Arthur Lewis, *Evolution of the International Economic Order* (Princeton: Princeton University Press, 1978), p. 31.

[38]Robert Gilpin, *The Political Economy of International Relations*, p. 32.

[39]The other region that changed dramatically in per capita GNP during this period — the Middle East — is interesting in another way. In the 1970s, with oil prices rising rapidly, per capita GNP rose quickly, but as prices declined, average per capita wealth suffered, too. Over those two decades, per capita GNP in the region actually declined.

FIGURE 10.2

Per Capita GNP for Developing and for Developed World

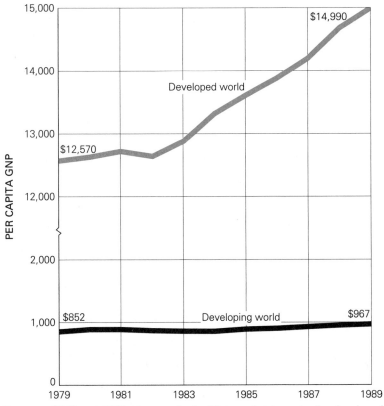

Between 1979 and 1989, the standard of living of citizens in the developed world, as measured by per capita GNP, increased substantially, far faster than the standard of living of citizens in the Third World.

Although GNP per capita is an important indicator, others can more vividly portray the division between the two worlds. Figures 10.3 and 10.4 show differences in life expectancy and literacy for low-income, middle-income, and high-income countries. The poor countries have recently improved, but they are still far behind the developed world. Infant mortality declined from 109 per 1,000 live births in 1970 to 71 per 1,000 in 1991 for the poorest countries. Yet those rates were still much higher than those of wealthier countries. Thus, in 1970, the infant mortality rate in the rich countries was 20 per 1,000 live births, declining to about 8 per 1,000 by 1991. Life expectancy rose from an average of about 50 years in 1965 to slightly more than 62 in 1991 in poor countries, but remained far behind the figure for most

1990 per capita GNP

☐ Low-income economies ($610 or less)
☐ Middle-income economies ($611–$7,619)
▨ High-income economies ($7,620 or more)

Low-income countries

Afghanistan	Haiti
Bangladesh	Honduras
Benin	India
Bhutan	Indonesia
Burkina Faso	Kenya
Burundi	Laos
Cambodia	Lesotho
Central African	Liberia
Republic	Madagascar
Chad	Malawi
China	Maldives
Comoros	Mali
Egypt	Mauritania
Equatorial	Niger
Guinea	Nepal
Ethiopia	Myanmar
Gambia	Niger
Guinea	Nigeria
Guinea-Bissau	Pakistan
Guyana	

Rwanda
São Tome
and Principe
Sierra Leone
Solomon
Islands
Somalia
Sri Lanka
Sudan
Tanzania
Togo
Uganda
Vietnam
Zaire
Zambia

Middle-income countries

Albania	Costa Rica	Isle of Man	North Korea
Algeria	Cuba	Ivory Coast	Oman
American	Czechoslovakia	Jamaica	Pacific Is.
Samoa	Djibouti	Jordan	Trust Terr.
Angola	Domincan Rep.	Kiribati	Panama
Antigua and	Ecuador	Lebanon	Papua
Barbuda	El Salvador	Libya	New Guinea
Argentina	Fiji	Macao	Paraguay
Bahrain	Former USSR	Malaysia	Peru
Barbados	French Guiana	Malta	Philippines
Belize	Gabon	Martinique	Poland
Bolivia	Gibraltar	Mauritius	Portugal
Botswana	Greece	Mexico	Puerto Rico
Brazil	Grenada	Mongolia	Reunion
Bulgaria	Guadeloupe	Morocco	Romania
Cameroon	Guam	Namibia	Saudi Arabia
Cape Verde	Guatemala	Netherlands	Senegal
Chile	Hungary	Antilles	Seychelles
Colombia	Iran	New Caledonia	South Africa
Congo	Iraq	Nicaragua	South Korea

St. Kitts
and Nevis
St. Lucia
St. Vincent
Suriname
Swaziland
Syria
Thailand
Tonga
Trinidad and
Tobago
Tunisia
Turkey
Uruguay
Vanuatu
Venezuela
Western Samoa
Yemen
Yugoslavia
Zimbabwe

High-income countries

Andorra	Hong Kong	United
Aruba	Iceland	Kingdom
Australia	Ireland	United States
Austria	Israel	Virgin Islands
Bahamas	Italy	
Belgium	Japan	
Bermuda	Kuwait	
Brunei	Luxembourg	
Canada	Mayotte	
Channel	Netherlands	
Islands	New Zealand	
Cyprus	Norway	
Denmark	Qatar	
Faeroe Islands	Singapore	
Finland	Spain	
France	Sweden	
French	Switzerland	
Polynesia	Taiwan	
Germany	United Arab	
Greenland	Emirates	

FIGURE 10.3

Classification of Economies by Income and Region
The largest number of poor countries is in the Southern Hemisphere, and most of
the rich countries are located in the Northern Hemisphere. This is why we refer to
the North-South conflict over global economic issues.

developed countries. The story is much the same for adult literacy rates. Literacy too
improved in poor countries, but levels remained far behind those of rich countries,
where the rate of illiteracy was 1 to 3 percent.[40]

[40]See *World Development Report 1993: Investing in Health* (New York: Oxford University
Press, 1993), pp. 238–239, for data on life expectancy. For infant mortality, see pp. 292–293.
"Averages" may hide a significant range within a group of actors. Even though the average life
expectancy for poor countries is 62 years, the range for those countries is substantial. In
Guinea-Bissau, average life expectancy in 1991 was only 39 years, but it was 71 years in Sri Lanka.

FIGURE 10.4

Infant Mortality

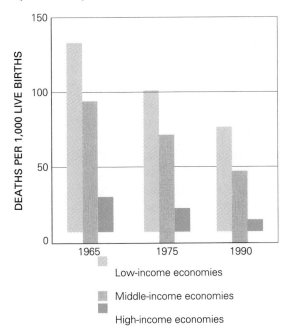

Low-income economies

Middle-income economies

High-income economies

Although infant mortality rates in poor countries in Africa, Asia, and Latin America
declined between 1965 and 1990, they still lag far behind wealthier countries,
especially in Europe and North America.

FIGURE 10.5

Life Expectancy

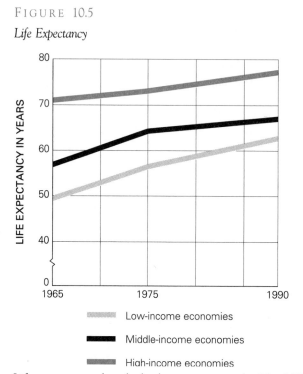

Low-income economies

Middle-income economies

High-income economies

Life expectancy, though slowly increasing in the Third World, also continues to lag behind the developing world owing to disease, malnutrition, and the absence of adequate medical facilities.

Several efforts have been made to combine indicators like those described above to arrive at a composite score for *quality of life*.[41] Each consists of a somewhat different basket of indicators. Economic and Social Rank lists states according to eleven variables—five involving health, five for education, and one for per capita GNP. A second, the Physical Quality of Life Index (PQLI), is based on infant mortality, life expectancy, and literacy. A third, the Index of Social Progress, consists of 44 indicators involving health, education, welfare, economics, political stability, and so on. A final scale, the Human Development Index, which includes life expectancy, literacy, and purchasing power, was developed by the U.N. Development Program. Table 10.1 shows the 1990 Human Development Index for 129 states with composite scores ranging from 0 to 1,000. In a summary way, it reveals how much the human condition differs and shows again that European states or those of European descent enjoy a much higher quality of life than states in Africa, Asia, or the Middle East.

[41]Michael J. Sullivan III, *Measuring Global Values: The Ranking of 162 Countries* (New York: Greenwood Press, 1991), pp. 218–219.

TABLE 10.1

HDI Ranking for Industrial Countries

Country	HDI value	Country	HDI value	Country	HDI value
Japan	0.983	Argentina	0.832	Honduras	0.472
Canada	0.982	Venezuela	0.824	Swaziland	0.458
Norway	0.978	Dominica	0.819	Solomon Islands	0.439
Switzerland	0.978	Kuwait	0.815	Morocco	0.433
Sweden	0.977	Mexico	0.805	Lesotho	0.431
USA	0.976	Qatar	0.802	Zimbabwe	0.398
Australia	0.972	Mauritius	0.794	Bolivia	0.398
France	0.971	Malaysia	0.790	Myanmar (Burma)	0.390
Netherlands	0.970	Bahrain	0.790	Egypt	0.389
United Kingdom	0.964	Grenada	0.787	São Tomé and Principe	0.374
Iceland	0.960	Antigua and Barbuda	0.785	Congo	0.372
Germany	0.957	Colombia	0.770	Kenya	0.369
Denmark	0.955	Seychelles	0.761	Madagascar	0.327
Finland	0.954	Suriname	0.751	Papua New Guinea	0.318
Austria	0.952	United Arab Emirates	0.738	Zambia	0.314
Belgium	0.952	Panama	0.738	Ghana	0.311
New Zealand	0.947	Jamaica	0.736	Pakistan	0.311
Luxembourg	0.943	Brazil	0.730	Cameroon	0.310
Israel	0.938	Fiji	0.730	India	0.309
Ireland	0.925	Saint Lucia	0.720	Namibia	0.289
Italy	0.924	Turkey	0.717	Côte d'Ivoire	0.286
Spain	0.923	Thailand	0.715	Haiti	0.275
Greece	0.902	Cuba	0.711	Tanzania, U. Rep. of	0.270
Czechoslovakia	0.892	Saint Vincent	0.709	Comoros	0.269
Hungary	0.887	Saint Kitts and Nevis	0.697	Zaire	0.262
Malta	0.855	Syrian Arab Rep.	0.694	Lao People's Dem. Rep.	0.246
Bulgaria	0.854	Belize	0.689	Nigeria	0.246
Portugal	0.853	Saudi Arabia	0.688	Yemen	0.233
Poland	0.831	South Africa	0.673	Liberia	0.222
Romania	0.709	Sri Lanka	0.663	Togo	0.218
Albania	0.699	Libyan Arab Jamahiriya	0.658	Uganda	0.194
Other countries		Ecuador	0.646	Bangladesh	0.189
Lithuania	0.881	Paraguay	0.641	Cambodia	0.186
Estonia	0.872	Korea, Dem. Rep.	0.640	Rwanda	0.186
Latvia	0.868	Philippines	0.603	Senegal	0.182
Russian Fed.	0.862	Tunisia	0.600	Ethiopia	0.172
Belarus	0.861	Oman	0.598	Nepal	0.170
Ukraine	0.844	Peru	0.592	Malawi	0.168
Armenia	0.831	Iraq	0.589	Burundi	0.167
Georgia	0.829	Dominican Rep.	0.586	Equatorial Guinea	0.164
Kazakhstan	0.802	Samoa	0.586	Central African Rep.	0.159
Azerbaijan	0.770	Jordan	0.582	Mozambique	0.154
Moldova, Rep.	0.758	Mongolia	0.578	Sudan	0.152
Turkmenistan	0.746	China	0.566	Bhutan	0.150
Uzbekistan	0.695	Lebanon	0.565	Angola	0.143
Kyrgyzstan	0.689	Iran, Islamic Rep.	0.557	Mauritania	0.140
Tajikistan	0.657	Botswana	0.552	Benin	0.113
Barbados	0.928	Guyana	0.541	Djibouti	0.104
Hong Kong	0.913	Vanuatu	0.533	Guinea-Bissau	0.090
Cyprus	0.890	Algeria	0.528	Chad	0.088
Uruguay	0.881	Indonesia	0.515	Somalia	0.087
Trinidad and Tobago	0.877	Gabon	0.503	Gambia	0.086
Bahamas	0.875	El Salvador	0.503	Mali	0.082
Korea, Rep. of	0.872	Nicaragua	0.500	Niger	0.080
Chile	0.864	Maldives	0.497	Burkina Faso	0.074
Costa Rica	0.852	Guatemala	0.489	Afghanistan	0.066
Singapore	0.849	Cape Verde	0.479	Sierra Leone	0.065
Brunei Darussalam	0.847	Viet Nam	0.472	Guinea	0.045

SOURCE: United Nations Development Program, *Human Development Report* 1993 (New York: Oxford University Press, 1993), pp. 11, 14.

In view of the gaps in wealth in the global system, it is hardly surprising that there are differences between North and South on monetary and trade issues. The distinction is geographic in the sense that most of the rich countries are in the northern hemisphere, and many of the less-developed countries in the southern hemisphere. The distinction is imperfect, however, for the southern hemisphere has such relatively rich countries as Argentina, Australia, and New Zealand. In time, the less-developed states translated these political differences between North and South into demands for an overhaul of the international economic order. In the early 1970s, at about the time the Bretton Woods system collapsed, the developing countries proposed a *new international economic order* (*NIEO*).

Call for a New International Economic Order

Demands that the global economic system be reformed date from the formation of the *nonaligned movement* in Belgrade, Yugoslavia, in 1961 and the establishment of the U.N. Conference on Trade and Development (UNCTAD) and the "Group of 77" in 1964.[42] The UNCTAD gathering was intended to deal with global economic issues from the poor countries' perspective and to challenge the GATT system, which seemed to favor developed states. Gradually, the nonaligned movement's platform "evolved from having a principally political orientation to one of economic reform, resembling in great measure the goals of . . . the Group of 77 (G-77)."[43] Late in the 1960s, the Group of 77 adopted the Charter of Algiers, which demanded global economic reform.[44] Similar proposals were discussed at meetings in the developing world during the early 1970s — in Zambia in 1970, Peru in 1971, and Guyana and Algeria in 1973. The last meeting was crucial because it instructed Algeria's President Boumedienne, then chairman of the nonaligned group, to deliver the Economic Declaration and the Action Programme for Economic Cooperation to the Sixth Special Session of the United Nations.

The passage of U.N. Resolutions 3201 and 3202 on May 1, 1974, at this special session of the General Assembly marked the formal call for the New International Economic Order. The resolutions set out principles and a program to improve global economic relations between rich and poor countries. These resolutions were also outlined as controversial demands in the *Charter of Economic Rights and Duties of States*, passed by the General Assembly in December 1974. These documents outlined six major areas of global economic reform that were necessary to forestall conflict between the developed and developing worlds. We consider first these "demands" and then the First World response to them. These were the demands:

[42]The nonaligned states remained outside Cold War alliances, seeking to avoid political entanglements while accepting economic assistance from both sides.

[43]Robert K. Olson, *U.S. Foreign Policy and the New International Order, 1974–1981* (Boulder, Colo.: Westview, 1981), p. 13.

[44]This chronology draws on James M. McCormick, "The NIEO and the Distribution of American Assistance," *Western Political Quarterly* 37 (March 1984), pp. 100–119.

1. Regulating transnational corporations.
2. Transferring technology from rich to poor.
3. Reforming the trading order to assist the development of poor states.
4. Cancelling or renegotiating poor countries' debt.
5. Increasing economic aid from rich to poor countries.
6. Revising voting procedures in international economic institutions to provide poor countries with greater influence.

Regulating Transnational Corporations

The NIEO proponents called for greater regulation of the activities of *transnational corporations* (TNCs) — Sony, Honda, Shell Oil — which have their headquarters in one country but operate in several.[45] This demand raises questions about the role of such corporations in and their effect on poor states. Many corporations originate in developed countries and, like the governments of those countries, advocate a free market. And, as we saw in Chapter 5, some have become pivotal global actors. For good reason, poor countries sometimes see them as agents of the rich.

The number, size, and clout of TNCs frighten the Third World. The number of TNCs has increased dramatically in the past three decades; more than 10,000 of them have 90,000 subsidiaries worldwide. Of these, the 500 largest control about 80 percent of the subsidiaries.[46] Many corporations now have a "global reach," with economic interests in almost every corner of the world.[47] They represent the range of corporate types from extracting minerals to providing services, and they enjoy access to resources and flexibility in policy that many states can only envy.

Critics of TNCs allege that these corporations often simply expropriate a local resource (such as bauxite) and export it for the company's benefit. In effect, poor countries lose control over their own assets. Such TNCs, the argument continues, return a disproportionate share of the profits to their home countries, plowing little back into their hosts. As a result, TNCs are less beneficial to the poor countries than they would be if they were locally controlled.[48] Critics also contend that TNCs create little employment in host countries and train and hire few locals for senior positions. As we saw in discussing *maquiladoras*, a variant of this argument is that TNCs not tied to

[45]For this discussion, we regard "international," "transnational," and "multinational" as identical.

[46]Walters and Blake, *Politics of Global Economic Relations*, pp. 108–109.

[47]See Richard J. Barnet and Ronald E. Muller, *Global Reach: The Power of the Multinational Corporations* (New York: Simon and Schuster, 1974). See also Commission on Transnational Corporations, "Supplementary Material on the Issue of Defining Transnational Corporations," U.N. Economic and Social Council, March 23, 1979.

[48]It is difficult to make the case that, when TNCs make decisions, they seek to benefit a home country because, as global entities, they seek to benefit themselves.

natural resources such as oil will seek cheap labor and move operations if labor costs rise. And even when they do create jobs, the result is greater local economic inequality and privileged urban elites with little stake in fostering local development. Finally, it is argued that the TNC's economic power is translated into political influence. Allegations have been made about TNC interference in local politics, ranging from outright bribery of government officials to illicit campaign contributions for local candidates.

A number of reforms have been suggested to curb these abuses. Developing countries sought to establish a code of conduct with norms limiting TNC activity in the Third World. Some countries have asserted a sovereign right to regulate corporations as they see fit and, if necessary, to nationalize foreign property. Compensation would be paid, but the host country would determine the amount owed.[49]

Technology Transfers and the Developing Countries

A second issue is the *transfer of technology* from rich to developing countries. Poor countries complain that high technology such as advanced computers is too costly to get from advanced countries or corporations, that the price is artificially high, and that no system exists to facilitate transfer of technology.[50] Because actors need high technology to compete in the global economy, the result, critics say, is that dependency of the developing countries on the developed world is perpetuated.[51]

Criticisms about technology transfer focus on four issues.[52] First, technology is expensive because patents are held by developed countries. By one estimate, only 30,000 of more than 3.5 million patents were held by nationals from developing countries. Second, the technology TNCs use in developing countries is *capital intensive*, not *labor intensive*, doing little to reduce chronic unemployment and underemployment. Third, the cost of the technology is either too high for developing countries to purchase or the manner in which it is sold reduces its value for the poor. Finally, developing states contend that research-and-development facilities are seldom located in their countries but primarily in the First World, resulting in a brain drain from the Third World as scientists, engineers, and technicians seek jobs in developed countries.

---

[49]"Charter of Economic Rights and Duties of States," as reprinted in Guy F. Erb and Valeriana Kallab, *Beyond Dependency: The Developing World Speaks Out* (Washington, D.C.: Overseas Development Council, 1975), p. 206. United States policy cutting off assistance to states that nationalize corporate property has been a deterrent to such action.

[50]A somewhat different criticism is that the high technology that TNCs use and the products they produce are inappropriate to local needs. For example, TNCs sell automobiles which only a few very rich people can afford and for which a poor country has to import expensive oil. Instead, local economies require "appropriate technology" such as bicycles or mopeds that can be used by poor peasants.

[51]Walters and Blake, *Politics of Global Economic Relations*, pp. 120, 169. The authors define technology transfer as "the flow of purposeful knowledge across national boundaries" (p. 167).

[52]See ibid., pp. 169–173.

To address these problems, developing states sought three reforms. First, they demanded that all countries facilitate technology transfer and create technology appropriate for them. Second, they asked developed countries to help poor countries strengthen scientific and technological institutions. Finally, "all states would co-operate in exploring with a view to evolving further international accepted guidelines or regulations for the transfer of technology."[53]

The NIEO and Trade Reform

The largest section in the Charter of Economic Rights and Duties of States was devoted to demands for reforming world trade. The main demand was that trading rules be revised to help develop the Third World. This reform would alter the pricing of commodities and raw materials, establish a system of *preferential trade* treatment for products from poor countries, and change the overall direction of global trade. Third World critics argued that the composition of global trade is disadvantageous to them. An overwhelming proportion (70 percent) was *among the rich*, and too little (25 percent) was between the developed and developing worlds.[54]

Another issue was the nature of the trade between rich and poor. In general, the North exports capital goods (for example, machine tools) and finished products (for example, computers and automobiles) to developing countries, and the South exports raw materials (for example, bauxite and gold) and agricultural products (for example, coffee, cocoa, sugar). Although this division of labor may seem reasonable, *terms of trade*—the relationship between the prices of imports and those of exports—have favored rich countries. The price of capital goods and finished products tends to rise more quickly than that of raw materials, and commodity prices fluctuate dramatically depending on conditions outside producers' control. This is one reason for the gradually widening gap between North and South.

Another source of friction between rich and poor was tariffs. Developed countries have historically tended to raise tariff barriers against products from developing countries. They bar not only manufactured goods (where one might expect rich countries to protect their industries from the products of cheap labor) but also agricultural products. Such barriers impede poor countries' efforts to modernize.

To improve the developing states' trade position, NIEO proponents sought several reforms. First, all states were asked to "cooperate . . . toward the progressive dismantling of obstacles to trade and the improvement of the international framework for the conduct of world trade." Second, the NIEO called for greater access to the world market for products from developing countries and for measures to stabilize prices for primary

---

[53]Charter of Economic Rights and Duties of States, as reprinted in Erb and Kallab, *Beyond Dependency*, p. 208.

[54]Developed countries produce more goods demanded by consumers in other developed countries than do less-developed countries.

products. Third, poor countries called for "preferential, non-reciprocal and non-discriminatory treatment to developing countries" to gain access to the markets of rich countries without granting the same privilege to those countries, thereby abandoning the principle of reciprocity in trade. Fourth, NIEO proponents called for addressing the terms-of-trade issue, arguing for "adjustments in the prices of exports of developing countries in relation to prices of their imports so as to promote just and equitable terms of trade for them." Finally, the NIEO Charter sought to establish commodity cartels and multilateral commodity agreements that would increase international trade.[55]

The NIEO and Global Debt

A fourth demand by NIEO proponents was aid for developing countries with debt burdens. Although the debt problem was already difficult in the early 1970s, it became a crisis early in the 1980s. The crisis deepened until early in the 1990s progress was achieved toward reducing the debt. The issue remains a source of friction between rich creditor and poor debtor states, however, and it has been complicated by the growing burden of debt in some of the developed countries, notably the United States, which owes others more than $4 trillion.

The *global debt crisis* originated in several trends in the 1970s and 1980s. First, steeply rising oil prices hurt both developed and developing countries. Poor countries needed loans to finance oil purchases and pay off earlier loans. This demand triggered higher global interest rates, exacerbating the problem. A second price rise in oil late in the 1970s helped push global interest rates and inflation to double digits, burying poor countries under mountainous debt and forcing them to devote much of their annual budgets to interest payments. A global recession in 1974–1975 and an accompanying decline in commodity prices made it even harder for these states to pay their bills. Finally, some developing countries like Mexico and Nigeria, counting on higher earnings from oil sales borrowed heavily for domestic projects. When oil prices plummeted early in the 1980s, they were left with enormous debt burdens. From 1970 until late in the 1980s, the poor countries' debt rose from about $67 billion to more than $1 trillion.

A global debt crisis became evident with one event: Mexico's inability to meet its debt-service obligations in 1982. Mexico admitted it was not earning enough from exports to meet payments, mostly to the big money-center banks like Bank of America and Citicorp. By the mid-1980s, other Third World countries—Bolivia, Brazil, Argentina, Nigeria, the Philippines—also found themselves close to bankruptcy. *Debt-service ratios*—the ratio of the principal and interest due on debts to export earnings—were estimated at between 20 and 50 percent for non–oil developing countries worldwide in

[55]Erb and Kallab, *Beyond Dependency*, pp. 206, 208, 209, 211.

1985.[56] Latin American countries had a debt-service ratio of 47 percent, African countries 27 percent, and Middle Eastern countries, 26 percent. As a result, between one-quarter and one-half of developing countries' export earnings had to flow back to developed countries to meet loan-repayment schedules.

The debt issue affects the welfare of both the developing and developed worlds. Poor countries, with less of their export earnings available to pay for new projects, find that their standard of living declines and domestic instability threatens. The developed countries are able to sell less in the developing world, costing jobs at home and increasing trade deficits. By one estimate, 400,000 U.S. jobs were lost early in the 1980s as the Latin America export market dried up.[57] The need to reschedule debt payments or make additional loans to finance repayments also threatens major banks in North America and Europe.

Well before global debt exploded early in the 1980s, the developing countries were making proposals to restructure debt burdens, reduce interest rates, and even cancel debt. Poor states sought case-by-case debt renegotiation to cancel or reschedule the debt owed. They argued that the debt burden was so onerous that dramatic action was needed if they were to have any chance of developing, and a one-time cancellation would be equivalent to a grant by the rich to the poor. Specifically, the NIEO sought debt relief for "the least developed" and those "most seriously affected by economic crises and natural calamities."[58]

The NIEO and Foreign Assistance

A fifth NIEO demand was for increased bilateral and multilateral assistance from rich countries. First and foremost, the poor states were dissatisfied that most of the rich states had failed to live up to the goals the U.N. set forth in its three Development Decades. For the first, the U.N. had called for an annual transfer of 1 percent of GNP from each developed state in the form of official development assistance to poor states. In the second and third decades, the U.N. lowered that target to .7 percent of GNP, hoping that the other .3 percent could be made up by private contributions.

In fact, the percentage of official aid from the developed world has declined. In 1965, the average official development assistance as a portion of GNP transferred from rich to poor was 0.47 percent. By 1970, it had declined to 0.34 percent, and by 1991 the

[56]Table B-3 in John W. Sewell, Richard E. Feinberg, and Valeriana Kallab, eds., *U.S. Foreign Policy and the Third World: Agenda 1985–86* (Washington, D.C.: Overseas Development Council, 1985), p. 174.

[57]"Opening Statement by Senator Bill Bradley," Subcommittee on International Debt, Senate Finance Committee, March 9, 1987.

[58]"Declaration and Action Programme on the Establishment of a New International Economic Order," in Erb and Kallab, *Beyond Dependency*, p. 194.

figure stood at 0.33 percent.[59] Some countries have done better than others. The Scandinavian countries and the Netherlands have approached or occasionally exceeded the 1 percent target, but the United States, Ireland, and New Zealand have often been near the bottom, with averages around 0.20 percent of GNP late in the 1980s.[60] Even as aid effort, measured by percentage of GNP, has declined, the overall amount has increased. In 1965, the developed countries provided about $6.5 billion to the developing countries. The amount rose to $14 billion in 1975, $29 billion in 1985, and $56 billion in 1991.[61] The leading providers have generally remained the same — the United States, Japan, France, Germany, Italy, and the United Kingdom — though the U.S. portion has declined from 62 percent in 1965 to 20 percent in 1991.

Beyond the general criticism of inadequate total assistance, developing countries expressed specific complaints about the aid that is provided. First, most of the aid is bilateral rather than multilateral and often has political strings attached by the donors. United States aid to Egypt and Israel was provided as a condition for concluding peace with each other late in the 1970s. Also, much of the aid is sent as loans, not grants, and much of it is tied to the recipients' purchase of goods from the donor country. Using loans as a vehicle for aid ensures that developing states will amass more debt. Although *tied aid* may make sense for the donor who wants to sell the idea of foreign aid to a dubious public, the requirement prevents developing countries from getting the best products and prices. Third, some donors, such as the former U.S.S.R., were criticized for emphasizing large-scale, highly visible projects that were less helpful to poor countries than modest projects that would focus on fundamental needs, especially in the agricultural sector. Third World leaders, especially those who after independence sought to build their reputations on such projects (for instance, Kwame Nkrumah of Ghana and Ahmed Sukarno of Indonesia), must assume some of the blame.

To address these criticisms, NIEO advocates called for several changes in the amount and composition of aid from rich to poor. They asked that states promote "increased net flows of real resources to the developing countries from all sources. . . ." They also sought "to increase the net amount of financial flows from official sources to developing countries and to improve the terms and conditions thereof."[62] In other words, they wished to rely less on private contributions and investments and more on government-to-government assistance. They also wanted grants, rather than loans, to be "a preponderant element for the least developed," and felt that "financial assistance should, as a general rule, be untied."[63] Finally, NIEO advocates asked major food-producing countries to extend special grants and assistance to poor countries in need.

[59]See Table 19 in *The World Development Report, 1993* (New York: Oxford University Press, 1993), p. 274.

[60]The U.S. aid effort declined from 0.58 percent of GNP in 1965 to 0.20 percent in 1991. Ibid.

[61]Ibid. This increase is significantly lower if one controls for inflation.

[62]Charter of Economic Rights and Duties of States, as reprinted in Erb and Kallab, *Beyond Dependency*, p. 210.

[63]These two quotations are from "'Consensus Resolution' of the Seventh Special Session of the U.N. General Assembly," reprinted in ibid., pp. 242 and 240, respectively.

International Organizations and the NIEO

A final demand by the NIEO was for restructuring international organizations to provide poor states with greater influence. Critics argue that because voting procedures in organizations like the World Bank and the IMF are based on the proportional financial contribution of states, these "clubs for the rich" are controlled by a few developed states. Decisions made by these organizations directly affect the poor states' welfare by determining, say, whether they receive loans and under what conditions, and so Third-World leaders demanded greater influence in those decisions.

The Charter of Economic Rights and Duties of States observed that all countries "have the right to participate fully and effectively in the international decision-making process in the solution of world economic, financial and monetary problems. . . . "[64] The developing states also sought to move discussions about reforming the global economic system out of international organizations dominated by the developed countries to those like UNCTAD where they have greater influence and voting power.

Developed States Respond to NIEO Demands

The First World's response to the NIEO agenda was initially negative. United States policy makers expressed anger at the idea of "demands." They saw the NIEO as a "screwball effort" and as a "rip-off" and as a way to "beat the West and the North over the head." Some of the initial NIEO proposals were described as "unrealistic," "economically meaningless," and "framed in a naive way."[65] In time, this harsh rhetoric has given way to efforts by developed states to address the issues raised by the NIEO. Denunciations have been replaced by dialogue between North and South. Still, the gulf remains between promise and performance. Let us review briefly the world's responses to the NIEO.

TNCs, Technology, and Development

The response to demands for regulating TNCs and for facilitating technology transfer between rich and poor has been minimal. Global standards for corporate behavior are almost nonexistent. Although the United Nations proposed a code of conduct early in the 1970s and a few national groups such as the U.S. Chamber of Commerce have done the same, only two major steps have been taken toward regulating TNCs. The first was

[64]"Charter of Economic Rights and Duties of States," as reprinted in Erb and Kallab, *Beyond Dependency*, p. 207.

[65]The quotations are from interviews with members and staff of the House Foreign Affairs Committee and officials at the U.S. Agency for International Development during the early 1980s. The results of the interviews are reported in James M. McCormick, "Congressional-Executive Attitudes Toward the NIEO," *International Studies Notes* 10 (Spring 1983), pp. 12–17.

a *voluntary* code of conduct among the Organization for Economic Cooperation and Development countries in 1976. Among other things, it prohibited some political activities and encouraged cooperation between TNCs and host countries. The code was very general and vague, and no mechanisms were provided to enforce it. A second step was establishing two centers in the mid-1970s to render TNC activity more "transparent." The Center on Transnational Corporations collects and disseminates information about TNCs to familiarize the global community with the range of activities of these corporations, and the Commission on Transnational Corporations checks on complaints against TNCs and manages the Center.[66]

Developed countries' efforts to regulate their own TNCs have also been minimal. The United States tightened laws against bribery late in the 1970s after reports were made public about corporate payments in a number of Third World countries. Some developed countries have tried another strategy, seeking to restrict or slow exporting jobs to the Third World. A special U.S. Senate subcommittee took a systematic look at TNCs to address this problem. United States labor unions, in particular, have sought to stem the exodus and have opposed the North American Free Trade Agreement (NAFTA) among the United States, Canada, and Mexico because they believe TNC expansion into Mexico will lose more U.S. jobs.

The most vigorous efforts to control and regulate TNCs have been undertaken by the host countries themselves. Some developing countries have joined in regional groups to establish their own codes of conduct for eliminating improper behavior by TNCs. Among the first of those to impose restrictions on TNCs was the *Andean Group*, founded in 1969 by Bolivia, Colombia, Ecuador, Peru, and Venezuela. The Andean Group stipulated limits on *repatriation of profits* from TNCs investing in their countries, set standards for transferring corporate technology to host countries, and required that, eventually, foreign ownership of local affiliates be surrendered.[67] In other instances, host countries such as Mexico have required at least majority local control before permitting TNC investments. Some countries have simply prohibited TNC investment in specified industries, believing that such investment would infringe upon their sovereignty and increase their economic dependency. Finally, a few countries have gone so far as to nationalize TNC property. Late in the 1960s and early in the 1970s, Peru, Libya, and Venezuela, among others, nationalized foreign petroleum industries in their countries, and Bolivia and Chile nationalized the tin and copper industries inside their borders.[68] *Nationalization* is a dangerous path, however, because it spurs conflict with the developed states and brings an end to investment and development assistance.

The threat of nationalization has lessened as developing countries' bargaining leverage toward TNCs has improved. As the number of TNCs increased, developing

---

[66]Spero, *Politics of International Economic Relations*, pp. 138–139.

[67]Walters and Blake, *Politics of Global Economic Relations*, p. 148. On the Andean Group, see also Barnet and Muller, *Global Reach*, pp. 207–208.

[68]Barnet and Muller, *Global Reach*, p. 188. Some of these industries were later returned to their corporate owners.

states became more selective about which they would permit to operate. Those countries can now exploit the competition among TNCs to get better contracts and more advantageous investments. Larger numbers of TNCs also reduce the prospect that corporations will pull up stakes because others can replace them. Finally, as the global economy becomes more competitive, the developing states will be better placed to improve their bargaining position.

If anything, the First World has been less responsive in facilitating technology transfer than in constraining TNCs. Although conferences on technology transfer have been sponsored by the United Nations, the rich countries and TNCs continue to protect their technological monopoly, for at least three reasons.[69] First, because costly technology is often developed by the private sector, it is not considered part of the "global commons." Protection of copyrights and patents is seen as a vital aspect of commercial success. Second, corporations believe that, when technology transfer does occur, it should be at a "fair market price" to enable the TNCs to recoup (and profit) from their innovations. Third, transferring technology to other countries may weaken the competitive edge of those who formerly enjoyed it exclusively. The controversy over technology transfer is evident in the Uruguay Round of the GATT, where protection of "intellectual property rights" is a major issue.

Trade and Debt

The developed countries have been more responsive to NIEO trade and debt demands than to demands for TNC regulation and technology transfer. In trade, the European Community in the mid-1970s began to provide preferential arrangements. In 1975, the EC concluded the first of the *Lomé Agreements* (named after the capital of Togo where it was negotiated), granting special access to Europe for products from a number of poor countries. Under these agreements, the ACP (African, Caribbean, and Pacific) countries — mainly former European colonies — were granted privileged access to the EC. The EC and the ACP countries also worked out an arrangement to stabilize prices for commodities purchased from these developing countries.

The United States has also granted preferential trading status to products from some poor states, albeit not as liberally as the EC. By the 1974 Trade Act, the United States established a general system of preference by granting access to 2,000 items from poor countries beginning January 1, 1976. The system was renewed and was to continue at least through 1994. Although critics argue that the items granted this status are minor, the principle of preferential access is important. In 1982, the Reagan administration proposed, and the Congress enacted, the Caribbean Basin Initiative (CBI), another preferential trading arrangement for countries bordering on the Caribbean (except Cuba). Under this plan, exports from these countries could enter the United States without duties for ten years, and tax incentives would be granted to U.S. firms

[69]Walter and Blake, *Politics of Global Economic Relations*, pp. 174–188.

investing in the Caribbean Basin.[70] In 1991, the Bush administration started the Enterprise for the Americas Initiative, which was also intended to promote freer trade between the United States and Latin America.[71]

Efforts to stabilize commodity prices, improve terms of trade between rich and poor, and institute general reform in the trading order did not, however, progress very far. A North–South conference (the Conference on International Economic Cooperation) convened in Paris for three years (1975–1977) to address these and other development issues. Although the developed states committed themselves in principle to establish a Common Fund to support the prices of various commodities, the idea never got off the ground because of inadequate funding. The Tokyo Round of the GATT (1973–1979) took up trading preferences for poor states, but results were minimal, leading to an almost complete Third-World boycott of the April 1979 concluding ceremony.

The North's early response to demands for debt relief were negative, but this attitude changed in the 1980s and 1990s. *Debt cancellation* was at first vigorously opposed, especially by Germany and the United States, using two major assumptions: First, they believed that canceling debt encouraged budgetary irresponsibility in developing states. If debts were canceled, states would engage in more deficit spending, expecting additional cancellation of debt. Second, it would disrupt the rich countries' economies. Cancellation would reduce profits and perhaps even endanger solvency of the private banks that had provided the loans. Instead, the developed countries preferred to allow *restructuring of debt* conditioned on stringent domestic reforms. This coupling of *conditionality* — reducing debt burdens conditioned on budget reform and reduced domestic spending — was often imposed by the IMF and entailed severe austerity in debtor countries. Such austerity, which in some countries included eliminating domestic subsidies for such staples as bread, produced strong resentment toward the IMF and the West and not a little agitation against governments that agreed to it.

As the debt issue festered in the 1980s, the developed countries took a number of initiatives. The Reagan and Bush administrations proposed two plans to cope with growing global debt. The first, the *Baker Plan* (named after the U.S. Treasury secretary), involved restructuring debt. Under Baker's proposal, commercial banks worldwide would aid the most deeply indebted countries by lending them up to $20 billion, and the international lending institutions would provide an additional $9 billion in new resources. The United States would provide additional funding for the international financial institutions and commit itself to further opening up its domestic markets to products from developing states.[72] Western leaders still expected the debt crisis would

[70]See President Ronald Reagan, "Caribbean Basin Initiative," Address before the Organization of American States, Washington, D.C., February 24, 1982.

[71]Patricia Lee Dorff, "Chronology 1991," *Foreign Affairs: America and the World 1991–1992* 71:1 (1992), p. 219.

[72]S. Karene Witcher, "Baker's Plan to Relieve Debt Crisis May Spur Future Ills, Critics Say," *The Wall Street Journal*, November 15, 1985, p. 1.

be eased by economic growth in the Third World. In fact, the crisis intensified, and, by late in the 1980s, the North decided to move more decisively in confronting the issue. Secretary of the Treasury Nicholas Brady acknowledged for the first time that cancelling debt might be necessary in dealing with the crisis. The so-called *Brady Plan* included a number of specific schemes, three of which were especially innovative.

One proposal was to encourage the international lending institutions to provide more assistance to poor countries to pay off a portion of their debt to commercial banks at a discount. The banks would get most of their money back even though they would have to write off some of the debt. A second strategy was for *debt–equity swaps* which entailed trading the debt owed to a bank or commercial institution for stock in a developing country's industry. A more sophisticated version of the idea was for banks to sell a portion of their loans to TNCs at a discount. The TNCs would convert the loans into local currency which could then be reinvested in host countries. According to this plan the poor countries would reduce their debt without having to sell off assets, and the banks would get much of the money owed them. A third idea was to institute *debt–commodity* swaps under which commercial banks would form companies to export the debtors' commodities, retaining some of the profits for repaying debt. This plan was designed to boost Third-World exports while allowing creditors to be repaid in hard currency.[73]

By mid-1992, the Brady Plan seemed to be working, especially in Latin America. After Brazil concluded an agreement with creditor banks in July 1992, Paul Volcker, former chairman of the U.S. Federal Reserve Board, declared: "I think you can say that the Latin American debt crisis is no longer a crisis. Most Latin American countries are hopefully back on a growth pattern, and the debts are manageable and should not be a threat to the financial system."[74] The Brazil agreement represented the sort of debt cancellation suggested in the Brady Plan. The package offered various ways for Brazil to write down its debt—a 35 percent reduction in principal and interest owed to commercial banks, immediate reduction in interest rates until economic conditions improved, lower interest and principal payments on the debt, and additional new loans if necessary.[75]

Although the debt picture had improved, the predicament of some countries was worse than ever. Little progress had been made toward relieving the debt burdens of African countries. Although the situation remained "a disaster for the Africans," declares Volcker, "[i]t is not a financial crisis in the same sense [as Latin America]. It is a development crisis."[76] Thus, abatement of the debt crisis has varied by region, with an eye toward reducing the threat to Western banks and stabilizing politically important societies.

[73]On these schemes, see ibid., p. 384, and Eric N. Berg, "Debt Crisis: Fresh Approaches," *The New York Times*, May 5, 1987, pp. D1, D4.

[74]Quoted in Jonathan Fuerbringer, "Brazil and Banks Reach Agreement on Reducing Debt," *The New York Times*, July 10, 1992, p. A1.

[75]Ibid., p. C2.

[76]Ibid., pp. A1 and C2.

Aid, International Organizations, and the Developed Countries

The First World has generally responded poorly to demands for greater foreign assistance. An economic slowdown in the West during the 1990s made foreign aid unpopular with voters and dampened any ardor to provide greater aid to the Third World. One important change, however, was growth in the amount of assistance Japan provides. Japanese assistance to the Third World jumped from about $458 million in 1970 to $3.4 billion in 1980. By 1989, its aid totaled $8.9 billion, making Japan the largest donor for that year.

Although amounts of aid have not increased significantly, some improvements have been made in the way in which aid is provided and in the kind of aid. In 1973, the U.S. Congress adopted a new aid strategy. One aim of new legislation was to "give the highest priority to undertakings submitted by host governments which directly improved the lives of the poorest of the poor and their capacity to participate in the development of their countries."[77] Aid projects would be directed toward meeting basic needs of the world's neediest people—food, health, and education. Another objective was to empower the poor by encouraging them to participate directly in planning projects. Two years later, the U.S. food aid program was altered to target aid to the "poorest of the poor," and Congress directed that 75 percent of food aid sales go to the world's neediest as defined by the World Bank.[78]

Partly in response to the U.S. initiative and to the NIEO, other developed countries too agreed to target more of their assistance to the world's poorest populations. In 1975, Great Britain issued a government white paper directing future aid in the form of grants to the world's neediest. In the same year Germany agreed to focus its assistance on the poorest and emphasize aid for rural development and agriculture. Two years later the Development Assistance Committee of the Organization for Economic Cooperation and Development approved a policy statement recommending that aid programs be directed toward meeting the basic survival needs of the poor in the Third World.

Initial assessments of these efforts are mixed. One analysis of the U.S. aid program concludes: "Neither the number of recipients receiving aid, the kind of assistance . . . nor the form of assistance—loans vs. grants—has changed appreciably in line with the NIEO requirements."[79] The "poorest of the poor" were still not the leading recipients, except for food aid, and grants were only about 20 to 30 percent of funding during the period examined. Another study concluded that much of the change was cosmetic rather than substantive.[80]

---

[77]AID's Challenge in an Interdependent World (Washington, D.C.: Agency for International Development, 1977), p. 11.

[78]See McCormick, "Congressional-Executive Attitudes Toward the NIEO," *International Studies Notes*, p. 14, and *Congressional Quarterly Almanac, 1975*, vol. 31 (Washington, D.C.: Congressional Quarterly, 1976), p. 342.

[79]McCormick, "NIEO and Distribution of American Assistance," p. 116.

[80]See Elliott R. Morss, *New Directions and Beyond: A Review of Accomplishments and An Agenda for the Future*. A paper prepared for the Congressional Research Service, November 1980.

During the 1980s, the U.S. government paid even less attention to NIEO preferences in foreign aid. The Reagan administration moved away from emphasizing basic needs and again focused on countries that were crucial to U.S. policy in the Cold War, and U.S. aid was tied to the recipients' establishing a free market. Increasingly, the administration took the position that private-sector investment should be the principal mechanism for producing economic development in poor countries. The end of the Cold War removed a primary domestic justification in the United States for providing assistance. Finally, astronomical domestic budget deficits during the Reagan and Bush years made foreign aid—which lacks a domestic constituency—even less popular politically than in the past. Other developed states have done little better than the United States. In Germany, a three-year study concluded that great obstacles confronted that country's effort to alter its aid strategy.[81] Although Japan has become a major donor, its behavior still does not measure up to NIEO standards. Complaints are regularly heard that Japan lavishes most of its aid on a few countries in Southeast Asia and that it is directed toward big industrial projects that benefit Japanese companies.[82]

About demands for reforming international organizations, no change has been made in voting procedures to ensure a larger voice for the world's poor. A flurry of conferences and meetings discussed NIEO demands—the Seventh Special Session of the U.N. General Assembly (September 1975), the Conference on International Economic Cooperation (North–South Conference, December 1975 to June 1977), and the Brandt Commission (1977, named after Willy Brandt, former West German Chancellor), and the Independent Commission on International Development Issues (1977). Although these meetings put the spotlight on NIEO demands and raised global consciousness about poverty, they accomplished little that was substantive.

Nowhere was the North's unwillingness to accede to the NIEO more evident than at a meeting of leaders from fourteen developing countries and eight developed countries in Cancún, Mexico in October 1981. President Ronald Reagan succinctly articulated his country's attitude toward the NIEO when he called for the developing countries to rely more on their own initiative and on the free market. He declared that he envisioned a development strategy enabling "men and women to realize freely their full potential, to go as far as their God-given talents will take them. Free people build free markets that ignite dynamic development for everyone."[83]

By the 1990s, the traditional international economic organizations—World Bank, GATT, IMF—had again become the principal forums for *North–South dialogue*, and the tone of the exchanges had moderated. It was clear as early as the 1983 meeting of the

[81]Brian H. Smith, *More Than Altruism: The Politics of Private Foreign Aid* (Princeton: Princeton University Press, 1990), p. 104.

[82]See Robert M. Orr, *The Emergence of Japan's Foreign Aid Power* (New York: Columbia University Press, 1990), pp. 109–131.

[83]"Excerpts from Reagan Speech on U.S. Policy Toward Developing Nations," *The New York Times*, October 16, 1981, p. A12.

nonaligned states in New Delhi, India, that the Third World had toned down its anti-West rhetoric and had decided to adopt a more conciliatory strategy.[84] Whether a softer tone would bring greater change in the order of things remained to be seen. The rich countries appeared unconvinced that restructuring the global economic order to enhance development of the Third World would benefit them. And, from time to time, Third-World frustration with failure by the rich to respond again bursts forth, as it did at the U.N. Conference on the Environment and Development held in Rio de Janeiro in June 1992. At that conference, one delegate after another from the developing states denounced the developed states for seeking environmental reforms that would hobble their efforts to achieve growth while failing to provide them with assistance.

For the near future, the developing world is likely to continue to experience frustration. Although the end of the Cold War made it easier for Western leaders to consider factors other than "strategic importance" in disbursing scarce aid and to seek humanitarian objectives, the Third World had little cause to be optimistic. First, the end of the Cold War reduced the visibility of many of these countries still further because they were no longer able to play one side against the other. Second, economic woes at home further reduced public sympathy in the developed world for foreign aid. The election of President Bill Clinton in November 1992 on a pledge to pay more attention to domestic economic issues than his predecessor might be a harbinger of declining U.S. interest in the Third World. Third, growing quarrels among developed states were likely to absorb disproportionate time and attention of First World diplomats. Finally, growing economic needs in Russia, Eastern Europe, and the other states of the former U.S.S.R. were competing for scarce resources.

Political Economy and the "Second World"

If the developed West and Japan together are the economic *First World* and African, Asian, and Latin American societies are the *Third World*,[85] the former Soviet Union and the members of its bloc were collectively known as the *Second World*. These states remained mostly isolated from the postwar global economy. This isolation was partly intentional, for Soviet leaders wanted to make their society self-sufficient and prevent dilution of Marxist "purity" by exposing their people to Western ideas and goods. It was also partly a result of the Soviet economic system's incompatibility with Western capitalism. As a result, the "command" (centrally planned) economies of the former U.S.S.R. and Eastern Europe were members of neither the IMF nor the GATT, and their currencies were not convertible into the hard currencies of the Western powers. And, with the collapse of the Soviet system, one of the greatest challenges in global politics was to integrate Russia and its former allies into the international economic system.

[84]See Mary Anne Weaver, "Nonaligned States, Seeking Economic Aid, Tone Down Anti-West Rhetoric," *Christian Science Monitor*, March 14, 1983, p. 5.

[85]In the 1970s, the label *Fourth World*, referring to the poorest of the poor, was added.

The Soviet System

The 1917 Bolshevik Revolution overthrew the capitalist order in Russia and led to a severing of economic ties with the West. Seventy-five years later the system that revolution ushered in was itself overthrown. Ironically, both events were triggered by the failure of Russia's economic system to satisfy popular demands or compete successfully with Western economies. Following the initial years of turmoil and civil war and Lenin's death (1924), the young Soviet regime set out to institute socialism in the Soviet Union and overcome the country's backwardness. Indeed, as an agricultural society seeking to industrialize, the Soviet Union faced many of the problems confronting Third World societies today. When Stalin assumed power late in the 1920s, the regime sought to advance its economic goals by a system of state ownership of the means of production and a centrally planned economy.

A series of five-year plans were instituted with government production targets emphasizing heavy industry and military goods. *Central planning* was an effort to dispense with the free market. Although highly inefficient, central planning and state management did permit the primitive Soviet economy to mobilize resources and labor for the country's rapid industrialization, but the human and environmental costs of the policy were staggering. Industrialization was accompanied by forcibly *collectivizing* agriculture, during which millions of peasants perished. The need for labor was met by forced emigration from rural to urban areas, and a vast system of labor camps and labor discipline was enforced by the Communist party. Although standards of living in the Soviet Union improved, most state investment was channeled to heavy industry that provided little direct benefit to Soviet consumers. The system established late in the 1920s and 1930s remained intact until the U.S.S.R. disintegrated.[86] It is aptly summarized by one observer:

> From the early 1930s onwards, the Soviet Union had a three-sector economy: heavy industry and defence as the priority sector, light industry a poor second, and then agriculture. Under Stalin it was a law of socialism that heavy industry should grow at a faster rate than light. . . . The economy was administered through a series of what we would call nationalized industries, run from Moscow by ministries, each responsible for a different branch of industry, and issuing plans and instructions to the enterprises below. . . . This was subsequently, post-1985, rightly referred to as the Administrative-Command System, a system under which the economy was run from above through the medium of a central plan, targets, and administrative orders.[87]

---

[86]Periodic reform efforts such as that initiated in 1965 were either half-hearted or met resistance from entrenched economic bureaucrats.

[87]Mary McAuley, *Soviet Politics 1917–1991* (New York: Oxford University Press, 1992), pp. 40–41.

Soviet GNP continued to rise rapidly through the 1970s,[88] and standards of living continued to improve. Nevertheless, overall economic performance was uneven. And, by the mid-1970s, Mary McAuley writes, "the momentum seemed to go; it was as though the system had run out of steam."[89] Mikhail Gorbachev's immediate predecessors, Leonid Brezhnev (1964–1982), Yuri Andropov (1982–1984), and Konstantin Chernenko (1984–1985) — all elderly and in poor health — were incapable of ending the stagnation that had engulfed the Soviet economy. Corruption, alcoholism, poor service, and cynicism were widespread. Agriculture remained a great problem, and, by the 1980s, the U.S.S.R. became increasingly dependent on Western imports of grain to make up shortfalls at home. Emphasis on meeting quotas meant that quality of goods got little attention. Finally, as the Soviet economy grew and became more complex, "muscle power" — the key to rapid growth of the economy in the 1930s and 1940s — grew less important, and access to high technology such as advanced computers became more critical.

Centralization of the economy was accompanied by a totalitarian political system built on a combination of police terror and ideological loyalty. All enterprises were controlled by party members with loyalty to the center, and they used all means to achieve the production quotas that were set for them. They also enjoyed special privileges including access to stores with foreign goods, housing, cars, and holiday resorts that were not available to ordinary Soviet citizens. These former managers of state enterprises continue to put up the strongest resistance to political and economic reforms in Russia.

In other words, central planning facilitated political control from the center. And, after 1985, first Mikhail Gorbachev and later Boris Yeltsin concluded that economic and political reform had to go hand in hand. Interestingly, Chinese leaders sought to separate the two, instituting economic changes that increased the role of the free market but resisting political democratization. Whether the Chinese experiment will succeed remains unclear, but, considering the goods and services its currency can buy, the Chinese economy has catapulted into third place behind the United States and Japan.[90] In the Soviet Union, Gorbachev's policies of glasnost ("openness") and perestroika ("restructuring") unleashed forces that finally brought the old system to collapse.[91] Gorbachev's objective was to introduce elements of the market economy, including some private ownership, but it was never to destroy the political and economic establishment from which he had grown. For the most part, economic reform failed, and political reform got out of control.

[88]During the 1960s, Soviet GNP grew an average of 5 percent a year. This rate declined to just above 2 percent in the second half of the 1970s and to below 2 percent for the period 1981–1987. Spero, *Politics of International Economic Relations*, p. 313.

[89]McAuley, *Soviet Politics 1917–1991*, p. 78.

[90]Steven Greenhouse, "New Tally of World's Economies Catapults China into Third Place," *The New York Times*, May 20, 1993, pp. A1, A6.

[91]See Chapter 12, p. 417–418.

East–West Economic Relations in the Cold War

Although the United States hoped the Soviet Union and especially the Eastern European states would join the postwar international economic regime, the Cold War and the chill in East–West relations prevented this from taking place. Instead, in 1949, responding to the Marshall Plan, in which they refused to take part,[92] the East bloc members created the *Council for Mutual Economic Assistance* (*Comecon*). This organization served three purposes: (1) facilitating Soviet control over its allies' economies, (2) creating a socialist trade bloc, and (3) dividing labor among the socialist states so that each specialized in producing items desired by the others.[93] By 1953, almost two-thirds of East-bloc exports went to other bloc members, and less than one percent went to the United States, Canada, and Latin America.[94] The Soviet system of central planning was imposed on other members of the bloc, and Eastern currencies were not convertible. In a word, the economies of Eastern Europe were isolated from the West and made to depend on the U.S.S.R.

Unlike economic relations among the developed capitalist states or between the First and Third Worlds, East–West trade during the Cold War was subordinated to political interests. The West used trade to induce the U.S.S.R. to modify its behavior and punish Moscow for anti-Western policies. During political thaws, East–West economic contacts would expand, but periods of East–West tension were often accompanied by reduced contacts. Following the Soviet invasion of Afghanistan in 1979, President Jimmy Carter placed an embargo on grain exports to the U.S.S.R. even though U.S. farmers stood to lose a lucrative export market. See Table 10.2.

Throughout the Cold War, the United States and its allies sought to deny the U.S.S.R. access to resources and technology that might contribute to Soviet military power. The 1949 U.S. Export Control Act, which was not revoked until 1969, gave the president authority to prevent exports to the Soviet Union and created a system for licensing exports. Also in 1949, a Coordinating Committee, known as *Cocom*, was established to coordinate the Western allies' policies on embargoing strategic goods to the East. Usually, U.S. allies were less willing than the United States to forego commercial opportunities to wage economic war against the U.S.S.R.

East–West Economic Relations After the "Second Revolution"

Revolutionary changes in the East created new economic challenges for the global system. As the former East-bloc members began to make strides toward democracy and create free-market economies at home, the developed West tentatively sought to help

[92]The U.S.S.R. prevented Poland and Czechoslovakia from accepting Marshall Plan aid.

[93]With the Soviet bloc and Comecon gone, trading patterns in Russia and Eastern Europe have been badly disrupted, and these countries no longer have guaranteed markets for the products Comecon assigned them to produce.

[94]Spero, *Politics of International Economic Relations*, p. 307.

TABLE 10.2

Soviet Grain Harvests, Exports, and Imports (millions of metric tons)

Year	Harvest	Export	Import
1950	81	2.9	0.2
1955	104	3.7	0.3
1956	125	3.2	0.5
1957	103	7.4	0.2
1958	135	5.1	0.8
1959	120	7.0	0.3
1960	126	6.8	0.2
1961	131	7.5	0.7
1962	140	7.8	—
1963	108	6.3	3.1
1964	152	3.5	7.3
1965	121	4.3	6.4
1966	171	3.6	7.7
1967	148	6.2	2.2
1968	170	5.4	1.6
1969	162	7.2	0.6
1970	187	5.7	2.2
1971	181	8.6	3.5
1972	168	4.6	15.5
1973	223	4.9	23.9
1974	196	7.0	7.1
1975	140	3.6	15.9
1976	224	1.5	20.6
1977	196	2.3[a]	18.9[a]
1978	237	2.8[a]	15.6[a]
1979	179	0.8[a]	31.0[a]
1980	189	0.5[a]	34.8[a]
1981	158	0.5[a]	46.0[a]
1982	187	0.5[a]	32.5[a]
1983	192	0.5[a]	32.9[a]
1984	173	1.0[a]	55.5[a]
1985	192	1.0[a]	29.0[a]
1986	210	1.0[a]	30.0[a]

[a]July to July of following year estimate of Department of Agriculture.

SOURCE: Marshall Goldman, *Gorbachev's Challenge* (New York: W. W. Norton, 1987), p. 39.

The impact of economic interdependence and the effort to integrate Russia into the global economic system after the Cold War is symbolized by this Russian sipping Pepsi Cola while reading his newspaper.

them make the necessary adjustments. Fear that economic dislocation would overthrow fragile democracies in Russia and elsewhere was the main source of this effort. Indeed, following Boris Yeltsin's introduction of free-market reforms in Russia in October 1991, the country's economy all but collapsed. Real incomes dropped by 50 percent in six months, and production fell by 24 percent in 1992 alone. *Hyperinflation* of more than 2,000 percent gripped Russian society,[95] and Moscow sought to reduce drastically the numbers of rubles in circulation to control inflation.

Three major tasks need to be addressed to help the Eastern European states and the states that were formerly part of the U.S.S.R. in making the transition to market economies: (1) integrate these states into the major global economic organizations, (2) establish convertible currencies in these countries, and (3) increase their trade with other countries and encourage investment in their economies. Some progress has been made in all these endeavors, but some in the West remain reluctant to move too quickly without assurances of fundamental domestic reform. Russia especially is caught in a vicious cycle. As long as the country appears to lack political stability, the West will hesitate to provide large-scale aid and investment. But as long as this hesitancy persists, Russia may remain unstable.

[95] Peter Reddaway, "Russia Comes Apart," *The New York Times*, January 10, 1993, Section 4, p. 23.

A first step was to integrate these states into the global economic system by admitting them to the IMF and the GATT. Progress has been significant in granting full membership to former Soviet-bloc countries and to the former U.S.S.R. republics. In July 1992, Russia and the IMF reached agreement on economic reforms needed within Russia for Moscow to qualify for IMF assistance.[96] Similar agreements to allow the others to join are under negotiation.

Another important step is to create a stable and convertible currency. In April 1992, the G-7 nations (the United States, Canada, Britain, France, Germany, Japan, and Italy) announced that they would support an IMF proposal to provide $24 billion in assistance, primarily to Russia but with a small portion to Ukraine. As part of that package, a $6 billion fund was established to stabilize the ruble and encourage confidence in Russian currency. At the 1992 Munich economic summit, the leaders of the United States, Japan, Germany, France, Italy, Britain, and Canada pledged $1 billion to Russia as a first step in this direction.[97] Following that meeting, however, the IMF declared that the full implementation of the aid package would be delayed until Russia carried out reforms, including cutting its budget deficit and reducing its runaway inflation.[98] The reason for this delay and the goal of this effort were to stabilize the Russian economy first so that the currency would be perceived as reliable when it did become convertible. Russia's leadership faced a dilemma. Cutting the budget and reducing inflation would increase unemployment and the reformers' unpopularity. Such unpopularity could provide opportunities for unrepentant communists or other authoritarian forces to seize power and undermine the reform movement. And, in October 1993, President Yeltsin had to use armed force to crush just such an effort in Moscow.

A third step in building this new economic relationship is to increase aid to and investment in the Eastern European countries and the former U.S.S.R. Germany and the EC have taken major strides toward providing economic assistance and investment for these countries. The United States has made tentative steps in this direction, and the Agency for International Development has encouraged investment, especially in Poland, the Czech Republic, Slovakia, and Hungary. The United States has also offered technical assistance to the U.S.S.R. successor states to help them institute a market economy.

---

[96]Louis Uchitelle, "I.M.F. and Russia Reach Accord on Loan Aid and Spending Limits," *The New York Times*, July 6, 1992, pp. A1, A6.

[97]Stephen Kinzer, "7 Leaders Promise $1 Billion for Russia," *The New York Times*, July 9, 1992, p. A4.

[98]On these developments, see Andrew Rosenthal, "Bush and Kohl Unveil Plan For 7 Nations to Contribute $24 Billion in Aid For Russia," *The New York Times*, April 2, 1992, pp. A1, A6, and Steven Greenhouse, "Ruble Support May Be Delayed to '93," *The New York Times*, July 13, 1992, p. A4.

Conclusion

Traditional theories of power politics often regard economic issues as separate from and less important than political and military issues. One purpose in this chapter has been to demonstrate how this view misses the mark. The economist C. Fred Bergsten understands the relationship between the political and economic spheres when, speaking of the United States, he declares:

> [T]he central task in shaping a new American foreign policy is to set priorities and select central themes. These choices must derive from America's national interests, which have shifted sharply in the direction of economics. . . . With the elimination of the principal threat to world peace, the priorities most countries attach to economic issues will rise substantially.[99]

President Bill Clinton and his Secretary of State, Warren M. Christopher, appear to share this view of global politics and have devoted much attention to issues like opening Japanese and European markets to U.S. exports and getting approval for NAFTA.

A second objective in this chapter has been to illustrate the tight relationship between the domestic and global arenas for many issues. Economic events and decisions within a country directly affect the global economy and vice versa. A third task has been to summarize, albeit briefly, the economic issues that produce conflict among the rich countries and between the wealthy North and the poor South and to review East-West economic relations. Although we approach these issues separately, they are closely linked. A positive response by the rich to the poor will ultimately enhance the economies of the former by creating greater purchasing power in the Third World. It will also reduce the prospect of instability in the Third World and the likelihood of conflict between the First and Third Worlds. And efforts to assist Russia and the other former members of the East bloc to cope with their current economic challenges are critical to future peace and stability.

[99]C. Fred Bergsten, "The Primacy of Economics," *Foreign Policy* No. 87 (Summer 1992), pp. 4, 5.

Key Terms

political economy	fixed exchange rates
liberal economic order	currency convertibility
beggar-thy-neighbor policies	most-favored-nation (MFN) status
Bretton Woods system	Nixon shock
exchange rates	floating exchange rates
balance of payments	expansionist economic policies

non tariff barriers
economic summits
new international economic order
   (NIEO)
Modern World System theory
economic nationalism
economic radicalism
nonaligned movement
transnational corporations (TNCs)
transfer of technology
capital intensive
labor intensive
terms of trade
preferential trade
global debt crisis
debt service ratios
First World
reserve currency
IMF
World Bank (IBRA)
Dillon Round
Kennedy Round
Tokyo Round
Uruguay Round
neomercantilists
tied aid
Andean Group
Lomé Agreements
Cocom
Second World
Third World

Fourth World
repatriation of profits
intellectual property rights
debt cancellation
debt restructuring
debt-equity swaps
debt-commodity swaps
North-South dialogue
collectivization
hyperinflation
Plaza accord
European Monetary System (EMS)
International Finance Corporation
International Development
   Association
General Agreement on Tariffs and
   Trade (GATT)
North
South
quality of life
Charter of Economic Rights and
   Duties of States
nationalization
conditionality
Baker Plan
Brady Plan
central planning
glasnost
perestroika
Council for Mutual Economic
   Assistance (Comecon)

PART THREE

Old and New Issues

Each chapter in Part III fleshes out and illustrates in a substantive manner some of the principles developed in Part II. Chapter 11 ("The Janus Face of Issues—Foreign Policy") illustrates how porous is the boundary between "interstate" and "intrastate" politics and how artificial is the barrier between them. Behavior is usually a result of a merging and blurring of domestic and foreign considerations.

Chapter 12 ("The Changing Security Dilemma: The End of the Cold War") uses several models to examine the changing balance between conflict and cooperation in global politics. Since the Cold War has ended, economic issues will assume center stage in global politics and economically powerful actors will play key roles. As a consequence, Chapter 13 ("Friendly Economic Adversaries: The United States, Japan, and Europe") examines the relations among the economic superpowers.

The end of the Cold War did not end conflict everywhere. Indeed, in some regions it has been accompanied by an upsurge in nationalist and ethnic violence. Nowhere is there such a clear confluence of diverse issues as in the Middle East. Chapter 14 ("The Middle East Cauldron: Terrorism, Nationalism, and Human Rights") concludes Part III by examining a region that is torn by issues of nationalism, war, human rights, and terrorism.

CHAPTER ELEVEN

Issues with a Janus Face — Foreign Policy

Invoking *Janus*, the two-faced Roman god, we suggest that it is necessary to focus simultaneously on events inside and outside the state to understand the sources of foreign policy.[1] Foreign policy results from domestic politics, global politics, and the interaction between them, and we must understand these forces. Each perspective helps us make sense of foreign-policy issues, but only by evaluating these forces *in combination* can we form a comprehensive picture. The challenge is to disentangle the political games simultaneously played among foreign-policy actors — governmental, nongovernmental, and transnational — and uncover both faces of foreign-policy issues.

To assist in this task, we identify and evaluate several ways of explaining foreign policy. Each relies on different *units of analysis* — the state or major decision-makers — to explain it, and each contributes something to our understanding of global politics, albeit in different ways. For a vivid portrait of foreign policy, we conclude by examining the foreign-policy decisions associated with the *Persian Gulf War* of 1991.

What Is Foreign Policy?

But first, we must specify what we mean here by *foreign policy*. At least three related conceptions have been suggested. The phrase denotes behavior that is external or foreign to the state, leading to the first version: "the general tendencies and principles that underlie the conduct of states." But this "national-interest" definition fails to focus on the *actions* or *behavior* that a state may undertake. A second definition further

[1]In Roman tradition, Janus is depicted as looking both to the future and to the past.

describes foreign policy as "the concrete plans and commitments" that leaders devise. But, though this definition anticipates purposive action, it fails to include the behavior itself. A third definition brings in behavior by identifying foreign policy as "the concrete steps that officials of a nation take with respect to events and situations abroad." Foreign policy is now more than an orientation, more than a tendency, and even more than an action program; it is "what individuals representing the state do or do not do in their interactions with individuals, groups, or officials elsewhere in the world."[2]

This last definition is more inclusive, but it too is flawed. It leaves the impression first, that sovereign states and their surrogates are the only actors, and second, it implies that only behavior external to the state is involved. As we have argued, the state is not and has never been the sole actor in global politics. Nongovernmental individuals and groups affect global politics, as do institutions above or beyond the state's control.

Consider Pope John Paul II's condemning destruction of the Amazon rain forests or the rich countries' material excesses. The moral consequences of this behavior probably matter more for global politics than actions by such "sovereign states" as Burkina Faso. Similarly, the European Community's collective decision to achieve greater political and economic union by the beginning of the twenty-first century is at least as influential as individual foreign-policy decisions made by some states in that organization such as Denmark. In short, foreign policy is carried out by a diverse cast of actors, not just by states.

Many definitions of foreign policy are flawed because they rely on foreign or external sources and consequences of behavior. Some apparent "domestic-policy" decisions may have dramatic foreign-policy consequences. Failure to appreciate how "foreign" and "domestic" are often two sides of the same coin and how the two arenas are linked can be costly. For example, the Japanese inspect imported U.S. auto parts themselves rather than rely on stated U.S. compliance, and they refuse to permit rice to be imported from overseas because of pressures from Japanese interest groups; in one sense, these are domestic decisions. Yet, these policies reduce U.S. exports to Japan, increase the U.S.–Japanese trade imbalance, and strain U.S.–Japanese relations.

A somewhat subtler illustration is Saudi Arabia's way of deciding how much oil to pump from its vast reserves. On the one hand, this decision involves domestic economic considerations, but its foreign-policy consequences can be enormous. Increasing Saudi oil production reduces world prices, harming economies in other oil-producing states, including those of some Saudi rivals, and enhances prosperity in industrialized societies, including those of Saudi friends like the United States. The foreign-policy objective may even be more specific. The high level of Saudi oil production in 1991–1992 probably reflected a conscious decision to assist President George Bush's bid for reelection. Following Bill Clinton's election, the Saudis announced they favored reducing production.

---

[2] These distinctions are drawn from James N. Rosenau, "The Study of Foreign Policy," James N. Rosenau, Kenneth W. Thompson, and Gavin Boyd, eds., *World Politics: An Introduction* (New York: Free Press, 1976), p. 16.

The distinction between domestic and foreign policy is blurred not just in economic matters but also for political, military, and environmental issues. For instance, the Israeli decision to expel twelve Palestinian activists from the occupied West Bank and Gaza early in 1992, presumably for internal security, temporarily delayed the separate peace talks between Israel and its neighbors and intensified suspicion between the Bush administration and the Shamir government. An Israeli decision later in that year to expel more than four hundred members of the Islamic fundamentalist Hamas organization further complicated U.S.–Israeli relations. Although this list of examples could be extended, it should already be evident that the dichotomy between the domestic and foreign spheres is artificial.

Foreign Policy and the Realist Tradition

The world has changed and become more complex, but *realist explanations* of foreign-policy behavior remain influential. Recently, however, other foreign-policy theories that try to account for this increased complexity have begun to appear. But first, let us review traditional realist approaches.

States, Billiard Balls, and Global Politics

Although significant differences appear in the power-politics tradition, it is held together by the belief that the global distribution of power determines actors' interests and that foreign policy is the rational power-maximizing response to this distribution. No one cares what goes on *within* the actor; it is *black-boxed*. One scholar says, "we see what comes out but not much of what happens inside."[3] Another metaphor describes power-theorists' model as *billiards*, in which states—all similar entities—are analogous to billiard balls, their behavior unaffected by anything other than competition for power in a zero-sum game.[4] Seen thus, states are the only actors in global politics, and their interactions are the sole source of global politics. Just as one would not explain a game of billiards by referring to anything other than Newtonian principles—action, reaction, balance, and equilibrium—so too theorists in this tradition ignore everything other than the efforts of states to exert influence on one another. Arnold Wolfers provides a classic exposition of the metaphor: "[T]he stage is preempted by a set of states, each in full

[3]Charles W. Kegley, Jr., "Decision Regimes and the Comparative Study of Foreign Policy," in Charles F. Hermann, Charles W. Kegley, Jr., and James N. Rosenau, eds., *New Directions in the Study of Foreign Policy* (Boston: Allen & Unwin, 1987), p. 248. See also Charles A. Powell, James W. Dyson, and Helen Purkitt, "Opening the 'Black Box': Cognitive Processing and Optimal Choice in Foreign Policy Decision Making"; and John A. Vasquez, "Foreign Policy, Learning and War," both in Hermann, Kegley, and Rosenau, eds., *New Directions in the Study of Foreign Policy*, pp. 205, 367–369 respectively.

[4]Stephen D. Krasner, "Regimes and the Limits of Realism: Regimes as Autonomous Variables," *International Organization* 36:2 (Spring 1982), p. 498.

FIGURE 11.1

The Billiard Model

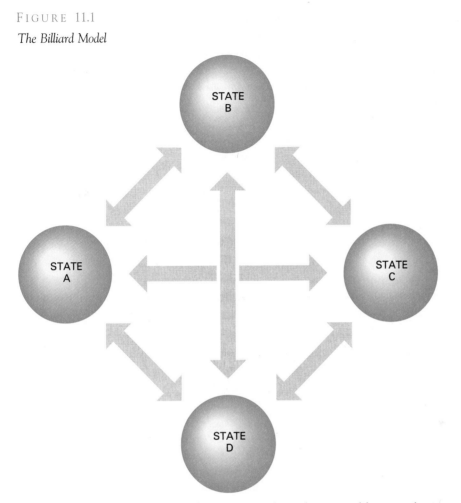

The billiard-ball model of global politics captures the realist view of foreign policy as little more than action–reaction.

control of all territory, men, and resources within its boundaries. Every state represents a closed, impermeable, and sovereign unit, completely separated from all other states."[5]

One state acts toward another (much as one billiard ball hits another), which, in turn, compels the second state (or billiard ball) to respond either by acting in a changed way or by deflecting the action of the first state (much as one billiard ball would do to another). Whether one state will be affected by another's action, in this perspective, depends on their relative geographic and political location in the global system (just as

[5] Arnold Wolfers, *Discord and Collaboration: Essays on International Relations* (Baltimore: Johns Hopkins University Press, 1962), p. 19.

a billiard ball's movement partly depends on its position on the billiard table). As the force and angle with which one billiard ball hits another determine the outcome, so too the amount of power one state brings to bear on another will, realists believe, determine the magnitude and kind of response and outcome.

Realists recognize that the configuration of states (like the arrangement and number of billiard balls on a table) will also affect their foreign-policy behavior. States calculate others' reactions and recognize that their options are constrained by such system-level factors as alliances. If several billiard balls (or states in alliance) are clustered and are struck by another, they may scatter in several directions, or they may all move in the same direction (much as in concerted alliance action). The billiard balls (or states) that were the targets may, in turn, affect others, a consequence that depends partly on the number of balls (states) remaining on the table as well as their location.

The analogy between billiard balls and states breaks down in the similarity or dissimilarity of the units. All billiard balls have the same size and weight, whereas states vary significantly in size and capability. Any differences among billiard balls pale compared with the difference between a superpower like the United States and *microsovereignties* like the Seychelles or Tonga. And, factors such as size probably are crucial in explaining differences in foreign-policy behavior. Small states probably act differently than large states, and developed states differently than developing states.[6]

A more sophisticated version of the power-politics tradition has recently evolved in which "the metaphor of *tectonic plates*" — the folds in the earth's crust whose movement causes earthquakes — better represents the image of foreign policy than does the billiard model. Stephen Krasner writes,

> The second realist tradition envisions a more complicated universe. Here the issue is the impact of the distribution of state power on some external environment. The interaction of states may, for instance, structure the pattern of world trade, the distribution of radio frequencies, the use of outer space, or the rules governing the exploitation of deep seabed nodules. Conflict is not ignored, but the world is not zero-sum.[7]

Despite this greater sophistication, however, most domestic factors are still ignored, and rational behavior is still assumed.

Realism and the Rational-Actor Model

Although metaphors like black box and billiard balls, oversimplify states' actual conduct,[8] they highlight the realist claim that foreign policy is really an *action–reaction*

[6]See James N. Rosenau, "Pre-Theories and Theories of Foreign Policy," in R. Barry Farrell, ed., *Approaches to Comparative and International Politics* (Evanston, Ill.: Northwestern University Press, 1966), pp. 27–92.

[7]Krasner, "Regimes and the Limits of Realism, p. 498.

[8]Simplification is desirable in models such as this as long as they accurately emphasize important attributes of reality and omit unimportant attributes.

or *stimulus–response* exchange between two or more states. What one state does is directly determined by the actions of another state or group of states. The underlying assumption is that a state's internal ways of reaching decisions are mostly the same (and hence irrelevant) in the sense that foreign-policy decisions everywhere are motivated by the desire to maximize the state's national interest. Power theorists regard the pursuit of national interest as determined by the distribution of power as the essence of a rational, value-maximizing process.[9] Thus, a weaker state will not attack a stronger one unless it has enough allies to ensure victory, and weak states will seek allies to protect them from the strong.

Power theorists who ignore the internal attributes of states explain U.S. and Soviet behavior during the Cold War as a function of their being superpowers. Possessing great power presumably explains U.S. intervention in the Dominican Republic (1965), Vietnam (1961–1973), and Grenada (1983) as well as Soviet intervention in Hungary (1956), Czechoslovakia (1968), and Afghanistan (1979). From this perspective, it does not matter that the United States was democratic and capitalist and that the Soviet Union was authoritarian and Marxist. Instead, U.S. and Soviet behavior is assumed to be a rational response to a *national interest* that is shaped by the relative size and capabilities of each.[10] Superpowers have more far-ranging interests than small states and greater capacity to defend those interests. Regional powers — India, China, Brazil, Egypt — may have ambitious regional interests and aspirations, and small powers have limited interest and capacity.

In short, in the realist tradition, foreign policy is not Janus-faced, but single-faced, looking only at actions taken by states toward each other. The essential guides to each state's foreign-policy behavior are other states' actions and the state's relative power in the global system. Neorealists have relaxed some of their predecessors' assumptions, recognizing, for one, the role of international regimes and organizations and the relationship between politics and economics. Nevertheless, they too treat the state as a black box. As scholars recognized how limited realism was, however, they began to look at other units of analysis.

Decision-Making Approaches to Foreign Policy

In 1956, economist Kenneth Boulding hinted at a new approach in arguing the simple but powerful proposition that "behavior *is dependent upon image*."[11] In other words, each

[9] A "rational" process generally assumes agreement on underlying values, perfect information about alternatives, and unfettered capacity to take advantage of that information. All these assumptions are flawed.

[10] The classic treatment of national interest and foreign policy is Hans J. Morgenthau, *Politics Among Nations* (New York: Alfred A. Knopf, 1948). More recent treatments of national interest and its role in foreign affairs can be found in Stephen D. Krasner, *Defending the National Interest: Raw Materials Investments and U.S. Foreign Policy* (Princeton: Princeton University Press, 1978), and Kenneth N. Waltz, *Theory of International Politics* (Reading, Mass.: Addison-Wesley, 1979).

[11] Kenneth E. Boulding, *The Image* (Ann Arbor: University of Michigan Press, 1956), p. 6. Emphasis in original. Also see Harold and Margaret Sprout, "Environmental Factors in the Study of International Politics," in James N. Rosenau, ed., *International Politics and Foreign Policy*, rev. ed.

of us for many reasons perceives the world differently and the action we take depends on our version of reality. Our *image* of the world is not the same as reality; instead, it is subjective knowledge, or what we believe to be true. For example, Americans' way of seeing the U.S.S.R.'s reality, not reality as defined by some objective standard, mainly determined U.S. foreign policy toward the Soviet Union. Thus, most Americans held a negative image of the Soviet Union after the 1917 revolution and during the Cold War, contrasting with the benign image of that country during World War II and again in the 1990s.

Internal Processes and Foreign Policy

At the heart of a second, competing approach to explaining foreign policy is the assumption that *perceptions* are critical. Instead of the billiard-ball metaphor for foreign policy, this approach simply says policy-makers in different states perceive reality differently (they have differing "belief systems"). Hence, the *decision-making approach*, as it came to be called, serves as a counterpoint to realism because it sees foreign policy as built less by interaction among states than by decisions reached within states.[12] This model equates the state with its decision-makers, and foreign policy is a product of *domestic* processes. The goal is to explain how decision-makers view the world and predict how they are likely to act in a specified situation.

Two concepts are at the heart of this approach: *key decision-makers* and *situation*. First, the analyst must identify the primary decision makers in a state and describe their motivations, information, and perceptions.[13] Second, the analyst must define the situation that conditions the decision makers' perceptions of the world. In the original formulation, many factors were identified as shaping this definition for an individual policy maker: the internal setting, the nature of the social structure within the nation, and the external setting.

The *internal setting* and the nature of the *social structure* refer to the domestic political and social environments facing policy-makers. Such factors affect the way in which decision-makers in each state define the same situation. Policy-makers in democratic societies may have different policy options than those in authoritarian societies and, as a result, may define the same situation differently. Leaders in democratic

(New York: Free Press, 1969), pp. 41–56. For the sort of research that this insight inspired, see Herbert C. Kelman, ed., *International Behavior: A Social-Psychological Analysis* (New York: Holt, Rinehart and Winston, 1965).

[12]Richard C. Snyder, H. W. Bruck, and Burton Sapin, "The Decision-Making Approach to the Study of International Politics," in Rosenau, *International Politics and Foreign Policy*, pp. 199–206.

[13]Lloyd Jensen, *Explaining Foreign Policy* (Englewood Cliffs, N.J.: Prentice-Hall, 1982), p. 7.

states generally need to calculate the domestic political costs of a policy more than do leaders of authoritarian states. Similarly, leaders in societies with several major ethnic or religious groups and political parties will define a situation differently than those in a society dominated by one ethnic group or political party. In a country like India, which is divided between Muslims and Hindus, the government has a more difficult time defining the situation in the Middle East than the government of Saudi Arabia, dominated by one religion — Islam — and one ruling family — the House of Saud.

American foreign-policy leaders keep at least one eye on changing domestic conditions. President George Bush, criticized late in 1991 for spending too much time on foreign policy, was forced to postpone a long-scheduled trip to Asia. When he finally made the trip early in 1992, he shifted from bolstering alliances in Asia to opening markets for U.S. exports and creating jobs back home. President Bush thus defined the situation differently and acted differently under pressure from domestic politics and an impending presidential election.

The *external setting* is the global system's influence on decision-makers' perceptions. In the decision-making approach, the external setting's effect is not direct but is filtered through decision-makers' perceptions. External events are relevant only after decision-makers notice and interpret them. When the People's Republic of China sells ballistic missiles to Iran, Argentine leaders may not notice, but Iraqi leaders will, because they fear Iran and know the violent historical relationship of their two countries. Thus, the impact of the global environment on foreign policy is mediated through the perceptual screens of decision-makers.

The distinction among types of "situations" that decision-makers face was subsequently added to the originally formulated definition of the situation. *Crises* that surprise leaders, strongly threaten the states' values, and give decision-makers only a short time for decisions challenge policy-makers more than expected, routine events that unfold slowly and carry low stakes. Situations that share some of these traits will elicit still other decision-making processes, definitions of the situation, and foreign-policy responses.[14]

Individuals and Foreign-Policy Analysis

Foreign-policy observers, facing the many factors that affect the definition of the situation, have devised theories of decision-making that, for simplicity, can be grouped into two general categories. One analyzes decision-makers' cognitive methods and the other their affective processes. The *cognitive approach* involves assessing distortions in perception due "to the difficulties a careful and logical person would have in making

---

[14]For an analysis of different situations and their hypothesized effect on policy, see Charles F. Hermann, "International Crisis as a Situational Variable, " in Rosenau, ed., *International Politics and Foreign Policy*, rev. ed., pp. 409–421.

inferences from an ambiguous environment under trying conditions," and the *affective approach* assesses distortions "due to personal emotions, such as insecurity, hostility, and humiliations."[15] Examples of studies in both traditions illustrate how they have been applied to foreign policy.

Cognitive Processes and Foreign Policy.[16]   Political scientist Ole R. Holsti's study of Secretary of State John Foster Dulles — a principal architect of U.S. foreign policy in the 1950s — shows how cognitive processes are assessed to understand foreign policy.[17] After examining Dulles's writings and statements, Holsti concluded that Dulles had a closed belief system about the Soviet Union. Dulles's personality, background, and negative experiences with the U.S.S.R. predisposed him to view that country in terms of "atheism, totalitarianism, and communism," and little could be done to alter that image. Holsti showed that, seeking *cognitive consistency* between this negative image and Soviet behavior that seemed to contradict it, Dulles so reinterpreted that behavior that the Soviets appeared sinister. When Soviet leaders proposed the Austrian State Treaty in 1955, which would withdraw all foreign forces in that state and establish a neutral regime, Dulles interpreted it, not as a conciliatory act, but as a sign that the Soviet system was weakening. Indeed, whenever he perceived a thaw in the Cold War, Dulles explained it away as a trick or as evidence that the U.S.S.R. was failing. Throughout his secretaryship (1953–1959), Dulles varied little in his general evaluation of the Soviet Union, always seeking the most negative interpretation of events in that country.

The Dulles study tells us two things about the decision-making approach to foreign policy. First, it shows how important individual decision-makers are in shaping foreign policy. Secretary of State Dulles was at the center of U.S. foreign policy, and his image of the Soviet Union was crucial and predicted how the United States would behave toward Moscow. Second, we see that other states' actual behavior may determine policy less than we assume and that factors within states mediate between action and reaction. Despite the ebb and flow of Soviet behavior — from conciliation to hostility — Dulles was unable or unwilling to alter his image of the Soviet Union. Little wonder that U.S. policy toward the U.S.S.R. changed minimally during the Dulles years.

Since Holsti, others have tried to study decision-makers' cognitive processes to account for foreign-policy decisions. Much has been said about how perceptions affect crises in global politics. One influential project sought to determine how much leaders'

---

[15]Robert Mandel, "Psychological Approaches to International Relations," in Margaret G. Hermann, ed., *Political Psychology* (San Francisco: Jossey-Bass, 1986), p. 253.

[16]For a useful collection involving cognitive approaches, see Christer Jonsson, ed., *Cognitive Dynamics and International Politics* (New York: St. Martin's Press, 1982); and Donald A. Sylvan and Steve Chan, eds., *Foreign Policy Decision Making: Perception, Cognition, and Artificial Intelligence* (New York: Praeger, 1984).

[17]Ole R. Holsti, "The Belief System and National Images: A Case Study," *Journal of Conflict Resolution* 6:3 (September 1962), pp. 244–252.

perceptions had to do with starting World War I. The project demonstrated how misperceptions shaped policy responses by both alliance systems. One conclusion was that: "The leaders of the Dual Alliance [Germany and Austria-Hungary] consistently overperceived the level of violence in the actions of the Triple Entente [Great Britain, Russia, and France]. On the other hand, the Triple Entente tended to underperceive the actions of the other coalitions."[18] In a subsequent study of the Cuban missile crisis, which did not lead to war, the same researchers reached a different conclusion about perceptions: "Unlike some of the key decision-makers in the 1914 crisis, those in October 1962 thought in terms of linked interactions — closely tied reciprocations — rather than two sides, each acting independently, *in vacuo.*"[19] That outcomes differ in similar situations shows how powerful images and perceptions are in shaping policy.

Affective Processes and Foreign Policy. The decision-makers' affective character-istics may also distort perceptions. Political psychologist Margaret Hermann has exam-ined various personality characteristics: degree of nationalism, belief in one's ability to control events, need for power, need for affiliation, conceptual complexity, and distrust of others. She also considered their relation to types of foreign-policy behavior: professed orientation to change, independence or interdependence of action, commitment, affect, and environmental feedback.[20] Her findings suggest that leaders who strongly need affiliation are more likely to follow change-oriented policies; those who need power are more likely to follow an independent course in foreign affairs; and those who deeply distrust others are unlikely to make high-level foreign-policy commitments. Hermann also reports that these personal characteristics were more likely in leaders with little foreign-policy training than those with substantial experience. Lyndon Johnson, who had little experience in foreign affairs prior to becoming president, greatly needed power and, this, Hermann suggests, led him doggedly to increase U.S. involvement in Vietnam despite growing doubts among those around him and among U.S. allies.

Lloyd Etheredge did a similar affective analysis for a group of U.S. policy makers between 1898 and 1968.[21] Etheredge focused on two personality traits — *dominance over*

[18]Ole R. Holsti, Robert C. North, and Richard A. Brody, "Perception and Action in the 1914 Crisis," in J. David Singer, ed., *Quantitative International Politics: Insights and Evidence* (New York: Free Press, 1968), p. 154. Also see Dina A. Zinnes, "The Expression and Perception of Hostility in Prewar Crisis: 1914," in ibid., pp. 85–119.

[19]Ole R. Holsti, Robert C. North, and Richard A. Brody, "Measuring Affect and Action in International Reaction Models: Empirical Materials from the 1962 Cuban Crisis," in Rosenau, ed., *International Politics and Foreign Policy,* rev. ed., p. 694. Emphasis in original.

[20]See, for example, Margaret G. Hermann, "Explaining Foreign Policy Behavior Using the Personal Characteristics of Political Leaders," *International Studies Quarterly* 24:1 (March 1980), pp. 7–46. Also see Mandel, "Psychological Approaches to International Relations," p. 256.

[21]See Lloyd S. Etheredge, "Personality Effects on American Foreign Policy, 1898–1968: A Test of Interpersonal Generalization Theory," *American Political Science Review* 72: 2 (June 1978), pp. 434–451. Also see Etheredge, *A World of Men: The Private Sources of American Foreign Policy* (Cambridge: MIT Press, 1978). See also Alexander L. George, "The 'Operational Code': A

subordinates and *extroversion* — of thirty-six U.S. presidents, secretaries of state, and advisers to discover if personality differences predicted variations in their foreign policies. Etheredge found that officials who score high on dominance are more likely to favor force and that those who are extroverts are more likely to pursue cooperative foreign policies.

Evaluating Internal Processes as Foreign-Policy Explanations

Despite the interest generated by the decision-making approach, it has proved less useful than proponents had hoped. First, the approach is almost solely directed at internal conditions. Although the realists attended exclusively to the external environment, the opposite criticism can be made against the decision-making approach, which mainly omits external factors. Second, in some ways this approach is little more than a collection of diverse internal factors that are rarely easy to evaluate. Key decision-makers' perceptions are especially difficult to fathom. Third, the approach is more appropriate to large states with complex bureaucracies and may be more useful in America and Europe than in the Third World, where decision-making structures are smaller and less complex.

Nonetheless, these studies of foreign-policy making, and especially the cognitive and affective efforts, do question two important realist assumptions: the *rationality* of the underlying process and the objectivity of national interest in shaping outcomes. Even if we can demonstrate that two individuals act in the same way in similar conditions, one (or both) may be misperceiving reality and reaching "inappropriate decisions."[22] Or individuals may see reality in different ways and act appropriately, though differently. Either way, the factors that shape individual perception explain policy outcomes better than a rational cost–benefit calculus. As a result, it is difficult to identify an objective national interest because definitions of it are mostly subject to the cognitive and affective factors described above.

Bureaucratic and Organizational Models of Foreign Policy

Early in the 1970s, foreign-policy theorists proposed moving beyond analysis of just a few key decision-makers — as early practitioners of the decision-making approach had done — to focus on the broader decision-making environment in which policy-makers

Neglected Approach to the Study of Political Leaders and Decision-Making," *International Studies Quarterly* 13:2 (June 1969), pp. 190–222.

[22]See Robert Jervis, *Perception and Misperception in International Politics* (Princeton: Princeton University Press, 1976), pp. 28–31 for a two-step perceptual model. The phrase is at p. 29.

operate. They argued that the domestic decision-making environment should be viewed as an agglomeration of bureaucratic and organizational structures that shape the decision-makers' policy choices. Those structures would be crucial for understanding foreign policy.

Two complementary models eventually formed from this reassessment of the decision-making approach: the *bureaucratic politics* and the *organizational process models*.[23] Although both models continued to conceptualize foreign policy as mostly resulting from domestic politics, each emphasizes different aspects of that environment in accounting for behavior. They both abandoned assumptions of a unitary national actor and an objective national interest.

The Bureaucratic-Politics Model

Foreign-policy decisions, according to the bureaucratic-politics model, result from a *bargaining game* among competing domestic "players" (groups). Decisions are reached less by the rational choices made by individual decision-makers than by "the pulling and hauling that is politics" among groups of policy-makers.[24] To understand foreign-policy decisions from this perspective, one must untangle this web of participants, their relative policy positions and influence, and the bargaining that occurred among them prior to a decision. Even though a top decision-maker like the U.S. president may be offered a range of alternatives, his choices will have been narrowed by bureaucratic interests. Those powerful interests will have eliminated some options before the president is asked to make a decision and will have structured those which remain to make some appear more attractive than others.

In this tradition, policy analyst Morton Halperin sought to understand why the Johnson administration decided late in the 1960s to deploy an antiballistic missile (ABM) system against China, when in fact the Chinese had still not achieved ballistic-missile capability. Halperin shows that decision resulted from competition among organizations and individuals with a stake in it. On the side favoring deployment of a full-scale ABM system were powerful bureaucracies—Army, Navy, Air Force—and several prominent individuals, including John S. Foster, Director of Defense Research and Engineering, Senators Richard Russell (chairman of the Senate Armed Services Committee), John Stennis, and Henry Jackson. Opposed to ABM deployment were two Department of Defense offices—Office of Systems Analysis and Office of International

---

[23]The most accessible exposition of these models is found in Graham T. Allison, *Essence of Decision* (Boston: Little, Brown, 1971). Allison labels his bureaucratic-politics model the "governmental politics" model. Nevertheless, the former label is more widely applied to this approach in the literature. For a penetrating critique of Allison, see Jonathan Bendor and Thomas H. Hammond, "Rethinking Allison's Models," *American Political Science Review* 86:2 (June 1992), pp. 301–322.

[24]Allison, *Essence of Decision*, p. 144.

Security Affairs—and several individuals, including Secretary of Defense Robert Mc-Namara. President Johnson was somewhere in the middle.[25] The president cared about the issue mostly because of the intense feelings it produced in other participants with whom he had good relations. Hence, his decision was a compromise—a small ABM deployment (not a large-scale deployment across the country) directed against China (not the Soviet Union). The president's decision was "qualitatively different," and he was "not simply a very powerful player among less powerful players"; but his actions were greatly shaped by the environment in which he made the decision.[26] The decision was not rational as realists define the term, and it was not responsive to any objective idea about the national interest.

Another widely cited study of bureaucratic politics is Graham Allison's analysis of decision-making during the 1962 Cuban missile crisis. Allison declares that the members of the Executive Committee of the U.S. National Security Council "whistled many different tunes" as the decision-making process began over what to do about the Soviet missiles discovered in Cuba in October 1962. By the end, however, a consensus had formed to impose a naval quarantine around Cuba. "The process by which this consensus emerged is a story of the most subtle and intricate probing, pulling, and hauling, leading, guiding, and spurring" among the participants.[27]

The idea that bureaucrats compete with each other to get policies adopted that benefit them contrasts with the idea that bureaucracies function in routine, almost compulsive ways and that foreign policy is the unplanned result of "normal" bureaucratic routines and procedures. We now turn to this model.

The Organizational-Process Model

The organizational-process model also conceptualizes foreign policy as primarily driven by processes internal to the state. Here, unlike to the bureaucratic-politics model, however, policy results less from bargaining among bureaucracies and more from the *standard operating procedures* (SOPs) that large organizations follow. These procedures are policies designed for *classes* of situations and are efficient ways for organizations to deal with complex but similar and repetitive problems. They provide guidance in responding to problems without having to reach a new decision in each case, and they help an organization draw upon expertise from all its divisions. Immigration authorities in all countries require prospective immigrants to fill out standardized forms and answer standard questions, regardless of who the prospective immigrants are and what their

---

[25]Some foreign-policy bureaucracies are actually left out of the decision-making procedure. For the ABM, the Arms Control and Disarmament Agency, State Department, and President's Science Advisory Committee did not have "a major role in the decisions." See Morton H. Halperin, "The Decision to Deploy the ABM: Bureaucratic and Domestic Politics in the Johnson Administration," *World Politics* 25:1 (October 1972), p. 72.

[26]Ibid., p. 91.

[27]Allison, *Essence of Decision*, p. 200.

personal situation is. The steps in immigration are standard operating procedures, and violations of these are "exceptions to the rule."

Such procedures are common in any large organization, and we need to decipher how they operate to understand the organizational-process model. The theoretical source of that model is the work of organizational theorists and such economists as Herbert Simon. Taking exception to the traditional "*comprehensive-rationality*" assumption of economists, Simon argues instead for "*bounded rationality*" in discussing decision-making in organizations.[28] This principle recognizes human limitations that make rationality less likely in decision-making. Instead of considering *all* possible alternatives, evaluating each, and making a decision as required by comprehensive rationality, the decision-maker seeks to "*satisfice*." The decision-maker searches among options and seeks the *first* that supplies minimal satisfaction, even though it may not be the "best" of all possible choices. In making a selection, the decision maker employs *uncertainty avoidance* — focusing on alternatives with assured outcomes rather than trying to estimate the probabilities in different choices — and follows *institutional repertoires* — plans for dealing with types of situations — to reduce time and uncertainty.

These insights into organizational behavior are integrated into the *cybernetic model* of foreign-policy decision making.[29] According to the cybernetic model, bureaucrats try to control uncertainty by relying on a simplified procedure, in which only information relevant to the issue, combined with established responses, is used to guide decisions. Rather than seeking to maximize a value outcome, the decision-maker seeks to preserve existing values. The cybernetic decision maker acts like Simon's "satisficer."[30] The cybernetic model advances the organizational-process model in one important way. Bureaucratic organizations have the capacity to change internally to deal with complex problems. Such problems attract attention from more individuals in the organization, and subgroups are formed to cope with them.[31]

These approaches apply to foreign-policy procedures in many societies. States are often confronted with complex decisions, in situations fraught with uncertainty. For dealing with such complexity, the norm is collective, not individual, decision making. The organizational-process model (and its underlying assumptions about individual behavior) provides ready routines to knit together the collective process and manage complexity and uncertainty. At the same time these routines also provide the basis for an *incremental bias* to the approach. Graham Allison says, "The best explanation of an organization's behavior at t is $t - 1$. The best prediction of an organization's behavior at $t + 1$ is t."[32] In other words, large bureaucratic organizations are conservative and risk-averse and are likely to support policy changes only at the margin. Thus, despite

---

[28] Herbert A. Simon, *Models of Man* (New York: John Wiley, 1957), p. 198.

[29] See John D. Steinbruner, *The Cybernetic Theory of Decision* (Princeton: Princeton University Press, 1974).

[30] Ibid., pp. 66–67.

[31] Ibid., p. 69.

[32] Allison, *Essence of Decision*, p. 88.

promised reductions, President Clinton's proposed 1993 "post–Cold War" defense budget strongly resembled President Bush's last Cold War budget. Even dramatic external disturbances may fail to produce change in organizational routines.

Applying the Models to American Foreign Policy

In the U.S. foreign-policy establishment, a number of *senior interagency groups* (SIGs) and *interagency groups* (IGs) address any foreign-policy issue that may arise. These structures are hierarchic, in that they were created by the president and the National Security Council (NSC) and in turn are responsible to the president and NSC. They also incorporate expertise from the various foreign-policy bureaucracies. At any time, an IG or a SIG may be composed of representatives from the State Department, the Defense Department, the CIA, the Treasury Department, or the National Security Council. Their composition can change as necessary. (If an agricultural-aid issue arises, the Department of Agriculture and the Agency for International Development might have representatives on an IG.) After an IG reviews and develops policy options, it passes its recommendations on to the SIG, where the procedure is repeated. In turn, the SIG's recommendations are forwarded to the National Security Council, and ultimately the president.

Organizational and cybernetic models help make sense of specific cases. Using these approaches, policy analyst Graham Allison was able to explain apparent *anomalies* in the sequence of events for both actors during the Cuban missile crisis. Organizational complexities seem to explain why Soviet surface-to-air missile (SAM) defenses were not operational in Cuba before the medium-range ballistic missiles (MRBMs) were functional and thus why the MRBMs were vulnerable to a potential U.S. air strike. Apparently the Soviet Air Defense Forces were responsible for constructing the SAM sites, but the Soviet Strategic Rocket Forces were responsible for constructing the MRBM sites.[33] The different organizations had different schedules and, in this instance, lacked mechanisms for coordination. Similarly, President Kennedy's public warnings to Soviet leaders not to install offensive missiles in Cuba "were too late; the Soviet decision to deploy had been made months before, and the relevant machinery had been set in gear."[34]

Turning to the United States, organizational routines seem to have dictated decisions connected with imposing the quarantine around Cuba. To give the Soviet Union more time to contemplate its response to U.S. actions, President Kennedy

[33]Ibid., pp. 109–111.

[34]James G. Blight, Joseph S. Nye, Jr., and David A. Welch, "The Cuban Missile Crisis Revisited," *Foreign Affairs* 66:1 (Fall 1987), p. 181. This article gives a taste of the additional information that became available about the missile crisis when the Cold War thawed. See also David A. Welch and James G. Blight, "The Eleventh Hour of the Cuban Missile Crisis: An Introduction to the ExComm Transcripts," *International Security* 12:3 (Winter 1987/88), pp. 5–29.

decided within a day of ordering the blockade to pull it closer to Cuba. Orders went out to the U.S. Navy to make this change and should have been obeyed. Allison's reconstruction of events (including calculation of where the first ship, the *Marucla*, was stopped and boarded) leads him to conclude that the blockade "was *not* moved as the President ordered."[35] Standard operating procedures in the U.S. Navy proved more compelling than the commander-in-chief's directives.

Reservations About the Models

The organizational-process and bureaucratic-politics models have intuitive appeal because they move beyond the model of a unitary rational state with an objective national interest. Multiple actors with multiple and often competing interests shape foreign-policy outcomes either through the "pulling and hauling" of bureaucratic competition or the routines and programs of organizations' structures. Appealing though these approaches are, they too have generated questions and criticisms.

One criticism is whether these models can be applied in other settings. These approaches seem most applicable to developed states with complex bureaucracies and democratic institutions. Are they really useful outside the American context, where they have usually been applied? At least one critic has doubts: "[T]he characteristics that make bureaucratic politics an important feature of foreign policy-making in the United States are not to the same extent or degree in other national systems."[36]

Parliamentary systems in Western Europe, Canada, and Australia have some of the same characteristics as the U.S. political system that might encourage struggles among "players in positions." All face foreign-policy issues that cut across ministries; they have agencies with different responsibilities that try to coordinate policy; and some — Canada and Australia — have a federal political structure like that of the United States. Yet research on Canada suggests that these models do not work well in these settings. The reason is that "in parliamentary systems the concentration of political authority in cabinet allows the political executive to impose constraints on legitimate conflict between policy-makers at lower levels in the decision-making process."[37]

The question about whether these models are generally applicable is even more appropriate for developing and nondemocratic countries. Developing countries can afford only small bureaucracies. Some small countries cannot even afford representation abroad and depend on their U.N. representative in New York or the good offices of larger countries to keep them informed about global developments. In such countries,

[35] Allison, *Essence of Decision*, p. 130. Emphasis in original.

[36] Kim Richard Nossal, "Bureaucratic Politics and the Westminster Model," in Robert O. Matthews, Arthur G. Rubinoff, and Janice Gross Stein, eds., *International Conflict and Conflict Management* (Scarborough, Ont.: Prentice-Hall of Canada, 1984), p. 122.

[37] Ibid., p. 125.

bureaucratic competition and organizational routines can hardly explain policy. In nondemocratic societies the problem is different. The views of dominant individuals or elites are likely to shape foreign policy, and the bureaucracy is left to implement the leadership's wishes.[38]

These models have been criticized even in the American context. One critic argues that presidential preferences and domestic politics are more pivotal than bureaucratic politics, especially in such major decisions as using military force. Only in decisions affecting "institutionally grounded issues," which usually are not critical, does bureaucratic politics explain the outcome.[39] It is also argued that, despite claims by organizational and bureaucratic theorists, it is unlikely that a U.S. president can be captured by Washington's bureaucracies.[40] After all, a president is accountable to the electorate for his actions and is likely to ensure that foreign policy reflects his wishes. As a result, the president is likely to select foreign-policy advisers who are dedicated to his interests, and to use agencies only if he believes they will operate in a way compatible with those interests. Finally, despite bureaucratic-politics theorists who assume that *role* determines outlook, bureaucrats can adopt positions divorced from the role they occupy. They are influenced by general "culture and values" in arriving at their views on an issue, and are susceptible to presidential influence. These considerations lead some critics to argue that foreign policy is more likely to be explained by top decision-makers' values than by the parochial values of lower-level bureaucrats:

> Neither organizational necessity nor bureaucratic interests are the fundamental determinants of policy. The limits imposed by standard operating procedures as well as the direction of policy are a function of the values of decision-makers. . . . The failure of the American government to take decisive action in a number of critical areas reflects not so much the inertia of a large bureaucratic machine as a confusion over values which afflicts the society in general and its leaders in particular.[41]

Foreign Policy and Complex Interdependence

The realist and decision-making approaches fail to identify all the *units of analysis* that can help us understand foreign policy. Both rely on the state as the unit of analysis. Neither the effect of international institutions or regimes nor the influence

[38]There are exceptions. Allison was able to use his models to explain Soviet actions in the Cuban case. Another scholar who has used this approach effectively to explain Soviet policy is Jiri Valenti. See "The Bureaucratic Politics Paradigm and the Soviet Invasion of Czechoslovakia," *Political Science Quarterly* 94, 1 (Spring 1979), pp. 55–76.

[39]Robert J. Art, "Bureaucratic Politics and American Foreign Policy: A Critique," *Policy Sciences* 4 (1973), pp. 467–490.

[40]Stephen D. Krasner, "Are Bureaucracies Important? (Or Allison Wonderland)," *Foreign Policy* No. 7 (Summer 1972), pp. 159–179.

[41]Ibid., pp. 169, 179.

of *subnational actors* is adequately captured by these approaches. Yet these other units of analysis are critical in explaining foreign policy today. Including these additional actors in foreign-policy analysis is partly justified by the "complex-interdependence" critique of realism offered in the mid-1970s.[42] Global politics stems from many sources and not just one—the realist state. Many actors, or "multiple channels," flow among societies beyond governments' formal relations. Although government-to-government behavior is important, the contacts between government and nongovernment elites and masses and among nongovernmental groups also shape global politics. Actors such as corporations, revolutionary movements, intergovernmental and nongovernmental organizations, and prominent individuals can also shape foreign affairs.

Adherents of complex interdependence offer still more reasons for enlarging the galaxy of actors to understand contemporary foreign policy. First, global politics is not confined to issues of military power. The global agenda has expanded to take in economic and social issues as well. Second, leaders have more ways of influencing each other today than even a few decades ago. Force and violence, so much a staple for the foreign-policy realist, just begin the list of instruments available to actors today. Third, because capabilities are not easily converted from one use to another, different issues have different casts of actors who enjoy varying degrees and types of influence in each issue.[43]

The *complex-interdependence model* perspective forces us to move beyond the state and the unitary actor model, just as the bureaucratic-politics and organizational-process models did. But it does more. It also forces us to look to actors outside the state's government apparatus that may help explain foreign-policy outputs. The number of these actors is growing and their importance has yet to be fully assessed. Let us briefly sum up some of their roles.

The Global System and Foreign Policy

One kind of actor to consider in analyzing the sources of foreign policy are international and regional organizations such as the United Nations and the European Community. Interstate actors have been around for centuries but were usually assumed to be subservient to states, neglecting their role as independent actors. Now, however, we finda more nuanced view of international organizations, identifying at least three

---

[42]Robert O. Keohane and Joseph S. Nye, *Power and Interdependence,* 2nd ed. (Glenview, Ill.: Scott, Foresman, 1989). Also see Richard W. Mansbach, Yale H. Ferguson, and Donald E. Lampert, *The Web of World Politics* (Englewood Cliffs, N.J.: Prentice-Hall, 1976).

[43]Keohane and Nye, *Power and Independence,* pp. 29–37, and Joseph S. Nye, Jr., *Bound to Lead: The Changing Nature of American Power* (New York: Basic Books, 1990), pp. 174–201.

foreign-policy roles: (1) as instruments of foreign policy by states or groups, (2) as intermediaries in global politics that can modify actions by states or groups, and (3) as autonomous global actors.[44]

States commonly use international organizations as *instruments* of national policy. The United States and its allies used the United Nations to legitimize their reversal of Saddam Hussein's seizure of Kuwait. A few studies have explained how states use international organizations for their own ends, but our knowledge is confined to such applications as using the United Nations.[45] Foreign-policy analysts need to study closely how extensively states actually rely on international institutions as they seek foreign-policy options and how they achieve their goals.

International organizations also serve as intermediaries between actors and may modify foreign-policy actions undertaken by states or groups. Institutions like the United Nations and European Community certainly do both restrain and facilitate some members' foreign-policy behavior. After the Persian Gulf conflict, Iraq had to agree to international inspection of its nuclear facilities and limit its foreign-policy activities as conditions for ending hostilities. After the Warsaw Pact collapsed, the European Community (EC) became crucial for shaping relations between Western Europe and the newly democratic states in Central Europe. In this way, international institutions may change their roles. Thus, the Conference on Security and Cooperation in Europe is composed of almost fifty states in Europe plus the United States and Canada. In November 1990 it added a function designed to increase confidence among members: maintaining peace in Central Europe. But steadily escalating civil strife in the Balkans suggests that the CSCE may be poorly suited to its new task.

International organizations are vital intermediaries for small states. Many African states cannot afford to maintain diplomatic missions except at the United Nations. With that as their forum, however, they can bring issues to the attention of the world community and try to shape policy at that highest level. These states have been able to use the U.N. forum to focus world attention on such issues as racial discrimination in Rhodesia and South Africa and independence for Namibia, Angola, and Mozambique. Regionally, the Organization of African Unity (OAU) serves a similar function for these states. These fifty or more states together can adopt a unified (or nearly so) position on issues and wield more influence than their individual size might predict.

International economic institutions also serve as foreign-policy intermediaries. The International Monetary Fund and the World Bank often provide aid to developing

---

[44]For more on these three roles, see James M. McCormick, "Alternate Approaches to Evaluating International Organizations: Some Research Directions," *Polity* 14:3 (Spring 1982), p. 532; and Charles Pentland, "International Organizations," in James N. Rosenau, Kenneth W. Thompson, and Gavin Boyd, eds., *World Politics: An Introduction* (New York: Free Press, 1976), pp. 621–659.

[45]See, for example, John G. Stoessinger, *The United Nations and the Superpowers: China, Russia, and America* 4th ed. (New York: Random House, 1977), and Alexander Dallin, *The Soviet Union at the United Nations: An Inquiry into Soviet Motives and Objectives* (New York: Praeger, 1962).

countries only on the condition that they adopt specified economic and political reforms. The states may have to reduce imports, devalue currency, or undertake other economic reforms such as reducing the number of state-run industries. But in return, poor states have relied on economic organizations to influence the wealthy states' policies. In the 1960s, when many developing states were dissatisfied with global trading arrangements set by the General Agreement on Tariffs and Trade (GATT), they pressured the United Nations to establish a Conference on Trade and Development (UNCTAD) as an institutional counterweight to GATT. In time, UNCTAD sought to reduce barriers to trade between developed and developing states, and earned the title of "a trade union of the poor against the rich."[46] The appeal of such an organization is that it gives weak states, acting in combination, the chance to place pressure on powerful states.

In other ways too, poor states get help from international organizations. Several African countries — Ethiopia, the Sudan, Somalia, and Mozambique — rely on specialized U.N.-affiliated agencies and organs for necessities like food. The Food and Agriculture Organization (FAO) and the World Food Council provide such assistance, as do private voluntary organizations including CARE and Catholic Relief Services.

As intermediaries, international organizations can become intrusive. For example, between 1969 and 1972, World Bank and International Monetary Fund officials subjected the Ghanaian government to so many requirements as conditions for continued economic help that the government in Accra found itself without domestic political support and in short order was overthrown.[47] International organizations not only directed the state's foreign-policy behavior but undermined its internal stability as well.

Finally, as we observed in Chapter 5, international organizations behave as *autonomous actors*. International regimes have been established in wide-ranging functions, from telecommunications and mail service to nuclear proliferation and trade.[48] Such regimes create rules, norms, and expectations, transferring policy making from states to regime. Such units of analysis are just now getting attention in global politics.

Subnational Actors and Foreign Policy

To explain foreign-policy behavior, students of complex interdependence also point to subnational actors. Among these are private individuals, organized interest groups (business, labor, and agriculture) political parties, terrorists and liberation groups, and

[46]Robert L. Rothstein, *The Weak in the World of the Strong: The Developing Countries in the International System* (New York: Columbia University Press, 1977), p. 145.

[47]Ronald T. Libby, "External Co-Optation of a Less Developed Country's Policy Making: The Case of Ghana, 1969–1972," *World Politics* 29:1 (October 1976), pp. 67–89.

[48]For a recent survey of regime theory in international politics, see Stephen Haggard and Beth A. Simmons, "Theories of International Regimes," *International Organization* 41: 3 (Summer 1987), pp. 491–517.

nongovernmental organizations. Such groups may affect foreign policy in two ways: they may indirectly influence foreign policy by lobbying their governments or interacting directly with foreign actors. The subnational group has interests beyond its frontiers primarily because many issues can no longer be isolated within the state's boundaries. Most major issues — global warming, AIDS, nuclear proliferation, international trade — defy state boundaries and attract multinational responses. Domestic actors recognize that such issues affect their interests and organize themselves more and more to manipulate them.

When American labor unions or the Big Three automakers put on the pressure to protect jobs and markets in the United States, they affect the global economy, not only in Japan but in countries like Korea and Mexico that have a stake in the U.S. market. And when General Motors decides to lay off workers or downsize or restructure its operations in the United States, its choices too touch individuals at home and governments and individuals abroad. Scientific research in one country often stimulates interest in other countries, as in 1988, when the French pharmaceutical company Roussel-UCLAF (a subsidiary of a German corporation) began to market an "abortion pill" (RU-486) in France. In the United States, those on both sides of the abortion issue were activated. Abortion opponents successfully lobbied the U.S. government to deny access, and the company, fearing it would be boycotted, did not seek to market the pill in the United States.[49] Such examples illustrate how issues may involve individuals, corporations, governments, and subnational groups across national borders.

Former U.S. Trade Representative and Ambassador to Russia, Robert Strauss, in describing negotiations during the GATT Tokyo Round in the 1970s, described the dual character of these subnational groups. Struck by the many domestic interest groups active on trade issues and the complications they caused in negotiations, Strauss quickly discovered that his negotiating role was really doubled: "I spend as much time negotiating with domestic constituents (both industry and labor) and members of the U.S. Congress as I did negotiating with our foreign trading partners."[50]

Other subnational actors may influence global politics even more dramatically and publicly than unions and corporations do. Two fundamentalist Islamic groups — Hizbal-lah (the Party of God) and Islamic Jihad (Holy war) — were leaders in seizing and holding Western hostages in Lebanon during the 1980s and early 1990s. States outside the Middle East seemed timid and states in the region apparently could do little about these

[49]After the 1992 election, President Clinton called for a review of this government ban, partly in response to subnational groups on the other side of this issue, and shortly thereafter the United States permitted women to bring the drug with them from abroad while the Food and Drug Administration conducted tests to ensure its safety.

[50]Cited in Robert D. Putnam, "Diplomacy and Domestic Politics: The Logic of Two-Level Games," *International Organization* 42:3 (Summer 1988), p. 433. See also Putnam, "Two-Level Games: The Impact of Domestic Politics on Transatlantic Bargaining" in Helga Haftendorn and Christian Tuschhoff, eds., *America and Europe in an Era of Change* (Boulder: Westview, 1993), pp. 69–83.

groups, suggesting how influential such actors can be. For almost a decade, no one could tell who had influence over whom. Did these groups act against the states' wishes, or were they really following orders from Iran and Syria?[51]

Competing Explanatory Units and Foreign-Policy Analysis

The approaches we have covered illustrate how many units of analysis contribute to understanding and explaining foreign policy. We have identified at least three: the state, bureaucratic organizations, and transnational processes, each model moving us further from assuming that foreign policy was produced by unitary rational actors. Each also added complexity to foreign-policy analysis.

Which are the appropriate units of analysis for understanding foreign policy? The question merits two responses. One is that the best unit depends on the questions you want to ask. For transnational issues such as environmental pollution, complex interdependence provides the richest picture. But if you seek a complete picture of foreign-policy sources, each unit of analysis has something to contribute.

Foreign-Policy Analysis and the Persian Gulf War

We conclude by examining how these approaches may be combined to help enrich our understanding of an important case: the allied forces' action against Iraq in the Persian Gulf War. Each unit of analysis helps us to fit together another piece of the global puzzle and further polish our view of foreign policy.

The Realist Perspective

For the realist, the Persian Gulf War might be explained by the challenge that Iraq's seizure of Kuwait posed to the system of state actors and the security of leading members in that system. For the realist, no challenge to the global system's stability must go unanswered. Iraq's actions threatened the principles of sovereignty and national interest for states both in the region and elsewhere and threatened Western interest in keeping unimpeded the oil flowing from the region. Although Kuwait and Saudi Arabia seemed the immediate victims of Iraqi aggression, it was feared that Iraqi domination of the Persian Gulf would give it immense oil leverage over other countries. The allies sought

[51]On the bargaining over the U.S. hostages late in 1991, see Elaine Sciolino, "Tea in Teheran: How Hostage Deal Was Born," *The New York Times*, December 6, 1991, pp. A1, A6.

to protect their oil supply and their economic prosperity. For realists, states must be willing to act to protect their national interests. If states were permitted to augment their power without opposition, the system as a whole would be unbalanced and other states placed in peril.

From Iraq's vantage, Kuwait's actions caused its invasion. Iraqis felt Kuwait had violated Iraq's territorial integrity by claiming border areas rich in oil and had engaged in "slant drilling" to tap into Iraq's oil reserve. Kuwait did not seize Iraqi territory, but its actions had the same effect. Iraq also had an historical claim to Kuwait whose borders had been determined by British colonial authorities.[52] Beyond these territorial quarrels, Iraq sought to defend its economic interests. Baghdad was vexed by Kuwait's refusal to cancel debts incurred in Iraq's eight-year war against Iran, in which the Iraqis felt they were protecting the "Arab nation" against "Persian aggression." Baghdad also sought to force an increase in global oil prices, which the Iraqis believed were being kept artificially low by Kuwaiti and Saudi overproduction. From a realist perspective, then, Iraq was defending its economic interests. Negotiations between the two countries failed, and Iraq felt compelled to force a resolution to these festering questions and, when it saw an excuse, did so.

The Decision-Making Perspective

Another explanation is possible for Iraq's decision to invade Kuwait and for the U.S. response to it. The conflict could have been caused by differing perceptions held by Presidents George Bush and Saddam Hussein and their advisers. Their perceptions about the Middle East situation and the events that led up to the conflict were so different that their decisions sent them headlong toward collision. Focusing on perceptions is an instructive way to understand how conflicts evolve.

We can summarize President Bush's foreign-policy values and beliefs as pragmatic and prudent, labels that, not coincidentally, are closely associated with political realism, an approach that informed the president's view of the world. His administration was generally cautious in foreign policy, carefully watching changes in power and threats to the global status quo. Within days of the invasion, however, President Bush's "definition of the situation" compelled him to undertake a decisive response. He saw Kuwait as a close ally and was sensitive to growing Saudi fears that it might be the next victim. First, Bush believed that Saddam Hussein had deceived him: "This aggression came just hours after Saddam Hussein specifically assured numerous countries in the area that there would be no invasion. . . . Only 14 days ago, Saddam Hussein promised his friends he would not invade Kuwait. And 4 days ago, he promised the world he would withdraw. And twice we have seen what his promises mean. His promises mean nothing." Second, Bush, recalling his own experience in World War II and the bitter fruit of Western

[52]Three decades earlier, Iraqi claims to Kuwait had been rebuffed by a British military presence in Kuwait.

appeasement of Hitler (to whom he compared Saddam), concluded that aggression must be answered. "There is no justification whatsoever," he declared, "for this outrageous and brutal act of aggression." Third, for the president, more than Kuwait was at stake: "This is not an American problem or a European problem or a Middle East problem."[53] It was, he believed, a problem for the global community. These perceptions led the president to order an embargo on U.S. trade with Iraq, freeze Iraqi assets in the United States, and deploy a U.S. military force to Saudi Arabia to protect that country from Iraqi aggression.

Saddam Hussein's definition of the situation was crucial in Iraq's decision to intervene in Kuwait. He believed the United States would not react; indeed, he saw the United States as indifferent to his dispute with Kuwait over territorial boundaries and oil prices. This perception was encouraged by American actions throughout the 1980s and immediately before the crisis in August 1990. After 1984, when U.S.–Iraqi ties were restored after being broken during the Six-Day War in June 1967, the United States sought to improve relations with Iraq. During the Iran–Iraq War (1981–1988), Washington tilted toward Iraq and shared with Baghdad intelligence about Iran. Even when Iraqi jets, perhaps by error, attacked the USS Stark in May 1987 in the Persian Gulf, killing thirty-seven American sailors, the Reagan administration was willing to accept the explanation that the episode was a mistake. Further, although the Reagan administration chided Iraq over its use of chemical weapons against Kurdish villages, it did little more. Indeed, both the Reagan and Bush administrations worked vigorously to forestall congressional economic sanctions against Iraq from 1988 through summer 1990 by removing Iraq from the list of states that supported international terrorism.[54]

Saddam Hussein's perception of the United States was no doubt reinforced by reassurances of American friendship offered by the U.S. ambassador to Iraq, April Glaspie. About a week before the invasion, Ambassador Glaspie told Saddam Hussein, "I have direct instructions from President Bush to seek better relations with Iraq," and observed that the United States had "no opinion on the Arab–Arab conflict, like your border disagreement with Kuwait."[55] In congressional testimony only days before the invasion, U.S. officials failed to issue a warning to Saddam.[56] Saddam Hussein undoubtedly held President Bush personally responsible for Iraq's subsequent expulsion from Kuwait. In revenge, he apparently organized an unsuccessful assassination attempt against Bush when the former president visited Kuwait early in 1993.[57]

[53]The quoted passages are from President Bush's speech to the nation, "The Arabian Peninsula: U.S. Principles," delivered August 8, 1990.

[54]Throughout the period Baghdad continued to host and assist some of the world's most notorious terrorists.

[55]The first quoted passage is cited in Tom Matthews, "The Road to War," Newsweek, January 28, 1991, p. 56. The second is from Elaine Sciolino with Michael R. Gordon, "U.S. Gave Iraq Little Reason Not to Mount Assault," The New York Times, September 23, 1990, p. 1.

[56]Matthews, "Road to War," pp. 54–65.

[57]In retaliation, President Clinton ordered a cruise-missile attack against Iraqi intelligence headquarters in central Baghdad.

With the end of the Cold War, U.S. foreign policy responded to new challenges, including the civil strife and famine that engulfed the East African country of Somalia. Photos such as this persuaded the American public that something must be done, and the United Nations authorized the landing of U.S. forces in Somalia to enable humanitarian relief to reach starving Somalis.

Organizational and Bureaucratic Perspectives

Theories on organizational and bureaucratic politics are especially helpful in explaining allied and Iraqi actions as the Gulf crisis deepened between August 1990 and mid-January 1991. As the allies sought to strengthen their forces in the Persian Gulf and deter further Iraqi aggression against Saudi Arabia, standard operating procedures were followed to determine the mix of naval, air-force, and army units dispatched to the area. One difficulty General Norman Schwarzkopf, allied commander in the Gulf, faced was that initially he had insufficient forces to deter Saddam. As the crisis began, Schwarzkopf estimated that it would take seventeen weeks to build up an effective deterrent force.[58]

[58]Bob Woodward, *The Commanders* (New York: Simon & Schuster, 1991), p. 252.

Thus, at first the allies were really trying to deceive the Iraqis about the allied armies' strength to make deterrence credible.

Coordination and bureaucratic bargaining among the allies became a more important requisite for action. Crucial bargains had to be consummated among Europeans, Japan, and the United States on funding the military effort. The United States wanted Europeans and Japanese to foot more of the bill, and it wanted the Europeans to provide more forces. As it turned out, Japan provided about $11 billion and Germany about $6.5 billion to support the operation, and the Europeans (principally British and French) provided large military contingents.[59]

We can glean more about the Persian Gulf events by applying the bureaucratic-politics approach to the U.S. decision on using force against Iraq. The U.S. Congress and the American public supported President Bush's decision to impose an economic embargo and send forces to the Persian Gulf, but agreement was less solid on actual use of force. The Bush administration sought an adequate rationale for initiating the use of force and trumpeted Saddam's development of weapons of mass destruction and allegations about Iraqi atrocities in Kuwait to set the stage for offensive operations. As the president took steps to double American forces in Saudi Arabia early in November 1990 to give the allies an "offensive capability," the Congress felt its constitutional prerogative to declare war was being infringed. Some members of Congress wanted to vote on the question promptly; others wanted to wait until the new Congress was seated in January 1991 and until the president made a formal request. Still others believed the president had the authority to go forward if he wished.[60]

Thus, pulling and hauling started between the two branches, and the characteristics of the bureaucratic-politics model were unmistakable. Congressional foreign-affairs and armed-services committees launched public hearings to assess the wisdom of continuing economic sanctions or authorizing the use of force against Iraq. The president argued that he did not need congressional authorization and that he had power as chief executive to use force if necessary. And the public tended to side with the Congress, as reflected in public-opinion polls late in autumn, 1990. Fifty-four members of Congress even filed a legal challenge to the president in a U.S. district court. The case was dismissed, pending a decision by the Congress itself. By January 8, 1991, however, President Bush had changed his mind and requested authorization from the Congress to carry out U.N. Resolution 678 to use force to end Iraq's occupation of Kuwait.[61] After three days of agonizing debate in both chambers, the Congress approved the president's request, but only by a narrow margin (250–183 in the House and 52–47 in the Senate). The fate of American policy in the Middle East was bound up in bargaining and debate between the two branches of government. To this extent, the bureaucratic-politics model provides a useful guide to events.

[59]Others making major financial commitments to the war effort were Saudi Arabia, Kuwait, the United Arab Emirates, and South Korea. Statement of Charles A. Bowsher, Comptroller General of the United States, before the Committee on Budget, U.S. House of Representatives, February 27, 1991 (Washington, D.C.: U.S. General Accounting Office, n.d.), p. 12.

[60]Adam Clymer, "Congress in Step," *The New York Times*, January 14, 1991, p. A11.

[61]Ibid.

The Complex-Interdependence Perspective

The complex-interdependence perspective on the Gulf War focuses on the global system, a broader range of actors, and the links among them to explain what transpired. From the beginning of Iraq's occupation of Kuwait, the U.N. was involved in the decision. Within hours of Iraq's invasion, the U.N. Security Council passed a resolution condemning the act and calling for swift Iraqi withdrawal. Through eleven other resolutions from August through November 1990, the Security Council imposed air, sea, and land sanctions against Iraq to compel it to leave Kuwait. The last of these resolutions, passed November 29, 1990, took the final step under the U.N. Charter of authorizing member states "to use all necessary means to uphold and implement" the previous resolutions.[62] The only reservation was that Iraq be given until January 15, 1991, to leave Kuwait before force was used.

These resolutions enjoyed broad support, and no more than two states voted against any of the twelve resolutions the Council passed. Hence, they signified consensus in the global community about Iraq's actions. It might be argued that these resolutions served only as instruments for implementing the policy desired by one country — the United States — but the resolutions also served as an intermediary role in many states' foreign-policy calculations. Some states were undoubtedly more likely to accept and contribute using force against Saddam because the global community voiced approval in the U.N. Security Council's actions. This approval was absolutely essential to obtain compliance from such Arab states as Syria.

Conclusion

In this chapter, we have exposed the Janus face of the foreign-policy process. We have looked at the traditional realist and decision-making approaches, in which the state or primary decision-makers are considered vital to foreign-policy analysis. These traditions roughly outline the Janus face of foreign policy by providing competing explanations that focus respectively on interactions among unitary states and on perceptions and interests of decision-makers within states. Each adds to the mosaic that explains foreign policy in contemporary global politics. Each omits important factors, however.

To fill in these gaps and to provide richer context for the making of foreign policy, we add the organizational-process, bureaucratic-politics, and complex-interdependence models of foreign policy. The first two models enable the analyst to appreciate the richness and complexity of decision-making within a state. These approaches also move us away from the unitary rational-state actor. Instead, they suggest a method that is more competitive (the bureaucratic-politics model) or much more cybernetic and routine (the organizational-process model) than realism admits. Complex interdependence prompts

---

[62]UN Security Council Resolution 678 (1990), reprinted in Marjorie Ann Browne, "Iraq–Kuwait: U.N. Security Council Resolutions — Texts and Votes," Washington, D.C.: Congressional Research Service, the Library of Congress, December 4, 1990.

us to look at actors other than the state to make sense of foreign policy. Both international organizations and subnational actors have interests that transcend state frontiers and the capacity to act autonomously. As we move from one unit of analysis to the next, we get closer to a complete picture of the sources of foreign-policy behavior.

To illustrate how these several perspectives can be applied to enrich our understanding of foreign policy, we examined the Persian Gulf War. Each perspective depicts somewhat differently the events that led up to the war because each points to different factors as critical. By combining those several perspectives, we come to comprehend the Janus face of foreign policy.

In the subsequent chapters in Part II, we apply these perspectives to deepen our understanding of other global issues, past and present. In Chapter 12, we summarize and explain the rise and demise of the Cold War between the Soviet Union and the United States, mostly applying realist and decision-making lenses. We analyze in Chapter 13 how international economic relations evolved among the United States, Japan, and Europe, from the vantage of the global system, the states involved, and subnational actors with interests in the issues. Finally, in Chapter 14, we approach the bloody issues in the Middle East, again applying various theoretical lenses to evaluate the complex issues and divisions peculiar to that region.

Key Terms

Janus face of foreign policy	crisis
units of analysis	dominance over subordinates
foreign policy	extroversion
national interest	rationality
black boxing	bureaucratic-politics model
billiard ball model	organizational process model
microsovereignties	standard operating procedures (SOPs)
tectonic-plates model	bounded rationality
action-reaction model	satisficing
image	uncertainty avoidance
decision-making approach	institutional repertoires
decision-makers	cybernetic model
definition of the situation	anomalies
internal setting	role
external setting	complex-interdependence model
perceptions	subnational actors
Persian Gulf War	cognitive consistency
realist explanations	bargaining game
stimulus-response	comprehensive rationality
social structure	incremental bias
units of analysis	senior interagency group (SIG)
cognitive approach	interagency group (IG)
affective approach	

CHAPTER TWELVE

The Changing Security Dilemma:
Exit Cold War

With the unification of Germany, the collapse of communism in Eastern Europe, and the dissolution of the multinational Soviet Union between late 1989 and the end of 1991, the *Cold War* was finished.[1] The central security dilemmas that filled the preceding forty-five years—communism and capitalism in conflict, Germany's fate debated, and central European security in question—had been addressed. Although the conflict had been waning in previous years, its abrupt end still shook global political foundations. The Cold War injected rigidity and tension into global politics, but for many actors it also produced regularity and predictability. Suddenly, by 1990, the old rules and standards no longer worked. What could political actors use as the benchmark against which to judge their actions? Had we reached the "*end of history*," from which democratic liberalism would triumph around the world?[2]

New issues would arise to shape foreign policy, but what those issues would be was far from clear. Would a dominant issue like the Cold War again arise to dominate global affairs, or would many discrete issues pull global politics in different directions? Would new actors arise as well? We offer some tentative answers to these questions in subsequent chapters, but first we examine the rise and demise of the Cold War, with special attention to its Janus-faced character.

[1]During the U.S.-Soviet détente early in the 1970s, the Cold War had prematurely been declared over, only to flare again late in the 1970s and early in the 1980s.

[2]Francis Fukuyama, "The End of History?" *National Interest* (Summer 1989), pp. 3–18.

The Issue Cycle and the Cold War

As we saw in Chapter 4, issues like the Cold War assume an identifiable process as they move on and off the agenda.[3] An issue passes through stages, entering the global agenda either from changes in the global environment or from changes in specific actors' behavior. Environmental catastrophe—reports of a growing hole in the ozone layer above the North Pole in February 1992—helped place global ecology on the agenda. Similarly, governments' violation of human rights—the crushing of democracy demonstrators in Tiananmen Square by Chinese authorities in June 1989—brought that issue back to the world community's attention.

Once an issue reaches the *global agenda*, it is still not sure to be recognized by the global community. It must move from the public agenda, where someone voices interest in it, to the policy-makers' agendas, where those who allocate resources can do something about it.[4] This process makes an issue "salient" for those in the leadership who have the authority and capacity to publicize and deal with it. Although *salience* is difficult to measure, any issue which raises costs to important actors, which is perceived as likely to affect their fate significantly, and which has widespread consequences will attain prominence on the global agenda. The attention of leaders is finite, so that relatively few issues can be on their formal agenda at any moment, and others compete for their attention. Thereafter, an issue passes through the four possible stages in the *issue cycle: genesis,* the birth of an issue; *crisis,* that is, moment(s) of danger in which adversaries seek to determine the rules of the game; *ritualization*, during which routine patterns of behavior and rules evolve among actors to address and manage the issue; and *resolution,* when final agreement is reached or the issue loses the attention of key actors.

The issue cycle is a useful framework for describing how the Cold War evolved. The conflict began in Europe as an ideological and strategic struggle between the United States and the Soviet Union shortly after World War II, became routine in the 1950s and 1960s as both sides learned the rules of the game in recurrent crises, and was finally resolved by developments between 1985 and 1991. In the following pages we focus on the Cold War issue cycle, emphasizing its genesis and resolution. At its peak, the Cold War dominated the global agenda by incorporating most other issues.

Stage 1: Genesis of the Cold War

For more than four decades the Cold War overshadowed profound changes in global politics. The number of states more than doubled and the number of intergovernmental

[3]See Richard W. Mansbach and John A. Vasquez, *In Search of Theory: A New Paradigm for Global Politics* (New York: Columbia University Press, 1981), pp. 87–142.

[4]The distinction between public and formal agenda is drawn from Roger W. Cobb and Charles D. Elder, *Participation in American Politics: The Dynamics of Agenda Building* (Boston: Allyn & Bacon, 1972), pp. 103–109.

and nongovernmental actors more than tripled. Military destructiveness increased geometrically for many states, but especially for the superpowers, and in economic capability all states grew impressively, but especially the United States, Japan, and the European Community. All the while, environmental and demographic problems quietly magnified, receiving little public attention except from a few experts.

The Soviet Union, the United States, and Postwar Europe

The Cold War dates back to the *Bolshevik* seizure of power in the Soviet Union in 1917. The young Soviet state was wary of Western intentions, especially after Western intervention in North Russia and Siberia in summer 1918. United States President Woodrow Wilson sought to justify intervention as part of an effort to keep the Russians fighting the Germans in World War I, but Western actions fed deeply a profound dislike for *communism*. The historian John Lewis Gaddis writes, "The fact is that a fundamental loathing for Bolshevism influenced all of Wilson's actions with regard to Russia and the actions of his Allied counterparts." This antipathy, Gaddis says, was mutual, for "the Bolsheviks made no secret of their fundamental loathing for the West."[5]

The enforced alliance between the U.S.S.R. and the West against the Nazis in World War II proved temporary, and the Cold War burgeoned from global conditions as that war ended. In 1945, the United States and the Soviet Union were the only powers still in a position to influence global politics. The other European states, traditional powers on the continent, had suffered indescribable economic and psychological damage. Great Britain had lost roughly a third of its wealth, and France suffered even greater damage. Defeated Germany, Italy, and Japan were in ruins, and Germany was divided and occupied by the victors.[6] All were heavily in debt, and all, to varying degrees, had to rely upon the United States for more or less assistance to meet basic needs.

Politically, too, Europe was in shambles. British Prime Minister Winston Churchill was unceremoniously voted out of office, and the new Labour government immediately confronted domestic and foreign troubles. The British Empire unraveled as "the jewels in the crown," such as India, clamored for independence, and the British Mandate in Palestine thrashed in civil war.[7] Britain lacked food and coal to feed and heat itself, its troops in Europe, and the Germans for whom the British occupation forces were responsible. Early in 1947, the British ambassador in Washington reported that his country could no longer help Greece and Turkey, both threatened by communist insurgencies, and asked the United States to assume this responsibility. France faced political instability: coalition governments were short-lived, and the powerful French Communist Party attracted many

---

[5]John Lewis Gaddis, *Russia, the Soviet Union, and the United States: An Interpretative History* (New York: John Wiley, 1978), p. 76.

[6]Richard Mayne, *The Recovery of Europe 1945–1973* (Garden City, N.Y.: Anchor, 1973), pp. 27–52.

[7]India was partitioned and along with its Muslim foe, Pakistan, was granted independence under chaotic circumstances in 1947.

French voters. France too had to deal with colonial rebellions abroad, first in Indochina and later in North Africa. The Netherlands too confronted an independence movement in Indonesia that would ultimately succeed in 1949.[8]

By contrast, the United States immediately after World War II was economically vigorous and politically stable. United States industry, a chief source of allied victory, was booming, accounting for 45 percent of world manufactures, and the United States enjoyed large trade surpluses and huge reserves.[9] United States military might was unsurpassed. Its troops occupied much of Western Europe and Japan, its navy was the world's largest, and it had a monopoly on a new and highly destructive weapon, the nuclear bomb. The Soviet Union had borne much in the war against Nazi Germany, suffering more than twenty million dead and the devastation of over two decades of socialist construction. Nevertheless, 175 Soviet divisions remained in the heart of Europe, a fact that grew meaningful as U.S. forces in Europe were demobilized. Politically, Stalin's ruthless regime had survived the Nazi onslaught, and no one dared oppose the aging tyrant. Finally, and most important, the Soviet Union, as one of the victors and with an army occupying Central Europe, expected to share in the spoils of war.

Continued United States–Soviet Postwar Cooperation?

The U.S.–Soviet alliance had won the war, and it seemed reasonable to believe their cooperation would continue. President Franklin D. Roosevelt had envisioned such agreement in his postwar plans. He expected the United States to remain an active participant in world affairs and assumed that the wartime allies would remain peacetime collaborators, especially in the U.N. Security Council. Roosevelt also believed that power politics (a phrase he would not have used) would be the guiding principle in the postwar world, and his grand design looked and sounded much like a global balance-of-power system. Under his "Four Policemen" proposal, Britain, China, the United States, and the Soviet Union would, in effect, be responsible for maintaining global peace in their areas of the world. Although "*spheres of influence*" and "power politics" were nowhere made explicit, they were implicit in the proposal.[10]

Several wartime conferences were held to iron out differences among the major powers. Meetings at Teheran (1943), Cairo (1943), Yalta (1945), and Potsdam (1945) addressed not only ways of prosecuting the war but also postwar arrangements in Europe and elsewhere. The most important of these, shaping postwar European politics and feeding the misunderstandings that accompanied the beginning Cold War, was the *Yalta*

[8]Although inhabitants of such European colonies as Malaya, Indochina, and Indonesia were victimized by brutal occupation, the Japanese defeat of the European powers destroyed the myth of European invincibility and energized national independence movements.

[9]Stephen E. Ambrose, *Rise of Globalism: American Foreign Policy 1938–1976* (New York: Penguin Books, 1976), p. 16.

[10]John Lewis Gaddis, *The Long Peace: Inquiries Into the History of the Cold War* (New York: Oxford University Press, 1987), p. 50.

Conference, held in that Crimean city in February 1945. Several significant bargains were struck at Yalta to shape the postwar world. Although the commitments made there bore the imprint of balance-of-power politics, they also foreshadowed continued cooperation. The spirit of the time was reflected in a letter from George Kennan to Charles Bohlen just prior to Yalta in which Kennan asked, "Why could we not make a decent and definite compromise with it [the Soviet Union] — divide Europe frankly into spheres of influence — keep ourselves out of the Russian sphere and keep the Russians out of ours?"[11]

One set of Yalta agreements covered representation and voting arrangements for the proposed U.N. organization.[12] The Soviet Union wanted all its republics seated in the United Nations, but Washington objected. A bargain was struck whereby the U.S.S.R. was granted three seats in the General Assembly and the United States could have the same number if it wished. A second agreement provided for veto power in the Security Council, the principal peacekeeping organ in the new organization. Under the veto arrangement, any of the five permanent members of the Council (the United States, U.S.S.R., Britain, France, or China) could halt any substantive action proposed by the United Nations. That arrangement ensured that the permanent members would have to work together if the United Nations were to function effectively.

Yet another agreement determined the four-power (Britain, France, United States, and Soviet Union) zones of occupation in Germany. This arrangement was a compromise (France was given a zone only after much wrangling), but it also ensured future U.S. participation in European affairs and made it less likely that America would return to prewar isolationism. The arrangement initiated the division of Germany among the victorious powers and was a first step in establishing spheres of interest between East and West in Central Europe.

Additional agreements were reached on German war reparations and on establishing a coalition government including communists and noncommunists in postwar Poland. The most controversial decision at Yalta, however, was the "Declaration on Liberated Europe," which pledged the Yalta participants to foster free elections and guarantee basic freedoms in all liberated countries. When the promise of Yalta was not honored by Stalin in Eastern Europe, it became a powerful rationale for U.S. suspicions about Soviet intentions and actions.[13] One impetus for the United States to strike these deals at Yalta was to get a Soviet commitment to enter the war against Japan.

---

[11]Cited in ibid., p. 48.

[12]On the Yalta agreements, see Robert H. Ferrell, *American Diplomacy: A History* (New York: W. W. Norton, 1975), pp. 594–603.

[13]Although Roosevelt has been accused of allowing himself to be taken in by Stalin, he recognized the realities of power politics both before and after Yalta. In January 1945, he pointed out to a group of senators that "the occupying forces had the power in the areas where their arms were present and each knew that the others could not force things to an issue. The Russians had the power in Eastern Europe." Shortly after Yalta, he made the same point: "Obviously the Russians are going to do things their own way in the areas they occupy." Cited in Daniel Yergin, *Shattered Peace: The Origins of the Cold War and the National Security State* (Boston: Houghton Mifflin, 1977), pp. 58, 66.

At the *Potsdam Conference*, held in a Berlin suburb in July 1945, further discussions were held on the future of Central Europe. Even though the question of Poland and its borders was to be a principal topic at Potsdam, the Soviet Union announced it had reached agreement with the Polish government on that country's new boundaries. This *fait accompli* reduced the prospects of bargaining among the parties, and disagreement was papered over in a protocol statement indicating that the boundary question "shall await the peace settlement."[14]

Expectations still remained high that the Soviet Union would be willing to bargain over the future of Central Europe. The hope was that the "Yalta Axioms" would continue to guide U.S.-Soviet relations.[15] One of these axioms was that the Soviet Union was much like any other state and thus driven fundamentally by power considerations. Derived directly from the realist perspective, this axiom implied that the Soviet Union would seek to advance its interests but that it would also recognize its power had limits. Rationally calculating its capabilities would thus restrain Soviet behavior. In fact, the United States had hoped to use prospective economic aid and international control of atomic energy as inducements to gain Soviet compliance with the Yalta Declaration on Liberated Europe and the agreement on unifying Germany.[16]

United States–Soviet ministerial meetings late in 1945 and early in 1946 proved disappointing, and Soviet actions in Eastern Europe began to raise doubt about its future intentions. Free and democratic elections were not held in Eastern Europe, as promised at Yalta. Instead, first coalition, and eventually communist-dominated governments, came to power in Poland, Hungary, Bulgaria, Romania, and Czechoslovakia. These events powerfully affected U.S. public opinion, especially among urban ethnic communities. The Czech coup in 1948 and the apparent murder of the country's foreign minister, Jan Masaryk, son of the country's founder, were the final steps in Sovietizing Eastern Europe.

By late in the 1940s, all of Eastern Europe had fallen under the shadow of Soviet power. In Germany, the major stake in postwar Europe, the Soviet Union in 1946 rejected a proposal for a disarmed, unified state and reinforced its hold over its occupation zone.[17] Subsequent Soviet actions limiting Western powers' access to Berlin in 1948–1949 (the first Berlin crisis) and establishing a separate German state (the German Democratic Republic) in its zone of occupation seemed to confirm Western suspicion that the Soviets intended to dominate Europe.

[14]Ferrell, *American Diplomacy*, p. 623. In a vain bid to maintain cooperation with the U.S.S.R. at Potsdam, the United States had withdrawn its forces from territory outside the occupation zones negotiated at Yalta.

[15]See Yergin, *Shattered Peace*, pp. 42–68.

[16]John Lewis Gaddis, *Russia, the Soviet Union, and the United States* (New York: John Wiley and Sons, 1978), p. 181.

[17]Gaddis, *The Long Peace*, p. 54.

Growing Mistrust and Suspicion

As early as 1946, Soviet actions had begun to move the United States away from the *Yalta Axioms* and toward the *Riga Axioms* instead.[18] Unlike the Yalta Axioms, the Riga Axioms assumed that the Soviet Union was driven by ideology rather than power. According to these axioms, the Soviet Union's totalitarian structure was the ultimate source of its actions at home and abroad, and a totalitarian state at home would follow a totalitarian foreign policy. One analyst said, "doctrine and ideology and a spirit of innate aggressiveness shaped Soviet policy. . . . The U.S.S.R. was committed to world revolution and unlimited expansion."[19]

The growing perceptions that Soviet and American decision-makers had of each other during that time are revealed in formerly classified documents. Nothing conveys more clearly the perception of the U.S.S.R. that was evolving in official Washington early in 1946 than the so-called *Long Telegram* sent by George F. Kennan, then a counselor in the U.S. Embassy in Moscow. Kennan's image of the Soviet Union was almost entirely negative: Mistrust and basic incompatibility between the two superpowers are dominant themes. We quote parts of the Long Telegram because it portrays the deep suspicion with which this influential policy adviser viewed the Soviet Union.

First, consider Kennan's assessment of the Soviet position toward the United States:

> We have here a political force committed fanatically to the belief that with the U.S. there can be no permanent modus vivendi, that it is desirable and necessary that the internal harmony of our society be disrupted, our traditional way of life be destroyed, the international authority of our state be broken, if Soviet power is to be secure.[20]

Next, consider Kennan's view of ideology's part in Soviet behavior and how it warps the Soviet view of reality:

> It [the Soviet Union] is seemingly inaccessible to considerations of reality in its basic reactions. For it, the vast fund of objective fact about human society is not, as with us, the measure against which outlook is constantly being tested and reformed, but a grab bag from which individual items are selected arbitrarily and tendentiously to bolster an outlook already preconceived.[21]

Finally, consider Kennan's view of the Soviet Union's challenge to the United States and the West generally:

---

[18]The expression "Riga Axioms" is Daniel Yergin's (*Shattered Peace*, pp. 17–41) and refers to the Latvian city of Riga, where the first American Soviet watchers were posted after the U.S.S.R. was established. These analysts were wary of Soviet intentions and believed Soviet foreign policy was driven by its Marxist–Leninist roots.

[19]Ibid., p. 35.

[20]George F. Kennan, *Memoirs 1925–1950* (Boston: Little, Brown, 1967), p. 557.

[21]Ibid.

Efforts will be made . . . to disrupt national self-confidence, to hamstring measures of national defense, to increase social and industrial unrest, to stimulate all forms of disunity. . . . Where individual governments stand in [the] path of Soviet purposes pressure will be brought for their removal from office. . . . In foreign countries Communists will, as a rule, work toward destruction of all forms of personal independence, economic, political, or moral.[22]

Although Kennan offered several general suggestions about what could be done to combat the Soviet threat in the Long Telegram, he had no specific prescription for U.S. foreign policy. That was to await publication of his "Mr. X" essay in *Foreign Affairs* a year later.

From documents released later, we learn that the Soviet Union at the time held an equally wary view of U.S. intentions. The Soviet ambassador to the United States, Nikolai Novikov, sent a secret report to Soviet Foreign Minister Vyacheslav Molotov in September 1946, outlining dangers from the United States.[23] The opening line in the "*Novikov Telegram*" sets the tone: "The foreign policy of the United States, which reflects the imperialist tendencies of American monopolistic capital, is characterized in the postwar period by a striving for world supremacy." United States' policy, Novikov argued, was particularly dangerous because its leadership had changed, and it had begun to embark on actions to achieve "global dominance." "The ascendance to power of President Truman, a politically unstable person but with certain conservative tendencies, and the subsequent appointment of [James] Byrnes as Secretary of State" gave power to "the most reactionary circles of the Democratic party." America had instituted a military draft, increased its defense expenditures, and placed military forces around the world, actions that, in Novikov's view, had one purpose: "All of these facts show clearly that a decisive role . . . for world domination by the United States is played by its armed forces."[24]

The Novikov Telegram declared too that, although U.S. policy extended to all corners of the world, it was principally focused on the Soviet Union, where the Truman administration's "objective has been to impose the will of other countries on the Soviet Union." According to Novikov, U.S. policy has been "directed at limiting or dislodging the influence of the Soviet Union from neighboring countries" and has sought to "secure positions for the penetration of American capital into their economies." Even more ominous, the United States has been undertaking preparations for a possible "war against the Soviet Union."[25]

[22]Ibid., pp. 555–556.

[23]The Novikov Telegram was released to Soviet and American historians in July 1990 at a meeting at the U.S. Peace Institute in Washington, D.C. See John Lewis Gaddis, "The Soviet Side of the Cold War: A Symposium," *Diplomatic History* 15:4 (Fall 1991), p. 525.

[24]"The Novikov Telegram, Washington, September 27, 1946," reprinted in *Diplomatic History* 15:4 (Fall 1991), pp. 529, 530.

[25]Ibid., pp. 535, 537.

The Novikov message is a *mirror image* of the Long Telegram. The Soviet Union saw the United States as driven by capitalist imperatives and bent on world domination. The United States saw the Soviet Union as driven by Marxist–Leninist imperatives and bent on world revolution. In part, then, the Cold War was triggered by each side's propensity to see the other as expansionist while failing to recognize that the other saw it in the same manner.[26] The private images of the policy advisers sent to their respective governments were reflected in public pronouncements by leaders in both East and West. On February 9, 1946, in an address before elections to the Supreme Soviet, Stalin resurrected the traditional Marxist view of the Western capitalist powers and the danger with which they threatened the global order:

> Marxists have repeatedly declared that the capitalist world economic system conceals in itself the elements of general crisis and military clashes as a result of which the development of world capitalism in our time proceeds not by smooth and even progress but by crises and military catastrophes.[27]

In effect, Stalin argued that war was inevitable among capitalist states and that a fundamental incompatibility separated capitalist and Marxist systems. Although only about one tenth of Stalin's speech was about foreign policy, that was the portion which captured American attention and gave impetus to the Cold War.[28]

The mirror image appears in a speech by Winston Churchill to a U.S. college audience in March 1946, doubtless interpreted by Moscow in the same way as Stalin's was by Washington the month before. Churchill responded to Stalin's suspicion of the West by assailing Soviet expansionism. Perhaps the speech is best recalled for introducing the world to the phrase peculiar to the Cold War:

> From Stettin in the Baltic to Trieste in the Adriatic, an *iron curtain* has descended across the Continent. Behind that line lie all the capitals of the ancient states of Central and Eastern Europe. Warsaw, Berlin, Prague, Vienna, Budapest, Belgrade, Bucharest and Sofia, all these famous cities and the populations around them lie in what I must call the Soviet sphere, and all are subject in one form or another, not only to Soviet influence but to a very high and, in many cases, increasing measure of control from Moscow.[29]

Churchill did more than introduce a powerful image; he also offered a new policy prescription for the West, built on confronting rather than cooperating with the Soviet

---

[26]William A. Gamson and André Modigliani, *Untangling the Cold War: A Strategy for Testing Rival Theories* (Boston: Little, Brown, 1971), p. 109.

[27]Cited in B. Thomas Trout, "Rhetoric Revisited: Political Legitimation and the Cold War, *International Studies Quarterly* 19:3 (September 1975), p. 264.

[28]Deborah Welch Larson, *Origins of Containment: A Psychological Examination* (Princeton: Princeton University Press, 1985), pp. 252–253, and Trout, "Rhetoric Revisited," p. 269.

[29]Robert Rhodes James, ed., *Winston S. Churchill: His Complete Speeches 1897–1963*, vol. VII: 1943–1949 (New York: Chelsea House, 1974), p. 7290.

Union. Free peoples should cooperate against the Bolshevik menace, a "fraternal association of the English-speaking peoples" and a "special relationship between the British Commonwealth and Empire and the United States." These actors, working under the "general authority" of the U.N., should stand up to the Soviet challenge. If they did so, "there will be no quivering precarious balance of power to offer its temptation to ambition or adventure. On the contrary, there will be an overwhelming assurance of security."[30] Such resistance was necessary because of the Soviet Union's treachery in Eastern Europe and elsewhere.

Interpreting the Genesis of the Cold War

The Realist Lens. From a realist perspective, the Cold War can be interpreted as the outcome of a sequence of moves and countermoves by two powerful states between 1945 and 1991 in which each pursued its *national interest*. A realist would argue that those interests were shaped and made incompatible by the postwar *power vacuum* in Central Europe and East Asia with Germany and Japan defeated and the other European powers weakened. Each superpower recognized that the only state powerful enough to do it real harm was the other. Neither wanted the other to enjoy a preponderance of power, and each sought to prevent this superiority by building its own internal power and forging alliances with friendly states.[31] As a result, endeavors by both sides to secure German occupation on its own terms, Soviet attempts to create a buffer zone of friendly states on its Western border,[32] and even later conflicts over Berlin and Korea could be interpreted in a balance-of-power framework.

The Perceptual Lens. If we use only a realist lens, much will not be explained, such as the ferocity with which the Cold War began, the deep ideological differences between actors and their leaders, and the role of many actors other than the two superpower governments. As we have seen, the image that each set of decision-makers had of the other may have been as pivotal in starting the Cold War as their actions. Kennan's Long Telegram, the Novikov Telegram, and Churchill's and Stalin's speeches convey the yawning perceptual abyss that had opened between the former wartime allies in a very brief time. Soviet–U.S. ideological hostility had been subordinated to the imperative of defeating a common foe, but once that task was accomplished, latent

---

[30]Ibid., pp. 7289, 7293.

[31]Historian John Lewis Gaddis points out that, despite their isolationist heritage, by the early 1940s Americans had begun to think that "the primary American interest in postwar international affairs would be to ensure that no single state dominates Europe." See *The Long Peace*, p. 49.

[32]From a realist perspective, there is little difference between Soviet behavior in Eastern Europe after World War II and the French design to create a *cordon sanitaire* in the same region after World War I.

suspicion and mistrust dating from the 1917 Bolshevik Revolution quickly resurfaced. Wedding misperception and ideological hostility to changing power relationships in Central Europe provides a potent explanation for conflict.

The Complex-Interdependence Lens.   This framework moves beyond the perceptions of each country's leaders and elites and focuses on the competing world views or ideologies that each society represented. Seen thus, Americans and their allies and Soviets and their allies held incompatible conceptions about how societies ought to be organized politically and economically. One group of actors looked on *capitalism* as the fundamental principle for economic organization, and the other favored *socialism*. One emphasized a version based on individual political freedom and rights, and the other another version based on economic equality and collective responsibility. Each regarded the other's version as a sham giving power to the few at the expense of the many, and each feared that the other intended to impose its version of truth on the entire world.

The universality of both world views sets the stage for the Cold War. Communists believed actions by the United States and its allies were part of a transnational "capitalist" effort to strangle socialism in general and the Soviet state in particular. "*Capitalist encirclement*" and "Western imperialism" summarized their belief that economic and class imperatives shaped U.S. and Western policies after World War II. From this perspective, giant transnational corporations and banks, protected by Western governments that they controlled, were the engines driving capitalist expansion. One analyst summarizes this perspective: "Because of the irresistible pressures of American capitalism and the power of economic elites in the shaping of foreign policy, the United States pursued a policy of imperial anticolonialism rationalized in the language of humanitarianism and national self-determination but motivated by the quest for free markets essential to America's prosperity and well-being."[33]

Communists believed capitalism's economic imperatives left little room for accommodation with socialism. Satisfying Soviet security interests in Eastern Europe necessarily challenged the free market and the economic open-door policies essential to capitalist interests.[34] From this perspective, the Cold War was caused by capitalism's transnational interests and its desire to maintain access to worldwide markets and resources. Because the U.S.S.R. and its socialist allies challenged those interests, conflict between the two ideologies was inevitable.

A reciprocal interpretation of the Cold War formed in the West. *Marxism–Leninism*, guided by the Soviet Union, which controlled a worldwide network of communist

[33]Kenneth W. Thompson, *Cold War Theories*, vol. 1 (Baton Rouge: Louisiana State University Press, 1981), pp. 44–45.
[34]Ibid., p. 46.

parties,[35] was "on the march," not only in Western Europe but globally as well. One piece of evidence was Stalin's creation in 1947 of the *Cominform* (Communist Information Bureau) in Belgrade, consisting of the Communist parties of the Soviet Union, Hungary, Romania, Czechoslovakia, Bulgaria, France, and Italy. The Western intellectual climate at the time is described by one observer:

> Never had the threat or promise of Communism loomed larger than it did three years after the conclusion of World War II. A century earlier two young German radicals introduced their fiery challenge to the old order on an exuberant note: "A specter is haunting Europe—the specter of Communism." But in 1848 Marx and Engels spoke for only a tiny sect, and publication of the *Communist Manifesto*, with its message of class war, was a little-noticed incident in the wave of revolutionary convulsions that shook the Old World that year. . . . But what in 1848 had been an expression of youthful bravado became one century later only too true. . . . [T]he representative and carrier of the Communist idea, the Soviet Union, was the *dominant* power on the Continent. Eastern Europe lay under Moscow's domination, its vassal regimes rapidly transforming their societies in the Soviet model. No West European state, or all of them together, could match the strength of the Red Army. . . . Nor was the threat to Western Europe purely military. The French and Italian Communist parties . . . enjoyed a wide following in their countries. . . . [36]

A National Security Council report labeled *NSC-68* written in 1950 perhaps best summarized the official Western perspective on the danger from the Soviet Union and international communism:

> The fundamental design of those who control the Soviet Union and the international communist movement is to retain and solidify their absolute power, first in the Soviet Union and second in the areas now under their control. In the minds of the Soviet leaders, however, achievement of this design requires the dynamic extension of their authority and the ultimate elimination of any effective opposition to their authority.[37]

According to this view, international communism sought absolute control worldwide and so universally threatened human freedom and individual liberty. Under these circumstances, Western responses to communist activities—whether in Europe or elsewhere—were necessary and justifiable.

From this perspective, the Cold War owed less to competing Soviet–U.S. national interests or misperceptions than to the transnational movements and ideologies that the

---

[35]Before World War II, communist parties had been organized into a Communist International or Comintern headquartered in Moscow. An organization of communist parties from around the world located in Moscow, the Comintern gave Stalin an instrument to control and use communists everywhere. The Comintern was abolished in 1943 as part of Stalin's wish to endear himself to his Western allies.

[36]Adam B. Ulam, *The Communists: The Story of Power and Lost Illusions: 1948–1991* (New York: Charles Scribner's Sons, 1992), pp. 1–2. Emphasis in original.

[37]A Report to the National Security Council, April 14, 1950, p. 5. Declassified February 27, 1975.

two societies represented. All three lenses have something to offer the analyst, and only by combining them can one understand why the Cold War began.

Stage 2: The Cold War as Crisis

The Cold War issue entered crisis stage late in 1946 and early in 1947. By enunciating the *Truman Doctrine*, the United States dropped the gauntlet and adopted a confrontational attitude toward the Soviet Union. The Truman Doctrine was the name given to a speech President Truman delivered to a joint session of Congress on March 12, 1947, in which he proclaimed a new policy and role for the United States in global affairs. Specifically, the president sought $400 million in economic and military assistance for Greece and Turkey, two strategic Mediterranean countries threatened by subversive forces supported by the Soviet Union, after the British said a month earlier that they could no longer provide the necessary support.

The Truman Doctrine

To justify aid requested for Greece and Turkey to a skeptical Congress, Truman placed the situation in the context of the broader changes that he saw taking place in global politics. "The peoples of a number of countries," he declared, "have recently had totalitarian regimes forced upon them against their will." Although the United States had "made frequent protests against coercion and intimidation, in violation of the Yalta agreement, in Poland, Rumania, and Bulgaria," those protests had proved insufficient. The United States must now be willing, Truman declared, "to help free peoples to maintain their free institutions and their national integrity against aggressive movements that seek to impose upon them totalitarian regimes."[38] The sweeping language, the worldwide U.S. commitment to assist any state threatened by totalitarianism, and the abrupt change in foreign-policy action following the speech gained it the status of a "doctrine" and a lasting policy for the United States. Yet the speech was more than that: It was a declaration of the Cold War. The issue was beginning to overshadow everything else on the global agenda.

Following Truman's declaration, George F. Kennan, author of the Long Telegram, published an influential article under the pseudonym "Mr. X" in the journal *Foreign Affairs*, in which he outlined a policy of *containment* against the Soviet Union. The strategy was meant to put enough pressure on the Soviet Union ("the application of counter-force at a series of constantly shifting geographical and political points," Kennan wrote) to produce a change in both its internal structure and its international conduct ("the break-up or the gradual mellowing of Soviet power").[39] As a result of the

---

[38]Congressional Record, Vol. 93, Part 2, March 12, 1947, pp. 1980–1981.

[39]The parenthetical passages are from Mr. X (George Kennan), "The Sources of Soviet Conduct," *Foreign Affairs* (July 1947), pp. 566–582.

proposal and of Soviet actions late in the 1940s, the United States embarked on a global strategy to confront and contain the Soviet Union. Notwithstanding changes in nuance and tactics, containment remained the basis for U.S. policy for four decades.

During the ensuing years, the United States concluded alliance commitments globally. The Inter-American Treaty of Reciprocal Assistance (Rio Treaty) was signed by Washington with twenty-one Western Hemisphere nations in 1947, the North Atlantic Treaty with twelve (later fifteen) European states in 1949, the ANZUS Treaty with Australia and New Zealand in 1951, and the Southeast Asia Treaty Organization with countries within and outside of the region in 1954. Bilateral pacts were completed with the Philippines, Japan, Korea, and Taiwan early in the 1950s.[40] The United States also undertook economic and military assistance programs worldwide,[41] and a vigorous campaign at home and abroad to warn against dangers from the Soviet Union[42] as ways to implement containment. Although these actions set in motion U.S. policy guidelines for the Cold War, two events clearly thrust the issue into a crisis stage — the *Berlin blockade* in 1948 and 1949 and the *Korean War*, 1950 to 1953.

In May 1948, anticipating the West's establishment of a new state from their zones of Germany, the Soviet Union began a rail, water, and road blockade around the former German capital, Berlin. The city, located in the Soviet zone, was also divided into occupation zones, and Western access was guaranteed by several agreements. Soviet anger had been sparked by a unilateral Western currency reform in its zones that had been instituted because of Soviet refusal to fulfill its obligation to treat Germany as a single economic unit. The blockade was in place by June 24, 1948, and the West responded vigorously to this violation of the Quadripartite Agreements.[43] Late in July, the Western powers began a massive airlift to the beleaguered city. By one estimate, U.S. and British aircraft transported "over 1.5 million tons of food, fuel and other goods into Berlin (the highest load in one day exceeded 12,000 tons)" during the ten months from July 1948 to the end of the blockade in May 1949.[44] The Berlin blockade was an important lesson in how West and East could confront each other without direct resort to arms.

[40]These formal commitments supplemented many informal arrangements between the United States and other countries that were deemed useful for containing Soviet expansionism.

[41]The Marshall Plan, named after a proposal first discussed by Secretary of State George C. Marshall in a June 1947 Harvard commencement address, was initiated to provide economic assistance to help rebuild and unite Western Europe. By early in the 1950s, the United States had a large foreign-assistance program that offered economic and military help labeled "mutual security" for nations threatened by international communism. Providing such aid linked U.S. security to that of the recipients.

[42]A secret National Security Council report (NSC-68) made it a high U.S. priority to alert other countries and the American public to the dangers of communism. Making recommendations for policy abroad, it also called for higher defense budgets at home, protecting U.S. institutions from subversion, rallying the public in opposition to the Soviet Union, and proceeding with the H-bomb.

[43]See Dennis L. Bark, *Agreement on Berlin: A Study of the 1970–1972 Quadripartite Negotiations* (Washington, D.C. and Stanford: American Enterprise Institute for Public Policy Research and Hoover Institution on War, Revolution and Peace, 1974).

[44]Peter Calvocoressi, *World Politics Since 1945*, 6th ed. (New York: Longman, 1991), p. 19.

The other event was the Korean War, which spread the Cold War to Asia and militarized the superpowers' policies. Like Berlin, divided Korea was also an anomaly — it was in neither the Western nor the Eastern camp. Indeed, in a January 1950 speech, U.S. Secretary of State Dean Acheson declared that South Korea was outside the U.S. defense perimeter in East Asia. Six months later, on June 25, 1950, war began when North Korean troops suddenly invaded the south. United States leaders believed the attack had been ordered by Moscow to test Western resolve, because the Soviet Union had previously occupied North Korea and was still allied with it. Following its containment strategy, the Truman administration believed it had few options except to help Syngman Rhee's anti-communist regime in South Korea. The United States and its allies intervened under U.N. auspices and were involved in a conflict that lasted three years and led to intervention by the Chinese communists.[45] In the end, an armistice between North and South Korea around the 38th parallel was arranged and remains to this day. Although the Korean War's military outcome was inconclusive, its political influence was profound. The war, thousands of miles from Europe, confirmed that the Cold War was global. For Americans, the Korean War ended "the incoherence which characterized U.S. foreign and defense efforts in the period 1946–1950"[46] and propelled the United States in the direction of fully implementing the containment doctrine.

To the Soviet Union, however, U.S. actions through the late 1940s and early 1950s supported a comparable view of Western goals. Harsh attacks on the U.S.S.R. by Presidents Truman, Eisenhower, and others suggested that the United States had forgotten their common struggle against the Nazis and was unwilling to continue cooperating with the Soviet Union.[47] Building alliances globally, funneling assistance to states along the Soviet perimeter, and rallying states against it, of course, reinforced the Soviet view.

Stage 3: Ritualizing the Cold War

At some time in the 1960s, the superpowers tacitly concluded that their relations had to be governed by rules and procedures that would reduce the likelihood of mutual annihilation and would allow them to coexist. Ritualization had set in. Ritualization

[45]Rapid American intervention was possible because U.S. occupation troops were in Japan under General Douglas MacArthur. See Allen S. Whiting, *China Crosses the Yalu* (Stanford: Stanford University Press, 1960); and John W. Spanier, *The Truman–MacArthur Controversy and the Korean War* (New York: W. W. Norton, 1965).

[46]Robert Jervis, "The Impact of the Korean War on the Cold War," *Journal of Conflict Resolution* 24:4 (December 1980), p. 563. Also see John Lewis Gaddis, "Was the Truman Doctrine a Real Turning Point?" *Foreign Affairs* 52:2 (January 1974), pp. 386–402, on dating the origins of the Cold War.

[47]That Western authorities in Germany quickly abandoned efforts at denazification to transform the Federal Republic into an anticommunist bastion reinforced this impression.

does not mean peace, however, and superpower relations were still dominated by the threat of force, bargaining from strength, and a generally hostile climate.

Both the presence and power of ritualization were evident in the spiraling defense burdens that both sides accepted, the interventionist policies that both pursued, and the fluctuations in tension between them. Despite such factors, which many observers feared would bring on World War III, U.S. and Soviet leaders learned what they could and could not do if they wished to avoid cataclysmic war and how to manage their mutual relations. Even amid the most dramatic East–West showdown in the Cold War — the missile crisis in October 1962 — the superpowers were able to modify their behavior to prevent the confrontation from escaping their control and igniting a global conflagration.[48]

Military Spending, Intervention, and Ritualization

By 1953, U.S. defense expenditures soared to more than 13 percent of GNP and remained above 8 percent during much of the 1960s and the Vietnam war.[49] These expenditures began to decrease in the 1970s, only to rise again early in the 1980s as the Reagan defense buildup began. For the Soviet Union the pattern of defense expenditures is more difficult to verify, but estimates range from 10 to 20 percent of Soviet GNP (and even higher) throughout the Cold War. These expenditures fueled both a conventional and a nuclear arms race, but, despite expectations that such races must end in war, they did not. Why? Because the U.S.-Soviet arms race was an expected and permissible ritual.

Direct military confrontation between the superpowers was too dangerous, and they tacitly agreed to avoid it. Less dangerous and therefore permissible under the rules of the game were conflicts involving superpower proxies (such as Israel versus Syria, Somalia versus Ethiopia) or conflicts between one superpower and a surrogate of the other (such as the United States versus North Korea or North Vietnam). Such conditions allowed intervention by the superpowers or their surrogates as long as such intervention was limited and avoided direct superpower confrontation.[50] The rules also allowed other

---

[48]Some might think it peculiar to place the Cuban missile crisis in the ritualization rather than the crisis stage. By this time, however, the two countries had done some learning and that experience assisted them during the confrontation.

[49]These data are for total national defense rather than only Department of Defense data. See Alice C. Moroni, *The Fiscal Year 1984 Defense Budget Request: Data Summary* (Washington, D.C.: Congressional Research Service, 1983), p. 13.

[50]Because communication in global politics is imperfect, these rules were endangered from time to time. United States bombing of the North Vietnamese port of Haiphong in May 1972 damaged Soviet vessels in the harbor and threatened U.S.–Soviet détente, and risk-taking by both sides during the 1973 Arab–Israeli war threatened to escalate out of hand.

forms of Soviet–United States conflict: propaganda, espionage, and subversion; overt and covert economic, political, and military assistance; and other techniques for "informal penetration."[51]

The threat of communist expansionism was the reason for U.S. military action in Korea (1950), Iran (1953), Guatemala (1954), Vietnam (1961), Cuba (1961), the Dominican Republic (1965), and Grenada (1983). In all these, the Soviet response was restrained and did not directly challenge the U.S. position.[52] Fear that socialist control would be undermined motivated Soviet intervention in East Berlin (1953), Hungary (1956), Czechoslovakia (1968), and Afghanistan (1979). The United States, despite rhetoric about "rolling back" communism in Eastern Europe early in the 1950s, did little more than offer moral support to Hungarian freedom fighters as Soviet tanks smashed into Budapest in November 1956. The United States again did nothing after the Warsaw Pact intervened in Czechoslovakia in August 1968 to crush the "Prague Spring." After Soviet intervention in Afghanistan in December 1979, Washington took several limited political and economic steps against the U.S.S.R. but did not confront Moscow directly.[53] In effect, Churchill's Iron Curtain became a line of demarcation between the two sides, and even responses to interventions were ritualized.

Ritualizing by Confrontation and Accommodation

Superpower confrontations were another manifestation of the ritualization of the Cold War. Kenneth Waltz argued in 1964 that the "nearly constant presence of pressure and the recurrence of crises" was a source of superpower learning and actually stabilized their relations by serving as a substitute for war.[54] Dangerous crises flared in areas that were not in either superpower's sphere of interest, such as Berlin, Korea, Vietnam, Cuba, and Afghanistan. In time, recognizing the enormous costs that they would have to pay for a misstep, both sides sought to work out rules for these gray areas as well.

The *Cuban missile crisis* illustrated the potential dangers in misunderstanding the rules of the game and the importance of crises for superpower learning. In 1962, the Soviet Union placed offensive missiles in Cuba—to help Fidel Castro's communist government, intimidate the United States, and alter the global balance of power. This surprising action violated U.S. expectations and the tacit understanding that neither superpower would meddle in its adversary's immediate neighborhood. The ensuing showdown lasted a few tense days until Moscow capitulated. By any assessment, this

[51] Andrew M. Scott, *The Revolution in Statecraft: Informal Penetration* (New York: Random House, 1965).

[52] A possible exception was Chinese intervention in the Korean conflict in 1950 as U.S. forces approached the Yalu River on China's border. The Soviets do not appear, however, to have been involved in Beijing's decision to intervene.

[53] Covert assistance, including Stinger antiaircraft missiles, was channeled to the Afghan rebels early, and overt aid was provided by 1986.

[54] Kenneth N. Waltz, "The Stability of a Bipolar World," *Daedalus* 93:3 (Summer 1964), p. 883.

episode was the most frightening confrontation in the Cold War, yet its termination peacefully demonstrated that both sides still had learning capacity. Indeed, this crisis, more than any other event, persuaded leaders that additional rules had to be created to lessen chances of a war that neither wanted.

Before and after the Cuban crisis, other confrontations contributed to ritualization. In 1958 and 1961, for example, the Soviet Union and the United States faced off again over access by the Western powers to Berlin. In August 1961, East Germany built the *Berlin Wall* to divide East and West Berlin. The wall became a symbol for the abyss separating East and West and visibly staked out in Europe spheres of interest over which the adversaries enjoyed exclusive authority. Ultimately, the two sides recognized it was safer to leave things alone in Berlin. Gradually and tacitly, therefore, "the main lines of expectations . . . converged around the rough status quo"[55] as Moscow and Washington ritualized their disagreement over Berlin and set the issue aside.

Although hostility colored the ritualization period, those years also had thaws between East and West and even a brief *détente* (relaxation of tensions) in the 1970s. These episodes, too, helped each side to accommodate the other. After Stalin died in 1953, superpower relations were warmed by the "spirit of Geneva" (named after a 1955 summit there). By late in the 1950s, "peaceful coexistence" entered the global-politics vocabulary, and a summit meeting was held at Camp David, Maryland, between President Dwight D. Eisenhower and Soviet Premier Nikita S. Khrushchev. After the Cuban missile crisis, too, President Kennedy proposed greater effort to reach arms-control agreements to help stabilize relations.

The first significant arms agreements limiting each side's nuclear arsenals were signed at a May 1972 summit in Moscow.[56] While they worked at stabilizing the arms race, the superpowers committed themselves to cooperate in reducing global tension. They also signed several economic and social-cultural agreements to promote trade and contacts between them, symbolizing their interest in coexistence. As a result, a period of Soviet-American détente began.

Détente was to be short-lived, however. Superpower relations were poisoned by a new Soviet arms buildup and by growing Soviet involvement in the Horn of Africa and southern Africa in the mid-1970s. The Soviets were surprised and angered by the Carter administration's human-rights policy and its intrusive efforts to influence Soviet domestic affairs, as in easing barriers to Jewish emigration from the U.S.S.R. Although a new arms-control agreement (SALT II) was eventually signed between Presidents Carter and Brezhnev, the Soviet invasion of Afghanistan in December 1979 sounded the death knell for détente. A new U.S. arms buildup began in the last year of the Carter administration and was accelerated by President Reagan, further burying détente.

[55]Joseph S. Nye, Jr., "Nuclear Learning and U.S.–Soviet Security Regime," *International Organization* 41:3 (Summer 1987), p. 394.

[56]See Chapter 8, pp. 271–274.

Domestic Politics and Ritualizing the Cold War

Domestic conditions in both societies also contributed to ritualizing the Cold War. As Soviet and American societies developed a mirror image of each other, leaders sought to socialize their citizens to the dangers from the other and mobilize support for the struggle. As new leaders in both societies gained power, the Cold War pattern remained, but it became more and more routine.

The anticommunism routine in the United States was manifested most dramatically by Senator Joseph McCarthy (R-Wisconsin) and the Army hearings that he held early in the 1950s. Senator McCarthy's aim was "to root out communists" inside and outside of government and expose subversive activities by individuals and groups. Although in the end McCarthy was censured by the Senate for some of his attacks on colleagues, his actions chilled the foreign-policy debate in the country as a whole. A similar witch hunt for suspicious activities was conducted by the House Un-American Activities Committee in the 1950s and into the 1960s. These hearings contributed to a charged and intimidating political atmosphere. Coupled with government warnings about communism, these witch hunts enforced a foreign-policy consensus that helped shape the Cold War.

The "*Cold War consensus*" encouraged and legitimized vigorous U.S. actions, ranging from economic and military assistance to regimes that appeared to be threatened by Communist takeover—whether or not they were authoritarian—to the use of force to reduce such threats.[57] It was also reflected in sustained support for high defense expenditures. In time, this consensus was modified by various American administrations and changing global events. Events like Yugoslavia's defection from the Soviet bloc in 1948, the Sino–Soviet split late in the 1950s, and progress in arms control in the 1970s affected public perceptions and modified views of the Soviet Union. Perhaps the event with profoundest effect on the Cold War consensus was the *Vietnam War* and America's defeat in that conflict.

United States involvement in Vietnam dated back to the French colonialists' defeat in 1954. American efforts to prop up a pro-Western government in South Vietnam took many forms and, after 1965, involved massive military intervention. The seemingly endless war challenged the Cold War consensus. Assumptions about "monolithic" communism, America's world role, the uses of military power, the power of the American presidency, and the absence of domestic debate on foreign policy were all challenged by the war. At the same time the American public became more receptive to accommodation with the Soviet Union, even as it remained wary of Soviet power. Thus, American attitudes, too, eventually became ritualized.

A parallel development occurred in the U.S.S.R. With propaganda and coercion just after World War II, Stalin instilled among the Soviet people great fear of the West and the United States. He sought to build "*socialism in one country*," reinforce his

[57]Eugene R. Wittkopf and James M. McCormick, "The Cold War Consensus: Did It Exist?" *Polity* (Summer 1990), pp. 627–653.

personal power, and intensify Soviet nationalism by painting a threatened "capitalist encirclement." A few years after Stalin's death, his successor, Nikita S. Khrushchev, shocked the Twentieth Congress of the Communist Party of the Soviet Union (CPSU) in 1956 by a secret speech in which he denounced Stalin's crimes, declared that war between the United States and U.S.S.R. was no longer inevitable, and initiated a policy of *peaceful coexistence* with the West. In succeeding party congresses, other doctrinal changes were announced permitting greater accommodation with the West.[58]

Other Soviet actions, however, seemed to contradict the relaxation that followed Stalin's death. Khrushchev boasted to Americans that "we shall bury you," meaning that the Soviet economic system would outperform America's capitalist system, but his harsh rhetoric and his melodramatic behavior — pounding his shoe on a desk during a United Nations debate, supporting *wars of national liberation* in the Third World, and belittling President Kennedy after a 1961 summit meeting in Vienna — fed East–West hostility.

Khrushchev's successor, Leonid Brezhnev, continued to encourage evolution in Marxism-Leninism, even as he asserted the U.S.S.R.'s growing military and political power. Soviet technological and scientific achievements were emphasized, and contacts with the West proliferated. As the Soviet economy faltered in the 1970s, though, Brezhnev sought to reaffirm that the Soviet way of life was superior, and the Soviet leadership again embraced Leninist orthodoxy.[59] Ultimately, the centrally planned economy could not modernize Soviet society and resolve mounting economic difficulties, a failure that proved too much for the Soviet state.

Stage 4: Resolving the Cold War

Between 1989 and 1991, the Cold War issue that had dominated the global agenda for four decades began to decline and finally evaporated. So quickly did Cold War hostilities disappear that, by 1992, no longer preoccupied by a "Red menace," the U.S. Congress debated how much foreign assistance it should authorize for the Russian economy in its difficult transition to a free market. Before this sea change in global politics, and perhaps as a prelude to it, however, the Cold War produced one last flurry of confrontation and crisis between the superpowers. Indeed, little happened early in the 1980s to make an observer predict anything but further chilly days in the Cold War.

[58]Paul Marantz, "Prelude to Détente: Doctrinal Change Under Khrushchev," *International Studies Quarterly* 19:4 (December 1975), pp. 501–528; and Gordon B. Smith, *Soviet Politics: Struggling with Change*, 2nd ed. (New York: St. Martin's Press, 1992), p. 80.

[59]Smith, *Soviet Politics*, pp. 80–81.

The Reagan Years and the Cold War Revived

The Reagan administration's initial strategy was to refocus U.S. policy on the Soviet "threat." It would "win" the arms race by taking advantage of America's economic and technological superiority and challenge the U.S.S.R. in regional conflicts by supporting anti-Soviet proxies. Secretary of State Alexander Haig acknowledged a tougher line in 1981 when he described Soviet power as the "central strategic phenomenon of the post–World War II era" and added that the "threat of Soviet military intervention colors attempts to achieve international civility."[60] President Reagan's antipathy toward the U.S.S.R. was evident in a 1982 speech to the British House of Commons in which he echoed Churchill's iron-curtain speech of four decades earlier:

> From Stettin on the Baltic to Varna on the Black Sea, the regimes planted by totalitarianism have had more than 30 years to establish their legitimacy. But none—not one regime—has yet been able to risk free elections. Regimes planted by bayonets do not take root.[61]

A year later, Reagan described the contest between the United States and the Soviet Union as a "struggle between right and wrong, good and evil."[62]

The heart of the renewed U.S. venture was a massive arms buildup. A $180-billion nuclear modernization program was proposed in which new land-based and sea-based missiles and long-range bombers were to be added to America's arsenal. New intermediate-range nuclear missiles were subsequently deployed in Western Europe to counter similar Soviet weapons and provide greater credibility to America's commitment to its allies. A new nuclear defensive system, the Strategic Defense Initiative, was also proposed to protect the U.S. homeland from nuclear attack.

At first, the Soviet Union responded in kind, continuing to deploy mobile intermediate-range missiles in the western part of the U.S.S.R., building new long-range nuclear missiles, and modernizing its nuclear submarine fleet. It also continued to support Marxist forces in Afghanistan, Angola, Kampuchea (Cambodia), and Ethiopia. Finally, it abruptly broke off arms-reduction talks after U.S. INF deployments began in Western Europe in November 1983.

Nevertheless, even as Moscow continued to command a military establishment equal to that of the United States and to underwrite numerous foreign-policy ventures, it was becoming clear that cracks in the country's social and economic foundations required dramatic remedy. Economically, the Soviet Union was becoming a second-rate

---

[60]Alexander Haig, "Opening Statement at Confirmation Hearings" (Washington, D.C.: Bureau of Public Affairs, Department of State, January 9, 1981), p. 2. This was Current Policy Statement No. 257.

[61]Ronald Reagan, "Address to Members of the British Parliament, June 8, 1982," in James M. McCormick, *A Reader in American Foreign Policy* (Itasca, Ill.: F. E. Peacock, 1986), p. 181.

[62]"Excerpts from President's Speech to National Association of Evangelicals," *The New York Times*, March 9, 1983, p. A18.

power. One Soviet economist admitted that, in 1980, more than 25 percent of the Soviet population (68.7 million) lived below the official poverty line, and that figure grew to about 28 percent by 1988.[63] The Soviet economy was afflicted by technological obsolescence, inadequate hard currency, low productivity, hidden inflation, underemployment, and scarcity in basic consumer goods.[64] And the decline was continuing with no end in sight. Between 1971 and 1975, Soviet GNP grew at more than 3 percent per year; between 1981 and 1985, that rate may have declined to less than 1 percent. In short, the Soviet economy was no longer able to support adventures around the world.

Gorbachev and the Cold War's End

Mikhail Gorbachev, who became General Secretary of the Soviet Communist Party in March 1985, recast domestic and foreign-policy priorities. He inaugurated a period of *"new thinking"* about domestic and foreign policy. For Soviet domestic policy, he proposed three important concepts — *perestroika, glasnost,* and democracy. *Perestroika* meant "restructuring" Soviet society to address pressing economic and social problems, including changes in the country's economic and political bureaucracies. *Glasnost* called for opening up society to achieve internal democracy. More information about Soviet society would be made available, and greater criticism of policies would be allowed. Increased political democracy, Gorbachev believed, would enhance the legitimacy of Soviet institutions, facilitating *perestroika* and *glasnost.* Gorbachev considered democratization a way of challenging and reforming (rather than destroying) the Communist Party's power.[65]

Domestic pressures were the incentive for Gorbachev to seek an end to the Cold War. Overseas adventures and unproductive investments in defense could not continue if domestic reform were to succeed. Gorbachev therefore set out to move Soviet thinking away from belief in the need for nuclear "superiority" toward acceptance of "sufficiency." He would reduce Soviet forces, adopt a new nonprovocative conventional-force posture, and scale back Soviet global commitments. All these actions provided greater flexibility to address the crisis at home. The barriers between domestic and foreign policy proved impossible to sustain and were to prove pivotal in ending the Cold War.

[63]See Bill Keller, "Soviet Economy: A Shattered Dream," *The New York Times,* May 13, 1990, pp. 1 and 13, and Keller, "How Gorbachev Rejected Plan to 'Shock Treat' the Economy," *The New York Times,* May 14, 1990, pp. A1, A6.

[64]Goods that were available were shoddy, and the Soviet media were filled with stories of exploding television sets and boots that fell apart.

[65]On the changes in the Soviet Union, see Michael Mandelbaum, "Coup de Grâce: The End of the Soviet Union," *Foreign Affairs* 71:1 (1992), pp. 164–183. Mandelbaum argues that Gorbachev was a communist reformer and "not a Western-style democrat" (p. 172) who lost control of the reform movement he had begun. As domestic reforms proceeded, they took on a life of their own, and, after the abortive August 1991 coup, "there was nothing left to reform" (p. 173).

By the second term of the Reagan administration (1984–1988), the stage was set for fundamentally reordering superpower relations. A new U.S. attitude developed for several reasons. The U.S. arms buildup was now under way and its effect on the American economy was evident in growing budget deficits. Continued increases in military spending no longer received wide support from the Congress or the American public, and their mood favored more cooperation with the Soviet Union, especially in arms control. Finally, the new leaders in Moscow too had begun to talk about change. Accommodative moves by both sides quickly followed. "New negotiations" on intermediate, strategic, and defensive nuclear weapons began early in 1985, and the first summit meeting since 1979 between American and Soviet leaders was held in November. Additional summits followed, providing the impetus for Soviet-American rapprochement on many global and regional issues.

Major agreements were reached on arms control that raised the nuclear threshold. Genuine efforts were also made to address old regional differences. Agreement was achieved on ending the war in Afghanistan and hastening the departure of Soviet troops. The superpowers cooperated in obtaining a cease-fire in the Iran-Iraq War and ending the civil war in Angola so that Cuban troops could leave that country.[66] Perhaps the most dramatic example of Soviet-US cooperation followed the Iraqi invasion of Kuwait in August 1990. Presidents Bush and Gorbachev hastily arranged a summit meeting in Helsinki, Finland, and jointly condemned Saddam Hussein's aggression. More important, the two continued to cooperate in passing U.N. resolutions demonstrating the global community's resolve to reverse this aggression. Such superpower cooperation was especially gratifying because in previous years the Soviet Union had been Iraq's principal arms supplier and political patron.

Solving the German Puzzle

The revolutionary changes that finally brought an end to the Cold War began with German reunification and communism's collapse in Eastern Europe and, ultimately, in the Soviet Union itself. Poland led the way. Early in 1989, the Polish government reversed its long-held policy of outlawing the trade union Solidarity, and a process that challenged the power of the Polish Communist Party was launched. By the end of 1989, a noncommunist government had come to power in Poland, and the Soviet Union did nothing to reverse the verdict. When it became clear that the U.S.S.R. would not intervene as it had in the past, the challenge to communist power quickly spread. Moscow seemed to have adopted the "Sinatra Doctrine," allowing its neighbors to pursue their "own way."[67] Within the year, Czechoslovakia, Hungary, East Germany,

[66]The agreement reached between warring factions in Angola broke down in 1993, but did not affect U.S.–Russian relations.

[67]The allusion is to American singer Frank Sinatra, who popularized a song entitled "My Way."

and other Eastern European countries had abandoned communist rule. All these states held democratic elections. The promise of Yalta had finally been fulfilled.

Internationally, the key to the Cold War lay in Germany, where it had all begun decades before. If dividing Germany had kindled the Cold War, reunifying the two Germanys was a prerequisite for ending it. But the German Democratic Republic, long regarded as the keystone in Moscow's empire, must disappear.[68] Political fissures in the GDR became apparent in spring 1989, when many young East Germans took advantage as barriers were dismantled between Austria and Hungary to travel to Hungary as tourists and then flee to West Germany. By August, a trickle had become a deluge of 5,000 emigrants a week, and many others camped in Hungary. Unlike 1961, when the U.S.S.R. prodded East Germany to build the Berlin Wall to halt a similar flight, the Soviet leadership did nothing to stop this massive emigration. Taking this silence as consent, more and more East Germans fled to Hungary, Poland, and Czechoslovakia. Mass demonstrations broke out in East German cities, notably Leipzig.

As demonstrations continued into autumn and opposition political parties formed, the East German communist leadership sought to save itself. The aged hard-line leader, Erich Honecker, was ousted;[69] competitive elections were scheduled; and, on November 9, 1989, the Berlin Wall was opened, with unmistakable symbolism: the Wall was the final piece of the Iron Curtain separating the "Free World" from the "Socialist Bloc."

German reunification, which had seemed unthinkable until then, suddenly looked possible, and, in November 1989, West German Chancellor Helmut Kohl unilaterally presented a plan for reunification. Six months later, free elections brought to power Kohl's conservative allies in East Germany who were committed to his plan. In summer 1990, Gorbachev agreed to a reunified Germany that would remain within a changed NATO. The Germans agreed to pay for keeping Soviet occupation troops in East Germany for a limited transition period. In October 1990, the two Germanys were officially reunited, and an all-German democratic government was elected in December 1990. A major step was the September 1990 agreement among the World War II victors (Great Britain, France, the United States, and the U.S.S.R.) formally renouncing further claims on Germany and turning Berlin back to the Germans. The German question had been formally and finally resolved.

A final element in resolving the Cold War was ending Soviet–U.S. ideological hostility. At the Malta Summit (December 1989) and the Washington Summit (June 1990), the formal ending to the Cold War was initiated with commitments and agreements between the two states for future cooperation. Two agreements reached late

[68]Soviet control over East Germany, the Soviets had long argued, prevented revival of a strong Germany similar to that which had almost conquered Russia in World Wars I and II. Thus, any sign of opposition to Moscow was firmly suppressed. For many years after 1945 the East German Communist Party was regarded as among the most loyal to Moscow and the most rigidly authoritarian in Eastern Europe.

[69]In summer 1992, Honecker was returned from Moscow to Germany to stand trial for ordering shot those trying to flee to the West. The trial was halted after he was diagnosed as having advanced cancer, and he was allowed to join his family in Chile.

in 1990 clarified the new superpower relationship. The first was a treaty drastically reducing and limiting conventional weapons in Europe, and the second was a nonaggression pact between NATO and the Warsaw Treaty Organization.[70] The nonaggression treaty included a formal declaration that the two sides were no longer adversaries.[71]

Three events in the Soviet Union provided a footnote to the end of the Cold War. An attempted coup in the Soviet Union, led by hard-liners who wanted to restore centralized communist control, collapsed in days in mid-August 1991, and Gorbachev was subsequently forced to renounce the Communist Party. Even more dramatic, the multinational Soviet state was formally dissolved December 25, 1991, and replaced by a loose federation of republics known as the Commonwealth of Independent States (CIS). Yet another effort by hardliners in Russia's parliament, led by its speaker Ruslan I. Khasbulatov and Vice-President Aleksandr V. Rutskoi, to overthrow President Boris Yeltsin was crushed on October 4, 1993.

Interpreting the End

The Realist Lens.   In one sense, the end of the Cold War reflects an accommodation in which the superpowers and their allies adjusted their national interests in resolving the old German question. The signing of formal pacts by these states renouncing further claims on Germany and permitting the country's formal unification supports this interpretation. Perceptions of national interest were also reflected in state-to-state decisions between Moscow and the Eastern European states in dissolving the Warsaw Pact and enabling each to pursue its own goals.

More broadly, a realist interpretation would focus on the changing power relationships in the global system as the basis for resolving the Cold War. America's containment strategy had been designed to place sufficient pressure on the Soviet Union to change both its internal structure and its international conduct. A realist might affirm that these efforts had succeeded. The massive arms buildup by both states had heavily burdened their economies, but the Soviet system ultimately proved less able to sustain the effort and was forced to seek accommodation with the United States. Similarly, because the United States stymied repeated and expensive Soviet efforts to expand influence in the Third World, the Soviet ability to project power was blunted. As viewed through a realist lens, United States power was instrumental in forcing the Soviet Union to end the Cold War.

The Organizational-Process–Bureaucratic-Politics Lens.   Our understanding of how the Cold War ended is deepened by looking at events through alternate lenses. For example, the organizational-process and bureaucratic-politics models of decision-making

[70]This treaty followed a Soviet-American agreement in principle (February 1990) for each to reduce troop strength in Central Europe to 195,000. In fact, for economic reasons, both sides were likely to reduce troop strength below that figure. Indeed, U.S. forces in Germany were rapidly sent to Saudi Arabia as part of the force to liberate Kuwait. The first treaty consisted mainly of unilateral Soviet concessions in which Moscow surrendered its massive advantage in numbers of tanks, armored vehicles, artillery, helicopters, and combat aircraft.

[71]Alan Riding, "The New Europe," *The New York Times*, November 20, 1990, p. A4.

remind us how important changes *within* the Soviet Union were in precipitating changes in Soviet foreign policy. As Gorbachev undertook to transform and revitalize Soviet society, organizational inertia and resistance by the many *apparatchiks* whose careers were endangered transformed his original goal of "reform" into something more fundamental. Whatever Gorbachev's original objectives, his policies of *perestroika, glasnost,* and democracy set off bureaucratic battles over which he ultimately lost control, and the end product for the Soviet state was demise. The abortive 1991 coup attempt was made by Soviet bureaucrats who wished to turn back the clock, and its failure actually accelerated the end of the old order and the Cold War.

Within the Soviet party and government bureaucracy, some flatly opposed the 1985 and 1986 Gorbachev reforms. Yegor K. Ligachev, the Communist Party secretary for agriculture, condemned Gorbachev's party reform as "thoughtless radicalism." Others, led by future Russian president Boris Yeltsin, wanted more rapid and radical party reform, and Yeltsin, along with others, would eventually quit the Communist Party when Gorbachev seemed to vacillate.[72] And Khasbulatov, Rutskoi, and others continued to sabotage reform efforts.

An important illustration of bureaucratic pulling and hauling in the Soviet government occurred late in 1990 when Gorbachev's economic advisers presented the "Shatalin Plan," outlining the transformation from a command to a market economy within five-hundred days. The plan met with a firestorm of opposition from a number of quarters. The KGB (secret police) and the military opposed it because it loosened central control too much for their liking and devolved too much power to the constituent republics. Others opposed the plan because they believed it would lead to high unemployment and rapid inflation. Gorbachev's own prime minister, Nikolai Ryzhkov, denounced the proposal and offered a more moderate one of his own. Ultimately, Gorbachev sought a synthesis of the two proposals as a compromise. Neither the original proposal nor the compromise was satisfactory, and confusion spread through the Soviet hierarchy.[73] These plans for reform, moreover, challenged many old assumptions, such as supremacy of heavy industry over consumer goods, and questioned whether one of the Cold War's pillars — competing conceptions of how societies ought to be organized — was about to fall.

Bureaucratic politics was dramatically illustrated by the failed coup attempt against Gorbachev in August 1991 as he was about to sign a treaty to enhance the authority of the constituent republics at the expense of the center. The plotters, antireform members of the Communist Party and disaffected government officials, placed Gorbachev under house arrest at his summer dacha and vowed to move the Soviet Union on a reverse course. After three days (August 19–21), however, the coup collapsed when Russian President Boris Yeltsin and his allies challenged the plotters' authority. Aided by massive

[72]Peter Hayes, ed., "Chronology 1990," *Foreign Affairs* 70:1 (1991), p. 218.

[73]Bill Keller, "Gorbachev Offers His Plan to Remake Soviet Economy, But Includes No Timetable," *The New York Times*, October 17, 1990, pp. A1, A9.

popular protests in central Moscow and other cities and failure by plotters and army to use force to support the takeover, reformers were able to face down the coup leaders. A politically enfeebled Gorbachev was restored to power, his days as head of the Soviet Union numbered.

Ironically, the coup that sought to halt the reform movement actually accelerated it. The Communist Party was soon disbanded; Gorbachev surrendered power to the leader of the Russian Federation, Boris Yeltsin; and the fifteen constituent republics seized the opportunity to declare their independence. Most of the new states quickly abandoned communism and rule by the Communist Party. With these stunning "domestic" events, the Cold War no longer had a *raison d'être*.

The Complex-Interdependence Lens.   A third possibility is to interpret the end of the Cold War as one social system, capitalism, triumphing over another, socialism. After more than seventy years, communism had shown itself to be a bankrupt political, economic, and social system. Anticipating communism's demise, Zbigniew Brzezinski, President Carter's National Security Adviser, argued that "communism will be remembered largely as the twentieth century's most extraordinary political and intellectual aberration."[74] In his judgment, communism had failed, not just in the U.S.S.R., but wherever it had been tried.

Nowhere were the failure of transnational ideology and the reassertion of nationalism more dramatic than in Poland. Early in the 1980s, the trade union, Solidarity, directly challenged Poland's stagnating socialist system. Led by the charismatic electrician (and future president), Lech Walesa, and supported by Poland's historically nationalist Catholic Church,[75] Solidarity called for massive reforms and power-sharing in the country. The communist government responded by imposing martial law in December 1981 and arresting many of the union's leaders. These repressive acts intensified popular resentment against the government and the Soviet-imposed system. This feeling was translated into "the revival of Polish political life" and "the rebirth of an alternative political elite, potentially capable of replacing someday the existing Communist rulers."[76] Early in 1989, Solidarity was again legalized, and Polish communist authorities capitulated peacefully to the rising tide of Polish nationalism.

Similar resentment spread to Hungary, Czechoslovakia, and East Germany through the informal and underground networks of political opposition in those states. Even in Romania, where government controls were much stricter than elsewhere in Eastern Europe, challenges to the political system arose. Elites increasingly wished to escape

---

[74]Zbigniew K. Brzezinski, *The Grand Failure: The Birth and Death of Communism in the Twentieth Century* (New York: Charles Scribner's Sons, 1989), p. 1.

[75]For more than three decades, the Polish Church had adamantly opposed the communist regime. The "Polish Pope," John Paul, strongly supported his Polish brethren and proved an important factor in overthrowing communism in Poland.

[76]Brzezinski, *Grand Failure*, p. 123.

their socialist isolation on the eastern fringe of Europe and reassert their traditional identity as "Central" Europeans in the heart of the continent. "Traditional nationalism" among these states was reborn, and "Marxist internationalism was dead."[77]

The political consequences of this rising tide of discontent and reasserted national identity gained full expression sooner than many had expected. In the end, all the former socialist states took steps to institute political democracy and market economies as solutions to social and economic woes. The ideological struggle between capitalism and communism was over. Marxism–Leninism had been defeated, not so much by capitalism, but by the nationalist forces it had suppressed for seven decades in the Soviet Union and four in Eastern Europe.

The final acts in the drama took place late in August 1991, immediately after the failed coup in the Soviet Union, when Boris Yeltsin suspended all activities of the Communist Party in Russia. Within the week the last general secretary of the Communist Party of the Soviet Union, Mikhail Sergeivich Gorbachev, called upon his party's central committee to dissolve itself, and shortly thereafter nationalism reigned triumphant as one Soviet republic after another declared its independence. Adam Ulam describes this momentous transition:

> What for seventy years had been hailed as "the pride and conscience of the nation," "the vanguard of the proletariat" — the celebrated and mighty Communist Party of the Soviet Union — for all practical purposes ceased to exist. . . . All over the vast land crowds were dismantling statues of Lenin and other Communist notables. . . . *Communism had drawn its strengths and appeal from the claim that it was the only ideology and movement that could rise above nationalism* and establish a peaceful and stable state. . . . [78]

An ideological movement that had been an essential element in the Cold War had ended. Its abrupt termination led to a changed world in which new issues and actors would replace it.

Conclusion

In this chapter we have reviewed the stages in the Cold War that shaped global politics for over forty years. The issue illustrates how critical are the rules of the game in global politics for avoiding catastrophe and the utility of examining global phenomena through different theoretical lenses. We are too close to the end of the Cold War to judge with certainty what sort of world we are entering, but we do know some of the issues that will dominate the global agenda in coming years.

[77]Ibid., p. 135. The emphasis on Central European identity connoted "a repudiation of the Soviet-sponsored notion of a shared 'socialist' culture" (p. 139).

[78]Ulam, *The Communists*, pp. 490, 494. Emphasis added.

The end of the Cold War and the division between East and West was marked by the opening of the Berlin Wall and the subsequent reunification of Germany. Germans dancing on the wall in front of the Brandenburg Tor, the symbolic heart of Germany, shows the euphoria of the time.

Economic issues are certain to grow in importance. In Chapter 13, we examine the economic issues that unite and separate Europeans, Americans, and Japanese and how these issues may affect global politics in the future. Are these issues likely to provide the cement that will provide unity of purpose for these states, or will they prove so divisive that they will inspire greater rivalry and conflict in the future? In Chapter 14, we turn to the festering rivalries in the Middle East. How did they start, and how are they sustained? Does the end of the Cold War affect prospects for peace in the region? Are the rivalries in this region typical of those the pessimists fear for the rest of the world, or is the Middle East an exception to the orderly community that optimists believe is assembling?

Key Terms

Cold War
end of history
issue cycle
genesis
crisis
ritualization
resolution
communism
Bolshevik
spheres of influence
Yalta Axioms
Riga Axioms
Novikov Telegram
mirror image
Marxist–Leninism
global agenda
salience
Yalta Conference
Potsdam Conference
Long Telegram
iron curtain
national interest

capitalist encirclement
Truman Doctrine
containment
détente
peaceful coexistence
Cold War consensus
socialism in one country
wars of national liberation
perestroika
glasnost
power vacuum
capitalism
socialism
Cominform
NSC-68
Berlin blockade
Korean War
Cuban missile crisis
Berlin Wall
Vietnam War
new thinking

CHAPTER THIRTEEN

Friendly Economic Adversaries: United States, Japan, and Europe

For the moment, judging by military power the world appears unipolar, but changes are afoot. From an economic perspective, the world already has three poles: the United States, Japan, and Western Europe. Economically, the United States no longer enjoys its postwar domination. Since 1970, America's economic position has declined, as two observers declare, "as measured in terms of the American share of world output, world exports, and most other indicators."[1] This decline has been accompanied by growing disputes among the United States, Japan, and the European Community that include "how to break remaining barriers to trade . . . how to integrate Eastern Europe and the Soviet Union into the global economic system; how to deal with a polluted environment and ward off the danger of global warming; how to fight the international drug trade; how to stimulate sufficient savings to meet the explosion of demand for capital all over the world. . . . "[2]

Will the bipolar political conflict between West and East be replaced by economic conflict among three competitive trading blocs: North America (with the United States as its leader), Western Europe (with Germany at its helm), and East Asia (grouped around Japan)? Will the United States seek to restore its ebbing status, and will Japan and Europe exercise their economic clout in parochial ways? Or will the end of the Cold War and economic interdependence for the United States and its friends in Europe and Asia produce a dynamic and open global economic system in which growing prosperity makes resort to arms irrational and obsolete? A German scholar expresses the issue:

[1]Helen Milner and Jack Snyder, "Lost Hegemony?" *International Organization* 42:4 (Autumn 1988), p. 749.

[2]Leonard Silk, "Triple Play: The Rich Nations Get Richer and Then?" *The New York Times*, July 1, 1990, Section 4, p. 1.

As the postwar international order dissolves, some of the initial concerns that informed and shaped it are resurfacing. One key objective of this old order was the containment of Japanese and German military expansionism. . . . This rationale is rapidly fading now, and old specters once more raise their ugly heads. . . . Some observers fear a return of either state (or both) to traditional temptations of military power politics. . . . Others worry about the implications of a changing distribution of economic power as a result of Germany's and Japan's single-minded pursuit of economic gain abroad and tendencies toward parochial and closed societies and economies at home.[3]

In this chapter we examine evolving relations among the economic top dogs and discuss the prospects for their future cooperation or conflict in this context: America's economic decline; rising Japanese and European (particularly German) economic power; and the effects such changes will engender as we reach the twenty-first century. Until recently, the United States, Japan, and Western Europe did not compete with one another directly. Instead, each occupied an economic niche in which the products one produced did not threaten producers and workers in the others. This condition has so changed that, economist Lester Thurow writes, the twenty-first century will be seen "as a century of head-to-head competition."[4]

[S]tarting from approximately the same level of economic development, each country or region wants exactly the same industries to insure that its citizens have the standards of living in the twenty-first century. . . . *Niche competition* is win-win. Everyone has a place where they can excel; no one is going to be driven out of business. *Head-to-head competition* is win-lose. . . . Some will win; some will lose.[5]

And many fear that the United States is losing the competition. During the 1980s the United States ran up huge trade deficits with its largest trading partners: Japan, Germany, Canada, Taiwan, and others. In other words, Americans were failing to compete effectively with other major developed economies.

Declining American Hegemony?

Is it possible for an actor to remain a *political* and *military* leader or *hegemon* without also enjoying dominant economic influence? Some scholars argue that *imperial overextension* brings economic decline, which spells the end of political influence. The historian Paul Kennedy declares, with historical examples, that "the difficulties experienced by

[3]Hanns W. Maull, "Germany and Japan: The New Civilian Powers," *Foreign Affairs* 69:5 (Winter 1990/91), p. 91.

[4]Lester Thurow, *Head to Head: The Coming Economic Battle Among Japan, Europe, and America* (New York: William Morrow, 1992), p. 29.

[5]Ibid., p. 30. Emphasis added.

contemporary societies which are militarily top-heavy merely repeat those which, in their time, affected Phillip II's Spain, Nicholas II's Russia, and Hitler's Germany."[6] Similarly, British hegemony in the nineteenth century ended when that country, where the industrial revolution began and center of the world's largest trading empire, was overtaken by new economic giants—the United States and Germany. The argument concludes that the same fate awaits the Cold War superpowers. The Soviet collapse in 1991 under extensive military burdens seems to lend weight to the argument.

The question of whether the United States is in decline is not a simple one. Is a country weaker because it is an international debtor rather than a creditor? Is foreign investment a source of economic vigor or weakness? Which high-technology areas are most critical for the future? Economists and political scientists debate these and other issues, which are at the heart of comparisons of economic performance. As World War II ended, the United States stood alone, an economic colossus dominating almost every major economic sector. That supremacy has disappeared. The dollar is no longer undisputed king of global currencies, and U.S. dominance of world financial markets, manufacturing, trade, and overseas investment too has diminished. Global economic clout is shifting to the Pacific Rim, especially Japan and the *newly industrialized countries* (*NICs*)—Singapore, Hong Kong, South Korea, and Taiwan—and to Europe, especially united Germany.

Is America's apparent economic decline an illusion based on the echo Joseph Nye calls the "*vanishing World War II effect*" in which "the American share of global power resources exaggerated by World War II went through a natural and steady decline during the next quarter century and then stabilized"?[7] The year 1945 was hardly typical. Europe was in shambles; Japanese cities were reduced to rubble; and, of all the world's industrial regions, only America remained unscarred by war. If Nye's view is correct, then the change that appears to be a sustained decline is really a return to normalcy after a rare moment of supremacy. Thus, the pessimists who warn of America's fall from grace may be drawing conclusions from faulty time periods. Looking at trends from the immediate postwar period may overstate America's "normal" dominance.[8]

---

[6]Paul Kennedy, *The Rise and Fall of the Great Powers: Economic Change and Military Conflict from 1500 to 2000* (New York: Random House, 1987), p. 444.

[7]Joseph S. Nye, Jr., *Bound to Lead: The Changing Nature of American Power* (New York: Basic Books, 1990), p. 72.

[8]United States hegemony is often seen as analogous to British supremacy during the past century. Robert O. Keohane points out, however, that the comparison may be flawed because "Britain had never been as superior in productivity to the rest of the world as the United States was after 1945." *After Hegemony: Cooperation and Discord in the World Political Economy* (Princeton: Princeton University Press, 1984), p. 37. See also Bruce M. Russett, "The Mysterious Case of Vanishing Hegemony; Or, Is Mark Twain Really Dead?" *International Organization* 39:2 (Spring 1985), p. 211.

As other regions, already blessed with skilled workers and access to advanced technology, rebuilt their shattered infrastructures after 1945, America's apparent pre-eminence necessarily declined. Indeed, one primary goal of U.S. postwar foreign policy was to assist allies, and the prosperity of allies including Japan and Germany reflect successful policies like the Marshall Plan (1948–1952) and preferential access to U.S. markets provided for Japanese and European products. Even using data on GNP, military expenditures, and manufacturing production from 1945, one observer concludes that "the United States retains on all these indicators a degree of dominance . . . that compares well with the U.S. position in 1938." Thus, "The basis of American hegemony may have declined, but it has hardly vanished."[9]

In sum, despite relative decline from the lofty economic heights it once occupied, the United States still enjoys a GDP of $5.6 trillion, significantly larger than the *combined* domestic product of Japan and Germany ($4.94 trillion).[10] Although America's per capita gross national product ($22,240), which is an indicator of standard of living, appears lower than Japan's ($26,930) and higher than that of the European Community ($15,000), the figures are distorted by fluctuating currency.[11] Other indicators, such as ownership of homes, leisure time, and accessibility of higher education suggest that Americans still enjoy a higher standard of living than their Japanese or German counterparts.

When we observe America's economic position from a longer perspective, the picture changes. Analyzing the U.S. percentage of world product from 1900 through 1987, as in Figure 13.1, it is clear that, although the U.S. share has dropped from its high water mark in the late 1940s and early 1950s, it has really only settled back to a position comparable to the early part of this century. As shown in Figure 13.2, the U.S. share of world manufacturing production has declined from its postwar high of almost 45 percent (1953), but only to what it had been in 1938. Finally, as reflected in Table 13.1, even the decline in America's share of exports of technology-intensive products—an area emphasized by some policy-makers—is modest.

Then too, the bases of influence have gradually shifted so that the history of former hegemons may be a poor guide to the future. Table 13.2 charts the resources necessary for global leadership in different eras.

There is a temptation to confuse others' growing prosperity with the U.S. decline. In recent years, Japan's great strides in various technologies have *not* been made at the expense of the United States. Japan's growing share of high-technology exports between 1980 and 1989 was accompanied by U.S. losses in computers, precision equipment, aerospace, telecommunications equipment, and machine tools. At the same time,

[9]Russett, "Mysterious Case of Vanishing Hegemony," p. 211.

[10]The World Bank, *World Development Report 1993* (New York: Oxford University Press, 1993), p. 243.

[11]Ibid., p. 239.

TABLE 13.1

World Export Shares of Technology-Intensive Products, 1970–1986

Country	1970	1980	1986
United States	27.0%	22.9%	20.9%
Japan	10.9	14.3	19.8
France	7.1	8.5	7.9
West Germany	16.8	16.3	16.0
Great Britain	9.8	10.8	9.0

SOURCE: Joseph S. Nye, Jr., *Bound to Lead* (New York: Basic Books, 1990), p. 77.

though, the United States gained larger shares of exports in microelectronics, medical and biological products, and organic chemicals.

Even if America has suffered a relative economic decline, "soft power" — "cultural attraction, ideology, and international institutions"[12] — is gaining, which means that Washington may enjoy new sources of influence and may not need to abdicate global leadership. The Soviet system collapsed because Marxist ideology was bankrupt. America's strength may lie less in its laboratories and factories than in its liberal democracyand

[12]Nye, *Bound to Lead*, p. 188.

FIGURE 13.1

The Shape of American Decline

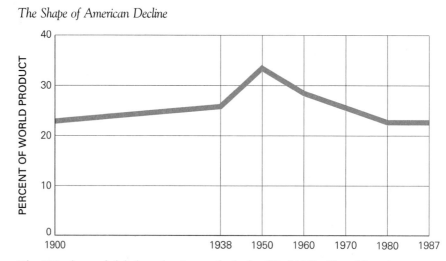

The U.S. share of global production peaked after World War II and has since declined to where it stood earlier in the century.

FIGURE 13.2

American Share of World Manufacturing Production

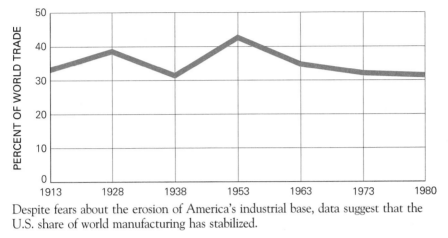

Despite fears about the erosion of America's industrial base, data suggest that the U.S. share of world manufacturing has stabilized.

free enterprise. If that is the reason, then, Nye says, America's future depends on whether the country "will have the political leadership and strategic vision to convert these power resources into real influence in a transitional period of world politics."[13]

[13]Ibid., p. 260.

TABLE 13.2

Leading States and Major Power Resources

Historical period	Leading state	Major resources
16th century	Spain	Gold bullion, colonial trade, mercenary armies, dynastic ties.
17th century	Netherlands	Trade, capital markets, navy.
18th century	France	Population, rural industry, public administration, army.
19th century	Britain	Industry, political cohesion, finance and credit, navy, liberal norms, island location (defensibility).
20th century		Economic scale, scientific and technical leadership, universalistic culture, military forces and alliances, liberal international regimes, hub of transnational communications.

SOURCE: Nye, *Bound to Lead*, p. 34.

Still, a nagging suspicion remains that something fundamental is behind America's economic trials. According to one gloomy assessment,

> The United States . . . has the world's biggest hole in its pocket. The national debt, just $1 trillion a decade ago, is now $3.5 trillion. The Federal budget deficit is expected to swell the national debt by $362 billion in the fiscal year 1992. . . . And the net foreign debt — foreigners' assets in this country minus Americans' assets abroad, measured at their current replacement value — swung from a surplus of $364 billion in 1982 to a deficit of $412 billion in 1990. . . . [14]

In less than a decade the United States has shifted from being the world's leading creditor to the world's leading debtor. From virtual self-sufficiency, the United States has grown increasingly dependent on world trade yet continues to suffer from a yawning trade deficit. Throughout the 1980s, America's productivity performance — output per hour of work — was poor (though it improved early in the 1990s).[15] Once self-sufficient in energy, the United States depends ever more on Middle East and other foreign oil. Perhaps most telling from the *declinist perspective* was America's need to go hat in hand to such allies as Japan, Germany, Saudi Arabia, and Kuwait to finance the 1991 Persian Gulf War.

Overall, America's global competitive position appears to be eroding because of such trends as decreasing educational standards and performance and reduced pools of skilled laborers. The United States has fallen far behind Japan in scientists and engineers per million in its population.[16] Low savings rates — roughly one-third as high as Taiwan, Malaysia, Korea, and Japan[17] — produce inadequate investment in the future. The weak U.S. dollar, combined with stronger economies elsewhere, encourages foreigners to purchase U.S. assets and creates fear of dependency on "outsiders" similar to that once common among Europeans and Latin Americans who feared the U.S. presence.[18] Anxiety about dependence on outsiders is produced by U.S. trade deficits in such vital industries as consumer electronics and semiconductors. The historian Paul Kennedy captures this anxiety:

[14]Leonard Silk, "Some Things Are More Vital Than Money When It Comes to Creating the World Anew," *The New York Times*, September 22, 1991, Section 4, p. 2.

[15]Thurow, *Head to Head*, p. 165. Between 1980 and 1990, U.S. productivity grew at 1.2 percent per year compared with 3.1 percent per year for Japan.

[16]Paul Kennedy, *Preparing for the Twenty-First Century* (New York: Random House, 1993), p. 216.

[17]Ibid., p. 199.

[18]See, for example, Thomas Omestad, "Selling off America," *Foreign Policy* No. 76 (Fall 1989), pp. 119–140. Typical of the earlier fear of U.S. dominance is J. J. Servan-Schreiber, *The American Challenge* (New York: Atheneum, 1968).

What if foreigners acquire a monopoly in industries that make strategic products for the Pentagon, or if an important military-related item is made only abroad? What if the country becomes ever more reliant upon foreign capital — will it one day pay a political price as well as a financial one for that dependency?[19]

Finally, what if America's competitors play by different rules? Lester Thurow tells of a secret meeting held in Singapore in 1990 between the two largest business groups in the world — the Mitsubishi group from Japan and the Daimler Benz–Deutsche Bank group from Germany — to consider a global alliance. Thurow writes:

> From an American perspective everything about that Singapore meeting was criminally illegal. . . . In the United States banks cannot own industrial firms and businesses cannot sit down behind closed doors to plan joint strategies. Those doing so get thrown into jail for extended periods of time. Yet in today's world Americans cannot force the rest of the world to play the economic game as Americans think it should be played.[20]

Challenge from the East: Rising Japan

Despite its deepest recession since World War II in the early 1990s, Japan remained the principal challenger to U.S. economic dominance. Japan's transformation from a devastated and occupied nation in 1945 to a prosperous power in the 1990s is a remarkable story about the second half of the twentieth century. The question remains, though, whether Japan has the will and capacity to become a hegemonic leader in the future and, if so, what sort of leader it would be.

Pre-World War II Japan

The prospect of Japan as a major power is not new. The country left feudal isolation[21] when a U.S. fleet arrived in Tokyo Bay in 1853 and Japan subsequently granted trading rights to the United States. It became "the first Asian industrialized nation" after defeating China in the Sino-Japanese War of 1894–1895.[22] As a result of that war,

---

[19]Kennedy, *Preparing for the Twenty-First Century*, pp. 299, 301.

[20]Thurow, *Head to Head*, p. 35.

[21]Japan had been closed to all foreigners except the Dutch since the seventeenth century.

[22]Ronald E. Dolan and Robert L. Worden, eds., *Japan: A Country Study*, 5th ed. (Washington, D.C.: U.S. Government Printing Office, 1992), p. 45. Also see Robert A. Scalapino, "The Foreign Policy of Japan," in Roy C. Macridis, ed., *Foreign Policy in World Politics* (Englewood Cliffs, N.J.: Prentice-Hall, 1992), pp. 187–189.

Japan seized Taiwan (called Formosa) and, like its imperial rivals in Europe, made territorial inroads in China. In 1902, Japan became the first Asian state to conclude an alliance with a European power (Great Britain), and this treaty (which aimed to balance Russian power in Asia) gave it a claim on German colonies in Asia after World War I. By defeating a European power in the Russo-Japanese War of 1904–1905, Japan's influence in Asia grew. By 1910, it had annexed Korea and extended its involvement in Manchuria at the expense of China and Russia.

During the following years, Japan continued to expand its influence in Asia, and early in the 1930s sought to widen its influence in China. A desperate search for markets during the Great Depression set off its seizure of Manchuria and growing involvement in the rest of China. Facing rivalry with China and Russia (in Mongolia), fear of Soviet communism, and friction with the United States and Britain, Japan cast its lot with the Axis in the Anti-Comintern Pact (1936).

With militarists controlling the cabinet, Japan pursued its war against China with renewed vigor despite growing opposition in the United States. In 1940, Japanese leaders began to plan to further extend Tokyo's influence in Asia and eliminate Western penetration of the region. Alarmed by U.S. economic sanctions, Japan called for a "Greater East Asia Co-prosperity Sphere" that would include Japan, Manchuria, China and the rest of Southeast Asia, with a Greater East Asia Ministry to promote this activity. On December 7, 1941, Japan attacked the U.S. Pacific fleet and sent its armies into Southeast Asia. At its peak, the Japanese Empire included all of Southeast Asia, Indonesia, and the island chains in the South Pacific and stretched to the frontiers of Alaska, Australia, and British India. The attack on Pearl Harbor was to prove the beginning of the end for Japan's attempt at global preeminence.

Japan's defeat was complete. The United States demanded Japan's unconditional surrender,[23] called for Tokyo to renounce war, and restricted Japan's sovereignty. During the wartime conferences, the victorious powers placed stringent conditions on Japan's reconstruction, calling for new political institutions and weakening the country's powerful *zaibatsu*, its giant industrial and financial institutions. The country remained under U.S. occupation until 1952, governed by General Douglas MacArthur, who directed Japan's reconstruction and its adoption of a new constitution.

As a consequence of defeat and occupation, Japanese society was restructured. First, the armed forces' influence on political life was eliminated. The new constitution was designed to prevent restoration of Japanese militarism. Article 9 proclaimed, "the Japanese people forever renounce war as a sovereign right of the nation and the threat or use of force as means of settling international disputes" and that "land, sea, and air

---

[23]In fact, Japan did not surrender unconditionally but negotiated to retain its emperor, even though he would no longer be regarded as divine.

forces, as well as other war potential, will never be maintained."[24] Second, a new generation was thrust into leadership, and the old prewar conservative elements were removed from power. Only in this way, it was believed, was it possible to instill commitment to democratic values. Third, efforts were made to increase workers' power with a revitalized trade-union movement. In this way, Japanese society would be restructured in a manner more compatible with Western values.

Postwar Reconstruction

The reconstruction of Japan after 1945 was rapid. Closely watched by U.S. and allied forces and the Supreme Commander of the Allied Powers (SCAP), the new democratic constitution was promulgated by early 1947. Political stabilization followed quickly with competing political parties. Economic recovery was a main objective, and plans were drafted to impose efficiency and combat inflation. Entrepreneurial activity was encouraged, emphasizing new technologies. By 1950, helped by the Korean War, Japan had embarked upon "a period of amazing economic development," writes one Asian expert.[25] Economic growth rates averaged about 10 percent in the 1960s and 1970s and continued to outpace most other industrial societies in the 1980s and 1990s.

With economic and political reform under way early in the 1950s, Japan was in a position to regain its independence. In 1952, fifty-one former enemies signed a Treaty of Peace with Japan,[26] and Washington and Tokyo signed a mutual-security pact. The occupation formally ended late in April 1952, and Japan simultaneously regained its sovereignty as well as a security umbrella from the United States. As part of the security pact, the United States committed itself to protect Japan from any external attack, a commitment that allowed Japan to emphasize rapid economic growth without burdening itself with military spending. The mutual-security treaty ushered in an extended period of close bilateral ties between the two countries.

For much of the Cold War, the United States was willing to provide security for Japan, even at significant cost. The arrangement not only served the U.S. policy of containment but permitted harnessing a mighty economic engine to the forces opposed

---

[24]Reprinted in Scalapino, "Foreign Policy of Japan," p. 194. The Japanese government gave Article 9 as its reason for not sending troops to join the U.S.–led coalition against Iraq. In September 1992, a controversy erupted in Japan when the government claimed that Article 9 did permit dispatching combat troops as part of a U.N. contingent helping Cambodia move toward free elections.

[25]Ibid., p. 197.

[26]John Foster Dulles, later U.S. Secretary of State, was the lead architect of the treaty. Of the major powers only the U.S.S.R. remained in a state of war with Japan. Russian efforts to end the state of war and attract Japanese investment have fallen victim to disagreement over four small islands in the Kurile chain north of Japan that the Soviet Union seized in 1945.

to Soviet communism. As Cold War pressure began to ease and the Japanese economic challenge grew, the United States became less willing to underwrite the security relationship.

Japanese Economic Power

The growth of Japanese economic power in recent decades, especially compared to that of the United States, can be illustrated in a number of ways. Measures of trade, investment, and currency especially indicate changing global economic relations.

In trade, Japan has become a superpower. As the U.S. trade deficit worldwide has increased, the Japanese continue to enjoy record trade surpluses. Throughout the 1970s and 1980s, except for the oil crises in 1973–1974 and 1979–1980, Japan had a positive trade balance. Following both crises, the Japanese export economy rebounded, and Japan's trade surplus ballooned, reaching $83 billion in 1986.[27] This pattern indicates the Japanese economy's overall strength in global affairs.

The United States went in the other direction during the same period. It experienced deficits in its merchandise trade account for seven of the ten years in the 1970s and for every year during the 1980s, a pattern that continues. In 1987, the trade deficit exceeded $160 billion before declining to about $100 billion in 1991.[28] Although deficits stabilized in the following years, the United States still struggles to remain competitive in trade because it continues to import more than it exports. "As a result of the hollowing of its industry," declares one caustic observer, "the United States no longer makes hundreds of products, ranging from ceramic semiconductor packages to bicycle tires to VCRs. . . . The composition of the trade has made the United States look ever more like a developing country. It imports high technology goods and capital from Japan and . . . exports to it mostly commodities, such as logs and soybeans. . . ."[29] This reading may overstate reality but not by much.

The volume of trade between the two countries is very high. Japan is America's second-largest trading partner (after Canada), and the United States is Japan's largest source of imports. In all, trade between the two totaled about $130 billion in 1988 and continues to rise. The imbalance in trade between the two that has grown over the years has, however, created friction in U.S.–Japanese relations. In 1982, the United States had a deficit with Japan of $19 billion. Five years later the deficit peaked at $60 billion,

---

[27]Dolan and Worden, *Japan: A Country Study*, pp. 272–273.

[28]See Table 2–1 in Joan E. Spero, *The Politics of International Economic Relations*, 4th ed. (New York: St. Martin's Press, 1990), pp. 38–39; and Bureau of the Census, *Statistical Abstract of the United States 1991* (Washington, D.C.: U.S. Government Printing Office, 1991).

[29]Clyde V. Prestowitz, Jr., *Trading Places: How We Are Giving Our Future to Japan and How to Reclaim It* (New York: Basic Books, 1988), p. 491.

declining to $41 billion by 1991.[30] The Japanese recession in 1992–1993 again exacerbated the U.S. trade deficit with Japan despite exertion on both sides to reduce it.

The Japanese economy is mobilized to promote exports by capturing and holding foreign markets in vital sectors, especially those at the high end of the technological chain. In the initial postwar decades, Japan dominated low-cost and low-technology sectors and, with each success, moved into more sophisticated sectors. The economy became a veritable export machine in which the Ministries of Finance and of International Trade and Industry (MITI) work hand in hand with big business to promote industries that will enhance the country's global competitiveness. Japan's *industrial policy* contrasts with America's free-market approach. Japanese economic ministries attract the country's most talented university graduates (unlike the United States), and bureaucrats singlemindedly pursue the goal of increasing exports.[31] "The real equivalent of the Japanese Ministry of International Trade and Industry (MITI) in the United States," declares one observer, "is not the Department of Commerce but the Department of Defense, which by its very nature and functions shares MITI's strategic, goal-oriented outlook."[32]

Japan's emphasis on exports is reflected in its dominance of key industries. On a worldwide scale, Japanese automobiles—Toyota, Honda, Mitsubishi, Mazda, Nissan, Isuzu—dominate the market in many countries and are highly regarded for quality and dependability. The same can be said for the electronics and communications industries, in which Japanese corporations like Sony and Matsushita are world leaders.[33] One critic says:

> Under the leadership of its elite bureaucracy, Japan's homogeneous, group-oriented society has striven to improve its standard of living and to avoid dependence on or intrusion by outsiders. It has done so by . . . focusing all of its enormous energy on building an industrial structure with comparative advantage and bargaining power. This strategy . . . has produced an industrial establishment of unparalleled efficiency which has conquered world markets but also engendered great resentment.[34]

Changing patterns of *foreign investment* are a second indicator of Japan's growing economic role. Although the United States still has more overseas investments than

[30]These data are taken from William H. Cooper, "Japan–U.S. Economic Relations: Cooperation or Confrontation?" *CRS Issue Brief* (Washington, D.C.: Congressional Research Service, April 18, 1989), pp. 2–3; and Steven R. Weisman, "Japan and U.S. Struggle with Resentment," *The New York Times*, December 3, 1991, pp. A1, A6.

[31]See Suzuta Atsuyuki, "The Way of the Bureaucrat," in Daniel I. Okimoto and Thomas P. Rohlen, eds., *Inside the Japanese System: Readings on Contemporary Society and Political Economy* (Stanford, Calif.: Stanford University Press, 1988), pp. 196–203.

[32]Chalmers Johnson, "Market Rationality vs. Plan Rationality," in ibid., p. 217. One reason for Japan's export orientation is to make use of surplus industrial capacity and maintain domestic employment. See Kozo Yamamura, "Japanese Industrial Policy: International Repercussions," in ibid., pp. 221–222.

[33]See Nye, *Bound to Lead*, p. 165.

[34]Prestowitz, *Trading Places*, pp. 489–490.

With the end of the Cold War, global economic issues assumed greater prominence, and some Americans believed that foreign imports, especially Japanese, posed a major threat to U.S. security. In this cartoon, Japanese bombers are seen dropping autos instead of bombs and using the same signal that marked the beginning of the Japanese attack on Pearl Harbor in 1941.

Japan, the rate at which Japanese global investment increases has outstripped the U.S. rate. In 1971, the book value of U.S. foreign investments was $86.2 billion, and in 1986 it had grown to $260 billion.[35] In 1970, Japan had only $3.6 billion invested overseas, a figure that rose to $36.5 billion by 1980. Eight years later Japanese overseas investments had increased fivefold, surpassing $186 billion. North America itself had become a magnet for such funds, accounting for more than 40 percent of Japan's global investments in 1988 (compared with 25 percent in 1970). High U.S. interest rates during this period were attractive to Japanese investors, and Japanese purchases of U.S. government securities helped pay the burgeoning cost of interest associated with America's spiraling budget deficit. [36]

[35]Spero, *Politics of International Economic Relations*, p. 107.

[36]Table 31, "Geographical Distribution of Cumulative Direct Investment, Selected Years, 1970–88," in Dolan and Worden, *Japan: A Country Study*, pp. 500–501.

Global financial power, as measured by dominance in *global banking* and *strength of currency*, is another indicator of Japan's growing global economic role. As recently as 1982, the two largest international banks were American. By 1990, the six largest world banks were Japanese, as were eleven of the top twenty. Only one, Citicorp, was American, and it ranked eighteenth. By 1993, nine of the ten largest banks were Japanese, and none were American.[37] By 1988, fifty-three of the world's largest corporations, including eight of the top ten, were Japanese, and only thirty-two were American.[38] Although these institutions may not directly serve Japan's interests, they reflect this society's vigor.

Aided by stable growth and low inflation, the Japanese currency — the yen — has challenged the U.S. dollar in investors' eyes. Wide fluctuations in the dollar's value and the continuing boom–bust cycle in the U.S. economy make the yen seem a desirable haven for investors. Although the yen has not replaced the dollar as the basis for global transactions, it did gain importance in the 1970s and the 1980s. In August 1993, the yen hit an all-time high against the dollar, nearly reaching parity with the U.S. penny.

The rapid growth in Japanese economic power frightens some observers. From the mid-1970s to the end of the 1980s, Japanese GNP increased sevenfold, doubling that of West Germany and surpassing that of the U.S.S.R. Two observers comment:

> At the end of the 1980s, the biggest problem the world economy posed to Japan was an embarrassment of riches — that is, the problem of how to recycle the staggering wealth of its external assets. These assets have been estimated to reach $470 billion in 1990, more than twice the combined external assets of the members of the Organization of Petroleum Exporting Countries (OPEC) at the height of the second oil crisis, and to soar to $1.3 trillion by the year 2000.[39]

Japan has the potential to transform its economic assets into political and military leverage. It has the technology to become a major nuclear and conventional military power. Japanese aid programs and the prospect of Japanese investment in economies that are starved for cash can provide political clout. Thus, Russia and China are competing for Japanese investment and technology; the United States relies on continued Japanese investment to pay its deficits; Southeast Asia depends on Tokyo for prosperity; and even the United Nations is trying to harness Japanese economic might to its peacekeeping efforts. Until now, Japan has been reluctant to assert itself politically, anxious that it might arouse memories of World War II. When in 1993 the *Liberal Democratic Party* (*LDP*) — the political party that had ruled Japan since World War II — splintered, the future became cloudier. But, if history provides any lessons, one is that an economic power — for example, the United States after 1919 — cannot long evade the political and military responsibilities that follow.

[37]Thurow, *Head to Head*, pp. 143–144.

[38]"Global Finance," *The Wall Street Journal Reports*, September 23, 1988, p. 18 R.

[39]Henrik Schmiegelow and Michele Schmiegelow, "How Japan Affects the International System," *International Organization* 44:4 (Autumn 1990), pp. 560–561.

United States–Japanese Economic Frictions

Japanese economic power has produced resentment among Americans and others, and the Japanese increasingly resent U.S. pressure. In reality, U.S.–Japanese frictions grow out of incompatible interests, genuine misperceptions, cultural differences, and a need to find scapegoats for domestic woes.

Many Americans blame Japan, particularly Japanese restrictions on access to their economy, for the U.S. trade imbalance. Typical of such *Japan-bashing* is James Abegglen's description of "Japan's trade interaction with the rest of the world," as "a monstrous burden on the world's trade system."[40] United States corporate executives, especially those in industries that fare poorly against Japanese competitors such as the Big Three[41] automakers, complain that the "playing field" is not even. Nontariff barriers, such as slow inspection of products entering Japan, quotas on commodities, chummy arrangements among Japanese firms, or outright bans on products such as rice, reduce America's ability to export to Japan. Complicated Japanese rules and procedures — excessive red tape, from the U.S. perspective — also prevent U.S. companies from investing in Japan. Although impediments also complicate entering the U.S. market, Americans argue it is relatively open to foreign trade and investment. A former official in the Department of Commerce writes,

> . . . Japan has . . . become the undisputed world economic champion with all the geopolitical power that implies. Desperate, but classically conventional measures aimed at salvaging the U.S. position have . . . not worked. Frantic demands for a "level playing field" . . . have not prevented the growing dependence on a Japanese technology that is systematically promoted as a matter of high national priority. A halving of the value of the dollar against the yen and stimulation of Japan's domestic economy were supposed to reduce the U.S. trade deficit and the Japanese surplus. They did not.[42]

Some Americans are disturbed that Japanese investment in the United States is so visible, giving the impression that Americans no longer control their own economic destiny. The Japanese have invested heavily in such prominent corporations as Columbia Pictures and have purchased gilt-edged real estate, including Rockefeller Center in New York City. In 1992, a Japanese investor became the largest shareholder in a major-league baseball team (the Seattle Mariners), which to some meant that even America's national pastime would somehow become less American. Such investments, coupled with the growing presence of Japanese nationals managing their investments in the United States; loss of jobs in U.S. industries unable to compete with Japanese

---

[40]James C. Abegglen, "Japan's Ultimate Vulnerability," in Okimoto and Rohlen, eds., *Inside the Japanese System*, p. 258.

[41]General Motors, Ford, and Chrysler. A weaker dollar and a heightened concern for quality on their part improved the competitiveness of U.S. automakers somewhat during the early 1990s.

[42]Prestowitz, *Trading Places*, p. 2.

firms; and comments by Japanese officials ascribing America's economic woes to poor work habits or racial factors, induce resentment.[43] All this adds up to anxiety in the United States, as reflected in a 1990 poll in which 63 percent of U.S. voters said it is very important for their country to be the world's leading economic power, and 69 percent believed Japan had already surpassed the United States.[44] Although such fears are probably exaggerated, they are politically potent.[45] Such anxiety and resentment have less to do with the actual extent of foreign investment than with prior national experience. Countries that have profited from a long history of foreign investment are less fearful than those with little memory of such investment.

American sensitivity to Japanese investment in the United States is intensified by perceived Japanese unwillingness to accept U.S. investment in Japan. Before the 1980s, the Japanese government strictly limited foreign investment in various ways, entirely excluding investment in some vital sectors. And even with some legal barriers to foreign investment eliminated, it is still restricted by exclusive national industrial associations, unavailability of stock in Japanese firms that is closely held by other Japanese firms, and nationalist sentiments that promote purchase of Japanese products. Between 1975 and 1991, direct foreign investment in Japan rose from less than $1 billion to less than $2 billion, while direct foreign investment in the United States soared from $6 billion to more than $45 billion.[46]

The real economic effect of growing Japanese investment in the United States remains to be seen. European and Canadian experience, as well as that of the United States in the nineteenth century, suggests that such investment is beneficial. It accelerates national growth, reduces balance-of-payments problems, and provides scarce capital, innovative management, and new technologies. This experience does not allay anxiety for some Americans, who fear that Japanese investment will heighten dependence on Japan for critical technology, reduce managerial opportunities for Americans, and create disadvantages for U.S. competitors of Japanese corporations.[47] Others complain that Japanese corporations, like other TNCs, avoid paying a fair share of taxes in the United States, are insensitive to U.S. traditions of labor–industry relations and, more generally, are unfeeling about U.S. social and cultural mores.

[43]Early in 1992, a high-ranking Japanese official described Americans as "lazy."

[44]Alan Murray and Urban C. Lehner, "U.S., Japan Struggle to Redefine Relations as Resentment Grows," *The Wall Street Journal*, June 13, 1990, p. A1. Sixty-three percent of those asked believe Japan leads the United States in science and technology, and 69 percent believe Japan invests too much in the United States.

[45]In fact, we have no reason to assume that Japanese transnational corporations in the United States care less about Americans' economic welfare than do U.S. TNCs. Both care principally about their own profits.

[46]"A Survey of the World Economy: Fear of Finance," *The Economist*, September 19–25, 1992, p. 17.

[47]Spero, *Politics of International Economic Relations*, pp. 115–116.

In time, some of the strain Japanese investment produces in the United States is likely to ease, for two reasons. Lower U.S. interest rates in the 1990s induced Japanese investors to look elsewhere for higher yields. More important, large Japanese corporations increasingly enter into "alliances" and joint ventures with former U.S. adversaries such as IBM rather than try to buy them up. Such alliances, involving research and marketing, are an innovative response to the high cost of getting new high-technology products to the market.

In a sense, the economic rivalries between the United States and Japanese exacerbate general cultural and social differences between the two societies. Americans emphasize individual achievement and Japanese emphasize collective success. Thus, Americans seek a higher personal standard of living but Japanese derive satisfaction through their corporation and nation. Americans are, as a rule, less willing than Japanese to postpone gratification and, as a result, spend more of their income on consumption and save less.[48] As a consequence, less money is invested in modernizing U.S. industries to make them competitive. The Japanese pay a steep price for saving as much as they do. Because they spend little on personal consumption, they continue to live in cramped housing and enjoy less leisure than American counterparts. Barriers to foreign imports raise prices and reduce the quality and variety of goods available to Japanese consumers. Japanese consumers, one observer says, "have enjoyed less than their full share of Japan's economic growth."[49]

One deplorable response by some U.S. corporations to their failure to compete effectively with Japanese firms has been to paint *racial stereotypes* and whip up painful memories of the past. It is reported that "American advertisers are stepping up their attacks on Japan and its people, attempting to thwart sales of Japanese products through commercials that feature ominous references to the late Emperor Hirohito, photographs of Samurai warriors, exaggerated accents and veiled ridicule of the Japanese physique."[50] Examples of Japan-bashing have been most prevalent in industries that have fared poorly against Japanese competition.

The Japanese have their own grievances toward the United States and their own explanations for American resentment. The Japanese place blame for America's current trade deficit on shortsighted economic policies pursued by the United States itself. The U.S. failure to address its huge budget deficit and the strong U.S. dollar in the early 1980s forced America to borrow abroad, especially from the Japanese, and made Japanese products more attractive to U.S. consumers. As a result, the U.S. trade deficit soared. Although the dollar has depreciated, the Japanese feel that U.S. budget deficits,

---

[48]In 1989, the Japanese savings rate was roughly five times that of Americans. *The New York Times*, July 1, 1990, Section 4, p. 1.

[49]Richard J. Samuels, "Consuming for Production: Japanese National Security, Nuclear Fuel Procurement, and the Domestic Economy," *International Organization* 43:4 (Autumn 1989), p. 625.

[50]Randall Rothenberg, "U.S. Ads Increasingly Attack Japanese and Their Culture," *The New York Times*, July 11, 1990, p. 1.

the high U.S. rate of consumption and low rate of saving, U.S. workers' poor education, and poor quality in many products continue to make American products uncompetitive. According to the Japanese, Americans should address these domestic problems rather than blame their trading partners for difficulties of their own making.

Most Japanese (70 percent) believe Americans "look down on the Japanese," and resent Japan's economic success.[51] Once again, the Japanese believe the problem is home-grown, not foreign born. American society is "deteriorating," one Japanese diplomat says, "Americans are losing their ability to communicate among themselves. Everyone is either fighting or hiring lawyers, and America's ability to integrate different elements into a melting pot is weakening. So Americans are looking for scapegoats and blaming Japan."[52] The real problem, then, is that Americans are unwilling "to respect the differences among people who live outside the United States." Americans should learn to respect the ways of others and "should stop lecturing Japan to change its ways."[53]

Resolving United States–Japanese Differences

Cooler heads in both countries recognize the costs to both of U.S.–Japanese hostility. A number of bilateral and unilateral initiatives have been undertaken to bridge the differences, going back at least to 1978 when the United States first asked Japan to increase its imports from the United States. Japan was persuaded to increase import quotas on beef and citrus and, in 1985, to cooperate in an orderly devaluation of the U.S. dollar to make U.S. exports more attractive.[54]

Leaders on both sides recognize that they must tame protectionist sentiment at home if they are to prevent relations from deteriorating, and to do so they have agreed to subtle forms of protectionism. Over the past decade, *orderly marketing agreements* have been reached limiting the number of automobiles imported into the United States from Japan, the sale of semiconductors, and U.S. access to the Japanese construction and auto-parts industries. These arrangements involve managing trade and are actually restrictions on free markets aimed at reducing political fallout.

In the same spirit, the United States and Japan agreed to the *Structural Impediments Initiative* (*SII*) in 1989 to study conditions in the two countries that affect free trade. The initiative involved analyzing impediments to U.S. economic efficiency and competitiveness such as savings and investment patterns, government regulations, and declining

[51]Steven R. Weisman, "A Deep Split in Attitudes Is Developing," *The New York Times*, December 3, 1991, p. A6.

[52]Cited in Steven R. Weisman, "Japan and U.S. Struggle with Resentment," *The New York Times*, December 3, 1991, p. A6.

[53]The first quotation is by Kazuo Ogura, director of cultural affairs in the Japanese Foreign Ministry, from ibid., and the second is from the analysis in ibid.

[54]James Sterngold, "Intractable Trade Issues with Japan," *The New York Times*, December 4, 1991, p. C4.

investment in research. Japanese impediments to free trade that are being studied include savings and investment patterns, land-use and distribution systems, and retail and distribution practices. The effect of SII has been mixed. Although it has focused attention on impediments to bilateral trade, it has also demonstrated how intractable are some of the social and cultural barriers to improving that exchange.[55] At the 1993 Tokyo summit, President Clinton and Japanese Prime Minister Kiichi Miyazawa papered over some of the differences with a vague "framework" calling for lower U.S. budget deficits and easier access to Japanese markets. Although the Clinton administration sought specific targets for reducing the Japanese trade surplus of $130 billion, it settled for a Japanese pledge of a "significant" reduction.[56]

United States–Japanese economic frictions have already had important political consequences for relations between the two countries that illustrate the close relationship among these several arenas. Because the Japanese were enjoying a robust economy and a trade surplus with the United States by the end of the 1980s and early 1990s, Washington increased pressure on Tokyo to devote more resources to defense and shoulder more of its security burden. The United States wanted Japan to exceed the 1 percent of its GNP spent on defense, assume greater responsibility for keeping Asian sea-lanes open, and pay a bigger share of the burden for basing U.S. military personnel in Japan. During the 1991 Persian Gulf War, Washington asked Japan to pay a significant amount to support that war; and, though Japan finally agreed, the issue was an excuse for a flurry of accusations in an already strained relationship.

Public-opinion data are mixed, reflecting, on the one hand, mutual anxieties associated with economic competition and, on the other, the basically friendly feelings of peoples who have cooperated for many decades.[57] Although some Americans fear that Japan will replace the Soviet Union as America's leading foe, most continue to have "friendly" feelings toward the Japanese. In December 1991, most Americans and Japanese did not expect relations between their countries to deteriorate over the "next few years." Two-thirds of the Japanese expected relations to "stay about the same," and 48 percent of Americans expected them to remain the same and 29 percent actually believed that relations would "get better." Nevertheless, growing Japanese resentment about U.S. pressure on Japan to reduce its trade imbalance was evident by the time of the Tokyo economic summit in 1993. In a poll conducted at that time, almost two-thirds of Japanese respondents described U.S.–Japanese relations as "unfriendly," and only 6 percent held "favorable" feelings about

[55]See William H. Cooper, "U.S.–Japanese Trade," in *Trade and Investment: The Changing International Framework* (Washington, D.C.: Congressional Research Service, February–March, 1992), p. 22.

[56]Paul Blustein, "Giving a Little, Taking a Little," *The Washington Post National Weekly Edition*, July 19–25, 1993, p. 20.

[57]Weisman, "A Deep Split in Attitudes Is Developing," p. A6.

FIGURE 13.3

Glaring Across the Pacific

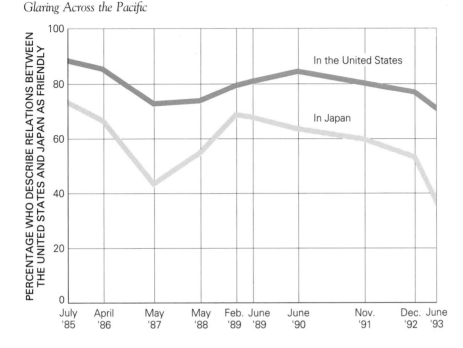

Based on polls conducted by *The New York Times*, CBS News and the Tokyo Broadcasting System. The latest poll is based on 1,363 telephone interviews conducted June 21–24 in the United States, and 1,395 face-to-face interviews conducted June 10–16 in Japan.

Between 1989 and mid-1993, there was a marked erosion in the numbers of Japanese and Americans who perceived their countries' relations as "friendly."

President Clinton. Furthermore, though 45 percent of U.S. respondents expressed the belief that Japanese companies were "competing unfairly with American companies," 85 percent of Japanese respondents thought "the United States is blaming Japan for its own economic problems."[58] As Figure 13.3 shows, Americans were less disturbed than the Japanese about the relationship between the two countries. It also shows, however, that on both sides of the Pacific resentment and mistrust are on the upswing, and, if leaders are careless, the countries could be on a collision course.

[58]David E. Sanger, "64% of Japanese Say U.S. Relations Are 'Unfriendly,'" *The New York Times*, July 6, 1993, pp. A1, A6.

Challenge from the West: European Community and Germany

Another economic challenger is an enlarged *European Community* (EC) based on renewed German economic power. The reconstruction of Europe (and Germany in particular) has parallels to Japan's rebirth after 1945. Like Japan, Europe had suffered devastation, and many of its famous cities lay in ruins. Germany was divided and occupied by foreign forces, and even the victors' economies were badly weakened. Reconstruction of Europe required massive infusions of U.S. economic aid.

The Growth of the European Community

The first step in helping Europe was creating an environment in which reconstruction could take place. Following a European initiative — the Brussels Treaty (1948) — the United States and its friends in Western Europe formed a military alliance — NATO (1949). Washington also began economic assistance with the Marshall Plan, contingent on European ability to coordinate their economies.[59] The two U.S. commitments — one providing the security environment in which reconstruction could occur and the other affording the tools for that reconstruction — enabled the Europeans to embark on their own campaign to regain prosperity. A primary U.S. objective was to encourage movement toward a united Europe as a counterweight to the threat from the East, as a tonic for the anemic postwar global economy, and as a way of preventing future European conflicts like the one just ended.

The idea of a united Europe — some spoke of a "United States of Europe" — was advocated by such functionalists as Jean Monnet, a former French government official, and was promoted by former British Prime Minister Winston Churchill in a speech in Basel, Switzerland, in 1946 as a way to assist Europe and prevent another war.[60] Although the idea did not immediately catch fire, it led, in 1951, to a proposal for establishing the *European Coal and Steel Community* (ECSC). That scheme called for Belgium, West Germany, France, Italy, Luxembourg, and the Netherlands to pool their coal and steel production under a supranational institution. The immediate aims of ECSC were economic and political: to rehabilitate the German economy within a larger European context that would prevent resurgence of German nationalism. For some of the ECSC founders, however, the goal was more ambitious: to launch European *regional integration*. Once established in 1952, ECSC had just that

[59]The Organization of European Economic Cooperation (OEEC) was the European response to this offer. In 1960, the OEEC became the Organization for Economic Cooperation and Development (OECD), with additional members, including the United States, Canada, and Japan.

[60]Klaus-Dieter Borchardt, *European Unification: The Origins and Growth of the European Community* (Luxembourg: Office for Official Publications of the European Communities, 1987), p. 11.

effect. Although the idea of an integrated European army (the European Defense Community) died in 1954,[61] the foreign ministers of "the Six" met in Messina in Sicily in 1955 to examine other ways of furthering European integration. The result was two treaties establishing the *European Atomic Energy Community* (*EURATOM*) and the *European Economic Community* (*EEC*) that were signed in Rome in March 1957 and went into effect January 1, 1958.[62]

The EURATOM group was established to coordinate European policy in a limited sector: peaceful uses of nuclear energy. By contrast, the EEC sought to expand economic cooperation into several areas of European life. It provided for common agricultural, industrial, and trade policies among the six, eliminating tariff barriers, and establishing a common external tariff. Taken together, the pacts had very ambitious aims: "to preserve and strengthen peace, to achieve economic integration for the benefit of all the peoples of Europe through the creation of a large economic area, and to work towards political union."[63]

Novel political institutions were created in the EEC framework: a dual executive (the Council of Ministers and a European Commission), a legislature with limited powers (the Assembly or European Parliament), and a judiciary (the European Court of Justice). Further institutional elaboration followed. The three European organizations (ECSC, EEC, and EURATOM) agreed to integrate their executive structures, and, in 1965, a treaty was signed establishing one Council of Ministers and Commission to govern all three communities, collectively renamed European Community (EC).

Institutional growth was accompanied by increased membership from the original six to twelve. In 1973, the members of a rival trading bloc, the European Free Trade Association (EFTA), were invited to join the EC,[64] and three—Britain, Ireland, and Denmark—elected to do so.[65] Greece followed in 1981, and Spain and Portugal were added in 1986. Later, three Scandinavian countries (Sweden, Norway, and Finland),

---

[61]The objective of rearming West Germany in a European context to help meet the Soviet threat was instead achieved by creating the Western European Union (WEU) with West Germany as a member and then admitting West Germany to NATO.

[62]Derek Unwin points out that the ECSC expanded partly because of problems posed by the sector-by-sector approach. Although the approach grew out of conscious political and economic calculations, it also reflects the neofunctionalist argument that integration entails a "snowballing effect." See Unwin, *The Community of Europe* (London: Longman, 1991), pp. 76–77.

[63]Borchardt, *European Unification*, p. 19.

[64]Established in 1959, EFTA eventually included Austria, Britain, Denmark, Iceland, Norway, Portugal, Sweden, and Switzerland. It was established to encourage free trade, but it rejected the degree of integration associated with the EC.

[65]Norway was also invited but, after a referendum, it rejected EC membership. British entry followed a long fight. Through the 1950s, Britain resisted supranational proposals; and, when the British changed their minds, their application for membership was vetoed by French President Charles de Gaulle in January 1963. De Gaulle argued that Britain remained too dependent on the United States and was insufficiently committed to Europe.

long a neutral (Austria),[66] and three Mediterranean countries (Malta, Cyprus, and Turkey) applied for membership.[67]

The European Community's greatest achievement was the continental prosperity that accompanied its creation. Several specific goals were associated with economic integration, and some met with greater success than others.[68] First, the EC sought to eliminate customs duties on member states' products and establish a common external tariff to deal with others. These goals were accomplished by 1968. Second, the Community sought to promote free movement by workers and capital among members and to give citizens of member states the right to provide services anywhere in the community. These goals have not yet been fully realized. Finally, the Community sought to push common EC policies in various areas: agriculture, corporate mergers, transport, energy, and research. Except for the *Common Agricultural Policy* (CAP), however, the policy-coordination goal has remained mostly unfulfilled.

Important barriers remain to coordinated community action. Although no tariffs obstruct trade or transport, national health standards and other regulations impede common policy and free trade. Recognizing these impediments, the EC proposed the *Single Market Act* of 1985 to create an area in "which persons, goods, and capital shall move freely under conditions identical to those obtaining within a Member State."[69] The EC would become a free internal market for all goods and services, unobstructed by tariff or nontariff barriers, or other national regulations. The target for eliminating all internal barriers was December 31, 1992, and by that time most barriers had been removed. The Single Market Act also called for closer political coordination of foreign and defense policies.[70]

Completing "Europe '92" proved a formidable task. This ambitious project required numerous specific community-wide changes to standardize laws ranging from governing corporate mergers to setting tax rates.[71] One part of the dual executive in the EC structure, the European Commission, developed 282 directives to eliminate "existing

[66]Switzerland also applied for membership, but the prospect of Swiss membership dimmed when the idea was defeated in a referendum.

[67]"EC Debates Its Nature as the Queue Outside Lengthens," *The German Tribune*, June 5, 1992, p. 3. The last three pose special problems for the EC because they are relatively poor and would probably drain resources from the community's wealthier members. The Turkish application is further complicated by the country's poor record in human rights and by the Turkish–Greek quarrel over Turkish occupation of part of Cyprus.

[68]These goals are summarized by Borchardt, *European Unification*, pp. 33–51.

[69]Cited in Unwin, *Community of Europe*, p. 231.

[70]Less formal political cooperation already exists in the EC in the form of an instrument called the European Political Cooperation (EPC).

[71]See "A Survey of the European Community: An Expanding Universe," *The Economist*, July 7–13, 1990.

technical, fiscal, and physical barriers to trade." These directives not only needed approval by the Council of Ministers but they also required that member states adopt and implement them. This was an immense task.[72]

The movement toward "Europe '92" got a push when the twelve members completed a 250-page draft treaty for supranational economic and political union at a meeting in *Maastricht*, the Netherlands in December 1991. By the treaty, members would establish common foreign and defense policies and create a single currency (the *ecu*) by the end of the century. The treaty would establish a European central bank to set monetary policy and would require all but the British to adopt common social policies. Under the new European *exchange-rate mechanism* (*ERM*), currencies could fluctuate only within a narrow range.[73] Its adoption would reflect genuine "spillover," for the EC would be granted greater authority over more issues than in the past.

The treaty, however, required unanimous ratification by members, and much opposition was mobilized against it, illustrating the difficulty in moving from economic to political union. One setback was delivered by Danish voters, who rejected the treaty in a referendum in June 1992. One explanation for the Danish rejection was popular fear that the proposed union would erode national independence and culture.[74] Later in the same month, Irish voters approved the treaty by a 2–1 margin, but French voters in September 1992 endorsed the treaty by the narrowest of margins.[75] By the end of the year, ratification was incomplete because the British Parliament postponed its decision and the German Bundestag agreed to Maastricht subject to final arrangements on Europe's monetary union—an improbable prospect. Thus, "western Europe stumbled badly in 1992."[76] Although the Danes endorsed the treaty in a second referendum in May 1993, they approved a watered-down version that did not require them to accept a single currency, a common defense policy, or common European citizenship and immigration policies.[77] Shortly afterward, the British Parliament also approved, with reservations.[78] Maastricht was alive but at the cost of dividing Europe into two groups, one moving faster than the other toward integration.

[72]Raymond J. Ahearn, *U.S. Access to the EC Market: Opportunities, Concerns, and Policy Challenges* (Washington, D.C.: Congressional Research Service, June 16, 1992), p. 1.

[73]The ERM gave muscle to the European Monetary System (EMS) that had been established in 1979 to tie the currencies of member states together.

[74]"Why the Danes Wouldn't," *The Economist*, June 6, 1992, p. 52.

[75]James F. Clarity, "Ireland Approves Europeans' Treaty on Move to Union," *The New York Times*, June 20, 1992, pp. A1, A5; and Alan Riding, "French Approve Unity Treaty, But Slim Margin Leaves Doubts," *The New York Times*, September 21, 1992, pp. A1, A6.

[76]Josef Joffe, "The New Europe: Yesterday's Ghosts," *Foreign Affairs* 72:1 (1992/93), p. 36.

[77]Alan Riding, "Union in Europe Strongly Backed by Danish Voters," *The New York Times*, May 19, 1993, pp. A1, A4.

[78]John Darnton, "British Legislators Approve Pact Forging Greater European Unity," *The New York Times*, May 21, 1993, pp. A1, A7.

The obstacles to progress were evident when Europe's exchange-rate mechanism (ERM) broke down in September 1992.[79] The crisis was perhaps inevitable because the leading members of the EC and the United States pursued divergent macroeconomic policies. The U.S. failure to control its budget deficit and the Federal Reserve Bank's reducing interest rates to stimulate the U.S. economy forced down the dollar's value compared to the German mark and triggered a flight of funds from the United States to Germany as investors sought Germany's high interest rates. For its part, the German Bundesbank held interest rates high to prevent inflation and to attract funds to pay the costs of reunification, especially reconstructing the former east zone. Other Europeans were caught in the middle. The British, French, and Italian economies continued to suffer from recession and their governments were forced to keep interest rates high to prevent the flight of funds to Germany. High interest rates, in turn, acted as a brake on economic growth at home.

Following a small reduction in the German interest rate on September 16, 1992, accompanied by hints from the Bundesbank that other European currencies were overvalued, an overwhelming attack on the Italian lira and the British pound took place as speculators dumped these to buy German marks. The ferocious assault showed that national governments no longer had the resources to control the international monetary system. After the Bank of England tried vainly to stem the tide by spending as much as one-third of its foreign-exchange reserves to defend the pound, the British and Italians pulled out of the ERM. This series of events and the animosity it engendered, especially between British and Germans, made it clear that the 1992 deadline for a single market would not be met and that movement toward a unified Europe, including a single currency, had a long way to go.

A similar event took place during the summer of the following year when the Bundesbank refused to reduce interest rates, and an ensuing frenzy of speculation put pressure on the French franc. In an effort to save what remained of the European Monetary System, the EC agreed to permit wider fluctuations among currencies. German behavior seemed to reflect an unwillingness or inability to provide political leadership for Europe.[80]

The EC's failure to act decisively in ending hostilities in the Balkans, the shadows clouding the Maastricht Treaty's future, and the ERM's collapse suggested that European integration was slowing. Ominous too was the EC's failure to achieve consensus on agricultural policy. Internally, subsidies for agriculture consumed most of the EC's budget and inflated food costs for European consumers. Externally, the problem showed up in quarrels with other agricultural exporters, especially the United States, and these

---

[79]"A Ghastly Game of Dominoes," *The Economist*, September 19–25, 1992, pp. 89–90.

[80]Craig R. Whitney, "Reluctant Giant: Germany Balks at Leading Europeans to Unity," *The New York Times*, August 1, 1993, Section 1, pp. 1, 10; and Craig R. Whitney, "Europeans Agree to Let Currencies Fluctuate Widely, *The New York Times*, August 2, 1993, pp. A1, C8.

quarrels prevented agreement in the *Uruguay Round* of the GATT. Josef Joffe describes how this issue strains EC unity:

> After six years of General Agreement on Tariffs and Trade negotiations, the EC had finally reached an oilseed agreement with the United States. . . . The French government, however, was facing national elections in March 1993, so it did not matter that France had been outvoted in the EC council. What did matter were French peasants who stood ready for yet another storm on the Bastille. . . . The French message in December [1992] was: our peasants are more important than Europe.[81]

The final movement toward European integration is impossible to predict. The process of integration has overcome setbacks and may do so again. If, in the end, that movement achieves its goal, the EC will be a formidable political and economic unit. It will consist of 320 million citizens in twelve countries, and possibly more.[82]

Reconstructing Germany

The "German problem" has haunted European politics for more than a century. Since unification in 1871,[83] Germany has sought dominance in Central Europe. First, it defeated France in the Franco-Prussian War of 1870–1871 in a contest for continental hegemony and used balance-of-power policies to stabilize Europe with such alliances as the promonarchic Three Emperors' League (1872), composed of Germany, Austria, and Russia, and the Dual Alliance of Germany and Austria-Hungary (1879). These alliances were to carry out Chancellor Otto von Bismarck's balancing act, but they also began dividing Europe into hostile military camps. Like other European states, Germany

---

[81]Joffe, "The New Europe," p. 40. In June 1993, the French finally agreed to the oilseed agreement but resistance to it among French farmers persisted. See Roger Cohen, "Yielding, French Accept Farm Pact," *The New York Times*, June 9, 1993, pp. C1, C2.

[82]See Alan Riding, "Europeans in Accord to Create Vastly Expanded Trading Bloc," *The New York Times*, October 23, 1991, pp. A1 and C18. With the EFTA countries added, the free-trade zone would expand to 380 million people.

[83]Unification was achieved by Prussian victories over Denmark (1863), Austria (1866), and France (1870).

FIGURE 13.4

The Changing Faces of Germany

The German issue has been a key factor in global politics since the nineteenth century. Between 1863 and 1870 Germany was united by a series of wars. Since then World Wars I and II and the Cold War have caused it to expand, shrink, and finally in 1990 be reunified.

1863–1870

SWEDEN

North Sea

DENMARK

Baltic Sea

SCHLESWIG
• Kiel
HOLSTEIN • Lübeck
Hamburg
• Bremen
MECKLENBURG
POMERANIA
WEST PRUSSIA
• Königsberg
EAST PRUSSIA
• Danzig

OLDENBURG

BRANDENBURG

HANOVER
• Hanover
Berlin •
POSEN
• Warsaw

NETHERLANDS
• Amsterdam

WESTPHALIA
Essen •
P R U S S I A
Oder
POLAND

RUSSIAN EMPIRE

• Antwerp

• Leipzig

BELGIUM
Bonn •
Cologne •
RHINE PROVINCE
• Weimar
SAXONY
Dresden •
Sadowa
1866 ╳
SILESIA
• Krakow

Sedan
1870
Luxembourg •
• Frankfurt
• Nuremberg
Prague •
BOHEMIA
• Olmütz

• Verdun

LORRAINE
• Karlsruhe
BAVARIA
MORAVIA
AUSTRIA-HUNGARY

Nancy •
Strasbourg •
ALSACE
WÜRTTEMBERG
• Stuttgart
• Vienna

A U S T R I A N   E M P I R E

Dniester

BADEN
• Munich

BESSARABIA

FRANCE
• Innsbruck

Buda • Pest
BESSARABIA

SWITZERLAND

Pruth

DOBRUJA
(To Romania)

Morava

Save
Danube

ROMANIA
(Independent)

ITALY

Adriatic Sea

BOSNIA
HERZEGOVINA

SERBIA
(Independent)

BULGARIA
(Autonomous)

Black Sea

EAST ROUMELIA
(To Bulgaria, 1885)

MONTENEGRO

ROUMELIA

ALBANIA
MACEDONIA
O T T O M A N   E M P I R E

GREECE

Mediterranean Sea

╳ Major battles

——— German Confederation boundary, 1815–1866

〰〰〰 Bismarck's German Empire, 1871

☐ Prussia before 1866

☐ Conquered by Prussia in Austro-Prussian War, 1866

☐ Austrian territories excluded from German Confederation, 1867

☐ Joined with Prussia to form German Confederation, 1867

☐ South German states joining with Prussia to form German Empire, 1871

☐ Won by Prussia in Franco-Prussian War, 1871

– – – Ottoman Empire before 1878

☐ Ottoman Empire after 1878

☐ Occupied by Austria-Hungary

☐ Independent or autonomous

0   100   200 Km.

0   100   200 Mi.

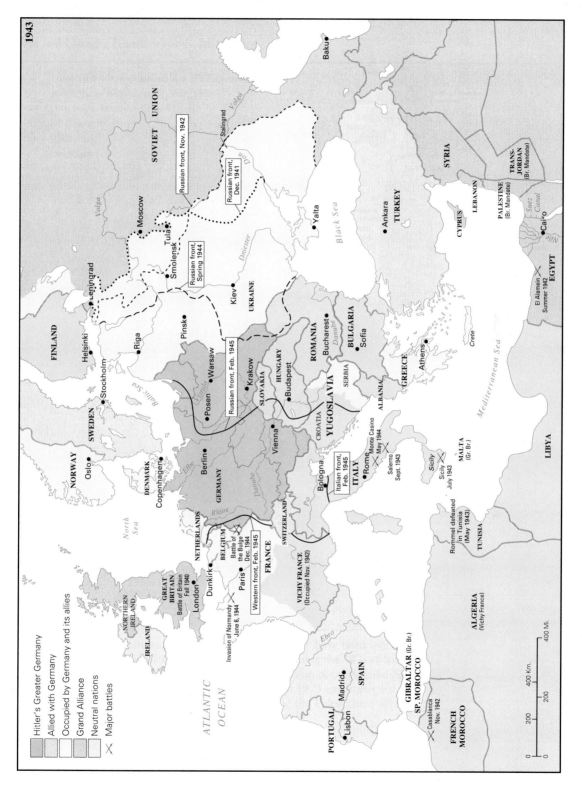

1943

Legend:
- Hitler's Greater Germany
- Allied with Germany
- Occupied by Germany and its allies
- Grand Alliance
- Neutral nations
- ✕ Major battles

IRELAND

NORTHERN IRELAND

GREAT BRITAIN
Battle of Britain
Fall 1940

London ●

ATLANTIC OCEAN

North Sea

NORWAY
Oslo ●

DENMARK
Copenhagen ●

SWEDEN
Stockholm ●

Baltic Sea

FINLAND
Helsinki ●

Riga ●

Leningrad ●

Moscow ●
Tula ●
Smolensk ●

Volga

SOVIET UNION

Volga

Stalingrad ●

Russian front, Nov. 1942

Russian front, Dec. 1941

Don

Baku ●

Pinsk ●

Russian front, Spring 1944

Kiev ●
UKRAINE

Dnieper

Dniester

Black Sea

Yalta ●

Ankara ●
TURKEY

SYRIA

LEBANON

CYPRUS

PALESTINE (Br. Mandate)

TRANS-JORDAN (Br. Mandate)

Suez Canal

Cairo ●

Nile

EGYPT

El Alamein
Summer 1942 ✕

Dunkirk ●

NETHERLANDS
BELGIUM
Battle of the Bulge
Dec. 1944 ✕

Paris ●
Invasion of Normandy
June 6, 1944 ✕
Western front, Feb. 1945

FRANCE

VICHY FRANCE
(Occupied Nov. 1942)

Rhine

Berlin ●
GERMANY

Elbe

Danube

SWITZERLAND

Posen ●
Warsaw ●
Russian front, Feb. 1945
Krakow ●

Vistula

SLOVAKIA

Vienna ●

Budapest ●
HUNGARY

ROMANIA
Bucharest ●

Danube

BULGARIA
Sofia ●

SERBIA

YUGOSLAVIA

CROATIA

ALBANIA

GREECE
Athens ●

Po

Bologna ●
Italian front, Feb. 1945

ITALY
Rome ●
Monte Casino
May 1944
Salerno
Sept. 1943

Sicily
July 1943 ✕
Sicily

MALTA
(Gr. Br.)

Crete

Mediterranean Sea

LIBYA

Rommel defeated
in Tunisia
(May 1943)

TUNISIA

ALGERIA
(Vichy France)

Casablanca
Nov. 1942 ✕

FRENCH MOROCCO

SP. MOROCCO
GIBRALTAR (Gr. Br.)

PORTUGAL
Lisbon ●

SPAIN
Madrid ●

Ebro

0   200   400 Mi.

0   200   400 Km.

M-14 b
Mansbach 13.03b

1945

NORWAY
Oslo
SWEDEN
Stockholm

FINLAND
Helsinki
From Finland, 1940–1956
Leningrad

North Sea

DENMARK
Copenhagen

Baltic Sea

ESTONIA to U.S.S.R., 1940
LATVIA to U.S.S.R., 1940
LITHUANIA to U.S.S.R., 1940

SOVIET UNION 1917

WHITE RUSSIA

U.S. Zone
NETHERLANDS
Amsterdam
Bremen
Soviet Zone
Berlin
British Zone
Brussels
BEL.
Bonn
EAST GERMANY
WEST GERMANY
LUX.
FRANCE
French Zone
U.S. Zone
Munich
Berne
SWITZERLAND
French Zone
U.S. Zone
Soviet Zone
Vienna
British Zone
AUSTRIA
Milan
From Italy, 1945
ITALY

Incorporated into U.S.S.R., 1945
Gdansk (Danzig)
Incorporated into Poland, 1945
Warsaw
POLAND 1947
Prague
CZECHOSLOVAKIA 1948
From Czechoslovakia, 1945–1947
HUNGARY 1949
Budapest
ROMANIA 1947

Brest
From Poland 1940–1947

UKRAINE

BESSARABIA
From Romania, 1940–1947

Corsica (Fr.)
Rome
Sardinia (Italy)

YUGOSLAVIA 1945
Belgrade
Bucharest
BULGARIA 1946
Sofia
Tirane
ALBANIA 1944
GREECE
Athens

From Romania, 1940–1947

Crimea
Yalta

Black Sea

Istanbul

TURKEY

Adriatic Sea

Sicily

Mediterranean Sea

Crete

CYPRUS

Legend:

—— Postwar national boundaries, to 1989
▨ Allied occupation of Germany and Austria 1945–1955
▢ Territory lost by Germany
▨ Territory gained by Soviet Union
1945 Year communist control of government gained
━━ "Iron Curtain" to 1989

EAST GERMANY
Soviet Sector
British Sector
West Berlin
U.S. Sector
East Berlin
Soviet Sector
EAST GERMANY
Potsdam
—— Berlin Wall (1961–1989)

0   400   800 Km.
0   400   800 Mi.

Post-1990

DENMARK
THE NETHERLANDS
Berlin
POLAND
BELGIUM
GERMANY
LUXEMBURG
CZECH REP.
FRANCE
LIECHTENSTEIN
AUSTRIA
SWITZERLAND

engaged in colonial expansion during the second half of the nineteenth century, and, by the early 1890s, the German Empire controlled large areas in East and Southwest Africa, as well as parts of China and island chains in the South Pacific.

After Wilhelm II became emperor in 1890 and dismissed the cautious Bismarck, Germany abandoned its balance-of-power policy for a more ambitious *Weltpolitik*, in which Berlin sought to challenge British supremacy at sea and seek the ideal Wilhelm called "a place in the sun." Germany's population grew rapidly after 1870, and the country was transformed from an agrarian society into Europe's largest producer of steel and chemicals. The German army was the best in the world, and its navy sought to challenge the British in their home seas. As a result, Germany's neighbors became anxious and sought security against German belligerence. In 1902, Britain entered an alliance with Japan. Two years later, Britain and France overcame colonial conflicts and entered into a "friendly understanding," and a few years later Russia joined them in a grouping that came to be called the Triple Entente.[84]

Germany continued to rattle sabers, thwarting French and Russian colonial ambitions and meddling in the tottering Ottoman Empire. When the Balkans were set aflame by wars and crises, Russia and Austria-Hungary squared off to claim the spoils from the Ottoman decline. The Balkans proved to be the fuse that lit the European powder keg. After Archduke Francis Ferdinand, heir to the throne of Austria-Hungary, was assassinated in June 1914, alliance politics brought Germany into the conflagration. Fearful of losing its only reliable ally, Germany gave the Austrians a free hand in the 1914 crisis.

In the war that followed, Germany was defeated and subjected to the harsh Treaty of Versailles. "This is not a treaty," observed French Marshal Ferdinand Foch. "It is an armistice for twenty years."[85] By its terms, Germany was forced to admit its war "guilt," disarm, give up its colonies, and cede territories that accounted for much of its wealth. Germany was also forced to pay large reparations, even while being deprived of the means to pay.[86] Britain and France used these reparations, financed by U.S. loans, in turn, to repay their debt to the United States. These events were a prelude to World War II. In 1933, Hitler was swept to power in Berlin on promises to overthrow the Versailles settlement and reverse the 1918 verdict.

Following its defeat in 1945, Germany was divided into zones of occupation and became the first battleground in the Cold War. With Europe divided, those zones became the basis for separate states. The Federal Republic of Germany (West Germany) and the German Democratic Republic (East Germany) were established within months of each other in autumn 1949. This division was to last only forty years, until October 3, 1990, when the two halves were reunited. During that time the two states went in

---

[84]A secret military alliance was signed between France and Russia in 1894.

[85]Cited in Winston S. Churchill, *The Gathering Storm* (Boston: Houghton Mifflin, 1948), p. 7.

[86]A young member of the British delegation to Versailles, John Maynard Keynes, denounced the treaty as a catastrophe. Keynes, *Economic Consequences of the Peace* (New York: Harcourt Brace Jovanovich, 1920).

very different social and political directions. In the end, West Germany's capitalist course became the model for a reunited Germany.

During its separate existence, West Germany succeeded in establishing democratic institutions and creating an "economic miracle." The Federal Republic accomplished these goals partly because of farsighted leadership by chancellors beginning with Konrad Adenauer (1949–1963) who appreciated how important were strong ties to the United States and Germany's European neighbors, especially France. Under Adenauer, the Federal Republic pursued policies that tied Germany tightly to the West (*Westpolitik*) by adherence to NATO and the European Community. The NATO commitment returned it to full sovereignty and ensured that reconstruction could be done in a secure context.[87] Adenauer was an early proponent of the EC. He believed German membership would demonstrate the country's commitment to the West. Adenauer's Germany became an advocate of enlarging the EC's membership and expanding free trade beyond the community's boundaries, and the German economy benefited significantly from these policies. By 1957, the economic miracle was under way. Economic recovery had been achieved, and prosperity was in sight. While West Germany was establishing a mutually beneficial partnership with its allies, East Germany was being bled by the U.S.S.R. and governed by a pro-Soviet puppet regime.

By late in the 1960s, the Federal Republic was in a position to expand *Westpolitik* and initiate an independent policy of *Ostpolitik* (Eastern policy). In 1969, the new German Chancellor, Willy Brandt, introduced a systematic policy of negotiation and accommodation with East Germany. This policy was possible, not only because of détente between the superpowers, but also because of West Germany's new economic vigor. Among the results of this initiative were the Basic Treaty of 1972, by which East and West Germany agreed to exist side by side in "one German nation"; a Soviet–West German agreement; and a new four-power agreement governing access to Berlin and reducing tension over the divided city. In the ensuing years, West Germany pursued a policy of establishing links to the East, including economic aid in return for a more liberal political climate.

Reunifying Germany

During the 1970s and 1980s, Germany continued to seek a political course to match its economic power. On a number of occasions, Germany was described as "an economic giant but a political dwarf," and it yearned to shake that label.[88] During the 1970s, Chancellors Brandt and Helmut Schmidt, both Social Democrats, sought to keep

[87]Although the Federal Republic was established in 1949, full sovereignty was not restored until 1955, when Bonn entered NATO and renounced atomic, biological, and chemical weapons. Allied legal involvement in German affairs did not end until September 1990, when Britain, France, the U.S.S.R., and the United States signed a treaty with the German states formally renouncing their postwar prerogatives.

[88]Cited in Jonathan Carr, *Helmut Schmidt: Helmsman of Germany* (London: Weidenfeld and Nicolson, 1985), p. 86.

détente alive and provide what assistance they could to compatriots in the East. Consequently, when U.S.–Soviet relations were deteriorating early in the 1980s, they worried that the U.S.–West German alliance too might unravel.

Europeans, especially West Germans, took vigorous exception when Presidents Carter and Reagan tried to use economic sanctions to bring the East to heel after the Soviet Union invaded Afghanistan in 1979 and the Polish government declared martial law in 1981. Although the Europeans agreed not to subvert these sanctions, their support for the policy was tepid. The United States, however, pressured Western Europe to abandon a deal with the U.S.S.R. to construct a natural-gas pipeline to bring Soviet gas to Western Europe, causing a deep political rift in 1982. The Reagan administration asserted the right to regulate subsidiaries of U.S. corporations in Europe. Infuriated Europeans saw this claim to *extraterritorial jurisdiction* as arrogant interference in their domestic affairs and an effort to overturn their laws. The crisis was resolved only when Washington backed off its threat to penalize European corporations involved in the deal. "To the Europeans," declares one observer, "Soviet natural gas was a means of necessary diversification of their imports of energy . . . For the Reagan administration, the pipeline was doubly condemned not only for the . . . dependency that it imposed on Western Europe . . . but also for the contribution that it made to Soviet economic well-being and ultimately to Soviet military gains."[89]

The selection of Christian Democrat Helmut Kohl as chancellor and his decision to limit the Federal Republic's overtures to the East, along with a warming trend in U.S.–Soviet relations during the last of the Reagan years, seemed to mend the U.S.–German tie. Kohl, however, also sought a larger role for Germany in European affairs, which necessitated building a special relationship with France. Franco-German ties increasingly became the fulcrum for actions in Europe, and Franco-German military cooperation provided the core for a European force that might become significant as the U.S. military presence in Europe is reduced. Combining German economic clout and French nuclear weapons provided a basis for potential political influence. In this way German influence could be exercised through "Europe," and Germany could serve as an economic engine for its EC partners.

By late in the 1980s, events in Central Europe began to unfold rapidly. In little more than thirteen months (November 9, 1989 to December 1, 1990), Germany was reunited and all-German democratic elections were held. Several events sparked this rapid change beginning with a mass exodus to the West of East Germans and other East Europeans in autumn 1989. In November, the Berlin Wall was breached, and revolutionary political change was under way.[90] By the end of 1989, Chancellor Kohl presented a plan for confederating the two Germanies.

---

[89]Miles Kahler, "The United States and Western Europe: The Diplomatic Consequences of Mr. Reagan," in Kenneth A. Oye, Robert J. Lieber, and Donald Rothchild, eds., *Eagle Resurgent? The Reagan Era in American Foreign Policy* (Boston: Little, Brown, 1987), p. 313.

[90]It is ironic that the Berlin Wall, originally erected in 1961 to halt the flight of East Germans to the West, was reopened to slow a new wave of emigration that reached 140,000 in November 1989 and threatened to bleed East Germany of skilled labor.

In February 1990, the four victor states and the two Germanys agreed on the outlines for reunification. On July 1, 1990, the economies of East and West Germany were reunited as the East German *Ostmark* was replaced by the West German *deutsche mark*. Not only did this act enlarge the German economy, it was a big step along the path of events toward political reunification. On October 3, 1990, reunification was declared and two months later, democratic elections were held in the newly unified Germany.

The end of the Cold War has not yet put Germany at the head of a united Europe as many had anticipated. Reunification turned German attention to the east, siphoned German resources into reconstructing its eastern territories and underwriting withdrawal of Soviet troops, and eroded coordination of economic and trade policy with other EC members. These differences were exacerbated by European dissension over the policy to adopt toward civil strife engulfing Yugoslavia, weakened support for the Maastricht agreement, Europe's monetary crises in 1992 and 1993, and French refusal to go along with the U.S.–EC compromise reached late in 1992 over agricultural subsidies. Finally, in Germany itself the events that accompanied reunification — recession, unemployment, and budget pressures, and rising right-wing and anti-foreigner violence — badly undermined German self-confidence. This violence, accompanied by right-wing gains in local elections, was intensified by 450,000 asylum seekers reaching Germany in 1992 and an additional 75,000 during the first two months in 1993.[91]

The Challenge of EC and German Economic Power

Like Japan, the EC with a united Germany has acquired great influence in the global economy. The great size of its market and its role in global trade provide the EC with clout. The EC countries account for two-fifths of global trade, and the EC has become the world's largest trading bloc. It is already a vast market for U.S. products. In 1991, 25 percent of U.S. exports — computers, machinery, telecommunication equipment, and agricultural commodities valued at $103 billion — were sent to the EC.[92] The EC, in turn, exported about $87 billion in goods to the United States in 1991, including automobiles, auto parts, chemicals, and aircraft. The United States has enjoyed a trade surplus with the EC since 1991, but did not in earlier years.

The EC has become a mecca for foreign investment, another indicator of its growing economic importance. Japanese investment in community countries grew from $7 billion to about $30 billion between 1984 and 1988. During the same period, U.S.

---

[91]Craig R. Whitney, "Right Wing Gains in Elections in State in Western Germany," *The New York Times*, March 8, 1993, p. A4.

[92]Raymond J. Ahearn, *U.S. Access to the EC Market*, pp. 1–2; and Glennon J. Harrison, *European Community Trade and Investment with the United States* (Washington, D.C.: Congressional Research Service, March 7, 1990), p. 2.

investment in the EC grew by $55 billion. Investments by EC countries in the United States have also been substantial. In one year (1987), EC investments in the United States—in such sectors as petroleum, manufacturing, finance, real estate, and publishing—totaled $325 billion.[93] Like the Japanese, Europeans have a huge stake in the U.S. economy.

Within the EC, Germany alone enjoys a GDP of more than $1.5 trillion, a population of 80 million, and a per capita income of about $23,650 (for West Germans), making Germany the largest economy in Europe.[94] Along with the U.S. dollar and the Japanese yen, the mark is one of the world's most desired currencies, and most European economies peg the value of their currency to it. Germany's strong economy has given it regional and global political influence. The country is the largest contributor to the EC budget, giving it a major voice in shaping EC policies. Typically it has used that voice to promote greater European integration. Germany has also taken the lead in linking Central European and Russian economies to the EC. Reunification increased Germany's potential economic and political power, but the initial period of adjustment, with low standards of living, high unemployment, and poor infrastructure in the east, also caused serious dislocation. Despite high hopes, united Germany remained mired in recession and unemployment (especially in the east) that helped touch off anti-foreigner violence.[95]

United States–European Community Economic Friction

United States–European relations are bedeviled by the same issues that cause friction between the United States and Japan. Bilateral negotiations between the EC and the United States have so far managed to overcome the frequent crises in their relations. Those relations, painfully reached, are complicated by the possibility that any European state might undermine an agreement.

Several possible approaches might manage this friction. One is to adapt common Atlantic institutions such as NATO and the Organization for Economic Cooperation and Development (OECD) to cope with post–Cold War issues or create links between such newer institutions as the EC and NAFTA. Although individual countries are tempted to bolt on some issues (as the French did in the December 1992 agricultural negotiations), nationalist and mercantilist solutions can only harm all participants. The GATT continues to provide a global forum for trade issues, but efforts to "manage" trade and investment between the European and North American blocs is more likely, especially because the two

---

[93]Ibid., pp. 4, 5, 9.

[94]*World Development Report 1993*, pp. 239, 243. The East Germans' per capita income was much lower than that of West Germans, reducing the per capita figure for Germany as a whole upon reunification.

[95]Craig R. Whitney, "Germans Feel Pain of Unity, Squabbling Over Who Pays," *The New York Times*, February 19, 1993, pp. A1, A4.

share political and economic interests toward third parties. *Managed trade* entails agreements that limit free trade (such as setting quotas on imports of selected products) and avoid uncertainty while eschewing the worst excesses of protectionism. Such arrangements are likely to flourish alongside government-corporate partnerships to develop high technology and increased economic espionage by government intelligence agencies.

Nowhere is U.S.–European friction more evident than in agriculture. On both sides of the Atlantic, farmers are small but politically important domestic interests. The EC's Common Agricultural Policy (CAP) limits the free market by maintaining artificially high domestic prices for European produce. Prices are kept high by purchasing agricultural surpluses and excluding commodities from outside the EC. In effect, inefficient farmers in some European countries such as France are kept in business by German and British contributions to the EC budget. Mountains of surplus food have resulted, yet the EC has refused to establish production controls. Instead, it has chosen to subsidize export of these surpluses, entering markets traditionally enjoyed by farmers from the United States, Canada, Australia, New Zealand, and other food exporters.

Both sides want to ensure prosperity and electoral support for their farmers, and each argues that the other's policies are protectionist. The Uruguay Round negotiations of the General Agreement on Tariffs and Trade (GATT) were stalled by acrimonious disputes over agricultural subsidies. The United States sought to eliminate or at least significantly reduce such subsidies, but the Europeans were reluctant to alter their arrangements.[96] United States hands were hardly clean, however: "Since the 1930s," declares Joan Spero, "the U.S. government has intervened in domestic agricultural markets to maintain agricultural prices and the income of U.S. farmers. It has supported domestic prices by purchasing domestic commodities, production controls, and deficiency payments, and further managed the domestic market through export subsidies and import quotas."[97] On the whole, however: government intervention in agriculture is less in the United States, and U.S. farmers are more efficient than European farmers.

In one sense, a united Europe should be welcomed by those committed to an open-market environment. Eliminating internal trade barriers in Europe would produce greater efficiency, stimulate growth, and bring greater trade among members. Uniform national standards and simpler government procurement of products from other countries would, according to some analysts, produce a net benefit for the United States. United States' investors in the EC would be likely to benefit as well. United States' companies in Europe would enjoy easier access to all member states under the Europe '92 arrangement, and, because they had already set up shop in Europe, these companies would also comply with requirements necessary to avoid the EC's uniform external tariffs.

---

[96]French farmers, among the most inefficient in the Western world, are a militant group, willing to use violent tactics to maintain their subsidies.

[97]Spero, *Politics of International Economic Relations*, p. 88.

Some Americans and Japanese fear, however, that growing European unity will boost European policies to protect the EC market. For several reasons, it will also mean costs for U.S. businesses.[98] Because the European states intend to liberalize their economies in a way that will benefit them, they will give little attention to the needs of "third countries" like the United States during political bargaining. As the Europeans change their definition of a European product ("rules of origin") and place *local content requirements* on them (that is, redefining the meaning of "manufactured in Europe"), oher countries' firms may be left out or may be forced to invest and locate inside the Europe '92 wall.

The EC also moved to provide greater public assistance to high-tech industries—computers, semiconductors, and telecommunications equipment. These industries compete directly with the largest U.S. exporters to the EC. The Clinton administration proposed a similar policy for the United States. The Europeans had sound reasons for their actions. Efforts to regulate and limit U.S. and Japanese economic penetration of the EC react to fear of technological backwardness, job losses, and a decline in European competitiveness. But, as a result, the open-trading order suffers.

A third general area of friction between Europe and North America results from incompatible macroeconomic policies. In recent years, the United States has urged its allies in Europe and Japan to pursue expansionist economic policies to energize the world economy and help end the lingering recession. If the Germans and Japanese were willing to increase government spending at home and accept more inflation, Americans argue, the number of jobs at home and abroad would be increased by greater overall international trade. European complaints about the United States mirror those of the Japanese, focusing on America's runaway budget deficits. They generally want Americans to exercise greater discipline by reducing those deficits. Such deficits, they argue, reduce funds available for European investments at home, harm the dollar, and reduce U.S. and European competitiveness. Despite U.S. rhetoric about protectionism, they declare—with truth—that the United States also indulges in protectionism for such inefficient industries as steel.

Like the United States and Japan, the EC and the United States have engaged in multilateral (e.g., GATT discussions), regional (e.g., yearly economic summits), and bilateral negotiations to iron out trade differences. Talks have been held on controversies including European imposition of import restrictions and duties on U.S. agricultural products, European barriers to importing U.S. beef that has been fed growth hormones, and European subsidies to domestic industries engaged in exporting. Such talks have narrowed differences, but significant gaps remain.

An agreement about the commercial airline industry illustrates efforts by both sides to make markets more orderly and competitive. In April 1992, the United States and the EC concluded five years of negotiations by agreeing to curb government assistance to their commercial aircraft industries. The EC's Airbus Industrie received 75 percent or

[98]Ahearn, *U.S. Access to the EC Market*, pp. 16–17.

more of its research support from the British, French, German, and Spanish governments, and its U.S. competitors — Boeing and McDonnell Douglas — received support from the U.S. government in lucrative military contracts. Both sides agreed to limit subsidies to make the industry more genuinely competitive.[99] Early in 1993, however, in a speech at Boeing, President Clinton threatened to reopen the controversy by charging that the Europeans continued to subsidize their aircraft industry unfairly.

Although one can imagine extensive economic conflicts between the United States and the EC in the coming years, leaders are likely to try to contain them. The Janus face of politics is again clearly visible in the contradictory imperatives from domestic constituencies fearing lost jobs and declining export markets and the global system in which free markets and greater trade produce benefits for all. More important is recognition that, if economic quarrels are not contained, they may infect the political bonds that helped win the Cold War and allowed Americans and Europeans to work closely together in supporting Russia's Boris Yeltsin, opposing Saddam Hussein, and promoting democracy in the Third World.

Free Trade and North American Economic Power

The United States has sought to meet the challenging economic power of Japan and the EC by establishing a regional *free-trade area* with its North American trading partners Canada and Mexico. These countries are, respectively, America's largest and (after Japan) third-largest trading partners. By building a new trade bloc, the United States seeks to create a larger market for its goods, pool resources with its neighbors, and limit inroads by Japan and the EC in North America. The project was begun in 1988 with the *U.S.–Canada Free Trade Agreement* (FTA), which went into effect January 1, 1989. In August 1992, the more ambitious *North American Free Trade Agreement* (NAFTA) was initialed by representatives of the United States, Mexico, and Canada. This agreement was scheduled to go into effect on January 1, 1994. NAFTA would create a larger free-trade area than the EC.

The United States–Canada Free-Trade Agreement

The FTA signed by U.S. President Ronald Reagan and Canadian Prime Minister Brian Mulroney January 2, 1988, was meant to eliminate trade barriers between the two countries over a ten-year period. The economic sectors covered by the pact were broad: agriculture, energy, autos, lumber, wine and distilled spirits, various services, and finance and investment. Under the treaty, U.S. firms in Canada and Canadian firms in the United States would enjoy the same treatment as indigenous enterprises. Some industries important to their country's *cultural sovereignty* — broadcasting, publishing, and

[99]Eduardo Lachica, "U.S., EC Agree on Terms to Curb Subsidies for Airbus and Its Rivals," *The Wall Street Journal*, April 2, 1992, p. A10.

films — were left out of the agreement. Any disagreement resulting from implementation of the pact would be handled by a binational commission.[100]

Each country had competing and complementary motives for pursuing the arrangement and was influenced by trends in the global economic system and their domestic economies. Policies followed by Japan and the EC, increased agricultural production in such developing countries as Brazil and India, and an overvalued dollar hampered expansion of U.S. agricultural markets. United States manufacturing was also suffering from increased foreign competition, and the U.S. service sector was proving something of an export disappointment.[101] The pact with Canada was an opportunity for the United States to stimulate its own economy and increase the competitive edge for industries in both countries. The FTA was also a model for more liberal trade worldwide in the way it addressed issues of nontariff barriers and trade subsidiaries.[102] The FTA was attractive to many Canadians because it promised to improve competitiveness for Canadian firms and give them access to the large U.S. market. In the midst of a deep recession, Canadian leaders concluded that, on balance, direct competition with U.S. industries would sharpen Canadian manufacturing's competitiveness.[103]

North American Free Trade Agreement (NAFTA)

The NAFTA, signed in August 1992, would enlarge the original free-trade area to take in America's southern neighbor, Mexico. The new pact was immediately hailed as one that "could unleash a surge of trading activity with Mexico, already [the U.S.'s] third-largest trading partner and fastest-growing export market."[104] Supporters argue that the enlarged free-trade area will enhance prosperity in all three countries. Under the pact, a regional bloc of 370 million people with a combined gross domestic product of more than $6 trillion would be created in fifteen years. All tariffs and other impediments to trade would be removed in sectors including advertising, agriculture, automobiles, banking, energy, insurance, textiles, and trucking.[105] At the same time, other countries would be prevented from eluding U.S. tariffs by going through Mexico and trinational panels would resolve disputes arising from the treaty.[106]

[100]See U.S.–Canada Free Trade Agreement (Washington, D.C.: U.S. Department of State, June 1988).

[101]Peter Morici, Making Free Trade Work: The Canada–U.S. Agreement (New York: Council on Foreign Relations Press, 1990), p. 3.

[102]Ibid., p. 15.

[103]Ibid., pp. 5–7, 13–14.

[104]Kay R. Whitmore, CEO of the Eastman Kodak Company as cited in Keith Bradsher, "Economic Accord Reached by U.S., Mexico and Canada Lowering Trade Barriers," The New York Times, August 13, 1992, p. A1.

[105]Ibid., p. C3.

[106]See ibid., and Keith Bradsher, "Free Trade Accord for North America Is Expected Today," The New York Times, August 12, 1992, p. A1.

More jobs and lower production costs, especially in agriculture, would probably result from the agreement, benefiting consumers and producers in the three countries. As Mexico spends more on imports, U.S. exporters would be the likely beneficiaries. At present, 70 percent of Mexican imports come from the United States, a figure likely to increase if NAFTA takes over. By one estimate, 175,000 new jobs would be created in the United States to meet demands from this new trade agreement.[107] Mexicans would benefit too. In a more open trading environment, Mexican workers would have a greater incentive to stay at home rather than emigrate across the Rio Grande. In time, their wages and working conditions would be more like those of their northern neighbors. Finally, variety and quality of agricultural produce in all three countries would improve.[108]

Benefits would not be distributed evenly, however, explaining opposition to the pact in the United States. Workers in inefficient industries would lose jobs to Mexican competition. Some fear that U.S. corporations would simply move south to get low-cost labor and evade strict U.S. environmental laws. For these reasons, President Clinton promised to obtain additional assurances from Mexico on these matters and met with Mexico's President Carlos Salinas shortly after taking office. Mexico's lower environmental standards are an especially thorny matter, and in June 1993 a U.S. federal court ordered a delay in U.S. ratification of the treaty until the U.S. government completed an environmental-impact study. The court order was later lifted. President Clinton also had to grant significant protection to U.S. groups like wheat and peanut growers to get narrow Congressional approval for the NAFTA pact in November 1993.

Strong Japanese and European reactions suggested NAFTA's potential effect. Japanese government and industrial officials expressed worry, and one described NAFTA as "outrageous," arguing that "the three countries are building a wall around themselves." Creating North American and European trading blocs may encourage the Japanese to form a similar bloc in Southeast Asia with such partners as Malaysia and Singapore. Some Europeans expressed unease lest NAFTA discriminate against their exporters. Whether the world is dividing into rival trading blocs, or whether the free-trade areas are stepping stones to global free trade remains to be seen.

Conclusion

Rapid change in global politics makes it difficult to discern the future shape of evolving relations among Cold War allies. What do the economic rivalries among the three economic centers of power portend for the twenty-first century? How will growing Asian economic dependence on Japan (and China's explosive economic growth) affect the

[107]Michael Boskin, "We Gain. Mexico Gains. Canada Gains." *The New York Times*, August 14, 1992, p. A15.

[108]See Keith Bradsher, "Free Trade Accord Expected to Trim Nation's Food Bill," *The New York Times*, August 15, 1992, pp. 1, 20.

other two? Will Europe's voyage toward integration produce greater economic cooperation or rivalry with the rest of the world? And what does NAFTA presage for the Western Hemisphere and the rest of the world? Will we see "islands of prosperity" sharply divided from and competing with each other — Pacific Rim versus NAFTA and NAFTA versus European Community? Or are we on the verge of greater global cooperation and prosperity as these actors recognize their global interdependence? Is a new world economy forming in which government and business will be closer partners and change things so that, as two observers say, "the choice is no longer between free trade and protectionism."[109]

If the past was prologue, then rivalry rather than cooperation would seem the order for tomorrow, but the future is not simply the past warmed over. Some trends promise greater cooperation. Japan suffered an economic recession in the early 1990s with steep declines in stock-market prices and domestic real-estate values making it recognize its stake in universal prosperity. Tokyo too is slowly recognizing that it has to face economic and social problems, such as integrating women into the workforce and growing demands for leisure, which are common to postindustrial societies. On the other side of the world, dramatic changes in Central Europe, especially the reunified Germany, are slowing European integration. Resolving the complex issues in unifying Europe will consume more time than originally anticipated and stretch those decisions toward the new century. For its part, U.S. ability to meet challenges from abroad is diminished by domestic problems, including the budget deficit and shortage of well-educated workers. Such problems may either accelerate divisions among economic powers or encourage the cooperation that the West enjoyed after 1945.

How will economic rivalries affect political ties among these regions and nations? Will economic friction reinforce political rivalries? Will Japan and Germany seek political and military power commensurate with their economic power? Economic rivalries have already created or exacerbated some political conflicts. Europeans and Americans are at odds over economic assistance to the newly democratic countries in Central Europe.[110] Yet unmet Central European economic needs could create deep political unrest and reverse their movement toward political democracy and free markets.[111] The Americans would also like the Europeans to assume a larger share in helping the newly democratic countries in Eastern Europe and ending bloodshed in the former Yugoslavia.

The inevitable question is whether these political frictions will stay within manageable limits. They have thus far, and prospects are good that they will continue to do so. Although Japan and Germany will grow more independent, they will continue to value their political and military ties to the United States. Both are constrained militarily

[109]Peter F. Cowhey and Jonathan D. Aronson, "A New Trade Order," *Foreign Affairs* 72:1 (1992/93), p. 183.

[110]In 1992 and 1993, the United States joined the other major democracies to support major aid programs for Russia and Ukraine.

by constitutional restrictions, and their commitment to democracy makes any rapid change in their global political role unlikely. Finally, both countries are deeply enmeshed in the web of global "complex interdependence."[112] Their commitments could be altered, but neither easily nor inexpensively. At the same time, though, Japan and Germany will become more active in their own regions and perhaps in the U.N. and other global organizations, but neither is likely to become a global adversary of the United States. Instead, Germany (and more generally the EC), Japan, and the United States are likely to remain friendly adversaries, less constrained than in the past (by a common foe) about bringing disagreements into the open but fearful of collisions that would harm them all.

Finally, do these changes in relations among Cold War allies add to or detract from America's preeminence in the global economy? In the short term, the United States will probably remain the leading player. For the future, more diverse actors will shape economic outcomes and diminish dominance by any one of them. In this sense, the notion of friendly rivalries will be more apposite.

Key Terms

head-to-head competition
niche competition
hegemon
imperial overextension
vanishing World War II effect
soft power
declinist perspective
zaibatsu
industrial policy
foreign investment
strength of currency
Japan-bashing
racial stereotypes
orderly marketing agreements
Structural Impediments Initiative (SII)
newly industrialized countries (NICs)
managed trade
Maastricht
European Coal and Steel
   Community (ECSC)
Liberal Democratic Party (LDP)

regional integration
exchange-rate mechanism (ERM)
Westpolitik (Western politics)
Ostpolitik (Eastern politics)
extraterritorial jurisdiction
Common Agricultural Policy (CAP)
Uruguay Round negotiation
local-content requirements
free-trade area
U.S.–Canada Free Trade Agreement
   (FTA)
North American Free Trade Agree-
   ment (NAFTA)
cultural sovereignty
European Community (EC)
European Economic Community
   (EEC)
European Atomic Energy
   Community (EURATOM)
Single Market Act

[111]For a useful summary of these issues, see Robert S. Jordan, *Atlantic Relations and the New Europe* (New Orleans: The Eisenhower Center for Leadership Studies, University of New Orleans, March 1992), especially pp. 21–33.

[112]For an argument on how the forces of complex interdependence may dampen rivalries among these actors, see Maull, "Germany and Japan," especially pp. 102–106.

CHAPTER FOURTEEN

The Middle-East Cauldron

In preceding chapters, we have surveyed the dominant issues in global politics during and at the end of the Cold War. We now turn to the Middle East, where political, military, and economic issues intersect. Their consequences are felt in many ways—in New York's World Trade Center bombing, in long lines at gas stations, in U.S. electoral politics. No region is as complex or dangerous as the Middle East, a vast arc stretching from North Africa eastward to Iran, and Middle Eastern issues have dominated the global agenda for years. The end of the Cold War may or may not bring them closer to resolution.

At the juncture of three continents—Europe, Asia, and Africa—birthplace of three of the world's great religions—*Christianity*, *Judaism*, and *Islam*—and site of about 60% of the world's proven oil reserves, the Middle East is a swirling cauldron of ancient hatreds. Since 1948, it has witnessed four major wars between Israel and its Arab neighbors, a bloody conflict between Iran and Iraq, Iraq's invasion and pillaging of Kuwait, and innumerable incidents of assassination and terrorist violence. One great puzzle is the possibility that the Cold War's end may actually increase the danger because the superpowers will no longer be willing or able to restrain their bellicose "clients," some of which have acquired or are developing weapons of mass destruction.[1]

---

[1]Israel almost certainly has nuclear weapons and may also have gas and bacteriological weapons. Iraq is trying to develop nuclear weapons, so worrying the Israelis that in June 1981 they launched a preventive air strike against Iraq's uncompleted Osirak nuclear reactor. Iraq used poison gas against Iranian soldiers and its own Kurdish minority. Libya too has been trying to acquire poison gas and has constructed a factory for making it.

In many ways the Middle East, with its clashing nationalisms, is today's equivalent to the Balkans before 1914—lands with "inflamed consciousness of nationality . . . with real injustice and maladministration"[2] reinforcing other grievances—out of which World War I exploded. Yet, Middle East politics are in many ways even more complex than Balkan politics. The region is home to a mosaic of actors and overlapping, reinforcing, and crosscutting issues. To fit the pieces together we briefly describe some of the key actors in context with the region's dominant issues and see how these issues are related.

Historical Overview

All issues have a historical dimension that must be recognized if they are to make sense.[3] In many ways, history probably weighs heavier on the Middle East than elsewhere. Some of the actors have been squaring off with each other since Biblical times. At the heart of Middle Eastern politics are two ethnically related peoples—Arabs and Jews— whose histories have been entwined for centuries. We now trace some past moments of these peoples.

Arabs and Islam

Early in the seventh century A.D., Muhammad (A.D. 571–632) launched a religious movement in Mecca in western Arabia. Islam was born as the third great religion in the Middle East. The religious revival Muhammad began owed much to Judaism and Christianity and, with those religions, shared the belief that God is one. Muslims believe that Moses and Christ were genuine prophets and that Muhammad was the third and final prophet of God. This debt is clear in the holy book of Islam, the *Koran*. One historian says, "The parallels between the Old Testament and the Koran are many and striking." [4]

Islam soon spread throughout the Middle East and northern Africa, eventually reaching Spain in the west and the borders of India in the east. The eighth to eleventh centuries A.D. were the peak of Arab power and Islamic civilization. Baghdad became the center for trade routes between Europe and Asia and Africa and saw an unparalleled flowering of the arts, literature, science, and philosophy.[5] "Arab scholars," declares Philip Hitti, "were studying Aristotle when Charlemagne and his lords were reportedly

---

[2]Laurence Lafore, *The Long Fuse: An Interpretation of the Origins of World War I*, 2nd ed. (New York: Lippincott, 1971), p. 46.

[3]For an excellent history of the Arabs, see Albert Hourani, *A History of the Arab Peoples* (Cambridge, Mass.: Harvard University Press, 1991). For a fine historical analysis of the Jews' relationship to Palestine, see Nadav Safran, *Israel—The Embattled Ally* (Cambridge, Mass.: Harvard University Press, 1978).

[4]Philip K. Hitti, *The Arabs: A Short History* (Chicago: Henry Regnery, 1956), p. 44.

[5]We owe much of our knowledge of classical Greece to the Arabic preservation and translation of Greek drama, philosophy, and science, including Aristotle's works.

learning to write their names. Scientists in Cordova, with their seventeen great libraries ... enjoyed luxurious baths at a time when washing the body was considered a dangerous custom at the University of Oxford."[6]

This brief moment of glory soon faded, for the Islamic Empire fragmented into competing dynasties by the end of the tenth century. Although the Arabs in the Islamic community remained influential, they were gradually eclipsed by Turks and Persians, and, during the fifteenth and sixteenth centuries, most Arabs lost their independence and were absorbed in another great empire, that of the Ottoman Turks. The *Ottoman Empire* was founded in modern Turkey next to the *Byzantine Empire*. In 1453, the Byzantine era ended when the Turks seized Constantinople (Istanbul), and by 1534 the Ottomans possessed Iraq, Egypt, and Syria and were the preeminent power in the Mediterranean basin. Most of Arabia, Palestine, and North Africa were also governed by the Ottomans, of whose empire Albert Hourani writes:

> The empire was a bureaucratic state, holding different regions within a single administrative and fiscal system. It was also, however, the last great expression of the universality of the world of Islam. It preserved the religious law, protected and extended the frontiers of the Muslim world, guarded the holy cities of Arabia[7] and organized the pilgrimage to them.[8]

This great multinational empire expanded to the gates of Vienna in 1698 but then was gradually enfeebled until, late in the nineteenth century, it had earned the title, "*sick man of Europe*." It was weakened by stagnation in the bureaucracy that had built the empire in the first place. Until the middle of the eighteenth century, the relationship between the Ottomans and the Europeans was still one of equality. Within a century, the societies of which the empire was composed were penetrated by the European powers and were becoming economically dependent on them. Mistreatment of Christians by the Ottomans provided the Europeans a handy excuse for intervening when they felt the desire to do so.

In 1798, Napoleon seized Egypt, but the British drove out his forces three years later. The French conquest of Algeria (1830–1847) was the first important conquest of an Arabic society by European imperialism, and the European powers also became deeply involved in the Ottoman Empire's European provinces. With their aid, Serbia gained independence in 1830 and Greece three years later. Thereafter, Tunisia (1881) and Egypt (1882), Morocco (1906), and Libya (1911)[9] were added to the European empires. World War I, which brought down the Ottoman Empire, was set off by the last

---

[6] Hitti, *Arabs: A Short History*, p. 5.

[7] Mecca and Medina.

[8] Hourani, *History of the Arab Peoples*, p. 207.

[9] These events were part of the mad scramble for empire that preceded World War I. Morocco was ceded to France after a tense crisis between France and Germany but was not secured for the French until after a second crisis with Germany in 1911. The Italian seizure of Libya was one of the final acts of prewar imperialism.

FIGURE 14.1

The Ottoman Empire at its Height, 1566

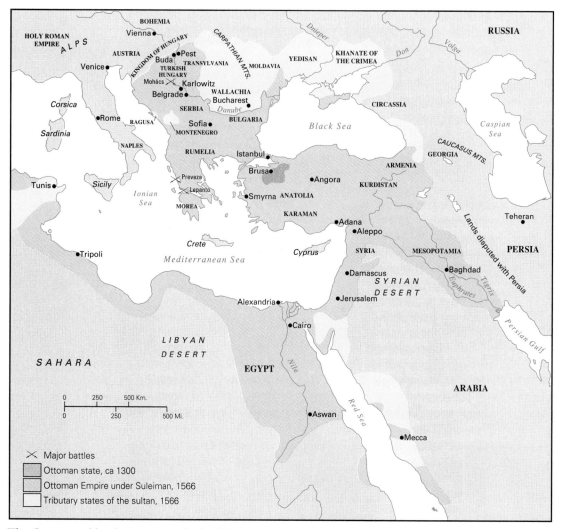

The Ottomans, like their great rivals the Habsburgs, rose to rule a vast dynastic empire encompassing many different peoples and ethnic groups. The army and the bureaucracy served to unite the disparate territories into a single state.

in a series of crises in the Balkans involving the struggle for control over areas being abandoned by the ebbing Muslim empire.[10] A flaming crisis in 1908 between Austria-Hungary and Russia over the former Ottoman province of Bosnia-Herzegovina brought the two powers to the verge of a war which finally erupted after the Austrian archduke was assassinated in 1914.[11]

Alliance with Austria-Hungary and Germany in World War I was a catastrophe for the Ottomans, and the war set off an eruption of Arab nationalism. The British waged war against the Ottomans in Palestine, Syria, and Iraq, triumphing everywhere. Among their local allies was Hussein, the governor (*sherif*) of Mecca and leader of the Hashemite clan of Arab Bedouins,[12] who launched an Arab revolt against the Ottomans in 1916. The revolt was encouraged by British promises of national independence, and its leaders were aided by an adventurer of mythic proportion, T. E. Lawrence, known as Lawrence of Arabia. The Ottoman Empire collapsed after the war (1923) when the sultanate was overthrown by army officers led by Mustapha Kemal (Kemal Atatürk), who then established the Republic of Turkey.

Arab hopes were soon dashed as European rule replaced the Ottomans. By agreement with the League of Nations in 1922, Britain was made responsible for Transjordan, Iraq, and Palestine and France for Syria and Lebanon. This partition reflected the spheres of influence to which the two powers had agreed in the secret Sykes-Picot Treaty in 1916. Only Saudi Arabia[13] and Yemen enjoyed independence, though Britain retained small *protectorates* along the Persian Gulf, including Kuwait, Oman, and Bahrain.[14] The Arab struggle for independence was to resume during and after World War II. Although the war ended with the British and French still in control, the days of European imperial rule were numbered. One outcome of the war was growing consciousness of "Arab" nationalism, a sense of community among Arabs living in different countries. By the end of 1946, French forces had left Syria and Lebanon. The British sought to encourage formal independence within a continued alliance between themselves and the Arabs. A potent combination of Arab nationalism and a new generation of Arab leaders and British inability to find a middle ground between Arabs and Jews doomed this effort.

[10]The end might have come sooner had it not been for the European balance of power. Only British and French intervention in the Crimean War (1853–1856) saved the Ottomans from disastrous defeat by Russia.

[11]The many Muslims still living in Bosnia are the remains of a community that once prospered under the Ottomans.

[12]The present king of Jordan is a Hashemite. His grandfather, Abdullah, was installed as ruler of Transjordan (1921–1951). Another Hashemite, Faisal, was king of Iraq (1921–1933).

[13]Much of this country was initially governed by the *sherif* Hussein of Mecca until he was overthrown by Ibn Saud, and Saudi independence was declared in 1932.

[14]Kuwait received independence in 1961; Muscat and Oman became an independent sultanate in 1951; Bahrain became an independent emirate in 1971.

Background to Jewish Nationalism

The Bible speaks of how God commanded Abraham to go to the land of Palestine, which would belong to his descendants after a long struggle. Jacob (or Israel), Abraham's grandson, was, the Bible says, forced by famine to emigrate to Egypt, where the Jews were enslaved. According to the Book of Judges, God appointed Moses to lead the Children of Israel out of bondage and back to Palestine. For forty years, Moses and his followers are said to have wandered in the desert until they arrived in "the Promised Land."

By 1100 B.C., the Jews—divided into (often conflicting) tribes—possessed much of Palestine. Although these tribes united for a time and a Temple was constructed in Jerusalem under Solomon, they remained independent. By about the sixth century B.C., the era of the First Temple ended with its destruction by the Babylonian king, Nebuchadnezzar, and the deportation of many Jews to Babylon.[15] Some of those who were deported returned to Palestine and rebuilt the Temple after the Persians conquered Babylon in 538 B.C., and in the ensuing years Jewish culture flourished under the Persians. In the following centuries, however, Jews faced persecution, first by the Seleucids of Syria who had replaced the Persians, and later by the Romans. Although the Romans tolerated local customs, Jewish nationalists fomented a general rebellion in 64 A.D. Twice again during the next seventy years, rebellions flared against the Romans. Finally, the Roman conquerors devastated Jerusalem in A.D. 135.

Many Jews had not returned to Palestine from Babylon, and others fled during the following centuries. Thus began the *Jewish Diaspora* (dispersion), during which Jewish communities lived in many countries around the world, always hoping to return to Palestine. Jewish communities in Egypt and Spain flourished under Arab rule in the centuries following Islam's birth, and, during the Middle Ages, Jews found greater tolerance among the Arab rulers in the Middle East, North Africa, and Spain than among the Christian rulers in Western Europe. Ghettos were created in European cities as places where Jews could live and which professions they could enter were restricted. Jews were not permitted to own land and were made scapegoats for societies' ills. In 1492, Spain expelled its Jewish and Muslim residents, and Jewish refugees fled eastward to Poland, southern Russia, and the Baltic states.

Wherever they went, Jews retained their distinctive customs and laws. The two factors that account for this durable sense of identity were the Jewish religion itself and refusal by other communities to welcome them. Although differences grew among customs and outlooks of the three major communities—*Ashkenazim* (those living in Europe outside Spain), *Sefardim* (those expelled from Spain), and *Orientals* (those living in the Middle East)—all were bound by belief that someday they would return to Palestine, the "Promised Land."

---

[15]Safran, *Israel—The Embattled Ally*, p. 8.

Late in the nineteenth century, this belief was transformed into a political doctrine — *Zionism*.[16] Zionists advocated creating a Jewish homeland in Biblical Palestine. How else, they asked, could the fourteen million Jews scattered around the world gain rights like other free peoples and protect themselves from persecution? Although most of Europe granted political and economic rights to their Jewish communities by the mid-nineteenth century, the country with the largest Jewish population — Russia — did not.[17] The belief that *anti-Semitism* was embedded in the psyche of Christian Europe influenced Jewish intellectuals led by Theodor Herzl to hold the First Zionist Congress in Basel, Switzerland (August 1897). The Congress established the World Zionist Organization.[18]

The legal basis for a Jewish state in Palestine was a letter written November 2, 1917, by British Foreign Secretary Arthur Balfour and known as the *Balfour Declaration*, declaring that: "His Majesty's Government view with favor the establishment in Palestine of a national home for the Jewish people, and will use their best endeavours to facilitate the achievement of this objective."[19] Another sentence, stating "that nothing shall be done which may prejudice the civil and religious rights of existing non-Jewish communities in Palestine," became a source of Arab opposition to the Jewish state.

Palestine was entrusted to Britain as a *mandate* by the League of Nations, and Britain was encouraged to carry out the Balfour Declaration. Having made promises to both Jews and Arabs, the British confronted a dilemma. Zionists sought to immigrate to Palestine, and Arabs feared becoming a minority in their own land. The British response was to permit limited immigration. During the 1920s and early 1930s, Jewish immigration to Palestine remained small, but the Jewish community in the country set up the institutions for statehood, including political parties, labor unions, and universities, and, most important, the Jewish Agency, which after 1948 became the government of the new state. With Nazi persecution of the Jews in the 1930s, emigration to Palestine soared, enlarging the Jewish community to 500,000.

With another war looming, the British in 1937 proposed a plan to divide Palestine into Jewish and Arab states, but the plan was unacceptable to the Arabs. Seeking to placate Arab nationalism on the verge of the war, the British in 1939 proposed to limit Jewish immigration and to establish one state with an Arab majority. This plan violated the Balfour Declaration and was violently opposed by the Jews in Palestine. It was the trauma of Hitler's genocidic effort against the Jews — *the Holocaust* — during which more

[16]After "Zion," the land of the Biblical ancestors.

[17]Jews were granted complete civil rights by the U.S. Constitution, making the United States the first country to do so.

[18]A minority of Jews were Zionists. Many became Marxists, believing that revolution would end anti-Semitism. Others, especially in Germany, believed they could assimilate into their societies.

[19]Cited in Safran, *Israel — The Embattled Ally*, p. 24.

than six million Jews were murdered, which gave birth to Israel. During the first years of Nazi rule in Germany, persecution led to the exodus of many Jews, including prominent figures like Albert Einstein and Sigmund Freud. Persecution soon became genocide when the policy known as *"the final solution"* was introduced under Adolf Eichmann,[20] who oversaw construction of death camps, including Auschwitz in Poland.

Although British authorities had restricted Jewish immigration, the Holocaust changed everything. On the one hand, global sympathy for the Jewish plight, especially in the United States, pressured British authorities to open Palestine to the wretched remains of European Jewry. On the other hand, a campaign for an independent Jewish state by members of an underground Jewish army consisting of veterans of World War II (the Haganah) and of terrorism by militants in the Irgun against British rule, created a cycle of violence.[21] Frustrated by their inability to find a political solution, the British in April 1947 turned the problem over to the United Nations.

Actors

The Middle East arena hosts a bewildering variety of actors beside national governments. The wall between external and internal politics is highly permeable, and domestic actors, like political parties, have a large role. Religious actors, ethnic and terrorist groups, transnational corporations and organizations, and even individuals also carry weight and may have decisive influence in some situations.

Political Parties

That political parties are influential in global politics is illustrated by Israel. That country has a parliamentary system with proportional representation; that is, political parties in the Knesset (parliament) are represented in proportion to the votes they receive. The largest parties are *Labor* and *Likud*, but the system requires that coalitions be formed with smaller parties to create a parliamentary majority. Likud, formerly led by Menachem Begin and later by Yitzhak Shamir, advocates a hard line toward Israel's adversaries, whether Palestinian residents of the *West Bank* and *Gaza Strip* or the governments in Syria and Iraq. Likud's refusal to compromise—accepting the principle of exchanging "land for peace" or halting construction of Israeli settlements in the territories seized in the 1967 war—appeals to Israeli hawks. The party's hard-line policies were responsible for its popularity with the Israeli electorate between 1977 and 1992. Labor, which until 1977 had provided Israel's most prominent leaders, suffered from widespread perceptions that it would pursue a flexible, perhaps even a dovish foreign policy. But in summer

[20]Eichmann was kidnapped from South America by Israeli agents and was tried and executed in Israel for war crimes in 1962.

[21]Former Israeli Prime Minister Menachem Begin was a member of the Irgun and participated in blowing up the King David Hotel in Jerusalem.

1992, Likud was voted out, and a Labor-led coalition took office with Yitzhak Rabin as prime minister. Israel's growing isolation from its main allies and improved prospects for peace persuaded Israelis that the time had come for a change.

Political parties are less crucial in the Arab world because democratic institutions are absent. In some cases, however, they are used effectively by authoritarian leaders for political and social mobilization. The Syrian *Baath Party* is an offshoot of a regional political movement that began in 1940 and exists elsewhere in the Arab world, especially in Iraq. It promotes socialism and secularism and is an instrument for the ambitions of the Syrian leader, Hafez al-Assad. The Iraqi branch of the Baath is a bitter enemy of its Syrian cousin, mainly because of the rivalry between Assad and Iraq's Saddam Hussein.

Religious Actors

No analysis of politics in the Middle East would be complete without reviewing religious actors. Not only is the region holy to three of the world's great monotheistic religions and Jerusalem the home of sites holy to each, but there are a variety of influential religious movements and actors.[22]

In Israel, small religious political parties enjoy influence because they often hold the balance of power in forming a government. In return for its support, the Sephardi Torah Guardians demand laws that require observance of many customs in orthodox Judaism. The National Religious Party promotes religious Zionism, and the Union of Israel is anti-Zionist and presses for strict observance of religious law.

Islam, too, is divided among contentious sects. Hostility between the Arab states and Iran has its roots in a schism within Islam that dates from the seventh century A.D. For a number of years following Muhammad's death, the Islamic community remained in the throes of a succession crisis. The fourth caliph, 'Ali (656–661), who was a cousin and friend of Muhammad and was married to the Prophet's daughter, was defeated in a civil war and then assassinated. The caliphs who succeeded 'Ali and those who supported them were known as *Sunni* ("*standard practice*") *Muslims*. Most Arabs were Sunni, and they permitted tribal ways and secular practices to dominate government and politics. A minority of Muslims, however, declared the caliphs after 'Ali to be illegitimate rulers, claiming that only the male heirs of 'Ali could govern the Islamic community.

Known as *Shi'a Muslims* (from *shi'at 'Ali* or "followers of 'Ali"), this sect advocated adherence to the original precepts of Islam and believed that the word of Allah alone provided sufficient guidance to govern Muslims. When the Shah of Iran was overthrown in 1979 by the followers of Ayatollah Ruhollah Khomeini, Shi'ite Islam became the official religion of the state and power was placed in the hands of the Shi'ite clergy, many

[22]Among the most important sites are the Wailing Wall (the remains of the Second Temple, which the Romans razed), the Dome of the Rock (Islam's first great mosque, built on the site of the Jewish Temple), and the Church of the Holy Sepulchre (built on the site where Christ is believed to have been buried).

The overthrow of Iran's Shah in 1979 brought to power a fundamentalist Shi'ite regime under Ayatollah Khomeini, and his death brought millions to mourn him as shown in the photo. Khomeini's 1979 triumph marked the onset of a wave of Islamic fundamentalism that threatened the stability of Muslim governments throughout the Middle East.

of whom were members of the Islamic Republican Party. The Ayatollah and his followers embarked on an effort to "purify" Islam and bring to power in other countries those who would rule according to these principles. Thus, the Iranian clergy or *mullahs* support *Islamic fundamentalism*; that is, the belief that Muslims should be governed in strict accordance with the Koran.

Sunni–Shi'ite antipathy was a factor in the Iraq–Iran war (1980–1988) as Iran tried to oust Saddam Hussein's Sunni regime and assist Iraqi Shi'ites.[23] Saddam repeatedly brutalized Iraq's Shi'ite community, as after the Persian Gulf War in 1991, and he continued to do so in defiance of U.N. resolutions demanding that he stop persecuting

---

[23]Many Iraqi Shi'ites live near the southern Iraqi port city of Basra, close to the border with Iran, and they rose up against Saddam in 1991.

this community. Because the Shi'ites are the poorest class in many Arab societies, many have been receptive to Iranian efforts to mobilize them and have been willing to serve Iran's purposes. Iran, with its Shi'ite majority, has been able to exert influence in Lebanon by supporting the terrorist group *Hizballah* (Army of God), mostly composed of Shi'ite followers in that country. This group was responsible for kidnapping Western hostages in Lebanon during the 1980s and for conducting raids against Israel's security zone in south Lebanon, as well as shelling towns in northern Israel that almost triggered war in 1993.

Another influential religious movement in the Arab world is the *Muslim Brothers* or *Brotherhood*. Founded in Cairo in 1928, the Society of the Muslim Brothers sought to evict the colonial masters who governed Egypt and opposed Western customs, believing that Muslim behavior should be in accord with the principles of Islam.[24] The Brotherhood supported the military regime in Egypt that overthrew King Farouk in 1952. Following an assassination attempt against President Nasser in 1954, some of its leaders were executed, and the group was forced to go underground. In 1981, the Muslim Brotherhood was involved in assassinating President Anwar Sadat of Egypt, and in the following year it sought to overthrow President Hafez al-Assad of Syria. Some of its adherents may have been involved in bombing New York's World Trade Center in March 1993. As this and other movements that demand the Arab world be "Islamized" acquired popularity in the 1980s, especially among the urban poor, Arab leaders increasingly invoked the rhetoric of Islam and made concessions to Islamic sensibilities. Followers of the Brotherhood hold power in the Sudan and are a threat to authorities in other countries: Algeria, Tunisia, and Egypt. Were they to succeed, these countries would become more anti-Western.

In Lebanon, the several religious communities continue to behave as autonomous actors. Major communities include Maronite Christians,[25] *Druses* (an Islamic sect that shares many doctrines of Shi'ism), and Shi'ite Muslims. These communities were adversaries and competed with one another for power during the Lebanese civil war. Their animosity, however, is not recent. In 1860, civil war engulfed Lebanon, leading to massacres of Christians.

In sum, Middle Eastern politics involves influential religious actors, some of which threaten stability in leading countries in the region. All hold deep and often conflicting views. Few are willing to compromise those ideas, which contribute to some of the bitterest cleavages in the region.

---

[24]Hourani, *History of the Arab Peoples*, pp. 348–349.

[25]The Maronites, though retaining their own customs and liturgies, have accepted papal authority since the twelfth century, when the Crusaders occupied the coastal areas in Lebanon and Syria.

Ethnic "Nations"

In a sense, Middle Eastern politics is "tribal," featuring conflicts between peoples who reside in artificial states created by colonial masters and who either are persecuted minorities within those states or separated from their brethren by the boundaries of those states. Kuwait, for example, was artificially created by Britain, and has long been claimed by Iraq as a province. A great deal of conflict in the region is rooted in ethnic tensions.

Indeed, Israel's founding—presumably the final chapter in a displaced people's search for a permanent home where they could live together—was an expression of ethnic aspiration. In many ways, the Palestinian Arabs' search for a national home is reminiscent of that earlier story.[26] Unfortunately, both Jews and Palestinians claim the same homeland—Palestine. The *Palestine Liberation Organization* (PLO), founded in Cairo in 1964 as a way "for the Arab states to control the nationalist guerrilla groups,"[27] expresses the Palestinians' aspirations for a national home. After 1967, the PLO gradually became an umbrella for groups like Yasser Arafat's Al Fatah organization and, since the late 1960s, it has evolved a complex bureaucratic structure to look after Palestinians' social and economic needs, as well as representing their political interests. Aided by Arab states and taxes and contributions from wealthy Palestinians, the PLO has accumulated large financial assets, which it invests overseas. The PLO has a military wing, the Palestine Liberation Army, as well as military forces organized by member groups. It also has a legislative branch, the Palestine National Council, theoretically its ruling body. Despite all this organization, the PLO remains a collection of often unruly militias with diverse ideologies and aspirations, and it is held together mainly by Arafat's political skill.

Jews and Palestinians are not the only significant ethnic groups in the region. The *Kurds* are an Islamic people who speak their own language and live as minorities mainly in Turkey, Iraq, and Iran[28] and for decades have been engaged in a struggle against the dominant peoples in those countries for an independent "Kurdistan." Under the Ottomans, the Kurds enjoyed a good deal of local autonomy, and many served in the imperial military forces. More recently, Kurdish minorities have missed out on the economic and social progress enjoyed by others in their countries and have been targets of efforts at forced assimilation. In recent decades, Kurdish unrest has been endemic in the three countries in which they live, and Kurdish aspirations have been repeatedly manipulated to serve others' interests. The Shah of Iran and his successors aided Kurdish resistance against Iraq. Saddam Hussein has repeatedly aided Kurdish rebels in Turkey

---

[26]Palestinians do not constitute a separate ethnic group. They are Arabs who live or used to live in Palestine.

[27]Deborah J. Gerner, *One Land, Two Peoples: The Conflict over Palestine* (Boulder, Colo.: Westview Press, 1991), p. 57.

[28]As many as 12 million Kurds live in Turkey (about 24 percent of the population) and 2.6 million in Iraq (15.5 percent). The number in Iran, though large, is uncertain.

FIGURE 14.2

Ethnicity and the Middle East

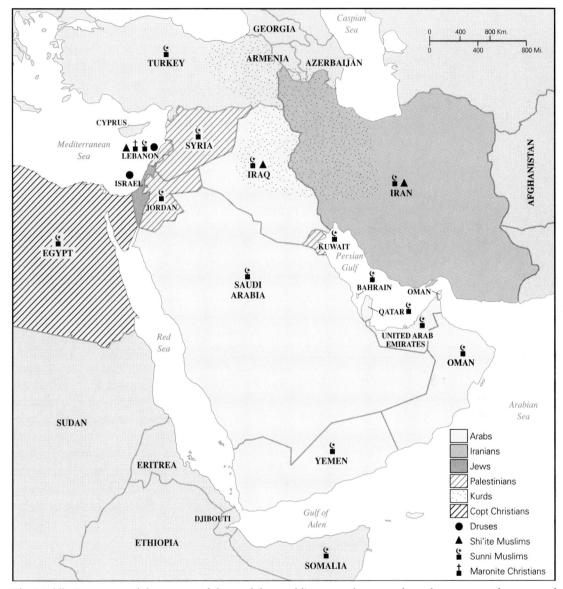

The Middle East—site of the origins of three of the world's great religions—also is home to a rich variety of ethnic and national groups.

and Iran even while murderously repressing the Kurds in his own country. And, since 1991, the Turks have allowed the United States to help the Kurds in Iraq while attacking Turkish Kurds who sought sanctuary in Iraq.

Terrorists

As we saw in Chapter 5, the Middle East has been host to many of the world's most violent terrorist groups and some of its bloodiest terrorist incidents in recent decades. *Terrorism* — the use of violence, usually against civilians — [29] is difficult to define in a way acceptable to all. Are violent acts directed against Israeli military authorities terrorism? What of the stabbing and shooting of Israeli civilians, including children and old people? Are Israeli reprisals against Palestinians in the occupied territories or in southern Lebanon terrorism or acts of self-defense?

Much terrorism in the Middle East, though by no means all, has been associated with Palestinian or Islamic extremists who have often received assistance from governments in Libya, Iran, Syria, and Iraq. Much of the terrorist violence is directed against Israel,[30] though with little success because of Israeli security measures. The difficulty terrorists have in striking Israel directly has encouraged them to strike at "softer" targets, especially the interests of Americans and Europeans whom the terrorists accuse of being pro-Israeli.[31]

The terrorist groups operating in the region sometimes cooperate and at other times compete among themselves. A brief description of a few will suggest how varied such organizations are. The Abu Nidal group, which split from the PLO in 1974, has been responsible for more than ninety attacks in more than twenty countries. The Armenian Secret Army for the Liberation of Armenia (ASALA) is a Marxist–Leninist group that conducts terrorism against Turkey in revenge for that country's massacre of Armenians in 1915. Hizballah (also known as Islamic Jihad — holy war — or the Party of God) operates in Lebanon and was responsible for seizing Western hostages in the 1980s and the suicide bombing of the U.S. Marine barracks in Beirut in 1983. Finally, several other groups (Popular Front for the Liberation of Palestine, Popular Front for the Liberation of Palestine–General Command, Popular Front for the Liberation of Palestine–Special Command, and Hamas) have employed terrorism against Israeli targets and those

---

[29]Brian Jenkins, "International Terrorism: The Other World War," in Charles W. Kegley, Jr., *International Terrorism: Characteristics, Causes, Controls* (New York: St. Martin's Press, 1990), p. 28. Also see Chapters 5 and 16.

[30]Among the notable exceptions to this aim have been efforts by Islamic fundamentalists against secular Arab leaders and the campaign of state terrorism Iran waged against the author Salman Rushdie and his "sacrilegious" novel, *The Satanic Verses*. Palestinian leaders themselves have frequently been victims of terrorist attacks initiated by other Palestinians in the struggle for power that characterizes Palestinian politics.

[31]Americans, Europeans, and Israelis have collaborated, especially in intelligence matters, in combating terrorism.

perceived to be pro-Israeli.[32] Members of one or another of these groups have committed such heinous acts as bombing Pan American Flight 103 over Lockerbie, Scotland in 1988 and in 1985 hijacking the cruise ship *Achille Lauro* and subsequently murdering a crippled U.S. citizen.

Middle Eastern terrorists pursue various objectives. Some seek to punish Israel directly for its "crimes" against the Palestinians. Others seek to punish those who assist Israel and influence them to reduce that assistance. Still others resort to terrorism to prevent Arab leaders from compromising with Israel. Such extremists use terrorism whenever the prospects for peace seem to grow so as to create "incidents" that will poison the atmosphere.

Transnational Corporations

Transnational corporations have long been involved in Middle East politics. In a regional context, the oldest and most important of these have been involved in extracting and processing oil. Shortly after the Standard Oil Trust was broken up in the United States in 1909, Standard Oil of New Jersey began to operate overseas, especially in Venezuela and the Middle East. It was followed by such European giants as Royal Dutch/Shell, and, by the late 1920s, seven corporations, known collectively as the "*seven sisters*," formed an *oligopoly* over production, refining, and distribution of oil.[33] This oligopoly was broken in the 1960s and 1970s by new firms entering the market and growing power among the oil-producing states. In recent years, however, as demand for oil and corporate profits declined, the number of independent firms has been reduced by mergers. Nevertheless, petroleum corporations remain in the global corporate elite, the largest group in the "billion-dollar club" (corporations with sales exceeding $1 billion).[34]

For many years the big oil companies have been players in the region's politics directly and indirectly (by pressuring governments). Their interest in maintaining close relations with countries on which they rely for oil has led them to lobby repeatedly for the Arabs. In 1948, they sought to keep the U.S. from recognizing Israel. In 1951, the Anglo-Iranian Oil Company exerted pressure to persuade the United States and Britain to support a clandestine operation that overthrew Iranian Premier Muhammad Mossadegh in 1953 and strengthened the Shah. Thereafter, a new international oil consortium concluded an agreement with Iran to develop its oil resources.

[32]For a list of major terrorist groups, see U.S. Department of State, *Patterns of Global Terrorism: 1992* (Washington, D.C.: Department of State Publication 10054, April 1993), Appendix B, pp. 29–54.

[33]The seven were Exxon, Royal Dutch/Shell, British Petroleum, Gulf Oil, Texaco, Chevron, and Mobil Oil.

[34]U.N. Centre on Transnational Corporations, *Transnational Corporations in World Development: Trends and Prospects* (New York: United Nations, 1988), p. 34.

The oil companies' influence relative to the oil-producing states began to decline early in the 1970s. Although we have more to say on this subject in discussing the Organization of Petroleum Exporting Countries (OPEC), the "seven sisters'" dominance has been weakened by new competitors such as Occidental, Marathon, Hunt, and Getty. These firms produced the 1959 oil-price reductions that inspired the creation of OPEC.

Oil is not the only way in which corporations have been involved in Middle East politics. Swiss, British, French, Italian, American, and, most important, German firms provided Saddam Hussein the technology and expertise for his attempts to produce weapons of mass destruction. German companies such as Karl Kolb, Rhein Bayern Fahrzeugbau, Thyssen GmbH, Gildemeista Projecta, Inwako, and Messerschmitt-Boelkow-Blohn are accused of providing the Iraqi war machine with lathes and presses to enrich uranium, plants and equipment to produce poison gas, equipment to make botulin toxin and mycotoxin weapons, and equipment for improving Scud ballistic missiles.[35]

International Organizations

For many decades, international organizations have been active in the Middle East. Few issues have preoccupied the United Nations as much as those in the Middle East. Year after year, the U.N. Security Council and General Assembly passed resolutions that, though often ignored, form the basis for attempts to resolve these issues. Israel was founded following U.N. adoption of a plan to partition Palestine (*U.N. Resolution 181*) put forward by the U.N. Special Committee on Palestine. The war that followed was punctuated by cease-fires demanded by the Security Council and was brought to a conclusion by bilateral cease-fires negotiated by the United Nations. The U.N. mediator, Count Folke Bernadotte, was assassinated in September 1948 by a Zionist terrorist group, the Stern Gang.

United Nations resolutions had vital roles in each of the subsequent Arab–Israeli wars and continue to provide a framework for such issues as the status of the territories occupied by Israel after 1967, Israel's right to exist, and the rights of the Palestinians. Some U.N. actions, however, have prompted much controversy, such as providing the PLO with observer status (1974) and equating "Zionism with racism" (1975).[36] Since 1948, too, the Middle East has hosted an alphabet soup of U.N. military observer and peacekeeping teams. Perhaps the most successful of these is a humanitarian rather than a peacekeeping organization—U.N. Relief and Works Agency for Palestine Refugees in the Near East (UNRWA)—which is responsible for providing food, housing, and

[35]R. Jeffrey Smith and Marc Fisher, "Saddam Hussein's German Connection: Exports of Nuclear Knowledge," *The Washington Post National Weekly Edition* (August 3–9, 1992), pp. 8–9.

[36]This resolution, widely regarded as anti-Semitic, was overturned in 1992 under U.S. pressure.

education for almost 800,000 Palestinian refugees scattered in 61 camps in the region, especially in Lebanon and Gaza.

One of the most important regional organizations in the Middle East is the *Arab League*, which was established as an expression of Arab solidarity in March 1945. All Arab states and the PLO are members. The League has a governing Council, a Joint Defense Council for collective security, a Permanent Military Commission, and an Economic Council. Owing to divisions among its members, however, the organization has never achieved its founders' aspirations. The League serves two major functions—as a forum to express differences among Arab governments and as an arena to rally the Arab world against Israel.

The *Organization of Arab Petroleum Exporting Countries* (OAPEC) is perhaps the best-known regional economic organization and an important expression of Arab economic solidarity (or lack thereof). Eight years after its umbrella organization OPEC was formed (the *Organization of Petroleum Exporting Countries*), OAPEC was established in 1968.[37] In regional politics OAPEC has had an important part, initiating an oil embargo against the West during the 1973 Middle East War. More generally, the "OPEC cartel" was feared in the 1970s as an oligopoly that could determine oil prices, and it enjoyed leverage over both the industrialized states for which oil is a major source of energy as well as developing countries in which cheap oil is critical for industrialization and agriculture. Two observers comment, "The dramatic success of OPEC between 1973 and the early 1980s is one of those seismic events in world affairs that directly affects virtually all dimensions of international political activity."[38]

Individuals

Individual *charisma* has always been important in the Middle East because of the tribal nature of society and the dominance of individual leaders in tribal politics. Moses, Jesus, and Muhammad all moved their followers by force of personality and ideas. In recent years, too, Middle East politics has been influenced by charismatic individuals who, whether heroes or villains, have left their imprint on their countries and altered history.

Among the Israelis in this category are Chaim Weizmann (the early Zionist leader), David Ben-Gurion (Israel's first prime minister), and Golda Meir (the former Milwaukee schoolteacher who served as prime minister during the dark days in October 1973). Another is the heroic one-eyed general Moshe Dayan, who (as a young major) during the 1948 war managed with a small, ill-equipped unit to repulse an invading Syrian army equipped with tanks and artillery. Dayan, a dashing figure, later masterminded Israel's

---

[37]The members of OAPEC are Algeria, Bahrain, Egypt, Iraq, Kuwait, Libya, Qatar, Saudi Arabia, Syria, Tunisia, and United Arab Emirates. Collectively, they account for about 90 percent of OPEC's reserves and 75 percent of its production.

[38]Robert S. Walters and David H. Blake, *The Politics of Global Economic Relations* (Englewood Cliffs, N.J.: Prentice-Hall, 1992), p. 205.

rapid advance to the Suez Canal in 1956 and was Israeli minister of defense during the decisive Six-Day War in 1967.

Surely the most charismatic Arab leader in his generation and the individual who came closest to uniting Arabs was Gamal Abdel Nasser of Egypt. Nasser was in a group of military officers who overthrew King Farouk in July 1952. He soon made himself master of Egypt, but he became the hero of the Arab masses throughout the Middle East by opposing the British, culminating in Egypt's seizure of the Suez Canal in 1956 and his acceptance of military assistance from the U.S.S.R. He retained his heroic status and died in 1970. Others would try to succeed Nasser: Anwar Sadat, who startled the world by flying to Jerusalem in November 1977 to make peace; Hosni Mubarak, who preserved peace with Israel while regaining acceptance in the Arab world, and others such as Hafez al-Assad of Syria and Saddam Hussein of Iraq. Finally, Yasser Arafat has been responsible for almost singlehandedly keeping world attention focused on the Palestinian issue.

Issues Between Arabs and Israelis

Newspaper stories tend to treat Middle Eastern politics as though it were built on a single relationship that pits Arabs against Israelis. In fact, Middle East politics is far more complex, consisting of contentious but related issues, some pitting Arabs against Israelis and some Arabs against Arabs. We begin by considering some of the issues between Arabs and Israelis, then turn to issues among the Arabs, and conclude by discussing oil as an issue in the region.

"From War to War"[39]

Four major wars set the stage for contemporary politics in the Middle East and shaped relations between Arabs and Israelis.

War of Independence or Palestine War.   The first major war began in November 1947 after the United Nations approved partitioning Palestine into two states, one Jewish, the other Arab. It is called either the War of Independence or the Palestine War. The Arabs immediately objected to the U.N. plan, and both sides began to jockey for control over areas desirable for a future state. Turmoil continued in Palestine until Israel declared its formal independence, May 15, 1948. At that moment, military forces from Egypt, Iraq, Syria, Transjordan, and Lebanon were sent to crush the new state. During

---

[39]See Nadav Safran, *From War to War: The Arab–Israeli Confrontation, 1948–1967* (Indianapolis, Ind.: Pegasus, 1969).

FIGURE 14.3

War and Changing Boundaries in the Middle East

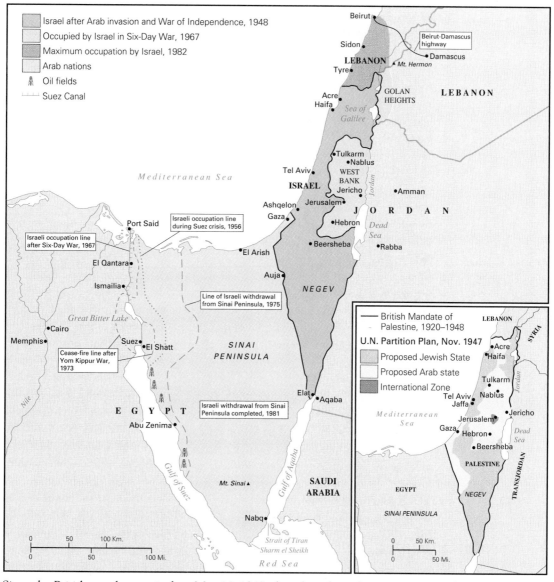

Since the British mandate expired on May 14, 1948, there have been four major wars and innumerable armed clashes in what was formerly Palestine. After winning the War of Independence in 1948, Israel achieved spectacular victories in 1967 in the Six-Day War, occupying the Sinai Peninsula, the Golan Heights, and the West Bank. The Yom Kippur War of 1973 eventually led to the Israeli evacuation of the Sinai and peace with Egypt. Finally, in 1993 Israel and the Palestinians achieved a breakthrough agreement to grant Palestinian self-rule in Gaza and the West Bank.

the following eight months of on-again–off-again warfare, the Arabs, despite their advantage in numbers and resources, were defeated, and a series of bilateral U.N.–brokered armistices ended the war.

The armistices did not bring real peace, however, and Israel's Arab neighbors refused to acknowledge their enemy's right to exist. Although Israel had survived (and was almost 50 percent larger than envisioned in the U.N. partition plan), it remained vulnerable. The war had also made refugees of many Palestinian Arabs, including 700,000 who had fled Israel.[40] Three-fifths of these became refugees in Jordan (including the West Bank), one-fifth in the Gaza Strip, and one-fifth in Lebanon and Syria.[41] Still others remained in refugee camps within the Jewish state. Their plight would become a major issue in later years.

One anti-Israeli policy still active is the Arab economic boycott of Israel. Not only were the Arabs unwilling to trade with Israel, but they listed non-Arab enterprises that did business with Israelis and declared that those companies could not do business with them.[42] Israeli shipping was also barred from the Suez Canal[43] and from the Gulf of Aqaba. "Such was the gravity with which the Israeli government viewed the Aqaba blockade," declares one scholar, "that in 1955 it decided in principle to go to war to remove it and left the execution to a convenient time, which came in October 1956."[44] Raids into Israel were launched from Egypt, Jordan, and Syria, and in 1953 a pattern began to unfold: Arab infiltration followed by Israeli retaliation. This tit-for-tat spiral intensified after 1955.

Suez Crisis.   These conditions contributed to the second Arab-Israeli war. The immediate spark was Nasser's seizure of the Suez Canal in July 1956 from an Anglo-French firm that had operated it. Without informing their U.S. ally, the British and French decided to regain control of the canal. A deal was struck with the Israelis by which an Israeli attack would provide the Europeans with an excuse to intervene to "protect" the canal. On October 29, that attack began, and, though the British and French got bogged down, the Israelis reached the canal in less than 100 hours. Furious at not having been consulted, U.S. Secretary of State John Foster Dulles marshaled opposition to the aggressors in the United Nations. On November 6, the British and French agreed to withdraw, and the Israelis did the same two days later. A U.N. Emergency Force (UNEF) was to separate the belligerents. Israel reaped little from its

---

[40]Arabs claim that Israel drove the refugees from their homes, and Israelis claim that the refugees left because Arab leaders ordered them to do so. Some truth lies in both claims.

[41]Safran, *Israel — The Embattled Ally*, p. 67.

[42]United States law forbids U.S. firms to participate in the Arab boycott.

[43]Egypt continued refusing to permit Israeli vessels to use the canal, violating a 1951 U.N. Security Council resolution.

[44]Safran, *From War to War*, p. 44.

triumph on the battlefield, eventually being forced to return the territory it had gained in the Sinai Peninsula. Its only tangible reward was access to the Gulf of Aqaba for shipping.

Six-Day War. Except for the War of Independence, the Six-Day War in June 1967 was the region's most decisive event since World War II, and any resolution of Middle East issues must confront its consequences. Although in the decade after the Suez crisis Israel's military and economic capabilities improved, the facts of geopolitics continued to bedevil the Jewish state: Israel was surrounded by enemies; it had a long frontier to defend (nearly 600 miles); much of its population and economic life was vulnerable to attack from Arab positions; its access to the Red Sea could easily be disrupted; and Syrian outposts in the *Golan Heights* dominated Israeli settlements below.

These facts of life would adequately explain Israel's strategy in rapidly preempting an Arab attack. Additional reasons were acquisition by Egypt and Syria of large stockpiles of modern Soviet weapons after 1956 and the Israeli economic disruption that would accompany a lengthy war, for which the country's large ready reserves would have to abandon their civilian pursuits.[45] At the same time, Arab frustration over Israel's continued existence and rising Palestinian nationalism helped ripen the region for more conflict. Although President Nasser of Egypt probably did not wish to trigger a war, provocative acts by Egypt and its allies made irresistible the temptation for Israel to preempt. On May 14, 1967, Egyptian armed forces went on maximum alert and began a buildup on the Sinai Peninsula. Two days later, Egypt demanded that the UNEF withdraw immediately. On May 21, Egyptian forces reached Sharm el Sheikh at the mouth of the Gulf of Aqaba, and next day Nasser announced that the gulf was closed to Israel. The last straw was probably that on May 30, Egypt, Jordan, and Syria established a joint military command (Iraq joined some days later), and Egyptian and Iraqi forces began a buildup in Jordan.

Nasser's actions put great pressure on Israel to strike before the balance of forces shifted irremediably against it. On June 5, Israeli air strikes just about destroyed the Egyptian, Syrian, and Jordanian air forces on the ground, and once more Israeli armor rolled into the Sinai and in four days demolished most of the Egyptian army.[46] The Sinai Peninsula and the Gaza Strip (a narrow band of territory on the Mediterranean formerly controlled by Egypt) were now in Israeli hands. In three days, the Jordanian Army too was crushed, and Israel was in command of the West Bank of the Jordan, including the whole city of Jerusalem. The battle against Syria began a few days later (June 9) and

---

[45]The extent of such disruption is clearer when we recognize that in 1967 Israeli mobilization expanded the armed forces to 300,000 in a Jewish population of 2.6 million.

[46]The extent of the victory shows in comparative losses: 12,000 Egyptian and 275 Israeli lives lost; 700 Egyptian and 61 Israeli tanks destroyed or captured. Safran, *Israel — The Embattled Ally*, p. 246.

ended with Israel seizing the strategic Golan Heights. In all, Israel had taken land from three of its neighbors, and these occupied territories remain a pivotal issue to this day.

Following the war, the U.N. Security Council, with U.S. and Soviet backing, passed *Resolution 242*, calling on Israel and its Arab neighbors to negotiate an exchange of "land for peace." The resolution did not require that *all* land seized in the Six-Day War be returned, and it made any outcome subject to negotiation among the parties. Nor did it mention "Palestinian," referring only to the refugee problem. The meaning of 242 has been in dispute ever since.[47] Despite an effort to implement the resolution, little progress was made, and a war of attrition broke out between Israel and Egypt across the Suez Canal. Egypt began to shell Israeli positions on the east bank of the Canal (March 1969), and the Israelis retaliated. Both sides suffered severe casualties, and the conflict escalated as massive Israeli air attacks drew growing Soviet involvement in defending Egyptian airspace. By July 1970, Soviet pilots were directly engaged in air combat against the Israelis, and Israeli air attacks were aimed at destroying sophisticated Soviet antiaircraft missile systems that were being moved toward the canal. The prospect of a flaming crisis was averted only by a U.S.-proposed cease-fire in August that lasted three years.

Yom Kippur War. The fourth war that shaped the current context of Arab–Israeli relations erupted in October 1973. It was a direct result of earlier events as Egypt sought to reverse the Arab "humiliation" of 1967. On October 6, 1973, Egypt and Syria launched a surprise attack against Israeli defenses along the Suez Canal and Golan Heights, beginning the conflict that came to be known as the Yom Kippur War.[48] Although the Israelis ultimately repulsed the attack, the Egyptian and Syrian leaders achieved their principal political purposes: restoring Arab dignity, regaining some land seized in the 1967 war, enhancing their popularity at home, and forcing the Israelis to consider diplomatic alternatives to the military stalemate.

The war did not solve the underlying conflicts between the parties, but it had one significant effect—quickening efforts to address the problems in the region, especially by the United States. In the eight months following the Yom Kippur War, U.S. Secretary of State Henry Kissinger brokered a series of negotiations among the belligerents that led to disengagement of military forces on the Egyptian and Syrian fronts and followed that with another agreement between Egypt and Israel in September 1975.[49] Although

---

[47]Resolution 338 (1973) called on the parties to implement Resolution 242 immediately.

[48]The name comes from the attack's being launched on the holiest day of the year for Jews, Yom Kippur, the day of atonement.

[49]Kissinger's repeated travels among Middle Eastern capitals earned the name "shuttle diplomacy," and such shuttling continued several years. Kissinger persuaded the foreign ministers of Israel, Egypt, Jordan, the United States, and the U.S.S.R. to meet in Geneva, under U.N. auspices, for the first time since the War of Independence.

the negotiations brought modest results, Arab and Israeli acceptance of the United States as an "honest broker" was a step that would have great consequences in the following years.[50]

The 1976 election of President Jimmy Carter brought a change in U.S. policy. For the first time a U.S. administration began to think about a distinct Palestinian issue, and U.S.-Israeli relations began to cool, especially after Israeli elections produced a right-wing government. The Carter administration sought a "comprehensive" settlement to the region's problems and succeeded in gaining Soviet joint sponsorship for an international conference. When President Anwar Sadat of Egypt announced in November 1977 that he would fly to Jerusalem and meet Israeli Prime Minister Menachem Begin, the Middle East logjam seemed ready to crack. On-again, off-again negotiations ensued, concluding on September 17, 1978, with the signing of the *Camp David Accords* between Israel and Egypt. The final details in the accords were mediated by President Carter in thirteen days of intensive negotiations at his retreat in Camp David, Maryland. One accord resulted in a peace treaty between Egypt and Israel signed March 26, 1979, calling for a swap of "land for peace." The Sinai Peninsula would be returned to Egypt (it was, in 1982) in return for full diplomatic relations between Egypt and Israel (which occurred immediately). The second—"A Framework for Peace in the Middle East"—called for establishing Palestinian self-government in the occupied territories, accompanied by negotiation to determine their final disposition.

The issues raised in the four Arab–Israeli wars and just partly resolved in the Camp David Accords are responsible for shaping the Middle East as we know it today. Despite other bloody events during the 1970s, 1980s, and 1990s—civil strife in Lebanon (1975–1991); successive Israeli invasions of that country (1978, 1982–1985); an Israeli preventive strike against an Iraqi nuclear reactor (1981); Palestinian insurrection in the occupied territories (after 1987); war between Iran and Iraq (1981–1988), and then between Iraq and the U.S.-led coalition (1991)—little has changed in relations between Israel and its Arab and Palestinian adversaries.

The Arab-Israeli-Palestinian Issues

Each participant in the Middle East—Arabs, Israelis, and Palestinians—holds differing views of what is at stake in their disputes. Let us review these perspectives.

Israeli Security and Recognition. For Israelis, the primary issue is the State of Israel's right to exist in secure borders. The state is geographically tiny with a small population. It sees itself as an island amid an ocean of hostile Arabs. Although Israel has had allies and friends since the state was founded in 1948 (the most important of which has been the United States), their history has convinced the Jews that they must depend

---

[50]To achieve this outcome, Kissinger had to make commitments to Israel that created a virtual U.S.–Israeli alliance.

on no one but themselves for survival. For this reason, Israel has created an effective military establishment (almost certainly armed with nuclear weapons) and intelligence service (the Mossad). For this reason, too, Israelis pursue a policy of negotiating from strength and refusing to deal with terrorists.

In a cultural sense, the Arab–Israeli cleavage reflects the clash between a traditional non-European and a modern European society. Modern Israel was established by European Jews who believed they could find safety only by gathering in the lands of their Biblical forefathers. The early Zionist settlers brought to Palestine vibrant culture, highly sophisticated technology and science, and a modern approach to problem-solving. Their arrival and rapid economic success, however, was considered threatening by Arab Palestinians and by traditional Arab leaders in the region who had been handed power by the British and French conquerors of the Turks. That perception of threat increased when, after World War II, the Jewish survivors of the Nazi Holocaust in Europe poured into Palestine.

Security of Arab States.   The Arab states, too, see the issue as security, though their position is far from monolithic. For some Arab states, especially the "front-line" states like Jordan, Syria, Lebanon, and Egypt, the fear is of Israeli military power. Further, the Arab states vary in opposition to the Jewish state's existence. Egypt has accepted Israel's right to exist, and Jordan tacitly cooperated with the Jewish state until entering into open negotiations in 1993. Other states, farther from Israel and with more ideological motivation (such as Libya) are more hostile, at least rhetorically, toward Israel.

Arab leaders have repeatedly used the "threat" of Israel to buttress their domestic political positions and explain away policy failures. In this way the domestic and interstate aspects of the Arab–Israeli question are inextricable. To some extent, Arab leaders became prisoners of their own rhetoric. Those who were soft on Israel risked alienating domestic opinion and attracting the ire of competing Arab leaders. Leaders like King Hussein of Jordan or King Fahd of Saudi Arabia had to tread with care lest their people saw them as insufficiently hostile to Israel. Other leaders like Saddam Hussein of Iraq and Hafez al-Assad (who detest each other) competed with each other (and other Arab leaders) in radical anti-Israeli rhetoric and behavior. Thus, during Iraq's conflict with the U.S.-led coalition that followed Saddam Hussein's invasion of Kuwait, the Iraqi dictator sought to rally support by explaining his act as an attack on Israel and on "dovish" Arabs. In this way, Saddam linked his aggression against Kuwait to the Arab–Israeli and Palestinian issues. That is why Saddam's two closest allies during this period were King Hussein, who feared the many Palestinians living in Jordan, and PLO leader Yasser Arafat, who feared his standing would be jeopardized if he appeared conciliatory toward Israel.

Several Arab states still have substantial border quarrels with Israel. Syria seeks return of the Golan Heights, which Israel seized during the 1967 war. Although the Rabin government has shown flexibility on this issue, Israelis are reluctant to return all the heights because the Syrians used them before 1967 to bombard Israeli settlements in the valleys below. The West Bank and Jerusalem also have security implications because Israel is so small. Some Israeli nationalists, many of them associated with the Likud Party, favor massive extension of Israeli settlements throughout the West Bank and incorporation of the territory, to which they give its Biblical name, Judea and Samaria, into Israel.

Before 1967, the West Bank and the city of Jerusalem[51] were governed by Jordan. For a number of years after the Israeli conquest, Jordan sought their return but has since given up any claim to them in favor of creating a Palestinian state. Consider the several reasons for this shift as well as Jordan's general inclination to disassociate itself from controversial policies. Jordan is an artificial creation of British imperial policy. Its ruler, King Hussein, is a member of a Bedouin family that supported the British against the Ottomans in World War I. Hussein was educated in British schools and universities and, after ascending the throne in 1953, pursued mostly pro-Western and pro-American policies. His political base is among the Arab Bedouins from whom the king's family is descended rather than the West Bank Palestinians. The king's policies are shaped by his country's weakness and vulnerability to its Arab neighbors, its volatile Palestinian population, and Israeli military might.

Jordanians try to walk a narrow line between doing anything that might provoke an Israeli military response — such as harboring terrorists — and doing anything that would be so conciliatory to Israel that it might bring on its stronger Arab neighbors' wrath.[52] Jordan refused to follow Egypt's lead in reaching a separate peace with Israel, yet after 1948 it cooperated quietly with Israel to control conflict. Jordan's policy after Iraq invaded Kuwait was dictated by its desire to steer a middle course. To maintain close economic ties with Iraq, avoid Iraqi anger, and placate its large Palestinian population, Jordan opposed isolating and subsequently warring against Iraq. In doing so, it alienated its chief supplier of oil — Saudi Arabia — and badly frayed its ties of friendship with the United States. However, once the Israelis and Palestinians reached agreement in 1993, Jordan could follow.

A Palestinian Homeland. For Palestinians, the fundamental issue is the desire for a homeland, and most want that homeland to be in the place now called Israel. The Palestinian question became a volatile issue after the Six-Day War, during which almost one million additional Palestinian Arabs in the West Bank and the Gaza Strip came under Israeli control. At an Arab summit in 1973, the PLO was designated official representative of the Palestinian people. Prior to that time, the Palestinians' fate was left mainly to other Arab leaders. After the Six-Day War, many Palestinians concluded that their Arab allies were a weak reed on which to lean. Despite rhetoric, the Arab states

[51]Until 1967, Jerusalem was a divided city. Since then Israelis have regarded it as their capital.
[52]Over the years, Jordan has been threatened with attack from Syria and Iraq.

and the Palestinians rarely had identical interests. Arab leaders used the Palestinian question to assail Israel but did little to assimilate Palestinians into their societies and took few risks to further the Palestinian cause when it seemed to endanger their own security.

Throughout its existence, the Palestinian movement has faced two main problems: where to establish a Palestinian state and where to operate until it was established. Although some Palestinian extremists still dream of driving Israelis into the sea and reclaiming the whole land of Palestine for themselves, for most this goal is no longer realistic. For the residents of the West Bank and Gaza and for Palestinian refugees living in squalid camps in Lebanon and Syria or cities such as Amman and Cairo, the question is acquiring an independent existence for the Palestinian "nation."

The West Bank appeared the obvious core for a future Palestinian state. Mainly inhabited by Palestinians who disliked King Hussein, the West Bank was never well integrated into Jordanian society, and some Bedouins saw its loss to Israel as a blessing in disguise. The Jordanians were wary lest a compromise on the Palestinian question be reached at their expense—fearful that, with a population more than half Palestinian, Jordan might become the Palestinian state sought by Palestinian nationalists.[53]

In December 1987, the Palestinian issue entered a new phase as the Palestinians in the West Bank and Gaza opened a popular campaign of resistance to Israeli rule known as the *intifada*. The resistance began without PLO foreknowledge and augured ill for that organization's future influence. The *intifada* was a source of pride for the Palestinians and, until the disastrous *Persian Gulf War* in which Palestinians supported Saddam Hussein, seemed to promise a brighter future. As Israel sought to suppress the resistance, it found itself the target of critical world public opinion. Israeli opinion itself was divided over the wisdom of refusing to make concessions on the issue of Palestine, and Israel was becoming estranged from the Bush administration by its policy of building Jewish settlements in the West Bank and Gaza.[54]

In an odd sense, Israeli and Arab hawks tacitly conspired to draw out the Arab-Israeli quarrel. Israeli hard-liners such as Likud leaders Yitzhak Shamir and Ariel Sharon were routinely cited to justify "rejectionist" Arab leaders like Saddam Hussein, and Arab belligerence, in turn, served Israeli politicians who advocated a "Greater Israel." The hawkish cycle could be broken only when leaders with courage on both sides stepped forward.

The logjam began to break in 1988. The stage was set for Arab–Israeli and Palestinian–Israeli negotiations by the PLO declaration of an independent Palestinian state in November 1988 and Yasser Arafat's public renunciation of terrorism. In 1991,

---

[53]This was known as the East Bank solution because Jordan is east of the Jordan River.

[54]United States annoyance was reflected in refusal to provide Israel with $10 billion in loan guarantees that had been promised to settle a huge influx of Jewish refugees from the former Soviet Union. After the Labor Party won the 1992 Israeli elections and promised a partial freeze on new settlements, the United States agreed to go ahead with these guarantees.

Presidents Bush and Gorbachev convened and co-hosted a conference in Madrid, Spain, and agreement was reached to hold bilateral face-to-face talks between Israel and its various adversaries including Palestinian representatives from the West Bank (though supposedly not members of the PLO). The first direct talks between the parties began in October 1991. The following year elections in Israel returned the Labor Party to power and ousted the hawkish Likud government. The removal of the Shamir government brought a change in Israel's settlement policy in the occupied territories and indicated a new willingness to negotiate flexibly about Palestinian self-government in those areas. Nevertheless, little progress seemed to take place in the peace talks which had moved from Madrid to Washington.

The breakthrough came in late summer 1993. A number of factors conspired to change fundamentally the nature of Israeli-Palestinian relations. For Israel's Labor Party and the government of Yitzhak Rabin, it had become necessary to make progress toward peace to reduce the growing violence directed at Israeli soldiers and citizens by Palestinian extremists in Gaza, the West Bank, and even Israel itself. Politically, it was also critical for Rabin and Foreign Minister Shimon Peres to show that their government could succeed where the hardline Likud government had failed.

For the secular PLO and its leader Yasser Arafat, a deal with the Israelis had become thinkable owing to the growing prominence of Palestinian hard-liners associated with Islamic fundamentalist groups. Groups such as Hamas began to challenge the status of the PLO as representative of Palestinian aspirations. Additional pressure was placed on Arafat by the PLO's growing financial straits that resulted from the cuts in aid from wealthy Arab countries that were retaliating for Arafat's support of Saddam Hussein during the Persian Gulf War. Thus, both Rabin and Arafat were moved by "domestic" considerations to alter their foreign policies, illustrating again the Janus nature of global politics.

After secret back-channel (behind-the-scenes) negotiations in Norway, Israel and the PLO reached an agreement by which both sides formally recognized each other as legitimate representatives of their respective people. Justifying his government's astonishing shift in policy, Israeli Prime Minister Rabin declared "Peace is not made with friends. Peace is made with enemies, some of whom . . . I loathe very much."[55] In a ceremony hosted in the White House Rose Garden by President Bill Clinton on September 13, 1993, that was televised around the world, the dramatic development was symbolized by a handshake between Prime Minister Rabin and Chairman Arafat. Under the Declaration of Principles signed that day, Israel agreed to grant self-rule (authority for education, health, welfare, direct taxation, and tourism) to "authorized Palestinians" in the Gaza Strip and an area on the West Bank around the town of Jericho. The parties also agreed that self-rule would be gradually extended throughout the West Bank over a period of five years. Israel would retain external security responsibilities for the

[55]Cited in Thomas L. Friedman, "Israel and the Palestinians See a Way to Co-exist" *The New York Times*, Section 4, September 5, 1993, p. 1.

Israeli Prime Minister Rabin and Chairman Arafat signed their historic agreement on September 13, 1993. President Clinton hosted the signing ceremony at the White House.

territory, while the PLO would police the territories granted self-rule. The PLO also formally renounced the use of violence. The agreement included formation of a Joint Israeli-Palestinian Liaison Committee and an Israeli-Palestinian Economic Cooperation Committee to plan regional economic development, and elections for a Palestinian Council by July 1994.[56]

Arab Against Arab

When analyzing Arab–Israeli and Israeli–Palestinian issues the propensity is to think of "the Arabs" as a monolithic group, but they are not. In fact, at least four major sources of conflict divide the Arabs themselves.

Pan-Arabism

Repeatedly, conflicts have arisen over whether or not the Arabs should unite into one nation and, if so, how it should be organized and who should control it. For decades, Arab politicians and intellectuals have forcefully argued that Arab weakness stems from

[56]"The Accord: What Comes Next," *The New York Times*, September 14, 1993, p. A7.

disunity. Earlier we saw how the *sherif* Hussein unsuccessfully sought to unify Arabs using traditional tribal values. Since World War II, some have advocated building unity on the basis of Islam, almost a restoring of the eighth-century Islamic community. Others, notably President Nasser of Egypt, have sought to unify the Arabs with secular socialism.[57] Whenever one leader seemed bent on unifying the Arabs under his leadership, however, rivals successfully opposed him.

Compared to Nasser, other Arab leaders who have sought to clothe themselves in a pan-Arab ideology have been less successful. Libya's Muammar Qadaffi has repeatedly espoused a confused ideology with elements of Islam, socialism, and populism, which he distributes in his *Green Book*. Hafez al-Assad of Syria and Saddam Hussein, each with "his" branch of the Baath party, claim vaguely socialist principles and do everything possible to undermine each other.

Iran–Iraq

Iraq and Iran, the ancient Medes and Persians, have long been competitors for influence in the Arab world.[58] Under its ruler Shah Muhammad Reza Pahlavi, Iran was a chief regional ally of the United States, and Iraq was aligned with the U.S.S.R. Both also have long quarreled over control of the Shatt al-Arab, the waterway that links the Persian Gulf to their main ports, and in 1975 the Shah forced Iraq to accept a demarcation of their boundary that favored Iran. In 1979, however, the Shah was overthrown, and a fundamentalist Shi'ite regime under Ayatollah Ruhollah Khomeini took power. United States–Iranian relations rapidly deteriorated, reaching their nadir after Iranian students illegally occupied the U.S. Embassy in Teheran on November 4 and sixty-six U.S. hostages were seized. The hostages were released only after 444 days of captivity, punctuated by an unsuccessful U.S. rescue attempt.[59]

Amid the chaos that followed the Shah's overthrow and growing hostility between Iran and the United States, Saddam Hussein in September 1980 abrogated the 1975 treaty and invaded Iran. Instead of achieving the lightning victory he had expected, however, Saddam found himself in a bloody military stalemate that lasted eight years.[60] Iran sought to overthrow Saddam and championed the cause of Iraq's large Shi'ite population. Saddam represented himself as protector of the Sunni Arabs from the Persian Shi'ite tide. So convincing was he that he received financial and other assistance from the entire Arab world except Syria and persuaded the United States to tilt toward

[57]Nasser's first tangible step toward creating a greater Arab state was unifying Egypt and Syria into the United Arab Republic in 1958, but this union ended in divorce three years later.

[58]Technically, this is not an inter-Arab issue because Iranians, though Islamic, are not Arabs.

[59]Failure to win their release contributed to Jimmy Carter's defeat in the 1980 presidential elections. They were released as President Reagan was being inaugurated, and the rumor surfaced that a deal had been made between Reagan campaign officials and the Iranians to prevent their release before the election. A congressional investigation in 1992 failed to reveal any such deal.

[60]Both sides hit population centers with missiles, and Iraq used poison gas against Iranian forces.

Iraq. Mutual exhaustion permitted a U.N.-brokered cease-fire to take effect in July 1988. Two years later, to secure his flank during the Kuwait crisis, Saddam conceded most of Iran's territorial claims.

"Modernizers" versus "Traditionalists"

Since achieving independence, several Arab states have overthrown their traditional rulers — kings, sheiks, emirs — whose power was based on tribal custom and replaced them with leaders who have sought to substitute nationalism for tribal and clan loyalties. The *modernizers* have usually found popularity among the urban poor, have governed through a single-party system, and have tried to bring about social and economic change. Groups of military officers deposed Egypt's King Farouk in 1952, Iraq's King Faisal II in 1958, and Libya's King Idris I in 1969, replacing *traditionalists* with modernizers.

Modernizers have also sought to oust the traditionalists from the states they continue to rule and replace them with progressives like themselves. As a result, Arab states with traditional rulers — Saudi Arabia, Kuwait, Jordan, the United Arab Emirates, Bahrain, Morocco, Tunisia, and the former Yemen Arab Republic (North Yemen) — have repeatedly clashed with states governed by modernizers — Egypt, Syria, Iraq, Libya, Algeria, and the former People's Democratic Republic of Yemen (South Yemen). During the Cold War, modernizers tended to align themselves with the Soviet Union and traditionalists with the United States.[61]

This cleavage has sometimes exploded into war. Between 1962 and 1969, the Saudis and the Egyptians became entangled in a civil war in North Yemen, with the Saudis supporting the royalists and the Egyptians the republicans. Egypt deployed 70,000 troops in Yemen and used poison gas against royalist forces. In another incident, the Syrians plotted to overthrow King Hussein and, in 1970, launched an abortive invasion of Jordan. The most important of these collisions, between Iraq and Kuwait, climaxed when Iraq invaded Kuwait in August 1990. Both countries were established by colonial fiat, and their common border was never satisfactorily demarcated. Iraq's Saddam Hussein considered Kuwait's emir a feudal remnant and claimed that Kuwait was more interested in oil profits than in supporting the Palestinian cause or in fighting Israel. Although some truth lay in these claims, they were hypocritical because Saddam also used pro-Palestinian rhetoric to justify actions that had nothing to do with the Palestinian question. The attack on Kuwait was also influenced by Saddam's desire to seize Kuwait's oil resources and push up the world price for oil so as to pay off the huge debt from Iraq's war with Iran. Much of this debt was owed to the Kuwaitis, who along with the Saudis had repeatedly paid "blood money" for "protection" from Iraq, Syria, and the PLO.

[61] A major exception was the close relationship between Egypt and the United States that was engineered by President Sadat late in the 1970s.

Saddam may have miscalculated how the world would respond to his aggression partly because of the large-scale U.S. and Soviet aid and trade that had buoyed his regime during the previous years and in part because of diplomatic attempts by Presidents Reagan and Bush to appease him. Led by President Bush, the United Nations declared economic sanctions against Iraq and, when these failed to do the job, formed a military coalition that drove Iraqi forces from Kuwait early in 1991. The U.N.-imposed peace specified that Iraq was to destroy all weapons of mass destruction, permit U.N. inspection of Iraqi facilities, compensate Kuwait and the other coalition members for the cost of the occupation and war, and cease persecuting Iraqi Kurds and Shi'ites. Economic sanctions were to continue until the terms were met. Nevertheless, Saddam managed to evade or delay many of these strictures.

Religious Cleavages

A growing source of conflict among Arabs involves Islam's role in society. Since the 1979 Iranian revolution, there has been a revival of Islam in a number of Arab societies, and some politicians have embraced Islamic fundamentalism as the road to Arab revival. They reject rule by those who wish to emulate Western practices and values and who seek to modernize Arab societies following secular principles. And they seek to alter the constitutions in countries like Algeria, Egypt, Iraq, Lebanon, Syria, and Turkey that were founded as secular states. The fundamentalists—already triumphant in Iran and the Sudan[62]—argue that society should be strictly governed according to the Will of Allah, as revealed in the Koran and in Muhammad's words and acts as interpreted by religious scholars. As a rule, such zealots are anti-Israeli and anti-Western, wish to return their people to simpler and more austere lives and values, including forcing women back into the home and making them subject to their father's and husband's will.

The struggle between partisans of secular and fundamentalist societies has brought violence to Arab societies. President Anwar Sadat of Egypt was assassinated by fundamentalists in 1981, and an antigovernment assassination campaign by fundamentalists in Syria elicited bloody revenge from President Assad, who razed large areas in the northern Syrian city of Hama in February 1982. Iranian efforts to spread Shi'ism have produced violence in Lebanon, Kuwait, Saudi Arabia, and elsewhere. For years, the Sudan's fundamentalist rulers have sought to crush Christian and animist tribes in the southern region of that country and Islamic fundamentalists have sought to undermine Hosni Mubarak's government in Egypt by attacking foreign tourists and by terrorizing Egypt's Coptic Christian minority.

[62]Elections in Algeria in 1992 would have brought Islamic fundamentalists to power there, but the results were reversed by a military coup.

Oil as an Issue

The oil question underlies other Middle East issues because that resource is so valuable to most actors. As Table 14.1 illustrates, the Arab states plus Iran account for almost 70 percent of the world's known oil reserves. Saudi Arabia alone accounts for more than a quarter of the world's total, explaining why U.S. policy-makers lavish so much care and attention on this sparsely populated desert kingdom.

Oil is essentially an economic issue — the oil-producing states wish to control their commodity and earn as much as possible while it lasts, and the industrialized societies want access to plentiful oil at stable prices — but it can quickly assume a political complexion too. Arab oil producers wish to show solidarity with the Palestinians and fellow Arabs against Israel and to protect themselves from Arab extremists; they have sought to use oil as a weapon and to use profits from its sale in assisting other Arab states and the PLO.

Libya was the first state to force companies to renegotiate previous arrangements. Threatening to seize company assets, Libyan leader Muammar Qaddafi in 1970 demanded that they raise the price of Libyan crude and reduce the amount being pumped. The companies' bid to defy Libya collapsed when Occidental Petroleum broke ranks and raised prices. Libyan success led other oil-producing states to demand similar increases, and, trying to stabilize prices, the oil companies themselves sought to involve the oil-producing states in multilateral negotiations to set a common price. Although an agreement was reached in 1971, several factors in the following years conspired to create an upward price spiral: global demand, devaluations of the dollar, and the Yom Kippur War and subsequent Arab oil embargo. Between 1970 and 1973, crude-oil prices jumped from $1.80 to $11.67 a barrel. In the same period, the oil-producing states seized control of price and production levels from the companies and assumed ownership of company concessions within their borders. The states would continue to rely on the companies for technology, expertise, capital, marketing, and distribution.[63]

Although the relationship between oil producers and consumers has been rocky from time to time, especially during the 1970s, dwindling American supplies of domestic oil and growing consumption made the United States increasingly dependent on foreign oil at this time. Oil prices began to edge up as OPEC presented a united front toward the oil companies and behaved oligopolistically, limiting supply by assigning production quotas to members. Devaluations of the dollar in 1971 and 1973, however, diluted profits because industrialized societies paid for oil in this currency. Although OPEC members had more dollars, those dollars were worth less.

After the 1973 Yom Kippur War, the Arabs tried to use the *oil weapon* to make the industrialized countries change their policies and pressure Israel to make concessions. A selective oil embargo was imposed on the United States, the Netherlands, and Portugal, and, although OPEC's brandishing of the oil weapon failed to change policies

---

[63]Robert S. Walters and David H. Blake, *The Politics of Global Economic Relations*, 4th ed. (Englewood Cliffs, N.J.: Prentice-Hall, 1992), pp. 199–203.

TABLE 14.1

Petroleum Production and Reserves

Production, % of world		Reserves, % of world		Years left
Europe				
Former U.S.S.R.	20.5%	Former U.S.S.R.	5.8%	13
U.S.	12.9	U.S.	2.6	10
U.K.	2.9	Norway	1.2	25
Canada	2.7	Canada	0.6	14
Norway	1.5	U.K.	0.4	5
		Middle East		
Saudi Arabia	8.3%	Saudi Arabia	25.5%	95
Iran	4.9	Iraq	10.0	131
Iraq	4.8	U.A.E.	9.7	188
U.A.E.	3.1	Kuwait	9.4	200
Kuwait	2.6	Iran	9.3	109
Libya	1.9	Libya	2.3	59
Algeria	1.2	Algeria	0.9	36
Qatar	0.7	Neutral Zone	0.5	45
Neutral Zone	n.a.	Egypt	0.4	13
Oman	n.a.	Qatar	0.5	n.a.
Egypt	n.a.	Oman	0.4	n.a.
South Yemen	n.a.	South Yemen	0.3	n.a.
		Africa		
Nigeria	2.7%	Nigeria	1.6%	32
		Asia		
China	4.7%	China	2.4%	23
Indonesia	2.0	Indonesia	0.8	20
India	n.a.	India	0.8	27
		Latin America		
Mexico	4.4%	Venezuela	5.8%	97
Venezuela	2.9	Mexico	5.6	54
Ecuador	0.5	Ecuador	n.a.	

SOURCE: Adapted from Michael J. Sullivan III, *Measuring Global Values: The Ranking of 162 Countries* (New York: Greenwood Press, 1991), Table V3.3b, p. 208.

FIGURE 14.4

Petroleum Production and Reserves

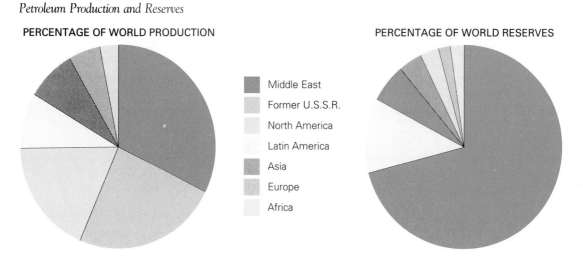

PERCENTAGE OF WORLD PRODUCTION   PERCENTAGE OF WORLD RESERVES

- Middle East
- Former U.S.S.R.
- North America
- Latin America
- Asia
- Europe
- Africa

The Middle East is not only the site of much of the world's petroleum production but also of much of its petroleum reserves.

in any major state, it did induce some to use caution.[64] Politics and economics combined to boost the price of oil, profits of the oil-producing states, and costs to oil consumers. In 1972, America paid $4.8 billion for oil imports; in 1980, it paid $80 billion.[65]

Between 1973 and 1980, supplies remained tight; OPEC discipline continued, and prices continued to soar. In 1979–1980, oil prices again shot up. They peaked in 1981 and then began to decline rapidly owing to global economic recession, conservation in the industrialized societies, broken discipline within the oil-producing cartel, and resulting overproduction. Non-OPEC countries — Norway, Mexico, and Great Britain — also began to account for a greater share of production.

The decline in oil revenues and in the political leverage that oil provided was a big factor behind the events leading to Iraq's occupation of Kuwait. Kuwait sought to get Iraq to repay the huge debts incurred during Baghdad's long war with Iran, and Iraq charged that Kuwait was profiting by exceeding its OPEC production quota. Iraq also claimed that Kuwait was pumping more than its share of oil from an oilfield that straddled their common border. Knowing the long United States preoccupation with

[64]A number of Third-World countries, especially in Africa, severed relations with Israel. Some assumed erroneously that they would receive cut-rate oil from OPEC. Most have since restored relations with Israel. Some developed societies, especially Japan, have gone out of their way to avoid giving offense to Arab oil producers.

[65]Walters and Blake, *Politics of Global Economic Relations*, p. 204.

Middle East oil, especially Saudi Arabia's security, few should have been surprised by the U.S. response to Iraq's invasion. Control of Iraq and Kuwait gave Saddam 20 percent of the world's oil reserves. More important, it placed the Iraqi war machine at the Saudi border, endangering an additional 25 percent.

A number of factors, however, have robbed OPEC of much of its former influence. The greatest is division among its members: conflicts between Iran and Iraq and between Iraq and the monarchies in Kuwait and Saudi Arabia. A second factor is economic, combining oversupply and falling prices for oil.

A Complex Web of Issues: Lebanon

The issues we have just described are linked, and the positions that actors occupy on each reinforce or dilute their cleavages on others. Figure 14.5 illustrates how these issues are related by superimposing these cleavages on each other and indicating how each produces hostility or friendship or both among actors. This illustration reminds us how complex Middle Eastern politics are.

That regional issues are connected can be seen in the story of Lebanon. Lebanese independence was based on the so-called National Pact of 1943, an understanding dividing government and legislative power between Christians and Muslims at a roughly 6–5 ratio. For several decades this pact ensured domestic stability and allowed the country to prosper and stay out of the region's quarrels. Lebanon's rapidly growing Muslim population and the Muslims' relative poverty began to undermine this stability. In 1958, U.S. Marines landed on Beirut beaches to prop up pro-Western President Camille Chamoun against Muslim and pro-Nasser adversaries. This intervention brought only temporary peace. In 1969, the PLO reached a secret agreement with the Lebanese Army to permit military action against Israel from Lebanese territory, and thereafter, with the PLO expelled from Jordan, Lebanon became an unwilling host to many PLO commandos and a target for repeated Israeli retaliation.

With the Lebanese state's integrity already in tatters, the country fell victim to a communal civil war in April 1975 between right-wing Christian members of the Phalangist Party and the Palestinians and their Muslim allies.[66] The Christians sought to get Palestinian forces removed and opposed efforts of Muslim nationalists to provide greater support to the Arab–Palestinian cause. The subtext, however, was that the National Pact was unraveled, and Lebanon's Muslims were determined to acquire greater power. As civil war continued, Syria intervened, and thus Israeli involvement also grew.

[66]The Phalangist Party, founded in 1936 by Maronite Christians, formed the core of a Christian alliance called the Lebanese Front. Its Muslim adversaries were loosely arrayed in an alliance called the Lebanese National Movement.

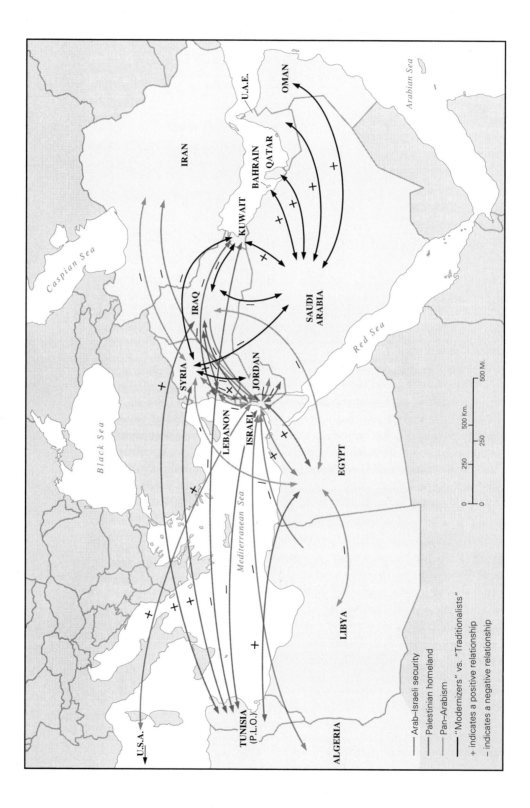

Arab–Israeli security
Palestinian homeland
Pan–Arabism
"Modernizers" vs. "Traditionalists"
+ indicates a positive relationship
– indicates a negative relationship

Palestinian guerrillas in Lebanon and their continued raids on Israeli targets prompted massive Israeli invasions of that country in 1978 and 1982. Divided by civil strife and with few friends, Lebanon was unable to discipline the Palestinians or prevent them from launching attacks against Israel (with inevitable Israeli retaliation). Israel was not alone in trying to limit Palestinian independence in Lebanon. Syria too sought to leash the PLO and supported attacks by a Palestinian Shi'ite force called Amal on Palestinian camps and bases in southern Lebanon. The three-year "War of the Camps" was part of the general anarchy that beset Lebanon during this time.

In March 1978, Israeli forces invaded Lebanon as far as the Litani River, then established a buffer zone in southern Lebanon. The Litani was a *red line* that neither Palestinian guerrillas nor Syrian troops were to cross. By 1981, more than forty private armies[67] were operating in Lebanon in addition to Syrian and Israeli military forces. They included Shi'ites backed by Iran and Syria; various Christian militias that opposed each other as well as Syrian occupation and Muslim goals; a number of loosely affiliated Muslim militias; and Palestinian militias that fought each other and Israel as well as, from time to time, the Syrians, Christians, and Shi'ites.

A second Israeli invasion in June 1982 sought to cripple the PLO. In a matter of days Israeli troops encircled Beirut, bent on forcing the PLO entirely out of Lebanon. But the Israeli campaign stirred world sympathy for the Palestinians, and a deal was struck in August, at U.S. insistence, in which a cease-fire would take hold, Palestinian guerrillas would leave Lebanon, and a multinational force would safeguard Palestinian civilians in Lebanon. Within a month the cease-fire broke down. Newly elected Lebanese President Beshir Gemayel was assassinated, setting off savage attacks by Israel's Lebanese Maronite Christian allies on Palestinian refugee camps. The resulting massacre of Palestinian civilians and allegations of indirect Israeli complicity, especially by Defense Minister Ariel Sharon, made Israel's position in Lebanon politically untenable. By June 1985, Israeli forces had withdrawn, maintaining a security zone in southern Lebanon occupied by Israel's Lebanese allies.[68]

The modest stability provided by Western military units between 1982 and 1984 abruptly ended with suicide attacks against U.S. and French units and their subsequent

---

[67]Whether Christian or Muslim, these militias were loyal to individual leaders rather than serious ideas; the struggle in Lebanon had come to resemble the violence waged over turf among organized crime families in the United States.

[68]In April 1978, 2,000 Israeli-backed Christian militiamen under Major Saad Haddad declared an "independent free Lebanese state" in an eight-mile-wide strip along the border with Israel.

FIGURE 14.5

The Complexity of Alignments in Middle East Politics
The Middle East is the scene of numerous crosscutting issues. Actors that are friends on some issues are adversaries on others.

withdrawal. Efforts to get the Syrians to withdraw from Lebanon after the Israelis withdrew failed, and the Syrians pursued a divide-and-conquer strategy by aiding selected Christian as well as Muslim groups. By the mid-1980s, battles raged between Muslim West and Christian East Beirut and within both sectors, and West Beirut became host to gangs of shadowy kidnappers.

The civil war was finally closed by an October 1989 agreement among Lebanese politicians meeting in Taif, Saudi Arabia, revising the National Pact in favor of Lebanon's Muslim majority. Resistance to the agreement by Christian General Michel Aoun and to the continued Syrian presence was crushed by the Syrians in October 1990. In the next year a Syrian-dominated Government of National Reconciliation was installed, and a parliament was elected in August 1992 for the first time in twenty years. Lebanon had become a Syrian puppet, with Syrian personnel running the country's security and military forces.

As you can see, every Middle Eastern issue (except oil) is present in Lebanon. The Arab–Israeli issue, from which Lebanon had remained aloof prior to its civil war, was evident in the Israeli–Syrian contest. Indeed, much of Israel's behavior toward other groups in Lebanon, including its 1978 and 1982 invasions, was meant to limit Syrian power. The Palestinian issue was reflected in constant battles between Palestinian guerrillas and Israeli security forces, especially after 1970. This issue was linked to the Arab–Israeli quarrel in Syrian efforts to walk a narrow line between supporting and trying to control the PLO and gaining a strategic foothold along Israel's northern border without provoking the Israelis into another major war, as well as the Lebanese struggle to restrain the Palestinians.

Arab–Arab issues were the most complex. The Syrians and Iraqis fought their feud by proxy in the winding alleys of Beirut and Tripoli, as did the Iranians in their conflict with Iraq and its Arab allies. Quarrels among religious factions were among the most prominent of inter-Arab tensions. Continued Muslim-Christian conflict masked violent struggles for power by factions in each community. Iranians supported Hizballah both to achieve greater influence for Lebanon's Shi'ite community and to give Iran dominance in that community (evident in Hizballah's conflict with the Syrian-backed Shi'ite group Amal). The Israelis backed Christian militias against Muslims, Palestinians, and Syrians to exploit Arab quarrels.

Conclusion

Great change is afoot in the Middle East. The shape of change that remains unclear, but the Cold War's end has affected this region as it has others. Movement toward peace may have begun, but it is, at best, fragile, and the region is a cauldron of conflicting passions. No clear resolution to many of the issues is in sight and the potential for violence remains high.

Since Israel was founded in 1948, it has sought to engage its neighbors in negotiations to force them to recognize its right to exist. Israelis have preferred bilateral negotiations and have been wary of international conferences to discuss Middle East issues lest they be outnumbered, outvoted, and pressured by global public opinion to compromise their security. Until the Bush years, the United States was unwilling to force the issue because it did not want a forum in which the U.S.S.R. might increase regional influence and did not want to alienate Israel or its domestic supporters in the United States. As the Cold War ended, however, all sides experienced greater U.S. pressure to reach a settlement. The United States was instrumental in persuading the PLO to renounce terrorism and accept U.N. Resolutions 242 and 338 in 1988, thereby implicitly recognizing Israel's existence and legitimacy. The Iraqi invasion of Kuwait and subsequent war in the Persian Gulf, along with the dissolution of the U.S.S.R. and the end of Soviet support for Iraq, Syria, and the PLO, dramatically shook up the status quo in the Middle East. The Palestinians were isolated and frustrated.

President George Bush and Secretary of State James Baker persisted until, in October 1991, Israel and its Arab and Palestinian foes joined in a peace conference co-sponsored by the United States and the Soviet Union. The resulting conference was less a multilateral gathering than a series of bilateral negotiations. Progress was slow, but the negotiations themselves gave reason for optimism. The less hawkish Israeli government elected in spring 1992 and Israel's removal of impediments to negotiation — among them proliferating Israeli settlements on the West Bank and the law preventing Israelis from talking directly to the PLO — augured well. The Clinton administration remained committed to negotiations, and progress took place despite opposition by extremists on both sides. Then came the dramatic events of September 1993, climaxing in mutual recognition by Israel and the PLO and their joint commitment to reverse decades of animosity and live together in Biblical Palestine.

Whether the Israeli–PLO agreement leads to regional peace remains to be seen. Extremists on both sides have a stake in continued hostilities, and serious issues of territory and trust remain to be overcome. So-called rejectionist Palestinians in groups like the Popular Front for the Liberation of Palestine and Hamas greeted the PLO-Israeli agreement with threats to assassinate Arafat, while Israeli settlers from Gaza and the West Bank demonstrated in Jerusalem. Nevertheless, it was clear that Arab leaders did not want to be left out of the accelerating process toward peace. Thus, the day after the Israeli-Palestinian agreement was signed, Israel and Jordan announced that they had achieved a framework for negotiating an end to their differences. One thing is certain: The landscape of the Middle East will never be the same after the signing of the Declaration of Principles in September 1993. That event, in President Clinton's words, was "an extraordinary act in one of history's defining dramas, a drama that began in a time of our ancestors when the word went forth from a sliver of land between the River Jordan and the Mediterranean Sea."[69]

[69]Cited in *The New York Times*, September 14, 1993, p. A7.

Key Terms

Christianity

Islam

Judaism

Koran

Ottoman Empire

Byzantine Empire

sick man of Europe

protectorates

Jewish Diaspora

Ashkenazim

Sefardim

Orientals

Zionism

anti-Semitism

Balfour Declaration

League of Nations mandate

the Holocaust

the final solution

Sunni Muslims

Shi'a Muslims

Islamic fundamentalism

Druses

Palestine

Kurds

terrorism

seven sisters

Labor Party

Likud Party

Arab League

Palestine Liberation Organization (PLO)

oligopoly

Organization of Petroleum Exporting Countries (OPEC)

U.N. Resolution 181

Organization of Arab Petroleum Exporting Countries (OAPEC)

charisma

West Bank

Gaza Strip

Six-Day War (1967)

Golan Heights

U.N. Resolution 242

Yom Kippur War (1973)

Camp David Accords

Persian Gulf War (1991)

intifada (1987–1993)

modernizers

traditionalists

oil weapon

red line

Baath Party

Hizballah

Muslim Brotherhood

PART FOUR

The Search for Solutions

Part IV consists of three chapters that explore emerging issues that challenge global politics as we approach the twenty-first century. Chapters 15 ("The State Versus the Species: Environmental Dilemmas") and 16 ("The State versus the Individual: Human Rights") reflect very different kinds of issues. The first involves problems, such as those producing environmental degradation, that challenge all humans whatever their nationality. These issues require collaborative and imaginative solutions that are beyond the capacity of any single state to impose. Pursuit of national interests will, in time, exacerbate these problems and generate threats to human survival itself.

The second type of issue pits states against their own citizens. The use of terrorism and violations of human rights by governments may, for example, serve the interests of those in power while exploiting the very individuals whom states are supposed to serve. Chapter 17 ("Solving the Puzzle: Some Alternate Futures") concludes this section by projecting two different scenarios for the future—one based on optimism for a brighter tomorrow and the other a world of danger and declining standards of living.

CHAPTER FIFTEEN

The State and the Species: Environmental Dilemmas

One observer succinctly captures our theme for this chapter: "Many of the new issues in international politics — ecology, drugs, AIDS, terrorism — involve a diffusion of power away from states to private actors and require organizing states for cooperative responses."[1] Individual societies cannot protect themselves from these problems, which do not respect "sovereign" boundaries. The classical tradition too, emphasizing states, national interest, and power, is unsuited for handling these issues, in which nonetheless everyone has a stake. We discuss here several highly political survival issues that you should keep in mind as you contemplate the future.

The State and Collective Goods

The most compelling threats to human survival are those which affect inhabitants in all countries and which individual governments cannot remedy by themselves. Such problems are exacerbated by separate actors working at cross-purposes and often pit individual actors' interests against those of humanity. Thus, U.S. reluctance to cooperate with Europe in rapidly limiting emission of gases that cause global warming because of American dependence on automobiles, a major source of such emissions, has delayed effectively responding to a critical environmental issue.

[1] Joseph S. Nye, Jr., *Bound to Lead: The Changing Nature of American Power* (New York: Basic Books, 1990), pp. 20–21.

Many issues to which we refer in this chapter involve *public* or *collective goods*.[2] This category, from economics, refers to benefits that, if made available to some, must be available to all. Clean air is a good or benefit that cannot easily be denied to some citizens even if they refuse to pay for it. If air pollution is reduced, it is difficult to limit that benefit to a few while depriving the remainder.[3] Other benefits such as *private goods* — private education or fire protection — can be enjoyed by some citizens and denied to others. Goods like these are available only to those who can afford them or who live in affluent areas.

Because collective goods benefit everybody, everyone has a stake in them. The paradox is that because so many individuals benefit, no one has an incentive to pay for them voluntarily. Each, wishing the benefit, would prefer that someone else pay and may conclude that, because the group is so large, no one will miss one contribution. The economist Mancur Olson, who is mainly responsible for the collective-goods idea, summarizes the paradox:

> It does *not* follow, because all of the individuals in a group would gain if they achieved their group objective, that they would act to achieve that objective, even if they were all rational and self-interested. Indeed, unless the number of individuals is quite small, or unless there is coercion or some other special device to make individuals act in their common interest, *rational self-interested individuals will not act to achieve their common or group interests.*[4]

In other words, a tension separates the collective interests of all from the individual interests of those who make up a collectivity. Most citizens benefit from a common defense, yet many prefer not to pay taxes to support it or to be drafted to fight for it.[5] Enforcing tax- and draft-evasion laws is required to ensure national defense. Or some additional private benefit, known as a *side payment*, may be necessary to get support from individuals or groups for a collective goal.[6]

In global politics, individual actors, though they favor the collective benefits that would flow from peace, a clean environment, and unfettered trade, may be averse to paying the price. The reluctance is especially great if actors who have to pay the highest cost do not expect to receive an equivalent share of the benefits. That is why the United States has dragged its feet even though all the planet's inhabitants would benefit by controlling global warming and preventing destruction of the earth's ozone layer.

[2]See Mancur Olson, Jr., *The Logic of Collective Action: Public Goods and the Theory of Groups* (New York: Schocken Books, 1965).

[3]In reality, no benefit is entirely collective. With sufficient ingenuity, it is even possible to deprive individuals of clean air and water.

[4]Olson, *Logic of Collective Action*, p. 2. Emphasis in original.

[5]Costs are not equally distributed. Those in higher tax brackets or with fewer exemptions have to pay higher taxes, and only the young are subject to conscription.

[6]In national security, defense contracts to local industries or military facilities that employ local residents are examples of side payments.

Americans would have to foot much of the economic bill but could expect no greater benefit than others. According to one estimate, reducing U.S. carbon-dioxide emissions by 20 percent from 1988 levels by the year 2020 would leave the U.S. economy 2.2 percent smaller than it would otherwise be.[7] In sum, trade-offs in politics make it difficult to carry out reforms or undertake programs that, on the surface, everyone favors.

Global trade in agriculture reveals similar tensions. Even though consumers everywhere would benefit from lower prices for food by ending government subsidies for farmers, Western European governments have opposed liberalizing world trade in agriculture because the relatively few citizens who farm would have to give up private benefits. The Japanese government has done the same in preventing importation of inexpensive foreign rice to protect relatively few inefficient Japanese rice farmers. These governments jealously protect private benefits for a minority (farmers) of their citizens and seem willing to forego the collective benefits that would flow from free trade in agricultural products.[8] *Special interests* face every issue, whether it is the lumber industry opposing efforts to save virgin forests or automobile manufacturers opposing stricter emissions standards.

The issues we discuss cast doubt on the value of nationalism and patriotism, suggesting that, far from being virtues, they may endanger human survival. Concepts like national interest may be *cognitive traps* for citizens, who are like residents of an earthquake zone—they cannot leave, even when dangerous tremors seem certain. National frontiers, border guards, tariffs, and nuclear weapons cannot keep disease and hunger from spreading, oceans and lakes from "dying," soil from eroding, or *salinization* from transforming fertile regions into deserts. If loyalty to governments is based on belief that such governments can deliver the goods and protect citizens from danger, then governments everywhere are in trouble.

Burgeoning Populations

As the Cold War came to its end and the threat of large-scale nuclear war declined, some analysts identified burgeoning populations and their strains on the environment as the greatest overall peril to human well-being. At best, population growth, if unchecked, will reduce standards of living and amenities for everyone. High birthrates in the poorest societies among people who live in crowded conditions with inadequate sanitary and medical facilities are associated with spreading diseases including AIDS (Acquired Immune Deficiency Syndrome), malaria, and cholera and resurgent death rates among children.[9] Citing greatly increased forecasts for world population growth, the U.N.

---

[7]Rose Gutfeld, "Agreement Is Near on Greenhouse Gases," *The Wall Street Journal*, May 8, 1992, p. A2.

[8]Neither is the U.S. government innocent, and U.S. farmers receive higher per capita government support than any comparable group in the country.

[9]Barbara Crossette, "Study Says Deaths Rise for World's Poor Children," *The New York Times*, May 9, 1992, p. 3.

Population Fund urged "a sustained and concerted program starting immediately" to limit the population explosion, which, according to the Fund's report, is intensifying hunger and poverty and straining the earth's resources.[10]

The population issue can be considered part of a larger problem, the gap between rich and poor. This view would have states emphasize meeting the development needs of the poor, as discussed in Chapter 10, to address population growth. As development takes place, population growth rates will decline and then stabilize. Indeed, some from the developing countries look with suspicion on efforts to limit population in their countries and point out that the pressures on global resources actually come from the developed, not the developing world.[11]

Two centuries ago, Thomas Malthus (1766–1834), an English economist and clergyman, described the growing imbalance between populations and food supply. He argued that world population would be kept in balance with resources only by natural regulation in catastrophes such as starvation, disease, and war. In fact, emigration, agricultural technology, and the industrial revolution greatly improved national productivity.[12] Indeed, even Malthus at the time left open the possibility that changes might forestall his dire predictions.[13] Whether or not a *Malthusian future* lies ahead we cannot tell.

Culture, Tradition, and Population

Discussions about population generate passion, for they touch personally individuals' cultural, economic, and ethical beliefs. In some developing societies, large numbers of male offspring are still wanted to help their parents in the fields, compensate for the high mortality rate among children, and provide *social insurance* for parents in old age. This preference for large numbers of children has deep roots. In some societies economic and social incentives are reinforced by patriarchal traditions treating children as symbols of prestige. Thus, women in Rwanda, a small African country, bear an average of 8.5 children, the highest rate in the world, and Rwandan men regard large families as a source of prestige.[14] From the individual's point of view, preferring many children may make sense even though it is harmful to society as a whole; that is, the individual's perceived private good and society's collective good are at odds.

[10]Cited in Paul Lewis, "U.N. Sees a Crisis in Overpopulation," *The New York Times*, April 30, 1992, p. A6. Also see Paul Kennedy, *Preparing for the Twenty-first Century* (New York: Random House, 1993).

[11]See Mahbub ul Haq, *The Poverty Curtain: Choices for the Third World* (New York: Columbia University Press, 1976), pp. 122–136.

[12]Kennedy, *Preparing for the Twenty-first Century*, pp. 6–8.

[13]Ibid., p. 348.

[14]Jane Perlez, "In Rwanda, Births Increase and the Problems Do, Too," *The New York Times*, May 31, 1992, pp. 1, 10.

The population issue is also linked to male dominance in many societies, especially traditional ones. That attitude shows in male control of "public" life and relegating women to "private" life—that is, the family. Women who remain pregnant during their years of fertility may find themselves politically and economicaly inferior to men who are being educated, earning money, and building careers. In Western societies, women have acquired greater independence and have assumed new roles as birth control has become available.[15] Nevertheless, in some societies, including such modern peoples as Japan, women are still denied equal status—they are refused education, kept in the kitchen, or relegated to menial jobs. In some areas, resurgent religious fundamentalism has entailed denying freedoms that women had previously won. Women were the main victims when the Shah was overthrown in Iran and a fundamentalist regime under Ayatollah Khomeini seized power.[16] Indeed, in some countries in which Islam dominates, women are subject to *purdah* (secluded in the home from the sight of men or strangers).

Traditional societies also value male children more than females because males are thought to be economically and militarily more valuable and serve to enhance the father's "macho" image. Females are considered burdensome dependents who must be fed and clothed until they can be married off. Such traditions reflect male dominance and have led to customs as "exposing" females (leaving them outside to die), which until recently was common in China, or *suttee*, a former Hindu practice in India in which a widow immolated herself on her husband's funeral pyre. Modern technology has not overcome these prejudices: Families in India and China increasingly use prenatal *amniocentesis* and *ultrasound scanning* to discover the gender of fetuses, thereafter aborting females.[17]

Because customs and values must be changed, birth control alone is not the answer, and limiting births forcibly, as in India during the 1970s, has had limited success. Social and economic upheavals are needed to alter individual incentives. Growing wealth, education, and urbanization often bring down birthrates, and some countries such as

---

[15]From a global perspective, reproductive issues are contentious problems, for they are shaped by cultural and religious values. In some poor societies, such as China and Russia, birth control devices are unavailable and population pressures, combined with grinding poverty and the specter of starvation and sometimes even governmental coercion, encourage widespread resort to abortion for birth control.

[16]Iran's birthrate went up dramatically after Islamic fundamentalists assumed power, until by 1985 it had reached 3.9 percent, the highest in the world. Recently, the Iranian government appears to have realized that this rate will produce impossible burdens on society. By changing course and advocating birth control, the government has managed to reduce the rate to 2.7 percent; even at this reduced rate, Iran's population will have grown from 37 million in 1979 when the Shah was overthrown to 85 million by 2000. Caryle Murphy, "Iran's Second Revolution: Population Control," *The Washington Post National Weekly Edition*, May 18–24, 1992, p. 15.

[17]In amniocentesis, a sample of amniotic fluid is taken from a pregnant woman's uterus to diagnose possible genetic defects. Information about the fetus's gender is a byproduct of the test. See Nicholas D. Kristof, "Peasants of China Discover New Way to Weed Out Girls," *The New York Times*, July 21, 1993, p. A1.

Singapore have enjoyed great success in lowering rates by combining economic incentives with coercion. Wealth and education arouse new interests outside the home and bring knowledge about opportunities for personal growth that are possible only with a small family. As women in developing societies increasingly join the work force, their interests (as well as those of spouses) change in ways that reduce birthrates. Finally, urbanization and government social-security policies reduce economic incentives to have large families and create practical constraints such as insufficient housing.

Combining economic development and coercion can make a significant difference, as reflected in China's recent experience. In 1988, the Chinese communist regime, with 22 percent of the world's population but only 7 percent of its arable land, imposed a harsh family-planning policy, setting population quotas for local officials. Between 1987 and 1992, China's birthrate dropped from 23.3 to 18.2 per thousand, and the country's fertility rate dropped to the lowest in recorded history.[18] This tremendous achievement has had human costs, for it includes compulsory sterilization and abortion; it was vigorously opposed by U.S. Presidents Reagan and Bush.[19]

At best, getting control over spiraling birthrates is painful. As industrialization proceeds and land-hungry peasants flock from countryside to city seeking jobs, urban services feel the pressure. Sewage, water, power, transportation, and police services break down under burdens larger than they were intended to bear. Even as population rates begin to decline, *shantytowns* with few amenities sprout up to house burgeoning numbers of urban poor. *Unemployment* and *underemployment* foster corruption and crime. Nevertheless, newly available cheap labor does attract foreign industry, which, in turn, draws more people from the countryside.

All this change has hastened global urbanization, drastically shifting big cities. London, the world's second-largest city in 1960, will drop out of the top twenty by the year 2000. Cities in Asia and Africa that were not among the top twenty in 1960 — Seoul (South Korea), Teheran (Iran), Manila (Philippines), Lagos (Nigeria), Delhi (India), Karachi (Pakistan) — will be up there by 2000. World population is shifting to the poorest developing societies.

A Crowded World

Fast-growing population is relatively recent. World population, as shown in Figure 15.1, remained roughly stable until the middle of the eighteenth century. Since then (about one-quarter of 1 percent of human history), population has increased sixfold, and the rate of increase is accelerating. At current U.N. projections, the world's population will soar from 5.48 billion in mid-1992 to 10 billion in 2050 and 11.6 billion in 2100, when it will level off. This translates into an increase of more than 90 million people *each year*

[18]Nicholas D. Kristof, "China's Crackdown on Births: A Stunning, and Harsh Success," *The New York Times*, April 25, 1993, Section 1, pp. 1, 6.

[19]United States policy between 1981 and 1993 was to withhold foreign aid for birth-control programs such as that undertaken by China.

FIGURE 15.1

World Population Growth

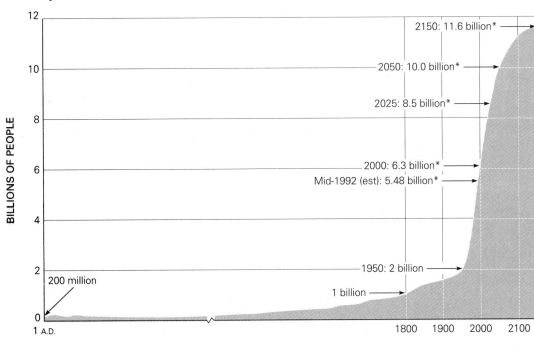

* Projected by United Nations Population Fund

Most of the world's burgeoning population growth has occurred in recent centuries. For much of human history, world population was stable.

during the 1990s,[20] an increase roughly equal to the combined population of the Philippines and Burma.

Population pressures are not evenly distributed. More people live in Asia than in the rest of the world combined. *Population density* in Asia and Europe is ten times that of North America and thirty times that of Oceania.[21] At one extreme is the South Asian country, Bangladesh, with a population of 111 million and a density of 768 people per square kilometer.[22] The United States, with a land area some 65 times that of Bangladesh, has a population only 2.5 times greater, with a density of only 27 per square kilometer. The implications of these differences are clearer when we realize that

[20]Paul Lewis, "U.N. Sees a Crisis in Overpopulation," p. A6.

[21]Oceania includes Australia, New Zealand, Melanesia, Micronesia, and Polynesia.

[22]World Bank, *World Development Report, 1993* (New York: Oxford University Press, 1993), p. 238.

Impoverished and densely packed shantytowns such as that in Rio de Janeiro exist in many Third-World societies as a result of migration from rural areas and high population growth rates.

North America has well over two acres of arable land[23] per inhabitant. Asia, however, has only a little more than a third of an acre of arable land to support each inhabitant.

At current rates, regional differences in population density will be greater by the year 2000. Population growth has pretty much stabilized in the developed regions in North America and Europe. But the less-developed areas, unless profound change comes, will experience significant population increases in coming decades. Almost all the projected population increase will take place in the Third World, more than a third in Africa alone. By the year 2000, the number of inhabitants per square kilometer is likely to increase by 45 percent in Africa, 29 percent in Latin America, and 25 percent in Asia.

Table 15.2 shows the disparity in population density and annual growth for a range of countries. Although countries such as the Netherlands and Japan have high population density, their growth (except by immigration) has mostly ceased. At the other extreme, the population in Uganda in Africa is increasing by 3.4 percent a year and in Bangladesh by 2.6 percent a year. At that rate, the Bangladesh population was expected to increase by more than 170 million people between 1987 and 2025.

[23]Land under temporary crops or meadows for pasture, land under gardens, and land lying fallow.

TABLE 15.1

Estimated Regional Population Densities, 2000

Region	Annual increase	Inhabitants/sq. km.	% increase from 1988
Asia	1.9%	136	25%
Europe	0.2%	103	3%
Africa	3.0%	29	45%
Latin America	2.1%	27	29%
USSR	0.8%	14	.7%
North America	0.8%	14	.7%
Oceania	1.4%	3.6	2%

SOURCES: *Food and Agriculture Production Yearbook* (1988), Table 1, p. 47; U.N., *1988 Demographic Yearbook,*
   Table 1, p. 161.

TABLE 15.2

Estimated Population Growth of Selected Countries, 1987–2025

Country	Population (1987)	Density (1987)	Annual increase	Projected population, 2025
Uganda	16,600,000	70	3.4%	58,800,000
Bangladesh	102,560,000	712	2.6%	274,390,000
India	781,370,000	238	1.8%	1,552,800,000
Indonesia	170,180,000	89	1.7%	326,760,000
United States	243,770,000	26	0.7%	319,260,000
Netherlands	14,660,000	359	0.4%	17,112,000
Japan	122,090,000	323	0.4%	142,940,000

SOURCES: UNESCO, *1989 Statistical Yearbook*, Table 1.1 and 1990 *Statistical Abstract of the United States*, Table
   1438, p. 8313.

Population Trends and Global Consequences

Population growth has political implications that affect societies and their relationships.
Historically, a large population was regarded as an element of base power that made it
possible to recruit large armies and support labor-intensive industries at low wages. For
some, a large population provided emigrants for overseas colonization that added to the
power of the metropolis (mother city). Overpopulation in the city-states of classical
Greece allowed for settlements in Asia Minor, North Africa, and elsewhere that spread

Greek influence to the corners of the known world. The poor from Great Britain settled North America and Australia, and excess population from a host of societies that, by emigration, contributed their talents to building the United States. For such reasons, countries competed to encourage growth in population. Thus, Mussolini's Italy in the 1930s offered rewards to mothers with many children. Today, Iran's Arab neighbors express fear of that country's burgeoning population. Palestinians denounce Russian Jews' immigration to Israel as a ruse to displace them and change the regional balance of power, and Jews in Israel are uneasy about the high birthrate in the country's Arab population.

An Increase in Young and Old.   Rapid population growth increases the numbers of young people in a society, and declining or stabilizing growth rates produce an aging or graying society. In areas where population has slowed or stabilized (North America and Europe), the percentage of young people has been declining rapidly, and the percentage of elderly has been increasing. Each trend entails different problems that have far-reaching consequences for global politics. Young people place special burdens on a society's economic and social infrastructure. The very young need medical care and day care so that their parents can work. If they are to contribute to society, they need education. Above all, they need land or jobs to survive, and, in much of the developing world, land and jobs are in short supply. If the educated have no opportunity to use their skills and realize their aspirations, they become disillusioned, often rejecting the political system that has failed them. Some may be ripe for radical movements and become terrorists or revolutionaries. The young were the backbone in European fascist and communist movements in the 1920s and 1930s, just as they are currently found in revolutionary groups in Latin America and Asia.

Aging populations also create problems for societies, such as labor shortages, high medical and social-security costs, and a reduced tax and investment base. Labor shortages in developed societies are helpful for developing societies because they provide an opportunity to "export" workers. During prosperous years, countries such as Germany, France, and Switzerland have hosted large numbers of "guest workers" from poor countries like Turkey and Algeria. Israel's problem with the Palestinians is complicated by the many Palestinians from Gaza and the West Bank who work in such vital sectors of Israel's economy as the construction industry. Finally, Middle Eastern countries that are wealthy in oil but small in populations (Kuwait, Iraq, Saudi Arabia) have development programs requiring that they "import" many foreign workers, including Palestinians, Egyptians, Filipinos, and Pakistanis. Indeed, some labor-rich countries such as South Korea and Taiwan have made deals with labor-short countries like Kuwait to send teams of workers for construction.

Perhaps the largest and most significant movement of laborers from a developing to a developed country is the Mexican migration to the United States, especially in California and Texas, to provide cheap labor for U.S. agribusiness. Despite recent reforms to ease their plight, many Mexican migrants continue to work for low wages, enjoy no health, unemployment, social security, or welfare benefits, and have no labor union to represent them. On the one hand, many Americans, especially labor unions, prefer more effective law enforcement to slow illegal migration. On the other, U.S. businesses that employ low-cost migrant labor have no interest in enforcing the laws. Finally, the Mexican government does not want the law enforced too vigorously because of the social and economic benefits Mexico obtains by exporting surplus labor.[24]

Large labor movements of this kind are mutually beneficial and work well until economic conditions worsen. Many guest workers settled in Western Europe, and by local law their children enjoy citizenship. With deepening recession in the 1990s, however, local resentment against guest workers intensified. Europeans who had been willing to let guest workers do work that they had spurned when unemployment rates grew came to see them as competitors. With economic hard times, racial hostility arose among Europeans against immigrant guest workers. Africans and Asians were accused of refusing to assimilate and of having large families that burdened Europe's generous social-welfare systems. Anti-foreign sentiment has boosted electoral fortunes for right-wing political parties in France and Germany.

A more striking example of hostility against guest workers took place in Kuwait following liberation of that country from Iraqi occupation in February 1991. Before the invasion, Kuwaitis had been a minority in their own country, and their economic life had depended heavily for muscle and brains on foreign laborers and entrepreneurs, especially Palestinians. During the war, however, the PLO expressed support for Iraq, and some Palestinians in Kuwait collaborated with the Iraqi occupiers. In revenge, after its liberation Kuwait expelled 400,000 Palestinians and treated with suspicion those who remained.[25] This reaction has historical parallels. In 1492, in the midst of *the Inquisition*, Spain's Christian rulers expelled its Jews and Moors (Muslim Spaniards), thereby losing some of their most talented citizens.

Increasing Conflict?   Rapidly growing population has been associated with conflict and war. One hypothesis is that a growing population translates into demands for resources, which, if not met, generate *lateral pressures*. Other countries may resist this pressure and tension may result.[26] Another aspect of this argument is that population density and economic inequality may combine to produce *land hunger* in agricultural

---

[24]In practice, the Mexican-U.S. border is so long that it is almost impossible to keep out Mexican migrants. Illegal Mexican immigration is an example of the link between domestic and international issues described in Chapter 11.

[25]Youssef M. Ibrahim, "A Peace That Still Can't Recover from the War," *The New York Times*, May 6, 1992, p. A4.

[26]Robert C. North and Nazli Choucri, *Nations in Conflict: National Growth and International Violence* (San Francisco, Calif.: W. H. Freeman, 1975); and North and Choucri, "Economic and Political Factors in International Conflict and Integration," *International Studies Quarterly* 27:4 (December 1983), pp. 443–461.

societies. Small elites own disproportionate amounts of arable land, leaving large numbers of poor peasants to share the rest, which is not enough to support them. Land hunger and economic and political inequality make an explosive combination that revolutionaries can exploit; it can breed civil strife.[27]

Land hunger was a main factor behind the civil war that raged in El Salvador during the 1980s. The U.S.-supported Salvadoran government resisted decisive land reform, and Marxist guerrillas seized large estates and distributed them to landless peasants. Although a political agreement in 1992 ended the war in El Salvador, continuing population pressures could rekindle social tension in the future.[28] Similar conditions afflict Guatemala and Honduras, and land hunger strongly abets the violent Maoist terrorist movement in Peru called *Sendero Luminoso* (Shining Path).[29]

Some analysts believe that crowding, a consequence of population density, spawns violence. One observer uses as a metaphor, the "human zoo":

> [O]nly in the cramped quarters of zoo cages do we find anything approaching the human state. If, in captivity, a group of animals is assembled which is too numerous for the species concerned, and they are packed too tightly together, then . . . serious trouble will certainly develop. . . . But even the least experienced zoo director would never contemplate crowding and cramping a group of animals to the extent that man has crowded and cramped himself in his modern cities and towns. *That* level of abnormal grouping, the director would predict with confidence, would cause a complete fragmentation and collapse of the normal social pattern of the animal species concerned.[30]

In this perspective, urban crime and war have common roots, and we would expect violence to be greater in densely populated societies than in sparsely populated ones. Although population pressures may contribute to such violence, keep in mind that other factors too are likely to contribute.

AIDS and Population. A recent offshoot of population growth has been the spread of AIDS. By one estimate, AIDS is likely to reach all societies in the next decade, but Asia, Africa, and Latin America will be especially hard hit. Sub-Saharan Africa will have more than 3 million adults infected by AIDS by 1995 and another 11 million infected with the *human immunodeficiency virus* (*HIV*) that produces the disease.[31] By

---

[27]Land reform may reduce social tension. Where peasant populations are large, however, as in Central America, resulting farms may be too small to be efficient, and failure to control population will renew tension.

[28]The Salvadoran population is projected to double between 1990 and 2025.

[29]Despite capture of the movement's leader, Abimael Guzmán, in September 1992, the conditions for social unrest remain: land shortage, inequality, and racial tension.

[30]Desmond Morris, *The Human Zoo* (New York: Dell, 1969), pp. 77–78. Emphasis in original.

[31]"The Future of AIDS," *The New York Times*, June 4, 1992, p. A8.

another estimate, almost one-third of pregnant women in some African countries are HIV positive, predicting a Malthusian fate for Africa: "If there is no cure found for AIDS in the next few years, then Africa's high fertility rates could be checked by worsening mortality rates."[32]

No region is immune to the epidemic. Asia will soon have more than 250,000 people with AIDS and 1.2 million with HIV. Latin America will have 420,000 cases of AIDS and almost 1.5 million cases of HIV infection. North America and Western Europe are estimated to have from 1 to 2 million HIV cases and from 250,000 to 500,000 AIDS-infected adults.[33] On a worldwide scale, the near-term projections were staggering: 17 million people infected with HIV and 5 million with AIDS itself. The disease has been attacked globally by research, treatment, and education, but with limited funds. Too few countries and their leaders have recognized how massive the problem is, and solutions extended across boundaries have been poorly coordinated.

Deteriorating Global Ecology

Population growth diminishes our physical space on earth, and it also strains to bursting the earth's physical, social, and political environments. Already the wealthy countries are running out of space in which to dump *solid waste*, some of it violently toxic, and are exporting it to land left to the poor. Where are the poor to dump their own waste, which will expand as their population grows and as economic modernization takes place? Environmental crises are not new. One popular explanation for the Roman Empire's fall was declining birthrates associated with the use of lead in water pipes. Industrialization in the West was, as we would expect, accompanied by environmental disasters. The Mad Hatter in *Alice in Wonderland* was based on an illness caused by mercury used in making hatbands. In the nineteenth century, entire species of animals such as the American bison were threatened by overhunting, and others were wiped out.

Nevertheless, the current global crisis appears to be unprecedented. According to the Worldwatch Institute, these are some current environmental trends:

The protective ozone shield in heavily populated latitudes of the northern hemisphere is thinning twice as fast as scientists thought just a few years ago.

A minimum of 140 plant and animal species are condemned to extinction each day.

Atmospheric levels of heat-trapping carbon dioxide are now 26 percent higher than the preindustrial concentration, and continue to climb.

The earth's surface was warmer in 1990 than in any year since record keeping began in the mid-nineteenth century; six of the seven warmest years on record have occurred since 1980.

---

[32]Kennedy, *Preparing for the Twenty-First Century*, p. 28.
[33]"The Future of AIDS," p. A8.

Forests are vanishing at a rate of some 17 million hectares per year, an area about half the size of Finland.

World population is growing by 92 million people annually, roughly equal to adding another Mexico each year; of this total 88 million are being added in the developing world.[34]

Water: Dying Seas and Drying Wells

Environmental stress is evident in the world's oceans and seas, which are used as open sewers, as if the oceans were so large that they could cope with any abuse. During the 1991 Persian Gulf War, Iraq's Saddam Hussein committed "eco-terrorism" by pouring Kuwaiti oil into the gulf; in March 1989, the captain of the supertanker *Exxon Valdez* lost enough oil to poison Prince William Sound in Alaska; and, for thirty years, the Soviet Navy dumped its radioactive waste in the Barents and Kara Seas in the Arctic.[35] Coral reefs, which support rich concentrations of life, have begun to die. Plastic debris and oil slicks have killed countless sea birds. Whales, seals, turtles, and fish are the victims of deadly toxins and viruses that are caused by chemical discharges. Common food fish such as tuna and swordfish are more and more heavily polluted, and species of food fish that were once common—cod, haddock, flounder, pollock, perch, and halibut—have been so overfished that extinction threatens them.[36]

Demands are also straining diminishing supplies of fresh water. Only 3 percent of the earth's water is fresh, and current demand is roughly 35 times as great as it was only 300 years ago. Inevitably, this scarcity has intensified competition for diminishing supplies. Agriculture currently accounts for about 66 percent of the fresh water that is used, industry 25 percent, and human consumption only about 9 percent. Figure 15.2 shows the global distribution of fresh-water resources.

More mouths and less water engender conflicts. During the severe drought that struck California early in the 1990s, state-sized cities like Los Angeles had to compete with the state's influential agricultural interests for diminishing supplies. Only after a long struggle were limitations placed on agriculture's extravagant consumption of water. Without long planning and care, California may find itself in the tragic position confronting the Central Asian regions in Kazakhstan and Russia from the polluted Aral

[34]Sandra Postel, "Denial in the Decisive Decade," in Lester R. Brown et al., *State of the World, 1992* (New York: W. W. Norton, 1992), p. 3.

[35]Patrick F. Tyler, "Soviets' Secret Nuclear Dumping Raises Fears for Arctic Waters," *The New York Times*, May 4, 1992, pp. A1, A4.

[36]Michael Specter, "The World's Oceans Are Sending an S.O.S.," *The New York Times*, May 3, 1992, p. E5; and David E. Pitt, "Fishing Countries Split On Harvest," *The New York Times*, August 1, 1993, Section 1, p. 6. In a highly innovative response to the problem, a consortium of public and private groups—the Atlantic Salmon Federation, the National Fish and Wildlife Foundation, and the U.S. State Department—pooled resources to pay the Greenland fishing industry not to catch salmon for two years to replenish stocks. Peter Bodo, "U.S. Buys 2-Year Timeout for the Atlantic Salmon," *The New York Times*, August 2, 1993, p. A7.

FIGURE 15.2

Annual Renewable Water Sources

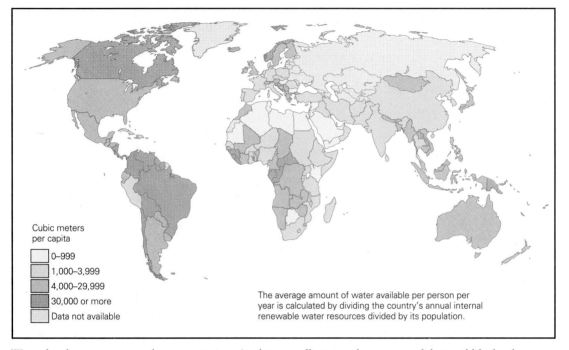

Cubic meters
per capita

☐ 0–999
☐ 1,000–3,999
☐ 4,000–29,999
☐ 30,000 or more
☐ Data not available

The average amount of water available per person per year is calculated by dividing the country's annual internal renewable water resources divided by its population.

Water has become a scarce human resource. As this map illustrates, large areas of the world lack adequate sources of renewable fresh water. As populations grow, conflicts over water resources will intensify.

SOURCE: *World Development Report, 1992* (New York: Oxford University Press, 1992), p. 217.

and Caspian Seas. For decades, so much water was diverted from rivers that feed the Aral Sea (Amu Darya and Syr Darya) to irrigate the region's cotton crop that the Aral is rapidly drying up. Toxic chemicals used to fertilize cotton have also leached into the region's groundwater, increasing infant mortality.

Water shortages have caused or are likely in the near future to stir political crises. One of the most dangerous is the conflict between Israel and its Arab neighbors over the Jordan River. Equally volatile is the conflict between Syria and Iraq over water from the Euphrates River. Rapidly growing populations throughout the region are intensifying quarrels over limited water supplies.

Too Little Food, Too Few Forests

Overfishing and diverted fresh water are part of an effort to sustain growing numbers. True, the mass hunger that demographers feared has been postponed by technology, including genetic engineering, new strains of plants, improved fertilizers, and mechanized agriculture.

Nevertheless, as shown in Table 15.3, in some regions per capita food consumption is outstripping increased food production. African food production in the early 1990s was 20 percent lower than two decades earlier.[37] The other side of the coin is that globally sufficient food is still available, but distributing it to those in need is very difficult. Both local and global political problems have shaped attempts to address that imperative demand.

Somalia is a shocking illustration. The U.S.-led intervention late in 1992 and early in 1993 was meant to arrest malnutrition and maldistribution of food assistance in that country. The global community's earlier response to the tragedy had been an "abject failure."[38] As in prior famines in Ethiopia and the Sudan, the world community chose to react late, only after starvation was clearly taking place. Part of the reason, of course, is that, in dealing with such issues, knotty local political issues have to be addressed. Ethiopia, the Sudan, and Somalia all suffer intractable political problems — petty warlords, weak central government, and ethnic rivalries — which negate external assistance. Thus, continued violence in Somalia persuaded President Clinton to announce that U.S. forces would be withdrawn by March 1994. Even if the global community wants to help, food assistance often fails to reach those who need it most. Finally, food aid can create local dependency, slowing agricultural reforms needed to make a country self-sufficient.

Sadly, food is a weapon in global politics. As more countries become dependent on a few food exporters, the latter may provide or withhold food exports to coerce political concessions, as did the Carter administration when it halted grain shipments to the U.S.S.R. to protest that country's invasion of Afghanistan in 1979. The United States provides inexpensive credits to countries it wishes to reward so that they can purchase surplus U.S. grain. Favored foreign leaders including Presidents Anwar Sadat and Hosni Mubarak of Egypt, Saddam Hussein of Iraq, and Boris Yeltsin of Russia have benefited by such credits. More dramatically, food has become a political football in civil wars. In Somalia, the Sudan, and Ethiopia, competing warlords have tried to withhold food from areas controlled by rivals. Food has also been used as a weapon in Afghanistan, Bosnia, and Iraq.

Local and global politics enter into the equation describing world food needs and so too do environmental factors. Intensive farming may contribute to soil erosion, salinization, and *deforestation*, and eventually even to spreading deserts. Already vast Third-World tracts have been denuded of forest to slake the demand for living space and fuel. Every year an area the size of Washington state or Belgium is cleared of jungles under pressure of population. Losing that much jungle reduces the earth's ability to produce oxygen, alters patterns of rainfall, and creates new deserts, and enlarges old ones. Among the most visible effects of deforestation is southward expansion by the Sahara in Africa and islands created in the Bay of Bengal by the silt runoff from the

---

[37]Marguerite Michaels, "Retreat from Africa," *Foreign Affairs* 72:1 (1992/93), pp. 95–96.
[38]Jeffrey Clark, "Debacle in Somalia," *Foreign Affairs* 72:1 (1992/93), p. 109.

Himalayas.[39] Another is the carbon dioxide, methane, and nitrous oxide poured ever faster into the atmosphere by burning trees and diminishing the ability of remaining forests to absorb carbon dioxide by *photosynthesis*. All these gases contribute to the *greenhouse effect*, and nitrous oxide also helps destroy the *ozone layer* that protects us from the sun's ultraviolet rays.[40]

Deforestation is most striking in Brazil's Amazon region, where national expansion's exigencies are colliding head-on with the imperatives of global survival. That region, drained by the Amazon River, covers 800 million acres, almost as large as Australia. Since 1975, some 11 percent of the jungle has been burned away — an area the size of Morocco — in fires that contribute to global air pollution.[41] As jungle is destroyed animal and plant life too are lost, and deforestation sends to extinction perhaps one-hundred species *every day*.[42]

A number of factors have combined to induce land hunger among Brazilian peasants. Steep population growth has been accompanied since World War II by agricultural unemployment caused by drought, mechanization,[43] and shifting crops (from rubber and coffee to soybeans). By 1989, about 81 percent of Brazil's farmland was held by fewer than 5 percent of the population.[44] Brazilian cities attracted many of the rural poor; between 1960 and 1980, 31 million Brazilians fled the countryside to cities like São Paulo. The cities could not absorb such numbers, and the political and social fabric of Brazilian society was headed toward collapse. To hard-pressed Brazilians, the enormous Amazon region seemed an answer. The Brazilian military supported the idea of opening the Amazon as part of their campaign to suppress guerrilla and drug-related violence. Brazilian entrepreneurs too were excited about riches from lumber, oil, bauxite, gold, and hydroelectric power.[45] In 1970, the government launched a vast program to

[39]Many thousands of Bengalis who have sought to live on these islands perish during annual cyclones.

[40]For a readable summary of the causes and effects of tropical deforestation, see Nicholas Guppy, "Tropical Deforestation: A Global View," *Foreign Affairs* 62:4 (Spring 1984), pp. 928–965.

[41]Edward Barbier, Joanne Burgess, and Anil Markandya, *Ambio* 20:2 (April 1991), p. 56; and Frederic Golden, "A Catbird's Seat on Amazon Destruction (Monitoring of Illegal Agricultural Burning by Remote Sensing Satellites)," *Science* 246, October 13, 1989, p. 201. Burning the Brazilian jungle has far more significantly affected global air quality than did burning Kuwait's oil fields by retreating Iraqi troops in 1991. Biomass burning produces not only carbon dioxide but also methane, a major contributor to global warming. See Reginald Newell, Henry Reichle, Jr., and Wolfgang Seiler, "Carbon Monoxide and the Burning Earth," *Scientific American*, October 1989, pp. 82–88.

[42]Among the most important of the plants pushed to extinction are those with high medical potential. Plants that may help cure or prevent cancer or AIDS tomorrow are being destroyed today.

[43]A tractor replaces about nineteen farm workers.

[44]Nicholas Hildyard, "Adiós Amazonia? A Report from the Altamira Gathering," *The Ecologist* 19:2 (1989), pp. 53–62.

[45]Prospective economic gain is a major challenge in environmentally sensitive regions like the Amazon. In the United States, political collisions have pitted environmentalists against business interests over felling trees in national forests and drilling for oil in the Alaskan tundra.

colonize the basin. Any farmer could have one-hundred acres free. Unfortunately, the land is poor and unsuited for agriculture. The rain-forest trees gather their own nutrients but store little in the soil, which, once cleared of jungle, can produce crops for only one or two seasons. Thereafter nothing grows; the remaining soil blows away and the farmer must move elsewhere.

The fight to reduce slashing and burning of the Amazon has been led by foreign and local ecologists and by those who use the jungle to tap rubber (a harvest that does not destroy trees). The violence has included the December 1988 murder of Chico Mendes, leader in protecting the rain forest and helping the rubber workers and the killing of indigenous Indians by gold prospectors in August 1993. Mendes's martyrdom turned Brazilian public opinion against the business interests that were profiting from exploitation of the Amazon. In June 1991, Brazilian President Fernando Collor de Mello announced steps to save the Amazon: abolishing tax subsidies for farmers and ranchers, removing the head of the Brazilian Indian Protection Agency, and, most important, willingness to embark on a new policy of exchanging debts for nature.[46]

The *debts-for-nature swap* is an approach to reducing friction with states that are being asked to bear a disproportionate share of the costs of global environmental reform. During the 1970s, countries in Latin America and elsewhere borrowed heavily at high interest rates from private banks in the United States and Western Europe to finance development. By the end of the decade, it became clear that they had overextended themselves, and some could not keep up with interest payments. A number of factors conspired to create this "debt" problem: global recession, lower oil prices (hurting oil producers like Venezuela and Mexico), and declining value of the U.S. dollar.[47] Thomas Lovejoy suggested the tactic in 1984, and it was applied for the first time three years later in Ecuador. The idea is that a government or environmental group will pay off part of a debtor's obligation at reduced interest. In return, the debtor will use the funds it would have paid in interest for environmental ends. The proposal attracted attention as it became apparent that some loans to debtor countries such as Brazil would never be repaid.[48] As a consequence, banks were willing to accept partial repayment of loans rather than confront a loan default.

In sum, producing food and distributing it generates global political controversy. Those who have food may extract a political price from those who need it, and may withhold it from rivals. And those who set out to reduce land hunger and increase food production risk leaving a damaged environment for future generations.

[46]These actions plus an economic recession have slowed but not halted deforestation of the Amazon rain forest. In 1991 an area the size of Delaware was burned and cleared. See James Brooke, "Homesteaders Gnaw at Edge of the Brazilian Rain Forest," *The New York Times*, May 22, 1992, pp. A1, A4.

[47]A decline in the dollar's value means that more dollars must be spent on needed imports of food, replacement parts for machines, and weapons.

[48]Peter Passell, "Washington Offers Mountain of Debt to Save Forests," *The New York Times*, January 22, 1991, p. C1.

Global Energy Needs and the Environment

Energy is an issue that illustrates how environmental and economic imperatives collide and create dilemmas for global politics in later decades. Actors in the global community have divergent views of trade-offs between the two demands. Third-World actors are willing to sacrifice environmental benefits to achieve rapid economic development at the same time as developed societies demand more stringent global environmental standards. We next discuss these trade-offs by identifying alternative sources of energy, evaluating their consequences for the environment, and describing attempts to balance safeguards for the environment with the need for energy.

Fossil Fuels and Economic Development

Harnessing new sources of energy tells much about how human society has modernized. The nineteenth-century industrial revolution was possible only because machinery was invented to replace human and animal labor, and that revolution was built on mountains of cheap, plentiful *fossil fuels* such as coal and coke. Transportation and distribution networks were built on the internal-combustion engine — trains, planes, and automobiles. In recent decades, the revolution in high technology has been brought about by computers that, using relatively little energy, can store and combine previously unimaginable quantities of information. If the engine of progress in earlier centuries depended on substitutes for human physical labor, the present revolution is fueled by substitutes for human mental labor.

Economic progress is never without cost, however. Inevitably, it changes life-styles and cultural traditions and destabilizes communities. Before labor unions, many people, including women and children, were forced to work long hours for little pay and to live in squalor.[49] Unfettered industrialism left terrible environmental consequences. Smog, toxic compounds, and other side effects of the workplace inflicted disease and premature death. Air and water were poisoned; coal miners contracted tuberculosis and *black lung*; and coal burned for heat made London notorious for its pea-soup fogs.

The global community today is more sensitive to the relationship between energy and environment and better understands how both are needed for prosperity and health. The economic and political sides of the equation received great attention during the *oil shocks* in 1973 and 1979. When oil was hard to find and its prices inflated following the Arab–Israeli war in 1973, interest picked up in alternative sources of energy such as solar, geothermal, wind, nuclear, and even thermonuclear power. The oil shocks showed the world it was depending ever more on oil from the Middle East, especially as old fields in places like Texas dried up. A few Arab states began to enjoy political leverage in the West.[50] All over the world, geologists feverishly sought new sources of oil, especially offshore in the North

---

[49]Working class conditions in nineteenth-century Europe and America influenced Karl Marx and Friedrich Engels (who wrote *The Condition of the Working Class in England*). Charles Dickens and Émile Zola vividly depicted in their novels how workers lived.

[50]See Chapter 14, pp. 496–499.

Sea, the South China Sea, the Pacific Ocean off California, and the Gulf of Mexico. Elevated oil prices in the 1970s also spurred conservation, especially in smaller cars with improved mileage. In fact, global use of oil dropped from 65 million barrels a day in 1979 to 59 million barrels in 1985.[51] Conservation and sources of cleaner energy promised to reduce air pollution. In the 1970s, the world seemed to learn it must become aware of and do something about environmental issues generally.

In the 1980s, though, new burdens were piled on the global environment. Efforts to cope with some challenges (e.g., local air pollution caused by sulfur) actually complicated programs for coping with others (e.g., *global warming* and holes in the ozone layer). The upsurge in oil exploration and production set off by earlier shortages and price rises, combined with reliance on market forces in the West and a weakened OPEC, brought prices down and created a global oil glut. One consequence was reduced interest in conservation. People again bought "gas-guzzling" cars and paid less attention to conservation. Again, dependence on Middle-Eastern oil began to climb.

Nuclear Energy

As rising oil prices awakened interest in alternative sources of energy, nuclear fission became a bigger source of energy in a number of countries. By the early 1990s, the world had 513 nuclear power plants, including 119 in the United States.[52] Even as the number of power plants grew, events made it appear that the cure might be worse than the illness. On March 28, 1979, a malfunctioning valve set in train events at the *Three-Mile Island* nuclear power plant near Harrisburg, Pennsylvania, uncovering the nuclear reactor core. Although little radioactive material escaped, the fear of *nuclear "meltdown"* gripped many in the United States. Then, on April 26, 1986, the *Chernobyl* nuclear power plant, near Kiev in the Soviet Union, blew up, sending toxic nuclear debris through much of Western and Central Europe. Although relatively few people were killed in the initial blast, estimates of future cancer deaths from radiation ranged as high as 45,000. If the Hiroshima and Nagasaki atomic bombings are a guide, rates of chromosome aberration, immune deficiency disease, and genetic disease in Ukraine and Belarus will also be abnormal because of Chernobyl. Memories of that incident and others since, such as the 1993 release of toxic debris from a Russian facility near the East Siberian city of Tomsk, one of ten secret nuclear sites in the former Soviet Union, have fired public fear about nuclear power in many countries.[53] This fear is fueled as publics

[51]Consumption has risen again since 1985 but at a modest rate. Christopher Flavin, "Building a Bridge to Sustainable Energy," in Brown, *State of the World*, p. 29.

[52]*Nuclear News Map*, as of June 30, 1991. In all, 27 countries have nuclear power plants, of which France, Germany, Japan, and the United States have most.

[53]Japan is likely to become a major battleground. The government is in the midst of a program of building "breeder" reactors (nuclear reactors that, during operation, make more fuel than they expend). Such reactors produce plutonium that can be used to make nuclear weapons.

begin to learn about earlier nuclear accidents such as the sinking of the Soviet nuclear submarine *Komsomolets* off the Norwegian coast in 1989.[54]

Even discounting dramatic events like Chernobyl, many suspect that nuclear power carries environmental hazards. Among the worst is low-level and high-level radioactive waste—"everything from piping-hot irradiated [used] fuel to mildly radioactive clothes worn by operators."[55] One issue is how to dispose of this "hot" trash safely. Some radioactive waste remains dangerous practically forever. Plutonium-239 will be poisonous for a quarter of a million years, and spent fuel rods from nuclear power plants must be stored for more than 100 years. Studies are under way on constructing a high-level radioactive-waste repository under Yucca Mountain in Nevada, and regional compacts are being sought among U.S. states to deal with low-level waste. None of these efforts has been wholly successful.

Another difficult problem with nuclear waste is created by the by-products from manufacturing nuclear weapons, especially by the United States and the Soviet Union during the Cold War. That problem is exacerbated because arms-control agreements require signatories to dismantle many of these weapons. Nuclear production plants in the United States are located at Piketown, Ashtabula, and Fernald, Ohio; Oak Ridge, Tennessee; Richland, Washington; Aiken, South Carolina; Denver, Colorado; and Amarillo, Texas.[56] These facilities are responsible for widespread contamination of soil and water. At least one defense contractor (Rockwell International), which operated the Rocky Flats Plant near Denver between 1975 and 1989, building atomic triggers for hydrogen bombs, was convicted of criminal felonies because of illegally incinerating nuclear waste and dumping radioactive water at the plant in the middle of the night.[57] In 1989, the U.S. Department of Energy closed several of these facilities and launched a multibillion-dollar cleanup operation. Since 1981, the government has been studying a permanent disposal site for nuclear-weapons waste in a salt formation in southeastern New Mexico. The proposed Waste Isolation Pilot Plant or WIPP would dispose of the "transuranic" waste from nuclear-weapons production facilities throughout the country permanently.

So far, though, no permanent solution has yet been found for disposing of different nuclear wastes, and few people want them in their back yard. At more than 400 facilities around the world, nuclear waste is being stored where it was produced. The problem

---

[54]William J. Broad, "Sunken Russian Sub to Be Tested For Leaks by Nuclear Warheads," *The New York Times*, August 1, 1993, Section 1, p. 11.

[55]Nicholas Lenssen, "Confronting Nuclear Waste," in Brown, ed., *State of the World*, p. 50.

[56]Ray Perkins, Jr., *The ABCs of the Soviet-American Nuclear Arms Race* (Pacific Groves, Calif.: Brooks/Cole, 1991), p. 35.

[57]Matthew L. Wald, "Rockwell's Guilty Plea Accepted on Nuclear Arms-Plant Charges," *The New York Times*, June 2, 1992, pp. A1, A8.

grows overwhelming as these temporary facilities reach capacity. Vast quantities of relatively low-level waste produced by hospitals and uranium mines must also be disposed of in the near future.[58]

Future Energy Needs and the Environment

Without viable alternatives, it appeared in the 1980s that, for the foreseeable future, the world would have to continue to rely on fossil fuels. Even individuals who know little about the issues cannot but notice the consequences of such fuels in the killer smogs that envelop Mexico City, Athens,[59] and other cities. Equally evident are some of the other consequences of air pollution caused by fossil fuels: *acid rain* that has denuded forests in eastern Canada, New England, Germany, and Central Europe and has eliminated fish from countless lakes, leaving them little "dead seas." Acid rain shows that no one society can cope with many environmental problems. Americans in the Midwest, where many of the pollutants that cause acid rain are produced, quarrel with its victims in New York, New England, and Canada, and airborne garbage from North America crosses the Atlantic to Western Europe.

Still worse are environmental problems that menace the earth as a whole. *Chlorofluorocarbons* (CFCs)[60] released at ground level threaten to destroy the earth's ozone layer, which protects us from the sun's dangerous ultraviolet rays. As a result, the rate of skin cancer is likely to rise greatly in coming decades. An international agreement in June 1990 (amendments to the 1987 Montreal Protocol) called for completely phasing out chlorofluorocarbon production and use by the year 2000 and was approved by 93 nations.[61] But the agreement may be too late to reverse ozone depletion, which has become noticeable in both Northern and Southern Hemispheres.

The carbon dioxide, CFCs, nitrous oxides, and methane that we release are mostly responsible for the growing threat from heating the earth's atmosphere, the *greenhouse effect*. These gases, produced especially by burning oil, coal, and other fossil fuels, trap heat just as a glass greenhouse does. As Figure 15.3 shows, carbon emission from fossil fuels continues to rise, especially in developing countries. Though sunlight can pass through these gases, they also reflect it back to earth's surface as infrared radiation, and it can no longer escape into space.[62] Even small changes in temperature may have big effects on the world as we know it. The earth 130,000 years ago was between 2° to 3°

[58]Radiation created by medical and dental x-rays and radiopharmaceuticals may actually produce higher doses of radiation for the population than do nuclear plants. See John R. Lamarsh, *Introduction to Nuclear Engineering*, 2nd ed. (Reading, Mass.: Addison-Wesley, 1983), p. 428.

[59]One footnote to automobile-generated air pollution in Athens is that it is eroding the Parthenon and other treasures of classical antiquity.

[60]These chemicals are released from air conditioners and other forms of refrigeration.

[61]"Amended Montreal Protocol Calls for CFC Ban by 2000," *Plastics Technology* 36 (August 1990), pp. 87–88.

[62]Richard Houghton and George Woodwell, "Global Climatic Change," *Scientific American* 260:4 (April 1989), pp. 36–44.

FIGURE 15.3

Carbon Emission from Fossil Fuels in Selected Regions

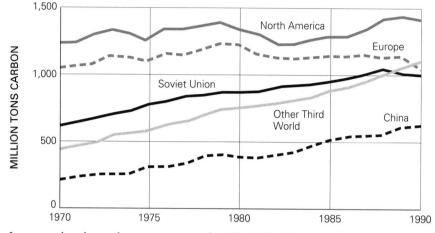

In recent decades, carbon emissions in the Third World have increased dramatically, but the West remains responsible for the bulk of these harmful emissions.

centigrade warmer than it is today, and tropical swamps thrived where London now sits. Sea levels were higher and areas in Europe and the United States that are now coastal dry land were then under water.

As the earth's temperature increases, the polar ice caps may melt and flood heavily populated coasts and islands. Studies suggest that island countries including the Marshall Islands, Tonga, and the Maldives may disappear beneath the waves.[63] Weather changes may make previously fertile areas in tropical zones desertlike, and crops that once thrived in temperate zones may become difficult to grow in those regions. Higher temperatures would probably cause droughts in the grain-growing areas of the American Midwest and deplete the underground aquifer on which the whole region depends. Massive coastal erosion would follow, and salt water would poison freshwater systems. Secondary effects would include death for freshwater life forms, reduced farmland, and immense property damage.[64] And the greenhouse effect would be intensified by continuous large-scale deforestation.

Issues such as global warming and deforestation reveal the tension between global needs and the individual society's perceived interests. For global warming as well as acid rain, the U.S. government has been a major impediment to collective action. As Table 15.3 shows, the United States is by far the world's leading source of carbon dioxide, yet

[63]Paul Lewis, "Danger of Floods Worries Islanders," *The New York Times*, May 13, 1992, p. A3.

[64]Edward Barbier, "The Global Greenhouse Effect," *Natural Resources Forum*, February 1989, pp. 20–29.

TABLE 15.3

National Sources of Carbon Dioxide

Country	1988 Total metric tons	Per capita metric tons
East Germany	327.4	19.8
United States	4,804.1	19.4
Czechoslovakia	233.6	15.0
Australia	241.3	14.7
Poland	459.4	12.1
West Germany	669.9	11.0
Great Britain	559.2	9.9
Japan	989.3	8.1
France	320.1	5.9
Korea	204.6	4.8
Spain	187.7	4.8
Mexico	306.9	3.7
China	2,236.3	2.1
Brazil	202.4	1.5
India	600.6	0.7

SOURCES: Environmental Protection Agency, "Policy Implications of Greenhouse Warming," National Academy of Sciences, in William K. Stevens, "At Meeting, U.S. Is Alone on Global Warming," *The New York Times*, September 10, 1991, p. B8.

the Bush Administration opposed adopting a firm timetable for limiting carbon dioxide emissions. The administration complained that, because of U.S. dependence on automobiles, Americans would bear a disproportionate part of the burden caused by reducing carbon dioxide emissions. Unfortunately, without U.S. cooperation, the world is almost certain to experience unpredictable but fearful consequences from global warming.

The brunt of a policy for conservation and limiting heavy industry and the internal combustion engine would fall on Latin America, Africa, and Asia. Western prosperity was built on intensive use of energy, and cities such as Pittsburgh, Manchester, and Glasgow were highly polluted during the industrial revolution. Today, many of the world's worst pockets of pollution are in societies that are beginning to modernize. Should they not enjoy the same "right" to develop as Europeans and Americans had in the nineteenth century and early in the twentieth? Energy use is currently lowest in poor societies, and demand will grow fastest in those regions. Nevertheless, citizens in wealthy societies still consume more resources and produce more waste per capita than those in poor societies. The economically advanced countries are responsible for three-quarters of the carbon released into the atmosphere, mainly from the fossil fuels they burn in automobiles.

Why, ask citizens in the Third World, should we not be permitted to exploit the Amazon jungles to feed, clothe, and heat our growing population? What right do others have to tell us how to use our own resources, especially because their societies already enjoy a high standard of living? Why should not the rich, whose societies have 20 percent of the world's population but account for 80 percent of worldwide carbon dioxide emissions, cut their standard of living for the common good rather than demand that we accept limits to growth? Former Brazilian President Jose Sarney said, "We cannot accept the developed world's manipulation of the ecology issue to resist Latin America's autonomy and progress."[65]

Such questions have no simple answer. Even prosperous societies encounter resistance at home to trade-offs between the environment and prosperity. The United States sees passionate conflicts between those who exploit forests and wetlands for jobs and profit and those who wish to preserve them; between those who wish to drill for offshore oil in the Arctic and off California and those who fear environmental damage; and between those who wish to develop "clean" nuclear power rapidly and those who fear new Chernobyls. Everyone bears some responsibility in such issues. On the one hand, consumers in developed societies use more resources, including energy, and produce more waste than the poor. On the other hand, the poor use energy less efficiently, invest little in controlling pollution, and have larger populations. Solutions require imaginative strategies enabling each actor to perceive that it will benefit by adopting measures to improve its economy and, at the same time, preserve the environment. Such proposals would have the rich agree to provide capital transfers to the poor in exchange for a greater environmental commitment, would create trade pacts to encourage development, even as environmental standards are raised, and would reduce debt for environmental clean-up.

Conclusion

Will individual states pursue their interests even though these will continue to imperil survival for the species by thwarting global cooperation to achieve collective goods? The multilateral venture to stop producing and applying chemicals that are destroying the earth's ozone layer is a hopeful sign. So too is the World Bank's establishing a Global Environmental Facility to support environmental programs in the developing world. The June 1992 international "Earth Summit" in Rio de Janeiro was at least evidence that people around the world were taking seriously the environmental threats to their survival and recognizing that,

---

[65]Cited in Andrew Hurrell, "The Politics of Amazonian Deforestation," *Journal of Latin American Studies* 23 (February 1991), pp. 197–215.

in the words of one observer, "Homo Sapiens rivals grand forces like the movement of continents, volcanic eruptions, asteroid impacts and ice ages as an agent of global change."[66]

Whether sovereign states can be persuaded to work for the common interest is a big question. Ecologists around the world appear to be ready to substitute vague voluntary aspirations for binding goals that would reduce greenhouse gases and preserve biodiversity to obtain U.S. cooperation, and it will not be known for years whether such aspirations will be met.[67] The world's wealthiest societies may or may not fully join the collective endeavor.[68] Thus, at Rio, the United States did not sign a treaty to ensure *biodiversity* — preserving diverse plant and animal life — and worked to weaken a treaty on global warming despite protests by the U.S. director of the Environmental Protection Agency. The Clinton administration set out to rethink that position, however, and seemed prepared to support the biodiversity treaty and endorse a timetable for reducing the global warming threat.[69]

The issues discussed in this chapter are so linked that trying to solve any one problem will affect others.[70] Feeding more mouths by clearing more land, growing new strains of crops, and using fertilizers to increase productivity all mean fewer trees to absorb carbon dioxide and produce oxygen, greater competition for scarce water supplies, more seepage of toxic chemicals into aquifers, and even more extensive soil erosion. Everything is tied to everything else. Cooperation on many issues and by the whole global community will be indispensable for ensuring survival. Some limited success has already been achieved for the environment — the Montreal Protocol to protect the ozone layer and the Rio summit agreement — but it has been so hard to get broad agreements that we will probably continue to see, as one analyst said, "piecemeal international agreements on environmental matters."[71]

A debate has raged for decades about earth's capacity to sustain continued growth. Although some disagree about defining that capacity and when it will be reached, consensus is growing about *limits to growth*, beyond which environmental collapse is inevitable.[72] Whichever answer is correct, it is clear that, one observer says, the "scale

[66]William K. Stevens, "Humanity Confronts Its Handiwork: An Altered Planet," *The New York Times*, May 5, 1992, p. B5.

[67]Rose Gutfeld, "Agreement Is Near on Greenhouse Gases." United States resistance to effective environmental controls led some to refer to President George Bush as "Uncle Grubby" and "Mr. Smoke." James Brooke, "U.S. Has a Starring Role at Rio Summit as Villain," *The New York Times*, June 2, 1992, p. A5.

[68]See, for example, Stephen Kinzer, "Bonn Criticizes U.S. Reluctance to Curb CO_2," *The New York Times*, May 21, 1992, p. A5.

[69]Richard L. Berke, "Clinton Supports Two Major Steps for Environment," *The New York Times*, April 22, 1993, pp. A1, A4.

[70]See Gareth Porter and Janet Welsh Brown, *Global Environmental Politics* (Boulder, Colo.: Westview Press, 1991).

[71]Kennedy, *Preparing for the Twenty-first Century*, p. 121.

[72]See William K. Stevens, "Humanity Confronts Its Handiwork," p. B6.

and pressure of human demands on the environment is little appreciated, and it is growing: in 1975 every single man, woman and child in the United States used on average 40,000 pounds of *mineral* matter alone. . . . And all this was used in commonplace ways—just in making buildings, roads, furniture, packaging, hamburgers . . . things we take for granted, [T]he majority represent destruction of the environment *somewhere*."[73]

No one should assume that solutions will be found to the problems we collectively confront. We have no guarantee that such solutions are possible or that actors have either the imagination or will to cooperate for the collective good. Most species that existed on this earth have already disappeared. Only the future can tell whether *Homo Sapiens* will be another casualty of failure to adapt to changing conditions.

Key Terms

acquired immune deficiency syndrome
   (AIDS)
collective goods
private goods
side payment
special interests
cognitive traps
salinization
Malthusian future
social insurance
purdah
suttee
amniocentesis
shantytowns
underemployment
population density
the Inquisition
lateral pressures
land hunger
Chernobyl

Three-Mile Island
human immunodeficiency virus
   (HIV)
solid waste
deforestation
photosynthesis
greenhouse effect
ozone layer
fossil fuels
oil shocks
black lung
global warming
nuclear "meltdown"
acid rain
chlorofluorocarbons (CFCs)
greenhouse effect
bio-diversity
limits to growth
ultrasound scanning
debts-for-nature swap

---

[73]Guppy, "Tropical Deforestation," pp. 930–931. Emphasis in original.

CHAPTER SIXTEEN

The State versus the Individual: Human Rights in the Global Arena

As a rule we think of governments as their citizens, servants, and guardians. In many democratic societies such as our own, that is the relationship, but in others, the government may actually be the citizen's enemy and a great danger to the individual's health and safety. For many reasons, from ideology to fear, governments may treat their citizens as adversaries from whom they must extract support and potential opposition whom they must repress. Some in power try to impose ideological, ethnic, linguistic, religious, and political views on their populations. Other governments are led by individuals whose thirst for power and glory or whose pathological personality make them behave despotically. Throughout the world, governments and leaders illegally imprison, torture, and kill their citizens.

Rogue regimes have carried out genocidal campaigns—deliberately and systematically exterminating national or ethnic groups—against segments in their population. During World War II, the German Nazis murdered more than six million European Jews and sought to exterminate other groups such as gypsies and homosexuals. Between 1975 and 1979, the communist Khmer Rouge government in Cambodia under Pol Pot murdered between one and one-and-one-half million of its eight-million citizens.[1]

Genocide is only an extreme in the scale on which governments can violate human rights. In Ethiopia in 1988, mass executions cut down civilians accused of supporting guerrilla movements in Eritrea and Tigre provinces. In neighboring Sudan, a Muslim

---

[1]Michael J. Sullivan III, *Measuring Global Values* (New York: Greenwood Press, 1991), p. 37. This atrocity is recorded in the book and film, *The Killing Fields*.

regime has sought to use war and famine to crush the mainly black and Christian population in the country's southern provinces. In Peru, large-scale "disappearances" of those seized by government troops in "counterinsurgency zones" have become common.[2]

Systematic violation of *human rights* was conducted during the 1992–1993 campaign by Serbian authorities in Bosnia-Herzegovina to force Croatians and Muslims from their homes by murder, starvation, and intimidation. The policy, euphemistically known as *"ethnic cleansing,"* has been compared to the fascist and Nazi policies in Yugoslavia during World War II. With acquiescence and assistance by Serbian authorities, including President Slobodan Milosevic and Serbian members of the former Yugoslav army, Bosnian Serbs employed terrorist tactics, including systematic rape, which violate human rights, to force Bosnian Muslims to flee their homes and villages. The Serbs meant to alter the map of Bosnia and get control of most of the country. By spring 1993, it appeared that Serbian aims would be realized, for U.N. efforts to halt the carnage by negotiation, economic sanctions against Serbia, and humanitarian relief for besieged Muslims in the capital city of Sarajevo and elsewhere, were conspicuously unsuccessful.

We will take the human-rights issue as exemplifying a more general problem: *citizens versus states in global affairs.* We begin by assessing the relationship between states and their citizens and how the human-rights idea fits into this relationship. Next, we consider the definitions encompassing the notion of human rights and survey the current state of global human rights according to these definitions. Third, we identify the factors that account for violations of human rights and discuss ways of monitoring, protecting, and improving human rights worldwide.

The State and the Individual

How is the state related to the individual and what rights does the individual have in the state? These questions have vexed political philosophers from Plato to Hobbes and from Locke to Marx. Do states determine the rights of individuals? Do individuals possess intrinsic rights, whether or not states recognize them? And, if individuals do have rights, what are they, and what are their limits? These questions have no definitive answers.

---

[2]The "disappearance" of real and imagined government foes at the hands of rightist "death squads" (often consisting of police and soldiers) was common practice in Argentina and Uruguay in the 1970s and in Guatemala, Honduras, and El Salvador in the 1970s and 1980s. Victims were called *los desaparecidos* ("the ones who disappeared"). See *Amnesty International Report 1989* (New York: Amnesty International U.S.A, 1989), pp. 9–11, 144, 200; and Neil J. Mitchell and James M. McCormick, "Economic and Political Explanations of Human Rights Violations," *World Politics* 40:4 (July 1988), p. 476.

Historical Sources of Human Rights

The modern conception of human rights derives from natural rights and natural law.[3] The idea of *natural law*, that God and nature confer dignity on all human beings, dates back to Greek Stoicism and Roman law. This tradition places obligations on both individuals and the societies of which they are a part. The demands of natural law were seen as duties of states whose rulers could not and should not violate those prescriptions.

During the late Middle Ages and the Renaissance, popular movements sought to limit rulers' arbitrary behavior. Natural-law doctrine as a basis for natural rights began to change its form. Instead of a code with which societies should comply, natural-law doctrine was seen as a basis for asserting the individual's "natural rights." At least two reasons might explain this transformed natural-law doctrine. First, states seemed to be flouting natural law more often. Second, the Renaissance, and later the Protestant Reformation and the Enlightenment, affirmed that the individual and individual liberty really mattered.

As early as the Magna Carta (1215), a new emphasis on individual rights suggested itself.[4] With the English Bill of Rights (1689), the American Declaration of Independence (1776), and the French Declaration of the Rights of Man (1789), the push for individual rights accelerated. Such events were, one observer suggests, "testimony to the increasingly popular view that human beings are endowed with certain eternal and inalienable rights, never renounced when humankind 'contracted' to enter the social from the primitive state and never diminished by the claim of 'the divine right of kings.'"[5] The doctrine of natural rights was transformed into a human-rights doctrine neither quickly nor smoothly. Political philosophers such as David Hume and Jeremy Bentham argued against basing human rights on natural law because such law lacked an empirical foundation. Others including John Stuart Mill and Friedrich Karl von Savigny contended that human rights could be grounded in their utility for society only as a whole and were necessarily bounded by *cultural relativism*. That which one society deemed a fundamental right might be denied by others so that human rights were limited to those society granted by law.

Nazi and Japanese atrocities renewed the call for enforcing human rights. The trial and conviction of Germans accused of crimes against humanity and war crimes by an international tribunal at *Nuremberg* were widely regarded as a path-breaking precedent in human rights, precedent reaffirmed by the U.N. establishment of a war-crimes

[3]See Burns Weston, "Human Rights," *Human Rights Quarterly* 6 (August 1984), pp. 257–283. For a review of evolving human rights, emphasizing cultural relativism, see David Forsythe, *The Internationalization of Human Rights* (Lexington, Mass.: D.C. Heath, 1991), pp. 1–26.

[4]Technically, this was less a new emphasis than a reaffirmation of the individualism emphasized in classical Athens. The Athenian conception was less than complete: women and slaves were denied the rights given other citizens.

[5]Weston, "Human Rights," p. 259.

tribunal in 1993 to try those who committed war crimes in Bosnia.[6] In 1948, the United Nations adopted the *Universal Declaration of Human Rights*.[7] Although that declaration was not legally binding on states, it set a tone for renewed attention to human rights that was reinforced by two further covenants passed by the General Assembly in 1966: *the International Covenant on Civil and Political Rights* and the *International Covenant on Economic, Social, and Cultural Rights*. Both imposed obligations on U.N. members and sought to codify human rights, but universal ratification has not yet been achieved.

During the Cold War, the superpowers often marginalized human rights when they got in the way of political objectives. Neither let the issue stand in the way of good relations with regimes that repressed individual rights. The United States maintained close relations with regimes like those of Francisco Franco in Spain, Chiang Kai-shek in Taiwan, Fulgencio Batista in Cuba, Syngman Rhee in South Korea, Ferdinand Marcos in the Philippines, Anastasio Somoza in Nicaragua, or Sese Seko Mobuto in Zaire despite their repressive policies. The Soviet government, too, was a major violator of human rights, as were communist regimes in Cuba, China, and Eastern Europe.

With a U.S. president committed to human rights, the issue gained new prominence in the mid-1970s. During the first year in President Jimmy Carter's administration, human rights seemed to dominate Washington's agenda.[8] Although the Carter administration argued for human rights, its behavior reflected the need to compromise with a difficult reality. Repeatedly, Washington was charged with being more willing to enforce its human-rights policy on small countries than on large ones and on enemies rather than friends. Consequently, even though countries like Indonesia committed severe human-rights abuses against the people of East Timor, the Carter administration refused to act against Jakarta because Indonesia was a strong U.S. ally. Subsequent U.S. administrations sought to play down the Carter administration's human-rights emphasis. The Reagan administration had to deal with complaints that its policy in Central America did not take human rights into account, including support for the El Salvador government and its *death squads* or the Nicaraguan *contras* and their violence against the Sandinista government. The Bush administration had to confront similar challenges over its continued political and economic ties with China after the June 1989 Tiananmen Square massacre of students demonstrating for democracy. Both the Bush and Clinton administrations were accused of indifference to atrocities being committed against Bosnian Muslims.

A nongovernmental organization, *Amnesty International (AI)*, has actively publicized human-rights violations. The group issues annual reports on global human-rights

---

[6]War crimes were also alleged during World War I, but few individuals were tried or convicted.

[7]Forsythe, *Internationalization of Human Rights*, p. 15.

[8]For a study of the Carter and Reagan administrations arguing that they differed little on human rights, see David Carleton and Michael Stohl, "The Foreign Policy of Human Rights: Rhetoric and Reality from Jimmy Carter to Ronald Reagan," *Human Rights Quarterly* 7 (May 1985), pp. 205–229.

conditions, has local chapters around the world, and engages in massive letter-writing campaigns to publicize abuses against human rights. Its work has been so influential that the organization was awarded the Nobel Prize for Peace in 1977. The AI scrutiny does make a difference in a government's way of dealing with political dissent because fear of publicity induces caution and restraint.

The Content of Human Rights

There is still no consensus about defining human rights. Do economic, social, and political rights qualify as human rights? Are some rights more important to protect than others? Can we identify a core of human rights? A good beginning is to define those rights more precisely. Political scientist Jack Donnelly declares that "[H]uman rights are the rights one has simply by virtue of being a human being."[9] Donnelly acknowledges that including humanness in the definition omits divine influence in their origin, and a long tradition conceives of rights as God given. Consider the passage in the American Declaration of Independence: "We hold these Truths to be self-evident, that all Men are created equal, that they are endowed by their Creator with certain unalienable Rights." Donnelly suggests that a right involves an entitlement that an individual can use to make a moral claim on others who are bound to respect that right. In this sense, violations of rights are fundamental wrongs.[10]

Human rights then are not merely goals that proper conduct directs us to follow, nor are they obligations that momentary expedience may make individuals feel compelled to obey. Rather, they are individuals' fundamental moral obligations toward each other. Rights are fundamental in another sense: they "logically and morally . . . take precedence over the rights of the state and society."[11]

Cultural Differences and Human Rights

Although human rights *as rights* derive mostly from Western traditions, demands that governments respect human *dignity* also have a basis in non-Western traditions. The source of this respect is mostly in reciprocal "duties" for rulers and ruled rather than a conception of inherent "rights."[12] Examples from Islamic culture, traditional African societies, Confucian China, and Hindu India can be adduced to support this judgment.[13] Islamic scholars contend that "the basic concepts and principles of human rights had

[9]Jack Donnelly, "Human Rights and Foreign Policy," *World Politics* 34:4 (July 1982), p. 575.

[10]Jack Donnelly, "Human Rights and Human Dignity: An Analytic Critique of Non-Western Conceptions of Human Rights," *American Political Science Review* 76:2 (June 1982), p. 304.

[11]Ibid., p. 305.

[12]Ibid., p. 306.

[13]The examples and passages are from ibid., pp. 306–309.

from the very beginning been embodied in Islamic law" and that "Muslims are enjoined constantly to seek ways and means to assure to each other what in modern parlance we call 'human rights.' " On closer inspection, these rights resemble the proper conduct that individuals should follow rather than fundamental entitlements.

In other cultures, the claims are much the same. The Chinese language did not have a word for "rights" until late in the nineteenth century. If rights were defended, they were placed among the ruler's duties toward the people as part of their heavenly and earthly responsibilities. The Confucian tradition in China, which dates back 2,500 years, implies reciprocal duties between rulers and ruled in which relations are dominated by human dignity and virtue without need for coercion. One historian writes, "Of crucial importance was the initiative of the ruler, who . . . could initiate benevolent government and win over the people. The people's confidence was essential to the state, more important than arms or even food."[14]

Is a universal claim for human rights thus undermined? Clearly the idea of individual human rights, even if Western in origin, has steadily gained global acceptance. One observer concludes that, "the connection to universal jurisdiction [of several global treaties] plus state public pronouncements and the bulk of applied policy clearly and universally indicate opposition to certain practices on grounds of a fundamental denial of human rights. . . . No exceptions are acknowledged because of culture or any other reason, such as stage of development or public disorder."[15] This claim is not, however, universally accepted. Thus, some authoritarian Third-World regimes argue that human rights should be interpreted differently in non-Western societies. They declare that the right of economic development for their countries as a whole may require limiting individual liberties or that women in Islamic societies must be treated differently than men. In reponse to such arguments, U.S. Secretary of State Warren Christopher, in a speech to the U.N.-sponsored World Conference on Human Rights in Vienna in June 1993, declared: "We cannot let cultural relativism become the last refuge of repression."[16]

One way to think about the individual's specific entitlements is to conceptualize human rights as negative or positive by their relationship to actions by states. *Negative rights* are those which prevent a government from interfering with the individual's independence and autonomy. In the U.S., these rights are readily familiar to us in the first ten amendments (the Bill of Rights) to the Constitution. Negative rights usually are *political* and *civil* rights and liberties.

[14]Conrad Schirokauer, *A Brief History of Chinese Civilization* (New York: Harcourt Brace Jovanovich, 1991), p. 31.

[15]David P. Forsythe, *The Internationalization of Human Rights* (Lexington, Mass.: Lexington Books, 1991), p. 9.

[16]Cited in Elaine Sciolino, "At Vienna Talks, U.S. Insists Rights Must Be Universal," *The New York Times*, June 15, 1993, p. A1.

But the idea of *positive rights* implies the government's obligation to provide for citizens' welfare — housing, employment, health care, education, and so on. Positive rights are often translated as *economic* and *social* rights. Nearly all governments today give some attention to these rights, but many disagree about how far they should proceed in securing and promoting positive rights.[17]

International Bill of Human Rights

Recently, attempts have been made to identify and codify human rights. Three documents — the Universal Declaration of Human Rights, the International Covenant on Civil and Political Rights, and the International Covenant on Economic, Social and Cultural Rights — are recognized as covering the core of universal human rights and are collectively labeled the *International Bill of Human Rights*.[18]

The first document, the 1948 Universal Declaration of Human Rights, declares that its aim was to set "a common standard of achievement for all peoples and nations" in observing human rights. Its thirty articles identify political, civil, economic, social, and cultural rights, including "the right to life, liberty, and the security of person," freedom from "torture or cruel, inhuman or degrading treatment or punishment," freedom from "arbitrary arrest," "the right to the freedom of thought, conscience, and religion," "the right to property," and "the right to take part in" government. The Declaration also identifies positive rights such as "the right to work," "the right to education," "the right to a standard of living adequate for health and well-being," and "the right freely to participate in the cultural life of the community."[19]

To make binding the rights set out in the Universal Declaration, the U.N. General Assembly adopted the other two covenants that focused on specific kinds of rights. The International Covenant on Economic, Social, and Cultural Rights identified many of the rights mentioned in the Universal Declaration, as well as several others such as the "right to work," and "the right of everyone to an adequate standard of living for oneself and one's family."[20] The second document, the International Covenant on Civil and

[17]For a discussion of economic rights, especially as they are associated with development, see Rhoda Howard, "Human Rights, Development and Foreign Policy," in David P. Forsythe, ed., *Human Rights and Development* (New York: St. Martin's Press, 1989).

[18] Some observers consider other agreements, such as the Covenants on Genocide and Torture as part of this International Bill of Human Rights. See Lawrence J. LeBlanc, *The United States and the Genocide Convention* (Durham, N.C.: Duke University Press, 1991).

[19]A description of the International Bill of Human Rights is in *The United Nations and Human Rights* (New York: Department of Public Information, 1984), pp. 241–261. The passages cited are from the Universal Covenant, reprinted in ibid., pp. 241–244.

[20]*Everyone's United Nations*, 9th ed., (New York: United Nations Department of Public Information, 1979), pp. 416–423.

Political Rights, outlined many of the negative rights in the Universal Declaration.[21] The International Covenant also established a Human Rights Committee, with signatories' as representatives to review the member country's report on human-rights compliance. The Optional Protocol to the International Covenant on Civil and Political Rights significantly added to the Human Rights Committee's work by recognizing individuals as subjects of international law who deserved protection from abuses by sovereign states.[22]

Although the United Nations passed these covenants and opened them for signature by the nations in 1966, they did not come into effect until 1976, when the required number of countries had formally acceded to them. By the end of 1991, 104 states had signed and ratified the International Covenant on Economic, Social, and Cultural Rights, and 100 had signed and ratified the International Covenant on Civil and Political Rights. Only 60 countries, however, had signed and ratified the Optional Protocol.[23] A few countries had signed, but not ratified, these covenants. The United States signed both, but only in 1992 did it ratify the Civil and Political Rights Covenant. But because many countries neither signed nor ratified these agreements, it is too early to conclude that these standards have been universally accepted.

The end of the Cold War again turned attention to human-rights issues. Neither the United States nor Russia felt the same pressure as in the past to support regimes that violate human rights to secure allies against the Cold-War adversary. As a result, countries like Turkey and Indonesia, in which human-rights violations are common, can no longer assume they will get unquestioning support from the United States or Western Europe. Human rights has also replaced anticommunism as something of a rationale for Western intervention in the Third World and elsewhere. Thus, the case for Western involvement in Somalia and Bosnia was partly based on human-rights violations in those countries.

The Global Human-Rights Record

Several analysts have tried to determine how well human rights are respected in global politics. Keep in mind that their results may be ambiguous. In some countries, regimes change quickly and so too do human-rights policies. In others, regimes are too weak to prevent police or military officials from committing human-rights abuses. We can see legitimate differences over what constitutes cruelty or suppression of political dissent. Many Westerners believe that punishments such as amputating a limb that are called for by the Koran are unnecessarily harsh, but many Muslims disagree. Some regimes

[21]Ibid., pp. 423–436.

[22]For the most part, international law recognizes only sovereign states as legal subjects.

[23]See *Amnesty International 1992* (London: Amnesty International Publications, 1992), pp. 300–304. The listing covers through December 31, 1991.

contend that allegations made by political enemies that they hold political prisoners are lies and that supposed political offenders are really common criminals. Whatever the ambiguities, however, the overall picture of human rights in contemporary global politics is bleak.

Protecting the "Integrity of the Person"

One examination of 122 countries discovered that more than half held political prisoners "often" or "very often."[24] Another third "sometimes" held political prisoners, and only eight did not commit human-rights violations of this kind. Torture was less frequently applied but still widespread. Forty-six countries "often" or "very often" resorted to torture, and another forty-seven countries used torture "sometimes" or "rarely." Only twenty-nine countries in the sample never used torture. When a similar analysis was conducted for 135 countries a few years later (1987), the results were equally discouraging.[25] Just under 60 percent of the countries in the sample often or very often held political prisoners, and only 10 percent never arbitrarily imprisoned individuals. About 37 percent frequently resorted to torture, and only 25 percent never engaged in such action.

Protecting Political and Civil Rights

Several assessments of compliance with political and civil liberties demonstrate that most nations do *not* allow free exercise of political and civil rights. Perhaps the best known was conducted by Freedom House, a U.S.-based nonprofit organization. Since 1978, this group has published a yearly worldwide assessment entitled "comparative survey of freedom," a country-by-country evaluation of political rights and civil liberties.[26] The 1990 results indicate how well these rights have been honored in recent decades.[27] Of the 169 nations in a recent survey, only 61 were considered "free," and 62 were declared "unfree." These results had changed little for nearly a decade.[28]

[24]See Neil J. Mitchell and James M. McCormick, "Economic and Political Explanations of Human Rights Violations," Table 1, p. 487. Coding for the countries and the number of a country's violations in each category are described and listed in note 17, p. 485.

[25]See Neil J. Mitchell and James M. McCormick, "Global Human Rights and the Reagan Administration," paper presented at the Annual Meeting of the International Studies Association, Vancouver, Canada, March 19–23, 1991.

[26]See *Freedom in the World: Political Rights and Civil Liberties, 1989–1990* (Lanham, Md.: University Press of America, 1990), pp. 19–20.

[27]*Freedom Review*, 22:1 1991, pp. 17–18. Freedom House is a strongly anticommunist organization with a conservative bias.

[28]Steve Chan, *International Relations in Perspective: The Pursuit of Security, Welfare, and Justice*, (New York: Macmillan, 1984), p. 372.

The U.S. government has undertaken to evaluate the status of human rights globally. Since the middle 1970s, the Congress has required the Department of State to report on human rights in countries that receive U.S. economic or military assistance, later enlarging its coverage to all U.N. members. Like the Freedom House reports, these focus on three components of human rights: "the right to be free from governmental violations of the integrity of the person," "the right to enjoy civil rights," and the right to "political rights, or the right of citizens to change their government."[29] In general, the portrait that these reports paint is that, despite lip service to human rights, they are not widely observed worldwide.

Promoting Economic and Social Rights

Most studies measure observance of economic and social rights indirectly, and, as with other human rights, the results are disappointing. To suggest how these rights have been evaluated, we consider several indicators and then a composite index that assembles a summary global portrait of the status of economic and social rights.

One measure of global economic rights is enjoyment of basic economic necessities, which compares per capita gross national product (GNP) for individual countries. In 1978, the average GNP per capita for the developed countries was $12,280, and for developing countries it was $870. During the following decade, the gap actually grew. In 1988, the comparable figures were $14,610 for developed countries and $976 for developing ones. In other words, individuals in developed countries enjoyed incomes fifteen times larger than those in poor countries.[30]

Other indicators of economic and social well-being address more directly some of the Covenant's rights, and these too are hardly encouraging. For example, as of 1990, low-income countries had only one medical doctor for every 6,760 citizens. For middle-income countries, the proportion improves to one for every 2,060 citizens, and, for wealthy countries, the ratio is one for every 420. The "health gap" between rich and poor is enormous. Other indicators of access to health care and education reflect the same disparity between rich and poor. *Infant mortality rates* vary greatly from rich countries (where only 8 in every 1,000 die) to poor ones (where 71 per 1,000 die). Life expectancy also varies. Citizens of poor countries can expect to live 62 years, but in the richest countries, life expectancy has climbed to 77 years. Literacy levels also vary

---

[29]Country Reports on Human Rights Practices for 1984, Report Submitted to the Committee on Foreign Relations and Committee on Foreign Affairs, U.S. House of Representatives by the Department of State (Washington, D.C.: U.S. Government Printing Office, 1985), p. 2.

[30]These data are calculated in constant 1988 dollars and are from U.S. Arms Control and Disarmament Agency, *World Military Expenditures and Arms Transfers, 1989* (Washington, D.C.: U.S. Arms Control and Disarmament Agency, 1990), p. 31.

dramatically across the globe. In high-income countries, average illiteracy is less than 5 percent, but in poor countries as many as 40 percent of the population may be illiterate.[31]

Since 1990, the U.N. Development Programme has published a *"human development index"* that measures progress in dealing with economic and social challenges. The index, sometimes described as "a measure of human happiness," is derived by averaging three indicators—life expectancy, education, and purchasing power—which are scored from 0 to 1 for ease of comparison.[32] The higher the score, the better off a country is in human development, as reflected by longer life expectancy, lower illiteracy, and higher income. Japan, Canada, Norway, and Switzerland do best, and impoverished African countries such as Burkina Faso, Niger, Mali, Guinea, and Sierra Leone do worst. As suggested in Table 16.1, income alone does not produce happiness. Overall, most countries score poorly, but some, including Australia, China, and Cuba, produce human development more effectively with limited resources than others like Brazil and Saudi Arabia. And some, such as Japan, Switzerland, and Canada, though they rank high overall, treat women poorly in comparison to men.[33]

The global record in protecting political rights and in promoting economic rights is poor. In some countries, human-rights violations by governments and opponents of governments are so systematic that their treatment deserves to be described as "terrorism," and that is our next subject.

Political Terrorism and Human Rights

Governments are not alone in violating individual human rights. Thus, shortly after assuming office in 1981, U.S. Secretary of State Alexander Haig declared that the "ultimate abuse of human rights" was international terrorism.[34] Is "private" terrorism, whatever the cause, less reprehensible than "public" terrorism? Are governments that assist terrorist groups for political ends less culpable than the groups themselves? Sympathizers see the violence done by revolutionaries and "freedom fighters" as different from human-rights violations. They may dismiss the former as political violence intended to achieve a desirable end and feel that therefore it does not deserve to be

[31]The data for physicians, infant mortality, life expectancy, and illiteracy are from *World Development Report, 1993: Investing in Health* (New York: Oxford University Press, 1993), pp. 238–239, 292–293.

[32]See United Nations Development Programme, *Human Development Report 1993* (New York: Oxford University Press, 1993), pp. 100–103.

[33]Ibid., Table 1.3, p. 16.

[34]Alexander Haig, "News Conference" (Washington, D.C.: Bureau of Public Affairs, Department of State, January 28, 1981), p. 5.

TABLE 16.1

Human Development Index Ranking (1993)

Rank	Selected countries	Score	GNP per capita rank
1	Japan	.983	3
2	Canada	.982	11
3	Norway	.978	6
4	Switzerland	.978	1
5	Sweden	.977	5
6	United States	.976	10
7	Australia	.972	20
8	France	.971	13
9	Netherlands	.970	17
10	Britain	.964	21
19	Israel	.938	27
22	Italy	.924	18
33	South Korea	.872	37
37	Russia	.862	47
53	Mexico	.805	60
70	Brazil	.730	53
75	Cuba	.711	101
84	Saudi Arabia	.688	31
85	South Africa	.673	57
87	Libya	.658	40
101	China	.566	142
103	Iran	.557	59
108	Indonesia	.515	122
124	Egypt	.389	120
132	Pakistan	.311	136
134	India	.309	146
157	Mozambique	.154	173
164	Guinea-Bissau	.090	165
165	Chad	.088	164
166	Somalia	.087	171
167	Gambia	.086	148
168	Mali	.082	154
169	Niger	.080	150
170	Burkina Faso	.074	149
171	Afghanistan	.066	169
172	Sierra Leone	.065	155
173	Guinea	.045	132

SOURCE: *Human Development Report, 1993*, Tables 1.1 and 1.2, pp. 11, 14.

labeled *terrorism*. This distinction probably misses the point. Terrorism, whether done by revolutionaries or secret policemen, is aimed at innocent civilians.[35] One analyst says that if we focus less on "the identity of the perpetrators or the nature of their cause," and more on the "quality of the act," we may begin to see terrorism for what it is.[36] Those who employ terrorism care little for human life and believe that the ends justify the means. Such violence, whether exercised by governments or private groups, represents disdain for human rights.

We have some idea about how widespread the phenomenon of nonstate terrorism has become. In 1992, 361 international[37] terrorist incidents were recorded, a 35 percent decline from the previous year.[38] In 1992, Latin America had the most casualties, including a spectacular bombing of the Israeli Embassy in Buenos Aires in March by Hizballah. Western Europe and the Middle East, long centers of terrorists' attacks in the 1970s and 1980s, suffered fewer casualties.[39] Overall, U.S. citizens and property were the most frequent targets of terrorist acts (40 percent) in that year. For the most part, however, U.S. territory has been spared the terrorism so frequent elsewhere, but the bombing of New York's World Trade Center in March 1993 by a group of Muslim radicals and the FBI's disruption of a plot to bomb major buildings in New York three months later may be omens of worse things to come. Cooperation among states, however, has reduced international terrorism in recent years.[40]

Political terrorism and common criminality may merge. Profits from international drug trafficking and sales sometimes help purchase weapons and support for revolutionaries. And the drug barons themselves use terrorist violence to produce political unrest, as do the Sicilian Mafia and the drug "families" in the Colombian cities of Cali and Medellín. The *narcotraficantes* in Peru and Colombia have used violence and terror without scruple to keep control of the coca industry and undermine local- and national-government challenges to them. They extend their violence overseas, where their cocaine, heroin, and other drugs are distributed and sold. Sometimes alliances between drug traffickers and political terrorists are overt, as in Burma and in Peru, where the *narcotraficantes* and *Sendero Luminoso* (Shining Path) are aligned in a sinister symbiosis. Shining Path, a Maoist group, needed a haven in which to coordinate its activities and chose the Upper Huallanga Valley, also home to *narcotraficantes*.[41] In the

[35]Brian Jenkins, "International Terrorism: The Other World War," in Charles W. Kegley, Jr., *International Terrorism: Characteristics, Causes, Controls* (New York: St. Martin's Press, 1990), p. 28.

[36]Ibid.

[37]"International terrorism" involves the citizens or territory of more than one country.

[38]United States Department of State, *Patterns of Global Terrorism: 1992* (Washington, D.C.: Department of State Publication 9743, April, 1993), p. 1.

[39]Ibid., p. 58.

[40]Steven A. Holmes, "U.S. Says Terrorist Attacks Dropped Sharply in 1992," *The New York Times*, May 1, 1993, p. 4; and Thomas J. Lueck, "New Threats Prompt Increases in Security," *The New York Times*, June 27, 1993, Section 1, p. 13.

[41]See Donald M. Snow, *Distant Thunder: Third World Conflict and the New International Order* (New York: St. Martin's Press, 1993), pp. 169–178.

resulting collaboration, the group provided military protection for the drug traffickers in return for financial support.

Governments and their opponents can become enmeshed in a vicious cycle of terrorism and counterterrorism. In South Africa, the white government used torture and detention for many years to enforce its racial apartheid policy. The discovery that the opposition African National Congress (ANC) had established prison camps to enforce discipline with staggering brutality was to be expected in view of this cycle. Even as the ANC fought for equality for blacks in South Africa, "from the late 1970's until 1991, suspected spies were imprisoned for up to eight years without any hearing, tortured to extract confessions, and beaten with sticks and wires in tortures eerily similar to those allegedly inflicted on blacks by the South African Police."[42] Where governments fail to respect human rights, their adversaries too are unlikely to do so.

Explaining Human-Rights Violations

What accounts for the repeated violations of human rights around the world? No one has a simple answer, and it is likely that a number of factors explain why states and others resort to repressive behavior and do not respect human rights. We can point to several economic, social, and political factors that have been offered as explanations for human-rights violations.

Economic Explanations

One explanation focuses on economic conditions in countries and how they affect resort to political repression. Thus, it appears that deteriorating economic conditions are associated with spreading debt slavery in some societies.[43] Former U.S. Secretary of Defense and World Bank President Robert McNamara declares, "There can . . . be no question but that there is an irrefutable relationship between violence and economic backwardness."[44] Following his reasoning, the poorer a country, the more likely it is that human-rights violations will occur. According to one political scientist, the greater the social and economic deprivation in a society, the more likely its government is to engage in repression. Similarly, economic inequality encourages a government to engage in repression.[45]

[42]"Inquiry by Mandela's Group Finds Abuses by Its Forces," *The New York Times*, August 24, 1993, p. A2.

[43]See, for example, James Brooke, "Slavery on Rise in Brazil, as Debt Chains Workers," *The New York Times*, May 23, 1993, Section 1, p. 3.

[44]Cited in Samuel Huntington, *Political Order in Changing Societies* (New Haven: Yale University Press, 1968), p. 41.

[45]Conway W. Henderson, "Conditions Affecting the Use of Political Repression," *Journal of Conflict Resolution* 35 (March 1991), pp. 124, 125.

The opposite claim is made by political scientist Samuel Huntington, who argues that the poorest countries are likely to be ultrastable because citizens are busy making ends meet and cannot imagine how they might alter their condition. "People who are really poor," Huntington contends, "are too poor for politics and too poor for protest."[46] But societies that are beginning to "modernize" and improve social, economic, and political conditions, such as Iran under the Shah or Iraq under Saddam Hussein, are susceptible to demands for change. As citizens make greater demands and as governments are less able to satisfy them, greater repression will follow.

Neo-Marxists provide an economic explanation for human-rights violations that goes beyond the conditions in one country to include that country's external ties. According to neo-Marxists, countries that are deeply enmeshed in the global capitalist system try to control the growth and influence of trade unions, repress revolutionary activities that threaten the influence of the regime in power, and control protest activities.[47]

Political Explanations

The first factor that many in the West think of in explaining respect for human rights is the state's type of political regime. Democratic or "liberal" states are assumed to have greater respect for human rights than authoritarian states.[48] The arguments are straightforward. Liberal regimes have the "requisite conception of human dignity" to make possible observance of human rights and are founded on a belief in individual dignity. Indeed, the concept of democracy is closely identified not only with the people's right to rule over their own affairs but with the belief that individual rights should be observed.[49] In some authoritarian societies, on the other hand, states are viewed as *more* than the sum of the interests of the individuals who comprise them, and the states' interests are given higher priority than those of citizens.

Back in 1979, Jeanne Kirkpatrick, U.S. Ambassador to the United Nations, sought to distinguish among nondemocratic states, arguing that some are worse than others in

[46]Samuel Huntington, *Political Order in Changing Societies*, p. 52. Huntington's argument is directed more at the general question of instability than at human-rights violations, but its implications are applicable to the study of human rights.

[47]See Neil J. Mitchell and James M. McCormick, "Economic and Political Explanations of Human Rights Violations"; Conway W. Henderson, "Conditions Affecting the Use of Political Repression"; and Kathleen Pritchard, "Human Rights and Development: Theory and Data," in David P. Forsythe, ed., *Human Rights and Development: International Views* (London: Macmillan, 1989), pp. 329–345. Pritchard examines political rights, civil rights, and socioeconomic rights and finds that economic factors are positively associated with greater respect for all three types of rights.

[48]Rhoda Howard and Jack Donnelly, "Human Dignity, Human Rights, and Political Regimes," *American Political Science Review* 80:3 (September 1986), pp. 801–818.

[49]Indeed, one problem in analyzing democracy as an explanation for human-rights violations is that it may be tautological or circular. The same factor that is used to explain human-rights violations (absence of democracy) is used to define democracy (respect for human rights).

observing human rights. *Totalitarian states* (which she tended to equate with states under communist control), she argued, leave the individual defenseless. *Authoritarian regimes* (such as Latin American military governments), she believed, though also repressive, do not penetrate so deeply into the fabric of society, exercise less than total control of individual conduct, and are more "susceptible of liberalization" than their totalitarian counterparts.[50] Events in the former Soviet Union and Eastern Europe cast doubt on the utility of her distinction because those societies have reformed further and faster than many authoritarian regimes.

Research does indicate that democratic or liberal states respect human rights better than nondemocratic states, though the relationship is not perfect.[51] The distinction between totalitarian and authoritarian regimes, however, is less useful.[52] In short, the type of political regime matters, but other factors also contribute to respect for human rights, including the society's cultural and ethnic background.

Cultural Explanations

Cultural divisions in a society also help explain violations of human rights. If a society is fractured along ethnic, racial, economic, religious, or ideological lines and if these cleavages reinforce one another, political repression is more likely. One analyst summarizes the reasoning behind this assumption:

> In ethnically and religiously diverse societies, social cohesion tends to be low; hence, challenges to the regime are more common and elites are more likely to respond violently. This is not only because of the frequency and intensity of challenges, but because compliance with regime policies is not likely to be given freely.[53]

Many states today are a patchwork of ethnic, religious, and racial groups. Indeed, most contemporary states are ethnically heterogeneous, and only a few are homogeneous. According to one analysis, only 35 of 135 states enjoyed a high degree of homogeneity and only 55 enjoyed moderate homogeneity. *In other words, slightly more than 40 percent of the states surveyed were split into two or more parts by ethnic diversity.*[54] Although systematic studies of the relationship between social cleavages and political instability and violence are few, evidence suggests that ethnic heterogeneity is linked to human-rights abuses.

[50]See Jeanne Kirkpatrick, "Dictatorships and Double Standards," *Commentary* 88 (November 1979), pp. 34–45.

[51]See, for example, Henderson, "Conditions Affecting Use of Political Repression."

[52]Mitchell and McCormick, "Economic and Political Explanations of Human Rights Violations," pp. 494–495.

[53]Ted Robert Gurr, "The Political Origins of State Violence and Terror: A Theoretical Analysis," in Michael Stohl and George A. Lopez, eds., *Government Violence and Represssion* (Westport, Conn.: Greenwood Press, 1986), p. 58.

[54]See the ethnic homogeneity rankings for the 135 nations listed in George Thomas Kurian, *The Book of World Rankings* (New York: Facts-on-File, 1984), pp. 48–49.

From its creation after World War I, Yugoslavia, for example, was a hodgepodge of ethnic adversaries. During World War II, Croatian and Serbian nationalists waged a cruel war against each other, and the country's integrity was maintained after the war only by the authoritarian policies imposed by Marshal Tito and the communist party. After the country broke up into its constituent republics, religious and ethnic cleavages contributed to widespread violations of human rights in Croatia and later in Bosnia-Herzegovina. Conflicts between the Tamils and the Sikhs in Sri Lanka, Hindus and Muslims in Kashmir and elsewhere, and Catholics and Protestants in Northern Ireland reinforce the impression that religious and ethnic divisions can have bloody political consequences. Unquestionably, ethnic hatreds are a major impediment to observance of human rights. New York Senator Daniel Patrick Moynihan expresses the issue:

> [W]hat is to be the basis of a legitimate political order? The will of the people? Well, yes. But which people? The cold war kept that question at bay. No longer. . . . The barbarians had gone; barbarism had returned. Europe . . . had become the setting of sealed trains, "ethnic cleansing," murderous hate. . . . In what had been Yugoslavia, a Serb militiaman . . . told of his village burnt, his brother-in-law dead, "Serbs, naked and tortured." He responded in kind. "I have cut the throats of three Turks[55] so far, and I don't ever have nightmares."[56]

Improving Human Rights

Efforts to protect individual human rights have been pursued through various channels. The issue mobilizes individuals, nongovernmental organizations, governmental agencies, and intergovernmental organizations including the United Nations. A brief survey of the groups and individuals and the kind of work that they undertake depicts global activity on behalf of human rights.

The Individual's Role

In many countries, improving human rights owes much to a few dedicated, courageous individuals, often risking imprisonment or worse at the hands of outraged officials. President Jimmy Carter's personal campaign to place human rights on the global agenda in the 1970s exemplifies what a major public figure can do, as well as the limits on such work. Nelson Mandela's exertions on behalf of South African blacks under a repressive regime reflected great personal courage. Mandela, himself imprisoned almost thirty years for his political activities, continued to wage his campaign to achieve political, economic, and social rights even while behind bars.

[55]Bosnian Muslims.

[56]Daniel Patrick Moynihan, *Pandaemonium: Ethnicity in International Politics* (New York: Oxford University Press, 1993), pp. 143–145.

One source of human rights abuse—South Africa's system of racial separation known as apartheid—came to an end. Negotiations also began to end white minority rule there. This photo shows Nelson Mandela, leader of the African National Congress, and Frederick W. de Klerk, South Africa's last white-minority president. These two South African leaders were jointly awarded the 1993 Nobel Peace Prize.

The quiet work by many individuals has begun to receive attention and recognition. Several recent winners of the Nobel Prize for Peace have been human-rights advocates. The 1992 recipient, Rigoberta Menchu of Guatemala, campaigned tirelessly for the rights of indigenous people in her country and sought to end the violence committed by the Guatemalan army against the rural poor. In 1991, the Burmese opposition leader, Day Aung San Suu Kyi (daughter of the country's founder), was awarded the same prize for her opposition to military rule in her country. Other human-rights activists who have received this award include two women from Belfast, Northern Ireland, who sought to start a dialogue between Catholics and Protestants, Mairead Corrigan and Betty Williams (1976); Mother Teresa of Calcutta (1979) for her work among the poor of India; Adolfo Pérez Esquivel (1980) for his advocacy of human rights in Argentina when that country was ruled by a military dictatorship; the former leader of the Polish trade union Solidarity (and later president of Poland), Lech Walesa (1983); the South African antiapartheid leader, Bishop Desmond Tutu (1984); the anti-Nazi activist Elie Wiesel (1986); and the exiled Tibetan leader, the Dalai Lama (1989).

Despite such recognition, much work by individuals goes unnoticed. These activities range from an Argentine mothers' campaign to locate and identify their sons and relatives who "disappeared" during the military regime's "dirty war" late in the 1970s and early in the 1980s to the many thousands of ordinary citizens who demonstrated for political freedom in Leipzig, East Germany, or Vilnius, Lithuania, early in the 1990s or gathered in Russia to thwart communist hard-liners' attempt to overthrow President Mikhail Gorbachev in a coup d'état. Clearly, individuals can make a difference.

Nongovernmental Organizations

More and more often, nongovernmental organizations do important work in monitoring human-rights compliance worldwide. Perhaps the most prominent of these and the most successful was started by several individuals in London in 1961. Amnesty International (AI), originally named the "Appeal for Amnesty, 1961," began as a campaign by several lawyers and writers in London. The campaign gained attention when one of them (a lawyer named Peter Berenson) wrote an essay in a London paper expressing his outrage at global human-rights violations and calling for worldwide action to stop them:

> Open your newspaper any day of the week and you will find a report from somewhere in the world about someone being imprisoned, tortured, or executed because his opinions or religion are unacceptable to his government. . . . The newspaper reader feels a sickening sense of impotence. Yet if these feelings of disgust all over the world could be united into common action, something effective could be done.[57]

The present AI charter summarizes its principal goal simply, "to secure throughout the world the observance of the provisions of the Universal Declaration of Human Rights and other internationally recognized human rights instruments."[58]

After three decades, this idea has grown into a worldwide movement with more than 1,100,000 members, subscribers, and donors in more than 150 countries worldwide. The local AI groups employ several methods to achieve the organization's goals: petitioning for changes in a country's constitution or seeking a government's adherence to international conventions. Amnesty International may also offer support for individuals held as "prisoners of conscience," work to improve the conditions under which such prisoners are held, and publicize the plight of political detainees worldwide. In 1991, AI was working on more than 2,400 human-rights cases involving more than 3,300 individuals.[59] In all, the organization assumes the burden of trying to protect individuals from brutal treatment and seeks to offer aid and assistance to improve the lot of those

[57]Peter Berenson, "The Forgotten Prisoners," *The Observer Weekend Review* (London), May 28, 1961, p. 21.

[58]Amnesty International Report, 1992, p. 293.

[59]Ibid., p. 311.

being improperly detained around the world. Some of its activities cause governments to alter their behavior, and its presence sometimes deters governments from violating human rights.

Other nongovernmental groups operate as human-rights monitors, seeking to improve global conditions. Three important regional human-rights organizations are Americas Watch, Asia Watch, and Africa Watch. Americas Watch was founded in 1981 to provide "a balanced, non-ideological approach to the promotion of human rights as a consideration in the formation of U.S. foreign policy toward Latin America and the Caribbean."[60] Its activities include carrying out fact-finding, research, and policy-writing missions in the Western Hemisphere, and testifying periodically before congressional committees in the United States. Asia Watch performs similar functions in Asia and has repeatedly complained about the treatment of Vietnamese refugees in Hong Kong and elsewhere. Africa Watch, too, monitors human rights and did much to focus world attention on famine in Somalia in 1992.

Other nongovernmental organizations focus on international law and legal advocacy as ways of protecting human rights worldwide. The Human Rights Advocates International is a New York-based group with "one hundred and fifty attorneys in forty countries who represent and advocate on behalf of individuals or groups in courts." Another, the International Human Rights Law Group, seeks "to promote and protect human rights around the world through the application of international human rights law." A third, the Lawyers Committee for Human Rights, relies upon "the international legal norms enshrined in the Universal Declaration of Human Rights and other widely accepted principles of international law" as the guideposts for its work.[61]

Church groups are also deeply involved in helping monitor and improve global human rights. In Central America, groups with church affiliations have been involved in monitoring human rights conditions and reporting on the abuses they have recorded. In El Salvador, a church group repeatedly challenged the Reagan administration's claim in the mid-1980s that the U.S.-supported government was improving its human-rights record. Finally, many nongovernmental organizations working for human rights have appeared in academic circles. Indeed, the study of human rights and human-rights violations has become a growth industry.

In sum, NGOs are doing more to curb abuses of human rights. Their ability to publicize abuses has sometimes helped mobilize international public opinion, and some governments have restrained their behavior to avoid such publicity and the resulting condemnation. Where governments are prepared to bear the cost of negative publicity, however, NGOs can do little.

[60]Thomas P. Fenton and Mary J. Heffron, *Human Rights: A Directory of Resources* (Maryknoll, N.Y.: Orbis Books, 1989), p. 3.

[61]Ibid., pp. 6, 9, and 10.

International Organizations

The United Nations has come to be recognized as the main international organization with responsibility for monitoring human rights. One of its principal organs, the Economic and Social Council (ECOSOC), has this specific responsibility. In 1946, shortly after the United Nations was founded, ECOSOC established the Commission on Human Rights, which continues to carry responsibility for evaluating human rights worldwide, for suggesting new initiatives to promote such rights, and for investigating alleged human-rights abuses, either by governments or by individuals. In recent years, the Commission and its principal subcommittee, the Sub-Commission on Prevention of Discrimination and Protection of Minorities, have sponsored meetings open to the public in which alleged human-rights violations are discussed. Private complaints and government responses to the Commission's enquiries, however, are usually held in confidence first and are made public only when the Commission issues a report to the ECOSOC.[62]

The Commission on Human Rights and the United Nations as a whole have initiated several other kinds of actions to promote observance of human rights worldwide. An international Human Rights Day is observed every December 10, and the International Day for the Elimination of Racial Discrimination is observed annually on March 21. The year 1968 was declared the International Year for Human Rights, and a conference was held on human rights on the twentieth anniversary of the adoption of the Universal Declaration of Human Rights. Finally, the United Nations provides governments with experts, training programs, and fellowships and scholarships to promote observance of human rights.[63]

Some regional international organizations also have committees or commissions for monitoring and addressing human-rights violations in their geographical area. Europe, Latin America, and Africa have human-rights organizations, although as yet no such group has been formed in either Asia or the Middle East.[64] Europe and, to a lesser extent, Latin America appear to have the most highly developed institutions for dealing with human-rights abuses. Both regions have human-rights courts in addition to human-rights commissions. In Europe, a Commission on Human Rights is responsible for implementing the European Convention on Human Rights and for investigating and evaluating human-rights violations brought to its attention by governments, individuals, or groups.[65] The Commission may investigate alleged violations and issue a report.

---

[62]*Everyone's United Nations*, 10th ed., (New York: Department of Public Information, United Nations, 1986), pp. 302, 306–307.

[63]Ibid., pp. 305–306.

[64]Jack Donnelly, "Human Rights in the New World Order," *World Policy Journal* 9 (Spring 1992), p. 252.

[65]A. Glenn Mower, *Regional Human Rights: A Comparative Study of the West European and Inter-American Systems* (Westport, Conn.: Greenwood Press, 1991), pp. 89–108, 131–145.

Where it seems necessary, the Commission can refer a matter to the European Court of Human Rights for further adjudication. The European Court has issued "binding legal judgments, with which states almost invariably comply."[66]

Governments

Governments can improve their human-rights records in two ways. First, they can undertake domestic reforms that demonstrate adherence to the norms of human rights. Second, a government or group of governments may take punitive action toward a state that violates human rights and demand that reforms be carried out in targeted states. Both strategies have been difficult to implement successfully, despite several partial successes.

The human-rights improvements in the former Soviet Union and Central Europe that resulted from Gorbachev's *glasnost* and *perestroika* and communism's subsequent demise illustrate how governments can make dramatic changes in their way of treating citizens. At no time in recent history have so many people's political and civil rights improved so quickly. Reforms in the former Soviet Union, so often portrayed as a violator of human rights,[67] demonstrate convincingly that a government (or, perhaps more accurately, a determined population) can significantly increase political freedom and put an end to repressive policies.

Less dramatically, in other recent cases governments have ended abuses and improved the climate for human rights in their own societies. With democracy restored, Argentina undertook a concerted campaign to publicize the abuses committed by the military regime during the dirty-war period late in the 1970s and early in the 1980s. A similar undertaking began in Chile when Patricio Aylwyn Azocar was elected president in December 1989, following sixteen years of repressive military rule under General Augusto Pinochet Ugarte. In the Philippines and Guatemala, governments have also come to power that are less oppressive than their predecessors. After a decade-long war in Central America, even El Salvador has sought to publicize and confront its past human-rights violations. A high official in the government of President Alfredo Cristiani hailed publicity on earlier human-rights atrocities as a signal that the "people of El Salvador . . . wish to live in democracy."[68] And when the president of Guatemala in spring 1993 tried to overthrow the democratic order in his country, he was thwarted by an alliance between human-rights activists and the military. Even South Africa has

[66]Jack Donnelly, "Human Rights in the New World Order," p. 252.

[67]Soviet leaders, including Stalin, routinely emphasized positive rights as prerequisites for negative rights. In general, Marxists argue that individual liberty is meaningless without economic and social equality.

[68]Tim Golden, "Bodies Attest to Salvadoran Atrocity," *Des Moines Register*, October 22, 1992, p. 8A. Even after efforts have been made to correct former abuses, however, it may be difficult to bring to justice those who perpetrated human-rights violations. The perpetrators may retain powerful positions in the army or the police, and bringing them to justice risks touching off a military coup.

begun to adopt internal reforms providing greater human-rights protection to its black majority population.

Nevertheless, major exceptions remain to the improving picture of human rights. Repressive regimes persist in power in many parts of the world, such as China, Cuba, Iraq, Haiti, and Zaire, and relying upon internal reform alone appears to be a weak reed for improving overall global human rights. Authoritarian leaders have few incentives for ceding power voluntarily, and, as for Saddam Hussein and Fidel Castro, outsiders have few levers that will bring about their overthrow.

A growing human-rights issue for governments is admitting refugees. With slow economic growth early in the 1990s, some countries have been less willing than in the past to accept the flood of refugees that accompany human-rights violations. Countries in Asia including Hong Kong, Malaysia, and Thailand routinely turn away Vietnamese "boat people." Western Europe is beginning to erect barriers to immigrants from Central Europe, the former Yugoslavia, and Africa.[69] In 1993, Germany tightened its liberal asylum law in response to a flood of refugees from the East and the rising neo-Nazi violence aimed at them, and the French government set a zero-immigration goal.[70] The issue has also surfaced in the United States, where President Clinton deployed the Coast Guard to return Haitian boat people trying to flee to U.S. shores and intercept boatloads of Chinese refugees.[71] This policy, which was upheld by the U.S. Supreme Court in June 1993, seems to violate the principle that people not be returned to a country where they may suffer persecution.[72] It also recalls U.S. policy of turning back shiploads of Jewish refugees from Nazi persecution prior to World War II.

The growing resistance to refugees is a painful problem because of the rapid increase in people fleeing civil disorder and repression. Between 1989 and 1993, refugee numbers soared by 4 million to almost 19 million, mostly fleeing turmoil in the former Yugoslavia, the Central Asian republics of the former U.S.S.R., Iraq, Somalia, Ethiopia, Mozambique, and Liberia.[73]

[69]Most often it is claimed that barriers to immigration are aimed at preventing "economic refugees" from taking advantage of laws permitting *political asylum*.

[70]Barry Newman, "Flooded by Refugees, Western Europe Slams Doors on Foreigners," *The Wall Street Journal*, July 8, 1993, pp. A1, A4.

[71]During 1993, one boatload of Chinese ran aground off New York City, costing a number of lives, and several others were interned in Mexico. See, for example, Anthony DePalma, "Refugees Are Sent Back to China Hours After They Dock in Mexico," *The New York Times*, July 18, 1993, Section 1, p. 1. Chinese and other Asian refugees have also fled to the U.S.-owned Northern Marianas, where they have been exploited. See Philip Shenon, "Saipan Sweatshops Are No American Dream," *The New York Times*, July 18, 1993, Section 1, pp. 1, 6.

[72]Deborah Sontag, "Reneging on Refuge: The Haitian Precedent," *The New York Times*, June 27, 1993, Section 4, p. 1. This is the principle of "non-refoulement" (after *refouler*, French for "to force back").

[73]Paul Lewis, "U.N. Refugee Official Seeks Pledges from Donors," *The New York Times*, June 20, 1993, Section 1, p. 3. The costs of caring for the refugees doubled between 1990 and 1992, and the main contributors to the U.N. High Commission for Refugees are less willing to give than in the past.

The other option that is available to governments is to use diplomatic, economic, and, rarely, military instruments against states that abuse human rights. Such ventures have generally had mixed success. For almost two decades the United States has had a legislatively mandated policy that denies foreign aid to states engaged "in a consistent pattern of gross violations of internationally recognized human rights." And, most evidence says that human rights worldwide have not been improved by this policy, for several reasons. Strategic considerations have interfered with consistently applying the policy, and target states have resisted interference in matters that they believe to be their domestic affairs.[74] Thus, in the 1980s, the U.S. government was prepared to impose sanctions on the Sandinista government in Nicaragua and the communist regime in Cuba but was disinclined to take strong action against anticommunist regimes in El Salvador and Honduras.

Governments have also tried to employ economic sanctions against offending states. Again, the overall record is mixed. Sanctions against the white minority government in Rhodesia (later Zimbabwe) ultimately were influential in bringing about majority rule, and sanctions against South Africa did encourage reform of the political system in that country. And tightened sanctions against Haiti in 1993 influenced that country's military regime to make concessions toward restoring democracy in their country though the Haitian army repudiated these concessions in October 1993. In many places, though, sanctions have had little effect. United States sanctions against the People's Republic of China over massacring prodemocracy demonstrators in Tiananmen Square or against the Iraqi and Serbian governments were blunted by intransigent targets. In sum, many governments are unwilling to pay a high political price to promote human rights and are reluctant to expend foreign-policy capital to pursue this goal.

Conclusion

We have described how global human rights have evolved and assessed the state of these rights in contemporary world politics. As we repeatedly observed, human rights in much of the world today remain precarious. Civil and political (negative) rights and social and economic (positive) rights are not widely respected. The reasons are rooted in political, economic, and cultural differences within and across political actors. Impediments to improvements in human-rights conditions remain formidable. Although in recent decades sensitivity has been greater toward individuals' rights in the international community and in some states, overall improvement in global human rights is disappointing.

[74]See James M. McCormick and Neil J. Mitchell, "Human Rights and Foreign Assistance: An Update," *Social Science Quarterly*, 70 (December 1989), pp. 969–979. United States aid decisions have sometimes been effective. The Carter administration's cutting off aid to the Somoza regime in Nicaragua reduced that regime's ability to survive, but human rights may not have greatly improved after the regime collapsed and was succeeded by the Sandinistas. The Bush administration's decision to cut off aid to Kenya over human-rights violations had more positive results.

With the end of the Cold War and the birth of a new era in global politics, have prospects for global human rights become any brighter? On the surface, the answer appears to be a cautious yes. With more democratic states presumably committed to human rights and with ever more government and nongovernmental agencies attending to human rights, future prospects should be good. Indeed, global sensitivity to the issue has never seemed greater. Human rights occupy a higher place on the U.S. agenda since the election of President Clinton. Indeed, in a major shift from Reagan and Bush policies, the U.S. government proposed appointing a U.N. High Commissioner for Human Rights and a special envoy to monitor abuses against women, and these matters were debated at a U.N. Conference on Human Rights in Vienna in June 1993.[75]

On the other hand, we should remain guarded in our conclusions for several reasons. First, governments remain primarily responsible for addressing the human-rights issue, and they continue to resist external pressure, especially pressure that would limit their domestic freedom of action. Nowhere was this more apparent than in the resistance of the Haitian military to the entry of U.N. observers in late 1993. Second, despite expansion in global human-rights institutions, their influence is still mostly limited to moral suasion, and they have little enforcement capability. That instrument, unfortunately, is relatively weak for persuading offending governments to alter their behavior. Third, even with new democracies in Europe, Latin America, and Asia, sustaining protection for human rights remains a tough problem for new regimes confronting immense economic and political difficulties. Finally, the end of the Cold War released powerful national and ethnic feelings that lead to human-rights violations.

Key Terms

genocide
human rights
ethnic cleansing
natural law
cultural relativism
death squads
negative rights
positive rights
International Bill of Human Rights
Nuremberg
Amnesty International (AI)
terrorism
infant mortality rate

human development index
narcotraficantes
totalitarian regime
authoritarian regime
political asylum
economic sanctions
Universal Declaration of Human Rights
International Covenant on Civil and Political Rights
International Covenant on Economic, Social, and Cultural Rights

[75]Steven A. Holmes, "Clinton Reverses Policies in U.N. on Rights Issues," *The New York Times*, May 9, 1993, p. 1.

CHAPTER SEVENTEEN

Solving the Puzzle:
Some Alternate Futures

Even as you read this book the time machine has continued to accelerate. For example, Americans, so used to worrying about Japanese economic competition, probably still do not know that China's economy is now as large as Japan's. Amid change so rapid we find it difficult to make sense of the world around us; the impression is ever-greater complexity. Then too, the past, present, and future are more tightly bound than ever before. From day to day our ancestors could expect that the society into which they were born—its technology, ethics, and modes of behavior—would remain more or less intact. As they grew older, they would notice gradual changes (about which they might complain because "things were better in the old days"), but the contours of life as they knew it in their youth would still be recognizable. We cannot do as they did. Accelerated change has telescoped the future, and each of us will experience not one but several generation gaps as the years pass.

Thinking About the Future

So great a change means we need to alter the lens through which we view the world. Does it make sense to use the same tools for interpreting events as Machiavelli or Thucydides did? In this "modern" world, persons, things, and ideas speed across frontiers; populations are more and more literate and urban; "security" and "insecurity" have so drastically altered their meaning that one prominent scholar declares we are entering an era of "*postinternational politics*," a phrase he likes "because it suggests flux and transition" and "allows for chaos."[1] Boundaries between domestic and global politics are falling, and security means more than safety from military attack.

National and *global* security are coming closer in meaning because "in a complex interconnected society *the conditions* of happiness for the mass of the people . . . involve a high degree of collective action. . . . "[2] Just as most individuals cannot by their own striving meet their needs for food, shelter, health, and old age, as their agrarian ancestors did in "simpler" times, individual states cannot shield their citizens from all threats, nor can they cope with emerging issues. But if they behave parochially and independently, states can only impede those equipped to confront grand challenges. As individuals diversify and specialize their occupation and role in society, the world mirrors them and we have global specialization. The fates of people everywhere have become linked. At the same time, though, the demands citizens make on society multiply, and they no longer meekly accept the status and destiny that come with birth.[3] Expanding claims tax national and international institutions, pressuring them to change the ways in which they operate. We are probably less secure in our collective existence than in earlier epochs, when our survival depended on our own exertion and imagination.

People now depend for prosperity and health on decisions arrived at far beyond their state frontiers. They are also enmeshed in global networks either as employees or as purchasers of goods and services. The trade in narcotics illustrates both that these networks are transnational and how futile it is for states to go it alone. Latin American peasants grow coca (for cocaine) because of the significant global demand for their product, and they will not cease doing so until they find an equally profitable substitute. If the supply of cocaine reaching the United States from one or another of these countries is reduced, street prices go up in U.S. cities, crime increases as users seek more money, and other countries find it profitable to get into the narcotics industry. Thus, America's *war on drugs* is doomed to fail until global solutions are found and enforced.

The tidy world of states pursuing narrow national interests was never an accurate depiction of reality. It is a dangerous image if people act as if it were real. More than national interest and power politics will be needed to fix such problems as the disease AIDS. Like ecological catastrophe, disease does not respect national frontiers. As of early 1992, almost 13 million people had been infected by the AIDS virus, of whom about 2.5 million had died.[4] By the year 2000, AIDS will infect between 40 and 110

[1]James N. Rosenau, "Global Changes and Theoretical Challenges: Toward a Postinternational Politics for the 1990s," in Ernst-Otto Czempiel and James N. Rosenau, eds., *Global Changes and Theoretical Challenges: Approaches to World Politics for the 1990s* (Lexington, Mass.: Lexington Books, 1989), p. 3.

[2]Daniel Bell, "The Study of the Future," *The Public Interest* 1 (Fall 1965), p. 120. Emphasis in original.

[3]Modern citizens enjoy many advantages that were unavailable to their ancestors, but their expectations have risen even faster. As a result, their *relative* satisfaction may decline even as their absolute well-being grows.

[4]Lawrence K. Altman, "Researchers Report Much Grimmer AIDS Outlook," *The New York Times*, June 4, 1992, pp. A1, A8.

million people worldwide. Nothing has been found to halt its spread. Sub-Saharan African societies are a shambles, with 6.5 million people infected by the virus that causes AIDS. Now exploding into Southeast Asia and Latin America, the disease is infecting women as well as men. *Between 1992 and 1995, more new infections will occur than in the entire previous history of the disease.* And still, few countries or their leaders are prepared even to speak publicly about the problem. Issues like this demonstrate that barriers between the international and domestic arenas are tumbling.

Even as the threat of nuclear war between the superpowers recedes, new conflicts are erupting over ethnicity and race. The species as a whole is threatened by environmental catastrophes, and environmental pressures will incite more conflicts—the so-called *green wars*. Growing scarcities of resources like water and fertile soil steer societies toward collisions that they can avert only by collaborating. Because of intense nationalism and larger segments of societies taking part in politics, political elites throughout the world find themselves forced into critical foreign-policy decisions as they respond to local pressures. At the very moment when critical issues demand global attention, coordination, and planning, actors continue trying to satisfy parochial constituencies and assess their well-being *relative to others*. If everyone fares poorly, though, what does it matter that some fare less poorly than others?

The "New World Order" or, Will We Miss the Cold War?

On May 6, 1992, in a speech at Westminster College in Missouri, where Winston Churchill had delivered his iron-curtain address four decades earlier, Mikhail Gorbachev declared, "[W]e live today in a watershed era. One epoch has ended and a second is commencing. No one yet knows how concrete it will be—no one."[5] His uncertainty suggests a more general doubt about the future. As in 1945, old expectations, rules, and norms have disappeared, and we do not yet know what the new ones will look like. Will coming global politics be more or less peaceful than the years of Cold War? Let us look briefly at two post–Cold War scenarios—one optimistic, the other pessimistic.

A Brighter Future

Optimists see the Cold War's passing as an opportunity to break out of power politics. They believe new issues will be unlike those of the past and that we can and must escape from the trap of the state and confront mushrooming global problems. Communism and the Soviet Union have failed; and unprecedented arms-control agreements have been

[5]"Gorbachev's Talk: Building on the Past," *The New York Times*, May 7, 1992, p. A6. President George Bush coined the phrase *"new world order"* to describe the world after the Cold War.

concluded between East and West, shrinking the specter of nuclear war and giving all a chance to reduce tensions worldwide. Conditions are now ripe to reduce still more national nuclear arsenals and to stop nuclear weapons from spreading as well.

Optimists point out that with no more Cold War to worry about, regional disputes have slackened in the Middle East, Central America, southern Africa, and Asia. After Saddam Hussein was defeated, unprecedented peace talks began among Arabs, Israelis, and Palestinians. In Africa, conflicts in Ethiopia and Mozambique came to an end; Namibia achieved independence; and the racial-discrimination system in South Africa began to crumble. In Asia, the Soviets ended their occupation of Afghanistan in 1988, and by the early 1990s, efforts were under way to form a coalition government. In 1989, Vietnamese troops left Cambodia, and shortly thereafter a U.N.-brokered agreement ended the civil war in that country and supervised the freest elections in that country's history. Even in Central America, which captured so much American attention in the 1980s, negotiated settlements ended conflicts in El Salvador and Nicaragua.

Optimists believe that these events have produced the conditions for unheard-of global political and economic cooperation. The United Nations found it could take decisive action against Iraq after that country invaded Kuwait, bring humanitarian aid to Somalia, and bring about elections in Cambodia. These are products of cooperation such as the sanguine envision. Reforming the United Nations to make it more efficient and effective, also suggests a new era of cooperation. Yet another sign of interstate collaboration is that regional economic organizations are expanding and new ones are forming. Leading this trend is the European Community, developing and expanding despite setbacks. With the Single Market Act (1985), the EC committed itself to create a "single market," with no barriers to trade. In December 1991, the EC seemed willing to go even further toward economic and political union, with a common currency, a central bank and common foreign and defense policies by the end of the decade.[6] Several additional countries (Norway, Sweden, Finland, and Austria) applied for admission to the EC, and some of the newly democratic Eastern European states gained associate membership.

Elsewhere, similar crusades were under way. Sparked by the U.S.–Canadian Free Trade Agreement, a North American Free Trade Area (NAFTA) with Mexico was negotiated, and it will have potential for further expansion. A "Southern Common Market" has been initiated among Argentina, Brazil, Paraguay, and Uruguay, and this union has sought cooperation with the United States. In Asia, the Association of Southeast Asian Nations (ASEAN) has expanded its economic cooperation to the political and military sphere. A new East Asian organization, the Asia-Pacific Economic Community (APEC), has also been forged in recent years. It seeks more liberal trade between Asia and the United States and continues to add members, including Hong Kong, Taiwan, and China.[7]

[6]Alan Riding, "Europeans Agree on a Pact Forging New Political Ties and Integrating Economies," *The New York Times*, December 11, 1991, pp. 1A and A10.

[7]James A. Baker, III, "America in Asia: Emerging Architecture for a Pacific Community," *Foreign Affairs* 70:5 (Winter 1991/92), p. 6. At present growth rates, the combined economies of

For optimists, this extending web of economic interdependence and cooperation means that nationalism and resort to force are increasingly irrelevant. Are the optimists on to something, or are they merely a new generation of idealists? The signs are mixed.

A Darker Future

Another scenario takes a less sanguine view of the future. In the *pessimists'* eyes, the dead Cold War portends rebirth for traditional power-politics issues and conflicting nationalisms. One doomsayer calls the Cold War something that "we will soon miss."[8] The U.S.–Soviet nuclear stalemate and the bipolar distribution of power, had made a "long peace" and provided order and stability for forty years. With that competition over, pessimists believe, world politics will return to a multipolar, conflict-prone world, reminiscent of the early twentieth century. It will then be a more dangerous place because nuclear weapons will be available to more and more actors.

The pessimists believe the spread of nuclear weapons was slowed because of U.S.– Soviet efforts. Without those restraints, nuclear weapons are more likely, not less likely to spread. Several actors in Europe and Asia (including Germany and Japan) can build nuclear weapons if they wish, and Third-World actors — Pakistan, Iraq, Syria, India, Iran, South Africa, Brazil — could quickly acquire or assemble nuclear weapons and effective delivery systems. Perhaps the most worrisome omen was North Korea's March 1993 announcement that it was withdrawing from the Nuclear Non-Proliferation Treaty rather than permit International Atomic Energy Agency inspectors to determine whether the country was producing weapons-grade plutonium in violation of the treaty.[9] In the late 1970s, the United States cooperated to prevent South Korea from acquiring nuclear weapons; at that time, the Soviet Union would probably have done the same with North Korea.

A second consequence of ending the Cold War (according to the pessimists) is that long-repressed ethnic and nationalist enmities were now unleashed. The most compelling evidence for this disastrous change has been ethnic violence in the former Yugoslavia and Soviet Union. The former Yugoslav army, mostly Serbs, sought to stop Slovenia, Croatia, and Bosnia-Herzegovina from declaring independence[10] and thereafter set out to expand

China, Hong Kong, and Taiwan will be larger than the U.S. economy by the twenty-first century. Steven Greenhouse, "New Tally of World's Economies Catapults China into Third Place," *The New York Times*, May 20, 1993, pp. A1, A6.

[8]The following pages draw upon John J. Mearsheimer, "Why We Will Soon Miss the Cold War," *The Atlantic Monthly* 266 (August 1990), pp. 35 ff. Also see his "Disorder Restored," in Graham Allison and Gregory F. Treverton, eds., *Rethinking America's Security* (New York: W. W. Norton, 1992), pp. 213–237.

[9]David E. Sanger, "North Korea Knew of West's Evidence on Atomic Program," *The New York Times*, March 13, 1993, pp. 1, 3; and David E. Sanger, "The Nonproliferation Treaty Bares Its Toothlessness," *The New York Times*, March 14, 1993, Section 4, p. 18.

[10]John F. Burns, "Confirming Split, Last 2 Republics Proclaim a Small New Yugoslavia," *The New York Times*, April 28, 1992, pp. A1 and A4. Yugoslavia has shrunk from six (Serbia, Montenegro, Slovenia, Croatia, Bosnia-Herzegovina, and Macedonia) to two republics (Serbia and Montenegro).

As this cartoon suggests, one of the major concerns of the post–Cold-War era is horizontal nuclear proliferation. One potential source of such proliferation is Russian sale of nuclear technology for desperately needed hard currency.

Serbian territory. Fierce fighting broke out in Croatia between Croats and the Serb minority in the Krajina region of that republic. The Yugoslav army joined the Serbs, and the war continued until ethnic Serbian areas had been wrested from Croatian control.[11] Savage ethnic violence also erupted among the Croats, Muslim Slavs, and Serbs in Bosnia. The European Community and the United Nations could not end the communal violence, and Bosnian Serbs resorted to the appalling policy of ethnic cleansing (forcibly removing non-Serbians from their homes and land). The dismemberment of Bosnia was not reversed, and the United Nations did not even succeed in creating genuine havens for Muslim survivors of the carnage.

Bloody clashes also broke out among ethnic and tribal groups in the former Soviet republics and the newly noncommunist Eastern European countries. In the Caucasus, Armenia and Azerbaijan went to war over the tiny area of Nagorno-Karabakh, which is inhabited mainly by Armenians but is within Azerbaijan. Azerbaijan itself was the scene of

[11]Serbian–Croatian hostility is not new. During World War II, a fascist republic was set up in Croatia, and both communities committed atrocities against each other.

coups and countercoups, and a secessionist movement in the isolated region of Nakhich-evan. Next door, Georgia was struggling to put down a secessionist movement in Abkhazia. In Tajikistan, the new government had to impose restrictions on Muslim activists seeking greater independence, and virtual civil war pitted former communists against Muslim fundamentalists. The Crimea, mostly inhabited by ethnic Russians, sought independence from Ukraine. Slavic separatists challenged the government of Moldova, a new country largely inhabited by ethnic Romanians. Civil War gripped Georgia, and tension was great between ethnic Russians and majority populations in the Baltic states of Latvia, Lithuania, and Estonia.

Ancient ethnic rivalries also menaced Eastern Europe. Hungary might again seek to protect ethnic Hungarians in Romania and Slovakia, and Moldovans might seek reunion with Romania. Economic and political differences severed Czechoslovakia and forced Czechoslovakia's popular poet-president, Vaclav Havel, to resign.[12] Turkey and Bulgaria might clash over ethnic Turks expelled from Bulgaria, and Bulgaria and Greece, with Macedonian minorities and unsatisfied territorial claims, eyed with suspicion newly independent Macedonia. Albanians, Serbs, Turks, and Greeks might find themselves in conflict if Serbia dealt with the Albanian majority in the "autonomous province" of Kosovo as ruthlessly as it did with Muslims in Bosnia.[13] Even Poles and Germans could clash over their nationals in the other's country and over the border between the two countries that was imposed by the U.S.S.R. after 1945.

Ethnic and religious strife also darkened the Middle East, India, and Africa. Afghanistan was breaking up into three ethnic regions—one in the north with Uzbeks and Tajiks, a second in the south around Kabul with Pathans, and a third in the west controlled by Afghans and with close ties to Iran.[14] Palestinians confronted Jews, Indian Hindus and Muslims were at each other's throats, Arabs and Kurds fought each other, and Shi'ite and Sunni Muslims continued to do battle in the Middle East. Tribal and clan conflicts were endemic in Africa, where Xhosa and Zulu killings in South Africa and Luo-Kikuyo tensions in Kenya seemed omens of a grim future.

Unlike the optimists, then, the pessimists believe virulent nationalism is alive and well and foresee a disorderly post–Cold War world of endemic regional conflict. And, if such nationalism continues unchecked, U.S. Secretary of State Warren Christopher says, "We'll have 5,000 countries rather than the hundred plus we now have."[15] Table 17.1 summarizes some of the most critical ethnic, religious, and national tensions and conflicts confronting the global system.

[12]The Czechoslovak Republic was born in 1918 in the ruins of the Austro-Hungarian Empire and officially died January 1, 1993. Thereafter, Havel became President of the Czech Republic.

[13]Kosovo is a part of Yugoslavia. More than three-quarters of its inhabitants Albanian, and the region is tightly controlled by Serbia. Episodic rioting by Albanians went on from 1989, and some feared that the Serbians might try to pursue ethnic cleansing in Kosovo.

[14]Edward A. Gargan, "Afghanistan, Always Riven, Is Breaking into Ethnic Parts," *The New York Times*, January 17, 1993, pp. 1, 6.

[15]Cited in David Binder with Barbara Crossette, "As Ethnic Wars Multiply, U.S. Strives for a Policy," *The New York Times*, February 7, 1993, p. 1.

TABLE 17.1

Major Ethnic, National, and Religious Tensions

Country	Main adversaries
Afghanistan	Pathan and Tajik
Belgium	Walloon and Flemish
Bosnia	Serb, Croat, and Bosnian Muslim
Burma	Burman, Karen, and Shan
Burundi	Tutsi and Hutu
Cambodia	Khmer and Vietnamese
Canada	French and English
China	Chinese and Tibetan
China (Taiwan)	Chinese and native Taiwanese
Cyprus	Greek and Turk
Djibouti	Afar and Issa
Egypt	Christian Copt and Muslim
El Salvador	Mestizo and Indian
Ethiopia	Amhara, Tigrai, and Eritrean
France	French, Corsican, Algerian and Breton
Germany	German and Turk
Guatemala	Ladino and Indian
Guinea	Fulani and Mandingo
Guyana	East Indian and Black
Hungary	Hungarian, Romanian, Slovak, and Gypsy
India	Hindu, Muslim, and Sikh
Indonesia	Indonesian and Chinese
Iran	Persian, Kurd, and Turk
Iraq	Sunni Muslim, Shi'ite Muslim, and Kurd
Israel	Jew and Arab
Jordan	Arab and Palestinian
Kenya	Kikuyu, Luo, and Masai
Kuwait	Arab and Palestinian
Lebanon	Sunni Muslim, Shi'ite Muslim, Maronite Christian, and Palestinian
Liberia	Bassa, Bella, Gbandi, Krahn, Mandingo, Mano, and Mende
Malaysia	Malay and Chinese
Mauritania	Arab, Toucouleur, Fulani, Sarakole and Wolof
Namibia	European, Ovambo, Kavango, Herero, Nama

TABLE 17.1 (contd.)

Country	Main adversaries
Nicaragua	White, Mestizo, Black, Indians
Nigeria	Hausa, Ibo, and Yoruba
Peru	White and Indians
Philippines	Catholic and Moro Muslim
Romania	Romanian, Hungarian, German, and Gypsy
Rwanda	Tutsi and Hutu
Sierra Leone	Mende and Temne
Singapore	Chinese, Malay, and Tamil
Slovakia	Slovak, Hungarian, Gypsy
South Africa	Afrikaner, British, Xhosa, Zulu, Sotho and East Indians
Spain	Spanish, Basque, and Catalonian
Sri Lanka	Sinhales and Tamil
Sudan	Muslim Arabs and Christian or animist Black
Thailand	Thai and Chinese
Trinidad and Tobago	East Indian and Black
Turkey	Turk and Kurd
United Kingdom	Irish Catholic and Irish Protestant
United States	White, Black, and Hispanic
Vietnam	Vietnamese and Chinese
Zimbabwe	Shona, Ndebele, European, and East Indian

One consequence of civil strife has been an explosion in the world's refugee population—from about 4.6 million in the early 1970s to nearly 15 million in 1989[16] and more than 18.9 million in 1993.[17] More than 6 million Afghans alone were displaced by the war that raged in that country after 1979. The heaviest refugee burden was in South Asia, Africa, and the Middle East. Strife in the former Yugoslavia and the broken-up Soviet Union added heavily to the refugee burden in Europe as well. Figure 17.1 summarizes the growing global burden imposed by the flood of refugees.

[16]"Voting with Their Feet, Their Trabants, and Their Oars," *The Economist*, December 23, 1989, pp. 17–19.

[17]*The Wall Street Journal*, April 23, 1993, p. A1, and *The New York Times*, June 20, 1993, Section 1, p. 3.

FIGURE 17.1

A Growing Tide of Refugees

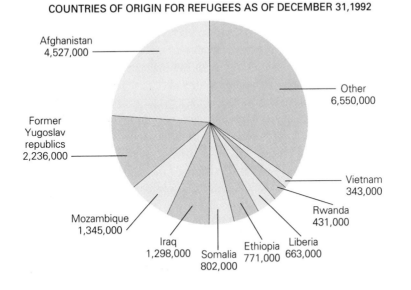

COUNTRIES OF ORIGIN FOR REFUGEES AS OF DECEMBER 31, 1992

Afghanistan 4,527,000

Other 6,550,000

Former Yugoslav republics 2,236,000

Vietnam 343,000

Rwanda 431,000

Mozambique 1,345,000

Iraq 1,298,000

Somalia 802,000

Ethiopia 771,000

Liberia 663,000

NUMBER OF REFUGEES WORLDWIDE

The tide of refugees has grown in the 1990s, as people seek to flee savage civil strife.

Civil conflicts threaten to break down order and basic services in a host of countries. Two observers write, "From Haiti in the Western Hemisphere to the remnants of Yugoslavia in Europe, from Somalia, Sudan, and Liberia in Africa, to Cambodia in Southeast Asia, a disturbing new phenomenon is emerging: the failed nation-state, utterly incapable of sustaining itself as a member of the international community."[18] And the end of the Cold War may have exacerbated this phenomenon because it also ended competitive economic and military assistance from the rival superpowers, reduced public willingness in the economically developed areas to become embroiled in foreign adventures and spend scarce resources to prop up corrupt regimes.

The pessimists also foresee economic conflict, not cooperation. Trying for economic integration and creating larger economic groupings, they believe, will inflame rather than extinguish economic rivalry. Although members may initially cooperate, eventually they will become rivals because some will be perceived as gaining more than others from free trade. Several regional economic organizations have already taken this path, and their experience may be more relevant to the future than that of the EC. The East African Common Market, established in 1963 among Kenya, Tanzania, and Uganda, initially enjoyed economic success, but Kenya's relatively greater gains, combined with ideological differences, soon undermined the grouping. The Central American Common Market, composed of Guatemala, El Salvador, Honduras, Costa Rica, and Nicaragua, met much the same fate after making economic progress at first. The "soccer war," a conflict that broke out between El Salvador and Honduras some years ago after a soccer game, reflected economic and population tensions. Economic transactions may breed economic and political conflict rather than harmony.

And, at the same time as economic institutions and regimes prove weak, economic conflicts among the European Community, Japan, and North America may also intensify. John Mearsheimer says, "Interdependence . . . is as likely to lead to conflict as cooperation, because states will struggle to escape the vulnerability that interdependence creates."[19]

Conclusion

We have no grounds for assuming that global politics will yield better outcomes in the future than in the past. Naive optimism is as out of place as paralytic pessimism. Changes in global politics brought about by factors like technological innovation do not necessarily improve our lot. If every problem has a solution, every solution creates new problems. Thus, as medical science overcomes old diseases, it accelerates population growth, intensifying pressure on the environment. As nuclear power reduces energy costs, it produces serious environmental risks. Policies that were intended to improve our lives will always have *unintended consequences*, and trends that seem to promise a

[18]Gerald B. Helman and Steven R. Ratner, "Saving Failed States," *Foreign Policy*, No. 89 (Winter 1992–93), p. 3. For an eloquent discussion of the havoc caused by ethnic conflict in contemporary global politics, see Daniel Patrick Moynihan, *Pandaemonium: Ethnicity in International Politics* (New York: Oxford University Press, 1993). See also Paul Johnson, "Colonialism's Back — and Not a Moment Too Soon," *The New York Times Magazine*, April 18, 1993, pp. 22, 43, 44, for a provocative analysis of why many states are unable to govern themselves.

[19]Mearsheimer, "Why We Will Soon Miss the Cold War," p. 45.

brighter future may in combination throw up unanticipated dilemmas. Hence, growing economic productivity improves standards of living but generates more waste and exhausts finite natural resources.

As change accelerates, the world becomes in many ways a more dangerous place. The great mathematician-philosopher Alfred North Whitehead wrote, "It is the business of the future to be dangerous. . . . "[20] The faster change moves, the more difficulty leaders have in understanding its implications and grappling with it effectively. In the best of times, policy makers have short time horizons. Busy coping with the crises of the instant, they are thinking about what they can accomplish in the few years they will be in office. They guess, follow their political instincts, and use shallow analogies to past events when they lack information or when (more often), they are overwhelmed by information but have no way of sifting the important from all the rest. The short-run and long-run imperatives have always collided, but that collision's cost is growing ominously. Of course leaders have blundered in the past. It is sobering to recall the *"law of gambler's ruin,"* as Karl Deutsch describes it:

> If one looks over the major decisions about initiating war . . . the probability of a major decision being realistic may well have been less than one-half, on the average. That is to say, if in the last half-century statesmen made major decisions on matters of war and peace, the chances were better than even that the particular decision was wrong.[21]

Key Terms

postinternational politics	pessimists
green wars	unintended consequences
new world order	law of gambler's ruin
optimists	war on drugs

[20] Alfred North Whitehead, *Science and the Modern World* (New York: Macmillan, 1929), p. 298.
[21] Karl W. Deutsch, "The Future of World Politics," *Political Quarterly* 13 (January–March 1966), p. 13.

GLOSSARY

Acid rain: Precipitation made acidic by sulfur dioxide and nitrogen oxides produced by industry, automobiles, and power plants. Acid rain and snow devastate forests and acidify lakes and streams, leaving them uninhabitable for fish.

Acquired immune deficiency syndrome (AIDS): A fatal disease involving the destruction of the body's immune system that is spread mainly by sexual contact or injection with infected blood.

ACP countries: A group of less-developed countries in Africa, the Caribbean, and the Pacific region that enjoy preferential trade and other links to the European Community.

Action-reaction model: A simplified view of foreign policy focused on states' actions toward others and the reactions that are elicited. Sometimes called the *stimulus-response model.*

Actors in global politics: Individuals or groups who seek to enhance their value satisfaction by participating directly in global politics.

Adjudication: A legal procedure by which a third party tries to resolve conflict between adversaries by making a binding decision.

Affective approach: Analyzing leaders' perceptual distortions caused by emotions such as insecurity and hostility.

African National Congress: The leading black organization in the struggle against the white government in South Africa. Under Nelson Mandela's leadership, the ANC is the core of a racially mixed South African government.

Aid burden: The foreign aid that a donor state provides as a percentage of its gross national product.

Alliances: Groupings of actors who pool their resources and coordinate their policies.

Amniocentesis: A surgical procedure applied in diagnosing genetic defects of a fetus in the womb.

Analogies from the past: The propensity of leaders reacting to crisis but having no information to draw comparisons between historical and present events.

Anarchy: In global politics, the absence of central government. Widely considered a source and cause of conflict.

Anomaly: Deviation from common expectations, rules, or types. Outcome that an observer, from contemporary knowledge, did not expect.

Anti-Semitism: Prejudice against Jews.

Apartheid: The racial-separation policy followed in South Africa until the early 1990s.

Apparatchik: Rank-and-file member of the Soviet Communist Party.

Appeasement: A policy designed to satisfy a potential belligerent by making concessions. Policies so labeled acquired a pejorative meaning by association with the concessions Western leaders made to Hitler before World War II. See **Munich complex** and **Munich Conference**.

Arab League: An organization of twenty-two Arab states established in 1945 to strengthen political, cultural, economic, and social relations among members.

Arab modernizers: Arab leaders who seek to industrialize and secularize their societies. See **Arab traditionalists**.

Arab traditionalists: Arab leaders who seek to maintain traditional tribal political and social customs.

Arbitration: The hearing and determining given a dispute between adversaries by a third party whom they choose or agree to.

Arms control: Any approaches designed to regulate levels and types of arms in a manner that reduces adversaries' incentives to initiate war.

Arms race: Rivalry among actors trying to outdo each other in quantity or quality of their armaments.

Arrogance of power: The idea that power can pervert a democratic society, encouraging its leaders to act undemocratically, especially when national security is threatened.

Ashkenazim: Jews with origins in Eastern and Central Europe.

Association of Southeast Asian Nations (ASEAN): A grouping of six countries in Southeast Asia established in 1967 to accelerate economic growth, social progress, and cultural development in the region.

Atlantic Charter: The 1941 declaration of principles to guide postwar security that was agreed to by U.S. President Franklin D. Roosevelt and British Prime Minister Winston Churchill.

Atrocity: Savage and illegal act toward civilians or prisoners of war.

Attitudinal power: Power derived from an actor's ability to alter a target population's attitude by using legitimate authority, expertise, or charisma.

Authoritarianism: A political system in which individual freedom is subordinate to the power of the state, concentrated in one person or small group that is not accountable to the people.

Authority: Power that is regarded as legitimate and right.

Autonomy: An actor's ability to formulate and pursue its own goals.

Baker proposal: An initiative by Secretary of State James Baker to overcome the Third-World debt crisis by domestic economic reform and loans from private banks.

Balance of payments: A summary of a country's financial dealings with other countries, usually over a year, indicating whether more funds are leaving the country ("deficit") or entering ("surplus").

Balance-of-power theory: The belief that peace or stability or both are most secure under conditions in which power is more or less equally distributed among five or more actors. Under such conditions, it is believed that no one actor or group of actors can dominate the others because defensive alliances are formed and re-formed.

Balancer: Under a balance-of-power system, the role played by an actor that decisively throws its support to a defensive coalition. This role was often Great Britain's choice in the eighteenth and nineteenth centuries.

Balance of trade: The difference in value between a country's imports and exports. When exports are worth more than imports, the country has a *trade surplus;* when imports are worth more than exports, it has a *trade deficit.*

Balfour Declaration: A letter written in 1917 by British Foreign Secretary Arthur Balfour that formed the basis for a Jewish state in Palestine.

Bantustans: Politics within South Africa that were set up by the white South African government as "homelands" for the country's majority black (Bantu-speaking) population. The international community did not recognize these states as legitimate.

Barbarian: A label that the ancient Greeks and Chinese applied to those who did not speak their language and whom they considered uncivilized.

Bargaining power: Coercion applied to influence actors.

Bargaining reputation: The reputation actors have for standing behind or reneging on their commitments.

Beggar-thy-neighbor policies: Policies meant to alter a country's trade balance by devaluing its currency and raising barriers to imports from other countries.

Beliefs: Actors' convictions about the world around them and about what is right or wrong in that world.

Bhopal: A city in India that was the site of a deadly 1984 accident in which highly toxic chemicals were released into the atmosphere.

Bilateral foreign aid: Foreign assistance that one country provides directly to another.

Billiard-ball model: A metaphor depicting global politics as a game in which billiard balls (unitary states) collide with each other in a continuous sequence of action and reaction. The model disregards factors within the actors.

Biodiversity: Greatly varied flora and fauna in a habitat.

Bipolarity: A political system divided into two centers of power.

Black-boxing a state: Analyzing a state's foreign policy as though its internal setting had no influence on behavior.

Black-lung disease: A disease of the lungs caused by inhaling coal dust.

Blitzkrieg (*lightning war*)**:** An offensive strategy devised by Nazi Germany employing close cooperation between armored units and bombers.

Bluffing: A tactic meant to mislead by bold action.

Boat people: Refugees who seek to flee their homelands in small boats. Specifically, those fleeing Vietnam and Haiti.

Bolsheviks: Members of the radical majority in the Russian Social Democratic Party (1903–1917) and followers of Vladimir Lenin. The Bolsheviks carried out the communist revolution in Russia and formed the Communist Party of the Soviet Union (CPSU).

Bolt from the blue: A surprise attack.

Boundaries of a system: The demarcation between that part of a system which is within and that which lies outside it.

Bounded rationality: A definition of rationality recognizing that human limitations constrain a decision-maker's ability to select the best alternatives.

Brady Plan: A plan that U.S. Secretary of the Treasury Nicholas Brady put forward to resolve the debt crisis in the Third World by renegotiating or reducing overall debt burden of Third-World countries.

Bretton Woods system: The postwar agreement reached at Bretton Woods, New Hampshire, which shaped international monetary arrangements until 1973. The agreement led to establishment of the International Monetary Fund (IMF) and the World Bank (IBRD).

Brinksmanship: A sequence of threats and counterthreats with bluffing, at extreme risk of war.

Buffer zone: An area that separates two potentially hostile actors.

Bureaucracy: A hierarchically-organized body of officials and administrators.

Bureaucratic-politics model: An approach to the study of foreign policy focused on bargaining and compromises among governmental organizations and agencies pursuing their own interests.

Byzantine empire: The Eastern Roman Empire, its capital Constantinople, which lasted from A.D. 473 to 1453.

Camp David Accords: An agreement between Egypt and Israel, reached with help from U.S. President Jimmy Carter, by which Egypt recognized Israel, the Sinai Peninsula was restored to Egypt, and a peace treaty was signed between the two countries.

Capabilities: Resources available to actors that can be used to influence other actors.

Capacity of a state: A state's ability to tap and use its citizens' resources.

Capital-intensive industry: An industry, such as computers, which depends on infusions of capital investment to acquire, say, the technology necessary to be competitive.

Capital investment: The resources invested in products that are used to produce other products.

Capitalism: An economic system based on private ownership of property and the means of production and a free market that allows competition.

Capitalist encirclement: Soviet dictator Stalin's allegation that the West sought to destroy the Soviet Union by surrounding it with hostile capitalist states. Stalin used this claim to justify rapid military and economic growth and violation of individual liberties in the U.S.S.R.

Cartel: A group of producers that set out to limit competition among their members, often by restricting production to keep prices high.

Central American Common Market (CACM): A common market among five Central American states established in 1961.

Charisma: The quality that gives an individual influence over large numbers of people.

Chernobyl: The Ukrainian nuclear plant hit by a meltdown in 1986.

Chicken game: A game-theory relationship in which actors find themselves in a dangerous conflict spiral.

Chivalry: The combined qualities of gallantry, courtesy, and courage expected of medieval European knights.

City-state: An independent political entity consisting of a city and its outskirts that dominated international politics in ancient Greece and Renaissance Italy. Singapore is among the few contemporary examples.

Civil war: Organized violence among citizens within a society.

Class struggle: The Marxist–Leninist theory that history is a struggle between economic classes such as the proletariat and the bourgeoisie.

Cocom (coordinating committee): A Cold-War arrangement enabling the United States and its allies to review and limit trade in high technology with the U.S.S.R. and its allies.

Coercion: Negative incentives such as threats or punishment for generating influence.

Coercive diplomacy: Using force or threats of force to make an adversary cease doing something or undo something it has already done. See **Compellance**.

Cognitive approach: Analyzing how leaders' perceptions are distorted by ambiguous information.

Cognitive consistency: The balance between feelings about and attitudes toward a phenomenon and the information that is received about it. If feelings and information seem to contradict each other, the result is *cognitive dissonance*.

Cognitive trap: A belief or system of beliefs that is dangerous and dysfunctional.

Cold War: A period of intense conflict and competition short of open war between the United States and its allies and the Soviet Union and its allies that lasted from the mid-1940s until 1991.

Cold-War consensus: The general fear and loathing of communism and acceptance of the national-security burden in the United States that accompanied the Cold War.

Collective good: A benefit such as clean air and water or military security from which individuals cannot be selectively excluded. Beneficiaries may wish the good but have no incentive to pay for it.

Collective security: A security system designed after World War I under which any actor's aggression would be met by all other actors' combined might.

Collectivized agriculture: Centralized organization in the Soviet bloc of agricultural enterprises under government control or ownership.

Colonialism: Rule imposed on a country or region by another country, often from another region.

Common Agricultural Policy (CAP):   A European Community policy to maintain common, artificially high prices for local agricultural products by purchasing surpluses and placing tariffs on agricultural imports. The policy stimulates overproduction and the exporting of food surpluses with help from export subsidies. Such exports eat into traditional overseas markets of the United States and other agricultural exporting countries.

Commonwealth of Independent States (CIS):   A loosely federated political entity consisting of most republics from the former Soviet Union, established January 1, 1992.

Communism: A political and economic system prescribing government ownership and management of production and distribution and relying on central planning rather than markets to achieve economic goals.

Comparative advantage: The theory that every country can benefit from international trade if it concentrates on goods that it can produce less expensively than its trading partners.

Compatibility of goals: The degree to which the aims of actors in a system do not conflict.

Compellance: Thomas C. Schelling's name for the use of force or threats of force to make an adversary cease doing something or undo something it has already done. See **Coercive diplomacy**.

Compensation: Conciliating a potential adversary by providing it with gains equivalent to one's own.

Competitiveness: An actor's economic performance, especially its productivity and export, compared with that of other actors.

Complex-interdependence model: An approach to analyzing global politics that goes beyond the assumptions that territorial states are the only important actors, that conflict is the dominant characteristic in global relations, that actors must rely on self-help, and that anarchy is the dominant feature of the global system.

Compulsory jurisdiction: The right of a court or tribunal to administer justice over a specific set of individuals and groups or types of behavior.

Concept: A general idea about something formed by mentally combining all its features.

Concert of Europe: A security system formed after the Napoleonic Wars with regular conferences among Europe's great powers.

Conference on Security and Cooperation in Europe (CSCE):   A series of meetings initiated by the 1976 Helsinki Accords among NATO, the former Soviet bloc, and neutral European countries to build confidence among participants about their national security.

Confidence-building measures: Actions and agreements aimed at improving communication and trust between potential adversaries and reduce the possibility of misunderstandings and misperceptions that could lead to war.

Containment: A strategy George Kennan suggested to prevent Soviet expansionism by exerting counterpressure along Soviet borders.

Contract state: A state expending much money and manpower on defense. See **Garrison state**.

Contras: The name given U.S.-armed anticommunist rebels against the Sandinista government in Nicaragua during the 1980s.

Conventional weapons: Armaments other than nuclear, biological, and chemical weapons.

Correlates of War (COW) project: A major data-based research endeavor to describe and explain international war and its causes.

Costs of power: The tangible (such as budget and manpower) and intangible (such as time) costs associated with exercising power.

Council for Mutual Economic Assistance (Comecon): An international economic organization created in 1949 among Soviet-bloc members.

Counterforce strategy: A deterrence plan targeting an enemy's military forces and weapons systems.

Countervalue strategy: A deterrence scheme targeting an enemy's cities and industrial centers.

Credibility of deterrence: The degree to which others believe that an actor will carry out its deterrence threats.

Crisis: A situation threatening prized goals, imposing time constraints, and surprising decision-makers. A moment of danger, often at the second stage in an issue cycle, during which adversaries seek to determine the rules of the game.

Crisis of overproduction: A leading aspect in Vladimir Lenin's theory of imperialism, stating that capitalist economies produce more than citizens can afford to consume and so have to seek overseas markets.

Cruise missile: A pilotless plane with precision guidance that flies low to avoid radar and can carry either nuclear or conventional payloads.

Cult of the offensive: European belief before World War I that war could be won only by rapidly mobilizing armies and at once launching offensive operations.

Cultural imperialism: One culture imposing its tastes and norms on another.

Cultural relativism: The claim that ethical beliefs are different in different cultures so that there are few or no universal ethical principles.

Cultural sovereignty: A society's capacity to maintain its cultural traditions against "dilution" from overseas.

Currency convertibility: Interchangeability of one national currency into another or into gold. A country must have convertible currency to participate in international trade.

Currency stabilization: The effort to stabilize a currency's value relative to that of other currencies.

Cybernetic model: An approach to foreign policy focused on bureaucrats' attempt to control uncertainty by relying on simplified procedures, using limited information.

Death instinct: Psychologist Sigmund Freud's claim that human beings have an innate impulse toward destruction.

Death squad: A group that assassinates its political opponents.

Debt-commodity swaps: A strategy for dealing with international debt crisis under which commercial banks form companies to export the debtor's commodities, putting aside some of the profit for repaying debt.

Debt crisis: A prolonged financial crisis beginning in 1982 when it appeared that a number of Third-World states including Brazil might default on their loans.

Debt–equity swaps: A strategy for dealing with the international debt crisis under which debt owed to banks is traded for stock in the debtor's industries or loans are sold at a discount to transnational corporations.

Debt restructuring: Renegotiation between borrowers and lenders of a loan, usually to lengthen the repayment time or reduce interest rates.

Debt-service ratio: The ratio between the amount of interest and principal due on loans and export earnings.

Decision-making approach: An approach to foreign policy focusing on domestic factors, especially decision-makers and the setting and situations in which they find themselves. It is contrasted to the realist and unitary-actor models, which exclusively consider the external setting of states to explain foreign policy.

Declinist debate: A debate pitting those who believe the United States is a declining world power against those who believe such a decline is not occurring.

Defense of superior orders: Argument by those accused of war crimes or crimes against humanity that they were only following orders from military or political leaders.

Definition of the situation: A decision-maker's interpretation of a problem or an issue.

Deflationary macroeconomic policies: Programs designed to curb inflation, such as higher interest rates and lower government spending.

Deforestation: Massive loss of forests with environmental consequences such as reduced production of oxygen and extensive erosion of soil.

Democracy: A form of government in which political power is exercised by all the people or their elected surrogates.

Demonstration effect: The propensity of geographically separated individuals and groups to copy each other's behavior.

Dépendencia model: Approach claiming that the international economic system places less-developed countries at a disadvantage in dealing with developed countries and transnational corporations.

Détente: Relaxation of tensions between adversaries.

Deterrence: A strategy aimed at preventing an adversary from pursuing its aims by threatening to use military force in retaliation.

Diaspora: Scattering of the Jews to countries outside Palestine after the Babylonian captivity.

Dienbienphu: A decisive 1954 battle that led to the French withdrawal from Indochina.

Diplomacy: The art of conducting negotiations.

Disarmament: Agreements to reduce or eliminate weapons or categories of weapons. Such agreements arise from the assumption that possession of weapons is a cause of war.

Distribution of attitudes: The manner in which identities, expectations, beliefs, and goals are distributed among actors in a political system. This distribution predicts what is likely to take place within the system.

Distribution of influence: The distribution among actors in a system of a capacity to change the behavior of others.

Distribution of resources: Distribution within a system of factors that contribute to an actor's capability. This distribution predicts what is possible within a political system.

Divine right of kings: A doctrine, very popular in the eighteenth century, that kings rule by the grace of God and are accountable only to God for their acts.

Dollar convertibility: A commitment by the U.S. government until 1973 to exchange dollars for gold.

Domain of power: The persons or things over which an actor exerts influence.

Druses: A sect living in Lebanon, Israel, and Syria having a religious faith combining elements of Islam, Judaism, and Christianity.

Dual-track decision: The decision by NATO in 1979 to deploy intermediate-range nuclear missiles in Europe while trying to negotiate an INF arms-control agreement with the U.S.S.R.

Dynastic interests: Kings' interests in ensuring or improving the status of their families and heirs.

Economic nationalism: Theories about the international political economy stressing the need to reduce imports and increase exports using protectionist measures if necessary. Sometimes called *neomercantilism*. See **Mercantilism**.

Economic radicalism: Theories about international political economy, often from a Marxist perspective, holding that free trade and free markets perpetuate poverty and dependence in the Third World.

Economic sanctions: Efforts to exert influence on other actors by limiting or severing economic relations.

Ecoterrorism: Intentional destruction of the environment with the aim of terrorizing adversaries. The label was applied to the Iraqi forces' spilling of Kuwaiti oil into the Persian Gulf in January 1991.

Emergent property: Characteristic of a group of actors that is the unforeseen consequence of interaction among the actors.

Empirical theory: Knowledge that is derived from experiment and experience.

End of history: A phrase popularized by Francis Fukuyama to express his belief that the end of the Cold War marked the triumph of democratic liberalism around the world.

End-of-the-world game: An interaction that takes place only once and does not permit reciprocity.

Escalation: An upward spiral in level of conflict or violence.

Ethnic cleansing: A euphemism for the forced and brutal removal of members of one ethnic group from a city or region by members of another ethnic group. Applied to Serbians' and Croatians' campaign to remove each other and by both to clear areas of Bosnian Muslims during civil strife in the former Yugoslavia starting in 1992.

Ethnic group: A group of people of the same race or nationality who share a distinctive culture.

Ethnocentrism: Belief in the inherent superiority of one's group and tendency to evaluate other groups according to one's own.

Europe 1992: Commitment by the European Community to end all internal barriers to movement of goods, people, and services by the end of 1992.

European Coal and Steel Community (ECSC): An intergovernmental organization established in 1952 to ensure that Western Europe would have adequate supplies of coal and steel at a reasonable price.

European Commission: Executive organ of the European Community.

European Community (EC): A regional intergovernmental organization established in 1967 consisting of the European Economic Community (EEC), the European Atomic Energy Community (EUROATOM), and the European Coal and Steel Community (ECSC).

European Economic Community (EEC): A regional free market established in Western Europe in 1958.

European Free Trade Association (EFTA): A grouping of non-EEC states established in 1960 under British leadership to liberalize trade and counterbalance the EEC.

European Monetary System (EMS): Endeavor by European-Community members to stabilize the value of their currencies in relation to each other and the dollar.

Evil empire: Label applied by President Ronald Reagan in 1983 to the Soviet Union.

Exchange rate: The price of one currency compared to those of other currencies or gold.

Exchange-rate mechanism (ERM): An agreement among European-Community members to closely link the value of their currencies.

Expansionist macroeconomic policies: Policies designed to bring about economic growth and reduce unemployment, such as lower interest rates and higher government spending.

Expectations: The outcomes that actors in global politics anticipate.

Expected-utility theory: An approach to war predicated on the belief that leaders are rational and seek to maximize gains.

Expertise: Skills or knowledge that provide influence.

Export quota: An example of managed trade in which countries agree on amounts that can be exported from one to another.

Extended deterrence: The effort to deter an adversary from attacking one's allies.

External setting: Factors outside the state that influence foreign policy.

Extraterritoriality: One country's political rights over individuals or groups in another country.

Extroversion: Psychological proclivity to show interest in objects outside the self.

Fascism: An authoritarian political system headed by a dictator and based on aggressive nationalism and racism.

Feudalism: A social and economic system based on holding lands in fief or fee and on the resulting relations between superior (lord) and inferior (vassal).

Final solution: Nazi name for a plan to exterminate the Jews of Europe during World War II.

First-strike capability: A nuclear power's ability to launch an attack and successfully destroy an adversary's capability to retaliate.

First World: The wealthy industrialized countries, most of which are members of OECD.

Fission: The release of nuclear energy by splitting heavy atoms such as uranium. It is used in the atomic bomb.

Fixed exchange rates: Currency exchange rates that prevail when actors agree to maintain their relative value at established levels.

Flexible response: A NATO military doctrine instituted in the 1960s under which response to a military provocation would be adjusted to the level of the provocation and would change as necessary in response to an enemy's willingness to cease or escalate. Under the doctrine NATO would not use nuclear weapons in responding to the first stages of an enemy's conventional-weapons attack.

Floating exchange rates: Currency exchange rates that prevail when actors allow the market to determine their relative value.

Foreign direct investment: Purchase by citizens of other countries of property, stock, or other assets or provision of capital to start new enterprises.

Foreign policy: The sum of an actor's goals and purposive actions in global politics. In studying foreign policy we seek to explain and predict those goals and actions.

Fossil fuel: Fuel formed from organic remains, especially coal, petroleum, and natural gas.

Fourteen Points: The conditions outlined for the postwar world by President Woodrow Wilson in a 1918 speech. They included national self-determination, collective security, free trade, open diplomacy, and freedom of the seas.

Fourth World: The very poorest among the less-developed Third-World countries.

Free trade: Unrestricted movement of goods and services among actors in the international economic system.

Free World: Name applied by many in the West to countries allied against the Soviet Union during the Cold War. In fact, some of these countries were governed by authoritarian regimes.

French Revolution: The revolution in France that began in 1789, overthrew the Bourbon monarchy, roused French nationalism, and ended with Napoleon's assuming power in 1799.

Front-line states: Name applied to black states bordering South Africa and Arab states bordering Israel.

Frustration–aggression models: Theories that explain conflicts as caused by impediments in the path of human desires and inducing frustration that in turn causes aggression meant to eliminate those impediments.

Functionalism: A theory that conflict eventually can be eliminated if actors cooperate in dealing with relatively noncontroversial technical issues like health, communications, travel, and environmental protection. Functionalists believe that cooperative habits acquired in one area will spread to others and that functional international organizations will increasingly assume the responsibilities currently carried out by nation-states. See **Spillover** and **Neofunctionalism**.

Functional similarity: The degree to which the units in global politics are similar in the tasks they perform.

Fusion: Release of nuclear energy — radiation and high-speed neutrons — by fusing light atoms, especially hydrogen. Used in the hydrogen or thermonuclear bomb.

Game theory: A formal deductive approach to analyzing conflict by systematically enumerating players, capabilities, and alternative strategies and emphasizing the players' linked fates.

Garrison state: A state in which the military exercises undue influence and seeks to maintain international tension to preserve its status and privileges. See **Contract state.**

General Agreement on Tariffs and Trade (GATT): A U.N.-affiliated organization established in 1947–1948 as a forum for promoting international trade.

Genesis: The first stage in the issue cycle during which an issue is placed on the global agenda.

Geneva Conventions: A group of four legal agreements signed in 1949 to protect victims of war. The four deal with conditions of the wounded and sick, condition of those who are shipwrecked, treatment of prisoners of war, and protection of civilians.

Genocide: Deliberate or systematic extermination of a national or racial group.

Geopolitics: Study of the relationship between politics and geography.

Glasnost: Policy of openness initiated by Soviet President Mikhail Gorbachev.

Global agenda: Issues that attract the attention of major actors and to which those actors are prepared to devote resources.

Global norms: Behavior in global politics that significant actors consider appropriate.

Global system: The political system embracing actors worldwide among which a pattern of interaction is discernible.

Global warming: Warming of earth's climate caused by release of "greenhouse" gases trapping heat from earth that would otherwise escape into outer space. Also known as the *greenhouse effect.*

Goal: An outcome that actors in global politics seek.

Government: The group of persons and agencies that rule a state and act on its behalf.

Graduated reduction in tension (GRIT): A proposal meant to create trust by making unilateral concessions to the other side to elicit reciprocity.

Great Power: In the eighteenth century, the name for a European state that could not be conquered by the combined might of other European states. More recently applied to countries regarded as among the most powerful in the global system.

Greater East Asia Co-Prosperity Sphere: Japanese name for the areas they conquered in Asia between 1931 and the end of World War II.

Green war: A war fought over scarce resources such as fresh water.

Gross domestic product (GDP): A measure of a country's income that excludes foreign earnings. See **Gross national product.**

Gross national product (GNP): The monetary value of a country's total output of goods and services during one year.

Group of Seven (G-7): The world's seven leading industrialized states — Canada, France, Germany, Great Britain, Italy, Japan, and the United States — whose leaders meet annually at economic summit conferences.

Group of 77 (G-77): An alignment of the world's developing countries formed in 1964 to seek global redistribution of wealth from the wealthy countries. The original 77 members of the group have grown to more than 120.

Gulf Cooperation Council (GCC): Grouping of six Arabian Gulf states established in 1981 to enhance political and military cooperation among them.

Guest workers: Laborers who migrate from poor countries where unemployment is high, such as

Egypt and Turkey, to wealthier countries where unemployment is lower and wages are higher, such as Germany.

Hague Peace Conferences: International meetings held in 1899 and 1907 to promote peaceful methods of conflict resolution and limit the use of specified weapons. The conferences were precursors to the League of Nations.

Hard currency: A currency widely accepted, especially by private investors, which can be used to finance international trade. Such a currency is believed to be backed by a strong economy and is freely convertible.

Hard shell of impermeability: In the eighteenth century, the protection afforded inhabitants by the impenetrable frontiers of states.

Head-to-head competition: An international economic system in which different countries and regions seek the same industries, thereby threatening the economic status and security of each other's workers and producers.

Hegemon: A dominant state that uses its military and economic power to impose and maintain customs and rules aimed at preserving the current world order and its position in that order.

Hegemonic stability theory: A theory that a dominant state is necessary to enforce international cooperation and maintain international rules and regimes.

Hegemonic war: A war initiated by a hegemon to preserve its status or by a challenger seeking to overthrow the hegemon.

Helsinki Accords: An agreement reached in 1975 by the members of NATO, the Warsaw Pact, and a group of neutral European countries, meant to implement confidence-building measures, free flow of people and ideas, and increased economic and scientific cooperation.

Heterogeneous state: A state in which citizens are deeply cleaved by ethnicity, religion, language, or other differences.

Hierarchy: Units in global politics organized so that some are ranked above others.

High politics: War and peace issues that involve survival of the state.

Historical experience: Past relations among actors that affect their current behavior toward each other.

Holocaust: The murder of more than six million Jews in Europe by the Nazis during World War II.

Homogeneous state: A state with relatively few ethnic, religious, linguistic, or other cleavages among citizens.

Horizontal nuclear proliferation: An increase in the number of states or other actors that possess nuclear weapons.

Hot line: A system set up after the 1962 Cuban missile crisis to permit rapid communication between Soviet and American leaders.

Human Development Index (HDI): A summary index developed by the United Nations comparing countries by life expectancy, literacy, and income.

Human immunodeficiency virus (HIV): The viral infection that causes AIDS.

Human-nature theories: Theories about war and other behavior that start from a belief that such behavior is inherent in human beings and cannot be altered.

Human rights: The rights that individuals in all countries hold by virtue of their humanness.

Hyperinflation: Rapid rise in prices caused by a currency's declining value.

Idealism: Realists' name for a group of thinkers after World War I who believed in a basic harmony of interests among people making it possible to use reason to overcome war. Idealists, sometimes called *utopians*, advocated international law and organization and applying universal ethics to political issues. See **Legalistic-moralistic approach.**

Identities: The shared self-identifications or self-descriptions of peoples indicating how psychologically close they are.

Ideology: A closed system of closely linked concepts and theories purporting to offer a coherent and comprehensive explanation for reality.

Image: An individual's perception of reality that is influenced by experience and beliefs.

Imperialism: The policy of extending a country's rule over other countries. *Neoimperialism* connotes subtle forms of foreign influence such as control over exports or raw materials.

Imperial overextension or overstretch: A condition in which a country's overseas commitments exceed its ability to honor them.

Import quota: A nontariff barrier to free trade limiting the quantity of a product that is imported from other countries.

Import substitution: Encouraging domestic industries to produce goods that would otherwise have to be imported.

Incrementalism: A style of decision-making involving only small and discrete policy adjustments.

Individual-level analysis: An approach to understanding global politics focused on individuals as units of explanation.

Industrial policy: Joint planning by government and corporations to invest in and seek to export selected high-technology products.

Influence: See **Power**.

Inkatha: A conservative black organization in South Africa, mostly Zulu, and the main black opponent of the African National Congress.

Inquisition: A tribunal run by the Catholic Church in Spain from 1480 to 1834 that sought to combat and punish religious heresy.

Institutional deficiency: A weakness in international institutions such as absence of information or a framework of conventional law.

Intangible resources: Nonmaterial resources difficult to observe or measure that contribute to an actor's power.

Intellectual property rights: Ownership of ideas as reflected in patents. A contentious issue in the Uruguay Round of the GATT.

Intelligence community: The U.S. system of human and technical intelligence begun after World War II that includes the Central Intelligence Agency (CIA), National Security Agency (NSA), and the Defense Intelligence Agency (DIA), all led by a Director of Central Intelligence.

Interaction: Reciprocal behavior or influence between two or more actors.

Interdependence: A relationship in which two or more actors are sensitive and vulnerable to each other's behavior and in which actions taken by one affect the other.

Intergovernmental organization (IGO): An international organization consisting of representatives of sovereign states.

Intermediate-Range Nuclear Force (INF) Treaty: A 1987 agreement between United States and Soviet Union to remove intermediate-range nuclear weapons. The pathbreaking agreement was the first that entailed eliminating many nuclear weapons.

Internal setting: Factors within a state that influence foreign policy.

International Bank for Reconstruction and Development (IBRD): Sometimes known as the World Bank, the IBRD was established at Bretton Woods to offer loans to member countries at reasonable rates.

International Bill of Human Rights: Collective codification of global human rights in the Universal Declaration of Human Rights, the International Covenant on Civil and Political Rights, and the International Covenant on Economic, Social and Cultural Rights.

International Court of Justice (ICJ): A U.N. organ established to adjudicate disputes referred by member states and provide advisory opinions on legal questions to other U.N. organs. The I.C.J., often called the World Court, is the successor to the League of Nations Permanent Court of International Justice.

International Development Association (IDA): A specialized U.N. agency established in 1960 to provide development credits on special terms to less-developed states.

International Finance Corporation (IFC): A specialized U.N. agency established in 1956 to encourage private enterprise in less-developed states.

International Labor Organization (ILO): An early specialized U.N. agency responsible for improving conditions for workers.

International law: A body of principles and rules derived from custom and treaties commonly observed by global-community members in their dealings with each other.

International Monetary Fund (IMF): A U.N. agency established at Bretton Woods to provide a multilateral system of payments and help stabilize currency rates necessary for expanding international trade.

International nongovernmental organization (INGO): An organization whose members are individuals and private groups from more than one state.

International political economy (IPE): An approach to global politics emphasizing the close and reciprocal relationship between international economic factors such as ownership, trade, investment, and monetary policy and political factors and the political setting.

International regime: Rules, norms, and decision-making procedures that govern actors' behavior within an international area of activity.

Interstate relations: Global interactions that are initiated or sustained by nation-state governments.

Intifada: A popular, often violent Palestinian campaign against Israeli rule in the West Bank and Gaza between 1987 and 1993.

Iron curtain: A metaphor Winston Churchill coined in a 1946 speech to describe the line separating the Soviet sphere of interest from the "free" countries in Western Europe.

Islam: The religious faith of Muslims, as set forth in the Koran, which teaches that Allah is the only god and that Muhammad is his prophet.

Islamic fundamentalism: The belief by some Muslims that the tenets of Islam are the sole source of political authority.

Isolationism: A policy based on the belief that peace and security can be achieved best by avoiding alliances and other overseas commitments. The U.S. policy between 1919 and 1941.

Israeli–PLO Declaration of Principles: The September 1993 agreement reached by Israel and the PLO by which each recognized the other and by which self-rule was accorded Palestinians in the Gaza Strip and the West Bank.

Issue cycle: A cycle of four stages through which an issue passes between the time it is placed on the global agenda and the time it leaves that agenda.

Issues in global politics: Contentions among actors over proposals for distributing among them valued objects and ends.

Jackson–Vanik Amendment: A 1974 amendment to the U.S. trade act linking Soviet emigration policy to granting that country most-favored-nation trade status.

Janus face of foreign policy: The idea that foreign policy is produced by forces both within and outside of states. Janus was a two-faced Roman god.

Japan-bashing: Exaggerated attribution of economic woes to unfair Japanese trade practices.

Judaism: Religion of the Jews, based on the Old Testament.

Juridical statehood: The legal rather than empirical attributes of statehood.

Just-war doctrine: The belief that war may be initiated only for selected moral reasons and must be waged in an ethical manner.

Kellogg-Briand Pact (Pact of Paris): An international treaty signed in 1928 outlawing war as an instrument of national policy. The treaty is often cited as an example of "idealism."

Koran: The sacred text of Islam.

Kurds: Members of an Islamic people who live in areas of Turkey, Iraq, and Iran.

Labor-intensive industry: An industry, such as textiles, which depends on having plenty of cheap labor to compete.

La Marseillaise: The national anthem of France, written at the time of the French Revolution.

Land hunger: A country's condition when its land is inadequate to support its population.

La patrie: French word meaning "fatherland" and used in referring to the country after the French Revolution. Implied that France was owned by all its citizens, not merely the king and the aristocrats.

Lateral pressure: Stress or pressure that is directed sideways.

Law of gambler's ruin: A gambler who keeps betting double-or-nothing on the same outcome will ultimately lose all.

Leaders in mufti: National political leaders who are in their nation's military forces.

League of Nations: An intergovernmental organization established by the Versailles Treaty after World War I mainly to promote international peace and security.

League of Nations mandate: Colonial territories taken from Germany and Turkey after World War I, such as Palestine and Southwest Africa, and administered by the victors under supervision by the League of Nations.

Legalistic–moralistic approach: Another name for idealism. An approach emphasizing international law and morality as remedies for conflict.

L'état: French word meaning "state" used to refer to the country before the French Revolution.

Levée en masse: The general conscription introduced in France after the French Revolution.

Levels of analysis: The different perspectives from which to consider global politics. An observer may focus on "wholes" or "parts" of political systems.

Liberal economic theory: The belief that global prosperity can be achieved by establishing a free market and eliminating political impediments to the free movement of capital, goods, and labor.

Limited war: A war in which enemies avoid using specified weapons, try to limit civilian casualties, or restrict fighting to limited regions.

Limits-to-growth theory: A theoretical perspective on the global environment claiming that earth's ability to support life has inherent limits and that if any critical limits such as supplies of fresh water are reached large numbers of deaths will ensue.

Linked fate: The condition of individuals or actors whose futures and destinies are entwined.

Local-content requirement: The requirement that an imported product incorporate parts that are manufactured locally.

Long-cycle theory: A theoretical perspective focusing on the major influence exerted by the Great Powers' long-term rise and fall.

Low politics: Social and economic issues that do not seem to involve the state's survival.

Maastricht Treaty: An agreement signed by European Community (EC) leaders in December 1991 that outlined steps toward increased European political and economic unity.

Maginot Line: A zone of French fortifications built along the Franco-German frontier in the years preceding World War II.

Malthusian future: Thomas Malthus's grim prediction that unchecked population increases geometrically, outstripping subsistence, which increases arithmetically.

Managed trade: A policy to limit free trade by agreements among countries or export–import limits, goals, and quotas.

Manchukuo: A puppet state set up by Japan after it occupied Manchuria in 1931.

Maquiladora: American-owned enterprise established on the Mexican side of the U.S.-Mexico border with the aim of reducing production and labor costs.

Maronites: A Christian sect living in Lebanon.

Marshall Plan: A U.S. program of grants and loans conceived in 1947 to assist postwar Western European recovery.

Marxist internationalism: The doctrine that supporters of Marxism in any country are obliged to aid Marxists elsewhere.

Massive retaliation: The U.S. strategic posture during the Eisenhower administration under which the United States threatened to use nuclear weapons against the U.S.S.R. in response to conventional weapons challenges by the U.S.S.R. or its allies.

Maximin strategy: A strategy, derived from game theory, that allows players to minimize their potential losses. Also called *minimax.*

Mediation: A procedure by which a third party seeks to resolve conflict by providing adversaries with nonbinding solutions.

Melian Dialogue: A passage in Thucydides' *History of the Peloponnesian War* in which Athens threatens to destroy Melos unless the latter becomes an ally. The passage illustrates power politics in action.

Mercantilism: The doctrine that exports should be encouraged and imports discouraged to accumulate national wealth and power.

Mercenaries: Professional soldiers serving in a foreign army solely for pay.

Merchants of death: Name coined after World War I for corporations that sell arms overseas.

Microsovereignty: Countries like the Andorra, Monaco, or the Comoro or Maldive Islands that have tiny populations and territory.

Military–industrial complex: The idea articulated by President Eisenhower that private defense interests, Congress, and the Pentagon cooperate to keep U.S. defense spending high.

Mirror image: The propensity of groups and individuals to have similar perceptions of each other — that is, we see in others what they see in us.

Modernity: Substituting brain power for muscle power in economic development and acquiring secular and rational attitudes toward the outside world.

Monroe Doctrine: President James Monroe's 1823 proscription of European intervention in the affairs of the Spanish–American states.

Most-favored-nation trade principle (MFN): The principle that tariff preferences that are granted to one actor for its exports must be granted to all trading partners.

Multilateral foreign aid: Foreign assistance provided through such international organizations as the United Nations or groupings of countries like the G-7.

Multipolarity: A political system having three or more dominant power centers.

Munich complex: The belief among American leaders after World War II that the mistakes made in the 1938 Munich Conference should not be repeated, especially with the Soviet Union, and that an aggressor must never be appeased.

Munich Conference: The 1938 meeting at which British and French leaders capitulated to Hitler's demands for Czechoslovakia's Sudetenland region. Their behavior has become synonymous with appeasement.

Mutual Assured Destruction (MAD): A nuclear-deterrence strategy based on each nuclear state's ability to launch devastating nuclear retaliation even if an enemy attacks it first.

Napoleonic Wars: The French wars between 1796 and 1815 in which Napoleon Bonaparte unsuccessfully sought to dominate Europe.

Narcotraficantes: Those involved in the transnational traffic of narcotics.

Nation: A collection of people loyal to each other because of perceived ethnic, linguistic, or cultural affinity.

National budget deficit: A situation in which public spending exceeds government revenues.

National interest: The idea that a state has a corporate interest composed of its relative power, geographic location, or other factors that determine its political behavior.

Nationalism: Exclusive attachment to a national or ethnic group.

Nationalization: Takeover by the state of private property sometimes with compensation and sometimes not.

National-liberation movement: An organization thats seek a separate state for its ethnic or national group, often by resorting to violence.

National security: A state's capacity to ensure its fundamental economic and political independence and survival, and its citizens' safety and well-being. Sometimes used by politicians to justify policies and activities not related to national survival.

Natural-rights theory: Belief that human beings have inalienable rights which existed before societies and which states cannot deny them.

Negative or corrective feedback: Information that brings about a change in policy and produces different behavior.

Negative rights: Individuals' rights not to suffer from undue government interference in personal independence and autonomy. Sometimes called *political and civil rights.*

Negative-sum game: A relationship in which participating actors lose jointly.

Neocolonialism: Indirect influence exercised by wealthy countries over less-developed countries, especially by economic and cultural penetration.

Neofunctionalism: A revised version of functional theory positing that organizations established by agreements among states may create political interests and pressures for broadening or strengthening their own authority or even for establishing additional organizations.

Neorealism: A variant of realism emphasizing the causal importance of the global system's anarchic structure and the role of power as an *intervening* rather than an *independent* variable.

New International Economic Order (NIEO): A composite of demands by the Third World for reforming the international economic system and redistributing global resources.

Newly-industrialized countries (NICs): A group of rapidly industrializing export-oriented countries, including Singapore, Hong Kong, South Korea, Taiwan, and Malaysia.

New-World Information and Communication Order: A Third-World demand for access to mass media that are not owned or controlled by the rich countries.

New world order: Phrase popularized by President George Bush in 1990 and 1991 to denote the world after the Cold War.

Niche competition: A situation in which different countries produce goods that do not compete directly with those of producers and workers in other countries.

Nixon shock: The 1973 announcement by President Richard Nixon that the United States was suspending convertibility of dollars into gold. That move brought an end to the Bretton Woods system.

Nonaligned movement: A group, originally established in 1961, currently consisting of more than one hundred countries that do not wish to be associated with Great-Power alliances and try to further Third-World interests.

Noninterference principle: Sovereign states' obligation to refrain from intervening in the domestic affairs of other sovereign states.

Nonproliferation: Preventing transfer of nuclear weapons or technology to countries that do not have nuclear weapons.

Nontariff barrier: A restriction on free trade other than tariffs such as quotas or complex requirements and inspection procedures.

Normative theory: Beliefs about what is moral and immoral.

North American Free Trade Association (NAFTA): An agreement among the United States, Mexico, and Canada to form a free-trade zone. Strongly opposed by organized labor and some environmental groups in the United States that fear that jobs will move to Mexico and that corporations will use the treaty to get around tough U.S. environmental laws.

North Atlantic Treaty Organization (NATO): An organization of countries in North America and Western Europe established in 1949 to provide a system of collective defense in the event of attack on any member.

North–South dialogue: Conferences and institutions seeking to negotiate differences between the developing and developed states over international economic issues.

Novikov Telegram: A secret 1946 report from the Soviet ambassador in the United States claiming that the United States was an aggressive threat to Soviet security.

Nuclear club: Countries possessing nuclear weapons.

Nuclear-free zone: A region from which nuclear weapons or their development are excluded by treaty.

Nuclear meltdown: A significant portion of a nuclear-reactor core literally melts because the fuel elements are inadequately cooled, potentially releasing massive quantities of radiation.

Nuclear Nonproliferation Treaty: An international agreement signed in 1968 to prevent horizontal proliferation of nuclear weapons.

Nuclear parity: The relative equality in nuclear striking power enjoyed by the United States and Soviet Union during the 1970s and 1980s despite significant differences in their respective force structures. Sometimes referred to as *essential equivalence.*

Nuclear winter: A period of life-threatening darkness and cold on earth that could follow nuclear war.

Oil shocks: Rapid increases in the price of oil following the 1973 Arab–Israeli war, the 1979 revolution in Iran, and the 1990 Iraqi invasion of Kuwait.

Oil weapon: The OPEC threat to place an oil embargo on countries that support Israel.

Oligopoly: An economic condition with very few sellers in which prices tend to remain high.

On-site inspection: Verifying arms-control and disarmament agreements by stationing personnel from other countries to monitor at first hand limitations on manufacturing, testing, or deploying weapons.

Opportunity cost: An opportunity that is not taken because resources are used for other purposes.

Optimists: Those who believe that with the Cold War over the world will be more peaceful and secure.

Orderly marketing agreement: An agreement among states violating free-trade principles to set quotas on their importing and exporting of selected products from each other.

Organization for Economic Cooperation and Development (OECD): An organization with many of the most highly developed states established in 1961 as a replacement for the Organization for European Economic Cooperation (OEEC). The OECD seeks to coordinate and represent its members' international economic policies.

Organization of African Unity (OAU): A regional grouping of African states established in 1963 to foster political cooperation.

Organization of American States (OAS): A regional grouping of American states established in 1951 to foster political cooperation.

Organization of Arab Petroleum Exporting Countries (OAPEC): A grouping of Arab oil producers within OPEC established in 1968 to help coordinate members' petroleum policies.

Organization of Petroleum Exporting Countries (OPEC): A worldwide organization of petroleum-producing countries established in 1960 to coordinate and unify members' petroleum policies and stabilize international oil prices.

Organization–process model: An approach to studying foreign policy focused on routine output of large bureaucracies.

Ostpolitik (east policy): The policy initiated by West Germany toward East Germany in 1969 for systematic accommodation, negotiation, and economic aid with the aim of gaining influence over events there.

Ottoman Empire: A Muslim–Turkish empire founded in 1300 and surviving until 1919 that held sway over much of the Middle East. For much of the nineteenth and twentieth centuries it was referred to as the *sick man of Europe*.

Ozone depletion: Thinning by human release of chlorofluorocarbons of the upper-atmosphere ozone layer that protects human beings from skin cancer.

Palestinian Liberation Organization (PLO): An umbrella organization of Palestinian groups established in 1964 to bring about an independent Palestinian state.

Paradox of power: Actors with greatest capabilities may find it difficult to achieve objectives because their power sows fear, envy, and hatred among other actors.

Participation explosion: The growing interest of mass public's in and knowledge about foreign policy and their willingness to become directly involved in world politics.

Pawn: An actor used or manipulated to further a more powerful actor's purposes.

Peace dividend: Funds and other resources made available by cuts in defense spending following the end of the Cold War. The dividend appears to have been less than many optimists had hoped.

Peaceful coexistence: The doctrine made popular by Soviet leader Nikita Khrushchev in 1956 claiming that war between capitalist and socialist states was not inevitable and that the two blocs could compete peacefully.

Peacekeeping: Using military forces to prevent fighting, separate combatants, or ensure by observation that peace agreements are kept. The forces are provided by neutral third parties under an international organization such as the United Nations, NATO, or the Organization of American States, and must be invited by at least one of the belligerents.

Pearl Harbor: The U.S. naval base in Hawaii that was the victim of a surprise Japanese air attack on December 7, 1941. The attack brought the United States into World War II.

Pearl Harbor complex: Fear among American leaders after World War II that the Soviet Union could carry out a successful sneak attack against the United States as the Japanese had done at Pearl Harbor in 1941. During the Cold War U.S. weapons and strategies were designed with an eye toward avoiding such a possibility.

Perception: The version of reality held by an observer or decision-maker. If that version differs from reality, it is called *misperception*.

Perestroika: Economic-restructuring policy initiated by Soviet President Mikhail Gorbachev.

Persian Gulf War: A war waged in 1991 by a U.S.-led coalition that ended Iraqi occupation of Kuwait.

Pessimists: Those who believe that with the Cold War ended, global politics will see greater violence and disorder.

Photosynthesis: Synthesis by green plants and other organisms of complex organic materials from carbon dioxide, water, and salts, for which sunlight is the source of energy.

Plaza Agreement: A 1985 agreement among leading industrialized states to coordinate international exchange rates and domestic interest rates.

Polarity: Distribution of power centers in a political system.

Political asylum: A haven provided for refugees who are fleeing political persecution.

Political consciousness: Awareness of political conditions and events and of their implications and consequences.

Political culture: A society's practices and attitudes produced by its history and the values its citizens hold. Political culture is a primary domestic factor in explaining an actor's foreign policy.

Political pluralism: A political system featuring competition among competing domestic groups seek to pressure the government to enact policies favorable to their interests.

Political war: Using various tactics short of open war to harass and undermine an enemy.

Population density: Ratio of population to arable land.

Portfolio investment: Speculative investment intended to get capital gains by following fluctuations in the market.

Position-of-strength principle: The belief, held in the United States during much of the Cold War, that one can most effectively negotiate with an adversary when enjoying superior military power.

Positive or amplifying feedback: Information that reinforces policy and produces more of the same behavior.

Positive rights: Individuals' rights to have their essential needs such as food and health seen to by the government. Sometimes called *economic and social rights*.

Positive-sum game: A relationship in which participating actors win jointly.

Postinternational politics: Political scientist James N. Rosenau's name for the presence in global politics of new structures, processes, and relations other than sovereign states and relations among them.

Potential power: Capabilities that can be directed toward constructing a power relationship.

Power: A psychological relationship in which one actor influences another to behave differently than it would have if left to its own devices.

Power-cycle theory: An approach to understanding war focused on the factors and conditions that enable some states in a system to rise above others and aspire to hegemony.

Power elite: Individuals in a political system who enjoy disproportionate political influence either by occupying political and economic positions or by having access to those who do.

Power politics: An intellectual tradition affirming that outcomes in global politics are determined by distribution of political power and changes in that distribution. See **Realism**.

Power-preponderance theory: The belief that peace is ensured when one actor or group of actors in a political system enjoys hegemony.

Power-transition theory: Theory that war is most likely to break out when differences in power among rivals have narrowed.

Preemptive war: A war launched by one actor from fear that another actor is about to attack it.

Preferential trade: Affording special trade treatment to selected states.

Preventive diplomacy: Inserting U.N. peacekeepers in a conflict, especially in the Third World, to prevent intervention by and possible confrontation between the superpowers.

Preventive war: A war begun by one actor to prevent an enemy from becoming so powerful that it might be a military threat in the future.

Primary products: Raw materials and agricultural products.

Prisoner's-dilemma game: A relationship among actors described in game theory to illustrate the problem of trust under conditions of anarchy.

Prisoners of conscience: Individuals who have been imprisoned because of their political views.

Private good: A benefit that is enjoyed only by some and need not be shared with others.

Protectionism: Policies such as tariffs and quotas designed to shelter home industries from competition by imports.

Protectorate: Relationship between a strong state and a territory that it protects and controls.

Proxy: An actor that acts or speaks on behalf of another, often a Great Power.

Psychobiography: Analyzing a leader's political behavior by applying Freudian tools in studying the individual's personality.

Purdah: The practice among Muslims of secluding women from the sight of men and strangers.

Quasi-state: State in which incompetence, deflated credibility, and systematic corruption are so pervasive that it seems to bear little resemblance to traditional sovereign states.

Racial stereotype: A standardized, often denigrating conception applied to all members of a racial group.

Rational-actor approach: An approach to global politics assuming that actors and their decision makers select the best alternatives when formulating policy to maximize their goals.

Realism: A theoretical approach, dominant in the United States after World War II, that sees sovereign states as leading actors in global politics, power and its distribution as the main determinants of state behavior, and war as the primary issue in global politics.

Realpolitik: Policy based on power rather than ideals.

Reason of state: Idea that a state has a corporate interest that determines its policies.

Reciprocity: Strategy by which one actor behaves toward others as they have behaved toward it.

Recognition of states: Act by which states declare that a new state is legitimate and by which the new state acquires sovereignty.

Regional integration: The procedure or the result of endeavors in different regions to build political communities that transcend states.

Relative military-spending burden: The comparative burden of states as measured by the ratio of defense spending to GNP.

Relative power: An actor's power compared with that of other actors.

Repatriation of profits: The practice by which transnational corporations return profits to investors at home rather than reinvest them in host countries.

Resolution: The final stage in an issue cycle during which agreement is reached or the issue loses actors' attention.

Rewards: Positive incentives used to generate influence.

Riga Axioms: Unlike the Yalta Axioms, the belief that Soviet policy was driven by ideology rather than power.

Ritualization: The third stage in an issue cycle, during which routine patterns of behavior and rules for managing an issue evolve among actors.

Role: The manner in which an individual's official position affects the individual's attitudes and behavior.

RU-486: A pill developed in France that prevents pregnancy if taken after conception. Sometimes called an *abortion pill*, it arouses heated debate between "pro-choice" and "pro-life" sympathizers.

Rules of the game: Widely understood and accepted global norms that actors follow out of habit and self-interest.

Salami tactic: An aggressive strategy in which an actor makes small demands that collectively constitute something more significant.

Salinization: Causing infertile soil by adding excessive salt.

SALT I: The Strategic Arms Limitation Treaty, signed in 1972, which limited deployment of antiballistic missiles.

SALT II: The Strategic Arms Limitation Treaty, signed in 1979 but unratified by the United States because the Soviets invaded Afghanistan. Most of its provisions were honored by the signatories anyway.

Samurai: Member of the hereditary warrior class in feudal Japan.

Satisficing: Propensity of decision makers to select an alternative that meets minimally acceptable standards.

Schlieffen Plan: German military plan before World War I for a two-front war against France and Russia, in which victory would be achieved by rapidly invading France through Belgium.

Scope of power: Aspects of a target's behavior that are subject to an influence relationship.

Second-order feedback: Information that brings about a change in actors' goals, as well as their behavior.

Second-strike capability: A nuclear power's ability to absorb an enemy first strike and then launch a devastating retaliatory strike. Second-strike capability is achieved by making nuclear-weapons systems invulnerable to a first strike by hardening them or making them mobile.

Second World: Members of the former Soviet bloc.

Security dilemma: Actors' inability under anarchic conditions to trust each other because of the absence of reliable enforcement.

Self-determination: National and ethnic groups' right to govern themselves.

Self-help: The principle that, under anarchic conditions, actors must rely on themselves for security in global politics.

Sensitivity interdependence: The speed with which events in one part of the world affect other parts of the world and the magnitude of those effects.

Sephardim: Jews of North African and Middle Eastern origins.

Seven sisters: The seven petroleum corporations that controlled production, refining, and distribution of Middle East oil between the 1920s and the 1960s.

Shantytown: An extremely poor section in a city.

Shi'ite Islam: The smaller of the two major branches of Islam, consisting of those who regard Ali, son-in-law of Muhammad, as the Prophet's legitimate successor. Many Shi'ites believe the Koran is the only source of political authority. See **Islamic fundamentalism.**

Side payment: A special or private benefit provided to an actor or individual in return for supporting a policy involving collective goods. See **Collective good.**

Situational power: Power derived from an actor's ability to manipulate the situation of a target by using rewards and coercion.

Six-Day War: A war between Israel and its neighbors in 1967 that terminated in Israeli occupation of the West Bank, the Gaza Strip, Jerusalem, the Golan Heights, and the Sinai Peninsula.

Size: The absolute level of resources controlled by an actor, or to which it has access. Such resources predict the actor's potential influence in global politics.

Skyjacking: The seizure of airplanes by terrorists, who often use passengers and crew as hostages for their demands.

Social and economic development: The per capita level of resources controlled by an actor or to which it has access. Per capita resources predict how effectively an actor can use its resources.

Social insurance: The source of security for an individual's future.

Socialism in one country: A doctrine Stalin propounded during his rise to power in the 1920s that the Soviet Union had to strengthen itself to secure socialism at home before seeking to spread it to other countries.

Socialist Bloc: The Soviet Union and its allies during the Cold War. Interchangeable with either "Eastern" or "Soviet" bloc.

Soft power: Influence based on cultural attraction, ideology, and role in international institutions.

Sovereign equality: The principle that states are legal equals and under which threatening or using force against any state is prohibited.

Sovereignty: The status of states as legal equals under international law, according to which they are supreme internally and subject to no higher external authority.

Specialized agencies: A group of U.N.-affiliated organizations seeking to promote the common welfare by carrying out functional tasks.

Special relationship: Name for U.S.–British relations since the nineteenth century. For most of that time, the two countries have been close allies, sensitive to each other's problems and needs.

Sphere of influence: An area under the influence of a major state.

Spillover: In functionalist theory, the procedure by which successful cooperation in one sphere of human endeavor encourages cooperation on other issues and by which functional organizations' authority over such issues deepens.

Stability of a system: The ability of a system's structural features to maintain themselves with time and change slowly and predictably.

Stagflation: Inflation and recession combined.

Stag–hare parable: A parable told by political philosopher Jean-Jacques Rousseau to illustrate how anarchy produces conflict.

Standard operating procedures (SOPs): Established procedures that bureaucracies follow to carry out recurring tasks and duties.

State: A political entity that is sovereign and is said to control a defined territory and population.

State of nature: The political philosopher's imagined depiction of human relationships before society or state were created.

Status: An actor's ranking or prestige in the global hierarchy as defined by other actors.

Status inconsistency: An imbalance between an actor's ranking in the global hierarchy and its resources. Such inconsistency may be dangerous as actors seek to bring the two factors into balance.

Strategic Arms Reduction Treaty (START I): A 1991 U.S.–Soviet agreement to make major cuts in numbers of nuclear warheads.

Strategic Arms Reduction Treaty (START II): A 1992 agreement between the United States and Russia to reduce nuclear arsenals on both sides by 50 percent.

Strategic Defense Initiative (SDI or Star Wars): A plan President Ronald Reagan initiated to deploy an antiballistic missile system using space-based lasers.

Strategic stability: Condition in which leaders have few incentives to try to launch a military first strike.

Strong state: A state that has extensive autonomy and capacity.

Structural Impediments Initiative (SII): A 1989 agreement between the United States and Japan to study conditions in the two countries that affect free trade between them.

Structural realists: Another name for *neorealists,* who emphasize the primacy of system structure, especially the distribution of power and arrangement of the units, in determining behavior.

Subnational actor: A political actor located in one state.

Subsystem: Specialized group of actors whose relations show more interaction and interdependence than do those in the larger global system.

Sullivan principles: Rules suggested by black activist Leon Sullivan under which corporations agree to assure black employees in South Africa of the same treatment as that enjoyed by white employees.

Summitry: Meetings and negotiations between leaders of states.

Sunni Islam: The dominant branch of Islam consisting of those who regard the first four caliphs as legitimate successors of Muhammad.

Superpower: A country with military capabilities far beyond those of other states. First applied to the United States and the Soviet Union after World War II.

Supranational organization: A body with the authority to make decisions binding on member states without requiring their approval.

Suttee: A former Hindu practice by which a widow immolated herself on her husband's funeral pyre.

System: An abstraction referring to a set of units complexly interrelated by interaction.

System-level analysis: An approach emphasizing the causal influence of the global distribution of resources and attitudes on individual actors' behavior.

System structure: Distribution of resources and attitudes among the actors in a political system.

Tacit veto: The superpowers' ability to thwart U.N. action even without a legal veto in the Security Council.

Tangible resources: Material or substantial resources that contribute to an actor's power.

Tariff: A tax, known also as an *import duty*, which is added to the price of imported goods.

Technology transfer: The movement of advanced technology from wealthy, developed countries to poor, less-developed countries.

Tectonic-plates model: A metaphor associated with neorealists comparing foreign policy to the folds in the earth's crust whose movement causes earthquakes.

Terms of trade: The ratio between prices of exports and those of imports that determines a state's ability to prosper from international trade.

Territoriality: A political actor's possession of a defined territory or space.

Terrorism: Calculated use of violence against innocent civilians for political ends, especially to gain public attention. Terrorism can be undertaken by state authorities or nonstate groups and individuals.

Theocracy: A form of government based on religion and in which priests have a major part.

Theory: A set of related propositions that explain or predict phenomena.

Third World: All the less-developed countries, most of which are in Africa, Asia, Latin America, and the Middle East.

Thirty Years' War: The war fought from 1618 to 1648 in Central Europe between Catholic and Protestant supporters, creating the conditions for the modern sovereign state.

Tokyo Round of GATT: Multilateral trade negotiations held between 1973 and 1979.

Totalitarianism: A form of authoritarianism exercising control over even the minute details of individual lives, often by means of technology and an omnipresent political party.

Total war: A condition of unlimited violence caused by modern weapons and organizations envisioned by the Prussian military thinker Karl Maria von Clausewitz.

Traditional society: An agrarian society in which inhabitants follow preindustrial customs and in which religion and superstition continue to be highly influential in individual and group decisions.

Transnational corporation (TNC): A firm head-quartered in one country and having operations in one or more other countries.

Transnational relations: Direct interactions or transactions across national frontiers involving nongovernmental actors or social groups.

Treaty of Rome: A treaty signed in 1957 creating the European Common Market.

Treaty of Westphalia: The treaty ending the Thirty Years' War in 1648. It established the principle of sovereignty and the permanence of sovereign states in Europe.

Triad principle: The principle underlying the U.S. deterrence strategy of maintaining a retaliatory force consisting of three elements: land-based intercontinental ballistic missiles (ICBMs), nuclear submarines with sea-launched ballistic missiles (SLBMs), and long-range bombers.

Tribe: A political group united by descent from a common ancestor.

Truman Doctrine: The policy announced by President Harry S Truman in 1947 stating that the United States would support all countries threatened by external or internal communism. Many feel the policy marked the beginning of the Cold War.

Ultrasound: A procedure using ultrasonic technology to examine a fetus in the womb.

Uncertainty avoidance: Psychological propensity to focus only on alternatives with assured outcomes rather than estimating the probabilities in different choices when making a decision.

U.N. Conference on Trade and Development (UNCTAD): A U.N. organization created at a special 1964 conference to promote Third World economic development.

Underemployment: Employment of individuals in jobs that do not make full use of their skills and abilities.

U.N. Economic and Social Council: The U.N. organ with principal responsibility for eco-nomic and social issues and functional tasks. It consists of regional commissions and functional commissions.

U.N. General Assembly: An organization of all U.N. members with the power to discuss and make recommendations on any issue (except those before the Security Council).

Unintended consequences: Outcomes from foreign-policy initiatives that were not foreseen.

Unipolarity: Domination of global politics by one actor or power center.

Unit of analysis: The entity or unit whose behavior a theorist seeks to explain or predict. Sometimes called *unit of explanation*.

Unitary-actor approach: An approach to understanding global politics assuming that actors' internal attributes or differences among such attributes do not affect behavior.

United Nations (U.N.): A global intergovernmental organization established in 1945 to maintain peace and security and improve its members' economic and social conditions. The U.N. consists of six principal organs: the General Assembly, the Security Council, the Economic and Social Council, the Trusteeship Council, and the Secretariat and the World Court.

Uniting for Peace Resolution: A procedure adopted by the U.N. General Assembly at the time of the Korean War to get around the veto provision in the Security Council.

U.N. Office of High Commissioner for Refugees (UNHCR): A U.N. agency established in 1951 to provide protection and relief to international refugees.

U.N. Relief and Works Agency (UNRWA): A U.N. agency established in 1949 to assist Palestinian refugees.

U.N. Resolution 181: Endorsed partition of Palestine and triggered the first Arab–Israeli war in 1948.

U.N. Resolution 242: Called on Israel and its Arab neighbors in 1967 to negotiate an exchange of "land for peace."

U.N. Secretariat: The executive organ of the United Nations, consisting of the U.N. Secretary General and the U.N. staff.

U.N. Security Council: A U.N. organ with five permanent members and ten nonpermanent members whose principal responsibility is to maintain international peace and security.

U.N. Trusteeship Council: The U.N. organ whose primary responsibility is preparing former colonial territories for self-government and political independence.

Uruguay Round of GATT: Multilateral trade negotiations from 1986 to 1993 to consider such issues as nontariff barriers, agricultural trade, and intellectual property rights.

U.S.–Canada Free Trade Agreement: A 1989 agreement establishing a free-trade area between the two countries.

Verification: The procedure by which signatories' adherence to arms-control and disarmament agreements is confirmed.

Versailles Treaty: The treaty concluded in 1919 bringing an end to World War I. Its major provisions included establishing the League of Nations, placing the blame for the war on Germany, and forcing Germany to pay steep war reparations.

Vertical nuclear proliferation: An increase in the nuclear capabilities of actors that already possess nuclear weapons.

Veto: The prerogative held by permanent members of the U.N. Security Council to prevent action by the Council by voting against a resolution.

Vulnerability interdependence: The alternatives available to actors that seek to limit the effects of events and changes happening elsewhere in the world.

War of attrition: A war in which the outcome is a result of a slow but bloody attempt by each side to wear down the other.

Warsaw Treaty Organization (WTO): A military organization formed in 1955 by Soviet bloc members.

Weak state: A state that lacks autonomy and capacity.

Weapons of mass destruction: Nuclear, chemical, and biological weapons whose use is likely to produce massive civilian casualties and damage.

Weltpolitik (world policy): German policy under Kaiser Wilhelm II, challenging British supremacy at sea and seeking additional colonies.

West Bank: A region in Palestine between the Jordan River and Israel. Formerly a part of Jordan, it was occupied by Israeli forces in the 1967 Six-Day War.

Western European Union (WEU): Grouping of Western European states for collective self-defense and political collaboration, established in 1955 as successor to the Brussels Treaty Organization.

Westpolitik (west policy): The West German government's strategy for much of the Cold War, linking itself as closely as possible to the United States and the countries in Western Europe.

Window of vulnerability: Reagan administration's description for the period when the Soviet Union seemed to have the capability to destroy the U.S. land-based missile force in a first-strike attack.

World-system theory: A belief that global politics can be explained by an international division of labor between wealthy core states that produce capital-intensive products and poor peripheral states that produce raw materials and agricultural commodities.

Worst-case analysis: Foreign-policy planning based on the assumption that an adversary will seek to do as much harm as possible.

Xenophobia: Fear and hatred of foreigners.

Yalta Axioms: The belief of American leaders before the Cold War that it was possible to bargain with the Soviet Union and that the latter was much like other states that designed foreign policies based on power.

Yalta Conference: A 1945 summit meeting with Franklin D. Roosevelt, Josef Stalin, and Winston Churchill at which major postwar issues were discussed, such as the status of Poland and voting arrangements in the United Nations.

Yom Kippur War: The 1973 Arab–Israeli war that began with a surprise attack by Egypt and Syria against Israel, trying to reverse the outcome of the Six-Day War.

Zaibatsu: The great industrial or financial enterprises of Japan.

Zero option: A 1981 proposal by the Reagan administration for the worldwide elimination of INF missiles.

Zero-sum game: A relationship in which a gain for one actor is equal to a loss for another actor.

Zionism: A worldwide Jewish movement for establishing a national homeland for the Jews in Palestine.

Name Index

Licklider, Roy, 79n
Lie, Trygve, 306
Ligachev, Yegor K., 421
Lincoln, Abraham, 72
Lindblom, Charles E., 329n
Lippmann, Walter, 91n
Lipson, Charles, 194n, 207n
Litvinov, Maxim, 302n
Locke, John, 535
Lodge, Henry Cabot, 300
Loewenheim, Francis L., 196n
Lorenz, Konrad, 182n
Louis XIV (king of France), 84–85, 87
Louis XV (king of France), 217
Louis XVI (king of France), 89
Lovejoy, Thomas, 524
Luard, Evan, 301n, 302n
Ludendorff, Erich, 242, 244
Lueck, Thomas J., 546n
Luther, Martin, 44

Maasdorp, Gavin G., 172n
MacArthur, Douglas, 230, 410n, 434
McAuley, Mary, 359n, 360
McCarthy, Joseph, 8, 127, 414
McCormick, James M., 288n, 344n, 351n, 356n, 386n, 414n, 416n, 535n, 542n, 548n, 549n, 557n
McDougall, William, 218n
McGowan, Patrick J., 214n, 216
Machiavelli, Niccolò, 27, 43n, 79, 80, 82–83, 107, 213, 288, 559
MacIsaac, David, 237n
Mackinder, Sir Halford J., 60
McNamara, Robert, 380, 547
McNaughton, John T., 197
McNeill, William H., 24n, 221n, 226n, 227
Macridis, Roy C., 254n
Maginot, André, 235n
Mahan, Alfred Thayer, 60
Malan, Daniel F., 169
Malthus, Thomas, 510
Mandel, Robert, 220n, 376n, 377n
Mandela, Nelson, 171n, 175, 550, 551
Mandelbaum, Michael, 417n
Mansbach, Richard W., 27n, 110n, 111n, 112n, 132n, 189n, 385n, 397n
Mao Tse-tung, 8, 57, 160
Marantz, Paul, 415n
Marcos, Ferdinand E., 127, 220, 537
Marcum, John A., 175n
Markandya, Anil, 523n
Marshall, George C., 409n

Marx, Karl, 68–69, 129, 222, 324n, 407, 525n, 535
Masaryk, Jan, 401
Mathers, Todd, 165n, 168n
Matthews, Richard A., 293n
Matthews, Tom, 391n
Maull, Hanns W., 427n
May, Ernest R., 196n, 197n
Mayne, Richard, 398n
Mazarin, Cardinal, 84
Mazzeo, Domenico, 322n
Mead, Margaret, 221
Mearsheimer, John J., 72–73, 98n, 563n, 569
Meinecke, Friedrich, 82n
Meir, Golda, 483
Menchu, Rigoberta, 551
Mendes, Chico, 524
Mendez, Reuben P., 65n
Metternich, Klemens von (prince of Austria), 90
Michaels, Marguerite, 522n
Milgram, Stanley, 219
Mill, John Stuart, 222n, 536
Miller, Lynn H., 300n, 301n, 310n
Miller, Neal E., 219n
Mills, C. Wright, 247
Milner, Helen, 426n
Milosevic, Slobodan, 535
Mingst, Karen A., 298n
Mintz, Alex, 246n
Mitchell, Billy, 237n
Mitchell, Neil J., 535n, 542n, 548n, 549n, 557n
Mitrany, David, 296–297, 298
Miyazawa, Kiichi (Japanese prime minister), 331, 444
Mobuto, Sese Seko, 245, 537
Modelski, George, 85n, 224n
Modigliani, André, 404n
Molotov, Vyacheslav, 403
Monnet, Jean, 446
Morgenthau, Hans J., 87n, 91n, 93, 95n, 107n, 108–109, 109n, 117, 182n, 324, 373n
Morici, Peter, 463n
Morillon, Philippe, 163
Moro, Aldo, 159
Moroni, Alice C., 411n
Morris, Desmond, 518n
Morss, Elliott R., 356n
Mossadegh, Muhammad, 481, 196n, 481
Mother Teresa of Calcutta, 551
Mountbatten, Louis Earl, 161
Mower, A. Glenn, 554n

Subject Index

SADCC, *see* Southern African Development
Coordination Conference (SADCC)
"Salami tactics," 199–200
Salience, 397
Salinization, 509
SALT I, *see* Strategic Arms Limitation
Treaty I (SALT I)
SALT II, *see* Strategic Arms Limitation
Treaty II (SALT II)
Samurai, 244
Sanctions, 173, 292, 303, 457, 496, 557
Satellite effect, 99n
Satisficing, 381
Saudi Arabia, 369, 393, 471, 497
Savings rates, 432
SBLM, *see* Submarine-launched ballistic
missiles (SBLMs)
SCAP, *see* Supreme Commander of the
Allied Powers (SCAP)
Schlieffen Plan, 233
SDI, *see* Strategic Defense Initiative (SDI)
Seabed Arms Control Treaty (1971), 210,
272, 280
Sea-launched cruise missiles (SLCMs), 264n
Second-order feedback, 49
Second-strike capability, 257–258, 259, 263
Second World, 358–364. *See also* Eastern
Europe; Soviet successor states
Security
collective, 289, 295–296, 299, 300–302,
560–561; global, 113, 560–561; as Israeli
issue, 489–490; as issue for Arab states,
490–491; Japanese, during Cold War,
435–436; national, 127, 560–561; national
interest and, 124–125; new world
redefinition of, 13–14; nonmilitary threats
to, 13–14; Old World definition of, 9–10;
public vs. private goods and, 508; self-help
and, 181; terrorism and, 161; *see also*
Military resources
Security dilemma, 182–183, 187. *See also*
Prisoner's dilemma
Sefardim, 472
Self-help, 181
Sendero Luminoso (Shining Path), 159–160,
161, 518, 546–547
Senior interagency groups (SIGs), 382
Sensitivity, 135
Serbia, 286, 315, 316, 470, 535, 565
Seven sisters, 481, 482
Seven Years' War, 84n
Shantytowns, 512, 513
"Shatalin Plan," 421
Shi'a Muslims, 475–477, 495

Shining Path (terrorist group), 159–160, 161,
518, 546–547
"Shuttle diplomacy," 488n
Sick man of Europe, 470
Side payment, 508
SIGs, *see* Senior interagency groups (SIGs)
SII, *see* Structural Impediments Initiative
(SII)
Sinai Peninsula, 487, 489
"Sinatra Doctrine," 418
Singapore, 15, 62, 511–512
Single Market Act of 1985, 448, 562
Sino-Japanese War, 93, 433–434
Sino-Soviet rift, 8
Situation, definition of the, 374–375
Situational power, 102
Six-Day War, 191n, 484, 487–488
Size
foreign policy behavior and, 372; measure
for, 61; power and, 61–64
Skaggerak, 60
Skyjackings, 160
Slashing and burning, 523–524
SLCM, *see* Sea-launched cruise missiles
(SLCMs)
Slovenia, 118
Smog, 525, 528
Soccer War, 322, 569
Social change, *see* Traditional societies
Social insurance, 510
"Socialism in one country," 414–415
Socialist Bloc, 419
Society
distinguished from government and the
state, 116n; militarization of, in U.S.,
246–249; propensity to war and, 221–223
Socioeconomic class
balance of power politics and, 89; class
struggle and, 222, 337; loyalties and,
68–69; social propensity to war and, 222
Soft power, 430
Solidarity, 57, 418, 422
Solid waste, 519
Somalia, 145–146, 541
civil war in, 145–146; Cold War politics
and, 8, 145; food needs in, 522; U.N.
peacekeeping operation in, 311;
U.S.-French relations and, 113
SOP, *see* Standard operating procedures
(SOPs)
South Africa
apartheid in, 168–175, 547; government
of, 170–172; human rights progress in,
550–551, 555–556; IGOs in, 173; map of,

170; neighboring countries and, 170, 171,
172–173; NGOs and, 174–175; nuclear
weapons and, 280; terrorism in, 547
Southeast Asia, 189–191, 237, 357, 434. *See
also* Third World; *specific countries*
Southeast Asia Treaty Organization
(SEATO), 8, 409
Southern African Development Coordination
Conference (SADCC), 172
Southern Common Market, 165, 562
Southern Rhodesia, 173
South-West African People's Organization
(SWAPO), 172
Sovereign equality, 117
Sovereignty
concept of, 44, 117; cultural, 449; decline
of, 117–124; international benefits of,
122–123; Japanese, 434; legal vs. practical
consequences of, 122–123; recognition of,
117–119; transnational corporations and,
155–156; *see also* Independence;
Territorial states
Soviet successor states
ethnic tensions in, 564–565; global
economic issues and, 336, 363–364;
nuclear weapons held by, 254; *see also*
Baltic states; Commonwealth of
Independent States (CIS); Second World;
specific republics
Soviet Union
arms sales and, 244; civil war in
Afghanistan and, 9; collapse of, 2, 10, 14,
420; cooperative initiatives by, 292–293;
coup attempt in (1991), 420, 421–422;
development of nuclear weapons and, 253,
256, 257; economic crises in, 61, 415,
416–417; economic system in, 359–361;
end of Cold War and, 200–203; genesis of
Cold War and, 398–399; grain harvests in
(1950–1986), 361; human rights in, 535;
military expenditures in, 103, 104; nuclear
accidents in, 526–527; Riga Axioms and,
402; South Africa and, 171; U.N. Security
Council vetoes by, 307; *see also* Cold War;
Cuban missile crisis; Russia, republic of;
Soviet successor states
Space exploration, 10n
Special interests, 509
Specialization, 46
Specialized agencies, 163, 307, 318–321, 387.
See also specific U.N. agencies
Specialized global intergovernmental
organizations, 163–164
Specialized regional intergovernmental

organizations, 164–165
Special relationship, 69–70, 195–196, 405
Spheres of influence, 5n, 6, 399–400, 471
Spillover, 298, 321, 449
Sputnik, 263
Stability
balance of power politics and, 87, 93;
defined, 56; as emergent property of
systems, 56; exchange rates and, 329–330;
interdependence and, 52; as issue in global
politics, 56; polarity and, 87, 96–97;
Soviet successor states and, 363–364;
strategic, 262, 263–266
Stagflation, 13
Stag-hare parable, 181–182, 192, 194
Standard operating procedures (SOPs), 380,
383
START I, *see* Strategic Arms Reduction
Treaty I (START I)
START II, *see* Strategic Arms Reduction
Treaty II (START II)
"Star Wars," *see* Strategic Defense Initiative
(SDI)
State-centric world, 108, 132, 133, 143
"State of nature," 181–182, 194
states and, 294
States
collective goods and, 507–509; conquest
by, and mass participation, 130;
differences among, 119–124; distinguished
from government and society, 116n; failed
nation-state phenomenon and, 568;
federations of, 26; in global politics,
25–26, 114–116; homogeneous vs.
heterogeneous, 116; human rights issues
and, 534–558; juridical statehood and,
124; leading, resources of, 431; vs.
nations, 90–91; recognition of, 117–119;
relation to individuals and, 535–538;
strong vs. weak, 143–146; traffic in arms
among, 241; transnational challenge to
independence of, 127–139; transnational
corporations and, 148–150, 155–156; *see
also* City-states; Territorial states
State terrorism, 156
Status, 64–67
defined, 65
Status inconsistency, 67
Stern Gang, 482
Stimulus-response model, *see* Action-reaction
model
Stockholm Conference on Confidence and
Security-Building Measures and
Disarmament in Europe (1986), 275

Credits